SEXUAL VIOLENCE
AS AN INTERNATIONAL CRIME:
INTERDISCIPLINARY APPROACHES

SERIES ON TRANSITIONAL JUSTICE

The Series on *Transitional Justice* offers a platform for high-quality research within the rapidly growing field of transitional justice. The research is, of necessity inter-disciplinary in nature, drawing from disciplines such as law, political science, history, sociology, criminology, anthropology and psychology, as well as from various specialised fields of study such as human rights, victimology and peace studies. Furthermore, the research is international in outlook, drawing on the knowledge and experience of academics and other specialists in many different regions of the world.

The series is aimed at a variety of audiences who are either working or interested in fields such as crime and justice; human rights; humanitarian law and human security; conflict resolution and peace building. These audiences include academics, researchers, students, policy makers, practitioners, non-governmental organisations and the media.

All books published within the series are subject to a double-blind peer review by recognised authorities in the field.

Published titles within the series:
1. Stephen Peté and Max Du Plessis, *Repairing the Past? International Perspectives on Reparations for Gross Human Rights Abuses* (2007), 978-90-5095-492-1
2. Laura Stovel, *Long Road Home, Building Reconciliation and Trust in Post-War Sierra Leone* (2010), 978-94-000-0028-5
3. Andy Aitchison, *Making the Transition. International Intervention, State-Building and Criminal Justice Reform in Bosnia and Herzegovina* (2011), 978-94-000-0140-4
4. Stef Vandeginste, *Stones left unturned. Law and Transitional Justice in Burundi* (2010), 978-94-000-0115-2
5. Antoine Buyse (ed.), *Margins of Conflict. The ECHR and Transitions to and from Armed Conflict* (2011), 978-94-000-0157-2
6. Gaby Oré Aguilar and Felipe Gómez Isa (eds.), *Rethinking Transitions. Equality and Social Justice in Societies Emerging from Conflict* (2011), 978-1-78068-003-3
7. Richard Zajac Sannerholm, *Rule of Law after War. Ideologies, Norms and Methods* (2012), 978-1-78068-008-8
8. Nicola Palmer, Phil Clark and Danielle Granville (chief editors), *Critical Perspectives in Transitional Justice* (2011), 978-1-78068-035-4
9. Edda Kristjánsdóttir, André Nollkaemper and Cedric Ryngaert (eds.), *International Law in Domestic Courts: Rule of Law Reform in Post-conflict States* (2012), 978-1-78068-041-5
10. Bas van Stokkom, Neelke Doorn and Paul van Tongeren (eds.), *Public Forgiveness in Post-Conflict Contexts* (2012), 978-1-78068-044-6
11. Ilse Derluyn, Cindy Mels, Stephan Parmentier and Wouter Vandenhole (eds.), *Re-Member. Rehabilitation, Reintegration and Reconciliation of War-Affected Children* (2012), 978-94-000-0027-4

Series on Transitional Justice, Volume 12

SEXUAL VIOLENCE AS AN INTERNATIONAL CRIME: INTERDISCIPLINARY APPROACHES

Edited by

Anne-Marie de Brouwer
Charlotte Ku
Renée Römkens
Larissa van den Herik

intersentia

Cambridge – Antwerp – Portland

Intersentia Publishing Ltd.
Trinity House | Cambridge Business Park | Cowley Road
Cambridge | CB4 0WZ | United Kingdom
Tel.: +44 1223 393 753 | Email: mail@intersentia.co.uk

Distribution for the UK:
Hart Publishing Ltd.
16C Worcester Place
Oxford OX1 2JW
UK
Tel.: +44 1865 517 530
Email: mail@hartpub.co.uk

Distribution for the USA and Canada:
International Specialized Book Services
920 NE 58th Ave. Suite 300
Portland, OR 97213
USA
Tel.: +1 800 944 6190 (toll free)
Email: info@isbs.com

Distribution for Austria:
Neuer Wissenschaftlicher Verlag
Argentinierstraße 42/6
1040 Wien
Austria
Tel.: +43 1 535 61 03 24
Email: office@nwv.at

Distribution for other countries:
Intersentia Publishing nv
Groenstraat 31
2640 Mortsel
Belgium
Tel.: +32 3 680 15 50
Email: mail@intersentia.be

Sexual Violence as an International Crime: Interdisciplinary Approaches
Anne-Marie de Brouwer, Charlotte Ku, Renée Römkens and Larissa van den Herik (eds.)

Artwork on cover: Author Jan Jordaan, title 'Hurt', medium Linocut, 1999. From the *Universal Declaration of Human Rights – International Print Portfolio, Article 5*, published by Art for Humanity, South Africa, 1999

ISBN 978-1-78068-002-6
D/2012/7849/107
NUR 828

GPRC
Guaranteed
Peer Reviewed
Content

British Library Cataloguing in Publication Data. A catalogue record for this book is available from the British Library.

ACKNOWLEDGEMENTS

The editors would like to thank the sponsors and participants of the two colloquia, "Sexual Violence as an International Crime: Interdisciplinary Approaches" and "Systematic Sexual Violence and Victims' Rights" held in The Hague in 2009 and 2011 respectively that provided the content for this volume. Sponsors of the colloquia were the Center on Law and Globalization, the University of Illinois College of Law, the American Bar Foundation, the Department of Criminal Law and INTERVICT of Tilburg Law School (Tilburg University), the Grotius Centre for International Legal Studies of Leiden University/Campus The Hague, the Dutch Ministry of Foreign Affairs, the Peace Palace, and the Municipality of The Hague.

For their work in preparing the manuscript for publication, we thank the staff of the University of Illinois College of Law Office of Graduate and International Legal Studies and especially Administrative Honors Fellows Isabelle Liger and Kelly Ann Smith for their painstaking and careful work on the citations. Final formatting was completed by Jennifer Duffy and Molly Lindsey of the University of Illinois College of Law journal offices.

We also gratefully acknowledge the financial support and vision of the Center on Law and Globalization, a partnership of the University of Illinois College of Law and the American Bar Foundation and Tilburg Law School to pursue interdisciplinary projects and to facilitate the networking that made this project possible.

Lastly, we would like to thank the editors of this series, Prof. Stephan Parmentier, Prof. Elmar Weitekamp and Prof. Jeremy Sarkin, for their trust in this project; the anonymous peer reviewers for their insightful comments and suggestions to improve the quality of the book chapters; and the publisher Intersentia, in particular Tom Scheirs, for their help in finalizing the book.

The Editors
June 2012

FOREWORD

Patricia Viseur Sellers

"The act of rape, ... had a terrible effect on them. They could, perhaps, explain it to themselves when somebody steals from them, or even beatings or even some killings. When rapes started, everybody lost hope, everybody in the camp, men and women. There was such fear, horrible"
Mr. Gutic, inmate at Omarska Detention Center

Prosecutor v. Dusko Tadic, IT-94-I-T, 7 May 1997

International judicial institutions have shepherded in a "coming of age" of sexual violence prosecutions under international criminal law and humanitarian law. The task is promising yet tenuous: It requires vision and vigilance. The chapters in this book deliver both prerequisites by their articulation of tools to fortify enforcement of international criminal law's safeguards against sexual violence.

Enforcement is complex and entails more than well intended drafting of express legal provisions into a statute or convention. Edicts banning wartime sexual assaults were inserted into ancient warrior codes. International conventions, such as the 1929 Geneva Convention prohibited infliction of sexual assaults upon female and male prisoners of war. In the immediate aftermath of the World War II, martial law decrees such as Control Council No. 10 explicitly proscribed rapes as acts of crimes against humanity. Indeed, the Nuremberg and Tokyo international military tribunals investigated, prosecuted and handed down convictions for war crimes based upon sexual violence. Still, these precedents heralded no manifest undertaking of sexual violence prosecutions as international crimes in national courts and, along with other illicit conduct endured the dearth of adjudications at the international level. Derelict attention, unapologetic impunity and ignored or misconstrued jurisprudence openly paraded the inability to enforce prohibitions of sexual violence under international law.

During the past two decades, in a welcomed realignment of intent, the international community directed concerted scrutiny at the pervasiveness of impunity for war crimes, crimes against humanity and genocide. International and internationalized judicial institutions emerged to respond to the calls for enforcement and to conduct the tripartite process of investigations, prosecution and adjudications of international crimes. Whether generated by Chapter VII of the United Nations Charter, by a United Nations agreement or by the multilateral consensus of a treaty, the responsibility of most of these judicial institutions was to redress the heretofore pithy enforcement of wartime prohibitions and acts of crimes against humanity or genocide related to specific geographical and time bound situations, with the exception of the International Criminal Court that will exercise prospective jurisdiction. Their constitutive instruments, namely the Rome Statute, the Statutes of the Yugoslav Tribunal, the Rwandan Tribunal, the Special Court for Sierra Leone and the Extraordinary Chambers in the Courts of Cambodia, each mandated the diligent pursuit of criminal conduct, including sexual violence that could be susceptible to characterization as genocide, war crimes, or crimes against humanity. Accordingly, sexual violence investigations, prosecutions and adjudications cloaked in the mantel of these internationally endorsed institutions are integral to the litmus test of enforcement.

Redress, *cum,* enforcement of sexual violence, and other gender-based conduct actionable under international crimes merit an analysis, to discern, if you will, the "*supra*-national enforcement" obligations and to detect a gendered approach to such obligations. Enforcement of sexual violence proscriptions interacts with the dual nature of the international crimes – meaning the crimes' status amid international laws and its internal doctrinal nature. War crimes, crimes against humanity and genocide, as international offences are accepted peremptory norms. They prescribe human created scourges that are recognized as *erga omnes,* of concerned to all. The judicial pursuit of peremptory norms violators gives voice to the international community's highest values. As a consequence of their peremptory norm status, genocide, crimes against humanity and war crimes bind States to fulfill procedures that are non-derogatory duties, or *obligatio erga omnes.* Every State must exercise jurisdiction to investigate, to prosecute and to adjudicate alleged perpetrators of war crimes, genocide or crimes against humanity. In the alternative, a State unable to perform its duties is bound to extradite alleged perpetrators to a State who shall perform these obligations. Acts characterized as genocide, crimes against humanity or war crimes must be pursued at all times, irrespective of the factual basis of an act, be it a massacre or rape. The non-derogatory duties activate an interdependent enforcement mechanism among States. Each State's execution of their obligations ensures redress of the harm to the international community, or otherwise stated, redress of the international crime.

Significantly, modern international and internationalized judicial institutions are recipients of a mandated "transfer" of States' peremptory norm obligations. The governing statutes of today's international judicial institutions expressly include war crimes, crimes against humanity and/or genocide. These international judicial institutions act on behalf of states and the international community through the exercise of jurisdiction under the respective governing statutes, whether jurisdiction is complimentary, concurrent or *via* primacy to national courts. As such, these judicial institutions execute similar non-derogatory duties – namely investigation, prosecution and adjudication of peremptory norm recognized crimes. The synchronized functions of the peremptory norm status and of the non-derogatory duties erect a type of "supranational-enforcement," that underpins the redress mechanism that has been transferred to international judicial institutions.

Examination of the internal doctrinal nature of crimes designated as peremptory norms surfaces and confirms the compulsory responsibility to redress sexual violence, and other gender based violence. The crime of genocide is illustrative. To thoroughly comply with the "supranational enforcement" triggered by the peremptory norm status of genocide acts committed against an ethnic, racial, national or religious group demands a gendered analysis of the group and an understanding of the genocidal conduct perpetrated upon group members, such as sexual violence. The legal rationale of the Genocide Convention forthrightly encompassed gender-based violence. Article 2(b) recalls the egregious Nazi torture regime replete with the sexual and reproductive experiments conducted upon males and females, while the Article 2(d) outlaws the imposing of measures to prevent births, as a direct consequence of the Nuremberg laws that controlled the sexual reproduction of non-Aryans. Factually, the Rwandan genocide was comprised of killings and rapes, and the alleged genocide in Darfur is replete with a mixture of sexual violence, massacres and debilitating conditions. Thus, historically, the internal doctrinal nature of the genocide, legally and factually contemplated sexualized violence within the context of genocide.

Possibly, future manifestations of genocide might entail rapes against females and male genital mutilations intertwined with acts of direct, public incitement in the form of sexual propaganda against the group. Such acts might be judged to be inextricable from the massacres of both sexes. Each act that potentially qualifies as a manifestation of genocide, compels the non-derogatory duties to ensure its prevention, suppression or its punishment by investigation, prosecution and adjudication. Moreover, activation of the non-derogatory duties to investigate, prosecute and adjudicate genocide do not countenance restrictions based upon gender identity or age. The only qualification for protection is that survivors and victims of the inflicted acts of genocide are members of the targeted group.

Females are not *per se* a separate protected genocide group, however, neither, are males. Genocides that solely target gender identity are not recognized under international law. Notwithstanding, comprehension of the gender composition of a targeted group and acute analysis of the gender-based violence contained in the genocide is necessary to inform and drive the non-derogatory obligations that are executed by way of investigations, prosecution and adjudication.

Crimes against humanity, also compels an invocation of the attendant transfer of "*supra*-enforcement" at the aforementioned international judicial institutions. Internally, crimes against humanity has readily lent itself to prosecutions of sexual violence. The accepted jurisprudence of the Yugoslav and Rwandan Tribunals, the Special Court for Sierra Leone and Extraordinary Chambers in the Courts of Cambodia consistently, have ruled that females as well as males are potential victim/survivors of any of the provisions of crimes against humanity. The criminal conduct is often inflicted in an obviously gendered manner. For example, the males and females were routinely imprisoned and deported separately in the former Yugoslavia. Girl soldiers captured by rebel groups in Sierra Leone, unlike the boy soldiers, were invariably raped and frequently assigned to men as their slaves within the pretext of "marriage". Unhesitant findings of fact within the crimes against humanity prosecutions have held rapes to satisfy both underlying acts as well as evidence of an attack against the civilian population. Keen judicial observations has also ruled that sexual violence could fulfill the factual basis of other, non-sexually explicit provisions of crimes against humanity, such as enslavement, torture, inhumane acts and persecution. The Rome Statute of the International Criminal Court expanded the sexually explicit provisions of the crimes against humanity and included gender in the basis of persecution – a positive development for broadening enforcement. Jurisprudence on these, and other non-sexually explicit provisions is eagerly awaited.

The rationale for crimes against humanity, to protect the civilian population from attacks, again demands a gendered analysis of civilians as the targeted group. Statistically females constitute a majority of the population, and logically, comprise the majority of the civilian or non-militarized population destined to be shielded from crimes against humanity. Non-militarized males, including boys are also within the protected group. Enforcement proscriptions of crimes against humanity, thus, must be vigilant about the manner by which females and males are attacked as civilians. Enforcement measures must be cognate of the breadth of incidents and their toll on victim/survivors according to gender. If an attack against the civilian population is examined by its systematic nature, policies that impact female civilians could reveal the gendered contours of the attack. Absence of a gender analysis of the civilian population and of the design of the attack risks dilution of the outcome of investigation and the factual findings and legal conclusions in the judicial examination.

War crimes, in particular, the grave breaches of the Geneva Conventions trigger "*supra*-enforcement" for all States. International judicial institutions in receipt of the mandated transfer of the non-derogatory duties have rendered substantial jurisprudence on prohibitions concerning war crimes perpetrated in international and non-international armed conflict. While the peremptory norm status of humanitarian law aims at ensuring enforcement of the prohibitions, the internal, pre-breach functioning of humanitarian law demands special protection for women, children, the aged, those most vulnerable, *and* assurances of non-adverse distinction to secure humane treatment of the group. Prohibited conduct that might be characterized as war crimes, is not circumscribed by the sexual nature of the act. To the contrary jurisprudence confirms several, non-sexually explicit war crimes, such as torture, to be satisfied by sexually violent conduct that, readily traverses precepts of humane treatment. Likewise, gender-based violence would seemingly contravene the safeguard erected by disallowance of any adverse distinction that would impede humane treatment.

Among humanitarian law's overriding objective is protection of certain groups – civilians, prisoners of war, the wounded on land, the shipwrecked and persons *hors de combat* from exposure to inhumane treatment. Similar to the gender analysis of genocidal groups or the civilian population within crimes against humanity, females, undoubtedly, can comprise part of each protected groups. Protection from war crimes is determined solely by membership in the protected groups. Protection is comprehensive and exist irrespective of the gender, age, ethnicity or any other qualification of the protected person, as long as membership in the group is established. Similar to genocide and crimes against humanity, enforcement of war crimes compels investigation, prosecution and adjudication of alleged war crimes.

An overdue coming of age of sexual violence prosecution is materializing at the international judicial institutions. To be sustained and strengthened, compliance with non-derogatory obligations must be buttressed by the judicial institutions' consistent resort to apt methodologies of enforcement. To paraphrase from the human rights cannon, enforcement is reliant upon inter-dependent and indivisible pursuit of investigation, prosecutions and the adjudication of sexual violence. The authors in the present volume offer such adept methodologies regarding approaches to the investigation of sexual violence. Prosecutions are dependent upon rigorous investigation.

The chapters demonstrate how criminal investigators when partnered with forensic and social scientists, or other professionals are primed to develop pointed techniques that distill patterns of gender-based acts against males and females and that discard distracting stereotypes that serve only to abet the propagation of impunity. Social science studies can expose the synchronicity of events, such as hate speech, genocidal propaganda or other contemporaneous inhumane acts, with the occurrence of sexual violence, whether in displacement camps or in villages. Refinement of analytical tools is crucial to identifying the segments of group afflicted sexually and to revealing the myriad forms of sexual violence used by perpetrators. Furthermore, the development of productive relations with civil society groups and members who provide expertise, to indicate witness leads or to furnish other essential services can be paramount to securing sexual violence testimony. These intricate collaborative efforts increase an investigation's potential outcome while heightening the competence of investigators to uncover, inspect, collect, process and safeguard evidence of sexual violence. Such alliances assist investigators and other court personnel in their dealings with survivors and in the preservation of their own personal and profession persona.

Adjudications, in turn, depend upon skillful prosecutions, vigorous defenses and, more recently at the International Criminal Court, the conscientious representation of victims. Prosecutors, defense attorneys and victims' representatives need to submit relevant and pertinent evidence and to advancement persuasive legal arguments at proceedings concerning sexual violence. Judges need to ensure unfailingly fair trials and appeals. Several authors' contribution in the present volume acknowledge the challenges of litigating sexual violence at international judicial institutions. There are many instances of *de novo* legal situations wherein judges must craft decisions that resonate with customary law, emerging doctrine and the spirit of redress. Interpretation of substantive provisions of international crimes that are peremptory norms and their accompanying requirements of proof, such as the individual liability, especially of political and military leaders, as well as defenses and procedural issues is a solemn responsibility. The bench needs to deliver well-reasoned decisions that soberly examine the facts and the law that substantiate ultimate acquittals or conviction of alleged perpetrators of sexual violence. The judicial pronouncement and the release or imprisonment of the accused is the *sina qua non* of *supra*-national enforcement and completes the institution's non-derogatory duties to enforce the peremptory norm based international crimes.

The task to fortify enforcement of international crimes, and in particularly sexual violence prosecutions, is being honed at today's international and internationalized judicial institutions. These institutions have earnestly commenced a retreat from impunity and the march toward redress. Nonetheless, this goal must be shouldered broadly by State and members of the international community. This book – *Sexual Violence as an International Crime: Interdisciplinary Approaches* – represents a determined step.

CONTENTS

THE INTERNATIONAL TRIBUNALS AND COURTS

PART 2
SOCIAL, ARCHIVAL AND MEDICAL DATA COLLECTION AND ITS USE FOR THE CRIMINAL LAW PROCESS: METHODOLOGY ISSUES

ABBREVIATIONS

ADS	Atrocities Documentation Survey
BIH	Bosnian War Crimes Court
BWCC	Bosnian War Crimes Chamber
CAR	Central African Republic
CDR	Coalition for the Defence of the Republic
CIOMS	Council for International Organizations of Medical Sciences
CPK	Communist Party
DRC	Democratic Republic of Congo
ECCC	Extraordinary Chambers in the Courts of Cambodia
EMD	El Mujahed Detachment
ETO	École Technique Officielle (Official Technical School)
FARDC	Forces Armées de la République Démocratique du Congo
FDLR	Forces démocratiques de libération du Rwanda
FNI	Front des Nationalistes et Intégrationnistes
FPLC	Forces Patriotiques pour la libération du Congo
FRPI	Force de Résistance Patriotique en Ituri
FRY	Federal Republic of Yugoslavia
FWCW	Fourth World Conference on Women
GBV	Gender-Based Violence
GBVIMS	GBV Information Management System
GCU	Gender and Children Unit
GoS	Government of Sudan
HLM	Hierarchical Linear Modeling
ICC	International Criminal Court
ICPD	International Conference on Population and Development
ICRC	International Committee of the Red Cross
ICTR	International Criminal Tribunal for Rwanda
ICTY	International Criminal Tribunal for the former Yugoslavia
IDP	Internally Displaced Person
IHT	Iraq High Tribunal
IMT	International Military Tribunal
IMTFE	International Military Tribunal for the Far East
INTERVICT	International Victimology Institute Tilburg
IRB	Institutional Review Board
IWHRC	International Women's Human Rights Law Clinic

JCE	Joint Criminal Enterprise
KR	Khmer Rouge
LRA	Lord's Resistance Army
MLC	Mouvement de Liberation du Congo (Movement for the Liberation of Congo)
NGO	Non-Governmental Organization
OHCHR	Office of the High Commissioner for Human Rights
OSCE	Organization for Security and Cooperation
OTP	Office of The Prosecutor
PTSD	Post Traumatic Stress Disorder
RAF	Rwandan Armed Forces
RMA	Rape-Myth Acceptance
RPF	Rwandan Patriotic Front
RTLM	Radio Télévision Libre des Mille Collines
RUF	Revolutionary United Front
SCSL	Special Court for Sierra Leone
SGBV	Sexual Gender Based Violence
UDHR	Universal Declaration of Human Rights
UN	United Nations
UNFPA	United Nations Population Fund
UNHCR	United Nations High Commissioner for Refugees
UPC	Union des Patriotes Congolais
UPDF	Ugandan People's Defence Force
VRS	Bosnian Serb Army
VWU	Victim and Witnesses Units
WCC	World Criminal Court
WESU	Witness and Expert Support Unit
WWII	World War II

INTRODUCTION

CHAPTER 1

INTERDISCIPLINARY APPROACHES TO RECOGNIZING, INVESTIGATING AND PROSECUTING SEXUAL VIOLENCE AS AN INTERNATIONAL CRIME

Anne-Marie DE BROUWER, Charlotte KU, Renée RÖMKENS
and Larissa VAN DEN HERIK

The 1990s proved a turning point for international law and international institutions. In Europe the dissolution of the Soviet Union brought on the one hand hope that freedom and democracy would be restored in many countries, but also led to the destabilization of countries in Central Europe with unexpectedly bloody consequences. On a more global level, the aftermath of decolonization, in conjunction with shifting power balances after the end of the Cold War, ushered in unprecedented episodes of mass killing and brutality. It seemed to take the international community by surprise. The killing of an estimated 800,000 citizens in Rwanda in 1994 and the killing of an estimated 150,000 to 200,000 during the Yugoslav conflict are but two examples of the tremendous human toll taken by these post-Cold War conflicts. Embedded in these numbers are the many untold acts of sexual violence, predominantly against women and children, yet increasingly sexual violence against men is coming to the foreground. Despite the surge of international and non-international armed conflicts reflecting severe breakdowns of the rule of law, the 1990s will also be remembered as a decade which marks important and innovative steps towards advancing international justice through the development of new codes of law and legal institutions to uphold them.

Although crimes of sexual violence and efforts to punish them can be traced to ancient times, a focused international effort to end impunity for sexual violence and gender-based crime has been much longer in coming. Since the 1970s concerted efforts of the international women's movement to end the silencing and to politicize the problem of violence against women, eventually led to the recognition that sexual violence and rape are systematically used as weapons of war.[1] This historical shift in perspective on violence against women translated into international legal recognition of the discriminatory nature of violence against women and as a violation of the fundamental human rights of women. Since the early 1990s this is firmly established in binding international human rights law.[2]

It should furthermore be noted that the occurrence and severity of sexual violence in times of war and conflict cannot be isolated from wider cultural and social dynamics which to a large extent condone sexual violence against women as an unfortunate yet inevitable part of social life, particularly when the victim and perpetrators are intimate partners. The widespread reality of sexual abuse and violence in so-called peace time reflects, *inter alia*, how deeply rooted the sense of entitlement to women's bodies and their sexuality still is in many societies. The net result is the cultural normalization of rape and the silencing of victims. There are the conditions created during peacetime which facilitate rape in times of conflict, when impunity for perpetrators was historically guaranteed.

The abovementioned developments in recognising and addressing sexual violence are noteworthy in their own right, but besides this, the area of prosecution of sexual violence and gender-based crime specifically represent landmark developments in international criminal law. These are notably reflected in the 1998 Rome Statute establishing the International Criminal Court (ICC). The Rome Statute not only criminalizes a wide range of sexual violence and gender crimes, it also includes considerations for the well-being of victims and witnesses as well as provisions for varying forms of assistance and reparations. This pushes international criminal law beyond the prosecution of specific actions to that of providing forms of redress to victims of sexual violence and to their communities. This work is assisted by networks of non-governmental organizations and field workers trained in a variety of specialties from investigation to counseling. The development of this area of international criminal law has also created the need for considering different tools to establish the existence of mass brutality. The pioneering work of scholars and practitioners to develop credible means of collecting and interpreting data to present as

---

1 E.g. Susan Brownmiller, *Against Our Will: Men, Women and Rape* (New York: Fawcett Books, 1975); and Joanna Bourke, *Rape: Sex, Violence, History* (Berkley, Cal.: Counterpoint, 2007).

2 In 1979 when the UN Convention on the Elimination of All Forms of Discrimination Against Women (CEDAW) was adopted, it was politically still too contested to explicitly include violence against women in the treaty. This was amended in 1992 via the UN General Recommendation no. 19 of the CEDAW Committee, recognizing violence against women as a form of discrimination. The Inter-American Convention on the Prevention, Punishment and Eradication of Violence Against Women (1994), and the Protocol to the African Charter on Human and People's Rights on the Rights of Women in Africa (2003) provide dedicated international human rights instruments addressing violence against women as a violation of human rights. The most noteworthy recent development is the Council of Europe Convention on Preventing and Combating Violence against Women and Domestic Violence (effective as of September 2011).

evidence to support suspicions of international crime have helped to thwart impunity for committing mass crimes. In prosecuting sexual violence at the international level, the international criminal justice system therefore now draws from experts from a range of professions outside the law who work with victims or who can analyze large bodies of data which can serve as reliable and valid empirical evidence that can be presented in the court room.

In April 2011, Elisabeth Rehn, Chair of the Board of Directors of the Trust Fund for Victims of the International Criminal Court, noted that "12 of the 17 accused before the International Criminal Court are charged with crimes of sexual violence including rape both as a war crime and a crime against humanity."[3] A further important advance noted by Rehn is the growing recognition of the importance of women and girls "in establishing durable peace and security and lasting institutions."[4]

The recognition, investigation and prosecution of crimes of sexual violence by international courts have significantly increased in the past three decades. This is mainly because of the work of the International Criminal Tribunal for the Former Yugoslavia (ICTY, set up in 1993) and the International Criminal Tribunal for Rwanda (ICTR, set up in 1994), the first international criminal tribunals that recognized rape explicitly as a crime against humanity,[5] and the Special Court for Sierra Leone (SCSL, set up in 2000), which included several different forms of sexual violence in its Statute (e.g. rape, sexual slavery, enforced prostitution, forced pregnancy and any other form of sexual violence as a crime against humanity).

With regard to substantive international criminal law, arguably the most notable jurisprudential achievements the ICTY and the ICTR made are to acknowledge that rape and sexual violence can amount to genocide and that the definition of rape does not need to include lack of consent as an element of the crime.[6] The recognition that consent is virtually meaningless in a context of structural force and subjugation, would reflect an important achievement from a gender and victim's perspective. It reflects a recognition that the traditional burden of proof of the lack of consent is putting an unjustifiable burden on the victim/witness, notably in the context of conflict situations where conditions of force and threat preclude any freedom to consent.[7] In addition to these two

3 Elisabeth Rehn, Keynote Address, *Conference of Systemic Sexual Violence and Victims' Rights* (The Hague, the Netherlands, 2011), available at http://lexglobal.org/files/Press%20Release%20Elisabeth%20Rehn%20final.pdf.

4 *Ibid.*

5 The ICTR also recognized rape and enforced prostitution as the war crime of 'outrages upon personal dignity'.

6 E.g. Kelly Dawn Askin, "Gender Crimes Jurisprudence in the ICTR: Positive Developments," *Journal of International Criminal Justice* 3, no. 4 (2005): 1007; and Erik Møse, "Main Achievements of the ICTR", *Journal of International Criminal Justice* 3, no. 4 (2005): 920.

7 There seems to be no consensus on this definition yet as ICTY and ICTR Chambers have come up with different definitions of the crime, sometimes including lack of consent as an

jurisprudential advances, rape and sexual violence have been successfully prosecuted as war crimes and crimes against humanity, such as rape, torture, enslavement and persecution.[8] The Tribunals have also noted that other gender-related crimes, such as forced marriage, forced nudity, forced pregnancy, sexual mutilation, and forced abortion, may constitute an international crime, and that men and boys are also subjected to various forms of sexual violence. In fact, the SCSL has successfully prosecuted not only rape and sexual slavery, but also "forced marriage," as the crime against humanity of an "other inhumane act". Further, in 2011, the Extraordinary Chambers in the Courts of Cambodia (ECCC) convicted "Duch," the head of a notorious Khmer Rouge torture facility, of a number of crimes, including rape subsumed under torture as a crime against humanity. Furthermore, it is by now established that gender crimes may form part of a joint criminal enterprise (JCE), and that perpetrators and others participating in the JCE may be held responsible for not only intended, but also for persecutorial or foreseeable crimes committed in furtherance of the JCE. These are all major steps forward in the development of sexual violence and its different forms as self-standing crimes in international criminal law for which individuals can be held accountable under different liability modes.

With regard to international criminal procedural law, of particular importance to victims/survivors of sexual violence are several evidentiary rules of the Rome Statute of the ICC, in particular the rules specifying that, as for any testimony, the testimony of a victim/survivor of sexual violence does not need to be corroborated, that consent cannot be inferred from words or conduct undermined by coercive circumstances, and that evidence on prior or later sexual conduct is not admitted (Rules 63(4), 70–72 Rules of Procedure and Evidence (RPE)). While these rules are essentially concerned with the presentation of evidence, they also offer certain protective measures to victims/survivors of sexual violence when testifying. These rules, for the first time laid

element. Pursuant to the non-binding Elements of Crimes of the ICC, however, lack of consent is, in principle, not an element of the crime. *See e.g.* Patricia Viseur-Sellers, "The 'Appeal' of Sexual Violence: Akayesu/Gacumbitsi Cases", in *Gender-Based Violence in Africa*, ed. Karen Stefisyn (Pretoria, South Africa: University of Pretoria, 2007), 51–103.

8 Note that in the 2011 Council of Europe Convention on Preventing and Combating Violence against Women and Domestic Violence (2011) (Art. 60, addressing gender-based asylum claims) it is recognized "[T]hat gender-based violence against women may be recognised as a form of persecution within the meaning of Article 1, A (2) of the 1951 Convention relating to the Status of Refugees." This makes it the first dedicated international human rights instrument in the field of violence against women that acknowledges that gender based violence can amount to persecution as a basis for asylum. This touches on the ongoing discussion whether and under which conditions gender based violence can amount to torture as defined in Art. 3 of the 1951 Convention Against Torture; see *e.g.* Rhonda Copelon, "Intimate Terror: Understanding Domestic Violence as Torture", in *Human Rights of Women: National and International Perspectives*, ed. Rebecca J. Cook (Philadelphia, Penn.: University of Pennsylvania Press, 1994); and Amnesty International, *Broken Bodies, Shattered Minds: Torture and Ill-Treatment of Women* (London: Amnesty International, 2001).

down in the international criminal procedural rules of the ICTY and the ICTR (for both Tribunals in Rule 96 RPE), are a major achievement, particularly when compared with a number of national jurisdictions which, *inter alia*, use definitions of rape which allow defense counsel to introduce suggested consent of the victim as a defense strategy, even in the context of force. This discriminates against victims of sexual violence by allowing their credibility to be challenged, thus impeding them from participating in the legal process.[9] It also fails to take into account the fundamentally different circumstances when acts of sexual violence are committed under conditions of mass violence and when they occur in an otherwise stable and peaceful society.

The ICC is mandated to investigate and prosecute a wide range of sexual violence crimes. In addition to rape, sexual slavery, enforced prostitution, forced pregnancy, enforced sterilization and any other form of sexual violence are defined as crimes against humanity and war crimes (Articles 7 and 8 Rome Statute). In addition, gender based persecution as well as trafficking in women and children may be prosecuted under the Rome Statute as crimes against humanity. The Elements of Crimes furthermore recognize that rape and other forms of sexual violence can amount to the crime of genocide (Article 6(b), element 1, footnote 3 Elements of Crimes). As mentioned, the Rules of Procedure and Evidence of the ICC contain progressive procedural provisions for victims of sexual violence and also include provisions requiring geographical and gender balance among the staff of the Court, and expertise in sexual violence. For example, the Office of the Prosecutor of the ICC, *inter alia*, appointed a Special Gender Advisor, established the Gender and Children Unit, and provides training on the legal framework and methods of conducting interviews on sexual violence crimes. The available legal instruments and measures taken to enhance their implementation indicate that the ICC aims to carefully address sexual violence committed in conflict situations.

The successful prosecutions in the late 1990s of rape as a war crime, crime against humanity, and genocide by the ICTY and ICTR opened a new phase of development in this area of international criminal law. Although these and other tribunals have been applauded for several breakthroughs in international criminal law and procedure, they have also been criticized for their inadequate and incoherent investigation and prosecution policies, related to failing to include charges of sexual violence in the indictments against the accused,

9 Gerd Bohner, Friederike Eyssel, Afroditi Pina, Frank Siebler and G. Tendayi Viki, "Rape Myth Acceptance: Cognitive, Affective and Behavioural Effects of Beliefs That Blame the Victim and Exonerate the Perpetrator," in *Rape: Challenging Contemporary Thinking*, eds. Miranda Horvath and Jennifer M. Brown (Cullompton, Devon UK: Willan Publishing, 2009), 17–45; Barbara Krahé and Jennifer Temkin, "Addressing the Attitude Problem in Rape Trials: Some Proposals and Methodological Considerations," in *Rape: Challenging Contemporary Thinking*, eds. Miranda Horvath and Jennifer M. Brown (Cullompton, Devon UK: Willan Publishing, 2009), 301–324.

charges of sexual violence being dropped over the course of proceedings, and charges not being representative of the sexual violence committed.[10]

Following two decades of experience prosecuting crimes of sexual violence, it seemed timely to produce a volume not only to review the steps that have brought us to this point, but also to assess the work that has been done with a view to understanding the next steps that need to be taken. We have been fortunate to be able to convene two international colloquia that brought together scholars and practitioners – many who have played and continue to play key roles in the development of an international response to crimes of sexual and gender-based violence.

In 2009 and 2011, the Center on Law and Globalization (a partnership of the University of Illinois College of Law and the American Bar Foundation) in cooperation with The Grotius Centre for International Legal Studies, Campus The Hague (Leiden University) and the Department of Criminal Law and the International Victimology Institute Tilburg (INTERVICT) (Tilburg Law School, Tilburg University) organized two days of international colloquia on "Sexual Violence as an International Crime: Interdisciplinary Approaches (16–18 June 2009)" and "Systematic Sexual Violence and Victims' Rights (7–8 April 2011)" in The Hague, the Netherlands. The two colloquia brought together and worked to facilitate the development of a global network of activists, lawyers, journalists, (international) court and government officials, nonprofit leaders, and scholars who seek to combat and remedy the systematic sexual victimization of women and men and improve human rights and the rule of law in international settings. This book contains the results of the colloquia, in particular the first colloquium, in three clusters, which reflect the conference themes.

Although this edited volume acknowledges milestones reached, it will in particular expose the challenges in the investigation and prosecution of sexual violence still ahead. The prosecution of those cases raises new questions as to how to build evidence, but also how to address victims' concerns in that process. The chapters in this book will address innovations and questions of empirical and other new kinds of social scientific, archival and medical data collection

10 Marie-Bénédicte Dembour and Emily Haslam, "Silencing Hearings? Victim-Witnesses at War Crimes Trials," *European Journal of International Law* 15, no. 1 (2004): 151; Binaifer Nowrojee, *"Your Justice is Too Slow": Will the ICTR Fail Rwanda's Rape Victims?*, United Nations Research Institute for Social Development, Occasional Paper 10 (November 2005); Amanda Beltz, "Prosecuting Rape in International Criminal Tribunals: The Need to Balance Victim's Rights with the Due Process Rights of the Accused," *Saint John's Journal of Legal Commentary* 23, no. 1 (2008): 167; Doris E. Buss, "Rethinking 'Rape as a Weapon of War,'" *Feminist Legal Studies*, 17 (2009): 145; Chiseche Mibenge, *Show Me a Woman! Narratives of Gender and Violence in Human Rights Law and Processes of Transitional Justice* (Philadelphia, Penn.: University of Pennsylvania Press, 2011, forthcoming); Hilmi Mohammad Zawati, *Symbolic Judgements or Judging Symbols: Fair Labelling and the Dilemma of Prosecuting Gender-Based Crimes under the Statutes of the International Criminal Tribunals* (Philadelphia, Penn.: University of Pennsylvania Press, 2011, forthcoming).

techniques; the development of evidence in relation to charges ranging from sexual violence as a war crime, crime against humanity to genocide; and how we can raise awareness of these crimes.

In keeping with the approach of the colloquia, the book is interdisciplinary in character. It brings together contributions from lawyers, social scientists, medical personnel, psychologists, journalists and activists. The contributors are academics as well as practitioners working at international criminal courts and tribunals, NGOs or in domestic settings. The book seeks to document practices that non-lawyers and lawyers must confront when intervening in conflict situations that may result in legal action, non-legal or awareness-creating action.

The book is a unique collection as it includes contributions from a diverse community of professionals actively engaged with the issue of sexual violence particularly in times of conflict. This volume gives voice to the various concerns in this diverse community. In addition, we hope that it will help in understanding how these disparate elements can advance the normative agenda. From the legal perspective, the work against sexual violence may provide an important example of the wide-ranging community of interest required to support effective development of and compliance with international norms.

The first part deals with the milestones in international criminal law pertaining to the prosecution of sexual violence and with the challenges it still brings about. Before looking at major recent developments in international criminal law and procedure, one should not overlook the developments in criminalizing and prosecuting sexual violence prior to the 1990s. Although these developments were not always far-reaching or the prohibitions on sexual violence non-existent or vaguely worded, they did lay the groundwork for recognition of these crimes in the 1990s. In this volume, Askin, elaborates on these developments up to WWII, while also looking already to the challenges ahead.

The more recent milestones, yet challenges at the same time, highlighted in this part concern two recognitions of sexual violence crimes long overlooked: persecution based on gender as well as sexual violence committed against men. As for the ICC's recognition of the crime of gender-based persecution in its Statute, in her chapter, Oosterveld explores three potential areas of difficulty that the ICC will need to address in order to ensure a fulsome consideration of gender-based persecution, namely (1) how to interpret the Rome Statute's definition of the term 'gender' in relation to persecution; (2) how to approach the intersection of other forms of persecution with gender-based persecution, and (3) how to consider existing ICC case law on "cumulative" charging such that persecution is not incorrectly excluded from consideration by a Pre-Trial Chamber.

Another challenge – one could say a milestone in *statu nascendi* – pointed out by Sivakumaran in this volume, is the slow recognition of sexual violence perpetrated in conflict situations against men and boys. Sivakumaran argues that sexual violence against men and boys continues to be overlooked, downplayed, or re-characterized. He explains that sometimes this is a deliberate decision, taken so as to focus on sexual violence against women and girls, and that at other times, it is a by-product of the relative lack of knowledge of male sexual violence. Although considerable progress has been made, much remains to be done in order to have these crimes investigated, properly charged and prosecuted. His chapter clearly informs us that sexual violence can be committed by anyone (male and female) against anyone (female and male) and that we shouldn't shy away from these realities.[11]

The other milestones and challenges addressed in this part concern those reached and faced within the different international courts, namely the ICTY, ICTR, ICC, SCSL and ECCC. These chapters demonstrate a familiar paradox in legal developments: the many achievements already accomplished imply many challenges lying ahead.

According to Jarvis and Martin Salgado, who write about the ICTY, the biggest challenge for prosecuting sexual violence in the future is to prosecute senior officials (the "big fish"), who are far away from the crime scene. Before the ICTY, to date, most cases of sexual violence concern the more straight forward cases involving direct perpetrators of sexual violence crimes, or others close to the scene of the crime. They discuss how high-level political and military figures can be held responsible based on the theories of superior responsibility and the joint criminal enterprise, arguing that sexual violence cases should not be treated differently from other types of cases.

Bianchi, in her chapter on the ICTR, argues that despite the low number of ICTR convictions for sexual violence, the record thereof is not that bad when taking into account the totality of the record of cases tried at the ICTR. She discusses how the ICTR, having faced several challenges in the investigation and prosecution of sexual violence crimes, being a pioneer in the field, established a Committee for the Review of the Investigation and Prosecution of Sexual Violence in 2007. Based on their work they came up with recommendations to improve the investigation and prosecution of sexual violence, which she elaborates upon.

In his chapter on the ICC, Ocampo elaborates on the innovative aspects of the Rome Statute in including gender based violence as an integrated element to address, and the strategy which the Office of the Prosecutor has taken in the investigation and prosecution of sexual violence crimes. While illustrating this with pending cases, he discusses the institutional framework and underlines the

---

11 See also Lynn Lawry, Kristen Johnson, and Jana Asher, "Evidence-based Documentation of Gender-based Violence," in *Sexual Violence as an International Crime: Interdisciplinary Approaches*, eds. Anne-Marie de Brouwer, Charlotte Ku, Renée Römkens and Larissa van den Herik (Antwerp, Belgium: Intersentia), *infra*.

Prosecutor Office's determination to effectively investigate and prosecute sexual and gender-based crimes by taking a focused and integrated approach.

Doherty describes in her chapter the developments that took place before the SCSL as regards the prosecution of sexual violence, more particularly the forced marriage of women and girls in Sierra Leone during the civil war in that country. She mentions that before the AFRC and RUF cases, forced marriage had not been considered by any other international tribunal. Forced marriage was recognised in these cases as the crime against humanity of an "other inhumane act", although not without a (legal) fight.

In her chapter on the ECCC, Studzinsky discusses the unique role provided to victims as parties to the proceedings before the ECCC, but points to the (initial) decisions made by the prosecutor by not including sexual violence crimes at all. She voices concerns about inadequate and incoherent investigation, and argues that these reflect mistakes which are not easily remedied later on in the process. One major milestone that Studzinsky discusses is the inclusion of forced marriages in the 2010 indictment of case 002, which, she states, got included because of successful civil party participation.

The second part looks at the social, legal and medical data collection and its use for the criminal law process. It touches upon the topic of new methodological issues related to collection and use of data on sexual violence in conflict and how interdisciplinary partnerships may reduce impunity, strengthen law, and alleviate suffering for victims of sexual violence.[12] Maybe one day, some have argued, it may even be possible to bring cases before the ICC without physical evidence and without victims in the court.[13]

Part II opens with the chapter of Reis, discussing methods of research for sexual violence crimes, and draws our attention to ethical issues related to data collection, sharing and use, and discusses the development of recommendations to inform those who are collecting, using or supporting the collection of data on how to address these.

Marcus points to the reluctance that sometimes can be seen with investigators and prosecutors to investigating sexual violence crimes, even though these crimes have no greater evidentiary burden than any other non-sexual violence crimes. She discusses some of the strategies that can be used in order to have these crimes charged and prosecuted.

In their chapter, Lawry, Johnson and Asher discuss how a health and human rights framework allows for meaningful documentation of sexual violence crimes and their consequences. The essential and complementary roles that qualitative and quantitative data play in providing evidence of sexual violence

---

12 See also Terence C. Halliday, "Introduction: Symposium on Systematic Sexual Violence and International Criminal Law," *Law & Social Inquiry* 35, no. 4 (2010): 835.

13 See Luis Moreno-Ocampo, "Keynote Address – Interdisciplinary Colloquium on Sexual Violence as International Crime: Interdisciplinary Approaches to Evidence," *Law & Social Inquiry* 35, no. 4 (2010): 839.

crimes are outlined and the best methods for quantitative data collection on sexual violence are discussed in more detail. They argue that employing these methods provide a means to generate statistically significant data that can be generalized to the population as a whole for the purposes of evidence collection in the case of international crimes, such as before the ICC.

Hagan, Brooks and Haugh subsequently demonstrate how the innovative use of social science evidence has developed to meet the "reasonable grounds" standard of the Rome Statute. Use of techniques like hierarchical linear modelling can help to make both horizontal and vertical connections between the perpetrators of crime and those at a higher level in a chain of command. It can also provide evidence of actions and behaviour that may be precursors to genocide or mass brutality. Horizontal linear modelling can further document the targeting both of individuals, groups, and clusters of villages to establish the intent to destroy a group in whole or in part, i.e. to commit genocide. The challenge of using this kind of evidence is the ability of judges and other court officials to adequately interpret the information generated through these highly specialized statistical analyses and techniques.

The third part examines how we can create awareness about sexual violence as an instrument of warfare and how to alleviate shame and stigma and silencing surrounding sexual violence crimes, and how to achieve change on multiple levels.

Inder echoes some of the concerns with the way investigation and prosecution of sexual crimes have developed and discusses what NGOs can do in contributing to the pursuit of truth and address the wider experiences of victims when testifying before international criminal tribunals. She elaborates on what NGOs can do to make valid contributions to the testing of evidence, establishment of the facts and in describing, with greater human voice, the form and extent of victimization and the perseverance of communities until justice is satisfied.

Irwin, working as a journalist on international criminal law and transitional justice issues, interviewed the Van Velzen sisters on how they see their role as documentarists in bringing to light the sexual violence crimes that are being committed in the DRC. The Van Velzen sisters, *inter alia*, explain that they think it is important not only to talk to the survivors, but also to the perpetrators, as change also needs to come from them. Their documentary, shown not only worldwide, but also throughout eastern DRC, aims to create awareness on the impact of sexual violence and to change people's actions.

Sharratt, having interviewed court officials at the ICTY and the Bosnian War Crimes Court (BIH), shows the importance of creating awareness by training court officials on what sexual violence entails, its consequences, the impact testifying in court can have on victims, and how court officials should consider interacting with victims coming to court. Her chapter underlines the need to overcome the legacy of stereotypical gender assumptions that many court officials may still have.

Finally, in the concluding chapter of this volume we elaborate on future prospects concerning interdisciplinary approaches to the recognition, investigation and prosecution of sexual violence as an international crime.

We hope that the colloquia which provided the feeding ground for these chapters will continue to serve as a source of inspiration for the community of activists, practitioners, scholars and survivors who are presently engaged in the ongoing development of creating awareness, investigating and prosecuting sexual violence and gender-based crimes. As technology has helped with the monitoring and investigation of these crimes, we are using technology to keep those working in this area connected via social media and the internet.[14] We hope that creating awareness among those now working in this field of where investigations are taking place or cases prosecuted will help to leverage each of these efforts by connecting people and contributing to the development of a resource for understanding the nature of these crimes and the tools used to investigate, to prosecute, to redress, and ultimately to mitigate and end these crimes.

14 See www.lexglobal.org/?q=node/15&tid=15 for materials of the first two colloquia, and to find out how to connect via Twitter, LinkedIn, Facebook, the Newsletter, etc.

PART 1

OVERVIEW OF SEVERAL MILESTONES AND CHALLENGES CONCERNING INTERNATIONAL CRIMINAL PROSECUTION OF SEXUAL VIOLENCE

A HISTORICAL PERSPECTIVE, THE WAY FORWARD AND MILESTONES LONG OVERLOOKED

CHAPTER 2

TREATMENT OF SEXUAL VIOLENCE IN ARMED CONFLICTS: A HISTORICAL PERSPECTIVE AND THE WAY FORWARD

Kelly Askin

1. SUMMARY

War and atrocities are intricately interlinked. Armed conflict has occurred since the existence of humankind and with it, sexual violence is rampant, committed both opportunistically and strategically. With war comes misery and destruction paralleled only perhaps by the worst natural disasters unleashed by the power of nature. Weaponry and technology have become far more sophisticated in the past century and are used in many, but by no means all, of the contemporary wars. Violence, including against civilian women and girls, not only continues, it has increased as civilians have become the primary targets of armed conflict.

Traditionally, women were regarded as legitimate spoils of war or rape as an inevitable by-product of war. Although opportunistic rape continues during the atmosphere of violence, chaos, hatred, retaliation, and the breakdown of the rule of law common in armed conflict, various forms of sexual violence are also used as strategic weapons of warfare, committed as part of a calculated strategy to terrorize, demoralize, and destroy victims, families, and communities or associated groups.

After centuries of wars within nations and between nations, it took the monstrous atrocities committed in the 1940s during World War II for the international community to finally create two international war crimes tribunals to try those most responsible for serious crimes committed during the war. Hence, when the Second World War ended, the Allied victors established the International Military Tribunal (IMT) in Nuremberg, Germany to try vanquished

Nazi leaders,[1] and the International Military Tribunal for the Far East (IMTFE) in Tokyo, Japan to prosecute senior Japanese officials.[2] Some crimes of sexual violence were explicitly or implicitly prosecuted in these trials, although the primary focus was on prosecuting crimes against peace, considered the supreme crime.

Despite the historical significance of and legal precedent set by these groundbreaking efforts to establish individual accountability for massive crimes, impunity reigned for gender and non-gender crimes for nearly five decades afterwards in armed conflicts scattered throughout the world.

In 1993 and 1994 – nearly half a century after the Nuremberg and Tokyo trials – the United Nations Security Council created two *ad hoc* international war crimes tribunals to punish individuals responsible for serious violations of humanitarian law committed in the territory of the former Yugoslavia[3] and for genocide in Rwanda.[4] These two tribunals together created a new global paradigm shift which gained momentum for ending impunity for mass atrocity. These efforts culminated in the creation of a permanent International Criminal Court (ICC), as well as other internationalized war crimes tribunals or special chambers to prosecute atrocities committed in Sierra Leone, East Timor, Cambodia, Bosnia, and Kosovo. While none of these courts have prioritized prosecuting gender crimes in a meaningful way, they have nonetheless collectively recognized that sex crimes are amongst the most serious crimes committable, and in certain circumstances constitute genocide, crimes against humanity, war crimes, rape, torture, persecution, enslavement, sex trafficking, and other heinous crimes. Indeed, despite shortcomings inherent in international/ized trials, in less than two decades, there has been greater progress in acknowledging gender related crimes and addressing a wide range of sex crimes than in all of recorded history previously.

With concerted efforts and genuine commitments, the next two decades can make real and demonstrable progress on ending impunity for gender crimes and in providing true redress – justice, reparation, knowledge, security, and a reversing of sex crime stereotypes – for the victims.

---

1 Charter of the International Military Tribunal, Annexed to the London Agreement, 8 UNTS 279, 8 August 1945; 59 Stat. 1544, 8 AS No. 472. Reprinted in *American Journal of International Law* 39 (1945): 257 (1945) (Supp.) (IMT Charter or Nuremberg Charter).

2 "Special Proclamation by the Supreme Commander for the Allied Powers at Tokyo", 19 Janurary 1946, TIAS No. 1589, 4 Bevans 20. The Annex to the Special Proclamation contains the Charter of the International Military Tribunal for the Far East, 19 Jan. 1946, 4 Bevans 21. As *amended*, 26 April 1946, 4 Bevans 27, 18 (IMTFE Charter or Tokyo Charter). See generally *The Tokyo Judgments: The International Tribunal for the Far East,* ed. B Röling and C. Rüter (1977).

3 International Criminal Tribunal for the former Yugoslavia, Security Council Resolution 827, U.N. SCOR, 48th Sess., 3217th mtg. at 29, U.N. Doc. S/827/1993 (1993) (ICTY or Yugoslav Tribunal).

4 International Criminal Tribunal for Rwanda, Security Council Resolution 955, U.N. SCOR, 49th Sess., 3453d mtg. at 15, U.N. Doc. S/INF/50 Annex (1994) (ICTR or Rwanda Tribunal).

2. A HISTORICAL PERSPECTIVE OF SEXUAL VIOLENCE IN CONFLICT AND THE STATUS OF GENDER RELATED LAWS

As early as 500 B.C., codes of warfare existed in order to protect combatants, and to some extent noncombatants, in times of conflict.[5] For thousands of years, the laws or customs of war were not codified into an official code. Cicero (106–43 B.C.) urged soldiers to observe the rules of war, since obeying the regulations was the only thing that separated the "men" from the "brutes." He reminded his contemporaries that war was fought by humans and thus should be conducted with as little cruelty or inhumanity as possible, in order to reduce its implicit horrors.[6] It was Cicero's conclusion that wars for property or glory were "just" wars; yet if the goal was conquest or national glory alone, the war should be conducted with a "minimum of hatred."[7] If one nation wanted to invade another nation simply to conquer it for its riches or property, that was a legitimate reason to go to war.[8]

Domestically, women were considered to be under the lawful "property" or ownership of man, and could do little without his consent.[9] Thus, females had few rights, including over their own bodies or sexual integrity. Rape of a woman or girl was considered a property crime – a crime committed against whichever man "owned" her, father, husband or even son or brother.[10] During armed conflict, women fared even worse. For example, in Ancient Greece, rape was "socially acceptable behavior well within the rules of warfare" for combatants who considered the conquered women "legitimate booty, useful as wives, concubines, slave labor or battle-camp trophy."[11] 'To the victor goes the spoils' was a war cry for centuries, and women were regarded as the spoils of warfare; rights over women and girls often served as an added incentive to capture a town.[12]

---

5 M. Cherif Bassiouni, "International Criminal Law," *A Draft International Criminal Code 5* (1980) (Bassiouni, *Draft Code*).

6 Cicero, *Marcus Tullius, Cicero's Three Books of Offices, or Moral Duties* (*reprinted* in 1897), 21–25.

7 Cicero at 161, *supra* 6.

8 Every area of the globe was establishing codes of warfare. By the seventeenth century, particularly in Western civilizations, strong philosophical foundations would be established "for the limitation of war (and its conduct)." Bassiouni, *Draft Code*, *supra* 5 at 4.

9 See*Women and Property – Women as Property*, ed. Renee Hirschon (London: Croom Helm, 1984); Lewis Okun, *Woman Abuse, Facts Replacing Myths* (Albany, New York: State University of New York Press, 1986), 3–5.

10 Roy Porter, "Rape – Does it have a Historical Meaning?" in *Rape: An Historical and Social Enquiry*, eds. Sylvana Tomaselli and Roy Porter (Oxford, UK: Basil Blackwell, 1986), 217.

11 Susan Brownmiller, *Against Our Will, Men, Women and Rape* (New York: Fawcett Books, 1975), 33.

12 Peter Karsten, *Law, Soldiers, and Combat* (Westport, Connecticut: Greenwood Press, Inc., 1978), 5.

During the Middle Ages, as jurists, writers, and scholars pontificated on war, most concluded that as long as war was "just," the methods towards victory were without bounds.[13] Accordingly, if there was an acceptable reason to be involved in the armed conflict, including self-defense, the war could be waged as brutally and ruthlessly as possible. With no limitations existing as to what the warriors could do to the conquered enemy, atrocities committed against civilians were pervasive and relentless. Women and children were sexually assaulted as "part and parcel" of the war.[14] Progress was slow in affording legal protections to women in "peacetime" domestically, and the treatment of women during wartime was even slower.

As the distinction between the right to wage war, the *jus ad bellum*, and the rights and duties invoked once a war began, the *jus in bello*,[15] became more pronounced, greater restrictions on warfare were imposed. Hence, even if a nation was involved in war for a permissible reason, there became limits as to how the war could be fought. Most of the restrictions applied only to weapons and the treatment of combatants, not to the protection of women or civilians more generally.

In the fifteenth and sixteenth centuries, scholars, jurists, philosophers, and theologians examined and systemized wartime practices.[16] Whether war was considered just or unjust, whether for conquest, self-defense, God's glory, or man's revenge, in practice, women tended to be considered little more than chattel, to be used by the conquering males in any way he chose.[17]

A particularly noteworthy jurist, Alberico Gentili (1552–1608), insisted that all women, including female combatants, be spared from sexual assault in wartime. He proclaimed: "It is not lawful to do this wrong [rape], even if it is sometimes lawful to kill women… If a woman fights, why should she not allow war to be made upon her?… But there is no reason why she should suffer so signal an insult [as rape]."[18] Thus, Gentili advocated prohibiting rape in wartime, as in peacetime, and he did not limit his arguments to civilian women. He clearly intended that women who took up arms and participated in the conflict should

13 See generally Michael Walzer, *Just and Unjust Wars: A Moral Argument with Historical Illustrations* (New York: Basic Books, 1977); Sheldon M. Cohen, *Arms and Judgment: Law, Morality, and the Conduct of War in the Twentieth Century* (Boulder, Colo.: Westview Press, 1989).

14 See Brownmiller at 31–113, *supra* 11.

15 See William V. O'Brien, *The Conduct of Just and Limited War* 13–70 (Santa Barbara, California: Praeger Publishing, 1981); Theodor Meron, "Shakespeare's Henry the Fifth and the Law of War," *Am. J. Int'l L.* 87 (1992): 1, 5–12; Christopher Greenwood, "The Relationship Between jus ad bellum and jus in bello," *Rev. Int'l Stud.* 9 (1983): 221.

16 *The Law of War – A Documentary History*, ed. Leon Friedman (2 vols.), 11.

17 Maurice Hugh Keen, *The Laws of War in the Late Middle Ages* (London: Routledge & K. Paul, 1965), 192; Geoffrey Best, "Restraints on War by Land before 1945," in *Restraints on War*, ed. Howard (Oxford, UK: Oxford University Press, 1979), 26; Brownmiller, *supra* 11 at 31–51.

18 Alberico Gentili, *De Iure Belli Libri Tres* (trans. John Rolfe, Vol II, 1995) (1612), 258–59.

not be raped, even though these same women might lawfully be killed.[19] These interpretations of the law of war did not prevail in practice. One reason for this was the notion pervasive throughout military circles that all persons, including unarmed women and children, were still the enemy, with the belligerent having conquering rights over them.[20]

Lucas de Penna, a fourteenth century jurist and judge, also advocated for the protection of noncombatants, including women. He insisted that "[i]n war, the belligerents are not at liberty to act without restraint. Soldiers may not be given license to murder, rob, plunder, rape, or constrain civilians; those who do such things should be as severely punished as if the crimes had been committed in peacetime. Once the enemy has been captured and is therefore incapable of doing further harm, he [or she] should be treated humanely."[21] Pierino Belli, a sixteenth century soldier and jurist, noted that although wartime rape could be punished by death, soldiers were not deterred. His treatise on military law was one of the most comprehensive examinations of the rules of war in the 1500s.[22]

With each passing decade, the rules of war became more specific and regimented. Formal prosecution for violations of war crimes rarely took place until the late Middle Ages.[23] As noted by Professor Wells: "Before there could be crimes of war there had to be laws of war. Before there could be laws of war there had to be customs of war. Before there could be customs of war there needed to be some sense that war had limits."[24] Over the years, the laws and customs of war changed and expanded, generally increasing in universality with the passing centuries. The first record of a formal international trial for violations of the rules or customs of war consists of the following account,[25] when twenty-eight international judges tried Sir Peter Hagenbach for murder, rape, and perjury, amongst other crimes:

> In the trial of Sir Peter Hagenbach in 1474, he was accused of having instituted a reign of terror in the town of Breisach. The charge against him was that he had instituted this terror without first having declared war. Had he declared war the acts

19 *Ibid* at 251–54. He advocated that all civilians should be treated humanely, and even if it was lawful to kill women, it was unlawful to rape the women before killing them.

20 See generally, Richard Shelly Hartigan, *The Forgotten Victim: A History of the Civilian* (Chicago: Precedent Publishing, 1982), 155.

21 *Ibid*, at 50. Thus, once soldiers were captured, they should not be mistreated, regardless of whether the soldier was male or female. See also Meron, *Shakespeare's Henry the Fifth and the Law of War*, *supra* 15 at 25.

22 Pierino Belli, *A Treatise on Military Matters and Warfare* (*De Re Militari Et Bello Tractatus*) (Herbert C. Nutting trans., Vol II, 1995) (1563), 178.

23 Donald A. Wells, *War Crimes and Laws of War* (Lahman, Md: University Press of America, 2nd ed., 1991), 91. In 1419, Seigneur de Barbasan was tried by a military court for breaches of the laws of war. Lyal S. Sunga, *Individual Responsibility in International Law for Serious Human Rights Violations* (London: Martinus Nijhoff Publishers, 1992), 18.

24 Wells, *supra* 23 at 91.

25 Bassiouni, *Draft Code*, *supra* 5 at 8.

> would have been proper. Thus the declaration of war brought the rules of war into play... Once war had been declared rules took effect... [S]oldiers could kill and wound, but they could not burn or take spoil. In war to the death every man, woman, and child could be slain. *In the case of cities which had refused to surrender when surrender had been demanded, the women occupants could be raped.* Each warring group had its own banners and pennons and any deception in their use was an offense of war.[26]

This case illustrates that during this period of history, there remained instances when it was considered acceptable, even legal, to rape women. It was because this particular war was undeclared, and thus unjust, that the abuses were deemed illegal, so Hagenbach was tried and convicted of rape committed by his troops.

In the seventeenth century, Hugo Grotius (1583–1645) conducted the first comprehensive work on systematizing the international laws of war.[27] He concluded, based on views of states, natural law, and historical practice, that sovereign defense, recovering property, and deserved punishment were the three just causes for going to war. Unacceptable reasons included the desire to conquer other lands and other peoples.[28] Grotius asserted that while natural law and the law of nations did not forbid all wars, conflicts which violated the rights of others would not be tolerated.[29] Regarding wartime sexual assault, he concluded:

> You may read in many places that the raping of women in time of war is permissible, and in many others that it is not permissible. Those who sanction rape have taken into account only the injury done to the person of another, and have judged that it is not inconsistent with the law of war that everything which belongs to the enemy [including the women] should be at the disposition of the victor. A better conclusion has been reached by others... and consequently [rape] should not go unpunished in war any more than in peace.[30]

Thus, Grotius insisted that men who committed rape, whether in war or in peace, should be punished. While the more progressive nations forbade wartime sexual assault during this period, rape in war "continued to flourish."[31]

---

26 Wells, *supra* 2 at 93–94 [emphasis added], citing Keen, *The Laws of War in the Late Middle Ages* (1965).

27 See Hugo Grotius, *The Law of War and Peace* (reprinted in 1925) (1646); *The Law of War* (Friedman ed.), *supra* 16 at 14.

28 *Ibid*; Wells, *supra* 23 at 20–25.

29 Remigiusz Bierzanek, "War Crimes: History and Definition," in *A Treatise on International Criminal Law*, eds. Bassiouni & Nanda (Springfield, Ill.: Thomas, Vol. I, 1973), 560.

30 Grotius, *De Jure Belli Ac Pacis Libri Tres* (trans. Francis W. Kelsey, Vol II, 1995)(1646), 656–57. See Leslie C. Green, "What One May Do in Combat – Then and Now," in *Humanitarian Law of Armed Conflict*, eds. Delissen & Tanja (London: Martinus Nijhoff Publishers, 1991), 283.

31 Brownmiller, *supra* 11 at 35. See also, Meron, *Shakespeare's Henry the Fifth and Law of War*, *supra* 15; Keen, *The Laws of War in the Late Middle Ages*, *supra* 17.

One of the most important figures insisting that civilians should be immune against the ravages of war was Emmerich van Vattel (1714–1767).[32] As a rule, noncombatants were to be unharmed during periods of armed conflict.[33] While Vattel urged protection of women and others he considered weak, he was patriarchal in doing so:

> Women, children, feeble old men, and the sick are to be counted among the enemy, and a belligerent has rights over them... But these are enemies who offer no resistance, and consequently the belligerent has no right to maltreat or otherwise offer violence to them... If occasionally an enraged and unrestrained soldier goes so far as to outrage female virtue, or to massacre women, children, and old men, the officers regret such excesses and endeavor to check them, and a wise and humane general even punishes the offenders when he can. But if women wish to be spared they must keep to the duties of their sex, and not assume the position of men by taking up arms.[34]

Concepts of the purposes and restraints of war continued to evolve under the eighteenth century impact of enlightenment thinking. Nonetheless, since the incentives for allowing wartime rape and other abuse of women continued, gender crimes were rarely punished. Largely as a result of municipal norms and military incentives, commanders rarely punished their men for wartime rape. While many domestic laws did prohibit rape, the violence was typically considered either justified or inconsequential. Further, laws against spousal rape were inconceivable. A wife was considered under the complete authority of her husband and had no right to refuse sex with him; she had even fewer rights than slaves, since slaves technically had the legal right to refuse sex with their masters.[35] In one incident committed during the French Revolution, women were slaughtered by General Westermann because of their reproductive capacity. He said: "I have... massacred the women who... will breed no more brigands."[36]

3. DEVELOPMENT OF CODIFIED LAWS OF WAR ON GENDER-RELATED CRIMES

In the late eighteenth and nineteenth centuries, treaties and war codes began including vague yet important provisions for protecting women and girls. The

---

32 See Emmerich de Vattel, *The Law of Nations or the Principles of Natural Law* (*reprinted* in 1916) (1758); Emmerich de Vattel, *The Law of Nations* (Fenwick trans., 1995), at Book III, War.

33 Hartigan, *supra* 20 at 107–09.

34 Vattel, *The Law of Nations or the Principles of Natural Law*, *supra* 32 at 282–83. Jean-Jacques Rousseau (1712–1778) expressed similar views on the protection of noncombatants. Jean-Jacques Rousseau, *On The Social Contract* (1978), Book I, Chap IV, at 51.

35 John Stuart Mill, *The Subjection of Women*, (1870), 32–33. It would be over 100 years later, the mid-1970s, before marital rape was finally recognized as a crime in some states in the US. Okun, *supra* 9 at 4–5.

36 Hoffman Nickerson, *The Armed Horde*, 1793–1939, (New York: G.P. Putnam's Sons, 1940), 91.

Treaty of Amity and Commerce (1785) specified, in case of war, "women and children… shall not be molested in their persons."[37] The Declaration of Brussels (1874), on the laws and customs of war stated, "honour and rights of the family… should be respected."[38] The Oxford Manual (1880) on the laws of land warfare asserted, "human life, female honour, religious beliefs… must be respected. Interference with family life is to be avoided."[39] Although the language is unnecessarily vague, the provisions were generally intended to protect women and children against sexual assault.

During the Civil War in the United States, the U.S. military took the first step in codifying international customary laws of land warfare. This code, drafted by Francis Lieber in 1863 as General Orders No. 100,[40] was derived from international custom and usage and became the official U.S. Army regulation guide on the laws of land warfare.[41] Immunity for civilians, including women, was an important theme. Regarding sexual assault, the Lieber Code mandated, "all rape… [is] prohibited under the penalty of death."[42] The Lieber Code was both comprehensive and comprehensible. While not purporting to be an international document, it nevertheless "shaped and laid the cornerstone on which the laws of war… are based."[43] Other militaries adopted similar instructions for their soldiers.[44] These written codes of warfare made an exceptional contribution to humanitarian law. It is notable that this first codified regulation of soldier's conduct expressly criminalized rape under penalty of death, suggesting prohibitions on rape had a firm status in customary international law at that time.

---

37 Treaty of Amity and Commerce, signed at The Hague (on behalf of Prussia) 10 September 1785, and previously (on behalf of the United States) at Passy (signed by Benjamin Franklin) 9 July 1785, at Paris (signed by Thomas Jefferson) 28 July 1785, and at London (Adams) 5 August 1785.

38 International Declaration Concerning the Laws and Customs of War, adopted at Brussels, 27 August 1874, 4 Martens (2d) 219, reprinted in *American Journal of International Law* 1 (1907) (Supp.), 96.

39 *The Laws of War on Land*, Manual published by the Institute of International Law (Oxford Manual), Adopted by the Institute of International Law at Oxford, 9 September 1880.

40 "Instructions for the Government of the United States in the Field by Order of the Secretary of War," 24 April 1863 (Lieber Code; also known as General Orders No. 100); *Rules of Land Warfare*, War Dept. Doc. No. 467, Office of the Chief of Staff, approved 25 April 1914 (G.P.O. 1917); Army Field Manual, *The Law of Land Warfare* (FM 27–10, 1956).

41 Telford Taylor, *The Anatomy of the Nuremberg Trials* (New York: Knopf, Inc., 1992), 8–9. Lieber spoke of the difficulties in achieving his unique objective: "I have earnestly endeavored to treat of these grave topics conscientiously and comprehensively… [N]othing of the kind exists in any language. I had no guide, no groundwork, no textbook." Hartigan, *supra* 20 at 113–14.

42 Lieber Code, *supra* 40 at Article 44. See *The Laws of Armed Conflict: A Collection of Conventions, Resolutions and Other Documents*, eds. Dietrich Schindler & Jiri Toman (Dordrecht, the Netherlands: Martinus Nijhoff Publishers, 3rd ed, 1988), 10.

43 *The Laws of War* (Friedman ed.), *supra* 16 at xv (in Foreword by Telford Taylor).

44 *Ibid.* at 152.

The original Geneva Convention on the rules of war was promulgated in 1864,[45] one year after the Lieber Code. Twelve European nations signed the convention, which played a crucial role in the development of international humanitarian law. It was considered unique since it "aimed at regularizing in a permanent manner, a situation which until then had only been haphazard."[46] The Geneva Convention was revised and expanded in 1906 and 1929 (and eventually in 1949, with additional protocols developed in 1977.) The Geneva Conventions codified before the end of World War II did not provide protections to the civilian populations.

The Hague Peace Conferences of 1899 and 1907 resulted in the establishment of thirteen international conventions governing war on land, at sea, and neutrality, and, to some extent, the peaceful settlement of disputes.[47] Drafted in 1899 and revised in 1907, the "Convention with Respect to the Laws and Customs of War on Land" was signed in The Hague by the major world powers, with the exception of Russia.[48] The Hague Conventions dealt predominantly with prisoners of war and the relationship between military personnel of an occupying power and noncombatant civilian inhabitants. The Hague Conventions of 1907, aimed at preventing unnecessary suffering in war, primarily regulate the *methods* of warfare.[49] As such, they do not distinguish between offensive and defensive wars, nor do they make aggressive war illegal. But, they "outlawed [war] in certain respects, at certain times, and with certain formal obligations."[50] The Preamble of the 1899 Hague Convention contains the famous 'Martens Clause,'[51] which states:

---

45 "Geneva Convention for the Amelioration of the Condition of the Wounded and Sick of Armed Forces in the Field" (22 August 1864), 129 CTS 361 (Parry, ed); 22 Stat. 940; 1 Bevans 7.

46 Perry Gulbrandsen, "A Commentary on the Geneva Conventions of August 12, 1949," in *A Treatise on International Criminal Law*, eds. Bassiouni & Nanda (Springfield, Ill.: Thomas, Vol I, 1973), 375 quoting Louis Renault, *Acts of the Geneva Conference* (1906), 243.

47 "Convention with Respect to the Laws and Customs of War on Land" (First Hague, II), (29 July 1899), 32 Stat. 1803, T.S. No. 403 (entered into force 4 September 1900); "Convention Respecting the Laws and Customs of War on Land" (Second Hague, IV), (18 October 1907), 36 Stat. 2277, T.S. No. 539 (entered into force 26 January 1910). Reprinted in *Documents on the Laws of War*, eds. Roberts & Guelff (Oxford, UK: Clarendon Press, 1989).

48 See generally A. Pearce Higgins, *The Hague Peace Conferences and Other International Conferences Concerning the Laws and Usages of War: Texts of Conventions with Commentary* (Cambridge, UK: Cambridge University Press, 1909); Sheldon M. Cohen, *Arms and Judgment: Law, Morality, and the Conduct of War in the Twentieth Century* (Boulder, Colo.: Westview Press, 1989), 21–46.

49 See 1907 Hague Convention, *supra* 47; Ingrid Detter De Lupis, *The Law of War* (Cambridge, UK: Cambridge University Press, 1987), 178.

50 Ahmed M. Rifaat, *International Aggression, A Study of the Legal Concept: Its Development and Definition in International Law* (Stockholm, Sweden: Almqvist & Wiksell International 1979), 29.

51 Professor Martens was the principle Russian negotiator at the Hague Peace Conferences of 1899 and 1907. Hilaire McCoubrey, *International Humanitarian Law: The Regulation of Armed Conflict* (Hanover, New Hampshire: Dartmouth Publishing Company, 1990), 190–91. The 1907 convention also contains this language.

> Until a more complete code of the laws of war is issued, the High Contracting Parties think it right to declare that in cases not included in the Regulations adopted by them, populations and belligerents remain under the protection and empire of the principles of international law, as they result from the usages established between civilized nations, from the laws of humanity and the requirements of the public conscience.

Due to inadequate laws of war, in cases of legal uncertainty, notions of decency and humanity were expected to prevail. The 1907 Hague Convention IV Respecting the Laws and Customs of War on Land is the most important of the Hague Conventions in regards to protecting women. Article XLVI states: "[f]amily honour and rights... must be respected."[52]

The crimes of the First World War (1914–1918) resulted in a concerted effort by several nations to determine if there could be international accountability for atrocities committed during the war, when Kaiser Wilhelm II conducted German war operations in a way that raised "a worldwide storm of hate and fear."[53] Invading soldiers raped women and massacred opponents by the thousands.[54] During the German invasion of Belgium in August 1914, sexual assault was "catapulted into prominence as the international metaphor of Belgian humiliation."[55] There, it was reported that "[o]utrages upon the honour of women by German soldiers have been so frequent that it is impossible to escape the conviction that they have been condoned and indeed encouraged by German officers."[56] Particularly appalling and sordid rape reports were used for propaganda purposes to incite anti-German fervor; once this purpose was served, "Allied countries no longer bothered to tally rape reports or tried to verify the rumors. There was no need."[57] When reports of rapes, murders, and other atrocities continued, "voices were raised insisting upon trial and punishment by law" of the alleged war criminals, preferably before an international tribunal.[58] Rarely before World War I had accounts of wartime sexual violence been so well documented.[59]

52 See Hague Conventions, *supra* 47.
53 Taylor, *The Anatomy of the Nuremberg Trials*, *supra* 41 at 12.
54 *Ibid.* at 12–13.
55 Brownmiller, *supra* 11 at 40, 41–48.
56 Brownmiller, *supra* 11 at 42, *quoting* Professor J.H. Morgan.
57 Brownmiller, *supra* 11 at 43. Nevertheless, in the early 1900s, rape was considered a war crime, subject to criminal penalties. James W. Garner, "Punishment of Offenders Against the Laws and Customs of War," *American Journal of International Law* 14, (1920): 70, 71–72 (rape a violation of the laws and customs of war).
58 Taylor, *The Anatomy of the Nuremberg Trials*, *supra* 41 at 14.
59 Brownmiller, *supra* 11 at 40–42.

3.1. WORLD WAR I WAR CRIMES COMMISSION (1919)

The major Allied powers had greatly differing views surrounding the establishment of an international war crimes tribunal. In 1919, a War Crimes Commission of fifteen persons was established to report on the issue.[60] The War Crimes Commission's report charged Germany and the other Axis powers with "extensive violations of the laws of war" and recommended that war crime suspects be tried before an international tribunal.[61] The report listed thirty-two violations of the laws and customs of war for which suspects could be tried. Rape and forced prostitution were two of the enumerated offenses, ranked high on the list, as offense numbers five and six, respectively.[62] Thus, by 1919, rape and enforced prostitution were clearly considered violations of the laws and customs of war. In the report, the War Crimes Commission established:

> (i) That there were in many parts of Belgium deliberate and systematically organized massacres of the civil population, accompanied by many isolated murders and other outrages.
> (ii) That in the conduct of the war generally innocent civilians, both men and women, were murdered in large numbers, women violated, and children murdered... Murder, lust, and pillage prevailed over many parts of Belgium on a scale unparalleled in any war between civilized nations during the last three centuries.[63]

The War Crimes Commission concluded that "these disclosures will not have been made in vain if they touch and rouse the conscience of mankind, and we venture to hope that... the nations of the world in council will consider what means can be provided and sanctions devised to prevent the recurrence of such horrors as our generation is now witnessing."[64]

Yet the sole recommendation of the Commission followed by the Allied Powers was in drafting the Treaty of Versailles:[65]

---

60 The War Crimes Commission is also referred to as the "Peace Conference Commission," the "Commission on Responsibility of Authors of the War," and simply the "1919 Commission." The War Crimes Commission report which was presented to the Preliminary Peace Conference is reproduced in 14 *American Journal of International Law* (1920): 95.

61 Taylor, *The Anatomy of the Nuremberg Trials*, *supra* 41 at 14–15.

62 See UN War Crimes Commission, *XIII Law Reports of Trials of War Criminals* (1949), 122–124; "Commission on the Responsibility of the Authors of the War and on Enforcement of Penalties," Report Presented to the Preliminary Peace Conference, 29 March 1919, *American Journal of International Law* 14, (1920): 95, 114; Bierzanek, (Bassiouni & Nanda eds.), *supra* 29 at 563–64, citing *History of the UN War Crimes Commission* (1948), 34. The list started with crimes against the person, such as murder, and moved down the list toward property crimes.

63 Sheldon Glueck, *War Criminals, Their Prosecution and Punishment* (New York: Knopf, Inc., 1966), 68.

64 *Ibid.*

65 "Treaty of Peace with Germany (Treaty of Versailles)," signed at Versailles, 28 June 1919, 11 Martens Nouveau Recueil (3d) 323 (entered into force 10 January 1920).

> Under Article 227 of the Treaty, Wilhelm II Hohenzollern, former German Emperor, was to be publicly arraigned 'for a supreme offense against international morality and the sanctity of treaties,' and to be tried before a specially constituted international tribunal. Under Article 228 of the Treaty, the Allied and Associated Powers had the right to bring before military tribunals persons accused of having committed acts in violation of the laws and customs of war... Article 229 provided for the trial of war criminals before military tribunals of the state against whose nationals the alleged crimes had been committed...[66]

Efforts to prosecute and punish the war criminals on the basis of these provisions failed. The Netherlands refused to surrender ex-Kaiser Wilhelm II and thousands of people actively protested against extradition of the accused war criminals; the Germans used the lack of consensus among the Allies to present a formidable front.[67] The Americans refused to agree to the creation of an international tribunal because an international criminal court lacked precedent and individual criminal responsibility varied with national laws.[68]

Individuals accused of war crimes were ultimately tried before the Supreme Court of Germany in Leipzig, in a compromise reached between the Allies and Germany.[69] Concerning the travesty of these trials: "[t]he result of the Leipzig trials was that of the 901 persons on the list of war criminals accused of the most appalling crimes, 888 were either not tried, acquitted or summarily released, and only thirteen were convicted to sentences ranging from six months to four years and even they were not made to serve their terms."[70] Undoubtedly, attempts to hold trials of accused war criminals of World War I for serious war crimes, including sex crimes, failed miserably.

3.2. SUMMARY OF LAWS PROHIBITING SEX CRIMES PRIOR TO WORLD WAR II

From Cicero's urgings in the first century B.C. to conduct warfare with as little cruelty as possible, through Vitoria's conclusion in the Middle Ages that war should be entered into only as a last resort, to Grotius' attempt in the seventeenth century to systematize the laws of war, rules of warfare expanded and became

---

66 Bierzanek, (Bassiouni & Nanda eds.) *supra* 29 at 565–66. See also William B. Simons, "The Jurisdictional Bases of the International Military Tribunal at Nuremberg," in *The Nuremberg Trial and International Law*, eds. Ginsburgs & Kudriavtsev (Dordrecht, the Netherlands: Martinus Nijhoff Publishers, 1990), 40.

67 Bierzanek, *supra* at 566–67.

68 See Simons, (Ginsburgs & Kudriavtsev eds.), *supra* 66 at 40.

69 For a detailed account of the Leipzig Trials and a discussion of their historical significance, see generally Claud Mullins, *The Leipzig Trials, An Account of the War Criminal Trials and a Study of German Mentality* (London: Witherby, 1921).

70 Bierzanek, (Bassiouni & Nanda eds.), *supra* 29 at 567–69.

more specific. Throughout these centuries, sexual violence against women in both wartime and peacetime was pervasive.

Various international treaties formally adopted certain principles and rules for war and explicitly limited or forbade certain acts or particular methods of warfare. The first among these, the 1863 Lieber Code, uncompromisingly demanded severe punishment for rape. A year later, the original Geneva Convention was promulgated, in an attempt to provide international guidelines for the protection of the individual, particularly the combatant, against abuse. Some thirty five years later, the 1899 Hague Convention was signed, advocating the wartime protection of "family honours and rights."[71]

After the four years of World War I, the 1919 War Crimes Commission concluded its report on the violations of the laws and customs of war committed by the Axis forces. Rape and forced prostitution were two of the thirty-two crimes listed as prosecutable. There is thus strong evidence that sexual assault was considered a clear violation of the laws of warfare.

During the twenty-one year period between the end of the First World War and the beginning of the Second, efforts were concentrated on attempting to regulate wars and outlaw aggression. If aggression was illegal, conceivably there would be no more wars, and thus, no need for further conventions regulating the methods of warfare or protecting individuals.

War has long been considered 'man's business,'[72] so war's regulations and protections were centered on males. In surveying the laws and conduct of land warfare prior to 1945, one author concluded:

> Ideas about women and sex obviously have always taken a large place in a [military] culture which is as wholly male a culture as one could hope to find...[I]mplications for the observation of the laws of war are serious. Women have not yet much appeared as armed combatants, but have usually been the larger part of that non-combatant world to which both the law of war and ordinary military discipline ostensibly offer protection...[There is a] clash between the requirements of the law and the probable expectations of the common soldier. A free hand with the girls seems always to have been a basic component of what the common soldier hopes for, believes he deserves, and feels entitled, when circumstances permit, to get; forcibly, if nothing else will get it.[73]

---

71 "[1899] Hague Convention (II) With Respect to the Laws and Customs of War on Land", at Art 46. See *supra* 47. The language of this article differs only slightly from the 1907 version.

72 General Barrow, former Commandant of the U.S. Marine Corps, in arguing against allowing women to participate in combat, stated: "War is man's work... [Women in combat positions] trample[] the male ego. When you get right down to it, you have to protect the manliness of war." Kenneth L. Karst, "The Pursuit of Manhood and the Desegregation of the Armed Forces," 38 *UCLA Law Review* 38, (1991): 499, 534, quoting from Wright, "The Marine Corps Faces the Future," *N.Y. Times (Magazine)*, 20 June 1982 at 16, 74.

73 Best, (Howard ed.), *supra* 17 at 26. Best concludes that this attitude continues amongst both the military and nonmilitary society. In his reasoning, he quotes the following statement from a lawyer in the *House of Lords Weekly Hansard* in 1976: "When I practised [law], I never

3.3. WORLD WAR II WAR CRIMES TRIALS IN NUREMBERG AND TOKYO: TREATMENT OF SEX CRIMES

World War II involved all the world's superpowers and affected virtually every other nation. The global military conflict lasted from 1939–1945, and cost over sixty million lives, the vast majority being civilian. The massive atrocities directed against civilians during the Second World War were unprecedented in scope.

On 8 August 1945, the U.S., France, England, and the U.S.S.R., meeting in London, reached a mutual agreement to establish an International Military Tribunal for the purpose of holding a joint international war crimes trial to prosecute the major Nazi war criminals whose crimes did not have a particular geographic locale.[74]

Attached to the London Agreement was the Charter for the IMT, the document on which the Nuremberg Trial would be based. The four major Allied powers invited other governments to adhere to the Agreement, and nineteen nations accepted, effectively expressing their approval of the Nuremberg Tribunal.[75] Therefore it was not now solely the United States, Britain, France, and the Soviet Union that had the political will to prosecute the alleged Axis war criminals. The landmark International Military Tribunal[76] at Nuremberg was established by the victorious Allied nations to try European Axis war criminals. Prior to this time, war criminals had been punished only by their own state, or more commonly, by their adversary, *if* punished at all.[77] Summary execution, not trial, had been a common form of punishment of those deemed guilty by the victors.

The IMT Charter failed to include any form of sexual violence in its articulation of crimes within the jurisdiction of the court, and the IMT did not *expressly* prosecute such crimes. However, various forms of sexual violence were

---

lost a case of rape when I was defending [a man accused of wartime rape] because juries in the past were more predominantly male. If one got on the right note one would always invite them to conclude that either they got up to that sort of thing when they were servicemen or they would have, had they had the courage." Ibid.

74 "Agreement for the Prosecution and Punishment of Major War Criminals of the European Axis," London, 8 August 1945 (hereinafter, the London Agreement) 8 UNTS 279; 59 Stat. 1544, 8 AS No. 472. at preamble. Reprinted in *American Journal of International Law* 39(1945) (Supp), 257. Attached to the London Agreement is the "Charter of the International Military Tribunal, Annexed to the London Agreement", 8 August 1945 (IMT Charter or the Nuremberg Charter).

75 William J. Bosch, *Judgment on Nuremberg, American Attitudes Toward the Major German War Crime Trials* (Chapel Hill, N.C.: University of North Carolina Press, 1970), 11.

76 The official documents of the Nuremberg Trial are contained in the forty-two volume work, *Trial of the Major War Criminals Before the International Military Tribunal,* 14 November 1945–1 October 1946 (42 Vols., 1947) (hereinafter *IMT Docs.*).

77 Antonio Cassese, *Violence and Law in the Modern Age* (Princeton, N.J.: Princeton University Press, 1986), 108.

included as evidence of the atrocities prosecuted during the trial, and sex crimes *can be considered* subsumed within the IMT Judgment, particularly within the crimes against humanity of "other inhumane acts" and "persecution on political, racial or religious grounds."[78]

Throughout the war, sexual violence was committed with a vengeance. Documentation of various forms of sex crimes committed by Axis troops was submitted to the Nuremberg Tribunal.[79] The transcripts of the trials contain evidence of rape, sexual slavery, sexual torture, forced prostitution, forced sterilization, forced abortion, pornography, sexual mutilation, forced nudity, and sexual sadism.[80]

There were no high level women at Nuremberg[81] and the evidence of sexual violence was often given short shrift during trial.[82] Whether it was out of discomfort, prudishness, confusion, or other reason, the lack of both public documentation and official prosecution gave impetus to the notion that sex crimes were less important or that sex crimes were not prosecuted at the IMT. Indeed, the comprehensive, 732-page Index to the forty-two volume set reporting the proceedings of the Nuremberg Trial does not even bother to include "rape," "prostitution," or "women" among either the headings or subheadings. In contrast, "looting" warrants three and one half pages in the Index alone.[83]

Nonetheless, as noted below, various forms of sexual violence were documented by the Nuremberg Trials and can be considered subsumed within the Judgment.

---

78 IMT Charter, *supra* 74 at Ch II, Art 6.

79 This chapter only considers sexual violence committed by the Axis nations at trial. Professor Robertson states that the Allies declined to indict Nazi war criminals for sexual violence because they themselves committed the worst abuses: "The worst example of tolerated and systematic rape was during the Russian army advance on Germany through eastern Europe, during which an estimated two million women were sexually abused with Stalin's blessing that 'the boys are entitled to their fun.'" Geoffrey Robertson, *Crimes Against Humanity, The Struggle for Global Justice* (UK: Allen Lane, 1999), 306.

80 See *IMT Docs, supra* 76 at Vol II, transcript p. 139 (pornography); Vol VI, transcript, 170 (torture), 178 (torture/rape), 212 (forced sterilization, forced abortion, infanticide), 213-214 (forced prostitution), 404-407 (rape); at Vol VII, transcript 453-457 (rape), 467 (rape), 494 (rape/torture), 505 (torture, sexual mutilation), 548 (pornography); at Vol XX, transcript, 381 (sexual assault).

81 See Diane Amann, Portraits of Women at Nuremberg, available at http://papers.ssrn.com/sol3/papers.cfm?abstract_id=1654732.

82 See, for example, *IMT Docs, supra* 76 at Vol VI, transcript, 404 (after reporting a rape, the prosecutor avows "I will not mention any more of the atrocities described in this document."); transcript, 405 ("'54 women or young girls from 13 to 50 years of age were raped by maddened soldiers.' The Tribunal will forgive me if I avoid citing the atrocious details which follow."); transcript, 407 ("'rapes were committed against three women in that area.' I pass on.").

83 *IMT Docs, supra* 76 at Vol XXIII. Volume 23 is the Chronological and Subject Matter Index. Even searching under "civilian population", in its sub-index of "crimes committed against," no gender related crime is mentioned.

3.3.1. *Evidence of sexual violence in Nuremberg Trial*

3.3.1.1. Rape, forced prostitution/sexual slavery, forced nudity, forced pornography

There was compelling evidence of various forms of sexual assault.[84] Witnesses recounted horrendous sex crimes committed during the war, including the outright rape and slaughter of all women and girls in some villages. A deposition given by an eyewitness to two separate rapes noted that, as Germans stormed the Soviet Union, reports declared "Everywhere the lust-maddened German Gangsters break into houses, they rape the woman and girls under the very eyes of their kinfolk and children, jeer at the women they have violated, and then brutally murder their victims."[85] According to evidence presented to the IMT:

> Women and young girls are vilely outraged in all the occupied areas. In the Ukrainian village of Borodayevka... the fascists violated *every one* of the women and girls. In the village of Berezovka... drunken German soldiers assaulted and carried off *all* the women and girls between the ages of 16 and 30. Near the town of Borissov in Bielorussia, 75 women and girls... fell into their hands. The Germans first raped and then savagely murdered 36 of their number... [T]he soldiers marched... a 16-year-old girl[] into the forest, where they raped her [and then nailed her to some boards]... and cut off her breasts. [I]n the Leningrad region, a 15-year-old girl... was raped by a group of German soldiers and died as a result of the assault.[86]

According to trial documents: "[i]n the city of Smolensk the German Command opened a brothel for officers in one of the hotels into which hundreds of women and girls were driven; they were mercilessly dragged down the street by their arms and hair."[87] In the village of Bassmanova, a large group of school girls were abducted and forced to sexually service German officers.[88] At concentration camps like Auschwitz and Ravensbruck, women enslaved in the camps were forced into "brothels" to provide sexual services to officers or male workers at the camp. In order to determine which women to prostitute, men would observe the women during "disinfection" when the women were naked, and then make their selections.[89]

Another report reveals that on one particular night, twenty-four Jewish girls were raped and ultimately murdered by SS soldiers. After being raped, they were "offered their lives if they would agree to 'live with the German guards.' They

84 See *IMT Docs, supra* 76 at Vol II, transcript, 139; at Vol VI, transcript, 170, 178, 211–14, 404–07; at Vol VII, transcript, 449–57, 467, 494, 548; at Vol XX, transcript, 381.

85 *IMT Docs, supra* 76 at Vol VII, transcript, 456.

86 *IMT Docs, supra* 76, at Vol VII, transcript, 456–57.

87 *IMT Docs, supra* 76 at Vol VII, transcript, 456.

88 *IMT Docs, supra* 76 at Vol VII, transcript, 455.

89 *IMT Docs, supra* 76 at Vol VI, transcript, 213–14.

refused. They were then put on a truck and taken to the cremation site. The truck backed up to the roaring fire. Each girl was then shot in the head and her body was kicked into the flames."[90] Had these young women been willing to provide ongoing sexual services to the military men, their lives would have been spared, at least for a time. Yet as have many other rape survivors who came before and after these victims, they chose death as preferable to living, either because they had already been sexually assaulted and could not live with this gross bodily invasion, or because they could not bear the reality that they might have to endure more sexual assault. Whether forced into a formal brothel or taken to a hotel, home or other location for the soldier's exclusive use, thousands of women were forced into sexual servitude in wartime Europe.[91]

Some women were photographed nude prior to being killed. According to the transcripts, "Condemned to death, these [naked] women were forced... to pose before the camera."[92] And, "Russian girls were deloused by men, nude photos in forced positions were taken."[93] Others were simply singled out for rape or sexual services, never to be heard from again.[94]

3.3.1.2. Forced sterilization

During World War II, and the Nazi aim to exterminate the Jews, many not outright murdered or worked to death, were prevented from producing a Jewish or non-Aryan offspring,[95] by being forcibly sterilized.[96]

The IMT Indictment alleged that the defendants "conducted deliberate and systematic genocide, viz., the extermination of racial and national groups... in order to destroy particular races and classes of people."[97] Indeed, an employee

---

90 Moshe Pearlman, *The Capture and Trial of Adolf Eichmann* (New York: Simon and Schuster, 1963), 285.

91 Theodor Meron, *Henry's Wars and Shakespeare's Laws* (Oxford, UK: Clarendon Press, 1993), 113.

92 *IMT Docs, supra* 76 at Vol VII, transcript, 548.

93 *IMT Docs, supra* 76 at Vol II, transcript, 139.

94 *IMT Docs, supra* 76 at Vol XX, transcript, 381 (The SS men "inspect our column and take away three young, pretty girls... The car drives off, the girls cry out, trying to defend themselves against molestations of the SS officers.").

95 *IMT Docs, supra* 76 at Vol XX, transcript, 272–73 (The Nazi party "proposed to sterilize all Jews and all half-Jews".).

96 For documentation related to sterilization experiments, see *IMT Docs, supra* 76 at Vol I, transcript, 45–46, 252; at Vol VI, transcript, 211. Experiments were also done to attempt to manipulate "sex hormones." *IMT Docs, supra* 76 at Vol VI, transcript, 310.

97 *IMT Docs, supra* 76 at Vol I, Indictment, 43–44. When Adolf Eichmann was eventually captured, he was convicted on Count 4 of taking "measures to prevent births among Jews by directing that births be banned and pregnancies interrupted among Jewish women in Theresienstadt, with intent to exterminate the Jewish people." He was acquitted of charges relating to forced sterilization. Pearlman, *supra* 90 at 613. Note that at the time of the IMT Indictment, the term 'genocide' was used but not yet defined in the 1948 Genocide Convention.

of the Auschwitz infirmary testified, "The Jewish women… were subjected to abortion… [But if] their pregnancy was near the end… the babies were drowned."[98] Similarly, another person testified, "[The Nazis] proposed to sterilize all Jews and all half-Jews."[99]

Thus Jewish and other "undesirable" women and girls were subjected to several forms of reproductive crimes, including forced abortion, forced sterilization, and infanticide, as well as being forbidden to reproduce. According to an official announcement received into evidence by the IMT, forced abortion of non-Germans was included as part of official Nazi policy: "[E]very case of pregnancy of non-German women was to be reported, and in all such cases these women were to be obliged to have their child 'removed by operation in a hospital.' The announcement itself explains that in cases when non-German women give birth to their children this 'creates difficulties for their use in work,' and besides, it is also 'a danger for the population policy.' Furthermore, this announcement states that the Office of Labor Service should try to influence these women to commit an abortion."[100]

Sterilization experiments at Auschwitz were barbaric, resulting in loss of ability to reproduce, while also causing extreme physical pain, emotional trauma, or death. The following testimony provides evidence of forced sterilization:

> As to the experiments, I have seen… the queue of young Jewesses from Salonika who stood waiting in front of the X-ray room for sterilization. I also know that they performed castration operations in the men's camp… They sterilized women either by injections or by operation or with rays. I saw and knew several women who had been sterilized. There was a very high mortality rate among those operated upon… *They said that they were trying to find the best method for sterilizing so as to replace the native population in the occupied countries by Germans after one generation*, once they had made use of the inhabitants as slaves… The Jewish women, when they arrived in the first months of pregnancy, were subjected to abortion. When their pregnancy was near the end, after confinement, the babies were drowned in a bucket of water… After a while another doctor arrived and for 2 months they did not kill the Jewish babies. But one day an order came from Berlin saying that again they had to be done away with. Then the mothers and their babies were called to the infirmary. They were put in a lorry and taken away to the gas chamber.[101]

---

98 *IMT Docs*, *supra* 76 at Vol VI, transcript, 211–12.

99 *IMT Docs*, *supra* 76 at Vol XX, transcript, 272–73.

100 *IMT Docs*, *supra* 76 at Vol VIII, transcript, 133.

101 As described by Vaillant-Couturier, an employee of the Auschwitz infirmary, *IMT Docs*, *supra* 76 at Vol VI, transcript, 211–12.

The evidence also demonstrates that in addition to the sexual violence, women were subjected to the same non-sexual crimes as men, including torture and murder.[102]

3.3.2. Control Council Law No. 10 (CCL10)[103] *– Rape included as a crime against humanity*

Signed in Berlin on December 20, 1945 by the four allied victors of the war, this document provided for the trial of war crime suspects in the zones of occupation. These were essentially to be the trials for the lower level accused whose crimes had a specific locale – generally, war crime suspects who were not the primary architects of the war (for instance, it would include a commander of a concentration camp or a doctor who conducted unethical experiments on victims.) In addition to crimes against peace, war crimes, and crimes against humanity, CCL10 also allowed for indictment for membership in an organization which the IMT declared criminal. Control Council Law No. 10 was the document from which the twelve subsequent U.S. trials at Nuremberg, held for the "lesser" war criminals, drew their authority.[104]

The preamble to CCL10 stated that it was enacted to give effect to the terms of the Moscow Declaration, London Agreement, and Nuremberg Charter, and "to establish a uniform legal basis in Germany for the prosecution of war criminals and other similar offenders, other than those dealt with by the International Military Tribunal."[105]

In the subsequent Nuremberg trials held by the Allied forces under the auspices of Control Council Law No. 10, rape is specifically enumerated as a crime against humanity.[106] Nevertheless, while rape was explicitly recognized as a crime, gender related crimes were given only cursory treatment in the trials. Most, but inadequate, attention to gender crimes was in the context of trials of medical doctors performing unethical experiments and concentration camp guards facilitating the commission of grave crimes within the camps. In these

102 *IMT Docs*, *supra* 76 at Vol VII, transcript, 452 ("women interned in the camp were subjected to the same ill-treatment and torture; they suffered the same forms of control, of work beyond their strength, of beating, and ill-treatment."); at Vol VI, transcript, 170 ("women were subjected to the same treatment as men.") Similarly, *IMTFE Docs*, *supra* 76 at Vol 6, transcript, 13192–13193 (forms of torture included lighting paper to "pass the flame over the thighs and private parts of the accused, men and women both being treated in this fashion.").

103 "Allied Control Council Law No. 10 Punishment of Persons Guilty of War Crimes, Crimes Against Peace and Humanity," 20 December 1945, Official Gazette of the Control Council for Germany, No. 3, Berlin, 31 January 1946 (hereinafter CCL10).

104 These twelve trials were: Case No. 1, Medical Case; Case No. 2, Milch Case; Case No. 3, Justice Case; Case No. 4, SS, Pohl Case; Case No. 5, Flick Case; Case No. 6, Farben Case; Case No. 7, Hostages Case; Case No. 8, Rusha Case; Case No. 9, Einsatzgruppen Case; Case No. 10, Krupp Case; Case No. 11, Ministries Case; and Case No. 12, High Command Case.

105 CCL10, *supra* 103 at Preamble.

106 CCL10, *supra* 103 at Article II(1)(c).

cases, forced sterilization, forced abortion, and sexual mutilation were at least mentioned.[107]

3.3.3. *Establishment of the IMTFE and other war crimes trials in Asia*

3.3.3.1. The International Military Tribunal for the Far East:[108] Its treatment of sex crimes

On July 26, 1945, the Potsdam Declaration announced the joint Allied decision to punish individual war criminals from Japan, proclaiming: "There must be eliminated for all time the authority and influence of those who have deceived and misled the people of Japan into embarking on world conquest... We do not intend that the Japanese shall be enslaved as a race or destroyed as a nation, but stern justice will be meted out to all war criminals."[109]

Eventually, the Allies decided to hold a trial to punish the Japanese war criminals.[110] On May 3, 1946, five months before the verdicts were rendered at Nuremberg, the trial of the International Military Tribunal for the Far East (IMTFE) began in Tokyo.[111] The Tokyo Trial was considered a "natural and unavoidable consequence of the Nuremberg Trial."[112] Whereas the Nuremberg Trials were held to prosecute the Nazi war criminals of Europe, the Tokyo Trials were held to prosecute the top war criminals from Japan. However, whereas the Nuremberg Charter was produced at the London Conference after long negotiations between the US, Great Britain, the USSR, and France, the Tokyo

107 See, e.g., *U.S. v. Brandt*, in 2 Trials of War Criminals Before the Nuremberg Military Tribunal Under Control Council Law No. 10 (1946) (forced sterilization and castration); *U.S. v. Pohl*, in 5 Trials of War Criminals Before the Nuremberg Military Tribunal Under Control Council Law No. 10 (1947) (evidence of forced abortion and concentration camp "brothels"); *U.S. v. Greifelt*, in 4–5 Trials of War Criminals Before the Nuremberg Military Tribunal Under Control Council Law No. 10 (1947) (forced abortion, gender/ethnic persecutions, genocide, and reproductive crimes).

108 "International Military Tribunal for the Far East," Proclaimed at Tokyo, 19 January 1946 and amended 26 April 1946, TIAS No. 1589 (entered into force 19 January 1946) (IMTFE or Tokyo Tribunal), Annex, Charter of the International Military Tribunal for the Far East (Tokyo) (IMTFE Charter or Tokyo Charter).

109 Documents of the Tokyo Trial are reproduced in *The Tokyo War Crimes Trial: The Complete Transcripts of the Proceedings of the International Military Tribunal for the Far East*, eds. R. Pritchard & S. Zaide (New York: Garland Publishing, 22 Vols, 1981) (hereinafter *IMTFE Docs*). *IMTFE Docs*, Vol 20, reproduces the Potsdam Declaration.

110 The Tokyo Tribunal was established by virtue of the Cairo Declaration of 1 December 1943, the Declaration of Potsdam of 26 July1945, The Japanese Instrument of Surrender of 2 September 1945, and the Moscow Conference of 26 December 1945. *IMTFE Docs, supra* 109, at Vol 20, transcript p. 48415.

111 The Nuremberg Verdict was rendered on 1 October 1946 at the Palace of Justice.

112 Bert V.A. Röling, "The Nuremberg and Tokyo Trials in Retrospect," in *A Treatise on International Criminal Law*, eds. Bassiouni & Nanda (Springfield, Ill.: Thomas, 1973), 596.

Charter was promulgated merely by an executive decree of General Douglas MacArthur.[113]

Rape was one of the war crimes with which some of the defendants were charged in these trials, despite "rape" being omitted from the IMTFE Charter. The Tokyo Indictment stated acts were "carried out in violation of recognized customs and conventions of war... [including] mass murder, *rape*, ... and other barbaric cruelties."[114] According to the prosecution, during the first six weeks of the Japanese occupation of the Chinese city of Nanking, in excess of 20,000 women and girls were raped by Japanese soldiers.[115] In alleging breaches of the laws and customs of war in the IMTFE Indictment, sex crimes were incorporated as follows:

> 1. **Inhumane treatment**, contrary to Article 4 of the Annex to the Hague Convention IV of 1907 and the whole of the Geneva Convention of 1929 and the said assurances. Prisoners of war and civilian internees were murdered, beaten, tortured and otherwise ill-treated, and **female prisoners were raped** by members of the Japanese forces.
> 5. Mistreatment of the sick and wounded, medical personnel and female nurses:
> (c) **Female nurses were raped**, murdered and ill-treated;
> 12. **Failure to respect family honour** and rights, individual life, private property and religious convictions... Large numbers of the inhabitants of such territories were murdered, tortured, **raped** and otherwise ill-treated...[116]

Thus at Tokyo, rape was charged in the IMTFE under prohibitions against "inhumane treatment," "ill-treatment," and "failure to respect family honour."

A notable difference between the IMT and IMTFE trials was the inclusion of three women as assistant prosecution counsel at the Tokyo Tribunal.[117]

---

113 *IMTFE Docs, supra* 109 at Vol I, Pre-Trial Documents, "Special Proclamation", at 1. MacArthur was a General of the U.S. Army and the Supreme Commander for the Allied Powers in Japan. He issued the executive decree under orders from the United States Joint Chiefs of Staff. Richard H. Minear, *Victors' Justice: The Tokyo War Crimes Trial* (Princeton, N.J.: Princeton University Press, 1971), citing Solis Horwitz, *The Tokyo Trial, International Conciliation* (New York: Carnegie Endowment for International Peace, 1950), 465–80. It went essentially unquestioned that MacArthur had the right to establish any rules, regulations, and procedures deemed necessary for military commissions within his jurisdiction. Richard L. Lael, *The Yamashita Precedent, War Crimes and Command Responsibility* (Lanham, M.D.: Rowman & Littlefield Publishers 1982), 60.

114 *IMTFE Docs, supra* 109 at Vol 1, Indictment, transcript, 29.

115 *IMTFE Docs, supra* 109 at Vol 2, transcript, 4592; International Military Tribunal for the Far East, Dissentient Judgment of Justice Pal 624 (1953) (hereinafter IMTFE, Pal Dissent.).

116 As reproduced in *Imtfe, Pal Dissent, supra* 109 at 601–03 (emphasis added).

117 According to the *IMTFE Docs, supra* 109 at Vol Index & Guide II, 424, the following women were each listed as Assistant Prosecution Counsel: Mrs. Lambert (US), Mrs. Grace K. Llewellyn (US), and Mrs. C.R. Strooker (Netherlands).

3.3.3.2. Evidence of sexual violence by Japanese troops

As in Europe, sexual assault atrocities committed in Asia during World War II encompassed the full gamut of horrific gender specific crimes. Reports of these acts by investigators, eye-witness testimony, and affidavits from survivors and witnesses, entered into the official record at the Tokyo Trial.[118] At one point in cross-examination of a witness who had testified extensively about sex crimes, the President of the IMTFE, Justice Webb, interrupted the cross-examination by reprimanding the defendant's attorney, who was advancing the theory that the Chinese had raped Japanese women. Webb admonished: "I must remind you that rape and the murder of women could never be just reprisals... and it is useless to continue your cross-examination along those lines."[119]

One of the most prolific occurrences of wartime rape ever recorded was perpetrated in Nanking, China during the war. The first three months of Japanese occupation of Nanking demonstrates a particularly egregious account of sexual violence documented at trial:

> ... [A]ll resistance had ceased as the Japanese Army entered the city on the morning of 13 December 1937. The Japanese soldiers swarmed over the city and committed various atrocities... Individual soldiers and small groups of two or three roamed over the city murdering, raping, looting, and burning. There was no discipline whatsoever. Many soldiers were drunk... There were many cases of rape. Death was a frequent penalty for the slightest resistance on the part of a civilian or the members of her family who sought to protect her. Even girls of tender years and old women were raped in large numbers throughout the city, and many cases of abnormal and sadistic behavior in connection with these rapings occurred. Many women were killed after the act and their bodies mutilated. Approximately 20,000 cases of rape occurred within the city during the first month of occupation... The barbarous behavior of the Japanese Army cannot be excused as the acts of a soldiery which had temporarily gotten out of hand when at last a stubbornly defended position had capitulated – rape, arson and murder continued to be committed on a large scale for at least six weeks after the city had been taken...[120]

As reports of gang rapes and violence spread, Generalissimo Chiange ordered a news blackout of the city. Nevertheless, Western reporters began breaching the order. Typically, stories of murder and looting were given priority, while accounts

---

118 See *IMTFE Docs* at Vol 2, transcript, 2568–2573, 2584, 2592–2595, 3904–3944, 4463–4479, 4496–4498, 4501–4503, 4504–4507, 4512–4515, 4518–4521, 4526–4531, 4533–4536, 4544, 4559, 4572–4573, 4594, 4602, 4615,4638, 4642, 4647, 4660; at Vol 6, transcript, 12521–12548, 12995, 13117, 13189,13641–42, 13652. For other accounts of rape and forced prostitution in Asia during the Second World War, see Yuki Tanaka, *Hidden Horrors, Japanese War Crimes in World War II* (Boulder, Colo.: Westview Press, 1996), 79–110.

119 *IMTFE Docs, supra* 109 at Vol 2, transcript p. 2595.

120 *The Law of War*, (Friedman ed.), *supra* 16 at 1061.

of rape were handled tentatively. Yet, even when reported in a statistical, unemotional manner, it was impossible to shroud the fact that savage, bloody sexual assaults were committed in inconceivable numbers. The reports of systematic rapes were so persistent that "the 'Rape of Nanking' soon passed into common usage as the world-wide metaphor" of the invasion.[121]

An American missionary from the Nanking International Relief Committee investigating criminal allegations wrote about the sexual atrocities in his diary. His account was entered into evidence:

> [The rapes are] a horrible story to try to relate; I know not where to begin nor to end. Never have I heard or read of such brutality... People are hysterical... Women are being carried off every morning, afternoon and evening. The whole Japanese army seems to be free to go and come anywhere it pleases, and do what it pleases... By day they [the soldiers] go into the buildings in our Safety Zone centers, looking for desirable women, and then at night they return to get them... Girls of eleven and twelve and women of fifty have not escaped. Resistance is fatal. The worst cases come to the hospital. A woman six months pregnant, who resisted, came to us with 16 knife wounds in her face and body, one piercing the abdomen. She lost her baby...[122]

The hospitals provided no refuge either. The IMTFE documents report that a group of Japanese soldiers entered a hospital in Java and, over a period of ten days, repeatedly raped several women, with the approval of the commanding officer, who often watched.[123] This was "mass, continuous merciless rape" committed "under threat" against women at the hospital.[124] A chaplain in the Canadian Army testified about the rape of nurses at a hospital in Hong Kong:

> A. [The nurses] were in a dreadful state and they had had a very bad time all through the night. They had been assaulted by Japanese soldiers and one of them told me she was forced to lie on two dead bodies and [be] used by the Japanese as they chose.
> Q. When you say they had been assaulted, what do you mean by the word "assault"?
> A. They had been raped by the Japanese.[125]

No place was safe from sexual assault, not even the church: "[The Japanese were] pulling girls outside of the cathedral, and I saw two Japanese raping those women right there in the cathedral, and one by my side she is pregnant five

121 Brownmiller, *supra* 11 at 57.

122 *IMTFE Docs, supra* 109 at Vol 2, transcript, 4467–4469; Arnold C. Brackman, *The Other Nuremberg* (New York: HarperCollins Publishers, 1987), 181–82.

123 *IMTFE Docs, supra* 109 at Vol 6, transcript, 13639–13642. When the rapes were reported, soldiers retaliated by raping more women.

124 *IMTFE Docs, supra* 109 at Vol 6, transcript, 13641.

125 *IMTFE Docs, supra* 109 at Vol 6, transcript, 13117.

months."[126] A Chinese woman who witnessed the heinous rape and murder of her family members by Japanese forces had her statement entered into evidence at the IMTFE:

> The first date the Japanese entered Nanking they fired and burnt our home, and we were proceeding to the refugee camp. There were the following in the party, my mother-in-law, my brother and his wife, two children of mine, and my brother-in-law's two children, aged 5 and 2...
> As we were proceeding... we were met by twelve Japanese soldiers, including some officers, who wore swords. One of the soldiers wearing a sword, whom I thought was an officer, grasped my sister-in-law and raped and then killed her in the presence of her husband and children, who were killed at the same time. The husband was killed for trying to defend his wife and the two children were killed because they wept when their mother was being raped. The five year old girl was suffocated by having her clothing stuffed in her mouth, and the boy was bayoneted. Their father and mother were both bayoneted and thereby killed. My mother-in-law was also bayoneted and died twelve days later... I was an eye witness to all of this. I went to the refugee camp, and on the way saw many corpses[,] women and civilian men. The women had their apparel pulled up and looked like they had been raped.[127]

Rape and forced prostitution/sexual slavery

Egregious episodes of forced prostitution – arguably, more adequately named sexual slavery – took place in Asia during the Second World War, and a small portion was prosecuted in the post World War II trials.[128] The Japanese government forced up to 200,000 Korean, Chinese, Filipino, Indonesian, and other women during World War II into sexual slavery to the Japanese military.[129]

---

126 *IMTFE Docs, supra* 109 at Vol 6, transcript, 12557.

127 *IMTFE Docs, supra* 118 at Vol 2, transcript, 4506–4507.

128 *IMTFE Docs, supra* 118 at Vol 6, transcript, 13652, reports an affidavit submitted to the tribunal attesting to rape and forced prostitution. This would indicate that the tribunal had knowledge of forced prostitution, even though only rape was included in the indictments. *IMTFE Docs, supra* 218 at Vol 2, transcript, 2584 refers to "whore houses" and "geisha houses," and somewhat implies that these housed involuntary prostitutes. Boling asserts that the IMTFE did in fact know of the "comfort women" system, in which some 200,000 women were forced into sexual slavery to the Japanese military. David Boling, "Mass Rape, Enforced Prostitution, and the Japanese Imperial Army," *Columbia Journal of Transnational Law* 32 (1995): 533, 546–47. While it was unclear whether the incidents cited in *IMTFE Docs, supra* 118 at Vol 6, transcript, 12520–12548, were part of the official "comfort system" or not, it is quite clear that many women were forced into facilities where they were repeatedly raped by a long succession of military men.

129 Since 1991, many survivors have come forward to testify about the sex crimes committed against them. See, for example, Yoshimi Yoshiaki, "Japan Battles Its Memories," *New York Times* (11 March 1992): 23; Jake Doherty, "Conference to Focus on Plight of Wartime 'Comfort Women'; Japan: Activists Say Victims Used as Sex Slaves in World War II Should be Compensated by the Government that Forcibly Recruited Them," *Los Angeles Times* (20 February 1993): B3; Teresa Watanabe, "Japan Admits that WWII Sex Slaves Were

> '[T]he roughest and saddest part of the whole picture' was Japanese conduct toward the women. Women in three neighboring homes were raped and, 'on five different occasions, which I can detail for you if desired, I, myself came upon soldiers in the act of rape.' Japanese soldiers, in gangs of fifteen or twenty roamed through the city in search of women. A friend witnessed the rape of a Chinese woman by seventeen soldiers in rapid succession. 'I do not care to repeat the occasional cases of sadistic and abnormal behavior in connection with the rapes...' On December 15, thirty college girls were raped... in one building alone. Three days later eighteen girls were raped in six different locations on campus.[130]

The high incidence of rape was reported to the IMTFE: "[i]t was again the same story, unbelievably terrible. The rapings continued day by day."[131] The reports indicated women were sexually assaulted for purposes of sport, forced prostitution, sexual slavery, terror, destruction, and humiliation:

> [W]itness after witness told similar stories – girls dragged off by gangs... in uniform; abducted women forced to wash clothes for the Army units by day and to "service" as many as fifteen to forty men at night; women forced to perform sex shows for troops at play; fathers forced at gunpoint to rape their own daughters. Many of the stories had similar endings. When a group of soldiers was finished with a captured woman, a stick was sometimes pushed up into her vagina; in some cases the woman's head was severed.[132]

The violence was against elderly women, young girls, pregnant women–no one was spared. One seventy-seven year old widow reported being raped over a dozen times.[133] Other testimony of various forms of sexual violence cited at the IMTFE included the following excerpts:

Coerced; Apology: Government Statement Overturns Decades of Denial; Yet the Questions of Redress for Victims Remains," *Los Angeles Times* (5 August 1993): A1. A speculation as to why it took so long for these victims to come forward has been ventured by Hicks:

Then as now, rape was never an easy charge to sustain. Given the high moral value attached to chastity, the comfort women invariably emerged from their wartime experiences defiled, yet unable to accuse their abusers. They had everything to gain by keeping silent and everything to lose by making accusations. From the patriarchal point of view, it was seen almost as a kindness to the comfort women to pretend that this systematic brutalisation had never taken place.

That local operators and recruiters collaborated in the comfort system was another good reason for silence. Many of them continued after the war in the same line of work, often using the former comfort women who, for economic reasons, were unable to break away from them. Until the late 1980s South Korea was also ruled by a succession of military men who did not countenance citizen demonstrations or lobbying.

George Hicks, *The Comfort Women* (New York: W.W. Norton & Company, 1995), xxi.

130 Brackman, *supra* 122 at 179–80.

131 *IMTFE Docs*, *supra* 109 at Vol 2, transcript, 3904.

132 Brownmiller, *supra* 11 at 59.

133 *IMTFE Docs*, *supra* 109 at Vol 2, transcript, 3905–3913.

- At a declared safety zone which held women and children refugees, soldiers routinely entered the grounds to take away women and girls, who were then "horribly raped and abused by Japanese officers".[134]
- "Rape! Rape! Rape! We estimate at least 1,000 cases a night, and many by day. In case of resistance... there is a bayonet stab or a bullet."[135]
- Five women were taken by Japanese soldiers "to wash their clothes by day, to be raped by night. Two of them were forced to satisfy from 15 to 20 men, and the prettiest one as many as 40 each night."[136]
- A baby of six-months was crying during the rapings of its mother, so "the soldier smothered it by putting his hand over its nose and mouth."[137]
- To torture women, they were stripped at the waist and made to "sit over a heated charcoal stove during the period of menstruation."[138]

Many reports referred to the horrific acts of sexual violence mere "disorder" by the soldiers; one referred to having to chase the "honorable soldiers" away because they were attempting to rape several women.[139]

The refugee and prisoner of war camps were also targeted for sexual violence. People were subjected to attack by either soldiers with apparently unlimited access to the areas, or by the men who were supposed to guard or maintain the camps. According to one account:

> At the time the Japanese entered the city on December 13, 1937, I and my father and my sister had already [been] removed to... the refugee zone. There were about 500 persons living in that house, and I often saw the Japs come to the house asking and searching for women. On one occasion one woman was raped in the open yard. This happened in the night, and all of us could hear her cry while she was raped. But when the Japs left we could not find her, they had taken her away with them. Twice I saw the Japs' truck come to the house and round up women living at the house. These women were taken away by the Japs and none of them returned with the exception of one girl who managed to get back home after having been raped by the Japs, and she told me that all the girls who had been taken in the truck had been raped many times by the Japs, one after the other. This one girl who managed to get back to the house told me that she had seen one other girl raped, and after being raped the Japs stuck weeds into her vagina, and the girl had died from this treatment.[140]

A prosecution report submitted to the IMTFE summarized the horrifying details of some of the sex crime cases: "The victims ranged from young girls to old women... One woman would frequently be assaulted by a number of soldiers.

---

134 *IMTFE Docs*, *supra* 109 at Vol 2, transcript, 4464–4465.
135 *IMTFE Docs*, *supra* 109 at Vol 2, transcript, 4467– 4468.
136 *IMTFE Docs*, *supra* 109 at Vol 2, transcript, 4476.
137 *IMTFE Docs*, *supra* 109 at Vol 2, transcript, 4477.
138 *IMTFE Docs*, *supra* 109 at Vol 2, transcript, 4642.
139 *IMTFE Docs*, *supra* 109 at Vol 2, transcript, 4512–4515; 4526–4528, respectively.
140 *IMTFE Docs*, *supra* 109 at Vol 2, transcript, 4501–4502.

A woman was killed for refusing intercourse. For amusement, a father was forced to assault his daughter. In another case, a boy was forced to assault his sister. An old man was forced to assault his son's wife. Breasts were torn off, and women were stabbed in the bosoms."[141] Clearly, degradation and demoralization were also intended by the aforementioned assaults.

One of the most positive aspects of the Tokyo Trials was its inclusion of rape as a serious war crime meriting inclusion in the prosecution's charges. While rape was not specifically enumerated in the Tokyo Charter, rape was charged in the indictment as a war crime, under "inhumane treatment," "ill-treatment," and "failure to respect family honour and rights." Further, it appears that the Tokyo Tribunal made an effort to ensure that rape crimes were included in the public records during the trial.

In the IMTFE Judgment, General Iwane Matsui, Commander Shunroku Hata, and Foreign Minister Hirota were held criminally responsible for crimes, including sex crimes, committed by persons under their authority.[142] Yet much of the evidence of gender crimes was obscured because the sex crimes apparently were deemed to not warrant coverage in the index. In the five supplementary indexes to the twenty-two-volume set documenting the Tokyo Trial, "rape" is only included under the subheading "atrocities." Even then, a mere four references are cited, representing but a minuscule portion of the number of times rape and other forms of sexual violence were included within the IMTFE transcripts.[143]

In 1948, the Batavia Military Tribunal held a war crimes trial to prosecute the forcible seizure for rape and enforced prostitution of Dutch women living in Dutch Indonesia, who had been forced into sexual servitude by the Japanese during World War II.[144] This trial was the only war crimes trial held after the war to prosecute forced prostitution or sexual slavery.[145] However, the names of both the victims and the accused were sealed. International attention on this

---

141 *IMTFE Docs*, *supra* 109 at Vol 2, transcript, 4544.

142 *The Tokyo Judgement: The International Military Tribunal for the Far East*, eds. B.V.A. Roling & C.F. Ruter (Amsterdam, the Netherlands: University Press Amsterdam 1977), 445–54.

143 See, e.g., *IMTFE Docs*, *supra* 109 at Vol. 2, transcript, 2568–73, 2584, 2593–95, 3904–44, 4463–79, 4496–98, 4501–36, 4544, 4559, 4572–73, 4594, 4602, 4615, 4638, 4642, 4647; at Vol. 6, transcript, 12521–48, 12995, 13117, 13189, 13641–42, 13652.

144 Hicks, *supra* 129 at 31; Nora V. Demleitner, "Forced Prostitution: Naming an International Offense," *Fordham International Law Journal* 18 (1994): 163, 181. Batavia is now Jakarta.

145 There were several lawsuits initiated in the 1990s on behalf of the former "comfort women." For legal analyses of the merits of two of these Complaints, see generally Boling, *supra* 128; Janet L. Tongsuthi, "'Comfort Women' of World War II," *UCLA Women's Law Journal* 4 (1994): 413. Even though the crimes were committed in the 1940s, war crimes and crimes against humanity can still be prosecuted. On 26 November 1968, the "Convention on the Non-Applicability of Statutory Limitations to War Crimes and Crimes Against Humanity" was adopted by G.A. Res 2391 (XXIII). The convention entered into force on 11 November 1970. United Nations, *Human Rights, A Compilation of International Instruments* (2 Vols, 1993) ST/HR/1/Rev.4/ (hereinafter, *Compilation of Int'l Instruments*).

trial was only gained in 1992, when the records, held in The Hague, were made available to the public.[146] While the trial was restricted to crimes against thirty-five Dutch women, it is estimated that between one to two hundred Dutch women were forced into sexual slavery by the Japanese.

3.3.3.3. The War Crimes Trial of General Yamashita

Although not included in the major war crimes trial of the Japanese, the trial of General Tomoyuki Yamashita, commander of the 14th Area Army, has generated much interest in humanitarian law. His trial, which was the first war crimes trial by Allied powers of World War II,[147] was a major development in the law of command responsibility.[148] MacArthur was not obliged to receive permission from the War Department before subjecting Yamashita to a military trial, because Yamashita was not charged with waging a war of aggression, the litmus test for trial before the IMTFE.[149] Thus, because he was not charged with crimes against peace, but instead with traditional war crimes, it was possible to try Yamashita before an American military commission in Manila. His trial began

146 As reported by Hicks, *supra* 129 at 153, who apparently managed to obtain the trial documents.

147 Philip R. Piccigallo, *The Japanese on Trial* 49 (1979).

148 The Yamashita Case, or the "Decision of the United States Military Commission at Manila, 7 December 1945," is reproduced in *The Law of War* (Friedman ed.), *supra* 16 at 1596 (hereinafter, the Yamashita Case); the "Order of General Douglas MacArthur Confirming Death Sentence of General Tomoyuki Yamashita, 6 February 1946," is *reproduced in The Law of War, supra* 16 at 1598. For the appeal to the US Supreme Court, including dissenting opinions, see "In re Yamashita," reproduced in *The Law of War, Ibid.* at 1599; "Judicial Decisions," *In re* Yamashita, *American Journal of International Law* 40 (1946), 432.

149 Lael, *supra* 113 at 68–69. While both Yamashita and Tojo were in American custody, most charges against Tojo were crimes against peace, whereas the charges against Yamashita were more traditional war crimes. Thus, to proceed against Tojo, MacArthur would have needed the permission of the War Department, which favored an international military tribunal instead of an American military commission. As such, Tojo's trial was postponed but Yamashita's case proceeded. Lael, *supra* 113 at xi, describes the impetus for the charge:

> General Douglas MacArthur, vividly remembering his harrowing flight from the Philippines, solemnly pledged in the dark days of 1942 that he would return. Fulfilling that promise in 1944, his forces invaded Leyte in October and Luzon, the most important island in the archipelago, in January 1945. His ensuing struggle with General Tomoyuki Yamashita's 14th Area Army, however, proved to be a long, bloody one. Indeed, by the time Tokyo accepted the terms of unconditional surrender imposed on it by the Allied governments, the number of American and Japanese soldiers who had lost their lives in the Philippines since MacArthur's invasion exceeded [265,000]. But it was the slaying of over thirty-five thousand apparently innocent Filipino civilians by Japanese soldiers during those same ten months that most shocked American and Japanese leaders... [R] eports surfaced, detailing the rape, murder, and torture of tens of thousands of civilians[.]... General MacArthur, angered that Yamashita had so clearly failed to exercise adequate control over his subordinates, ordered his trial as a war criminal.

on 8 October 1945.[150] The charges against him included both general and specific allegations involving command responsibility.[151] General allegations asserted:

> [B]etween 9 October 1944 and 2 September 1945, at Manila and at other places in the Philippine Islands, while commander of armed forces of Japan at war... [Yamashita] unlawfully disregarded and failed to discharge his duty as commander to control the operations of the members of his command, permitting them to commit brutal atrocities and other high crimes...[152]

The specific charges, which did include murder and rape,[153] alleged that as a superior officer he was responsible for the crimes committed by soldiers under his command and that he failed to maintain adequate supervision over the actions of his subordinates.[154]

Military law has long recognized that a leader is generally responsible for acts committed by those under their command. Indeed, an affirmative duty to stop or punish criminal behavior is imposed when a leader does know or reasonably should know of illegal acts committed by subordinates. The prosecution argued that the atrocities committed by Yamashita's troops were "so notorious and so flagrant and so enormous, both as to the scope of their operation and as to the inhumanity, the bestiality involved, that they must have been known to the Accused if he were making any effort whatever to meet the responsibilities of his command or his position; and that if he did not know of those acts, notorious, widespread, repeated, constant as they were, it was simply because he took affirmative action not to know."[155] The issues involved were of major significance regarding criminal liability of military commanders, and would have far reaching implications.

During trial, the prosecution presented strong evidence of Japanese atrocities committed by troops under Yamashita's command, including sexual violence:

150 The Yamashita Trial concluded before the Tokyo Trial even commenced.

151 M. Cherif Bassiouni, *Crimes Against Humanity in International Law* (The Hague, the Netherlands: Kluwer Law International, 1992), 80.

152 *Ibid.* at 80, quoting the Transcript, AG 000.5 (9–24–45) JA, "Before the Military Commission Convened by the Commanding General United States Army Forces, Western Pacific: Yamashita, Tomoyuki," at 31.

153 The specific charges included the murder and mistreatment of over 32,000 Filipino civilians and Americans who had been captured, the rape of hundreds of Filipino women, and the arbitrary destruction of property. Lael, *supra* 113 at 80. It was never alleged that Yamashita had personally committed these crimes.

154 This was not the case at Nuremberg, which did not focus on failing to control one's subordinates. Cassese explains: "[T]he judgement in Nuremberg did not pay much attention to the concept of responsibility for omission. There were so many 'criminal orders,' that they had no need to do so." Cassese, *Violence and Law, supra* 77 at 74.

155 Lael, *supra* 113 at 82–3, citing Transcript at 100.

> In whispers and in screams, [the court] heard how over thirty–two thousand Filipino civilians had died. It learned how Japanese soldiers executed priests in their churches, slaughtered patients in their hospitals, machine-gunned residents in their neighborhoods, and beheaded or burned alive American prisoners of war. It learned of Japanese torture, including the water cure, the burning of feet, and the removal of fingers. It learned how one Japanese soldier tossed a baby in the air and impaled it on the ceiling with his bayonet, and how others bayoneted an eleven–year–old girl thirty–eight times. It learned of rape and necrophilia; of how 476 women in Manila were imprisoned in two hotels and repeatedly raped over an eight–day period by officers and enlisted men alike; of how twenty Japanese soldiers raped one girl and then, as a grand finale, cut off her breasts; and of how drunken soldiers, after killing women civilians, then raped the corpses.[156]

Although the prosecution was unable to prove that Yamashita had ordered the atrocities or had even been made clearly aware of them, they argued that he must have known or should have known of the crimes, either because of the massive number of atrocities, the amount of time involved in committing them, or past knowledge that such crimes were likely. The only way he could not have known would be if he had made an affirmative attempt to remain ignorant, or uninformed. Therefore, it was determined that he should be held accountable.

On December 7, 1945, the fourth anniversary of the Japanese attack on Pearl Harbor, the Commission rendered its verdict.[157] Yamashita was found guilty and sentenced to death by hanging. The Commission held: "[i]t is absurd… to consider a commander a murderer or rapist because one of his soldiers commits a murder or rape. Nevertheless, where murder and rape and vicious, revengeful actions are widespread offences, and there is no effective attempt by a commander to discover and control the criminal acts, such a commander may be held responsible, even criminally liable, for the lawless acts of his troops, depending upon their nature and the circumstances surrounding them."[158]

The military Commission clearly considered certain offenses, including rape, war crimes. In confirming the sentence, MacArthur stated:

> Rarely has so cruel and wanton a record been spread to public gaze. Revolting as this may be in itself, it pales before the sinister and far–reaching implication thereby attached to the profession of arms. The soldier, be he friend or foe, is charged with the protection of the weak and unarmed. It is the very essence and reason for his being… This officer, of proven field merit and entrusted with a high command involving

156 Lael, *supra* 113 at 83–84.

157 Yamashita Case, *supra* 148. The court delivered its verdict within 48 hours after closing arguments were heard. Lael, *supra* 113 at 94–95.

158 Yamashita Case, *supra* 148 at 1597. Also reproduced in Lael, *supra* 113 at 95, citing Transcript at 4061–63. Continuing, the Commission concluded that the violations of the laws of war were "not sporadic in nature," and as a result, Yamashita had "failed to provide effective control… as was required by the circumstances." Yamashita Case, *supra* 148 at 1598.

> authority adequate to his responsibility, has failed this irrevocable standard; has failed his duty to his troops, to his country, to his enemy, and to mankind; he has failed utterly his soldier faith. The transgressions resulting therefrom as revealed by the trial are a blot upon the military profession, a stain upon civilization, and constitute a memory of shame and dishonor that can never be forgotten.[159]

Sex crimes were explicitly prosecuted at the IMTFE and Yamashita trial. Yet, the cases could have and should have gone much further in prosecuting various forms of sexual violence. The gender-related crimes committed were staggering both in their numbers and their barbarity. The cases prosecuted represent an important effort, yet a comparatively modest level of redress for the victims. The pervasiveness of sex crimes had been reported during the First World War and in countless wars before that. There was abundant notice that wartime sexual violence was foreseeable.

4. POST WORLD WAR II GENDER CRIMES REDRESS & A WAY FORWARD

As discussed extensively in this book and elsewhere,[160] after nearly 50 years of wartime impunity following the Nuremberg and Tokyo trials, jurisprudence on gender related crimes has been richly developed in the International Criminal Tribunals for the former Yugoslavia (ICTY)[161] and for Rwanda (ICTR),[162] and in

159 "Order of General Douglas MacArthur Confirming Death Sentence of General Tomoyuki Yamashita, February 6, 1946," *reproduced in The Law of War*, (Friedman ed.), *supra* 16 at 1598; see also Lael, *supra* 113 at 118.

160 In this book, see chapters by authors: Anne-Marie de Brouwer, Kelly Askin, Hon. Teresa Doherty, Valerie Oosterveld, and Patricia Viseur Sellers. For just a small handful of the many books and articles focused on the prosecution of gender crimes in international courts, see Anne-Marie L.M. de Brouwer, *Supranational Criminal Prosecution of Sexual Violence* (Antwerp, Belgium: Intersentia, 2005); Kelly Dawn Askin, *War Crimes Against Women, Prosecution in International War Crimes Tribunals* (The Hague, the Netherlands: Kluwer Law International, 1997); Kelly Askin, "Prosecuting Wartime Rape and Other Gender-Related Crimes Under International Law: Extraordinary Advances, Enduring Obstacles," *Berkeley Journal of International Law* 21 (2003), 288; Hon. Teresa Doherty, "Developments in the Prosecution of Gender-Based Crimes – The Special Court for Sierra Leone Experience," *American University Journal of Gender, Social Policy & the Law* 17 (2009), 327; Valerie Oosterveld, "Lessons From the Special Court for Sierra Leone on the Prosecution of Gender-Based Crimes," *American University Journal of Gender, Social Policy & the Law* (2009), 407; Dianne Luping, "Investigation and Prosecution of Sexual and Gender-Based Crimes Before the International Criminal Court," *American University Journal of Gender, Social Policy & the Law* 17 (2009), 431; Patricia Viseur Sellers, "Gender Strategy is Not a Luxury For International Courts," *American University Journal of Gender, Social Policy & the Law* 17 (2009), 301.

161 ICTY Statute, *supra* 3.

162 ICTR Statute, *supra* 4.

the Special Court for Sierra Leone (SCSL).[163] The permanent International Criminal Court (ICC)[164] specifically enumerated a broad range of sex crimes most of which had not previously been listed in other court's statutes. Because the gender crimes jurisprudence has already been detailed extensively, the leading jurisprudence will only be highlighted here.

In the contemporary war crimes tribunals, rape has been successfully prosecuted as a war crime,[165] a crime against humanity,[166] and an instrument of genocide;[167] the ICTY and ICTR have recognized rape as forms and means of torture,[168] rape and enslavement has been prosecuted as constituting sexual slavery,[169] as well as forms and means of persecution.[170] It is also established that gender crimes may form part of a joint criminal enterprise (JCE), and that perpetrators and others participating in the JCE may be held responsible for not only intended, but also persecutorial or foreseeable crimes committed in furtherance of the JCE.[171] The tribunals have also noted that other gender-related crimes, such as forced marriage, forced nudity, forced pregnancy, sexual mutilation, and forced abortion, may constitute an international crime,[172] and that men and boys are also subjected to various forms of sexual violence.[173]

In 1998, the Rome Statute of the ICC formally listed rape, sexual slavery, enforced prostitution, forced pregnancy, enforced sterilization, and "other forms of sexual violence of comparable gravity," as war crimes and crimes against humanity and also emphasized that gender based persecution as well as trafficking in women and children may be prosecuted.[174] While no judgments have yet been rendered in the ICC (as of March 2011), the court has accused a number of individuals of rape or sexual slavery as war crimes and crimes against

---

163 Special Court for Sierra Leone, UN Doc. S/2002/246, 8 March 2002; Statute of the Special Court for Sierra Leone, 16 January 2002, 2178 U.N.T.S. 145 (SCSL Statute).

164 Rome Statute of the International Criminal Court, U.N. Doc. A/CONF.183/9 (1998) (entered into force 1 July 2002) (Rome Statute or ICC Statute).

165 The leading precedent is *Prosecutor v. Delalic et al.*, IT-96–21-T, 16 November, 1998 (*Celebici Trial Chamber Judgement*); *Prosecutor v. Furundzija*, IT-95–17/1-T, 10 December 1998 (*Furundzija Trial Chamber Judgement*).

166 The leading precedent is *Prosecutor v. Akayesu*, ICTR-96–4-T, 2 September 1998 (*Akayesu Trial Chamber Judgement*); *Prosecutor v. Kunarac et al.*, IT-96–23-T & IT-96–23/1-T, 22 February 2001 (*Kunarac Trial Chamber Judgement*).

167 The leading precedents are *Akayesu Trial Chamber Judgement, supra* 166; *Prosecutor v. Muhimana*, ICTR-95–1B-T, 28 April 2005 (*Muhimana Trial Chamber Judgement*).

168 *Akayesu Trial Chamber Judgement, supra* 166; *Celebici Trial Chamber Judgement, supra* 165; *Furundzija Trial Chamber Judgement, supra* 165; *Kunarac Trial Chamber Judgement, supra* 166).

169 The leading precedent is *Kunarac Trial Chamber Judgement, supra* 166.

170 The leading precedent is *Prosecutor v. Kvocka*, IT-98–30-T, 2 November 2001 (*Kvocka Trial Chamber Judgement*).

171 The leading precedent is *Prosecutor v. Krstic*, IT-98–33-T, 2 August 2001 (*Krstic Trial Chamber Judgement*); *Kvocka Trial Chamber Judgement, supra* 170.

172 See *Kvocka Trial Chamber Judgement, supra* 170 at para 180 and note 343.

173 See *Kvocka Trial Chamber Judgement, supra* 170 at para 180 and note 343.

174 ICC Statute, *supra* 164 at Articles 7 & 8.

humanity committed in Uganda (Kony et. al), the Democratic Republic of Congo (Katanga & Ngudjolo; Mbarushimana), the Central African Republic (Bemba), and the Darfur region of Sudan (Harun & Ali Kushayb; Bashir). The genocide charge against President Bashir also includes sex crimes.[175] There will likely be sex crimes included in the situations in Kenya and Libya once charges are formalized and arrest warrants sought for these situations. Other ICC suspects who do not currently have sex crime charges against them, such as the BoscoNtaganda (aka The Terminator) from the DRC, will almost certainly have charges amended to include them.

Additionally, the Special Court for Sierra Leone (SCSL) has successfully prosecuted not only rape and sexual slavery, but also "forced marriage," as an inhumane act.[176] Further, the Extraordinary Chambers in the Courts of Cambodia (ECCC)[177] convicted "Duch," the head of a notorious Khmer Rouge torture facility, of a number of crimes, including rape.[178] There have perhaps been under-recognized efforts to prosecute rape as war crimes and crimes against humanity in the Bosnian War Crimes Chamber (BWCC). Some of the rape cases were sent from the ICTY down to the Bosnia court, as lower level indictees to be tried locally, but others have originated in the BWCC.[179]

As noted above, the Tribunals have prosecuted atrocity crimes, including sex crimes, under the Joint Criminal Enterprise (JCE) theory of responsibility. Under international law, individual criminal liability for participation in a JCE may ensue when there is i) a plurality of persons, ii) a common objective which amounts to or involves the commission of a crime within the governing statute, and iii) the accused participates in the crimes or the objective's implementation. There are three recognized forms of JCE: Essentially, JCE-I (basic) is when all co-defendants act pursuant to a common criminal design or plan and possess the same criminal intent. JCE-II (systemic) is characterized by an organized

---

175 These are all available on the court's website at www.icc-cpi.int/Menus/ICC/Situations+and+Cases/. The Women's Initiative for Gender Justice provides detailed coverage of each of these cases, with an emphasis on highlighting the advances and neglects of each case regarding the gender related crimes. See www.iccwomen.org. The American University's Washington College of Law's War Crimes Research Office is also working on a searchable gender jurisprudence database covering all tribunals. See www.wcl.american.edu/gender/wilp/gicl/.

176 *Prosecutor v. Sesay & Kallon*, SCSL-04-15-T, 25 Feburary 2009 (RUF Judgment); See also *Prosecutor v. Brima, Kamara & Kanu*, SCSL-04-16-T, 20 June 2007 (AFRC Judgment), Partly Dissenting Opinion of Justice Doherty on Count 7 (Sexual Slavery) and Count Eight ("Forced Marriages").

177 Law on the Establishment of Extraordinary Chambers in the Courts of Cambodia, UNGA Res. 57/228; UN Doc. A/RES/57/228 (18 December 2002) (ECCC or Extraordinary Chambers). The ECCC is also known as the Khmer Rouge Tribunal or KRT.

178 *Kaing Guek Eav alias Duch*, 001/18-07-2007/ECCC/TC, 26 July 2010.

179 Diane F. Orentlicher, *That Someone Guilty Be Punished: The Impact of the ICTY in Bosnia*, (July 2010, Open Society Justice Initiative), 118–125, and endnote 860, available at www.soros.org/initiatives/justice/focus/international_justice/articles_publications/publications/that-someone-guilty-20100707.

criminal system, such as a concentration camp or a system of persecution. JCE-III (extended) is used in situations when someone in a joint criminal endeavor commits an act which, while outside the common plan, is a natural or foreseeable consequence of the plan, for which the defendant willingly takes the risk.[180]

While the jurisprudence on gender crimes is groundbreaking and rich in development, it is also far from adequate. Many investigative missions wholly fail to include sex crime investigations despite clear evidence of the crimes, many indictments drop sex crime charges, and acquittals on these crimes occurs far too frequently. Women's activists and scholars as well as court and human rights monitors focused on ensuring that gender related crimes are not ignored can claim credit for a huge amount of the jurisprudence that has been successful in addressing these crimes. The presence of experts in women's issues and gender crimes, and competent women in decision-making positions, within these courts is also a key reason for the success. Yet sexist attitudes and ignorance surrounding sex crimes continue to be common, alongside harmful stereotypes and archaic practices. There is much room for improvement in all organs of the courts, and certainly all spheres of life outside the courts.

There is a grave need to prosecute senior military and civilian leaders far from the battlefield for sex crimes, particularly when the crimes have been committed consistently over an extended period. The Trial Chamber judgment in the ICTY's Krajisnik case was a long overdue step forward in this respect,[181] but the Appeals Chamber Judgment[182] in the case unfortunately reversed the significant legal advances made by the Trial Chamber, which included recognizing sex crimes as part of JCE-I (basic/intended), instead of simply JCE-III (extended/foreseeable). With the reversal, sexual violence was yet again relegated to being treated as a by-product of war or an opportunistic crime, not a strategic tool of warfare. Even if not originally contemplated in devising a plan of attack, if sex crimes occur and continue and authorities make no effort to put a plan in place to prevent the crimes, eventually they should be considered incorporated into the attack strategy. When such crimes are ignored they are acquiesced and tacitly approved. More often, however, sexual violence as a weapon of terror and destruction is part of the original attack strategy. Reports, including UN reports, as well as Security Council resolutions, recognize the use of rape warfare,[183] but pitifully few tribunal judgments do.

---

180 The JCE parameters were first articulated by the ICTY, using Nuremberg jurisprudence, in *Prosecutor v. Tadic*, IT-94-1-A, 15 July 1999 (*Tadic Appeals Chamber Judgement*), paras 185–229. See also the lengthy discussion of JCE and its historical usage, in *Kvocka Trial Chamber Judgement, supra* 170.

181 *Prosecutor v. Krajisnik*, IT-00-39-T, 27 September 2006 (*Krajisnik Trial Chamber Judgement*).

182 *Prosecutor v. Krajisnik*, IT-00-39-A, March 17, 2009 (*Krajisnik Appeals Chamber Judgement*).

183 See e.g. Security Council Resolutions 1325, 31 October 2000; 1612, 26 July 2005; 1674, 28 April 2006; 1820, 19 June 2008; 1882, 4 August 2009; 1888, 30 September 2009; 1889, 5 October, 2009; 1894, 11 November 2009; and 1960, 16 December 2010.

The courts should place an emphasis on investigating and prosecuting some of the reproductive crimes. Harming or killing the reproducers of a group has clear implications for the affected population. The international and domestic courts must make an effort to prosecute reproductive crimes, including enforced sterilization and forced pregnancy. The courts should also consider prosecuting sexual mutilation and forced abortion under the 'other forms of sexual violence of comparable gravity' language of the Statutes.

The crime of 'forced marriage' is essentially a more intimate form of sexual slavery (the women and girls typically are essentially forced to cook, clean, provide sexual services and perform other so-called 'wifely duties' for a single male instead of being held in a location where they are raped by dozens of different men and boys) and should be prosecuted under either 'sexual slavery' or 'other forms of sexual violence' instead of 'inhumane acts.' Victims conscripted into 'forced marriage' are often treated differently by society than victims of sexual slavery or rape, as those forced into so-called 'marriage' are frequently rejected as collaborators. Treating 'forced marriage' as a serious crime allows survivors their right to be a victim. It also identifies the sexual nature of the crime which is not obvious in broader umbrella language, such as inhumane acts.

Sentences should reflect the heinous and repeated nature of many sex crimes. Each and every act of sexual penetration should be considered a separate rape, and courts should recognize that crimes such as sexual slavery may represent hundreds of rapes, as well as loss of freedom and broader slavery treatment. Five or ten year sentences for such crimes are unjustly low. When children are victimized, sentences should be even more severe.

The UN Independent Expert on Combatting Impunity confirmed that victims of serious human rights violations have a right to know the truth of what happened, a right to justice, and a right to reparation, including guarantees that the violations will not be repeated.[184] Each of these rights needs to be realized. Both the ICC and the ECCC allow for reparations. Most victims of gender related atrocities are incredibly poor and among the most marginalized in their societies, living in a patriarchal community where women and girls are considered disposable or useless if they do not perform their primary 'function' or 'role' of serving men and taking care of the household. Their primary needs tend to be survival and security. Reparations can help them secure more independence and a better future, and courts should be encouraged to make every effort to grant reparations for the wrongs the victims have suffered and put measures in place to ensure these rights and remedies are realized. Often too, community reparations are more effective and fair than individual reparations.

---

184 Diane Orentlicher, *Commission on Human Rights, Updated Set of Principles for the Protection and Promotion of Human Rights Through Action to Combat Impunity*, U.N. Doc. E/CN.4/2005/102/Add.1 (8 February 2005).

The shame and stigmas wrongly attached to survivors of sex crimes should be reversed, and placed instead on the weak, cowardly, and dishonorable who commit sex crimes or allow them to occur by those under their authority. The perpetrators, not the victims, should be shunned and rejected by society. Only then will the crimes see a reduction and the use of rape warfare decreased.

For thousands of years, sex crimes have been committed during war. An affirmative duty to put in place and monitor steps to prevent such crimes should fall to state authorities or other responsible agencies in any armed conflict situation. Failures should be punished and otherwise remedied.

The international war crimes tribunals established since 1993 have investigated and prosecuted some of the most common forms of wartime sexual violence and the most widely reported occurrences. Domestic courts and regional human rights courts should step up and take responsibility for prosecuting the mid and lower level suspects, as well as the higher level suspects when possible. In eastern Congo, mobile gender justice courts have been very effective in going to remote communities otherwise without access to formal justice, and holding rape and crime against humanity trials against civilians and military personnel.[185] Holding trials in the community where the crimes occurred is an important feature of local courts.

International courts need to be far more efficient and effective. Victims resent the tens of millions poured into international courts, and the rights and perceived luxuries extended to defendants, when they struggle daily to simply survive. The courts need to be able to investigate and prosecute senior officials for serious crimes within months, not years, without sacrificing fair trial rights. This may be a decade away, but it is surely achievable. The higher level suspects convicted of crimes should systematically have their resources tracked and illicit funds returned to the society from which they've been plundered. Rich and powerful leaders should also not be allowed to plead indigency and require the international community to pay millions for their defense, when these resources can more usefully and more justly go toward other needs, including protective measures which prevent the crimes from occurring in the first place, and community reparations.

Under the ICC's core principle of complementarity – that the primary responsibility to investigate and prosecute atrocity crimes rests with states – domestic systems must do far more to ensure that atrocity crimes, including sex crimes, are redressed. As noted above, mobile courts have been quite effective in the DRC. In February 2011, a mobile military court in eastern DRC tried eleven soldiers, including a Lieutenant Colonel, for rape as a crime against humanity in

185 See, for example, Kelly Askin, *Fizi Diary: Mobile Court Hears Landmark Rape Case*, 17 February 2011, available at http://blog.soros.org/2011/02/fizi-diary-mobile-court-tries-landmark-rape-case/.

a trial that was found to meet fair trial standards.[186] More mobile courts, including mobile gender justice courts, which go out to people in remote locations far from justice centers, can help bridge the impunity gap by providing access to justice and ensuring local terrorizers are locked up.

Women's NGOs which monitor courts and demand adequate gender justice play an indispensible role in getting rape crimes investigated and prosecuted. And it is impossible to overemphasize how crucial it is to women's issues, gender crimes, and the law in general to have experienced, capable women in decision-making positions in international and local fora, particularly within the United Nations structure, and as judges, prosecutors, registrars, legal advisers and peacemakers. Women's empowerment is a necessary tool to remedy many of the crimes committed exclusively or disproportionately against women and girls. More can and must be done to end the centuries of near universal impunity for sex crimes committed during armed conflict and to ensure that women's bodies are not the battlefield and that sex crimes are no longer used systematically as weapons of warfare and terror.

186 See e.g., Kelly Askin, "Fizi Mobile Court: Rape Verdicts," *International Justice Tribune* 123 (2 March 2011).

CHAPTER 3
PROSECUTING GENDER-BASED PERSECUTION AS AN INTERNATIONAL CRIME

Valerie Oosterveld[1]

1. INTRODUCTION

The Rome Statute of the International Criminal Court (ICC) explicitly codified, for the first time in international criminal law, the crime against humanity of persecution based on gender.[2] The ICC will therefore be the first international criminal tribunal to prosecute gender-based persecution as a crime against humanity. This may occur in the case of Callixte Mbarushimana, a senior leader of the Forces Démocratiques pour la Libération de Rwanda (FDLR) charged with, *inter alia*, persecution in the Democratic Republic of the Congo achieved through means including rape.[3] It may also occur in the case of three other

1 The author thanks Marc Kitay for his research assistance. The author also thanks the Social Sciences and Humanities Research Council of Canada for its research funding.

2 Rome Statute of the International Criminal Court, arts. 7(1)(h), opened for signature 17 July 1998, UN Doc. A/CONF.183/9 (1998) (entered into force 1 July 2002) (Rome Statute). 'Gender' was added as a specific persecutory ground in order to bring the Rome Statute "up-to-date": Georg Witschel and Wiebke Rückert, "Article 7(1)(h) – Crime Against Humanity of Persecution," in *The International Criminal Court: Elements of Crimes and Rules of Procedure and Evidence*, ed. Roy S. Lee, Håkan Friman, *et al.* (Ardsley, New York: Transnational Publishers, 2001), 94–95. A similar provision on gender-based persecution was subsequently included in the Regulations of the United Nations Transitional Administration in East Timor (UNTAET), Reg. 2000/15, On the Establishment of Panels with Exclusive Jurisdiction Over Serious Criminal Offences, Section 5.1(h), 6 June 2000, crimes against humanity. In contrast, persecution on the ground of gender was not included in the Statute of the Special Court for Sierra Leone: Statute of the Special Court for Sierra Leone, annexed to Agreement Between the United Nations and the Government of Sierra Leone on the Establishment of a Special Court for Sierra Leone, 16 January 2002, available at www.sc-sl.org/LinkClick.aspx?fileticket=uClnd1MJeEw%3d&tabid=176.

3 *Prosecutor v. Callixte Mbarishumana*, ICC-01/04–01/10, Warrant of Arrest for Callixte Mbarushimana, 28 September 2010, paras 7(iii) and 10(xi), available at www.icc-cpi.int/iccdocs/doc/doc954979.pdf (Mbarushimana Warrant of Arrest). A majority of the Pre-Trial Chamber declined to confirm the charges against Mbarushimana on16 December 2011, but this decision is currently under appeal: *Prosecutor v. Callixte Mbarushimana*, ICC-01/04–

individuals – Ahmad Muhammad Harun ("Harun"), Ali Muhammad Ali Abd-Al-Rahman ("Ali Kushayb") and Abdel Raheem Muhammad Hussein – who have also been charged with persecution as a crime against humanity, including persecution in Darfur, Sudan, achieved through the intensely gendered act of rape.[4] It is an opportune time to consider the potential benefits and challenges currently facing the ICC in prosecuting gender-based persecution.[5]

This chapter begins by exploring judgments on the gendered dimensions of the crime against humanity of persecution issued by the International Criminal Tribunals for the Former Yugoslavia and Rwanda (ICTY and ICTR respectively). It finds that they provide helpful guidance to the ICC in identifying actions that might be considered to be directed against a group or collectivity (women, girls, men or boys) on the ground of gender. It then considers certain difficulties associated with the prosecution of gender-based persecution. The first difficulty comes from the way in which the term 'gender' is defined in the Rome Statute: "the two sexes, male and female, within the context of society."[6] This definition is not necessarily clear, and leaves room for judicial misunderstanding or misinterpretation.[7] The second challenge is that gender-based persecution often intersects with other forms of persecution: persecution can be carried out using acts directed simultaneously against a member of a group or collectivity because of his or her political affiliation, race, nationality, ethnicity, culture, or religion,[8] *and* due to his or her gender. Thus, the ICC's Prosecutor will need to clearly outline the nature of this intersectionality and, in so doing, explain why it is important for the Court to recognize not just one, but both, aspects of the intersection so as to avoid gender disappearing in favour of the more 'traditional' forms of persecution.

01/10, Prosecution's Document in Support of Appeal against the "Decision on the Confirmation of Charges", 12 March 2012, paras. 1–3, available at www.icc-cpi.int/NR/exeres/7C5318C0-122C-476A-8314-6A3C9144432D.htm (Mbarushimana Appeal).

4 *Prosecutor v. Ahmad Muhammad Harun* ("Ahmad Harun") *and Ali Muhammad Al Abd-Al-Rahman* ("Ali Kushayb"), ICC-02/05-01/07, Warrant of Arrest for Ahmad Harun, counts 10 and 39, 27 April 2007, available at www2.icc-cpi.int/iccdocs/doc/doc279813.PDF; *Prosecutor v. Ahmad Muhammad Harun* ("Ahmad Harun") *and Ali Muhammad Al Abd-Al-Rahman* ("Ali Kushayb"), ICC-02/05-01/07, Warrant of Arrest for Ali Kushayb, counts 10 and 39, 27 April 2007, available at www2.icc-cpi.int/iccdocs/doc/doc279858.PDF (Harun and Ali Kushayb Warrants of Arrest); and *Prosecutor v. Abdel Raheem Muhammad Hussein*, ICC-02/05-01/12, Warrant of Arrest for Abdel Raheem Muhammad Hussein, 6–7, 1 March 2012, available at www.icc-cpi.int/iccdocs/doc/doc1344965.pdf (Hussein Warrant of Arrest). Rape is an intensely gendered crime because it tends to be used against women, girls, men and boys in order to shame, punish and/or differentiate the victim as "other" in ways related to the perpetrators' and victims' understandings of social constructions of maleness and femaleness.

5 The Prosecutor's appeal against the decision of a majority of the Pre-Trial Chamber declining to confirm the charges against Mbarushimana is being considered in 2012.

6 Rome Statute, Article 7(3) *supra* 2.

7 Valerie Oosterveld, "The Definition of "Gender" in the Rome Statute of the International Criminal Court: A Step Forward or Back for International Criminal Justice?" *Harvard Human Rights Journal* 18 (2005) 55, 74, 77 and 82 (2005) (Oosterveld Definition of "Gender").

8 These are the other prohibited grounds of persecution listed in the Rome Statute, Article 7(1)(h), *supra* 2.

The final challenge is related to existing ICC case law on cumulative charging which raises the possibility that other gender-based crimes may be dismissed in favour of the persecution charge, or that persecution may be dismissed as a "cumulative" crime, at the confirmation of charges stage of the proceeding due to the fact that persecution is, by definition, linked with other prohibited acts.

This chapter concludes that the ICC will – beginning with its first prosecution of gender-based persecution – create important precedent. This precedent will set the tone for future prosecutions at the international level and could also profoundly influence the development of national crimes against humanity jurisprudence. Its influence may reach yet further, into international refugee law's consideration of gender-based persecution. It is therefore crucial that the ICC's Prosecutor and victims' counsel understand and properly explain the complex nature of gender, the ways in which gender-based persecution may differ from other forms of persecution, and the manner in which gender-based persecution can intersect with other forms of persecution. This will allow the ICC's judges to take the nascent findings of the ICTY and ICTR and profoundly deepen international criminal law's understanding of the role of gender in the crime against humanity of persecution.

2. CHARGES OF GENDER-BASED PERSECUTION BEFORE THE ICC

The newly-codified crime against humanity of gender-based persecution has not yet been prosecuted within the ICC. However, it may be considered in the near future, depending on the outcome of a prosecution appeal in the case of Callixte Mbarishimana, a senior FDLR leader accused of responsibility for crimes committed by the FDLR in the North and South Kivu provinces of the Democratic Republic of the Congo between January and September 2009.[9] The Prosecutor alleges that Mbarushimana, as Executive Secretary of the FDLR since July 2007 and heir to certain powers of the FDLR Presidency in November 2009, intentionally contributed to the commission of FDLR crimes under the mode of responsibility set out in article 25(3)(d) of the Rome Statute.[10] These FDLR crimes include, according to the Prosecutor, the crime against humanity of persecution, carried out by, among other acts, rape in a number of villages in both North and South Kivu.[11] A majority of the Pre-Trial Chamber declined to

9 *Mbarushimana Warrant of Arrest*, *supra* 3.

10 *Supra* 3 at paras 4 and 8.

11 *Supra* 3 at paras 7(iii) and 10(xi). These allegations are consistent with those also made in nongovernmental reports. For examples of reports of deliberate sexual violence by the FDLR from the same time period, see: *DR Congo: Brutal Rapes by Rebels and Army* (New York: Human Rights Watch, 8 April 2009), available at www.hrw.org/en/news/2009/04/08/dr-congo-brutal-rapes-rebels-and-army; and *Waking the Devil: The Impact of Forced*

confirm the charges against Mbarushimana, and the prosecution has appealed.[12] If successful in the appeal, the Prosecutor clearly intends to rely upon the gendered nature of FDLR violence – various forms of rape including forcing civilian men to rape women, as well as mutilation of genitals and slicing of pregnant women's bellies to remove fetuses – to establish the persecution charge.[13] He characterizes those acts as "intentionally and in a discriminatory manner targeting women and men seen to be affiliated with the FARDC [*Forces Armées de la République Démocratique du Congo*] on the basis of their gender, through torture, rape, inhumane acts and inhuman treatment".[14]

The ICC has also issued arrest warrants in the Darfur situation against three individuals – Harun, Ali Kushayb and Hussein – who are charged with persecution as a crime against humanity, including persecution achieved through rape.[15] These men are charged for their involvement in governmental and Janjaweed attacks directed against the primarily Fur population, including persecution achieved through rape in Bindisi town and surrounding areas, and Arawala town and surrounding areas.[16] The Harun, Ali Kushayb and Hussein arrest warrants are not clear as to exactly which ground, or grounds, of persecution listed in the Rome Statute is/are being pursued. However, the facts as presented by the Prosecutor with respect to rape – a gendered act focused in this case on women and girls[17] – support an argument based on persecution situated at the intersection of gender and ethnicity.[18] This approach is confirmed by reports in a number of other sources.[19]

Displacement on Civilians in the Kivus 1–2 (Oxford, UK: Oxfam, July 2009), 1–2, available at www.oxfamamerica.org/files/waking-the-devil.pdf.

12 *Mbarushimana Appeal, supra* 3.

13 *Prosecutor v. Callixte Mbarushimana*, ICC-01/04-01/10, Decision on the Prosecutor's Application for a Warrant of Arrest against Callixte Mbarushimana, 28 September 2010 at para 10 (Mbarushimana Decision on Arrest Warrant).

14 *Ibid.*

15 *Harun and Ali Kushayb Warrant of Arrest, supra* 4, at counts 10 and 39. *Hussein Warrant of Arrest, supra* 4, at 6–7.

16 *Ibid.*

17 While the focus of rape on women and girls is not entirely clear from the persecution counts, it is from the rape counts: *Harun and Ali Kushayb Warrant of Arrest, supra* 4 at counts 13, 14, 42 and 43, and *Hussein Warrant of Arrest, supra* 4 at 6–7.

18 While the arrest warrants issued against Harun, Ali Kushayb and Hussein are not clear as to how the Prosecutor will categorize the Fur population of Darfur – as a racial, ethnic or cultural group – in the second warrant of arrest issued against Sudan's President Al Bashir, the Prosecutor refers to the Fur, Masalit and Zaghawa groups as "ethnic": *Prosecutor v. Omar Hassan Ahmad Al Bashir* ("Omar Al Bashir"), ICC-02/05-01/09, Second Warrant of Arrest for Omar Hassan Ahmad Al Bashir, 12 July 2010, 5.

19 The International Commission of Inquiry on Darfur identified many forms of gender-based violence used by the Janjaweed militia and government forces in Darfur: rape of women and girls (including multiple rape, gang rape, public rape, rape in front of family, rape while being held in confinement and rape resulting in pregnancy), abductions and confinement of women and girls, executions of boys, forced nudity of women and girls, torture of women to prevent them from escaping, beatings during or leading to rape of women and girls, and murder

The ICC's indictments against Mbarushimana, Harun, Ali Kushayb and Hussein demonstrate that the ICC's Prosecutor is prepared to prosecute the crime against humanity of persecution carried out through rape and other gendered means. If it proceeds, the *Mbarushimana* case is likely to be precedent-setting within international criminal law, not only as the first international prosecution of gender-based persecution, but also for highlighting the fact that this form of persecution can be carried out against women, girls, men and boys.

3. DEFINITION OF PERSECUTION IN THE ICC AND JURISPRUDENCE OF THE ICTY AND ICTR

The Rome Statute of the ICC includes within its list of prohibited acts amounting to crimes against humanity "[p]ersecution against any identifiable group or collectivity on political, racial, national, ethnic, cultural, religious, gender… or other grounds that are universally recognized as impermissible under international law, in connection with any act referred to in this paragraph or any crime within the jurisdiction of the Court."[20] This codification expanded the list of prohibited grounds that had been included in earlier documents to include gender, cultural and other grounds that are universally recognized as impermissible under international law.[21] It also differed from the provisions of

---

following rape, and concluded that "the fact that rape and other forms of sexual violence were conducted against three "African" tribes is indicative of the discriminatory intent of the perpetrators": *Report of the International Commission of Inquiry on Darfur to the United Nations Secretary-General, Pursuant to Security Council Resolution 1564 of 18 September 2004* (Geneva, Switzerland: United Nations International Commission of Inquiry on Darfur, 25 January 2005), paras 333–60, available at www.un.org/news/dh/sudan/com_inq_darfur.pdf (International Commissions of Inquiry). See also: *Access to Justice for Victims of Sexual Violence* (United Nations High Commissioner for Human Rights, 29 July 2005), paras 27–28, available at www.ohchr.org/Documents/Countries/darfur29july05.pdf (which also notes the rape of boys); *Sudan, Darfur, Rape as a Weapon of War: Sexual Violence and its Consequences* (London: Amnesty International, July 2004), available at www.amnesty.org/en/library/info/AFR54/076/2004; *Five Years On: No Justice for Sexual Violence in Darfur* (New York: Human Rights Watch, 6 April 2008), available at www.hrw.org/en/reports/2008/04/06/five-years-0; and *The Crushing Burden of Rape: Sexual Violence in Darfur* (Gevena, Switzerland: Médecins Sans Frontières, 8 March 2005), available at www.msf.org/msfinternational/invoke.cfm?objectid=99CD9F41-E018-0C72-09C703FCC9098A2B&component=toolkit.report&method =full_html. Surprisingly, these reports do not identify the crime against humanity of gender-based persecution as one of the potential crimes in Darfur.

20 Rome Statute, Article 7(1)(h), *supra* 2.

21 For example, the Charter of the International Military Tribunal, Control Council Law No. 10 and the Statute of the International Criminal Tribunal for the Former Yugoslavia list political, racial and religious grounds: Charter of the International Military Tribunal, Article 6, in the Agreement for the Prosecution and Punishment of the Major War Criminals of the European Axis, 8 August 1945, 82 U.N.T.S. 279; Control Council Law. No. 10, Punishment of Persons Gui-lty of War Crimes, Crimes Against Peace and Against Humanity, 20 January 1946, 3 *Official Gazette of the Control Council for Germany* 50; and Statute of the International

the ICTY and ICTR Statutes because it added a requirement that persecutory acts be connected with other crimes within the jurisdiction of the ICC – a requirement that first appeared in the Charter of the World War II International Military Tribunal, but which had not been included in the ICTY and ICTR Statutes.[22]

Persecution is defined in the Rome Statute as "the intentional and severe deprivation of fundamental rights contrary to international law by reason of the identity of the group or collectivity."[23] As well, the ICC's Elements of Crimes document sets out the elements of persecution as:

1. The perpetrator severely deprived, contrary to international law, one or more persons of fundamental rights.
2. The perpetrator targeted such person or persons by reason of the identity of a group or collectivity or targeted the group or collectivity as such.
3. Such targeting was based on political, racial, national, ethnic, cultural, religious, gender as defined in article 7, paragraph 3, of the Statute, or other grounds that are universally recognized as impermissible under international law.
4. The conduct was committed in connection with any act referred to in article 7, paragraph 1, of the Statute or any crime within the jurisdiction of the Court.[24]

While the ICTY and ICTR Statutes do not themselves contain as detailed a definition of the prohibited act of persecution,[25] the ICC's definition largely reflects the approach taken in the ICTY and ICTR's extensive case law.[26] For

---

Criminal Tribunal, Article 5(h), 25 May 1993, 32 I.L.M. 1192 (1993) (ICTY Statute). The Statute of the International Criminal Tribunal for Rwanda lists the same persecutory grounds, but also requires that the crime against humanity be based on national, political, ethnic, racial or religious grounds: Statute of the International Criminal Tribunal for Rwanda, Article 3, 8 November 1994, 33 I.L.M. 1602 (1994) (ICTR Statute).

22 Many commentators have noted that this addition does not reflect customary international law. See, for example, Darryl Robinson, "Defining "Crimes Against Humanity" at the Rome Conference," *American Journal of International Law* 93 (1999): 43, 46 and Gerhard Werle, *Principles of International Criminal Law* (The Hague, the Netherlands: T.M.C. Asser Press, Second Ed., 2009), para 898 (Werle). The ICTY's Trial Chamber has also made a similar observation: *Prosecutor v. Kupreškić et al.*, IT-95-16-T, 14 January 2000, para 580 (Kupreškić Trial Judgment). This linkage was added to allay fears of conservative Arab states that the ICC would become a human rights, rather than an international criminal court: Robinson, *Ibid.* at 53.

23 Rome Statute, Article 7(2)(g), *supra* 2.

24 Elements of Crimes of the International Criminal Court, ICC-ASP/1/3 at 108, U.N. Doc. PCNICC/2000/1/Add.2 (2000) art. 7(1)(h) (footnotes excluded) (ICC Elements of Crimes). The final two elements relate to the overarching requirements of all crimes against humanity, namely: that the conduct was committed as part of a widespread or systematic attack directed against a civilian population, and that the perpetrator knew that the conduct was part of or intended the conduct to be part of a widespread or systematic attack directed against a civilian population: *Ibid.* at Article 7(1)(h), elements 5 and 6.

25 Werle at para 888, *supra* 22.

26 See, e.g., *Kupreškić Trial Judgment* at para 621, *supra* 22; *Prosecutor v. Krstić*, IT-98-33-T, 2 November 2001, para 534, (International Criminal Tribunal for the Former Yugoslavia)

example, the ICTY's Appeals Judgment in *Prosecutor v. Krnojelac* defined persecution as "an act or omission which discriminates in fact and which: denies or infringes upon a fundamental right laid down in international customary or treaty law (the *actus reus*); and was carried out deliberately with the intention to discriminate on one of the listed grounds, specifically race, religion or politics (the *mens rea*)."[27] This was confirmed in 2010 in *Prosecutor v. Popović et al.*[28]

The crime of persecution can be committed by a single intentional act or omission or a series of intentional acts or omissions.[29] The underlying discriminatory act(s) or omission(s) need not constitute a crime in international law, but must be of the same level of gravity as the crimes listed in the ICTY or ICTR Statutes.[30] As noted by William Schabas, "the whole point of having such a category is to enable the prosecution of acts not addressed elsewhere by international criminal law."[31] A number of discriminatory acts have been found to amount to persecution, such as infliction of physical or mental harm through murder, torture, beatings, harassment, humiliation, psychological abuse, hate speech, inhumane conditions, and targeting of property, as well as infringements on individual freedom, such as forced labour, unlawful detention, and deportation of civilians.[32]

Gender-based violence has also been found to amount to a persecutory act by the ICTY and ICTR. For example, the ICTY found that orders given to detained men to perform fellatio on each other amounted to persecution.[33] The ICTR held that the rape of Tutsi women at Kigali area roadblocks and in two religious

---

(Krstić Trial Judgment); *Prosecutor v. Kvočka et al.*, IT-98–30/1-T, 2 November 2011, para 184 (International Criminal Tribunal for the Former Yugoslavia) (Kvočka Trial Judgment); and *Prosecutor v. Krnojelac*, IT-97–25-T, 15 March 2002, para 434 (International Criminal Tribunal for the Former Yugoslavia) (Krnojelac Trial Judgment).

27 *Prosecutor v. Krnojelac*, IT-97-25-A, 17 September 2003, para 185 (International Criminal Tribunal for the Former Yugoslavia).

28 *Prosecutor v. Popović et al.*, IT-05–88-T, 10 June 2010, para 964 (International Criminal Tribunal for the Former Yugoslavia) (Popović Trial Judgment).

29 *Ibid.* at para 965. See also *Prosecutor v. Vasiljević*, IT-98–32-A, 25 February 2004, para 113 (International Criminal Tribunal for the Former Yugoslavia).

30 *Kupreškić Trial Judgment* at paras 614 and 621, *supra* 22 *Prosecutor v. Kvočka et al.*, IT-98–30/1-A, 28 February 20005, para 323 (International Criminal Tribunal for the Former Yugoslavia) (Kvočka Appeals Judgment); *Popović Trial Judgment* at para 966, *supra* 28; and *Prosecutor v. Nahimana et al.*, ICTR-96–11-A, 28 November 2007, paras 985–88 (International Criminal Tribunal for Rwanda) (Nahimana Appeals Judgment).

31 William A. Schabas, *The UN International Criminal Tribunals: The Former Yugoslavia, Rwanda and Sierra Leone* (Cambridge, UK: Cambridge University Press, 2006), 218 (Schabas).

32 *Ibid.* at 218–19. See also, for e.g., *Prosecutor v. Blaškić*, IT-95–14-T, 3 March 2000, paras 227 and 233 (International Criminal Tribunal for the Former Yugoslavia); *Kvočka Appeals Judgment* at paras 324–25, *supra* 28; *Nahimana Appeals Judgment* at paras 987–88, *supra* 30; and *Krnojelac Trial Judgment* at paras 128–72, *supra* 26.

33 *Prosecutor v. Todorović*, IT-95–9/1-S, Sentencing Judgment, 31 Jul 2001, paras 9, 12 and 38–40 (International Criminal Tribunal for the Former Yugoslavia).

buildings amounted to persecution.[34] The ICTY has also found that the rape of Bosnian Muslim and Bosnian Croat women by Bosnian Serb soldiers or policemen in a number of municipalities was "discriminatory in fact."[35] Similarly, the ICTY held that rape committed in the Trnopolje, Keraterm and Omarska camps was committed with discriminatory intent.[36] Both of the latter judgments noted that acts short of rape amounting to sexual assault or serious abuses of a sexual nature may also amount to persecution.[37] The case of *Prosecutor v. Brđanin* provided these examples of such acts: a Bosnian Croat woman forced to undress in front of cheering Bosnian Serb policemen and soldiers; a Bosnian Muslim woman who had a knife run along her breast; and forced sex among detainees demanded by their captors.[38] Rapes considered to be incidental, as opposed to systematic, were also recognized by the ICTY in *Prosecutor v. Krstić* to be persecutory because they were a foreseeable consequence of persecution.[39] As well, the Tribunals have recognized that gendered language can be used to carry out persecution.[40] For example, the ICTR recognized that "[t]he portrayal of the Tutsi woman as a femme fatale, and the message that Tutsi women were seductive agents of the enemy was conveyed repeatedly [in the media]."[41] This portrayal "articulated a framework that made the sexual attack of Tutsi women a foreseeable consequence of the role attributed to them."[42]

The Tribunals have also considered the tests that must be met by the Prosecutor in order for the Tribunals' judges to find that gender-based violence (most notably sexual violence) is an underlying act of persecution. In the 2009 trial judgment in *Prosecutor v. Milutinović et al.*, the ICTY found sexual assault to be an underlying act of persecution when it met the following elements:

---

34 *Prosecutor v. Bagosora et al.*, ICTR-98-41-T, Judgment and Sentence, 18 December 2008, para 2210 (International Criminal Tribunal for Rwanda).

35 *Prosecutor v. Brđanin*, IT-99-36-T, 1 September 2004, paras 1010–11 (International Criminal Tribunal for the Former Yugoslavia) (Brđanin Trial Judgment).

36 *Prosecutor v. Stakić*, IT-97-24-T, 31 July 2003, para 806 (International Criminal Tribunal for the Former Yugoslavia) (Stakić Trial Judgment).

37 *Brđanin Trial Judgment* at para 1012, *supra* 35; and *Stakić Trial Judgment* at para 757, *supra* 36.

38 *Brđanin Trial Judgment* at para 1013, *supra* 35.

39 *Krstić Trial Judgment* at para 617, *supra* 26. See also *Kvočka Trial Judgment* at para 327, *supra* 26. This is landmark jurisprudence: Patricia Viseur Sellers, "Individual(s') Liability for Collective Sexual Violence," in *Gender and Human Rights*, ed. Karen Knop (Oxford, UK: Oxford University Press, 2004), 153, 184.

40 The ICTY noted that the direct perpetrators of rape and sexual assault used pejorative language to propel discrimination, for example when one said that he wanted a Bosnian Muslim woman "to give birth to a little Serb": *Brđanin Trial Judgment* at para 1011, *supra* 35.

41 *Prosecutor v. Nahimana et al.*, ICTR-96-11-T, 3 December 2003, para 1079 (International Criminal Tribunal for Rwanda).

42 *Ibid.*

(a) The physical perpetrator commits an act of a sexual nature on another, which includes requiring the person to perform such an act;
(b) That act infringes the victim's physical integrity or amounts to an outrage to the victim's personal dignity;
(c) The victim does not consent to the act;[43]
(d) The physical perpetrator intentionally commits the act; and
(e) The physical perpetrator is aware that the act occurred without the consent of the victim.[44]

These elements are to be interpreted broadly.[45] Thus, while rape would amount to an act of a sexual nature, so too would a humiliating and degrading act where there is no physical contact between perpetrator and victim, such as forced nudity.[46] Beth Van Schaack notes that, in this respect, persecution can be particularly useful for charging acts of gender-based violence that are not captured in the other prohibited acts, like forced nudity.[47] The *Milutinović* Trial Chamber opined that, "[i]n the context of an armed conflict, the sexual humiliation and degradation of the victim is a more pertinent factor than the gratification of the perpetrator, and it is this element that provides specificity to the offence."[48] The Trial Chamber also noted that sexual assault qualifies as persecution because it violates a victim's fundamental rights to physical integrity and personal dignity.[49]

Given the ICC's explicit recognition of gender as a prohibited ground of persecution, the ICTY and ICTR's findings described above are likely to be carefully considered by the ICC. The main difference between the ICTY and ICTR case law, and the potential case law of the ICC, is that the ICTY and ICTR only consider gender-based violence in the context of its intersection with persecution motivated by race, religion or politics. The ICC, on the other hand, can consider persecution solely on the ground of gender. When it does so, it can be expected that the ICC will need to overcome a number of challenges.

---

43 Note that, in the ICC's Elements of Crimes, lack of consent is not an element of rape and thus differs from the ICTY's approach: ICC Elements of Crimes at Article 7(1)(g)-1, *supra* 24.

44 *Prosecutor v. Milutinović et al.*, IT-05–87-T, 26 February 2009, para 201 (International Criminal Tribunal for the Former Yugoslavia) (Milutinović Trial Judgment).

45 *Ibid.* at para 199.

46 *Ibid.*

47 Beth Van Schaack, "Obstacles on the Road to Gender Justice: The International Criminal Tribunal for Rwanda as Object Lesson," *American University Journal of Gender, Social Policy and the Law* 17, (2009): 361, 380 (Van Schaack).

48 *Milutinović Trial Judgment* at para 199, *supra* 44.

49 *Supra* 44 at para 192.

4. POTENTIAL CHALLENGES IN THE ICC'S PROSECUTION OF GENDER-BASED PERSECUTION

There are three main challenges to the ICC's prosecution of gender-based persecution. The first difficulty arises as a result of the opacity of the Rome Statute's definition of gender. The second challenge arises due to the intersectionality of gender-based violence with other forms of discrimination. The final challenge relates to existing ICC jurisprudence in the case of *Prosecutor v. Jean-Pierre Bemba Gombo* which raises a serious concern that ICC judges might, in the future, choose to dismiss charges of rape and other forms of gender-based violence in favour of gender-based persecution, or dismiss a charge of gender-based persecution in favour of other crimes against humanity charges such as rape. Both outcomes, if based on the *Bemba* reasoning, would ultimately weaken the ICC's understanding of gender-based crimes in general and gender-based persecution in particular. Each of these three concerns will be explored in turn.

4.1. ICC'S DEFINITION OF GENDER

The Rome Statute defines the term 'gender' as "the two sexes, male and female, within the context of society."[50] The negotiations on this provision were extremely contentious.[51] A number of states felt that the term 'gender' must be included in the Rome Statute, including in the listing of grounds relating to persecution, in order to ensure that the ICC is prepared to thoroughly, fairly and sensitively prosecute gender-based crimes.[52] A number of states were opposed to the inclusion of the term 'gender'.[53] These tended to be conservative Catholic or Arab states. They raised two main concerns: first, that the term could imply rights more expansive than those currently recognized in their states, especially that the term might sanction rights based on sexual orientation; and, second, that the term could not be adequately translated into all six official United Nations languages.[54] When the debate came to an impasse, the Chair of the Diplomatic Conference's Working Group on Applicable Law asked a selection of individuals from the first and second groups to come up with a definition that

50 Rome Statute at Article 7(3), *supra* 2.

51 For a detailed history of the provision, see Oosterveld, *Definition of "Gender"*, *supra* note 7.

52 A listing of some of those states is included *Ibid.* at footnote 48. Many in this group, including Canada (on whose delegation this author served), wished to avoid mistakes made by the ICTY and ICTR in the prosecution of rape and other crimes of sexual violence, and to implement lessons learned from these experiences.

53 Some of those states are listed in *supra* 7 at footnote 48.

54 *Supra* 7 at 63.

would be acceptable to both sides.[55] The group therefore worked through a series of possibilities, adopting the definition reflected in article 7(3).[56] The definition is meant to indicate that gender is a contextual and socially-constructed norm of maleness and femaleness. The definition was made as skeletal as possible in order to gain agreement, with the mutual understanding that the ICC's judges would decide the exact content of the term (and therefore the applicable gender norms) in any given case.

This definition has been criticized by some international criminal legal commentators. For example, Christine Chinkin states that the definition "refers primarily to the biological differences between women and men rather than an understanding of gender as the ascribed, social and cultural nature of distinctions between men and women", which "has the effect of excluding issues of sexuality from the definition."[57] Hilary Charlesworth expresses a similar opinion.[58] Brenda Cossman reads the definition as being limited to the two biological sexes and feels that it is not even clear that the definition is intended to include the more typical understanding of gender as socially constructed roles and values.[59] Other commentators have concluded that the ICC's definition of gender excludes the possibility of prosecution of persecution based on sexual orientation.[60]

This author disagrees both with the conclusions that the definition is somehow limited to biological sex, and that the definition excludes the possibility of prosecution of persecution based on sexual orientation. The definition does take biological sex as its starting point, as did many United Nations definitions of gender in the 1990s and early 2000s.[61] However, the ICC definition goes beyond biological sex by indicating that gender is a norm created "in the context

---

55 The author participated in this group.

56 See Oosterveld, *Definition of "Gender"*, *supra* 7 at 63–65 for further details.

57 Christine Chinkin, "Gender-Based Crimes," in *Max Planck Encyclopedia of Public International Law*, ed. Rüdiger Wolfrun (Oxford, UK: Oxford University Press, 2008-online edition), para 13, available at www.mpepil.com.

58 Hilary Charlesworth, "Feminist Methods in International Law," *American Journal of International Law* 93, (1999): 379, 394; and Hilary Charlesworth, "The Gender of International Law," *American Society of International Law* 93, (1999): *Proceedings* 206–07 (Charlesworth, *Gender*). Charlesworth and Chinkin have also jointly come to a similar conclusion: Hilary Charlesworth and Christine Chinkin, *The Boundaries of International Law: A Feminist Analysis* (Manchester, UK: Manchester University Press, 2000), 335 (Charlesworth and Chinkin).

59 Brenda Cossman, "Gender Performance, Sexual Subjects and International Law," *Canadian Journal of Law and Jurisprudence* 15 (2002) 281, 283.

60 E.g. Charlesworth, *Gender*, *supra* 58 at 207; Rana Lehr-Lehnardt, "One Small Step for Women: Female-Friendly Provisions in the Rome Statute of the International Criminal Court," *Brigham Young University Journal of Public Law* 16 (2002): 317, 340 and 351; Stephanie Farrior, "The Rights of Women in International Human Rights Law Textbooks: Segregation, Integration, or Omission?" *Columbia Journal of Gender and the Law* 12 (2003): 587, 598; and Werle at para 905, *supra* 22.

61 See Oosterveld, *Definition of "Gender"* at 67–68 and footnote 104, *supra* 7.

of society", thereby bringing in socially-constructed understandings of maleness and femaleness. The Special Rapporteur on Contemporary Forms of Slavery has recognized the definition as being "consistent with other, more clearly stated formulations" of the term adopted within the United Nations.[62] The current High Commissioner for Human Rights, Navanethem Pillay, has stated that the definition "recognizes the social construction of gender, distinguishing biology and social roles, and encompasses both male and female persons."[63] Other commentators have come to a similar conclusion.[64]

As the late Rhonda Copelon noted, the "words [of the definition] do not support an exclusion of sexual orientation."[65] There was no consensus either way.[66] The lack of consensus on the issue "effectively leaves the term open for the Court to interpret and apply to the circumstances under consideration, as appropriate."[67] As Copelon convincingly stated, it is "dubious to argue that any

---

62 Special Rapporteur on Contemporary Forms of Slavery: Systematic Rape, Sexual Slavery and Slavery-Like Practices During Armed Conflict, *Update to the Final Report Submitted by Ms. Gay McDougall, Special Rapporteur*, U.N. ESCOR, Commission on Human Rights, Sub-Commission on the Promotion and Protection of Human Rights, 52nd Session, Agenda Item 6, para 26, U.N. Doc. E/CN.4/Sub.2/2000/21 (2000).

63 Navanthem Pillay, "Protection of the Health of Women Through International Criminal Law: How Can International Criminal Law Contribute to Efforts to Improve the Health of Women?" *Emory International Law Review* 22 (2008): 15, 20 (2008).

64 Rhonda Copelon, "Gender Crimes as War Crimes: Integrating Crimes Against Women into International Criminal Law," *McGill Law Journal* 46 (2000): 217, 236–37 (Copelon); Machteld Boot as revised by Christopher K. Hall, III, "Paragraph 3: Definition of Gender," in *Commentary on the Rome Statute of the International Criminal Court: Observers' Notes, Article by Article*, ed. Otto Triffterer (Oxford, UK: Hart Publishing, Second edition 2008), 273 (Boot); Barabara Bedont and Katherine Hall-Martinez, "Ending Impunity for Gender Crimes Under the International Criminal Court," *Brown Journal of World Affairs* 6 (1999): 65, 68; and Pam Spees, *Women's Advocacy in the Creation of the International Criminal Court: Changing the Landscapes of Justice and Power, Signs: Journal of Women in Culture and Society* 28, no. 4 (2003): 1233, 1244.

65 Copelon at 237, *supra* 64. See also Spees at 1244, *supra* 64 at 1244.

66 Oosterveld, *Definition of "Gender"* at 77, *supra* 7.

67 Cate Steains, "Gender Issues," in *The International Criminal Court: The Making of the Rome Statute – Issues, Negotiations, Results*, ed. Roy S. Lee (The Hague, the Netherlands: Kluwer Law International, 1999), 357, 374. This author argues that the ICC is more likely than not to interpret the term 'gender' to include persecution based on sexual orientation and gender identity: Oosterveld, *Definition of "Gender"* at 77–81, *supra* 7. This would be in keeping with developments in international refugee law – which, while not binding on international criminal law, can provide helpful guidance on the link between gender and persecution of sexual minorities: Valerie Oosterveld, "Gender, Persecution, and the International Criminal Court: Refugee Law's Relevance to the Crime Against Humanity of Gender-Based Persecution," *Duke Journal of Comparative and International Law* 17 (2006): 49, 79–8 (Oosterveld, *Persecution*). The link between gender, sexual orientation and gender identity has been recognized by the United Nations High Commissioner for Refugees, *UNHCR Guidance Note on Refugee Claims Relating to Sexual Orientation and Gender Identity*, para 2 (21 November 2008), available at www.unhcr.org/refworld/pdfid/48abd5660.pdf, read in conjunction with the United Nations High Commission for Refugees, *Guidelines on International Protection No. 1: Gender-Related Persecution Within the Context of Article 1A(2)*

ambiguity [in the definition] should be resolved in favour of discrimination."[68] Those who argue otherwise seem to do so for one of two reasons: they are relying on an uncorrected version of an influential summary of the Rome negotiations by Australian delegate Cate Steains,[69] or they are simply assuming that the view of those states fearing the inclusion of sexual orientation in 'gender' must be the prevailing interpretation, without explaining why the views of states in favour of an interpretation including sexual orientation must be ignored.

Machteld Boot makes the interesting observation that, although the term 'gender' has a specific meaning within the Rome Statute, "persecution on gender grounds as the term is generally understood in other international instruments and UN usage may still fall within the jurisdiction of the Court to the extent that such discrimination would be based on one of the "other grounds that are universally recognized as impermissible under international law" or involved "other inhumane acts" within the meaning of paragraph 1(k)."[70] In other words, perhaps concern over the Rome Statute's definition of gender is misplaced: if the Statute's definition is considered too opaque to address specific circumstances, the Prosecutor or the Court could potentially rely instead on, for example, the Convention on the Elimination of All Forms of Discrimination Against Women as a basis for interpretation in cases of discrimination against women.[71] On the other hand, Boot stresses the limiting nature of *nullum crimen sine lege* on the interpretation of crimes originally derived from human rights law.[72]

---

of the 1951 Convention and/or its 1967 Protocol Relating to the Status of Refugees, 2 and 4 (7 May 2002), available at www.unhcr.org/publ/PUBL/3d58ddef4.pdf.

68 Copelon at 237, *supra* 64.

69 Steains, *supra* 67 at 374: Steains' chapter originally concluded that "[t]he second sentence [of the gender definition, which reads "The term 'gender' does not indicate any meaning different from the above"] was included upon the insistence of the 'anti-gender' delegations, despite arguments by the 'pro-gender' delegations that it was superfluous." This sentence was radically changed in meaning by the book's editor, without consulting Ms. Steains, to state in the published version that the second sentence in the definition of 'gender' was "ultimately included to forestall any implication that the issue of sexual orientation could be raised in connection with article 7(3)." Ms. Steains rejects this editorial change. E-mail from Cate Steains, Permanent Mission of Australia to the United Nations in New York, to author (January 22, 2004) (on file with the author). Copelon, at footnote 60, *supra* 64, also noted this key editorial change. For example, Machteld Boot cites Steains for the proposition that the wording "within the context of society" was included "to forestall any implication that the issue of sexual orientation could be raised in connection with Article 7(3), and thus also in connection with the crime of persecution": Machteld Boot, *Genocide, Crimes Against Humanity and War Crimes: Nullum Crimen Sine Lege and the Subject Matter Jurisdiction of the International Criminal Court* (Antwerp, Belgium: Intersentia, 2002), para 497 and footnote 256 (Boot 2002). As well, Charlesworth and Chinkin, and de Brouwer, cite Steains for the same proposition: Charlesworth and Chinkin, at 335, *supra* 58, and Anne-Marie L.M. de Brouwer, *Supranational Criminal Prosecution of Sexual Violence: The ICC and the Practice of the ICTY and ICTR* (Antwerp, Belgium: Intersentia, 2005), 160 and footnote 353.

70 Boot at 220, *supra* 64.

71 As suggested by Werle at para 905, *supra* 22.

72 Boot 2002 at para 510, *supra* 69.

Boot's observation does raise a key issue. There is a risk that the controversy, both in Rome and since, around the definition of the term 'gender' may mean that the term itself is viewed within the ICC as too difficult[73] or too unsettled to permit a clear formulation of persecution charges or convictions. Add to this the fact that the term is already widely misunderstood within the United Nations and elsewhere,[74] and prosecutors or judges may turn instead to other, more traditional or more easily recognizable and explainable grounds of persecution. This possibility is explored in the next section.

4.2. PROSECUTION OF INTERSECTIONALITY

In ICTY and ICTR cases identified above, individuals were targeted as Bosnian Muslim women, Bosnian Croat women or Tutsi women – identities with both ethnic/racial and gender components. Kelly Askin has noted that, during periods of war, oppression or mass violence, many individuals are targeted on the basis of gender as well as on other grounds.[75] This is reflective of the relational quality of gender.[76] Thus, an intersectional prosecution is needed: each of the bases for prosecution should be highlighted by the prosecutor.[77] However, there is the possibility that a dual analysis will not actually take place. Instead, one form of the intersected harm (for example, ethnicity) might be used as the prism to analyze the other (gender). This has been the case in the ICTY and ICTR, such that ethnicity is constructed to include gender, but not vice-versa, in order to fit within the prohibited persecutory grounds in the Statutes. The effect of this causes concern: as argued by Buss, in those Tribunals, "the complexity of sexual violence and inequality is maneuvered out of the decisions."[78] Gender is

---

73 The concept of gender contains many sub-components. Gender is a social construct; the construction of gender is complex and is influenced by culture, the roles women, men, boys and girls are expected to play, the relationship among those roles, and the value that society places on those roles; and the content of gender can vary within and among cultures, and over time: Oosterveld, *Definition of "Gender"* at 67–70, *supra* 7. This nuanced concept is not necessarily easy to convey.

74 Within the United Nations, the term "gender" is often misunderstood or misused as shorthand for "women": Hilary Charlesworth, "Not Waving But Drowning: Gender Mainstreaming and Human Rights in the United Nations," *Harvard Human Rights Journal* 18 (2005): 1, 14.

75 Kelly Askin, "The Jurisprudence of International War Crimes Tribunals: Securing Gender Justice for Some Survivors," in *Listening to the Silences: Women and War*, eds. Helen Durham and Tracey Gurd (Leiden, the Netherlands: Martinus Nijhoff Publishers 2005), 125, 143 (Askin).

76 Dianne Otto, "Lost in Translation: Re-Scripting the Sexed Subjects of International Human Rights Law," in *International Law and Its Others*, ed. Anne Orford (Cambridge, UK: Cambridge University Press, 2006), 318, 354.

77 Askin at 143, *supra* 5.

78 Doris E. Buss, *"The Curious Visibility of Wartime Rape: Gender and Ethnicity in International Criminal Law," Windsor Yearbook of Access to Justice* 25 (2007): 3, 6.

discussed in the context of ethnicity in such as way that the Tribunals fail to explore the complex range of factors that structure sexual violence. Instead, they consider "rape and gendered harm only within the tightly scripted dominant narratives of the conflict: rapes as extensions of nationalism; rape as one modality of ethnic harm."[79] Another case in point can be seen in the report of the International Commission of Inquiry on Darfur, which – even though the Rome Statute provides for persecution on the basis of gender – classified various acts of rape and sexual violence only as persecution on the basis of membership in "African" tribes.[80]

The ICC's charges against Harun, Ali Kushayb and Hussein raise the issue of the characterization of persecution when it occurs at the intersection of gender and another prohibited ground of discrimination, such as ethnicity. At present, it is not clear as to whether the ICC's Prosecutor is going to argue gender as a specific ground of persecution alongside ethnicity, or whether the rape crimes are planned to be argued solely as examples of ethnic persecution. The former is the better route, because to do otherwise risks obscuring the gendered nature of the crimes, or rendering them less salient.[81] Therefore, if and when these cases enter the pre-trial and trial stages, the Prosecutor and his staff should be prepared to explain in their pleadings and through their evidence why it is important for the Court to recognize not just one, but both, aspects of intersection, so as to avoid gender disappearing in favour of an understanding of ethnic persecution. In the *Mbarushimana* case, the Prosecutor has clearly indicated that he will rely upon gender as a ground of persecution, if he is successful in his appeal of the decision on the confirmation of charges. He has also identified the fact that the gendered persecutory acts intersect with persecution based on assumed political affiliation, in identifying the victims of the FDLR's gender-based persecution as "women and men seen to be affiliated with the FARDC."[82] Thus, the *Mbarushimana* case raises a similar risk that the Court may choose to 'read' gender through the prism of assumed political affiliation, as opposed to either focusing on gender directly or analyzing both gender and assumed political affiliation separately but as intersecting.

Intersectionality raises two related concerns. First, given the much more developed international jurisprudence on other forms of persecution, there is a potential that investigators and prosecutors will more clearly see – and charge –

---

79 *Ibid.* at 22.

80 International Commission of Inquiry at para 360, *supra* 19.

81 Van Schaak at 380, *supra* 47. Note, however, that the Prosecutor has largely taken the less-preferred route, charging the intersection of gender and political, national, ethnic or religious persecution solely as the latter: for example, see *Prosecutor v. Laurent Gbagbo*, ICC-02/11-01/11, Public Redacted Version of "Decision on the Prosecutor's Application Pursuant to Article 58 for a Warrant of Arrest Against Laurent Koudou Gbagbo," 30 November 2011, paras. 62 and 65, available at www.icc-cpi.int/iccdocs/doc/doc1291604.pdf.

82 *Mbarushimana Decision on Arrest Warrant* at para 10, *supra* 13.

those grounds and not identify the additional gendered persecutory aspects. Gender-based violations – especially those with a sexual component – may be more difficult to investigate.[83] "In particular, locating physical, documentary, and testimonial evidence that proves commission of sexual violence may present unique challenges as compared with other crimes of violence that may be more visible or publicly documented."[84] For example, investigators may not be trained to "listen to the silences" of what a victim is leaving out,[85] or may be reluctant to press for sensitive information from victims.[86] In addition, "there is a tendency to view acts of gender violence committed during armed conflicts or repression as simply opportunistic or as private crimes reflecting personal motives and desires that are unconnected to, or simply capitalizing on, the prevailing state of war."[87] This is why it is so important for the ICC to approach each investigation with a consistent and coherent strategy with respect to uncovering gender-based crimes, including keeping alert to the possibility of gender-based persecution directed against females and males, even in the context of other forms of persecution.[88] Ease of investigations must not be used as a reason to avoid the kind of in-depth investigatory work needed to squarely focus on gender-based persecution.[89]

---

83 Van Schaack at 368, *supra* 47.

84 Van Schaak at 368–69, *supra* 47. See also Alex Obote-Odora, "Rape and Sexual Violence in International Law: ICTR's Contribution," *New England Journal of International and Comparative Law* 12 (2005): 135, 140 (Obote-Odora).

85 This phrase is taken from the title of Eds. Helen Durham and Tracey Gurd, *Listening to the Silences: Women and War* (Leiden, the Netherlands: Martinus Nijhoff Publishers, 2005). Violations such as rape are often concealed by victims to avoid further emotional anguish, stigmatization and retaliation from perpetrators: Obote-Odora at 140, *supra* 84.

86 Van Schaak at 369, *supra* 47 at 369; and Binaifer Nowrojee *We Can Do Better: Investigating and Prosecuting International Crimes of Sexual Violence* (November 2004), available at, www.unictr.org/Portals/0/English/News/events/Nov2004/nowrojee.pdf. On this point, see also Sarah Sharratt, "Voices of Court Members: A Phenomenological Journey – The Prosecution of Rape and Sexual Violence at the International Criminal Tribunal for the Former Yugoslavia (ICTY) and the Bosnian War Crimes Court (BIH)," in *Sexual Violence as an International Crime: Interdisciplinary Approaches*, eds. Anne-Marie de Brouwer, Charlotte Ku, Renée Römkens and Larissa van den Herik (Antwerp, Belgium: Intersentia), *infra*.

87 Van Schaak at 376, *supra* 47 at 376, noting that this invisibility of gender-based crimes mirrors the public/private divide that runs through much of law and society.

88 To this end, Professor Catharine MacKinnon may play a part, as the Office of the Prosecutor's Special Adviser on Gender Crimes: see Office of the Prosecutor, *ICC Prosecutor Appoints Prof. Catharine A. MacKinnon as Special Adviser on Gender Crimes*, ICC-OTP-20081126-PR377 (26 November 2008), available at www.icc-cpi.int/Menus/Go?id=30484f06-076a-4e20-935a-8e603475cc37&lan=en-GB.

89 This comment stems from the ICC's Office of the Prosecutor, *Annex to the "Paper on Some Policy Issues Before the Office of the Prosecutor": Referrals and Communications* 1 (September 2003), which notes that ease of investigations is a factor taken into account when deciding on which situations to focus, as cited in Van Schaak, at footnote 28, *supra* 47. On the issue of investigating sexual violence crimes, see also Maxine Marcus, "Investigation of Crimes of Sexual and Gender-Based Violence Under International Criminal Law" and Chen Reis, "Ethical Safety and Methodological Issues Related to Collection and Use of Data on Sexual Violence in Conflict" and Lynn Lawry, Kirsten Johnson and Jana Asher, "Evidence – Based

The second concern is somewhat the opposite of the first: that gender-based persecution might be overlooked by investigators and prosecutors as a possible charge in favour of charges related to underlying prohibited acts such as rape, sexual slavery, forced pregnancy, enforced sterilization and other forms of sexual violence. This would be unfortunate, because "gender violence is regularly employed alongside and to exacerbate other forms of violence and repression",[90] and therefore gendered forms of violence may be used to "complete" the persecution of a group.

In sum, the gendered nature of intersectional forms of persecution must be properly contextualized within any given prosecution. When examining intersecting persecutory grounds, the ICC should consider each ground separately and not simply default to the more 'traditional' ground. Similarly, when examining underlying gendered acts, the query should always be made as to whether these form part of gender-based persecution. When considering the ground of gender, the Court should ask: what role did the social construction of masculinities and femininities play in the persecution? How did the perpetrators use male and female norms to shape or carry out the persecution? How were men, women, girls and boys targeted? Were men targeted in different ways than women? If men and women were targeted in similar ways, were the underlying persecutory acts carried out in a different ways based on gender? Was sexual violence used as one of the underlying persecutory acts? In considering the intersecting ground, the Court should ask: in what manner did gender intersect with (for example) religion? Was this intersection a key aspect of the persecution? Did the intersection compound the gendered harms? Asking these and related questions will help the Court to understand persecution on the basis of gender and the harm flowing therefrom, but will also help the Court to understand the wider picture of where targeting on the basis of gender fits within the particular conflict or oppressive situation under consideration.

4.3. REJECTION DUE TO CUMULATIVE CHARGING

Experience to date at the ICC raises a legitimate concern that, where gender-based persecution is charged alongside underlying gender-based acts such as rape, sexual slavery and other forms of sexual violence, some of these charges may be rejected by the Pre-Trial Chamber at the confirmation of charges stage. In the ICC's case involving Jean-Pierre Bemba Gombo, the Prosecutor charged Bemba, the alleged President and Commander in Chief of the *Mouvement de*

Documentation of Gender-Based Violence," in *Sexual Violence as an International Crime: Interdisciplinary Approaches*, eds. Anne-Marie de Brouwer, Charlotte Ku, Renée Römkens and Larissa van den Herik (Antwerp, Belgium: Intersentia), *infra*.

90 Van Schaack at 376, *supra* 47.

Liberation du Congo (MLC), with responsibility for a number of gender-based acts committed by MLC members in the Central African Republic in 2002–2003. Specifically, Bemba was charged with the crime against humanity and war crime of rape, the crime against humanity and war crime of torture, and rape and other acts as the war crime of outrages upon personal dignity.[91] In its 2009 decision, Pre-Trial Chamber II confirmed the charges of rape as a crime against humanity and as a war crime.[92] However, the Chamber, in a confusingly reasoned decision, declined to confirm the torture or outrages upon personal dignity charges on the grounds that the latter charges were cumulative to the rape charges.[93] Specifically, the Pre-Trial Chamber held that torture and outrages upon personal dignity were fully subsumed by the rape charges and were not "distinct crimes,"[94] despite the fact that the ICC's Elements of Crimes document sets out different elements of crimes for rape, torture and outrages upon personal dignity.[95] As well, the Pre-Trial Chamber held that the charges of rape, torture and outrages upon personal dignity were based on the same conduct, and therefore rape was the most appropriate characterization as it was the only charge with an additional material element, that of penetration.[96] Contrary to the extensive case law of the ICTY and ICTR,[97] the Pre-Trial Chamber also reasoned that responding to several charges based on the same conduct is "detrimental to the rights of the Defence since it places an undue burden on the Defence."[98] Based on this reasoning, the Pre-Trial Chamber held

91 *Prosecutor v. Jean-Pierre Bemba Gombo*, ICC-01/05–01/08, 10 June 2008, Warrant of Arrest for Jean-Pierre Bemba Gombo, Replacing the Warrant of Arrest Issued on 23 May 2008, paras 5, 15, 17 and 24, available at www2.icc-cpi.int/iccdocs/doc/doc535163.pdf.

92 *Prosecutor v. Jean-Pierre Bemba Gombo*, ICC-01/05–01/08, 15 June 2009, Decision Pursuant to Article 61(7)(a) and (b) of the Rome Statute on the Charges of the Prosecutor Against Jean-Pierre Bemba Gombo, 184–5, available at www.icc-cpi.int/iccdocs/doc/doc699541.pdf (Bemba Confirmation of Charges).

93 *Ibid.* at paras 190, 202, 302 and 310.

94 *Supra* 92 at paras 202, 204–5, 310 and 312.

95 ICC Elements of Crimes at Articles 7(1)(f), 7(1)(g)-1, 8(2)(a)(ii)-1, 8(2)(b)(xxii), 8(2)(b)(xxii)-2, 8(2)(c)(i)-4, 8(2)(c)(ii), 8(2)(e)(vi)-1, *supra* 24. Note also that Pre-Trial Chamber I, in its Decision on the Confirmation of Charges for *Prosecutor v. Katanga and Ngudjolo Chui,* adopted the opposite approach, confirming charges of sexual slavery and rape based on the same set of facts and, indeed, finding that rape can occur within sexual enslavement: *Prosecutor v. Germain Katanga and Mathieu Ngudjolo Chui*, ICC-01/04–01/07, 30 September 2008, Decision on the Confirmation of Charges, paras 347–345, and 350, available at www.icc-cpi.int/iccdocs/doc/doc571253.pdf.

96 *Bemba Confirmation of Charges* at paras 202–04 and 302–12, *supra* 92.

97 For example, see *The Prosecutor v. Jean-Pierre Bemba Gombo*, ICC-01/05–01/08, 31 July 2009, Amicus Curiae Observations of the Women's Initiatives for Gender Justice Pursuant to Rule 103 of the Rules of Procedure and Evidence, paras 18 and 28, available at http://212.159.242.181/iccdocs/doc/doc719028.pdf (Women's Initiatives Amicus); War Crimes Research Office, *The Practice of Cumulative Charging at the International Criminal Court* (Washington College of Law, May 2010), 7–10 and 29 (War Crimes Research Office); and *Prosecutor v. Delalić et al*, IT-96–21-A, 20 February 2001, para 412 (International Criminal Tribunal for the Former Yugoslavia).

98 *Bemba Confirmation of Charges* at para 202, *supra* 92.

that it would only be appropriate to confirm the charges directly referred to as "rape."[99]

The Prosecutor, supported by the ICC's Office of Public Counsel for Victims, requested leave to appeal this "cumulative" charging reasoning of the Pre-Trial Chamber.[100] Pre-Trial Chamber II rejected the Prosecutor's request and reasoning, as well as that of *amicus curiae* Women's Initiatives for Gender Justice,[101] repeating its original view that, where the Prosecutor relies on the same body of evidence "pertaining to acts of rape to substantiate two or more legal characterizations, the specific elements of the crime of torture and outrages upon personal dignity were congruent with those of the crime of rape and, therefore, fully subsumed by the count of rape."[102] The reasoning of the Pre-Trial Chamber raises the possibility that it may have strayed into an evaluation of its own original decision.[103] This is of concern because, if not remedied, the associated harms resulting from the various gender-related charges will not be fully captured in the trial judgment.

Given the Pre-Trial Chamber's reasoning and the lack of Appeals Chamber guidance in this regard, there is a risk that underlying acts such as the crime against humanity of rape charged alongside the crime against humanity of persecution might be rejected as "cumulative" by future Pre-Trial Chambers of the ICC because persecution contains one additional element, that of targeting a

99 *Ibid.* It also appears that the Prosecutor failed to clearly set out the link between the conduct of various types of rape, and the harm resulting from that conduct, in order to demonstrate that the physical and psychological harms were outrages upon personal dignity (these harms appeared to be humiliation, psychological distress due to powerlessness to stop the rapes, the breakage of familial units and therefore cultural binds): *supra* 92 at para 312.

100 *Prosecutor v. Jean-Pierre Bemba Gombo*, ICC-01/05-01/08-427, 22 June 2009, Prosecution's Application for Leave to Appeal the Decision Pursuant to Article 61(7)(a) and (b) on the Charges against Jean-Pierre Bemba Gombo; and *Prosecutor v. Jean-Pierre Bemba Gombo*, ICC-01/05-01/08-428, 26 June 2009, Office of the Public Counsel for Victims, Réponse du Représentant légal des victimes a/0278/08, a/0279/08, a/0291/08, a/0292/08,a/0293/08, a/0296/08, a/0297/08, a/0298/08, a/0455/08, a/0457/08, a/0458/08, a/0459/08, a/0460/08, a/0461/08, a/0462/08, a/0463/08, a/0464/08, a/0465/08, a/0466/08 et a/0467/08 à la demande d'autorisation d'interjeter appel déposée par le Bureau du Procureur à l'égard de la Décision sur la confirmation des charges.

101 Women's Initiatives Amicus, *supra* 97.

102 *Prosecutor v. Jean-Pierre Bemba Gombo*, ICC/01/05-01/08, 18 September 2009, Decision on the Prosecutor's Application for Leave to Appeal the "Decision Pursuant to Article 61(7)(a) and (b) on the Charges of the Prosecutor against Jean-Pierre Bemba Gombo," paras 52 and 54.

103 Under the Rome Statute, the Prosecutor must seek leave from the Chamber that rendered the original decision and that Chamber is not meant to evaluate the correctness of its own original decision, but rather whether the Prosecutor has raised an issue involving the Decision Confirming the Charges that "would significantly affect the fair and expeditious conduct of the proceedings or the outcome of the trial, and for which… an immediate resolution by the Appeals Chamber may materially advance the proceedings.": Rome Statute, Article 82(1)(d), *supra* 2.

specific group.[104] This would be unfortunate, not only because non-confirmation of the charges related to "connected" prohibited acts could undermine proof of persecution, but also because a narrowing of the range of gender-based criminal charges to exclusively include gender-based persecution will naturally result in under-identification of gender-based harms suffered in a given situation. For many women and girls, the violations they endure during conflict are part of a continuum of gender-based discrimination that they suffered prior to the conflict. Prior to the conflict, women and girls may suffer from or fear "ordinary daily physical violence", which is "intersect[ed] with sporadic communal cultures of violence, overlaid by institutions and structures that enforce and support such formal and informal violence in multiple ways."[105] Armed conflict can bring with it "an escalation of specific catastrophic and life-changing violence," such as rape.[106] The targeting of men and boys during conflict for gender-based violence, including sexual violence, may occur for similar or different reasons, and the harms may also be similar or different.[107] Thus, specific conduct fitting within the ICC's differing elements of crimes should be named several different ways – for example, as rape, torture, enslavement and persecution – because that conduct was multilayered in its function and in its range of harms.[108] To intimate, as the *Bemba* reasoning does, that specific conduct can result in one type of crime, and therefore harm, is incorrect. This view diminishes "the effective access of victims to justice"[109] and reduces the proper contextualization and breadth of gender-based crimes.

While less likely, on the *Bemba* Pre-Trial Chamber's reasoning, a charge of gender-based persecution could potentially be dismissed in favour of underlying charges related to gender-based violence for two reasons. First, persecution is

104 The Bemba Pre-Trial Chamber ostensibly recognized that different charges based on the same conduct were permitted as long as the prohibited acts contained "one additional material element not contained in the other", but then ignored the fact that the elements of torture are different from those of rape: *Bemba Confirmation of Charges* at para 202, *supra* 92.

105 Fionnuala Ni Aoláin, "Women, Vulnerability and Humanitarian Emergencies," *University of Minnesota Law School Legal Studies Research Paper No. 10-27* (2010): 8, available at http://papers.ssrn.com/sol3/papers.cfm?abstract_id=1611818.

106 *Ibid.*

107 Dustin A. Lewis, "Unrecognized Victims: Sexual Violence Against Men in Conflict Settings Under International Law," *Wisconsin International Law Journal* 27 (2009): 1, 6–17; Sandesh Sivukumaran, "Sexual Violence Against Men in Armed Conflict," *European Journal of International Law* 18 (2007): 253, 263–67; and Sandesh Sivukumaran,"Lost in Translation: UN Responses to Sexual Violence Against Men and Boys in Situations of Armed Conflict," *International Review of the Red Cross* 92 (2010): 259, 266.

108 Gender-based violence can result in a number of different, but interlinked, harms, such as death, physical injury, psychological injury, lasting stigma and discrimination, loss of familial, social and cultural bonds and imposition of new familial and social situations (for example, in the case of women and girls who give birth as a result of sexual violence crimes). See Fionnuala Ni Aoláin, "Exploring a Feminist Theory of Harm in the Context of Conflicted and Post-Conflict Societies," *Queen's Law Journal* 35 (2009): 219, 239–43.

109 Women's Initiatives Amicus at para 39, *supra* 97.

defined as "the intentional and severe deprivation of fundamental rights contrary to international law by reason of the identity of the group or collectivity."[110] Virtually any of the other prohibited acts within the crimes against humanity provision, and those listed in the genocide provision, could be viewed as amounting to an "intentional and severe deprivation of fundamental rights contrary to international law." As well, it is not uncommon for crimes against humanity to occur in situations in which groups or collectivities are targeted, especially in cases also charging genocide. Second, persecution is defined as being committed "in connection with" other prohibited acts listed within the crimes against humanity provision or other ICC crimes.[111] Persecution is proven using conduct that will also likely be used to prove other specifically-named prohibited acts, such as torture or rape, and thus, under the *Bemba* reasoning, the Court may prefer the more "direct" charges.

While the *Bemba* reasoning is not binding on other Pre-Trial Chambers, if it is followed, it could result in a narrowing of charges based on gender-based violence by collapsing the understanding of gender-based acts solely into consideration of gender-based persecution. The opposite could also occur. Either scenario would end with a diminished jurisprudential understanding of the role of gender in a given conflict or situation of mass or systematic violation.

5. CONCLUSION

The explicit codification in the Rome Statute of gender-based persecution for the first time in international criminal law is an exciting, and potentially revolutionary, development. This chapter has explored three potential difficulties that could stand it the way of the full development of this crime. First, the definition of the term 'gender' included within the Rome Statute is subject to differing interpretations, which may cause the ICC's prosecutors or judges to prefer other charges, such as rape and sexual slavery, rather than those of gender-based persecution. Second, in the case of intersectional forms of persecution, there may be an inclination to focus on the more 'traditional' persecutory grounds, to the detriment of a full understanding of gender as a ground in and of itself in any given case. Finally, existing ICC jurisprudence from the case of *Prosecutor v. Jean-Pierre Bemba Gombo* raises the possibility that charges for gender-based prohibited acts may be improperly dismissed as "cumulative" to a charge of gender-based persecution, or vice-versa. Both outcomes are potentially inimical to a full understanding of the gendered nature of the case, and the gendered harms that resulted from the crimes being considered. All of these

110 Rome Statute, Article 7(2)(g), *supra* 2.
111 *Ibid.* at Article 7(1)(h).

challenges can be overcome with a committed, coherent and consistently-applied prosecutorial strategy on gender-based crimes.

The potential of progressive jurisprudence on gender-based persecution by the ICC could have far-reaching effects. The ICC's approaches would not only be persuasive inside the ICC, but also could influence any other international or internationalized criminal tribunals with a mandate to prosecute crimes against humanity. As well, the ICC's consideration of gender-based persecution could also assist states undertaking domestic prosecutions of ICC crimes. Finally, the ICC's approaches may influence consideration of gender-based persecution in other areas of international law, such as refugee law: this would be fitting, as the inclusion of 'gender' as a persecutory ground in the Rome Statute was inspired by this area of international law.[112] With its inclusion in the Rome Statute, gender-based persecution is poised to expand the charging options available to the ICC's Prosecutor. It is an important, and timely, addition.

---

112 Oosterveld, *Persecution* at 50–51, *supra* 67.

CHAPTER 4

PROSECUTING SEXUAL VIOLENCE AGAINST MEN AND BOYS

Sandesh SIVAKUMARAN

1. INTRODUCTION

Sexual violence has been inflicted upon men and boys for centuries. This issue has been acknowledged in recent years in the context of the efforts being made to address sexual violence against women. Yet, sexual violence against men and boys continues to be overlooked, downplayed, or re-characterized. On occasion, this is a deliberate decision, taken so as to focus on sexual violence against women and girls. At other times, it is a by-product of the relative lack of knowledge of male sexual violence.

The prosecution of male sexual violence as an international crime is, in many ways, an allegory to the broader issue of male sexual violence. The recent prosecutions of male sexual violence, in particular by the International Criminal Tribunal for the former Yugoslavia (ICTY), reflect the very real advances that have been made on the subject more broadly in recent years. However, just as there is much distance yet to be covered as regards male sexual violence, the prosecution of male sexual violence reveals certain tensions and limitations. The state of prosecutions of sexual violence against men and boys thus reflects the state of affairs on the subject of sexual violence against men and boys more generally.

This chapter is divided into three substantive parts. Part two presents an overview of sexual violence against men and boys. The forms, prevalence and dynamics of male sexual violence are explored. The chapter then turns to international prosecutions. Part three identifies the advances that have been made as a result of prosecutions, focusing on the substantive law, the procedural law and the prosecutions themselves. Although considerable progress has been made, much remains to be done. Accordingly, the existing limits on prosecutions are the subject of Part four. These limits exist at two principal levels – at the level of investigations and at the level of charging, including the characterization of the charges. The chapter focuses on sexual violence against men and boys committed by other men and boys. Male sexual violence committed by female perpetrators is even less well known; buried still deeper are the instances of female perpetrators of sexual violence against female victims.[1]

2. OVERVIEW OF MALE SEXUAL VIOLENCE

That sexual violence is committed against men and boys in times of peace is reasonably well-known. Such instances of sexual violence fall outside the scope of this chapter unless they amount to crimes against humanity or genocide. What is less well known is that sexual violence is committed against men and boys in periods of political repression, internal tensions and disturbances, and armed conflicts. It has taken place in at least 25 such situations in the last three decades alone: in Argentina, Burundi, Central African Republic, Chechnya, Chile, Democratic Republic of the Congo (DRC), East Timor-Indonesia, El Salvador, Greece, Guatemala, Iran, Iraq-Coalition, Iraq-Kuwait, Kenya, Liberia, Northern Ireland, Peru, Rwanda, Sierra Leone, South Africa, Sri Lanka, Sudan, Turkey, Uganda, the former Yugoslavia, and Zimbabwe.[2] It is sometimes carried out on an *ad hoc* basis; at other times, the practice is widespread and systematic. Provided you are looking for it, reports are numerous; if you are not, they can remain hidden. Given the subject of this collection, there will be a focus on those countries that have benefitted from an international criminal tribunal (the armed conflicts in Yugoslavia and Sierra Leone; the armed conflict and genocide in Rwanda) as well as three country situations before the International Criminal Court (ICC) at the time of writing (DRC, Central African Republic, and Kenya).

Sexual violence against men and boys takes a number of different forms.[3] It includes rape of all sorts – by male and female perpetrators; through the person of the perpetrator or with objects; by individuals or gangs; forcing the victim to rape a fellow victim (enforced rape), where the latter is male or female, family member or stranger, alive or dead. Sexual violence is by no means limited to rape. Particularly prevalent in armed conflict are enforced sterilization, beatings administered to the genitals, enforced nudity, and enforced masturbation. Men and boys are also forced to act as sex slaves and forced to marry fellow victims.

---

1 The best known example of sexual violence committed by women against men is probably that of the abuse at Abu Ghraib. See *AR 15-6 Investigation of the 800th Military Police Brigade* (2004) (*the Taguba Report*). Sexual violence is also committed by and against women. For documented examples of the practice, see, e.g., Human Rights Watch, *We'll Kill You if You Cry* (New York: Human Rights Watch, 2002), 41–42.

2 For further detail on these situations, see S. Sivakumaran, "Sexual Violence against Men in Armed Conflict," *European Journal of International Law* 18 (2007), 257–58.

3 See generally, *Ibid.* at 261–67.

Sexual violence is carried out against men and boys for many of the same reasons as it is inflicted upon women and girls. Male sexual violence is committed in order to humiliate or degrade victims. Thus, the Waki report on post-election violence in Kenya refers to the 'humiliation of the violations' experienced by male victims.[4] It is conducted so as to prevent procreation on the part of victims. For example, genital beatings may be accompanied by statements such as "Muslims should not propagate."[5] Male sexual violence is also carried out for reasons that, although not identical to sexual violence against women, have parallels thereto, namely to disempower, emasculate, or feminize victims. Thus, one victim of male sexual violence in the DRC reports that "I'm laughed at', 'The people in my village say: "You're no longer a man. Those men in the bush made you their wife."'[6] The DRC country director for the non-governmental organization 'Women for Women' notes that "rape had been used like a weapon to exercise power and to have control over a community. The men who have been victims of rape, it's like they no longer exist. It's like, I am a man, but I am no longer a man because of what happened to me."[7] Male sexual violence is also committed for reasons that are not comparable to sexual violence against women, namely to cast aspersions of homosexuality. For example, a Human Rights Watch report notes that "[d]ue to the stigma attached to homosexuality in Sierra Leone, male victims of rape feared they would be perceived as homosexuals and therefore few boys were willing to report it."[8] Victims themselves may question their sexuality, particularly if they were forced to rape other men.[9]

The problem of male sexual violence remains a hidden one. As with sexual violence more generally, lack of reporting is a problem. Men may suffer from fear, stigma, shame, confusion, guilt, loss of masculinity, or a combination thereof.[10] Individuals on the ground may not be aware that men and boys are also subjected to sexual violence and may lack training to detect signs of abuse, compounding the hidden nature of the problem.[11] Survivors of male sexual violence have no natural constituency to advocate on their behalf; the issue

---

4 *Report of the Commission of Inquiry on Post Election Violence* (2008), 243 (Waki Report).

5 See *Prosecutor v. Simić, Tadić and Zarić*, IT-95-9-T, 17 October 2003, para 771.

6 J. Gettleman, "Symbol of Unhealed Congo: Male Rape Victims," *New York Times*, 5 August 2009.

7 J. De Capua, *Both Women and Men Victims of Rape in Eastern DRC*, 26 November 2008, available at www.VOAnews.com.

8 *We'll Kill You if You Cry*, *supra* 1 at 42.

9 Peel *et al.*, "The sexual abuse of men in detention in Sri Lanka," *The Lancet* 355 (2000): 2069–70; Peel, "Men as Perpetrators and Victims," in *Rape as a Method of Torture*, ed. M. Peel (2004) 61, 67.

10 S. Sivakumaran, "Male/Male Rape and the "Taint" of Homosexuality," *Human Rights Quarterly* 27 (2005): 1274, 1288; *Sexual Violence against Men*, *supra* 2 at 255–56.

11 See e.g. Oosterhoff *et al.*, "Sexual Torture of Men in Croatia and Other Conflict Situations: An Open Secret," *Reproductive Health Matters* 12 (2004), 68.

remains a cause without a voice.[12] Further, much of the attention – for hitherto understandable reasons – is focused on sexual violence against women. When the issue of male sexual violence is raised, there is sometimes concern that it will infringe upon, or take up the limited time, attention and resources devoted to tackling sexual violence against women.[13] Few prevalence studies exist on the subject of male sexual violence, although these are slowly starting to emerge. This means that the issue can be downplayed, the now-classic statement being that although there are instances of male sexual violence, the vast majority of victims are women.[14] This may well be true, but we simply do not know. And the prevalence studies on point are astonishing: 32.6% of male combatants surveyed in Liberia reported being subjected to some form of sexual violence;[15] 80% of 5000 male detainees of a camp in the Sarajevo canton reported being raped.[16] Thus, the issue cannot be dismissed for want of victims.

3. PROSECUTIONS: ADVANCES

The prosecution of sexual violence that is directed at men and boys as an international crime has made some important inroads into the lack of visibility surrounding the subject. The most important advancement to have been made relates to the law itself. Unfortunately, attitudes still lag some way behind the state of the law, and the clarity of the law has not always resulted in an attitudinal shift. These limits to prosecutions will be explored in Part 4; this part focuses on the advances that have resulted from prosecutions.

3.1. SUBSTANTIVE LAW

In the domestic law of numerous states, the crime of rape is defined by reference to a female victim and a male perpetrator. As such, for these states, rape is a crime against women. It was only in 1994, for example, that England and Wales

---

12 *Male/Male Rape*, *supra* 10 at 1280–85.

13 See e.g. the concern expressed in *OCHA-Policy Development and Studies Branch, Use of Sexual Violence in Conflict: Identifying Research Priorities to Inform More Effective Interventions* (New York: UN, 2008), 6.

14 See e.g. A-M. Goetz, *Introduction*, in *Women Targeted or Affected by Armed Conflict: What Role for Military Peacekeepers?* (Wilton Park, 27–29 May 2008), 3.

15 K. Johnson *et al.*, "Association of Combatant Status and Sexual Violence with Health and Mental Health Outcomes in Postconflict Liberia," *Journal of the American Medical Association* 300, no. 6 (2008): 676.

16 Ž. Mudrovčić, "Sexual and Gender-Based Violence in Post-Conflict Regions: the Bosnia and Herzegovina Case," in *The Impact of Armed Conflict on Women and Girls: A Consultative Meeting on Mainstreaming Gender in Areas of Conflict and Reconstruction* (New York: United Nations Population Fund, 2001), 64.

extended the law of rape to include male victims.[17] The precursor, the Sexual Offences Act 1956, provided quite simply: "It is an offence for a man to rape a woman."[18] Even the most recent legislation on point limits the offence of rape to male perpetrators,[19] and does not include penetration by objects.[20] Similarly, it was only in 2006 that the rape legislation in the DRC was extended to include male and female victims and various forms of penetration.[21]

It is not only that the law is oftentimes framed in an overly-narrow manner. The law may also be used to punish male *victims*. In states in which homosexual activity is a criminal offence, reporting of male sexual violence can lead to prosecution. Reporting of sexual violence crimes by male victims of male sexual violence may result in charges of (consensual) homosexual conduct being brought.[22] Thus, in many states, there exists a very real disincentive to report instances of male sexual violence.

It would be nice if we could explain these problems away by reference to their status as domestic legislation and to say that international law is rather more enlightened. Alas, historically, international law has not been immune to some of these problems. For example, on occasion, international humanitarian law limited protections against rape to women. Thus, Geneva Convention IV provides that '[w]omen shall be especially protected against any attack on their honour, in particular against rape, enforced prostitution, or any form of indecent assault.'[23] Similarly, the relevant provision of Additional Protocol I reads: '[w]omen shall be the object of special respect and shall be protected in particular against rape, forced prostitution and any other form of indecent assault.'[24] Even instruments that are otherwise progressive suffer from this problem. Thus, the Cape Town Principles relating to child soldiers, which otherwise provides a broad definition, includes as child soldiers '*girls* recruited for sexual purposes and forced marriage,' ignoring boys who are recruited with one of those purposes in mind.[25] For their part, the Guiding Principles on Internal

17 Criminal Justice and Public Order Act 1994, Section 142.

18 Sexual Offences Act 1956, Section 1(1).

19 A female perpetrator can be prosecuted for the offence of 'causing a person to engage in sexual activity without consent': Sexual Offences Act 2003, Section 4.

20 Sexual Offences Act 2003, Section 1(1), refers to penile penetration.

21 See C. Rodriguez, "Sexual Violence in South Kivu, Congo," *Forced Migration Review* 27 (2007), 45, 46.

22 See e.g. M. Scarce, *Male on Male Rape* (Cambridge, UK: Perseus, 1997), Chapter 11; W. Russell, "Sexual Violence against Men and Boys," *Forced Migration Review* 27 (2007): 22, 22.

23 Geneva Convention IV Relative to the Protection of Civilian Persons in Time of War, Article 27.

24 Protocol Additional to the Geneva Conventions of 12 August 1949 and Relating to the Protection of Victims of International Armed Conflicts, Article 76(1).

25 *Cape Town Principles and Best Practices* (New York: United Nations, 1997) (emphasis added). Cf. *The Paris Principles: The Principles and Guidelines on Children Associated with Armed Forces or Armed Groups* (New York: United Nations, 2007) para 2.1, which is more inclusive in this regard.

Displacement refer to 'gender-specific violence.'[26] However, the point should not be overstated. Protection to all individuals can be read into other provisions of international humanitarian law such as those on humane treatment.[27] And other instruments frame the protection in gender-neutral terms.[28]

The very creation of the International Criminal Court has played an important role in this area. The Rome Statute lists as crimes against humanity and war crimes, "[r]ape, sexual slavery, enforced prostitution, forced pregnancy, enforced sterilization, or any other form of sexual violence of comparable gravity."[29] The 'other form of sexual violence' is defined, in part, as "an act of a sexual nature against one or more persons or caused such person or persons to engage in an act of a sexual nature by force, or by threat of force or coercion."[30]

Two important sets of points should be noted here. First, the crimes themselves are framed in gender-neutral terms. Thus, aside from forced pregnancy, it has been recognized that each of the listed crimes is capable of being committed against men and boys. The Elements of Crimes, intended to 'assist the Court in the interpretation and application' of the crimes,[31] are also framed in gender-neutral terms. In one instance, this is even made explicit. One of the elements of rape, both as a crime against humanity and as a war crime, is that "[t]he perpetrator invaded the body of a person by conduct resulting in penetration, however slight, of any part of the body of the victim or of the perpetrator with a sexual organ, or of the anal or genital opening of the victim with any object or any other part of the body."[32] A footnote to the word 'invaded' reads: "[t]he concept of 'invasion' is intended to be broad enough to be gender-neutral."[33] That puts beyond any doubt that men and boys can be raped. The particular definition is important for another reason – it captures many of the forms of male rape documented to date. It is broad enough to include the rape of a male committed through the person of a male perpetrator or a female perpetrator; committed by a male or female perpetrator against a male victim through an object; and, importantly, the phrasing is such that it includes the

---

26 Principle 11(2)(a). The Annotations to the Guiding Principles recognise that: "Even if 'gender-specific violence' as prohibited by subparagraph (a) affects in particular women and girls, the term refers to violence against individuals of either sex." See W. Kälin, *The Guiding Principles on Internal Displacement: Annotations* (Washington, D.C.: American Society of International Law, 2008), 55.

27 For example, Article 3 common to the four Geneva Conventions of 1949; Additional Protocol I, Article 75(2); Additional Protocol II, Article 4.

28 See e.g. Instructions for the Government of Armies of the United States in the Field, General Orders No. 100 (Lieber Code), Article 44.

29 Rome Statute, Article 7(1)(g). See also Article 8(2)(b)(xxii); Article 8(2)(e)(xi).

30 Elements of Crimes, Article 7(1)(g)-6.

31 Rome Statute of the International Criminal Court, Article 9.

32 Elements of Crimes, Article 7(1)(g). See also the Elements of Crimes for Article 8(2)(b)(xxii) and Article 8(2)(e)(xi).

33 *Ibid.*

rather common situation of enforced rape, where a male victim is forced to rape a fellow victim.

The second reason why the list of crimes is an important one is because it is not limited to rape. It includes other forms of sexual violence, again reflecting the documented sexual violence that has taken place. This is particularly important insofar as men are concerned given that rape is not the predominant form of sexual violence to which they are subjected. Enforced sterilization is broad enough to cover castration or other violence against the genitals, provided, of course, that the other elements of the crime are satisfied. The 'other form of sexual violence' includes such abuses as genital beatings, enforced nudity, enforced masturbation, and enforced incest – all documented as taking place against men and boys in situations of armed conflict, or on a widespread or systematic basis. Although there has been some suggestion that this residual category requires a degree of penetration,[34] there is no reason why penetration should be required. All that is required is that the *gravity* of the offence be comparable to the other offences, not that the *acts* be comparable. The crimes of enforced prostitution and sexual slavery are also broad enough to cover male victims. The gender-neutral framing of each of these crimes should thus put to rest any arguments that, as a matter of law, these crimes can only be committed against women and girls. It is to be hoped that domestic legislation implementing the Rome Statute will transform domestic law along similar lines, given that domestic law in the vast majority of states lags far behind international law in this area.

Thus, today, there can be no question that sexual violence against men and boys can amount to war crimes and crimes against humanity. The question of whether it can also amount to genocide is yet to be tested; however, we can surmise that it would. As is well known, the underlying acts that could amount to genocide are limited to: killing members of the protected group; causing them serious bodily or mental harm; "deliberately inflicting on the group conditions of life calculated to bring about its physical destruction in whole or in part"; "imposing measures intended to prevent births within the group"; and "forcibly transferring children of the group to another group."[35] For our purposes, the principal acts that are brought into question are serious bodily or mental harm and imposition of measures intended to prevent births, though this is not to say that the other underlying crimes have no relevance.[36] Male sexual violence certainly could prove of such severity as to amount to serious bodily or mental harm. Indeed, the ICC Elements of Crimes note that serious bodily or mental harm 'may include, but is not necessarily restricted to, acts of torture, rape,

34 See A-M de Brouwer, *Supranational Criminal Prosecution of Sexual Violence* (Antwerp, Belgium: Intersentia, 2005), 148–51.

35 Convention on the Prevention and Punishment of the Crime of Genocide, Article II.

36 See D. Lewis, "Unrecognized Victims: Sexual Violence against Men in Conflict Settings under International Law," *Wisconsin International Law Journal* 27 (2009): 101, 129–32.

sexual violence or inhuman or degrading treatment.'[37] There is no reason why this would be limited to female sexual violence, nor does the Elements of Crimes limit it in this manner. Indeed, the *Akayesu* Trial Chamber held that "rape and sexual violence certainly constitute infliction of serious bodily and mental harm on the victims and are even, according to the Chamber, one of the worst ways of inflict[ing] harm on the victim as *he or she* suffers both bodily and mental harm."[38] Castration and, in certain situations, genital violence may be considered physical measures intended to prevent births. Again, the *Akayesu* Trial Judgment is instructive, noting that the physical measures may include 'sexual mutilation, the practice of sterilization, forced birth control, separation of the sexes and prohibition of marriages.'[39] Thus, depending on the circumstances, sexual violence against men and boys could also amount to genocide, again, provided that the other elements of the crime are satisfied.

3.2. PROCEDURAL LAW

Advances have not taken place solely at the level of the substantive law. Many of the procedural protections are afforded to all victims of sexual violence, rather than female victims of sexual violence alone. The UN Secretary-General, in his report on the creation of the ICTY, noted that:

> [i]n the light of the particular nature of the crimes committed in the former Yugoslavia, it will be necessary for the International Tribunal to ensure the protection of victims and witnesses. Necessary protection measures should therefore be provided in the rules of procedure and evidence for victims and witnesses, especially in cases of rape and sexual assault.[40]

The matter was thus phrased in gender-neutral terms, perhaps in light of the numerous instances of male sexual violence recounted in the reports of the UN Commission of Experts.[41] The procedural protections have proven important

---

37 Elements of Crimes, Article 6(b), footnote 3. For some of the mental harm that may result from male sexual violence, see World Health Organization, *Guidelines for Medico-Legal Care for Victims of Sexual Violence* (Geneva, Switzerland: World Health Organization, 2003), 16 (listing fear, depression, suicidal ideation, anger, sexual and relationship problems, and rape trauma syndrome).

38 *Prosecutor v. Akayesu*, ICTR-96-4-T, 2 September 1998, para 731 (emphasis added; footnote omitted).

39 *Ibid.* at para 507.

40 *Report of the Secretary-General pursuant to Paragraph 2 of Security Council Resolution 808* (Security Council Resolution 808, S/25704), 3 May 1993, para 108. On protective measures for victims of sexual violence, see generally de Brouwer, *supra* 34 at chapter 4.

41 See e.g. *Final Report of the Commission of Experts established pursuant to Security Council Resolution 780* (Security Council Resolution 780, S/1994/674/Add.2 (Vol V), 28 December 1994, Annex IX.

for male victims. In the *Tadić* trial, for example, male victims of sexual mutilation were afforded certain protective measures.[42] In the *Čelebići* case, a male victim of sexual violence requested that confidentiality measures be granted due to "a desire for privacy [and] a wish not to be publicly associated with the alleged sexual assaults upon his person and that of another."[43] In acceding to the victim's request and holding a closed session hearing, the Trial Chamber noted that "[t]estifying about the event can be a most difficult and humiliating experience for him."[44] The Trial Chamber had no trouble drawing on domestic legislation to support its conclusion, even when some of that legislation proved particular to female victims alone.[45]

This is not to say that male victims and female victims have precisely the same needs and should be treated exactly alike in international trials. It is often thought that a female victim of sexual violence would prefer to speak to a person of the same sex – a female investigator, counsellor, or the like – given that they may be more comfortable speaking to someone not of the same sex as the person who abused them.[46] It is often thought that male victims would also prefer to speak to someone of the same sex.[47] However, it is not at all clear that this is true of all male victims, at least those who are sexually abused by male perpetrators. On the one hand, men may not be comfortable speaking to women about such matters; on the other hand, the rationale for investigation by a person of the same sex no longer applies. The situation becomes even trickier if the abuse is committed by a female perpetrator. There remains much work to be done in this area.

3.3. ACTUAL PROSECUTIONS

Against this backdrop, the actual prosecutions of male sexual violence have been rather disappointing. This is not to suggest that the international criminal tribunals have not made important advances in the area. The ICTY has prosecuted several instances of male sexual violence. Indeed, its first indictment charged the accused with *inter alia* forcing two prisoners 'to commit oral sexual

---

42 *Prosecutor v. Tadić*, IT-94-1-T, Decision on the Prosecutor's Motion Requesting Protective Measures for Victims and Witnesses, 10 August 1995.

43 *Prosecutor v. Delalić, Mucić, Delić and Landžo*,IT-96-21-T, Decision on the Motions by the Prosecution for Protective Measures for the Prosecution Witnesses Pseudonymed "B" through to "M," 28 April 1997, para 30.

44 *Ibid.* at para 40.

45 *Ibid.* at para 41.

46 See e.g. *Co-Lawyers for the Civil Parties' Fourth Investigative Request concerning Forced Marriages and Sexually Related Crimes*, 002/19-09-2007-ECCC/OCIJ, 4 December 2009, para 6; Waki Report, *supra* 4 at 241.

47 T. Bouta, G. Frerks and I. Bannon, *Gender, Conflict, and Development* (Washington D.C.: World Bank, 2005), 48.

acts' and forcing one of them to 'sexually mutilate' the other.[48] Other cases have involved prosecutions for sexual assault. These have included charges for such acts as beatings to the genital area, "'bit[ing] into the penis,' forced 'oral sex,' and forcing two 'brothers to perform fellatio on each other.'"[49] However, there has been a dearth of prosecutions for the crime of male rape. The International Criminal Tribunal for Rwanda (ICTR) has been far less active in prosecuting male sexual violence. This is not because the issue has never come before it. Instances of male sexual violence have been documented in the jurisprudence of the Tribunal, though these have been few and far between. And subject to one exception, even these limited references have been at the level of background, informing the situation under consideration, or have not attracted any findings.[50] For its part, the Special Court for Sierra Leone (SCSL) did not prosecute any instances of male sexual violence. This was due to a failure of the Prosecutor to charge such offences. To its credit, despite not being charged, the *RUF* Trial Judgment sets out certain instances of male sexual violence committed during the armed conflict in Sierra Leone.[51] It also notes expressly that the definition of rape "is broad enough to be gender neutral as both men and women can be victims of rape."[52]

This varying degree of prosecution may reflect the evidence with which the Tribunals had to work. The ICTY had the benefit of the work of the UN Commission of Experts, the final report of which set out various forms of sexual violence to which men were subjected:

> Men are also subject to sexual assault. They are forced to rape and sexually assault women, they are forced to perform fellatio on guards and on each other, they are forced to perform other sex acts on each other, and they suffer castrations, circumcisions, and other sexual mutilations.[53]

There was also documented evidence of male sexual violence in Sierra Leone and in Rwanda,[54] but to a more limited extent. This is not to suggest that instances of male sexual violence committed in those two conflicts were far less. Indeed,

48 *Prosecutor v.Tadić*, IT-94-1-I, Indictment (Second Amended), para 6.

49 *Prosecutor v. Todorović*, IT-95-10/1-S, Sentencing Judgment, 31 July 2001, paras 36–40; *Prosecutor v. Stakić*, IT-97-24-T, 31 July 2003, para 241; *Prosecutor v. Cesić*, IT-95-10/1-S, Sentencing Judgment, 11 March 2004, paras 13–4.

50 *Prosecutor v. Muhimana*, ICTR-95-1-T, 28 April 2005, paras 441–4; *Prosecutor v Bagosora et al*, ICTR-98-41-T, 18 December 2008, para 1908. The exception is *Prosecutor v. Niyitegeka*, ICTR-96-14-T, 16 May 2003, paras 462–67.

51 See e.g. *Prosecutor v.Sesay, Kallon and Gbao*, SCSL-04-15-T, 2 March 2009, paras 1205, 1207–08 (*RUF* Trial Judgment).

52 *Ibid.* at para 146.

53 *Final Report of the Commission of Experts*, *supra* 41 at Annex IX, para 20.

54 On Sierra Leone, see e.g. D. Keen, *Conflict and Collusion in Sierra Leone* (Oxford, UK: James Currey, 2005), 60. On Rwanda, see e.g. L. Melvern, *A People Betrayed* (London: Zed Books, 2000), 186.

contemporaneous accounts suggest that instances of male sexual violence in both those conflicts were more numerous and more systematic than the jurisprudence of the ICTR or SCSL would suggest.[55] However, there are specific reasons for this relative lack of documentation,[56] and the differing pre-histories of the various tribunals may have played a part in the instances of sexual violence prosecuted before them.

Today, there is increasing recognition that men and boys are subjected to sexual violence. This is in large part due to the work of the international criminal tribunals and the very creation of the ICC. For example, in acknowledging the problem of sexual violence against men, the UN Secretary-General relied on the work of the International Criminal Tribunal for the former Yugoslavia (ICTY) and the Special Court for Sierra Leone (SCSL).[57] When definitions of sexual violence crimes were put forward at the level of international (criminal) law, these were framed in gender-neutral terms. Accordingly, today, it is beyond question that male sexual violence is a serious issue and that it can amount to war crimes, crimes against humanity and genocide.

4. PROSECUTION: LIMITS

Part 3 has shown that tremendous inroads have been made into the lack of visibility of male sexual violence and the lack of prosecution of perpetrators. In particular, we have moved beyond the idea that sexual violence is a problem for women and girls alone. However, despite these advances, remnants of this earlier way of thinking remain. The problem sometimes continues to be characterized as 'sexual violence against women' rather than as sexual violence, or sexual violence in particular against women. At other times, when the problem of sexual violence against men is recognized, its acknowledgment is often relegated to a footnote, or considered in passing in a sentence or two, before the 'real' issue is tackled.[58] It also seems that when sexual violence against men is reported, the issue is met with surprise.[59] Insofar as prosecutions are concerned, two particular aspects are in need of further consideration: investigations and charging.

---

55 On Sierra Leone, see e.g. *We'll Kill You if You* Cry, *spura* 1 at 42. On Rwanda, see e.g. D. Buss, "Rethinking 'Rape as a Weapon of War,'" *Feminist Legal Studies* 17 (2009): 145, 159 (referring to interviews with ICTR investigators).

56 See *infra*, Part 4.1.

57 *Report of the Secretary-General pursuant to Security Council Resolution 1820*, (Security Council Resolution S/2009/362), 15 July 2009, para 6.

58 See e.g. *Ibid.*

59 See e.g. Security Council, 5916th Meeting, 19 June 2008, S/PV.5916, 33 (Delegate of Slovenia); Security Council 6180th Meeting, 7 August 2009, S/PV.6180, 14 (Delegate of Mexico); Waki Report, *supra* 4 at 243.

4.1. INVESTIGATIONS

Much work remains to be done at the level of investigations of male sexual violence. Attempts at investigation sometimes are stonewalled or met with caution. This caution is understandable, but what is interesting for the purposes of this chapter is that the caution tends to put the investigations on hold. The matter simply is not pursued. Two examples usefully demonstrate the point.

During the armed conflict in Sierra Leone, Human Rights Watch issued an important report on sexual violence committed therein.[60] Human Rights Watch was told by a non-governmental organization active in the area that men and boys were raped during the armed conflict alongside women and girls. Some fourteen boys between the ages of 9 and 15 had been treated, but it was suspected that there were many more cases. The NGO noted that few boys were willing to report that they had been raped "[d]ue to the stigma attached to homosexuality in Sierra Leone" and the consequent fear that the victims "would be perceived as homosexuals."[61] The NGO also indicated that it "did not want Human Rights Watch to interview the boys they had treated as they feared that interviewing them would re-traumatize them."[62] This reaction and this fear are understandable. However, what is less understandable is that no attempts were made to try and tackle the underlying perceptions that gave rise to this fear so as to debunk some of the stigma and allow for investigation. This lack of visibility of male sexual violence and the consequent lack of investigation likely had some role to play in the failure of the Prosecutor of the SCSL to charge the accused in respect of the male sexual violence inflicted during the conflict.

The Waki Report on post-election violence in Kenya is similarly on point. The Report notes:

> [C]ases of sexual violence against men that took place after the 2007 elections were hitherto unheard of and new to the Commission and to Kenya. The tragic novelty of this experience meant that there were even fewer support groups available to men than to women. That, added to the humiliation of the violations meant that no male victims came forward to testify to the Commission, something the Commission understood, but nevertheless found regrettable.[63]

In many ways, the passage is a model one. It recognizes that sexual violence against men did take place; it suggests sensitivity to the feelings of victims; and it indicates regret that there was a lack of resources in place to help them. However, it is a shame that attempts were not made to try and ameliorate the 'humiliation' of victims and to put support mechanisms in place. This is particularly

---

60 *We'll Kill You if You Cry*, *supra* 1.

61 *Ibid.* at 42.

62 *Ibid.*

63 Waki Report, *supra* 4 at 243.

unfortunate in light of the fact that the Task Force mandated some five years earlier to determine whether a Truth, Justice and Reconciliation Commission was needed in Kenya had documented instances of male sexual violence.[64] It is to be hoped that any ICC prosecutions resulting from the post-election violence take on board lessons that should have been learned from the Sierra Leonean experience.

The reader also gets a certain déjà-vu when reading passages such as those of Human Rights Watch or from the Waki Report. In recent years, the problem of male sexual violence has been oft-noted and reports frequently castigate the dearth of available mechanisms for male victims.[65] Yet few inroads are made into combating outdated perceptions and providing support. This leads to a vicious cycle: a lack of support and a sense of humiliation lead to few victims coming forward; few victims coming forward leads to a lack of support and feelings of humiliation. One wonders quite how many times such passages will be written before attempts are made to break the cycle, let alone for the cycle to actually be broken. Investigators need to be sensitive to these dynamics and concerns. However, attempts must also be made to try and tackle some of the underlying problems in order to allow investigations properly to take place.

Care also needs to be taken that investigations do not focus on a certain subset of the population. To date, the few international prosecutions of male sexual violence that exist have tended to focus on civilian victims. Yet it is important to bear in mind that sexual violence also takes place against detained combatants or fighters; and it is equally important to bear in mind that the prohibitions against sexual violence extend to persons *hors de combat*. It suffices to recall the study on sexual violence in the internal armed conflict in Liberia, which found that 32.6% of the male combatants surveyed had been subjected to sexual violence.[66] Similarly, child soldiers would be omitted from consideration if investigations were limited to the civilian population. Yet they too face sexual violence, from their own side as well as from the side against which they are fighting. Thus, a report of the Special Representative of the Secretary-General for Children and Armed Conflict notes that "boys are especially vulnerable to sexual violence… during military conscription or abduction into paramilitary forces."[67] Certain international initiatives have an exclusive focus on civilians and sometimes on female civilians alone.[68] It would be unfortunate were such a focus to transpose across to the level of international prosecutions.

---

64 *Report of the Task Force on the Establishment of a Truth, Justice and Reconciliation Commission* (Nairobi: the Republic of Kenya, 2003), 31.

65 See e.g. *Gender, Conflict, and Development*, *supra* 47at 47–88; Mudrovčić, *supra* 16 at 64.

66 Johnson *et al.*, *supra* 15.

67 *Report of the Special Representative of the Secretary-General for Children and Armed Conflict*, (A/64/254), 6 August 2009, para 17.

68 See e.g. Security Council resolution 1820, 19 June 2008, on which see S. Sivakumaran, "Lost in Translation: UN Responses to Sexual Violence against Men and Boys in Situations of Armed Conflict," *International Review of the Red Cross* 92 (2010), 259.

It is also important that investigations do not simply perpetuate the dominant script. If the conventional wisdom is that an armed conflict is an ethnic one, that one side is systematically dominating the other side, and that the men of the former are inflicting sexual violence on the women of the latter, the temptation in investigation will be to follow this script. Yet this would have the unfortunate effect of overlooking the abuses that do not fit neatly within that paradigm, which would in turn lead to the exclusion of principally, but not exclusively, sexual violence against men and boys. Thus, it has been shown how, in the context of the Rwandan genocide, the international community has had some difficulty viewing Hutu women as victims.[69] Similarly sexual violence against Hutu and Tutsi men is frequently overlooked. Yet sexual violence was inflicted on Hutu men as a "device to humiliate and shame men who were not willing to join in the killing."[70]

4.2. CHARGING AND CHARACTERIZATION OF THE CHARGES

The hangover from earlier times, that only women and girls are subjected to sexual violence, has had serious consequences in the area of charging. The *RUF* case is illustrative of the point. The Indictment in that case refers to "[w] idespread sexual violence committed against *civilian women and girls* included brutal rapes, often by multiple rapists, and forced 'marriages.'"[71] The Indictment lists various instances of sexual violence committed against women and girls in various locations across Sierra Leone and at various points in time. Limiting the charges to 'civilian women and girls' had the effect that witness testimony on sexual violence against men could not form the basis of any conviction. Thus, the Trial Judgment details instances of male sexual violence recorded in witness testimony but expressly notes that "[t]he Prosecution... restricted its pleadings on sexual violence in the Indictment to crimes committed against 'women and girls,' thereby excluding male victims of sexual violence."[72] In the future, care needs to be taken that male victims of sexual violence are not ruled out right from the outset.

When male sexual violence *is* prosecuted, it should be characterized (at the very least) as sexual violence. It is no longer doubted that sexual violence can amount to torture as well as other criminal offences.[73] This means that the offence can be charged in a multitude of ways. Rape may be prosecuted as rape,

69 Buss, *supra* 55.

70 *Ibid.*, referring to correspondence with a human rights investigator working in refugee camps in Western Tanzania in the aftermath of the genocide.

71 *Prosecutor v. Sesay, Kallon and Gbao*, SCSL-04-15-T, Indictment, para 54 (emphasis added).

72 *RUF* Trial Judgment, *supra* 51 at para 1303.

73 See e.g. *Akayesu Trial Judgment*, *supra* 38 at para 597.

torture, or both; castration may be prosecuted as torture, enforced sterilization, wilfully causing great suffering, or a combination thereof; enforced nudity could be prosecuted as inhuman treatment, an 'other inhumane act,' an 'other form of sexual violence,' or a combination thereof. The danger is that, insofar as men are concerned, the act would be prosecuted in the general form (torture, inhuman treatment, and the like) rather than the specific (rape, or another form of sexual violence). This would reinforce stereotypes along the lines that only women are raped or that men cannot be raped, thus perpetuating the hidden nature of male sexual violence.

This is not simply a theoretical concern with little or no practical consequence. International prosecutions suffer from precisely such a deficiency. For example, in *Tadić*, the 'oral sexual acts' and the 'sexual mutilation' were charged in the Indictment as torture or inhuman treatment, wilfully causing great suffering or serious injury to body and health, cruel treatment, and inhumane acts.[74] Charges were not entered for any sexual violence crimes in respect of the acts. In *Blagoje Simić et al.*, a Trial Chamber of the ICTY characterized the "ramming [of] a police truncheon in the anus of a detainee" and "forcing male prisoners to perform oral sex on each other and on [one of the perpetrators], sometimes in front of other prisoners" as torture.[75] No doubt the acts did constitute torture, but it may be queried why the Prosecutor did not charge those acts also as rape. Along similar lines, in *Niyitegeka*, a Trial Chamber of the ICTR characterized the castration as an inhumane act.[76] Charges tend not to be characterized as *male rape*.[77] This is problematic.

Such limited characterization may not be intentional. Rather, it may be a reflection of the subconscious view that men cannot be raped. Alternatively, it may be a side-effect of the manner in which a report is drawn up. For example, the Report of the Sierra Leone Truth and Reconciliation Commission contains a chapter on youth, children, and women. The chapter on women details the various and numerous ways in which women were subjected to sexual violence. Given that that chapter was devoted to women, men and boys as victims of sexual violence were not considered. Yet, a perusal of the list of victims contained under the heading of 'sexual violence and forced conscription' reveals many instances of male sexual violence reported to the Truth and Reconciliation Commission. Thus, for example, numerous male victims are listed as having been 'stripped,' or 'tortured and stripped,' or 'assaulted, tortured and stripped.'[78] But there is little sense of what the assault or torture consisted. On other occasions, there is greater detail of the abuse suffered, but this is contained in the

---

74 *Prosecutor v.Tadić*, Indictment, *supra* 48 at counts 8–11.

75 *Simić, Tadić and Zarić*, *supra* 5 at paras 728, 772.

76 *Niyitegeka Trial Judgment*, *supra* 50 at paras 462, 467.

77 An exception is *Prosecutor v. Češić*, IT-95-10/1-S, Sentencing Judgment, 11 March 2004.

78 *Report of the Sierra Leone Truth and Reconciliation Commission*, Volume 2, Chapter 5: List of Victims.

section on the general military and political history of the conflict, and nowhere are the abuses characterized as sexual violence.[79] The Commission's report is too nuanced than to say that women were grouped with sexual violence and men with general violence. However, there is a danger of reinforcing the separation of the general abuse (suffered by men) and the specific abuse (suffered by women) and it is not altogether clear that there was an appreciation that men too were subjected to sexual violence.

As noted above, the fact that male rape has not been prosecuted as rape is problematic. However, at the other end of the spectrum, it is important that the focus not be limited to rape alone. For example, the Peruvian Truth and Reconciliation Commission focused on rape to the exclusion of other forms of sexual violence.[80] This meant that only a portion of the sexual violence that was committed during the armed conflicts in Peru was recorded by the Commission under the rubric of sexual violence.[81] Yet, as discussed above, rape is only one form of sexual violence committed in armed conflict and insofar as men and boys are concerned, it may not be the predominant form of sexual violence committed against them. For example, the Report of the Commission for Reception, Truth and Reconciliation in Timor-Leste notes that there were three reported cases of male rape.[82] However, it documents a far greater number of reported instances of sexual torture and sexual humiliation.[83]

Indeed, the precise forms of sexual violence that are committed against men and boys and the incidences of each of them will vary from conflict to conflict. Thus, it has been alleged that men have been forced to enter into marriage in Cambodia;[84] men were forced into sexual servitude during the armed conflict in Liberia;[85] and boys are held as sexual slaves by warlords and leaders of armed groups in Afghanistan.[86] The Report of the Commission of Experts investigating violations of international humanitarian law in the former Yugoslavia documents numerous instances of castration and genital violence.[87] Enforced nudity is also prevalent.[88] Thus, even if rape is the atrocity that springs to mind when speaking of sexual violence, the two are not synonymous with one

79 *Ibid.* at Volume 3A, paras 1134, 1477–79.

80 M. Leiby, "Digging in the Archives: The Promise and Perils of Primary Documents," *Politics and Society* 37 (2009): 75, 79.

81 See generally *Ibid.*

82 *Commission for Reception, Truth and Reconciliation in East Timor* (CAVR), Chapter 7, para 33.

83 *Ibid.*, Chapter 7.7.4.

84 See e.g. *Second Request for Investigative Actions Concerning Forced Marriages and Forced Sexual Relations*, 002/19-09-2007-ECCC/OCIJ, 15 July 2009, para 9.

85 Johnson *et al.*, *supra* 15.

86 *Report of the Secretary-General on Children and Armed Conflict in Afghanistan*, (S/2008/695), 10 November 2008, para 50.

87 *Final Report of the Commission of Experts*, *supra* 41 at paras 18(g) and 20.

88 See e.g. *Taguba Report*, *supra* 1 at Part One (Detainee Abuse): Findings, para 6.

another and the perception that rape is the predominant form of sexual violence committed against men in armed conflict is not always reflected in the practice.

5. ALL EYES ON THE INTERNATIONAL CRIMINAL COURT

As with international criminal law more generally, attention is shifting from the work of the *ad hoc* international criminal tribunals towards the ICC on the subject of prosecuting sexual violence. It is still early days and there is little work by the ICC on point to allow us to draw any conclusions. However, the ICC has given some indication that it will prove rather more promising insofar as male victims of sexual violence are concerned. It should be cautioned that early positive signs frequently give rise to dashed expectations rather than being brought to fruition, especially as the Prosecutor seems to be taking different approaches to the different country situations before him.

Instances of male sexual violence are within the ICC's activities in the Central African Republic. The background overview issued by the Prosecutor on the Situation in the Central African Republic reads in relevant part:

> [c]redible reports indicate that rape has been committed against civilians, including instances of rape of elderly women, young girls and men. There were often aggravating aspects of cruelty such as rapes committed by multiple perpetrators, in front of third persons, with sometimes relatives forced to participate. The social impact appears devastating, with many victims stigmatized and, reportedly for a number of them, infected with the HIV virus.[89]

And *Bemba* was charged with the rape of men, women and children.[90] In confirming the charges against him, the Pre-Trial Chamber found that "civilian women and men were raped from on or about 26 October 2002 to 15 March 2003 by MLC soldiers on the CAR territory."[91]

However, this approach should be contrasted with the ICC's activities in respect of the situation in the DRC. The Special Representative of the (UN) Secretary-General on Sexual Violence in Conflict has described the DRC as 'the rape capital of the world.'[92] It is generally recognized that a large number of

89 *Background: Situation in the Central African Republic*, ICC-OTP-BN-20070522-220-A_EN, 22 May 2007.

90 Situation in the Central African Republic, *Prosecutor v. Jean-Pierre Bemba Gombo*, ICC-01/05-01/08, Public Redacted Version of the Amended Document containing the Charges filed on 30 March 2009, 30 March 2009, para 39.

91 Situation in the Central African Republic, *Prosecutor v. Jean-Pierre Bemba Gombo*, ICC-01/05-01/08, Decision pursuant to Article 61(7)(a) and (b) of the Rome Statute on the Charges of the Prosecutor Against Jean-Pierre Bemba Gombo, 15 June 2009, paras 171–72, 286.

92 Security Council, 6302nd Meeting, 27 April 2010, S/PV.6302, 4.

men have been raped in the DRC. The exact figures remain unknown; a recent figure puts the proportion of male rape cases at 10 per cent.[93] However, it is generally recognised that there is a lack of reporting. If we move beyond rape to include other forms of sexual violence, it is likely that the figure would be far higher. Yet the first case arising out of the situation in the DRC, that of *Lubanga*, involved charges for recruitment and use of child soldiers alone.[94] This caused some consternation that charges for *inter alia* sexual violence had not been brought,[95] and it has been suggested that the charges should have been amended to include sexual violence. Any such amendment should have included charges for male sexual violence given that there is evidence suggesting that persons associated with Lubanga were involved in committing sexual violence against men.[96]

It should be noted that it is not just the Prosecutor and Chambers of the ICC that are involved with issues of sexual violence against men and boys. The Trust Fund for Victims is also active in the area. An announcement and donor appeal by the Trust Fund for Victims noted that:

> It is well known that armed conflict and sexual violence against women and girls often go hand in hand. What is less widely recognized is that armed conflict and its aftermath also bring sexual danger for men and boys. Sexualised violence against men and boys can emerge in any form of conflict. Both adult men and boys are also vulnerable during military operations in civilian areas and in situations of military conscription or abduction into paramilitary forces. In addition to acts of individual sadism, the main overt purposes of sexualised violence against men and boys appear to be torture, initiation and integration into military/paramilitary forces, punishment of individuals and a strategy of war designed to terrify, demoralise and destroy family and community cohesion.[97]

And since then, in the specific situation of the Central African Republic, the Trust Fund notified Pre-Trial Chamber II of its intended work. The Trust Fund indicated that "the crimes falling within the qualification of sexual violence are a

93 Gettleman, *supra* 6, referring to a figure of the sexual violence legal clinic in Goma, run by the American Bar Association. Older figures put it at 4 per cent and 6 per cent. See, respectively, C. McGreal, "Hundreds of Thousands of Women Raped for being on the Wrong Side," *The Guardian* (12 November 2007); *Shattered Lives: Immediate Medical Care Vital for Sexual Violence Victims*, (Brussels, Belgium: Médecins Sans Frontières, March 2009), 11.

94 Situation in the Democratic Republic of the Congo, *Prosecutor v. Thomas Lubanga Dyilo*, ICC-01/04-01/06, Warrant of Arrest, 10 February 2006.

95 See e.g. M.A. Drumbl, "*Prosecutor v. Thomas Lubanga Dyilo*, Décision sur la Confirmation des Charges, Case no ICC-01/04-01/06," *American Journal of International Law* 101 (2007): 841, 846–47.

96 See e.g. K. Glassborow, "Call for Lubanga Charges to Cover Rape," *Institute for War and Peace Reporting* (12 May 2008).

97 *Announcement of the Trust Fund for Victims Board of Directors*, Donor Appeal: Rehabilitating and Supporting Survivors of Sexual Violence, 10 September 2008.

priority for providing assistance" and that it "considers it important to target crimes of sexual violence as key steps in achieving its mission."[98] Importantly, it continues: "[m]en and children were also victims of sexual violence in the CAR. The UNFPA report... underlines that 'sexual violence affected both sexes.'" Amnesty International also reported that "even though the risks of being injured, killed or tortured, men in some situations have been victims of sexual violence."[99] Thus, the Trust Fund has made clear that not only are victims of sexual violence one of its priorities, but those victims include female victims as well as their male counterparts. Thus, the picture presented by the ICC is a hopeful one, albeit not uniformly so.

6. CONCLUSION

The international legal framework is in place for the prosecution of male sexual violence as an international crime. Sexual violence against men and boys in its various forms may be prosecuted as war crimes, crimes against humanity, and genocide. The substantive law on point is in advance of domestic law and procedural protections are also in place for male victims of sexual violence. Yet, despite the existence of this legal framework, actual prosecutions of male sexual violence are few and far between. Even in such instances, prosecutions tend to be for the general form (torture or cruel treatment) rather than for the specific sexual crime. All this suggests that the law can take us only so far. What is really needed is an attitudinal shift and that is something that is far more difficult to achieve.

---

98 Situation in the Central African Republic, Notification from the Board of Directors of the Trust Fund for Victims in Accordance with Regulation 50 of the Regulations of the Trust Fund for Victims, ICC-01/05, 30 October 2009, paras 26 and 27.

99 *Ibid.* at para 34.

THE INTERNATIONAL TRIBUNALS AND COURTS

CHAPTER 5

FUTURE CHALLENGES TO PROSECUTING SEXUAL VIOLENCE UNDER INTERNATIONAL LAW: INSIGHTS FROM ICTY PRACTICE

Michelle JARVIS
Elena MARTIN SALGADO[1]

1. INTRODUCTION

When the International Criminal Tribunal for the Former Yugoslavia (ICTY) was established in 1993, there were signs of the international community's determination to open a new chapter in the treatment of war-time sexual violence and to leave behind the inadequacies of past approaches. The Security Council singled rape out as one of the particularly reprehensible crimes committed during the conflicts in the former Yugoslavia and expressed its commitment to establishing accountability for these crimes as a core part of the ICTY's mandate.[2] Rape was specifically mentioned in the ICTY Statute as a crime against humanity[3] and, from early on, the Rules of Procedure and Evidence contained provisions to ensure sensitive approaches to evidence in sexual violence cases.[4] A Victims and Witnesses Section was also established to provide support for victims appearing before the Tribunal, "in particular in cases of rape and sexual assault."[5]

---

1 The views expressed in this Chapter are those of the authors and do not necessarily represent the views of the ICTY or the United Nations.

2 Security Council resolution 808, 22 February 1993 ("*Noting also* with grave concern the 'report of the European Community investigative mission into the treatment of Muslim women in the former Yugoslavia'...."); Security Council resolution 827, 25 May 1993 (expressing "grave alarm" at the "systematic detention and rape of women").

3 ICTY Statute (adopted by Security Council Resolution, 25 May 1993), Article 5(g).

4 ICTY Rules of Procedure and Evidence, IT/32/Rev.45, 8 December 2010 (Rules), Rule 96.

5 *Ibid.* at Rule 34.

Nevertheless, those who were familiar with the historical silences surrounding war-time sexual violence watched vigilantly and with some trepidation as the ICTY spread its fledgling wings. Even with the best of intentions, it would be difficult to dismantle centuries of inaction concerning war-time sexual violence and to travel a new more visionary path.

Part of the difficulty historically has been conceptions of rape and other sexual violence crimes as sexual acts – rather than violent acts – that are personal in nature and separate from the main activity of war.[6] For example, these mischaracterisations are visible in key international humanitarian law treaty provisions. Article 27(2) of the Fourth Geneva Convention states that "[w]omen shall be especially protected against any attack on their honour, in particular against rape, enforced prostitution, or any form of indecent assault." The ICRC Commentary to this provision states that these acts are incompatible with the honour, modesty and dignity of women.[7] Additional Protocols I and II perpetuate the perception that rape and other sexual assaults are outrages upon personal dignity rather than violent crimes.[8]

These mischaracterisations reflect the historical failure to recognise the gravity of sexual violence crimes. For example, rape and sexual assaults were not expressly listed among the grave breaches in the Geneva Conventions and Additional Protocol I, which set out the most fundamental provisions of the international humanitarian law regime.[9] These crimes were also inadequately dealt with in the post-World War II war crimes trials.[10]

Nineteen years after the ICTY's creation, we have much to reflect on. Although the progress has not been perfect,[11] the ICTY has made real strides

---

6 E.g. J. Gardam and M. Jarvis, *Women, Armed Conflict and International Law*, (The Hague, the Netherlands: Kluwer Law International, 2001), 135–176 (especially 172–173), 227; A Levy, "International Prosecution of Rape in Warfare: Nondiscriminatory Recognition and Enforcement," *UCLA Women's Law Journal* 255, no 4(2) (1994): 261–62; M. Bassiouni and P. Manakus, *The Law of the International Criminal Tribunal for the Former Yugoslavia*, (Ardsley, New York: Transnational Publishers, 1996), 577–588, note 154. See also L. Bianci, The Prosecution of Rape and Sexual Violence: Lessons From Prosecutions at the ICTR, 5 (commenting on the investigation of sexual violence by the ICTR and concluding that "[t]he strategy seemed to perceive and portray sexual violence as crimes being committed by individual persons on a random basis, as opposed to it being viewed holistically, as part of the greater atrocity that was taking place – genocide.").

7 *Geneva Convention Relative to the Protection of Civilian Persons in Time of War*, eds. J. Pictet *et al.* (1958), 206.

8 Additional Protocol I, Article 75(2); Additional Protocol II, Article 4(2).

9 E.g. J. Gardam and M. Jarvis, *Women, Armed Conflict and International Law*, (The Hague, the Netherlands: Kluwer Law International, 2001), 74, 183–84.

10 E.g. J. Gardam and M. Jarvis, *Women, Armed Conflict and International Law*, (The Hague, the Netherlands: Kluwer Law International, 2001), 204–205. See generally, K. Askin, *War Crimes against Women: Prosecution in International War Crimes Tribunals*, (Leiden, the Netherlands: Martinus Nijhoff, 1997).

11 E.g. M. Jarvis, "An Emerging Gender Perspective on International Crimes," in *International Criminal Law Developments in the Case Law of the ICTY*, eds. G. Boas and W. Schabas, (Leiden, the Netherlands: Martinus Nijhoff, 2003), 178–79.

towards debunking some of the historical myths about war-time sexual violence. ICTY case-law confirms that sexual violence is among the most serious crimes of war. Even the language used reflects this change. The term "sexual violence" has become the almost standard phraseology, replacing other terms like "sex crimes" which tend to obscure the fact that these crimes are less about sex and more about violence and control.

Still, it remains the case that most of the ICTY's sexual violence cases to date concern direct perpetrators of sexual violence crimes, or others close to the scene of the crime. One of the biggest challenges for prosecuting sexual violence crimes in the future is to ensure sensitive and accurate approaches to sexual violence as the complexity of cases further increases. The complex cases we refer to will typically involve high-level officials who are removed from criminal conduct on the ground and/or who are charged with crimes that require proof of links between sexual violence and a campaign of other violent crimes.

Complex cases necessarily depend upon prosecutors and fact-finders seeing connections between sexual violence and other violent crimes, being alert to patterns of sexual violence in the broader context of the conflict and understanding the indicators of sexual violence that make its occurrence foreseeable to high-level officials. Unless we can further dismantle the historical assumptions that tend to pull our thinking in the opposite direction, they will present significant obstacles to successful prosecutions in highly complex cases.

This Chapter begins with a brief overview of some of the advances in prosecuting sexual violence crimes in the ICTY context. We then move on to explore the potential pitfalls for sexual violence prosecutions in highly complex cases in the future.

2. ICTY ADVANCES IN THE PROSECUTION OF SEXUAL VIOLENCE

The ICTY has generated a solid body of jurisprudence that acknowledges the seriousness of war-time sexual violence. It has also exhibited sensitivity in interpreting the elements of crimes, such as rape, and handling procedural and evidentiary matters in sexual violence cases. In this section we briefly highlight some of these advances.[12]

The fact that the ICTY has entered convictions for sexual violence is *per se* recognition of the seriousness of sexual violence. Pursuant to its Statute, the

12 See further e.g. S. Brammertz and M. Jarvis, "Lessons Learned in Prosecuting Gender Crimes under International Law: Experiences from the ICTY," in *Protecting Humanity: Essays in International Law and Policy in Honour of Navanethem Pillay*, ed. C. Eboe-Osui (Leiden, the Netherlands: Martinus Nijhoff, 2010), 96–117; M. Jarvis, "An Emerging Gender Perspective on International Crimes," in *International Criminal Law Developments in the Case Law of the ICTY*, eds. G. Boas and W. Schabas (Leiden, the Netherlands: Martinus Nijhoff, 2003), 157–91.

ICTY's jurisdiction is limited to serious violations of international humanitarian law[13] and the seriousness of sexual violence crimes has been reinforced in ICTY case-law. In the *Kunarac* case, the accused were charged with rape as a violation of the laws or customs of war under Article 3 of the ICTY Statute.[14] Under ICTY case-law, to fall within Article 3, a crime not expressly enumerated in that provision must be a serious crime entailing individual criminal responsibility under customary international law.[15] The Appeals Chamber considered that the determination of what constitutes a war crime is "dependent on the development of the laws and customs of war at the time when an act charged in an indictment was committed,"[16] and found that rape met the requirements to be punishable under Article 3 of the Statute.[17]

The ICTY has acknowledged the reality that sexual violence crimes can satisfy the elements of a variety of serious international crimes that, historically, were not interpreted to include sexual violence. For example, ICTY case-law recognizes sexual violence as torture.[18] The Appeals Chamber in *Kunarac* found that, even if the perpetrator is motivated by the desire for sexual gratification, this does not rule out proof of intent for torture. In these circumstances, the perpetrator may still intend to cause severe pain or suffering in pursuit of a prohibited purpose such as to obtain information or to discriminate against the victim.[19]

The ICTY has also recognised that evidence of sexual violence is relevant in determining whether the elements of enslavement have been proved.[20] In doing so, the ICTY has moved away from traditional conceptions of enslavement that are closely associated with the forced labour of men, to an interpretation of the crime under international law that more accurately reflects the experiences of both women and men.

When it comes to the definition of rape, the ICTY has adopted a traditional position by requiring proof of non-consent.[21] At the same time, it has prescribed

---

13 ICTY Statute, Article 1 ("The International Tribunal shall have the power to prosecute persons responsible for serious violations of international humanitarian law committed in the territory of the former Yugoslavia since 1991 in accordance with the provisions of the present Statute.").

14 See *Prosecutor v. Kunarac et al.*, IT-96-23 & IT-96-23/1-A, 12 June 2002 (Kunarac Appeal Judgement), paras 190–93.

15 *Ibid.* at paras 66, 194.

16 *Ibid.* at para 67.

17 *Ibid.* at para 195.

18 See e.g. *Ibid.* at para 150 ("Sexual violence necessarily gives rise to severe pain or suffering, whether physical or mental, and in this way justifies its characterisation as an act of torture").

19 *Ibid.* at paras 153, 155.

20 *Prosecutor v. Kunarac et al.*, IT-96-23-T & IT-96-23/1-T, 22 February 2001 (Kunarac Trial Judgement), 281–82, paras 542–43; see also *Kunarac Appeal Judgement*, 125–26, paras 116–24 (upholding Kunarac and Kovac's convictions for enslavement as a crime against humanity).

21 *Kunarac Appeal Judgement* at paras 127–28; see also *Kunarac Trial Judgement* at paras 457–60 (requiring proof that, among other things, sexual penetration occurred without the consent of the victim).

a common sense approach to proof of non-consent that minimises the focus on the victim's conduct. The Prosecution need not introduce specific evidence from victims that they did not consent. Rather, non-consent can be inferred from the background circumstances such as an ongoing genocide or the victim's detention. The Appeals Chamber emphasised that, in the types of prosecutions being brought before the ICTY, the Prosecution's burden of proving coercive circumstances under which meaningful consent is not possible will generally not be difficult to discharge.[22]

Procedural advances emerging to deal with cases of sexual violence reflect sensitivity to the difficulties encountered by rape survivors during criminal proceedings, while at the same time safeguarding the rights of the accused. For example, notwithstanding evidence of post-traumatic stress disorder, Trial Chambers have accepted victims of sexual violence as credible and reliable witnesses.[23] They have also swiftly dismissed unmeritorious defence requests for sexual violence victims to undergo intrusive and unnecessary procedures, such as medical examinations.[24]

Finally, the ICTY's case-law on applications for pardon or commutation of sentence by persons convicted of sexual violence further reflects the seriousness of these crimes. For Zelenović, who pleaded guilty to personally committing rapes and torture through rapes, the President of the ICTY found that the gravity of his offences weighed against granting him pardon or commutation of sentence after he had served one-third of his sentence, even if he had displayed some evidence of rehabilitation.[25] In the case of Radić, both President Pocar and President Robinson took into consideration, in weighing the gravity of Radić's crimes, that he physically perpetrated crimes of rape and torture against several detainees in the Omarska camp.[26]

22 *Kunarac Appeal Judgement* at para 130 (finding that the prevailing circumstances in most cases where rapes are charged as either war crimes or crimes against humanity will be almost universally coercive so that true consent will not be possible); See also *Prosecutor v. Gacumbitsi*, ICTR-2001–64-A, 7 July 2006, paras 152–157.

23 E.g. *Prosecutor v. Furundžija*, IT-95–17/1-T, 10 December 1998 (Furundžija Trial Judgement), para 109; *Kunarac Trial Judgement* at para 564.

24 E.g. *Kunarac Trial Judgement* at para 917 (denying the defence's application to order the medical and psychological examination of certain witnesses).

25 *Prosecutor v. Zelenović*, IT-96–23/2-ES, Decision of President on Application for Pardon or Commutation of Sentence of Dragan Zelenović, 10 June 2010, paras 15–17, 20.

26 *Prosecutor v. Radić*, IT-98–30/1-ES, Decision of the President on Commutation of Sentence, 22 June 2007, para 14. Confidentiality was removed by *Prosecutor v. Radić*, IT-98–30/1-ES, Order Withdrawing Confidential Status of the 22 June 2007 Decision of the President on Commutation of Sentence of Mlađo Radić, 9 October 2008. *Prosecutor v. Radić*, IT-98–30/1-ES, Decision of President on Application for Pardon or Commutation of Sentence of Mlađo Radić, 23 April 2010, para 15.

3. REMAINING CHALLENGES: SUCCESSFUL SEXUAL VIOLENCE PROSECUTIONS IN HIGHLY COMPLEX CASES

The examples given above show that credible progress has been made in prosecuting sexual violence crimes over the past two decades. There are positive signals that we now recognise sexual violence as among the most serious of crimes committed during armed conflict, requiring a decisive response. However, the progressive approaches we have documented mostly concern comparatively[27] straightforward cases involving direct perpetrators of sexual violence crimes, or others close to the scene of the crime. For example, in the case of *Kunarac et al.*, the ICTY's most substantial and significant sexual violence case to date, the Trial Chamber specifically commented that none of the three accused played a significant role in the broader context of the former Yugoslavia conflict.[28]

As stated above, the challenge is to consolidate the progress made to ensure successful outcomes in complex cases involving high-level officials and/or crimes that require linking sexual violence with a broader campaign of crimes.[29] To guide the discussion in this section, we examine some of the key legal principles commonly applied at the ICTY in such cases. We consider how these principles might be specifically applied to future sexual violence prosecutions. In particular, we focus on holding high-level military and political figures responsible for crimes pursuant to superior responsibility and joint criminal enterprise theories and prosecuting sexual violence as genocide. Our discussion of the latter topic is supplemented by references to case-law from the International Criminal Tribunal for Rwanda.

3.1. HOLDING HIGH-LEVEL POLITICAL AND MILITARY FIGURES RESPONSIBLE FOR SEXUAL VIOLENCE CRIMES

As the ICTY has moved further into its case-load, the focus of prosecutions has changed from lower-level direct perpetrators towards holding senior political and military figures responsible for atrocities. This has been particularly so since

27 We say "comparatively" because few prosecutions under international criminal law are devoid of complexity. Nevertheless, as explained further below, some are more complex than others.

28 *Kunarac Trial Judgement* at para 858.

29 See also L. Bianci, The Prosecution of Rape and Sexual Violence: Lessons From Prosecutions at the ICTR, 7 (noting the difficulty of linking sexual violence to high-level accused persons before the ICTR and stating that "[t]he obstacle has been to link the highest-level accused to the sexual violence, where often no rape victim can directly tie them to the crimes").

2003, when the Security Council endorsed deadlines for the Tribunal to complete its investigations, trials and appeals.[30] As part of this strategy, the cases of lower-level perpetrators accused of less serious crimes were transferred back to the region of the former Yugoslavia.[31] This ensured that ICTY resources were allocated towards the more senior figures from the conflict alleged to bear greatest responsibility for the crimes.

This revised mandate has highlighted the general challenges associated with holding senior figures responsible for crimes. Very often it is obvious that a massive campaign of crimes must have been directed, or at least tolerated, by senior political and military figures. However, proving culpability to exacting criminal law standards may not be easy. These cases frequently depend on a large and complex web of circumstantial evidence and the inferences that can reasonably be drawn from this evidence.

At the ICTY, theories of superior responsibility and JCE responsibility have formed the backbone of the Prosecution's efforts to hold senior officials accountable. Both theories of liability entail their own challenges.[32] Many of the difficulties confronting prosecutors in sexual violence cases are symptomatic of these general challenges that apply to the prosecution of high-level offenders under international criminal law. Nevertheless, as we explain below, in cases of sexual violence, these challenges are often heightened and take on unique dimensions.

While the focus of this Chapter is on potential pitfalls in prosecuting sexual violence in future complex cases, there have been some encouraging early signs at the ICTY. Although now moving into the most intensive phase of high-level prosecutions, the Prosecution has already successfully prosecuted some mid-to high-level officials for their role in ethnic cleansing campaigns during the war in Bosnia and Herzegovina. In particular, convictions have been secured for

30 Secuirty Council resolution 1503, 28 August 2003, para 7 (calling on the ICTY and the ICTR to take all possible measures to complete investigations, all trial activities, and all work in accordance with the completion strategies).

31 See Rule 11 *bis* (Referral of the Indictment to another court): "(C) In determining whether to refer a case to authorities of a State for trial, the Referral Bench shall, in accordance with Security Council resolution 1534 (2004), consider the gravity of the crimes charged and the level of responsibility of the accused." See also Security Council resolution 1534, 26 March 2004 (calling on "each Tribunal, in reviewing and confirming any new indictments, to ensure that any such indictments concentrate on the most senior leaders suspected of being most responsible for crimes within the jurisdiction of the relevant Tribunal as set out in resolution 1503 (2003)"). See further Rule 28 (Reviewing and Duty Judges): "(A) On receipt of an indictment for review from the Prosecutor, the Registrar shall consult with the President. The President shall refer the matter to the Bureau which shall determine whether the indictment, prima facie, concentrates on one or more of the most senior leaders suspected of being most responsible for crimes within the jurisdiction of the Tribunal."

32 See below sections 3.1.1 and 3.1.2.

persecution based on sexual violence as an integral part of the ethnic cleansing campaigns.[33]

In the *Brđanin* case, the Appeals Chamber expressly dismissed defence arguments that rapes were "individual domestic crimes" unconnected to the armed conflict and to the widespread or systematic attack against the civilian population.[34] It found that the rapes of Bosnian Muslim women by Bosnian Serb soldiers and policemen occurred in the context of the armed conflict and as part of a widespread or systematic attack. The integral role played by sexual violence was reflected in the fact that the rapes took place during weapons' searches in a municipality where, over the same period, Bosnian Serb forces detained and beat numerous Bosnian Muslim men, Bosnian Muslim businesses were damaged, and a number of mosques were destroyed.[35]

While a positive start, there is still a long road ahead to entrench successful approaches to sexual violence prosecutions in complex cases. We turn now to some of the challenges before us.

3.1.1. *Superior responsibility*

Superior responsibility cases at the ICTY have confronted many obstacles and it has been difficult to secure convictions at the ICTY based on this theory of responsibility. For example, in the absence of traditionally functioning military chains of command, the Prosecution has had limited success in establishing the requisite effective control of the superior over the subordinate.[36] Similarly, notwithstanding broadly formulated *mens rea* standards for inquiry notice in theory,[37] evidence of quite specific notice regarding crimes has been required in practice.[38]

One of the key issues in future cases is likely to be proving that the superior knew or had reason to know of the risk of subordinates committing sexual

---

33 E.g. *Prosecutor v. Stakić*, IT-97-24-T, 31 July 2003 (Stakić Trial Judgement), paras 234–236, 240–241, 244, 757, 791–806, 818–826, 872, 881–882 (convicting Stakić of persecution as a crime against humanity based on, among other things, rapes and sexual assaults).

34 *Prosecutor v. Brđanin*, IT-99-36-A, 3 April 2007 (Brđanin Appeal Judgement), paras 253, 256–257.

35 *Brđanin Appeal Judgement* at paras 256–257.

36 E.g. *Prosecutor v. Blaškić*, IT-95-14-A, 29 July 2004, paras 349–422; *Prosecutor v. Hadžihasanović and Kubura*, IT-01-47-A, 22 April 2008, paras 194–232.

37 *Prosecutor v. Delalić et al.*, IT-96-21-A, 20 February 2001 (Čelebici Appeal Judgement), para 238 (finding that general information that subordinates have a violent or unstable character, or have been drinking prior to being sent on a mission, may suffice to put a superior on notice).

38 *Prosecutor v. Krnojelac*, IT-97-25-A, 17 September 2003 (Krnojelac Appeal Judgement), para 155; *Prosecutor v. Delić*, IT-04-83-T, 15 September 2008 (Delić Trial Judgement), para 514. See also L. Bianci, The Prosecution of Rape and Sexual Violence: Lessons From Prosecutions at the ICTR, 8 (noting similar difficulties in prosecuting superior responsibility cases before the ICTR).

violence specifically.[39] According to ICTY case-law, the Prosecution must prove that the superior had notice of the risk of the specific type of crime in question occurring. Thus, in *Krnojelac*, the Appeals Chamber found that a superior cannot be convicted of torture if he only had reason to know of beatings. To be convicted of torture, it is necessary to prove that the superior had reason to know of the risk of his subordinates carrying out beatings for one of the prohibited purposes of torture.[40]

The ICTY has applied this principle strictly. For example, Delić was the Commander of the Main Staff of the Army of the Republic of Bosnia and Herzegovina (ABiH) and a member of the Presidency of the Republic.[41] The Trial Chamber acquitted Delić of the murders of Bosnian Serb Army (VRS) detainees by the *El Mujahed* Detachment (EMD) (comprised of foreign and Bosnian Muslim Mujahedin) on the basis that the information which put him on notice of the risk of his subordinates committing cruel treatment, was insufficient to put him on notice of that same risk regarding murder. The Trial Chamber found that the instances of EMD violent behaviour and crimes reported in the bulletins reaching Delić did "not constitute a sufficient evidentiary basis to show beyond reasonable doubt that Rasim Delić was also alerted to the commission of murder by EMD members."[42]

When it comes to sexual violence crimes, the challenge may be to satisfy a fact-finder that an accused person at least had reason to know of the risk that his subordinates would commit sexual violence crimes specifically, as opposed to other types of mistreatment. As for the level of risk, it is sufficient that the superior knew of the possibility of crimes being committed. ICTY case-law confirms it is not necessary to prove a higher risk threshold such as a substantial likelihood of the crimes occurring.[43]

Given historical knowledge about the prevalence of sexual violence in most conflict situations,[44] the argument could be made that superiors are always on notice of the possibility that their subordinates will commit sexual violence crimes during conflict. Such a generalised level of risk may be insufficient for grounding criminal responsibility under the standards of superior responsibility adopted by the ICTY.[45] However, many of the factual situations at issue in

---

39 E.g. *Prosecutor v. Milutinović et al.*, IT-05-87-T, 26 February 2009 (Milutinović Trial Judgement), vol. III, paras 472, 1135 (finding that Šainović and Lukić were not responsible for sexual assaults pursuant to superior responsibility under Article 7(3) of the ICTY Statute as they "did not have reason to know of them").

40 *Krnojelac Appeal Judgement* at para 155.

41 *Delić Trial Judgement* at para 5.

42 *Delić Trial Judgement* at para 514. See also paras 513, 515–517.

43 *Prosecutor v. Strugar*, IT-01-42-A, 17 July 2008, para 304.

44 E.g. Susan Brownmiller, *Against our Will: Men, Women and Rape*, (New York: Fawcett Books, 1975); "War's Overlooked Victims: Rape is Horrifyingly Widespread in Conflicts all Around the World," *The Economist*, 13 January 2011.

45 E.g. *Delić Trial Judgement* at para 514.

international war crimes prosecutions disclose more concrete indicators of the risk of sexual violence crimes. These indicators include the separation of men from women during deportation and forcible transfer campaigns and the detention of women (or men[46]) in camps or other facilities where subordinates have uncontrolled access to them. The risk of sexual violence crimes is heightened where superiors fail to put in place systems for monitoring the treatment of prisoners by their subordinates.[47] Most of the sexual violence cases at the ICTY concern crimes committed in a detention setting.[48]

Other indicators that could be considered include knowledge that sexual violence has been prevalent in the recent past in a particular conflict zone,[49] the existence of particularly prejudicial attitudes towards women within a military hierarchy or indeed within communities,[50] and the use of sexualised representations of women as war propaganda.[51] Any factor showing that the risk of sexual violence crimes occurring was more than the generalised risk of sexual violence in any conflict zone may potentially be relevant.

Holding superiors responsible for sexual violence crimes will depend on prosecutors and fact-finders understanding the prevalence of sexual violence in a particular conflict zone and the propensity of subordinates to commit sexual violence, particularly when indicators are present such as those listed above. This in turn will depend upon the time and resources available to conduct investigations and prosecutions. As pressure increases to confine the scope of

46 E.g. K. Campbell, "The Gender of Transitional Justice: Law, Sexual Violence and the International Criminal Tribunal for the Former Yugoslavia," *International Journal of Transitional Justice* 1 (2007): 411–32 (describing ICTY cases involving sexual violence against men).

47 E.g., *Prosecutor v. Kvočka et al.*, IT-98–30/1-T, 2 November 2001 (Kvočka Trial Judgement), para 327.

48 E.g., *Prosecutor v. Delalić et al.*, IT-96–21-T, 16 November 1998; *Kunarac Trial Judgement*; *Kvočka Trial Judgement*; *Furundžija Trial Judgement.*

49 For similar reasoning see *Milutinović Trial Judgement*, vol. III, (Judge Chowhan, partial dissent). Opinion of Judge Chowhan, discussed further *infra*.

50 E.g. *Witness to Truth: Report of the Sierra Leone Truth and Reconciliation Commission* (2004),Volume 3A, Chapter 3, para 326 ("The patriarchal hegemony that had existed in Sierra Leone continued and worsened during the conflict evolving in the most macabre manner. The cultural concept that a woman was "owned" by a man played itself out in many of the violations that women suffered during the conflict").

51 E.g. "War's Overlooked Victims: Rape is Horrifyingly Widespread in Conflicts all Around the World," *The Economist*, 13 January 2011 (describing the prelude to massive sexual violence in the Rwandan genocide "In the weeks before the killings began, Hutu-controlled newspapers ran cartoons showing Tutsi women having sex with Belgian peacekeepers, who were seen as allies of Paul Kagame's Rwandan Patriotic Front"). *Prosecutor v. Akayesu*, ICTR-96–4-T, 2 September 1998 (Akayesu Trial Judgement), para 732 ("As part of the propaganda campaign geared to mobilizing the Hutu against the Tutsi, the Tutsi women were presented as sexual objects... This sexualized representation of ethnic identity graphically illustrates that Tutsi women were subjected to sexual violence because they were Tutsi."). See also L. Bianci, The Prosecution of Rape and Sexual Violence: Lessons From Prosecutions at the ICTR, 14 (describing sexualised representations of women that have been documented in ICTY case-law).

international investigations and prosecutions and to conduct them more quickly, the risk of failing to appreciate sexual violence in its proper context also increases. As a result links to senior officials will be more difficult to establish.

3.1.2. Joint Criminal Enterprise

JCE theory is one of the key available avenues for linking criminal conduct on the ground to the high-level officials who generally control the structures of power (usually political, military and/or police) used to implement massive criminal campaigns. As reflected in ICTY case-law, the application of JCE theory to sweeping crime-bases is complicated. For example, the ICTY has exhibited some reluctance in concluding that an accused person shared the common purpose of the JCE, sometimes convicting instead for aiding and abetting the crimes.[52] Further, to circumscribe the potential breadth of JCE liability, ICTY case-law requires proof of links between each crime on the ground and identified members of the JCE.[53] It also requires specificity concerning the evolution of crimes forming part of the common criminal purpose over the indictment period.[54]

It is against this general backdrop that we consider how sexual violence crimes can be addressed within JCE theory. In training courses we have conducted outside of the ICTY, concern is frequently expressed by participants about whether it is possible to include sexual violence crimes in JCE prosecutions. The concern apparently stems from the fact that high-level accused have seldom been direct perpetrators of the crimes and are not usually present at the scene. While there is generally little difficulty understanding how to prosecute direct perpetrators of sexual violence, there remains doubt about whether prosecuting sexual violence under theories like JCE is viable.

However, there is no reason to treat JCE cases where the crime-base includes sexual violence crimes differently from other JCE cases. No matter what types of crimes are involved, the key issue is always to link the crimes on the ground with the high-level accused person who may be physically removed from them. If linkage can be established, sexual violence should be prosecuted under JCE theory in the same way as other crimes.

The first step is to establish that sexual violence was part of a common criminal plan in which the accused participated (JCE categories I and II[55]), or

52 E.g. *Prosecutor v. Vasiljević*, IT-98-32-A, 25 February 2004, paras 115–135; *Prosecutor v. Krstić*, IT-98-33-A, 19 April 2004 (Krstić Appeal Judgement), paras 80–144.

53 E.g. *Prosecutor v. Krajišnik*, IT-00-39-A, 17 March 2009 (Krajišnik Appeal Judgement), paras 249–284.

54 E.g. *Krajišnik Appeal Judgement* at paras 163, 165, 171–78.

55 See *Prosecutor v. Tadić*, IT-94-1-A, 15 July 1999 (Tadić Appeal Judgement), para 228 (explaining that a category I JCE involves a common plan to commit a crime where all

that it was the natural and foreseeable consequence of the plan's implementation (JCE category III[56]).

3.1.2.1. Sexual violence as part of a common criminal purpose

In several large JCE cases before the ICTY, the common purpose has been limited by Trial Chambers to crimes of forcible transfer and deportation, with other categories of crimes such as murder, torture, beatings and sexual violence falling outside.[57] Nevertheless the ICTY Appeals Chamber has recognised that sexual violence can constitute part of a common criminal purpose, either at the outset of the JCE or over time.

Stakić, the President of the Crisis Staff of Prijedor municipality in Bosnia and Herzegovina, was convicted of the crime against humanity of persecution based on, among other things, rapes and sexual assaults (including rapes and sexual assaults in the notorious Omarska, Keraterm and Trnopolje detention facilities).[58] The Appeals Chamber found Stakić responsible as a participant in a JCE to ethnically cleanse Prijedor municipality by deporting and persecuting Bosnian Muslims and Bosnian Croats in order to establish Serbian control, where persecution, deportation and forcible transfer fell within the common purpose.[59]

Krajišnik, the President of the Bosnian Serb Assembly and member of the Presidency of the Bosnian-Serb Republic, was also convicted at first instance of persecution based on, among other things, sexual violence.[60] These crimes formed part of the common criminal purpose of the JCE in which Krajišnik participated. The Trial Chamber found that, over time, the common criminal plan to expel the non-Serb population developed to include sexual violence

---

co-perpetrators share the intent and that a category II JCE is a variant of a category I JCE and involves a system of ill-treatment).

56 *Tadić Appeal Judgement* at para 228 (explaining that category III JCE crimes are those that fall outside the agreed upon common purpose but which are foreseeable consequences of the execution of that purpose). See also *Prosecutor v. Karadžić*, IT-95-5/18-AR72.4, Decision on Prosecution's Motion Appealing Trial Chamber's Decision on JCE III Foreseeability, 25 June 2009 (Karadžić Interlocutory Appeal Decision).

57 *E.g. Prosecutor v. Martić*, IT-95-11-T, 12 June 2007, paras 445, 454; Milutinović Trial Judgement, vol. III, paras 89–96.

58 *Stakić Trial Judgement* at paras 234–36, 240–41, 244, 757, 791–806, 826.

59 *Prosecutor v. Stakić*, IT-97-24-A, 22 March 2006 (Stakić Appeal Judgement), paras 73, 84–85, 92–98, 104 (finding that murder and extermination were natural and foreseeable consequences of the common purpose's execution). The Appeals Chamber replaced the Trial Chamber's analysis of Stakić's responsibility as "co-perpetratorship" with responsibility pursuant to a joint criminal enterprise. It found that, contrary to the doctrine of joint criminal enterprise, co-perpetratorship as defined and applied by the Trial Chamber did not have support in customary international law or in the Tribunal's case-law: *Stakić Appeal Judgement* at paras 62–63.

60 *Prosecutor v. Krajišnik*, IT-00-39-T, 27 September 2006 (Krajišnik Trial Judgement), paras 4, 1126, 1145, 1182.

crimes. Sexual violence was committed against persons in and out of detention and was reported to the Bosnian-Serb leadership.[61] Despite this, the leadership, including Krajišnik, continued its forced displacement programme and persisted in their territorial conquests and demographic recompositions. Acceptance of this greater range of criminal means, coupled with persistence in implementing territorial goals signalled an intention to pursue the common objective through the expanded means.[62]

The Appeals Chamber, while accepting the theoretical possibility of an expanded JCE, overturned the Trial Chamber's findings due to insufficient detail.[63] Krajišnik's persecution conviction following appeal did not ultimately include sexual violence crimes, although the Appeals Chamber acknowledged the theoretical framework for such an outcome. The Appeals Chamber found that a JCE can come to embrace expanded criminal means, including sexual violence, as long as the evidence shows that the members of the JCE agreed on the expanded means.[64] While this agreement "may materialise extemporaneously and be inferred from circumstantial evidence,"[65] the Appeals Chamber signalled that it will require findings on precisely "how and when the scope of the common objective broadened in order to impute individual criminal responsibility for those crimes that were not included in the original plan, *i.e.* the expanded crimes."[66]

These developments in ICTY case-law contain positive signals regarding the prosecution of sexual violence as part of a common criminal purpose either from the outset of the JCE or over time. Nevertheless, in practice, there are still relatively few large ethnic cleansing cases at the ICTY where this has occurred. This situation is not unique to sexual violence crimes. The same is also true of other types of crimes apart from deportation and forcible transfer. When it comes to sexual violence crimes, however, there is a particular risk of failing to appreciate how they fit within an over-arching campaign of crimes due to the historical assumptions outlined above. Extra attention is likely to be required on the part of investigators and prosecutors to locate relevant witnesses and ask the right questions to uncover the extent to which sexual violence crimes fall within the broader pattern of crimes attributable to the JCE members.

3.1.2.2. Sexual violence as a natural and foreseeable consequence

It may be considered easier for prosecutors to prove that a crime was a natural and foreseeable consequence of a JCE than to prove that it formed part of the

61 *Ibid.* at paras 789, 800, 804, 965–966, 972, 1034, 1105.
62 *Ibid.* at paras 1096–1119.
63 *Ibid.* at paras 163–78.
64 *Ibid.* at para 163.
65 *Ibid.*
66 *Ibid.* at para 176.

common criminal purpose to which all JCE members subscribed. Common purpose crimes in the large ICTY ethnic cleansing cases have been largely limited to deportation and forcible transfer crimes. Other crimes, including sexual violence crimes, have then been dealt with under JCE III theory.

The inquiry into whether sexual violence is a natural and foreseeable consequence of the implementation of a JCE bears similarities to the risk assessment for the "reason to know" test forming part of superior responsibility.[67] ICTY case-law confirms that the risk threshold for both inquiries is similar. In the case of JCE III, the Prosecution must prove that the accused "with the awareness that such a crime was a *possible* consequence of the implementation of that enterprise, decided to participate in that enterprise."[68] Similarly, as explained above, for superior responsibility the Prosecution must prove that the superior had reason to know of the possibility of sexual violence crimes being committed.

At least two senior-level accused persons have been found responsible for sexual violence falling outside the JCE members' common plan, but amounting to a natural and foreseeable consequence of its implementation. In the first of these cases, Krstić, the Commander of the Drina Corps of the VRS, was convicted at the trial-level as a member of a JCE where the objective was to forcibly transfer the Bosnian Muslim civilians out of Srebrenica.[69] The Trial Chamber found that the creation of an attendant humanitarian crisis was "so closely connected to, and so instrumental in" the forcible evacuation of the civilians that it fell within the object of the criminal enterprise as a prelude to their forcible transfer.[70] The lack of food, shelter and necessary services accelerated the Bosnian Muslims' fear and panic and ultimately their willingness to leave the territory.[71]

The Trial Chamber was not convinced that the rapes, murders and beatings committed against the refugees in the midst of the humanitarian crisis had also been agreed upon as part of the JCE's common purpose. However, it did find that these were their natural and foreseeable consequences, "given the lack of shelter, the density of the crowds, the vulnerable condition of the refugees, the presence of many regular and irregular military and paramilitary units in the area and the sheer lack of sufficient numbers of UN soldiers to provide protection."[72] As

---

67 See section 3.1.1, *supra*.

68 *Karadžić Interlocutory Appeal Decision* at para 15 (affirming the *Brđanin Appeal Judgement*). See also para 18 (finding that the possibility standard is not satisfied "by implausibly remote scenarios," but requires that the possibility a crime could be committed is sufficiently substantial as to be foreseeable to an accused).

69 *Prosecutor v. Krstić*, IT-98-33-T, 2 August 2001 (Krstić Trial Judgement), paras 3, 615.

70 *Krstić Trial Judgement* at para 615.

71 *Ibid* at para 617.

72 *Ibid* at para 616.

a result, the Trial Chamber found that Krstić incurred liability for these crimes, pursuant to JCE III liability.[73]

The Appeals Chamber upheld Krstić's conviction. It dismissed the argument that Krstić could not be held accountable for these crimes because he was not aware of them.[74] His responsibility for the "incidental" murders, rapes and beatings arose from his participation in a JCE to forcibly transfer civilians. These crimes were natural and foreseeable consequences of that enterprise.[75]

Pavković was the second accused person to be convicted of sexual violence as a natural and foreseeable consequence of a JCE. Pavković, who was the Commander of the 3rd Army of the VJ (Army of Yugoslavia), was one of six accused persons tried as part of the *Milutinović* case, concerning the ethnic cleansing of Kosovar Albanians in 1999.[76] As a result of the ethnic cleansing campaign, at least 700,000 Kosovar Albanians were expelled from Kosovo in the short period of time between the end of March and the beginning of June 1999.[77] The Trial Chamber found that members of the forces of the Federal Republic of Yugoslavia (FRY) and Serbia sexually assaulted Kosovar Albanian women while detaining them during the mass expulsions.[78]

Based on the clear pattern of displacement of the Kosovar Albanian population, the Trial Chamber found that the common purpose of the JCE was achieved by deportation and forcible transfer.[79] The Trial Chamber was not satisfied that murder, sexual assault and destruction of cultural property also fell within the common purpose and these crimes were assessed pursuant to JCE III principles.[80]

The Trial Chamber concluded that Pavković was responsible for all of the JCE III crimes, including sexual assault.[81] The Chamber was satisfied that, given Pavković's detailed knowledge of events on the ground in Kosovo in 1998 and 1999, he was on notice that murders and sexual crimes would be committed by the VJ and the Serbian Ministry of Interior (MUP) as a result of the displacements taking place in 1999. The Trial Chamber also referred to evidence

73 *Ibid* at para 617.

74 *Ibid* at paras 145–46, 149–50.

75 *Ibid* at paras 150–51 (finding that it was sufficient to show (1) that the accused was aware that those acts outside the agreed enterprise were a natural and foreseeable consequence of it, and (2) that the accused participated in that enterprise aware of the probability that other crimes may result), In a latter decision, the Appeals Chamber clarified that the applicable standard was one of possibility and not of probability: see *Karadžić Interlocutory Appeal Decision* at para 15.

76 *Milutinović Trial Judgement*, vol. III at para 636.

77 *Ibid* at vol. II, para 1178.

78 *Milutinović Trial Judgement*, at vol. II paras 61–65, 68, 631–32, 688–90, 1158, 1187–88, 1224 (finding persecution through sexual violence in Beleg and Cirez/Qirez); *Ibid*. at vol. III, paras 472, 1135.

79 *Ibid*. at vol. III paras 89–96.

80 *Ibid*. at vol. III, para 94.

81 *Ibid*. at vol. III, paras 767–90.

that he knew rapes were occurring prior to the sexual assault crimes with which he was charged.[82] None of the other accused were convicted of sexual violence crimes and we will return to this below.

The *Kvočka et al.* case provides further support for holding accused persons responsible for sexual violence crimes pursuant to JCE III theory. The accused in that case were found responsible for persecutions, including through rape and sexual assault, committed in the Omarska camp in Prijedor.[83] One of the accused, Radić, was found to have personally committed sexual violence against female detainees.[84]

The Trial Chamber found that Omarska camp functioned as a system of ill treatment (JCE II) designed "to rid the territory of or subjugate non-Serbs" by persecuting non-Serbs held there through various forms of physical, mental, and sexual violence.[85] Although it did not hold any of the accused responsible for crimes beyond the common purpose of the joint criminal enterprise,[86] the Trial Chamber contemplated that:

> any crimes that were natural and foreseeable consequences of the joint criminal enterprise of the Omarska camp, including sexual violence, can be attributable to participants in the criminal enterprise if committed during the time he participated in the enterprise. In Omarska camp, approximately 36 women were held in detention, guarded by men with weapons who were often drunk, violent, and physically and mentally abusive and who were allowed to act with virtual impunity. Indeed, it would be unrealistic and contrary to all rational logic to expect that none of the women held in Omarksa, placed in circumstances rendering them especially vulnerable, would be subjected to rape or other forms of sexual violence.[87]

The Appeals Chamber upheld this theoretical possibility, stressing however that:

> [w]hat is natural and foreseeable to one person participating in a systemic joint criminal enterprise, might not be natural and foreseeable to another, depending on the information available to them… A participant may be responsible for such crimes only if the Prosecution proves that the accused had sufficient knowledge such that the additional crimes were a natural and foreseeable consequence to him.[88]

---

82 *Ibid.* at vol. III, para 785.

83 *Kvočka Trial Judgement* at paras 752, 755, 758, 761, 764 (convictions entered for persecution as part of a joint criminal enterprise based on, among other things, sexual violence). On appeal, Kvočka's conviction as a co-perpetrator of persecution through sexual violence was overturned because it could not be established that rape and sexual assault had taken place during the time he participated in the joint criminal enterprise as deputy commander of the camp's guard service: *Prosecutor v. Kvočka et al.*, IT-98-30/1-A, 28 February 2005 (Kvočka Appeal Judgement), paras 334, 339, disposition.

84 *Kvočka Appeal Judgement* at para 6 (citing *Kvočka Trial Judgement*, para 575).

85 *Kvočka Trial Judgement* at para 323.

86 See *Kvočka Appeal Judgement* at para 86.

87 *Kvočka Trial Judgement* at para 327. See also *Ibid.* at para 326.

88 *Kvočka Appeal Judgement* at para 86.

There are also examples in ICTY case-law where a Trial Chamber has not been satisfied that sexual violence was a natural and foreseeable consequence for the purposes of JCE III liability. In the *Milutinović* case, while convicting Pavković for sexual assaults under JCE III theory, the Trial Chamber acquitted (by majority) two other accused – Šainović and Lukić – of responsibility. Šainović was a Deputy Prime Minister of the FRY.[89] Lukić was the Head of the MUP Staff for Kosovo.[90] In their case, the Trial Chamber was not satisfied of a sufficiently strong connection between the sexual assaults and the ethnic cleansing campaign in Kosovo in 1999. The majority found that, while acts of murder and destruction or damage to religious property were sufficiently foreseeable consequences of the ethnic cleansing campaign to ground liability under the JCE III doctrine, sexual assaults were not.[91] The Majority expressly "examined the *Krstić* and *Kvočka* Trial Chambers' findings in relation to the foreseeability of rapes in those cases" but found that the particular facts of those cases with regard to foreseeability "were significantly more compelling" than those in relation to Šainović and Lukić.[92]

Judge Chowhan issued a partially dissenting opinion concerning the treatment of sexual assault as a JCE III crime in the *Milutinović* case. It is a short and straightforward statement of disagreement with the Majority's approach. In Judge Chowhan's view, in the context of the conflict under consideration and in the midst of carrying out an ethnic cleansing campaign, including the removal of women from their homes, it was foreseeable that sexual assaults would happen. Judge Chowhan considered this to be a matter of "prudence and common sense, as well as the past history of conflicts in the region."[93] The Prosecution has appealed the Majority's analysis of sexual violence as a JCE III crime in the *Milutinović* case.[94]

3.2. PROSECUTING SEXUAL VIOLENCE AS GENOCIDE

To date at the ICTY, no person has been convicted of genocide based on acts of sexual violence. However, it would be misleading to view this statistic in isolation, without regard to the overall picture of genocide cases at the ICTY. At

89 *Milutinović Trial Judgement* at vol.III, para 285.

90 *Milutinović Trial Judgement* at vol.III, para 945.

91 *Ibid.* at vol. III, paras 470–473 (finding, in respect of the accused Šainović, that murder and destruction of or damage to religious property was reasonably foreseeable but that sexual assault was not), *Ibid.* at 1134–36 (finding, in respect of the accused Lukić, that murder and destruction or damage to religious property was reasonably foreseeable by that sexual assault was not).

92 *Ibid.* at vol. III, paras 472, 1135.

93 *Ibid.* at vol. III, (Judge Chowhan, partial dissent).

94 *Prosecutor v. Šainović et al.*, IT-05-87-A, Notice of Filing of Public Redacted Version of Prosecution Appeal Brief, 21 August 2009, paras 60–82.

the ICTY, the Prosecution has issued far fewer indictments containing genocide charges than at the ICTR. The reasons for this are obvious. The 1994 genocide in Rwanda bears many of the hallmarks of historical genocides such as the Holocaust: a clear policy or plan to physically destroy the targeted group; hundreds of thousands killed and subjected to physical or mental harm during a sustained campaign of destruction engulfing most of the country; and men, women and children targeted for destruction without distinction. The events in Rwanda fit the historical genocide formula so indisputably that the ICTR has taken judicial notice of the 1994 genocide in Rwanda, thereby recognising it as a fact of common knowledge.[95]

The ICTY's genocide cases have been more complicated. To date, the successful genocide prosecutions have been confined to the July 1995 events in Srebrenica.[96] The Prosecution has not yet succeeded in proving that other aspects of the violent ethnic cleansing sweeping Bosnia and Herzegovina during the war constituted genocide,[97] although there are still opportunities to do so in the remaining cases.[98] We must view the record of prosecuting sexual violence as genocide at the ICTY against this backdrop of limited genocide convictions more generally.

In training courses that we have conducted external to the ICTY, the notion that sexual violence can constitute genocide is by far the most discussed aspect of developments in sexual violence prosecutions over the past two decades. Questions range from concerns that prosecuting sexual violence as genocide will water-down the seriousness of genocide to genuine confusion in understanding how sexual violence could meet the elements of genocide. These perceptions confirm the continued tendency to mischaracterise sexual violence as incidental, non-violent crimes.

In addition, our understanding of genocide is heavily informed by historical examples, particularly the Holocaust, where killing is seen as the overwhelmingly dominant feature. Yet the definition of genocide indisputably covers other violent acts, such as serious bodily and mental harm, provided they are carried out with genocidal intent.[99] If the necessary intent can be proved, there is no reason why sexual violence should not be considered as part of the *actus reus* of genocide.

---

95 E.g. *Prosecutor v. Karemera et al*, ICTR-98-44-AR73(C), Decision on Prosecutor's Interlocutory Appeal of Decision on Judicial Notice, 16 June 2006, paras 33–38.

96 See *Krstić Appeal Judgement* at paras 5–38; *Prosecutor v. Popović et al.*, IT-05-88-T, 10 June 2010, paras 837–866.

97 E.g. *Stakić Trial Judgement* at paras 535–561; *Stakić Appeal Judgement* at paras 37–57; *Prosecutor v. Brđanin*, IT-99-36-T, 1 September 2004 (Brđanin Trial Judgement) paras 963–91; *Krajišnik Trial Judgement* at paras 867–69.

98 See further section 4 *infra*.

99 Convention on the Prevention and Punishment of the Crime of Genocide, Article II(b)-(e), 9 December 1948, (reflected *verbatim* in ICTY Statute, Article 4(b)-(e)).

Prosecuting sexual violence as genocide generally requires persuading fact-finders of a link between sexual violence and a broader campaign of crimes. While it is possible that a small number of underlying acts could amount to genocide,[100] usually genocide cases will involve a broad campaign of crimes. Proving that acts of sexual violence were carried out with genocidal intent may require linking the sexual violence crimes with a broader criminal campaign. Convictions for sexual violence as genocide will be more likely if prosecutors establish that the sexual violence crimes were not isolated events but rather were connected to other crimes aimed at destroying members of the group.

The most ground-breaking development on this issue to date has taken place in the case-law of the International Criminal Tribunal for Rwanda (ICTR). In the *Akayesu* case, the Trial Chamber confirmed the classification of sexual violence as serious bodily and mental harm.[101] The Chamber went on to convict Akayesu, the bourgmestre of the Taba commune, of genocide based, in part, upon acts of sexual violence. After analysing the evidence in that case, the *Akayesu* Trial Chamber concluded that "[s]exual violence was an integral part of the process of destruction, specifically targeting the Tutsi women and specifically contributing to their destruction and to the destruction of the Tutsi group as a whole."[102]

ICTY case-law also recognises the theoretical possibility that sexual violence could form part of a genocidal campaign. Although the *Furundžija* Trial Chamber was not called upon to decide the issue, it noted in passing that rape could constitute genocide under the ICTY Statute.[103] Furthermore, during the

100 *Krstić Trial Judgement* at para 584 ("any act committed with the intent to destroy a part of a group, as such, constitutes an act of genocide within the meaning of the Convention"); *Prosecutor v. Semanza*, ICTR-97–20-T, 15 May 2003, para 316 ("there is no numeric threshold of victims necessary to establish genocide").

101 *Akayesu Trial Judgement* at para 731.

102 *Akayesu Trial Judgement* at para 731. See also e.g. *Prosecutor v. Muhimana*, ICTR-95–1B-T, 28 April 2005, paras 502, 513(c), 517 (confirming that serious bodily harm equals "any serious physical injury to the victim, such as torture and sexual violence" and convicting the accused of genocide based in part on his participation in attacks where he raped Tutsi women and shot refugees); *Prosecutor v. Musema*, ICTR-96–13-T27 January 2000, paras 158, 908, 933, 936 (finding that "measures intended to prevent births within the group" should be construed as including "sexual mutilation, enforced sterilization, forced birth control, forced separation of males and females, and prohibition of marriages" and entering a conviction for rape as genocide based on serious bodily and mental harm); *Prosecutor v. Gacumbitsi*, ICTR-2001–64-T, 17 June 2004, paras 291–92 ("Serious bodily harm means any form of physical harm or act that causes serious bodily injury to the victim, such as torture and sexual violence" and convicting the accused of genocide for instigating the rape of Tutsi women and girls, which constituted serious bodily harm); *Prosecutor v. Seromba*, ICTR-2001–66-A, 12 March 2008, para 46 (finding that rape is a quintessential example of serious bodily harm and that nearly all convictions for the causing of serious bodily or mental harm involve *inter alia* rapes).

103 *Furundžija Trial Judgement* at para 172 (confirming that rape can constitute genocide if all the required elements are met). See also *Stakić Trial Judgement* at para 516; *Brđanin Trial*

Karadžić and Mladić Rule 61 hearing,[104] the ICTY heard evidence about the physical and psychological harm inflicted as a result of sexual violence against women in Bosnia and Herzegovina and the proximity of the sexual violence to the killings. The Trial Chamber expressly recognised that systematic rape could be a relevant factor in determining genocidal intent.[105] In the *Karadžić* trial, the Prosecution has charged Karadžić with an ethnic cleansing campaign amounting to genocide. The genocide charge is based, in part, on sexual violence.[106] Ratko Mladić faces similar charges.[107]

In addition, gender considerations have been factored into existing ICTY genocide convictions to a degree. In particular, in confirming that the mass execution of the Muslim men from Srebrenica was an act of genocide, the *Krstić* Appeals Chamber drew support from the fact that the massacre of the men took place at the same time as the forcible transfer of the women and children.[108] The Appeals Chamber considered that the execution of the men had "severe procreative implications" for the Srebrenica Muslims, "potentially consigning the community to extinction."[109]

By contrast, the *Rukundo* case before the ICTR is an example of an unsuccessful outcome in prosecuting rape as genocide. Rukundo was a military chaplain for the Rwandan army during the genocide that engulfed Rwanda in 1994.[110] The Trial Chamber convicted Rukundo of genocide based on the sexual assault of a woman who had sought shelter at a seminary where Rukundo was present. According to the woman, who testified as Witness CCH, Rukundo locked her in his room and forced her on to his bed, with a gun set down on his bed-side table. Rukundo lay on top of Witness CCH with his trouser zipper opened and attempted to have sexual intercourse with her. Witness CCH

Judgement at para 690; *Krajišnik Trial Judgement* at para 859 (finding that sexual violence including rape amounts to "causing serious bodily or mental harm").

104 Rule 61 provides a procedure for a Chamber to review the evidence prior to the arrest and transfer of the accused and was used during the early phase of the Tribunal's existence when many accused persons remained at large.

105 *Prosecutor v. Karadžić & Mladić*, IT-95-5-R61 and IT-95-18-R61, Review of Indictment Pursuant to Rule 61 of the Rules of Procedure and Evidence, 11 July 1996, para 94 (referring to evidence of "camps... specifically devoted to rape, with the aim of forcing the birth of Serbian offspring, the women often being interned until it was too late for them to undergo an abortion... aim of many rapes was enforced impregnation" and to the use of systematic rape as a measure for transmitting a new ethnic identity to the child).

106 *Prosecutor v. Karadžić*, IT-95-5/18-PT, Third Amended Indictment, 27 February 2009 (Karadžić Indictment), para 40(b) and (c).

107 *Prosecutor v. Mladić*, IT-09-92-PT, Fourth Amended Indictment, 16 December 2011 (Mladić Indictment), para 39(b) and (c).

108 *Krstić Appeal Judgement* at paras 31, 33. See also *Prosecutor v. Blagojević and Jokić*, IT-02-60-A, 9 May 2007, para 123.

109 *Krstić Appeal Judgement* at paras 28–29.

110 *Rukundo v. The Prosecutor*, ICTR-2001-70-A 20 October 2010 (Rukundo Appeal Judgement), para 2.

managed to resist and so "Rukundo gave up trying to have intercourse, but rubbed himself against her until he ejaculated."[111]

The *Rukundo* Appeals Chamber by majority overturned Rukundo's conviction for genocide based on this sexual assault, finding insufficient proof of genocidal intent.[112] The Majority referred to the assault of Witness CCH as "qualitatively different" from the other acts forming part of the genocide.[113] This conclusion rests on the assessment that the sexual assault "appears to have been unplanned and spontaneous" and could "reasonably be construed as an opportunistic crime that was not accompanied by the specific intent to commit genocide".[114] Overall, the Majority considered that "Rukundo's sexual assault, while taking place during a genocide, was not necessarily a part of the genocide itself."[115]

In his partially dissenting opinion in *Rukundo*, Judge Pocar concluded that the sexual assault of Witness CCH was properly regarded as part of the genocide. In his assessment, Rukundo's sexual assault of Witness CCH was of similar gravity to the crime of rape and at the very least caused serious mental harm.[116] Judge Pocar challenged the Majority's classification of the assault as "opportunistic" and recalled that, even if the perpetrator's motivation is entirely sexual, this does not necessarily negate intent.[117] Judge Pocar put the sexual assault of Witness CCH into its broader context and saw concrete links with the genocidal campaign:

> Witness CCH was a Tutsi and sought refuge at the Saint Léon Minor Seminary fleeing violence against Tutsis in the surrounding area. In the context of the prevailing violence in the area and at the seminary, she sought Rukundo's assistance to hide her. Rukundo knew the victim, was aware that she was a refugee, and suggested that her entire family had to be killed because one of her relatives assisted the "*Inyenzi*". This evidence reasonably demonstrates Rukundo's *mens rea*, in particular in the context of 'mass violence against the Tutsi[s]' in the area as well as the specific evidence of his role in the repeated abductions and killings of Tutsis from the Saint Léon Minor Seminary.[118]

The mere fact that an act of sexual violence occurs during a genocidal campaign is insufficient to prove that it was carried out with genocidal intent. There may be examples of contemporaneous sexual violence that are not connected with the

111 *Rukundo Appeal Judgement* at para 227 (citing *Prosecutor v. Rukundo*, ICTR-2001-70-T, Judgement, 27 February 2009, para 373).
112 *Rukundo Appeal Judgement* at paras 227–38.
113 *Ibid.* at para 236.
114 *Ibid.*
115 *Ibid.*
116 *Rukundo Appeal Judgement* at para 9 (Judge Pocar, partial dissent).
117 *Ibid.* at para 10.
118 *Rukundo Appeal Judgement* at para 12 (Judge Pocar, partial dissent) (citations omitted).

prevailing genocide, just as other violent acts such as murder or torture could be committed during a genocide without being connected to it. Nevertheless, the risk remains that we are more likely to conclude that sexual violence crimes are "opportunistic" and disconnected from the prevailing context, than to reach these same conclusions for other violent crimes. The challenge for the future is to effectively guard against these tendencies. We must ensure that sexual violence is assessed in its proper context and, in appropriate cases, classified as genocide.

4. CONCLUSION

This Chapter has foreshadowed some of the challenges that remain in holding senior-level perpetrators accountable for sexual violence crimes in cases of high complexity. The ICTY has nine remaining cases involving sexual violence charges and all concern senior war-time officials.[119] Foremost among these are the cases of former Bosnian Serb political leader Radovan Karadžić and former Bosnian Serb military leader Ratko Mladić. The Prosecution has charged both Karadžić and Mladić with an ethnic cleansing campaign amounting to genocide. The genocide charge is based, in part, on sexual violence.[120] There is potentially a significant body of case-law on sexual violence prosecutions yet to be developed at ICTY and a final opportunity to establish a firm foundation for complex prosecutions of the future.

119 *Prosecutor v. Đorđević*, IT-05-87/1; *Prosecutor v. Karadžić*, IT-95-5/18; *Prosecutor v. Stanišić and Simatović*, IT-03-69; *Prosecutor v. Šešelj*, IT-03-67; *Prosecutor v. Prlić et al.*, IT-04-74; *Prosecutor v. Šainović et al.*, IT-05-87; *Prosecutor v. Župljanin and Stanisić*, IT-08-91; *Prosecutor v. Mladić*, IT-09-92; *Prosecutor v. Hadžić*, IT-04-75.

120 *Karadžić Indictment* at para 40(b) and (c); *Mladić Indictment* at para 39(b) and (c).

CHAPTER 6

THE PROSECUTION OF RAPE AND SEXUAL VIOLENCE: LESSONS FROM PROSECUTIONS AT THE ICTR

Linda BIANCHI[1]

1. INTRODUCTION

The International Criminal Tribunal of Rwanda (ICTR) was established as an *ad hoc* tribunal in the face of serious violations of international humanitarian law committed in the territory of Rwanda and neighbouring states between 1 January 1994 and 31 December 1994.[2] The establishment of the ICTR was momentous, as it was the first international criminal tribunal with a mandate to adjudicate violations of humanitarian law committed in a non-international armed conflict. The Office of the Prosecutor (OTP) has focused on bringing before the ICTR those persons bearing the greatest responsibility for genocide and violations of international human rights. During the 1994 conflict in Rwanda rape occurred on a massive scale. The ICTR's work has included the prosecution of the crimes of rape and other sexual violence perpetrated during the genocide. The recognition that sexual violence can constitute a war crime, a crime against humanity or a constituent act of genocide has been established in International Law through the work of the ICTR and the International Criminal Tribunal for the former Yugoslavia.

1 Linda Bianchi was a Senior Appeals Counsel in the Appeals and Legal Advisory Division for the Office of the Prosecutor at the ICTR where she worked since October 2003. She was the Chairperson and a founding member of the Committee for the Review of the Investigation and Prosecution of Sexual Violence, set up within the OTP in June 2007. This presentation is based on the work performed and materials composed by the Committee and its individual members. In particular, the author would like to thank the following two members, Inneke Onsea, Senior Appeals Counsel, and Renifa Madenga, Appeals Counsel at the ICTR for their contributions to the discussion in this paper. Ms. Bianchi is now working as a prosecutor for the Government of Canada in its Public Prosecution Service.

2 *Statute of the International Tribunal for Rwanda*, Security Council resolution 955, Annex, 8 November 1994, Article 1 (Statute).

The importance of ending impunity for acts of sexual violence has been stressed by the United Nations to be part of a comprehensive approach towards seeking sustainable peace, justice, truth and national reconciliation. The Security Council has very recently emphasized the responsibility of all States to put an end to impunity and to prosecute those responsible for genocide, crimes against humanity, and war crimes including those relating to sexual and other violence against women and girls. Resolution 1820, passed by the Security Council, requires all Member States to comply with their obligations for prosecuting persons responsible for such acts, to ensure that all victims of sexual violence, particularly women and girls, have equal protection under the law and equal access to justice, recognizing that, "[w]omen and girls are particularly targeted by the use of sexual violence, including as a tactic of war to humiliate, dominate, instil fear in, disperse and/or forcibly relocate civilian members of a community or ethnic group."[3]

Indeed, the prosecution of sexual violence crimes is a key component to stopping the global violence against women. Rape and other forms of sexual violence must be punished and be seen to be punished, if the cycle of sexual violence and other forms of violence is to be halted. The question is, how has the ICTR's work contributed to this effort? Has the ICTR delivered justice for the countless victims who suffered these egregious harms during the genocide in Rwanda in 1994? Much has been written about the ICTR's record on the investigation and prosecution of sexual violence crimes. In large part, commentators have criticized what has been seen as a very poor record, particularly in light of the fact that rape and sexual violence was widespread during the genocide that ravaged Rwanda in April, June and July 1994.

While the ICTR's history is somewhat storied in relation to the prosecution of these crimes, it nevertheless succeeded in securing numerous convictions for these atrocities, which, in itself, succeeds in not only making perpetrators finally account for these crimes and provide a sense of justice to the victims, but succeeds also in establishing a shift in paradigm of how these crimes are perceived in the international community – from the traditional view of being the spoils of war, to being crimes properly conceived of as international crimes worthy of prosecution. In addition, the entire record of the ICTR, regardless of whether convictions were entered in each individual case, creates a record of the existence of the crimes themselves. Critics condemn the ICTR for the low number of convictions for gender-based crimes, arguing that the convictions fail to paint the full picture of the pervasiveness of these crimes during the genocide. There is no denying that the OTP's low success rate for the prosecution of these crimes does not reflect the extensiveness of the rapes and sexual violence that occurred in Rwanda. However, a review of the entire jurisprudence of the ICTR, including those cases where acquittals were entered against charges of sexual

3 Security Council resolution 1820, 19 June 2008, page 1.

violence and those cases where no actual charges of sexual violence were even laid, reveals a much broader picture of what actually occurred. It is in the totality of the record of the cases tried at the ICTR where the pervasiveness of these crimes can be found that reflects their occurrence in the massacres of 1994.[4]

The challenges faced by the ICTR in its work on sexual violence have been many, and there remain several obstacles to overcome before justice is finally considered to be done for the victims of the Rwandan genocide. In this paper, I will discuss some of the many challenges faced by the ICTR in its work on sexual violence, some of the successes achieved despite these challenges, including a look at the development of the jurisprudence of the Tribunal which has significantly contributed to the recognition and prosecution of sexual violence crimes. Lastly, I will provide an overview of the jurisprudence of the ICTR generally to comment on the overall effectiveness of the ICTR cases to present a realistic picture of the true nature and scope of sexual violence crimes during the genocide.

2. THE RWANDAN EXPERIENCE

It is useful to briefly summarize the scope and nature of the sexual violence crimes that were committed in Rwanda in order to place the work of the OTP within its proper context.

The world witnessed the unfolding of a human tragedy of overwhelming proportions in Rwanda in the year 1994, when close to eight hundred thousand civilians – both *Tutsi* and moderate *Hutu* – were subjected to a range of human rights violations and/or were brutally killed within a space of one hundred days between April and June 1994. Violence during the genocide assumed gender specific forms, when members of the *Hutu* militia (known as the *Interahamwe*), the Rwandan Armed Forces (RAF) and civilians targeted Rwandan women and girls in a genocidal campaign of mass sexual violence.[5] The United Nations Security Council, in determining whether the conflicts in the Former Yugoslavia and Rwanda constituted a threat to international peace, accepted reports of massive and systematic rape of women.[6]

"Sexual violence has long formed part of armed conflicts and has empirically been shown not to be an incidental by-product, but a frequently used 'weapon of

---

4 This was a theory expounded by Professor Doris Buss, and which is more fully explored later in this paper.

5 *Struggling to Survive: Barriers to Justice for Rape Victims in Rwanda*, (New York: Human Rights Watch, September 2004 Vol. 16, No. 10(A)), 7 ("HRW Report of September 2004").

6 See Rene Degui-Segui, "Report of the Special Rapporteur on the situation of Human Rights in Rwanda," in *The United Nations and Rwanda 1993–1996*, (New York: Department of Public Information, United Nations, 29 January 1996), Document 167, paras 16–24, ("Degui Report").

war.'"[7] Rwanda was no exception. The pervasiveness of sexual violence and rape as means of committing genocide and as crimes against humanity and war crimes during the Rwandan conflict of 1994 is well-documented.[8]

It has been estimated that between 250,000 and 500,000 women were raped during the Rwandan genocide.[9] This is a staggering estimate that is reflected in the report by the United Nations Special Rapporteur that "Rape was systematic and was used as a 'weapon' by the perpetrators of the massacres... and according to consistent and reliable testimony... rape was the rule and its absence was the exception."[10]

Both rape and sexual violence were used during the Rwandan genocide to target Tutsi civilians and moderate Hutu, especially women. Rape and other forms of sexual violence were directed primarily against *Tutsi* women because of both their gender and their ethnicity.[11] One of the most poignant illustrations of the targeting of Tutsi women is seen in the case of *Mikaeli Muhimana*, who apologized to a young Hutu girl after raping her, stating he had raped her because he thought she was Tutsi.[12] Some *Hutu* women were also targeted with rape because they were affiliated with the political opposition, because they were married to *Tutsi* men or because they protected *Tutsi*.[13]

Women were raped in every *préfecture* of Rwanda, throughout the genocide, most often in the open in plain view, including at roadblocks, in official and governmental buildings such as military camps, churches, schools and university premises, hospitals, health clinics, stadiums, and marketplaces. The ages of the rape victims ranged from young girls to older women, even pregnant women were raped. Sexually subjugating and mutilating *Tutsi* women was both a way to punish the women and to attack the ethnic group.[14]

---

7 Judge Wolfgang Schomburg and Ines Peterson, "Genuine Consent to Sexual Violence Under International Law," *American Journal of International Law* 101, no. 1 (January 2007): 121.

8 See Degui Report at paras 16–24.

9 Alex Obote-Odora, "Rape and Sexual Violence in International Law: ICTR Contribution," *New England Journal of International & Comparative Law* 12, no. 1 (2005): 137, citing Rhonda Copelon, "Surfacing Gender: Reengraving Crimes against Women in Humanitarian Law" in *Women and War in the Twentieth Century: Enlisted with or without her Consent*, ed. N. Dombrowski (New York: Garland Publishing, 1999). It has been estimated that these numbers do not account for the women whose injuries prevented them from conceiving a child, or the number of women who experienced multiple rapes and gang rapes. Nor do the numbers account for women who either self-aborted or committed infanticide, who were mutilated by having breasts cut off or having implements brutally inserted into their genitals, or who were murdered after being raped.

10 See Degui Report at paras 16–24.

11 *Shattered Lives, Sexual Violence During the Rwandan Genocide and Its Aftermath,* (New York: Human Rights Watch, September 1996), 2 ("HRW Report: Shattered Lives").

12 See *Prosecutor v. Mikaeli Muhimana*, 95-1B-T, Judgement and Sentence, 28 April 2005, paras 517 and 552 ("*Muhimana* Trial Judgement").

13 HRW Report: Shattered Lives, at 2.

14 *Sexual Violence Crimes During the Rwandan Genocide, Expert Report of Binaifer Nowrojee*, (New York: Human Rights Watch, June 2004), paras 36 and 47.

It has also been documented that the forms of gender based and sexual violence were varied and included individual rape, gang-rape, rape with sticks, guns, or other objects, sexual enslavement, forced marriage, forced labour, and sexual mutilation.[15] Sexual violence was one of many injuries inflicted upon Rwandan women and girls, who were often abused after having witnessed the torture and murder of their family members and the destruction of their homes. According to many personal accounts of the genocide, a large number of victims were murdered directly following the sexual assaults.[16]

Rapes were committed by different categories of perpetrators. The emphasis of the ICTR has been on establishing the criminal responsibility of persons exercising the higher levels of responsibility and authority in Rwanda, that is, the political and military leaders who were the planners, instigators and commanders in Rwanda. The individual accused at the ICTR have come from all ranks of Rwanda's leadership, senior military commanders, top politicians, senior civilian administrators, the clergy and senior media practitioners. In some cases, though low-level militia men, soldiers and *Interahamwe* directly raped women and girls, these high ranking officials instigated, encouraged, supervised and, at times personally committed brutal acts of rape and sexual violence.

The sexual violence perpetrated against *Tutsi* women was a means of dehumanizing and subjugating all *Tutsi*.[17] As was stated in the *Akayesu* Trial Judgement, the "sexualized representation of ethnic identity graphically illustrates that tutsi women were subjected to sexual violence because they were Tutsi. Sexual violence was a step in the process of destruction of the tutsi group – destruction of the spirit, of the will to live, and of life itself."[18]

3. THE RECORD OF THE OFFICE OF THE PROSECUTOR – CHALLENGES ENCOUNTERED

There can be no question that crimes of sexual violence were used as weapons of conflict on a vast scale during the genocide in Rwanda, as has been true of nearly every armed conflict throughout history. Despite this being so, the success rate for prosecutions of these crimes has been low, due to numerous factors which make these types of prosecutions particularly challenging.

From the outset, the OTP adopted a policy to prosecute rape and sexual violence, alongside other crimes enshrined in the ICTR Statute, which differed

15 HRW Report of September 2004 at 7, citing HRW Report: Shattered Lives.

16 HRW Report of September 2004 at 7.

17 HRW Report: Shattered Lives at 2; See also Obote-Odora, "Rape and Sexual Violence in International Law: ICTR Contribution" at 131–32.

18 *Prosecutor v. Jean Paul Akayesu*, ICTR-96-4-T, 2 September 1998, para 732 ("*Akayesu* Trial Judgement").

from the traditional approach in which such crimes were normally not indicted.[19] As part of this comprehensive approach, the OTP has issued several indictments containing charges of rape and other sexual violence. Out of a total of 87 indictees, 40 of them have been charged with rape and other sexual violence crimes:

- 7 of these 40 cases involving charges of rape have not yet been fully adjudicated;
- There has been a charge of rape involved in the indictments of 33 completed cases;
- Of these 33 completed cases, 11 accused have been convicted of rape[20] and 1 accused convicted on a count of other inhumane acts as a crime against humanity for acts of sexual violence[21]; and,
- 22 Accused have been acquitted of rape and other acts of sexual violence.[22]

---

19 Obote-Odora, "Rape and Sexual Violence in International Law: ICTR Contribution" at 132.

20 Jean Paul Akayesu, Laurent Semanza, Mikaeli Muhimana, Sylvestre Gacumbitsi, Théoneste Bagosora, Augustin Bizimungu, Idelphonse Hategekimana, Pauline Nyiramasuhuko, Arsène Shalom Ntahobali. Edouard Karemera and Matthieu Ngirumpatse. The last seven cases are currently under appeal.

21 Eliézer Niyitegeka was convicted of a crime against humanity, other inhumane acts, for acts of sexual violence but acquitted on the count of rape as a crime against humanity. See *The Prosecutor v. Eliézer Niyitegeka*, ICTR-96-14-T, Judgement and Sentence, 16 May 2003, paras 458 and 467.

22 Ignace Bagilishema, *The Prosecutor v. Ignace Bagilishema*, ICTR-95-1A-T, 7 June 2001, Bagilishema was acquitted of all charges in his indictment; Alfred Musema, *Alfred Musema v. The Prosecutor*, ICTR-96-13-A, 16 November 2001, para 194, Musema was convicted at trial of rape, but his conviction was overturned on appeal; Eliézer Niyitegeka, *The Prosecutor v. Eliézer Niyitegeka*, ICTR-96-14-T, Judgement and Sentence, 16 May 2003; Juvénal Kajelijeli, *The Prosecutor v. Juvénal Kajelijeli*, ICTR-98-44A-T, Judgement and Sentence, 1 December 2003 ("*Kajelijeli* Trial Judgement"), In *Kajelijeli*, the Prosecution attempted to launch an appeal against the acquittals of rape and other inhumane acts, and filed a Notice of Appeal to that effect, however the Notice of Appeal was filed late and the Appeals Chamber would not validate the late filing. See *The Prosecutor v. Kajelijeli*, "Decision on Prosecution Urgent Motion for Extension of Time to File Notice of Appeal," 17 December 2003; Jean Bosco Barayagwiza, rape allegations were included in the indictment against Barayagwiza as part of the two charges of serious violations of Article 3 common to the Geneva Conventions and of Additional Protocol II. The Prosecutor conceded the dropping of these charges, stating "while the evidence adduced amounts to a prima facie case as to the War Crimes counts... the Prosecution does not resist the motions to strike these Counts 8 and 9 of the Barayagwiza indictment." See *The Prosecutor v. Ferdinand Nahimana, Jean-Bosco Barayagwiza, Hassan Ngeze*, ICTR-99-52-T, "Reasons for the oral Decision of 17 September 2002 on the Motions for Acquittal, Rule 98 *bis* of the Rules of Procedure and Evidence", 22 September 2002, para 21; Jean de Dieu Kamuhanda, *The Prosecutor v. Jean de Dieu Kamuhanda*, ICTR-1999-54A-T, Judgement and Sentence, 22 January 2004 ("*Kamuhanda* Trial Judgement"); Tharcisse Muvunyi, *The Prosecutor v. Tharcisse Muvunyi*, ICTR-2000-55A-T, Judgement and Sentence, 12 September 2006; Paul Bisengimana, Joseph Nzabirinda and Juvénal Rugambarara pleaded guilty and the rape charges were dropped during the negotiations for the guilty pleas: See, *The Prosecutor v. Paul Bisengimana*, ICTR-00-60-T, Judgement and Sentence, 13 April 2006, para 7; *The Prosecutor v. Joseph Nzabirinda*, ICTR-2001-77-T, Sentencing Judgement, 23 February 2007, paras 41 and 42; *The Prosecutor v. Juvénal Rugambarara*, ICTR-00-59-T, Sentencing Judgement, 16 November 2007, paras 2 and 3; Jérôme Bicamumpaka, Prosper Mugiraneza, Casimir Bizimungu, Justin Mugenzi, *The Prosecutor v. Bizimungu et al.*, ICTR-

Due to the seemingly low rate of conviction for crimes of sexual violence, particularly in light of the successful conviction rate for other crimes within the Tribunal's jurisdiction, the Prosecutor put in place a Committee for the Review of the Investigation and Prosecution of Sexual Violence in June 2007. The Committee's mandate was to look into all of the cases of the ICTR, as well as the experiences of the Office of the Prosecutor, to identify the successes and failures of the office, and the reasons attributable to these successes and failures. The Committee's work was divided into three phases: the first phase was a review of those completed cases where allegations of sexual violence had been included in the indictment to analyze what had been done correctly in those cases that resulted in convictions and to determine what had gone wrong in those that amounted to acquittals; the second phase included the same type of review with the cases that were ongoing at the Tribunal. Both phases included a thorough review of the paper record of the case as well as extensive interviews with the trial attorneys involved in each case to gain the insight and perspective of those working on the issues. The committee submitted two separate reports in relation to each phase to the Prosecutor. The committee then entered the third phase of its mandate, working on implementing strategies and procedures for the on-going and future prosecution of sexual violence crimes.

Upon completion of the first two phases of its work, the Committee submitted a Best Practices Manual on the Investigation and Prosecution of

---

99–50-T, 30 September 2011, all four accused in the *The Prosecutor v. Bizimungu et al.* case were acquitted of the charges of rape as a crime against humanity at the summary acquittal stage of the trial, as the Trial Chamber found that no evidence had been presented by the Prosecutor linking the accused to the rapes that had been committed. To establish the link, the Prosecutor had relied on the testimony given by the expert witness Binaifer Nowrojee. However, the Trial Chamber, in its "Decision on the Admissibility of the Expert Testimony of Dr. Binaifer Nowrojee" of 8 July 2005, declared inadmissible "those portions of Dr. Nowrojee's evidence that fall outside the scope of her expertise or express opinions on ultimate issues before the Chamber," which included her opinion regarding government authorities' knowledge of rapes throughout Rwanda in 1994. See "Decision on Defence Motions Pursuant to Rule 98 Bis," 22 November 2005, paras 85 to 96; Gratien Kabiligi, Aloys Ntabakuze, Anatole Nsengiyumva, *The Prosecutor v. Théoneste Bagosora et al.*, ICTR-98–41-T, Judgement and Sentence, 18 December 2008, paras 2124 and 2133 ("*Bagosora et al.* Trial Judgement"). Kabiligi was acquitted of all charges in his indictment. Tharcisse Renzaho, *Tharcisse Renzaho v. The Prosecutor,* ICTR-97–31-A, 1 April 2011. Renzaho's conviction at trial was overturned by the Appeals Chamber due to a failure in the manner in which the charges were pleaded in the indictment. See paragraphs 109 to 129 of the Appeal Judgement; Emmanuel Rukundo, *Emmanuel Rukundo v. The Prosecutor,* ICTR-2001–70-A, 20 October 2010. Rukundo's conviction at trial was overturned by the Appeals Chamber as a majority of the Chamber, Judge Pocar dissenting, found that the evidence failed to establish that he possessed the requisite genocidal intent when he committed the sexual assault. Jean Baptiste Gatete, *The Prosecutor v. Jean Baptiste Gatete,* ICTR-2000–61-T, Judgement and Sentence, 31 March 2011. While this case is currently under appeal, the Prosecutor has not appealed the acquittal; Francois Nuwonemeye and Innocent Sagahutu, *The Prosecutor v. Ndindiliyimana et al.*, Judgement and Sentence, 17 May 2011. The Prosecutor has not filed an appeal in relation to these acquittals.

Sexual Violence crimes to the Prosecutor, which was adopted. The OTP Best Practices Manual incorporates recommendations with respect to the lessons learned by the OTP in the investigation and prosecution of rape and sexual violence. It offers suggestions on how best to investigate and prosecute these crimes in an international setting. The Best Practices Manual has been distributed publicly at numerous conferences concerning global action against gender-based crimes in the hope that the ICTR's experiences can provide a lessons learned platform to assist future tribunals to achieve more successful prosecutions. I will now highlight briefly some of the more salient points arising from the Committee's work which have formed the basis for the Best Practices Manual.

3.1. INVESTIGATIONS

Crimes of a sexually violent nature have seemingly been overlooked in favour of prosecuting other crimes. This has been attributed to many factors, including to the perceived unwillingness of rape victims to talk to investigators, difficulties collecting evidence, as well as a general lack of understanding among prosecutors and investigators as to how sexual violence can be successfully investigated and prosecuted in the context of an armed conflict. However, if done in the context of the following specific considerations, investigating crimes of sexual violence need not be overly burdensome or difficult.

One of the main obstacles faced by the OTP at the beginning of its work was the fact that the ICTR, together with the ICTY, constituted the first institution to prosecute sexual violence as an international crime. There were no precedents or examples to follow with respect to investigation and prosecutions. In effect, the institution learned the hard way how best to proceed with these crimes and what methods and procedures would be inadequate and inappropriate in achieving successful prosecutions of these crimes.

3.1.1. The role of management

Underlying all considerations as to what helps or hinders these investigations is, of course, the political will to investigate and prosecute these crimes, without which, these crimes will not even form part of the prosecutorial mandate. Through its review of the OTP's history and the extensive interviews undertaken with members of the OTP, the Committee found that the political will to include these crimes within the OTP's mandate varied over the years. Senior Management should ensure that sexual violence crimes, including rape, sexual slavery and sexual mutilation are fully and fairly investigated and prosecuted, where appropriate, as crimes against humanity, genocide crimes, or war crimes. There must be a clear and comprehensive global strategy on how to proceed with charges of sexual violence crimes, and this strategy must be communicated to the entire office. In addition, the Best Practices manual recommends that Senior Management must determine a prosecution approach *at the outset* to ensure that sexual violence crimes are comprehensively integrated into the investigations and prosecution strategy for the overall office.

The Best Practices Manual also recommends that Senior Management must ensure gender parity in employment at the senior management levels, to ensure that women with experience in this area are working at senior levels of management. Gender parity also needs to be taken into consideration for all levels of employment. This is particularly so in light of the findings of the Committee, discussed in more detail below, that victims of sexual violence crimes will often only discuss these assaults with other women.

3.1.2. The methodology of investigations

Generally, investigations focused on areas where massive killings were committed, thereby focusing on such crimes as genocide, murder and extermination. From there, individuals were identified for prosecution of these crimes. It was from these already identified individual accused persons where the OTP then sought to establish whether those targeted persons had also been involved in rapes and sexual violence crimes. The target-based manner in which the OTP set of naming a target then finding an actual woman who had been raped by that target, was equivalent to looking for a needle in a haystack. The needle in some cases was eventually found, however, the main short-coming of this strategy was that the investigations failed to focus on the rapes that were committed by persons other than the targeted individuals, yet these rapes were numerous. The strategy seemed to perceive and portray sexual violence as crimes being committed by individual persons on a random basis, as opposed to it being viewed holistically, as part of the greater atrocity that was taking place – genocide.

One of the most important issues that arose from the Committee's review was that the ability to elicit the evidence and the quality of that evidence is dependent first and foremost on the manner of the conduct of the investigations and the interviewing of the witnesses. The Committee found that the Prosecutor may have had a low conviction rate, not because of the lack of evidence – since the rape witnesses and victims were there – but more because of the lack of understanding, know-how and training to elicit the necessary evidence that would support a conviction. In the early years of the Tribunal, the investigators received little or no training with respect to the methodology of investigating crimes of sexual violence in the context of the Rwandan genocide and crimes against humanity.

Special training was necessary in order for investigators to work within the unique circumstances present in Rwanda. Special considerations for the cultural aspects of the region and victims being handled is necessary if the investigators are to elicit accurate information from the victims and witnesses. Investigators need to understand how issues/topics of rape/body parts, especially genitalia and gender, are handled in order to be able to approach the victims well and to understand what any euphemisms used might mean. From a cultural standpoint, women who have suffered these crimes often talk around the event, such as using special phrases as "he made me sit down" or "he married me" to indicate they were raped. Investigators were often not aware that these women found it difficult to name the crime as such and so these clues to what was really being described were missed.

Also, in Rwandan society, sexual violence crimes carry strong stigmas and there is a powerful taboo against speaking about these crimes. As such, victims must be approached in a culturally-sensitive manner. Rwandan women, in general, felt a greater willingness to talk with other women than with men, however, the majority of the OTP's early investigators were male. Due to cultural factors, these women had great difficulty in relaying their experiences to men, so, often, they would not tell of their experiences at all when approached by a male investigator.

In addition, proper evidence that can withstand the rigours of the court room environment can only come from the necessary time and energy being spent with the witnesses. The Committee found that it often takes several interviews and meetings with a victim before she feels safe enough to open up about her experiences. For example, one Prosecuting counsel advised that she met with one witness four times before the witness trusted her enough to relate to her the anguishing story of her assault. Prosecutors and investigators, including interpreters, must be alive to this issue and approach these victims with the appropriate and necessary level of respect and care in order to be able to even elicit the evidence in the first place.

Furthermore, many investigators had not studied international humanitarian law, and had no prior experience in the investigation of sexual violence. Thereby, they were not familiar with the legal elements required for the proof of the crimes they were investigating. Investigations of rape and other forms of sexual assault should be conducted by teams that include trained prosecution counsel, that are skilled in interviewing women survivors. Investigators and prosecution counsel must work closely together to build a case based on a strategy that was designed through their joint input. Different prosecution strategies will require different evidentiary standards and investigative approaches. Prosecution counsel should provide direction to investigators on what sort of evidence needs to be collected: for example, should testimony be elicited from only rape victims or also rape perpetrators and other witnesses? Is the team looking for a qualitative approach or a quantitative one (for example, to establish that the rapes were widespread and systematic)? Are testimonies needed to fulfill the elements of a genocide crime or a sexual slavery crime against humanity?

Prosecution counsel and investigators should work closely together from the outset to analyze the strength of a case and of the evidence to ensure that victims are not unnecessarily dragged through the process and asked to recount very painful experiences unless there is a reasonable chance of obtaining a conviction for those crimes. This would require a thorough understanding of the law on sexual violence and the elements of the crimes that would need to be proved. For instance, for rape in international law, the prosecutors would not need to prove non-consent on the part of the victim, but could instead establish the existence of coercive circumstances surrounding the rapes under which meaningful consent is not possible.[23] A court is free to infer non-consent from the background circumstances, such as an on-going genocide campaign or the detention of the victim.[24] In this way the witness would not have to be questioned about any consent issues further traumatizing them.

Also, the early involvement of prosecution counsel would also enable them to gain the trust and confidence of the witnesses involved. This would not only provide comfort and support to the witness when it came time to provide the evidence in court, but it would strengthen the cogency of the evidence itself, as the witness's testimony would likely be more coherent and cohesive, having had the benefit of the constant involvement of the person who would eventually lead the evidence in court.

Given the unique circumstances surrounding the handling of victims of sexual violence, the Committee recommended the creation of a specialized unit to investigate and handle victims of rape and sexual violence. A specialized unit would help ensure that the necessary evidence is garnered while maintaining the appropriate care and safety of the victims. Successful prosecution and convictions are more likely to result from specially-trained investigators conducting their investigation under guidelines specially formulated particularly for the handling of rape and other forms of sexual violence. It should be noted that a Sexual Assaults Team did exist at the ICTR from about 1997, but was disbanded in 2000 by the then Prosecutor of the ICTR. In 2003, a new investigative sexual assaults team was formed with 3 female investigators. Given the Completion Strategy of the ICTR, the investigative stage of the Tribunal's work drew to an end all new investigations by 2005.

The specialized unit is envisaged as consisting of lawyers, investigators, doctors, nurses, counselors, interpreters and witness assistants, who would have undergone specialized training on how to handle the victims. It should be kept

---

23 *Prosecutor v. Sylvestre Gacumbitsi*, ICTR-2001-64-A, Appeal Judgement, 7 July 2006, para 155 ("*Gacumbitsi* Appeal Judgement").

24 *Ibid.* at para. 155.

in mind that, while many victims expressed a greater willingness and comfort level to engage with other women, men should be included in the unit and involved in the work to the extent possible in each circumstance. In creating a specialized unit, it would also have the added benefit of the witnesses having familiar and consistent faces that they are comfortable with and reduce the number of people the witness would have to encounter in the course of giving their evidence.[25]

3.2. PROSECUTION

3.2.1. Alternative strategies linking accused to crimes

Establishing criminal culpability for the accused at the ICTR for sexual violence crimes has proven to be a problematic task. The ICTR has pursued prosecutions against the "most responsible" for the genocide, which translates into the prosecution of military, governmental and civilian leaders and authority figures. These personalities often have been somewhat removed from the scene of the actual commission of the crimes, so, for the most part, were not committing the rapes themselves.[26] The obstacle has been to link the highest-level Accused to the sexual violence, where often no rape victim can directly tie them to the crimes, so that these persons do not go unpunished for their part in the widespread and systematic rapes. The strategy underlying investigations often failed to consider and account for establishing the necessary legal link between the rapes being committed on the ground and the ICTR's accused persons. While criminal procedure provides mechanisms for attaching criminal culpability to persons higher up in the command chain, these methods are weakened by evidential requirements that make successful prosecutions difficult. For example, the theory of command responsibility can be made use of to push responsibility for crimes committed by subordinates up to their superior commanders. Towards the proof of such superior responsibility, the indictments and the evidence that follows must make a case out for an accused who was in a position of authority where he exercised both effective control over subordinates and knew or should have known that his subordinates were involved in the commission of the crimes. This has proven to be a difficult hurdle. For example, in the *Muvunyi* case, the Trial Chamber accepted that sexual violence crimes took place as testified to by three rape victims, finding their evidence to be credible and reliable. However, the Trial Chamber did not accept that those

---

25 At the ICTR, the average witness encounters approximately thirty tribunal employees in the course of being a witness.

26 Of course, there are exceptions to this general rule. For example, Mikaeli Muhimana was convicted of personally raping seven women and directly encouraging and aiding and abetting the rapes of five other women.

committing the assaults were the legal subordinates of Muvunyi, thus acquitting him of those charges.[27] Again, in *Juvénal Kajelijeli*, the theory of command responsibility failed to attach liability to Kajelijeli, as the Trial Chamber failed to accept that Kajelijeli knew or had reason to know that *Interahamwe* under his control, who were found to have committed numerous rapes, had committed or were about to commit rapes.[28] Kajelijeli was convicted of genocide for the killings perpetrated by *Interahamwe,* with whom he was found to have been throughout the day while the *Interahamwe* killed Tutsi.[29] The Trial Chamber in this case accepted that rapes occurred at the same time as the killings, but did not accept the testimony of the two prosecution witnesses who directly implicated Kajelijeli in the rapes, even though the Trial Chamber accepted their evidence on the occurrence of the rapes themselves.[30] The Trial Chamber's attitude of treating rape as a separate crime was even reflected in the defence raised by Kajelijeli who called witnesses to say that while one of the victims was killed by the *Interahamwe*, she was not also raped.[31]

In its more recent prosecutions, the Office has been placing emphasis on putting the rapes *within* the context of the genocide so as to help Trial Chambers accept that the rapes were within the sphere of the genocidal campaign, not outside. In the *Bagosora et al.* case, the Trial Chamber stated that "[i]t is well known that rape and other forms of sexual violence were widespread in Rwanda during the events in 1994."[32] This is a breakthrough factual finding, which should facilitate the OTP in linking the accused to the crimes. It is hoped that this will help Trial Chambers draw the link between the orders and conduct of the accused and the commission of the rapes.

One legal theory that has been employed in an effort to attach responsibility to the leaders and authority figures for the widespread rapes is the joint criminal enterprise theory. In general, a joint criminal enterprise requires a plurality of co-perpetrators who act pursuant to a common purpose involving the commission of a crime.[33] Three categories of joint criminal enterprise have been identified in the jurisprudence of the *ad hoc* Tribunals, including the ICTR.[34] The *first category* is a "basic" form of JCE, represented by cases where all co-perpetrators, acting pursuant to a common purpose, possess the same

27 *Muvunyi* Trial Judgement at para 409. The Appeals Chamber dismissed the Prosecutor's appeal on this point. See *The Prosecutor v. Tharcisse Muvunyi*, ICTR-2000-55A-A, 29 August 2008, para 169.

28 *Kajelijeli* Trial Judgement at para 924.

29 *Ibid.* at paras 829–35.

30 *Ibid.* at paras 922, 680, 682, 683.

31 *Ibid.* at para 680.

32 *Bagosora et al.* Trial Judgement at para 1728.

33 *The Prosecutor v. Kvocka et al.*, IT-98-30/1-A, 28 February 2005, para 81.

34 *The Prosecutor v. Tadic et al.*, IT-94-1-A, 15 July 1999, paras 195–226; *The Prosecutor v. Elizaphan and Gérard Ntakirutimana*, ICTR-96-10-A & ICTR-96-17-A, 13 December 2004 ("*Ntakirutimana* Appeal Judgement"), para 463.

criminal intent.[35] The *second category* is a variant of the basic form, a "systematic" form of JCE, characterised by the existence of an organized system of ill-treatment.[36] The third category, an "extended" form of JCE, concerns cases involving a common purpose to commit a crime where one of the perpetrators commits an act which, while outside the common purpose, is nevertheless a natural and foreseeable consequence of executing that common purpose.[37] In the *Karemera et al.* case, the Prosecutor advanced the theory based on the third category of JCE that the two civilian authorities on trial are responsible for the rapes being committed throughout the country since the widespread nature of the rapes made them the natural and foreseeable consequence of the genocidal campaign.[38] The Prosecutor alleged that:

Although the Prosecutor will not offer evidence that Karemera, Ngiumpatse and Nzirorera personally committed rape themselves, the overwhelming objective evidence of pervasive, widespread and systematic rapes committed by militiamen, taken alone, will reveal an astounding tolerance, acquiescence, complicity and inferred intent on the part of the accused, and will form a basis for holding them individually criminally responsible for the natural, and foreseeable, crimes committed by their co-perpetrators in the joint criminal enterprise to destroy the Tutsi.[39]

This case is the only one thus far that has utilized the JCE concept to attach liability to authority figures for sexual violence crimes. As more fully described below, this theory was recently successful and the accused were found guilty on the basis that the rapes and sexual violence committed throughout Rwanda were a natural and foreseeable consequence of the genocidal campaign to destroy the Tutsi population. This case stands now as a strong precedent on how best to prosecute those leaders who sat apart from the actual brutal attacks but whose influence over them certainly ensured that they occurred. The rapes and sexual violence that occurred in Rwanda were found to be so widespread and systematic that these accused, while not on the ground committing the rapes themselves, undoubtedly knew about their occurrences and were liable for allowing them to continue. This theory should continue to be utilized to pierce the shield that these leaders and politicians attempt to use to distance themselves from the realities of the crimes committed on the ground. This is a powerful precedent to

35 *Ntakirutimana* Appeal Judgement at para 463.

36 *Ibid.* at para 464.

37 *Ibid.* at para 465.

38 The same theory had been advanced against Joseph Nzirorera but the proceedings against him have been stayed as he passed away during the defence phase of the trial.

39 *The Prosecutor v. Karemera et al.*, ICTR-98–44-T, Prosecutor's Pre-Trial Brief, 27 June 2005, para 76.

ensure liability for these crimes reaches those at the top of the hierarchy as those bearing the greatest responsibility for these crimes.

3.2.2. Other means of eliciting evidence

Many other challenges presented themselves in bringing the evidence of rape and sexual violence to Court, not least of which was providing an enabling courtroom environment to ensure witnesses felt safe and secure enough to give their evidence. The experience of testifying about sexual violence can be traumatic. Many witnesses became reluctant, and even unwilling, to provide their evidence when they realized that they would be sitting in an open courtroom, with judges and lawyers and the accused able to see them. Even when witnesses did give evidence, the courtroom environment seemed to intensify their anxieties and fears, which, in turn, would often affect the manner in which their testimony was delivered.

Despite these difficulties, in most cases, the witnesses who testified were for the most part found to be credible and their accounts believed. However, due to the extreme sensitivity of eliciting and obtaining this type of evidence, and the detrimental impact and re-traumatisation that providing such evidence often has on a victim, the OTP has developed alternative methods by which to bring evidence of sexual violence within the courtroom, in the context of the stringent evidentiary and procedural rules of the Tribunal, as set by the Rules of Procedure and Evidence. A variety of sources have been used at the ICTR, not just in-court testimony from rape victims.

The *Karemera et al.* case provides a significant example of alternative techniques that were successfully used to bring such evidence forward. First, the Prosecution had evidence admitted through the Judicial Notice provisions, that is, using facts as found in other cases, pursuant to Rule 94(B) of the Rules of Procedure and Evidence. The team in this case brought in evidence of rape through adjudicated facts from previous trials.[40] The Trial Chamber considered whether rapes had occurred in five specific prefectures and then the rest of

---

40 It is noteworthy that another crucial decision issued in the *Karemera et al.*, with respect to judicial notice, provides the requisite proof of the coercive background circumstances within which the sexual violence related crimes took place in Rwanda, in line with the *Gacumbitsi* Appeal Judgement, as discussed in more detail below. In *Karemera et al.*, the Appeals Chamber accepted as judicially noticed facts, under Rule 94(A), as facts of common knowledge: 1) Between 6 April 1994 and 17 July 1994, genocide against the Tutsi ethnic group occurred in Rwanda; 2) Between 6 April 1994 and 17 July 1994, there were widespread and systematic attacks throughout Rwanda against a civilian population based on Tutsi ethnic identification; and 3) Between 6 April 1994 and 17 July 1994, there was an armed conflict in Rwanda that was not of an international character. The judicially noticed facts can be used by the OTP to prove the background circumstances, which according to *Gacumbitsi*, would prove the existence of coercive circumstances. See *Prosecutor v. Karemera et al.*, ICTR-98-44-AR73(C), Decision on Prosecutor's Interlocutory Appeal of Decision on Judicial Notice, 16 June 2006, paras 22–28, and 57.

Rwanda.[41] In each of these categories, the Prosecution led evidence of two or three witnesses who gave *viva voce* evidence concerning the rapes, but then also led evidence of adjudicated facts from previous trials. The Trial Chamber accepted that evidence as proof of the occurrence of rapes in each location.

In addition to the alternative method of using adjudicated facts, the Prosecution also admitted evidence of rapes through the use of written statements of victims instead of calling their *viva voce* evidence. The written statements of 16 rape victims were admitted into evidence under Rule 92 of the Rules.[42] Interestingly, in relation to the Butare prefecture, no other evidence was called other than one statement from a victim was admitted as evidence on the rapes that occurred and the Trial Chamber accepted that statement on its own to find that "Tutsi women were raped on a large scale," and found that the statement of the victim had been corroborated by the pattern of evidence from other prefectures and the Defense had not sought to rebut her evidence.[43]

It is also worth noting that this Trial Chamber also accepted evidence on the occurrence of rapes from a broadcast that had been made on RTLM/Radio Rwanda on 21 June 1994 wherein the broadcaster stated that people were talking about rapes occurring in Rwanda and the Chamber relied on the findings in the report by René Degni-Ségui that women were raped and the rape was systematic and used as a weapon of war by perpetrators of the massacres.[44] The Court found that these two pieces of evidence corroborate the finding that Tutsi women and girls throughout Rwanda were subjected to widespread rapes and sexual assaults by the same persons that were attacking Tutsis as a group, namely *Interhamwe* and soldiers.[45]

Also, sexual violence evidence should be collected from a broad array of sources, not just from rape victims. Often observers or other eyewitnesses have powerful testimony that can be used in the courtroom. This was done in the *Bagosora et al.* Case, where the evidence of rapes and sexual violence crimes was elicited through witnesses who were not necessarily victims themselves. In that case, almost every witness was asked to relate what they saw with respect to the occurrence of sexual violence crimes. This strategy ultimately proved successful. The Trial Chamber in the *Bagosora et al.* Case found that sexual assaults occurred at civilian roadblocks in Kigali on the basis of the evidence of General Dallaire and Major Brent Beardsley who testified about what they saw at the roadblocks. No victim of sexual violence at these roadblocks was called in this trial. The defendant Bagosora was convicted on the basis of the evidence of

41 *Prosecutor v. Karemera et al.*, ICTR-98-44-T, Judgement and Sentence, 2 February 2012.

42 *Prosecutor v. Karemera et al.*, ICTR-98-44-T, "Decision on Reconsideration of Admission of Written Statements in Lieu of Oral Testimony and Admission of the Testimony of Prosecution Witness GAY", 28 September 2007.

43 *Karemera et al.* Trial Judgement at paras 1411 and 1412.

44 *Ibid.* at paras 1413 and 1414.

45 *Ibid.* at para 1424.

Dallaire and Beardsley for the sexual assaults carried out by his subordinates at these roadblocks.[46] Questions should therefore routinely be asked of all witnesses about their knowledge of sexual assaults. This strategy works particularly well in light of supporting a charge that the rapes were widespread or systematic.

Lastly, Prosecution counsel should, whenever possible, bring evidence from expert witnesses and medical professionals such as physicians, physicians' assistants, psychologists, psychiatrists, clinical social workers, psychiatric nurses, and other mental health professionals such as counselors, researchers, and college professors with expertise in the dynamics of sexual assault crimes and the impact of sexual assault victimization. Such testimony can be used in the following ways:

a) to assist the Chamber in better understanding and evaluating the evidence presented by factual witnesses to demonstrate that the victim's behaviour is consistent with that of someone who has been sexually assaulted and thus bolster witness testimony; and,
b) medical professionals such as physicians can be called to enhance evidence on the "mental harm" and "bodily harm" aspects of the crime of rape as genocide. Expert testimony can help to establish a proper record on the impact of sexual assault victimization and the long term physical and mental effects.

There are additional concerns that must be considered, particularly with respect to the care and well-being of victims and witnesses, but there is not enough room in this paper to go into all of the details. The OTP is in the process of finalizing a second Best Practices Manual that is being prepared specifically on the issue of the care and protection of victims and witnesses.

4. THE CONTRIBUTION TO THE LEGAL FRAMEWORK FOR THE PROSECUTION OF SEXUAL VIOLENCE – SUCCESSES ACHIEVED

The ICTR has made major and lasting contributions to the jurisprudence of gender related crimes. Despite the myriad difficulties associated with investigating and prosecuting sexual violence, the OTP has secured the conviction of several accused persons for rapes and other sexual violence offences.

The Statute of the ICTR lists the *ratione materiae* jurisdiction of the Tribunal as follows: crimes of genocide (Article 2), crimes against humanity (Article 3)

46 See *Bagosora et al.* Trial Judgement at paras 1908, 1920–24. The *Karemera et al.* case adopted a similar strategy eliciting such evidence through eye-witnesses other than victims.

and war crimes (Article 4: Violations of Article 3 Common to the Geneva Conventions and of Additional Protocol II). As such, these provisions define which sexual violence related charges are available to the OTP under international law.

In the ICTR Statute, rape is specifically defined as a *crime against humanity* (Article 3 (g)). In addition, instances of sexual violence have been charged as a crime against humanity under the provisions criminalizing torture, persecutions on political, racial and religious grounds, and other inhumane acts (Article 3 (f), (h), (i), respectively). Similarly, crimes of sexual violence have been prosecuted as a *war crime* (Article 4). In this respect, sexual violence may be charged under section (e) "outrages upon personal dignity, in particular humiliating and degrading treatment, rape, enforced prostitution and any form of indecent assault," and under (a) "violence to life, health and physical or mental well-being of persons, in particular... torture, mutilation or any form of corporal punishment." And last but not least, rape and other forms of sexual violence can constitute the crime of *genocide* under Article 2 of the ICTR Statute.

The OTP has succeeded in prosecuting and in holding accused criminally culpable for acts of rape, either as constituent acts of genocide (*Akayesu,*[47] *Gacumbitsi,*[48] *Muhimana,*[49] *Bagosora,*[50] *Karemera and Ngirumpatse*[51]), or crimes against humanity (*Akayesu,*[52] *Semanza,*[53] *Gacumbitsi,*[54] *Muhimana,*[55] *Bagosora,*[56] *Hategekimana,*[57] *Augustin Bizimungu,*[58] *Nyiramasuhuko,*[59] and *Ntahobali*[60] *and Karemera and Ngirumpatse*[61]), and as a war crime (*Augustin*

47 *Akayesu* Trial Judgement at paras 706 and 707.

48 *The Prosecutor v. Sylvestre Gacumbitsi,* ICTR-2001–64, Judgement, 17 June 2004, para. 292 ("*Gacumbitsi* Trial Judgement").

49 *Muhimana* Trial Judgement at paras 513 and 517.

50 *Bagosora et al.* Trial Judgement. This case is currently under appeal.

51 *The Prosecutor v. Edouard Karemera and Matthieu Ngirumpatse,* ICTR-98–44-T, Judgement and Sentence, 2 February 2012, para.1670 ("*Karemera et al.* Trial Judgement").

52 *Akayesu* Trial Judgement at paras 691 to 695.

53 *The Prosecutor v. Laurent Semanza,* ICTR-97–20-T, Judgement and Sentence, 15 May 2003 paras 476–79 and paras 481–84 where a conviction for torture was entered for the instigation of rapes ("*Semanza* Trial Judgement").

54 *Gacumbitsi* Trial Judgement at paras 321–32.

55 *Muhimana* Trial Judgement at para 562.

56 *Bagosora et al.* Trial Judgement at para 2203.

57 *The Prosecutor v. Idelphonse Hategekimana,* ICTR-00–55B-T, Judgement and Sentence, 6 December 2010, paras. 722–29.

58 *The Prosecutor v. Ndindiliyimana et al.,* ICTR-00–56-T, Judgement and Sentence, 17 May 2011, para 2127 ("*Ndindiliyimana et al.* Trial Judgement").

59 *The Prosecutor v. Nyiramasuhuko et al.,* ICTR-8–42-T, Judgement and Sentence, 24 June 2011, paras.6074–94 ("*Nyiramasuhuko et al.* Trial Judgement").

60 *Nyiramasuhuko et al.* Trial Judgement at paras 6074–94.

61 *Karemera et al.* Trial Judgement at paras 1682–84.

Bizimungu as rape,[62] *Bagosora*,[63] *Nyiramasuhuko*[64] *and Ntahobali*[65]) as outrages upon personal dignity, and *Semanza*, as violence to life, health and physical or mental well-being, the conviction being entered on appeal[66]).

Possibly the most significant application of international humanitarian law to crimes of sexual violence is the breakthrough interpretation provided by the first trial judgement issued by this Tribunal, the *Akayesu* Trial Judgement, namely that rape and sexual violence can constitute genocide, in much the same way as any other act. The only caveat, similar to other acts, is that such rapes and other sexual violence must be committed with the specific intent to destroy, in whole or in part, a particular group, targeted as such.[67] The Trial Chamber in the *Akayesu* case recognized that rape and other sexual violence can cause the infliction of serious bodily and mental harm to the victims, thus constituting genocide.[68] The significance of this groundbreaking judgement is that rape is not included as a prohibited act in the Genocide Convention of 1948 nor is gender included as a protected group. The Trial Chamber found that the rapes and other sexual violence were committed against *Tutsi* women, resulting in their physical and psychological destruction, their families and communities. It stated that sexual violence was an integral part of the process of destruction, specifically targeting Tutsi women and specifically contributing to their destruction and to the destruction of the *Tutsi* group as a whole.[69]

It should also be noted that, in the *Rukundo* case, the Trial Chamber for the first time, found that the sexual assault perpetrated by a clergy member on a young girl constituted genocide on the basis alone that she suffered mental harm from the attack – no finding was made that she also suffered any physical harm from the attack. In doing so, the Chamber held, "rape and sexual violence certainly constitute infliction of serious bodily and mental harm on the victims and are even… one of the worst ways of inflicting harm on the victim as he or she suffers both bodily and mental harm."[70] In considering what constituted mental harm, the Chamber stated that it did not have the benefit of any direct evidence on the victim's mental state, following the sexual assault, apart from her testimony that she could not tell anyone about the incident. The Chamber, however, recalled:

---

62 *Ndindiliyimana et al.* Trial Judgement at paras 2159–61.

63 *Bagosora et al.* Trial Judgement at para 2254.

64 *Nyiramasuhuko et al.* Trial Judgement at paras 6182, 6183.

65 *Nyiramasuhuko et al.* Trial Judgement at paras 6184, 6185.

66 *Laurent Semanza v. The Prosecutor,* Case No. ICTR-97-20-A, Appeal Judgement, 20 May 2005, paras. 370 and 371.

67 *Akayesu* Trial Judgement at para 731.

68 *Ibid.*

69 *Ibid.*

70 *Rukundo* Trial Judgement at para 386.

> that it may draw inferences from the evidence presented. The Chamber finds it necessary to look beyond the sexual act in question and finds it particularly important to consider the highly charged, oppressive and other circumstances surrounding the sexual assault on Witness CCH. The Chamber notes in particular the following circumstances:
>
> 1) Members of her ethnic group were victims of mass killings;
> 2) She and her family, fearing death in this way, sought refuge in a religious institution;
> 3) Upon seeing a familiar and trusted person of authority and of the church, *i.e.* the Accused, she requested protection for herself;
> 4) When the Accused refused her the protection she had requested, he specifically threatened her – that her family was to be killed for its association with the "*Inyenzi*";
> 5) Rukundo had a firearm;
> 6) Still hoping to be protected, Witness CCH sought to ingratiate herself to Rukundo by assisting him to carry his effects into a nearby room;
> 7) The Accused locked her in the room with him, put his firearm down nearby and proceeded to physically manhandle her in a sexual way; and
> 8) At the time of the incident, Witness CCH was sexually inexperienced.[71]

There was a dissenting opinion by Judge Park in regard to this finding. The opinion of the dissenting Judge was that the level of harm suffered by the victim did not rise to the level of seriousness required to constitute an act of genocide.[72]

This conviction was overturned by a Majority of the Appeals Chamber. The Appeals Chamber, however, did not comment on the findings made by the Trial Chamber regarding whether the acts constituted serious mental harm, but, rather, found that the evidence could not support the finding that Rukundo possessed the requisite genocidal intent when he committed the assault. The Appeals Chamber, Judge Pocar dissenting, found that Rukundo's sexual assault of Witness CCH was "unplanned and spontaneous" and "could reasonably be construed as an opportunistic crime that was not accompanied by the specific intent to commit genocide."[73] The majority opinion is heavily, and rightly, criticized by Judge Pocar in his dissent, where he states that their "attempt to differentiate Rukundo's sexual assault from other acts of genocide perpetrated by him is not reasonable."[74] Judge Pocar hit the proverbial nail on the head in noting that "the core of the Majority's reasoning on this point indicates that it does not fully appreciate the seriousness of his crime, which, in my view, is not 'qualitatively' different from other killings or serious bodily injury for which he

71 *Rukundo* Trial Judgement, para. 388.

72 See Dissenting Opinion of Judge Park, *Rukundo* Trial Judgement, 183.

73 *Rukundo v. The Prosecutor*, ICTR-2001-70-A, Judgement, 20 October 2010, para 236 ("*Rukundo* Appeal Judgement").

74 *Rukundo* Appeal Judgement, Partially Dissenting Opinion of Judge Pocar at para 4.

has been held responsible."[75] The Majority reasoning in this case poignantly illustrates the major obstacles still faced in prosecuting these crimes due to the manner in which these crimes can be easily mistakenly viewed as falling outside the sphere of the core crimes committed during these types of mass atrocities.

The *Akayesu* Trial Judgement was also a landmark decision in establishing the constituent elements of the crime of rape. The *Akayesu* case indeed moved away from a mere 'body parts' definition, and defined rape as a physical invasion of a sexual nature, committed on a person in circumstances that are coercive.[76] In the Trial Chamber's view, an act of thrusting a piece of wood into the sexual organs of a woman as she lay dying, therefore, constitutes rape.[77] Further, the Trial Chamber considered sexual violence, which includes rape, to be any act of a sexual nature which is committed on a person under circumstances which are coercive. Sexual violence is not limited to the physical invasion of the human body and may include acts which do not involve penetration or even physical contact.[78] According to the Trial Chamber, the incident in which a student was undressed and forced to do gymnastics in the public courtyard of the bureau communal, in front of a crowd, constituted sexual violence.[79] The Trial Chamber observed that coercive circumstances may be inherent in certain circumstances, such as armed conflict.[80] Following this interpretation, proving the non-consent of the victim was not a matter tasked to the Prosecution.

Nonetheless, some later ICTR Trial Chambers, such as in *Semanza*, *Kajelijeli*, *Kamuhanda* and *Gacumbitsi*, seemingly reverted to a more traditional understanding of rape with a mechanical approach as expressly rejected by *Akayesu*, and adopted a narrower consent-based definition endorsed by the ICTY Appeals Chamber in *Kunarac*.[81] This latter jurisprudence inserted the issue of non-consent as an element in the definition of the crime of rape.[82]

---

75 *Ibid.*

76 *Akayesu* Trial Judgement at para 688.

77 *Ibid.* at para. 686.

78 *Ibid.* at para. 688.

79 *Ibid.*

80 *Ibid.*

81 *The Prosecutor v. Dragoljub Kunarac et al.*, IT-96-23 & IT-96-23/1-T, Judgement, para 460; *The Prosecutor v. Dragoljub Kunarac et al.*, IT-96-23 & IT-96-23/1-A, Appeal Judgement, paras 129 and 130 ("*Kunarac* Appeal Judgement"). Several cases of the ICTR then followed the approach introduced at the ICTY: *Semanza* Trial Judgement, paras 344 to 346; *Kajelijeli* Trial Judgement, para 914; *Kamuhanda* Trial Judgement, para 708; and, *Gacumbitsi* Trial Judgement, paras 321–33, while others continued to follow *Akayesu*: *Alfred Musema v. The Prosecutor*, Case ICTR-96-13, Judgement and Sentence, 27 January 2000, para 226; and *Muhimana* Trial Judgement, para 551. In the ICTY, the first case to consider the *Akayesu* definition was *The Prosecutor v. Zejnil Delalic et al.*, IT-96-21-T, Judgement, 16 November 1998, which endorsed the *Akayesu* formulation of the definition. See: paras 478–79.

82 See *Kunarac* Appeal Judgement, paras 129 and 130. The Appeals Chamber endorsed the Trial Chamber's definition as follows: the *actus reus* of the crime of rape in international law is constituted by: the sexual penetration, however slight: (a) of the vagina or anus of the victim by the penis of the perpetrator or any other object used by the perpetrator; or (b) the mouth

Confronted with these different approaches to the requisite elements of the crime of rape, the OTP seized the opportunity in the case of *Gacumbitsi* to seek a clarification of the law relating to rape as an act of genocide, crime against humanity or a war crime.[83] The Prosecution argued that non-consent of the victim and the perpetrator's knowledge thereof should not be considered elements of the offence that must be proved by the Prosecution.[84] It added that the crime of rape only comes within the Tribunal's jurisdiction when it occurs in the context of genocide, armed conflict or a widespread or systematic attack against a civilian population – circumstances in which genuine consent is impossible.[85] The Prosecution submitted that rape should be viewed in the same way as other violations of international criminal law, such as torture and enslavement, for which the Prosecution is not required to establish absence of consent.[86]

The *Gacumbitsi* Appeals Chamber distinguished the following two questions: first, are non-consent and knowledge thereof elements of the crime of rape, and, second, if they are elements, how may they be proved. With respect to the first question, the Appeals Chamber adopted the *Kunarac* definition of rape, establishing non-consent and knowledge as elements of rape. As a result, the Prosecution does, in fact, bear the burden of proving non-consent and knowledge beyond reasonable doubt.[87] However, very importantly, with respect to the second question, the Appeals Chamber held that the Prosecution may prove non-consent by proving the existence of coercive circumstances under which meaningful consent is not possible.[88] It is not necessary for the Prosecution to either introduce evidence on the words and conduct of the victim or his/her relationship with the perpetrator, or introduce evidence on force.[89] The Trial Chamber is instead free to consider all relevant evidence, and infer non-consent from background circumstances such as an ongoing genocide campaign or the detention of the victim.[90] Similarly, knowledge of non-consent on the part of an accused may be proved if the Prosecution establishes beyond reasonable doubt that the accused is aware, or had reason to be aware, of the coercive circumstances that undermined the possibility of genuine consent.[91]

---

of the victim by the penis of the perpetrator; where such sexual penetration occurs without the consent of the victim. Consent for this purpose must be consent given voluntarily, as a result of the victim's free will, assessed in the context of the surrounding circumstances. The *mens rea* is the intention to effect this sexual penetration, and the knowledge that it occurs without the consent of the victim.

83 *Gacumbitsi* Appeal Judgement at para 147.

84 *Ibid.*

85 *Ibid.* at para 148.

86 *Ibid.* at para 149.

87 *Ibid.* at para 153.

88 *Ibid.* at para 155.

89 *Ibid.*

90 *Ibid.*

91 *Ibid.* at para 157.

Following this progressive approach to prosecuting rape, it is absolutely not required to question any victim of sexual assault or rape whether, or not, he/she consented to the sexual activity. Such questions would serve to re-traumatize the victim and would likely be quite offensive to a victim who underwent such brutal treatment in these coercive circumstances. According to this standard, the Prosecution need only establish the existence of coercive circumstances which vitiates the possibility of meaningful consent. Instead of discussing the personal circumstances of the victim, such as to ask whether or not the victim did consent, the line of questioning can focus on eliciting the existence of coercive circumstances to create the presumption that there was a lack of consent. The Appeals Chamber acknowledged that genocide, crimes against humanity and war crimes in general and conditions of detention constitute coercive circumstances.

Another noteworthy milestone in the prosecution of sexual violence at the ICTR recently occurred in the *Karemera et al.* trial judgement. In that case, both accused persons[92] were convicted for genocide and crimes against humanity for rapes and sexual violence on the basis that these violations were a natural and forseeable consequence of the joint criminal enterprise that the accused were members of whose purpose was the destruction of the Tutsi population.[93]

The Chamber found that the rapes and sexual violence that occurred were a natural and forseeable consequence of the campaign to destroy the Tutsi ethnic group. The Chamber found that during such a campaign, soldiers and militias who participate in the destruction "will resort to rapes and sexual assaults unless restricted by their superiors."[94] This statement is recognition of the rampant use of sexual violence in times of conflict.

The Chamber then went on to consider whether the two accused persons were aware of this risk and accepted the risk that rapes would occur as a consequence of the JCE whose purpose was to destroy the Tutsi population in Rwanda. The Chamber found that in light of the participation of both accused in the MRND political party and in light of Karemera's role as Minister of the Interior of the Interim Government from 25 May 1994, both accused were aware that widespread rapes and sexual assaults on Tutsi women were at least a possible consequence of the JCE and they willingly took the risk of further rapes and sexual assaults on Tutsi women and girls by continuing to participate in the JCE despite the widespread occurrence of rapes and sexual violence.[95] (Here, it is worth mentioning the Chamber found that most of the rapes and sexual assaults in three of the prefectures occurred in April 1994). As part of its reasoning, the Chamber found that while it did not find evidence of actual reporting of the

92 The third accused person, Joseph Nziorera, passed away prior to the completion of the case.

93 The accused were also found to be liable for these crimes as superiors for the rapes and sexual assault committed by the Kigali and Gisenyi Interahamwe during the genocide, which was taken into account during sentencing as aggravating factors.

94 *Karemera et al.* Trial Judgement at para 1476.

95 *Karemera et al.* Trial Judgement at para 1483.

rapes to these accused, it concluded the accused must have been aware of the occurrence of these offences given the circumstances present in the country, their access to information and their positions of authority. The Court also made note that in his testimony, Karemera actually acknowledged that he assumed that women would be raped during this conflict.[96]

In its legal findings, the Chamber found that the sexual assaults, mutilations and rapes that Tutsi women endured "certainly" constituted acts of serious bodily and mental harm.[97] In coming to this conclusion, the Chamber took note of the nature of the crimes and the brutal and often public manner in which they were carried out, often repeatedly and by more than one assailant. The Chamber found that the rapes and sexual violence were widespread and systematic and the women were subjected to severe humiliation and physical injuries, thereby not only causing harm to the women but also, by extension, to their families and communities. The Chamber concluded that the women were raped and sexually assaulted in order to increase their suffering before they were killed.[98] As such, the rapes and sexual assaults were found to be acts of genocide. These findings made by the Chamber are a huge step forward in the prosecution of sexual violence crimes as a clear acknowledgement that the rapes and sexual assaults were a part of the overall attack against the Tutsi and were used as a form of destruction in that genocidal campaign.

5. OVERALL REPRESENTATION OF SEXUAL VIOLENCE IN THE ICTR JURISPRUDENCE

As one commentator has recently observed, while the ICTR's record on convictions for sexual violence crimes can hardly be said to accurately reflect the pervasiveness of the crimes, a close review of the jurisprudence of the ICTR demonstrates that the cases actually do chronicle the widespread nature of these assaults.[99] To expand upon the theory put forth by Professor Buss, I point to several examples in the cases of the ICTR. First, the case of Juvénal Kajelijeli was discussed above where it was noted that the Trial Chamber failed to enter a conviction against Kajelijeli, finding the link between the perpetrators and Kajelijeli to be lacking such that the rapes could not be attributed to Kajelijeli. Nevertheless, the Trial Chamber accepted the evidence concerning the commission of five separate instances of rape and concluded that "between 7 April and 10 April 1994 some rapes were committed by members of the

---

96 *Ibid.* at para 1485.

97 *Karemera et al.* Trial Judgement at para 1666.

98 *Ibid.* at paras 1667 and 1668.

99 Doris Buss, "Learning our Lesson? The Rwanda Tribunal record on prosecuting rape," in *Rethinking Rape Law: International and Comparative Perspectives*, eds. Clare McGlynn and Vanessa Munro (London: Routledge Cavendish, 2010).

Interahamwe in Mukingo and Kinigi *Communes*, Ruhengeri *Préfecture*. Furthermore, given the circumstances under which these acts were committed, the Chamber finds that these rapes were committed in the course of a widespread attack upon the Tutsi civilian population."[100] The Chamber thereby established for the general record that rapes indeed did occur in that commune.

Similarly, in the early case of *Kayishema and Ruzindana*, where there were no charges of rape or sexual violence included in the indictment, the Trial Chamber nevertheless heard evidence that "On their way to the gathering places [in Kibuye] many witnesses saw roadblocks where the perpetrators separated Tutsis from the Hutus. Once the Tutsis reached these places they were injured, mutilated and some of the women were raped."[101] The Trial Chamber also found that "Men and women, old and young, were killed without mercy. Children were massacred before their parents' eyes, women raped in front of their families. No Tutsi was spared, neither the weak nor the pregnant"[102]

Again, in the *Ntakirutimana* case, where no charges of rape and sexual violence had been brought, the witnesses nevertheless referred to the fact that rapes had been occurring:

> Witness II sought refuge in Bisesero after 7 April through May 1994. He testified that on 20 May 1994 he saw Elizaphan Ntakirutimana among attackers at Dege, which is part of Muyira Hill in the area of Bisesero. He testified that he was hiding in a bush with three women when Interahamwe discovered them. The four captives were taken to the Gisovu-Gishyita road. There he saw Elizaphan Ntakirutimana standing very close to his vehicle, dressed in a black suit and wearing spectacles. The women were then taken approximately 15 meters away and raped, out of view of the witness, by the bourgmestre of Gisovu commune and by Alfred Musema. Two of the women were killed.[103]

Similarly, in the case of *Rutaganda*, no charges of sexual violence had been laid, but the Trial Chamber nonetheless included findings regarding the occurrence of rape within its factual conclusions. The Trial Chamber found:

> Many of the refugees who escaped or survived the attack at ETO headed in groups towards the Amahoro Stadium, where they thought they would be safe as it was under RPF control. These groups were stopped en route by soldiers, gathered together near the Sonatube factory and diverted, having been told that Colonel Rusatila had ordered them to Nyanza where their safety would be ensured. Some women were taken forcibly from the group and subsequently raped.

---

100 *Kajelijeli* Trial Judgement at para 922.
101 *The Prosecutor v. Clement Kayishema, Obed Ruzindana*, ICTR-95-1-T, 21 May 1999, para 294.
102 *Ibid.* at para 532.
103 *The Prosecutor v. Elizaphan and Gérard Ntakirutimana*, ICTR-96-10 & ICTR-96-17-T, Judgement and Sentence, 21 February 2003, para 645.

> The *Interahamwe* then began killing people with clubs and other weapons. Some girls were selected, put aside, and raped before they were killed. Clothing had been removed from many of the women who were killed.[104]

One final case worth mentioning is what is known as the *Media* case, involving three accused charged with their involvement in the perpetration of the genocide, including their use of the mass media to exhort violence against the Tutsi. The Trial Chamber noted that the evidence revealed that "throughout the killing, Tutsi women were often raped, tortured and mutilated before they were killed."[105] Significantly, it chronicled that:

> Tutsi women, in particular, were targeted for persecution. The portrayal of the Tutsi woman as a femme fatale, and the message that Tutsi women were seductive agents of the enemy was conveyed repeatedly by RTLM and Kangura. The Ten Commandments, broadcast on RTLM and published in Kangura, vilified and endangered Tutsi women, as evidenced by Witness AHI's testimony that a Tutsi woman was killed by CDR members who spared her husband's life and told him "Do not worry, we are going to find another wife, a Hutu for you." By defining the Tutsi woman as an enemy in this way, RTLM and Kangura articulated a framework that made the sexual attack of Tutsi women a foreseeable consequence of the role attributed to them.[106]

This is just a sample of the many references made in the jurisprudence of the ICTR to the nature and scope of the sexual violence that took place in Rwanda. Although the convictions entered at the ICTR may not, in themselves, accurately portray the extensiveness of the rapes, the entirety of the jurisprudence reveals that witness testimony throughout the cases does consistently and continually expose the insidious sexual assaults that occurred throughout the genocidal campaign.

6. LEGACY OF THE ICTR

Not only will the jurisprudence of the ICTR leave a historical record of the vast sexual violence that occurred in Rwanda, but the evidence collection of the OTP will serve to achieve the same end. In 2003, the OTP undertook to document the occurrence of crimes of sexual violence throughout Rwanda for use in its prosecutions. The OTP collected 405 statements from rape victims, eye-witnesses to rape and other corroborative witnesses. These testimonies – referred to as the

---

104 *The Prosecutor v. Georges Anderson Nderubumwe Rutaganda*, ICTR-96-3-T, Judgement and Sentence, 6 December 1999, paras 301–02.

105 *The Prosecutor v. Ferdinanda Nahimana, Jean-Bosco Barayagwiza, Hassan Ngeze,* ICTR-99-52-T, Judgement and Sentence, 3 December 2003, para 114.

106 *Ibid.* at para 1079.

OTP Rape Database – represent a sample of a larger number of rape statements collected by the OTP. The database also includes:

- U.N Reports, such as those of special rapporteurs (e.g. Degni Segui) describing the widespread and systematic phenomenon of rape during the 1994 events in Rwanda;
- Ms. Binaifer Noworjee's independent research and report on rape; and;
- Evidence on rape from completed trials, such as *Akayesu, Musema, Gacumbitsi, Muhimana, Semanza, and the Government I and Butare cases.* The evidence in those cases includes findings on the occurrence of rape, as well as on stereotyping of Tutsi women as part of the demonization of the Tutsi ethnic group.

Although the ICTR has completed its investigations, and is in the final stages of prosecutions, the information currently held in the database should be available for use in national prosecutions where access to the material is sought through the appropriate channels and granted by a Trial Chamber of the ICTR. On a broader level, the Tribunal is putting in place mechanisms for the archiving of its documentary collections to be maintained when the Tribunal eventually closes down. It must be noted that issues of witness protection are raised in the storing of this database and there is a need and requirement to protect these witnesses who gave evidence to the ICTR. The actual method of storage has not yet been determined and the eventual access to the material has not been confirmed. It may be that it will be sometime until these documents become open for public use. However, the collection will remain intact and will stand as testament to the sexual violence that pervaded Rwanda in 1994.

7. CONCLUSION

The ICTR has brought, and continues to strive to bring, perpetrators to account in order to bring justice to Rwandan victims of rape and sexual violence committed during the genocide, and to carve out a path for the future prosecution of such crimes for other armed conflicts. Through its pioneering work, the OTP has developed, despite the challenges it faced, experience in the investigation and prosecution of sexual violence. This experience, and the lessons learned, together with the successful contribution of the ICTR to the creation of a body of law relating to the prosecution of such crimes, can serve as a template for future prosecutions on a national and international level, especially in light of rapes and other sexual violence taking place daily around the globe in places such as the Democratic Republic of the Congo and in Darfur, just to name a few. Ending impunity for such crimes is an essential element in seeking sustainable peace, justice, truth and national reconciliation.[107]

---

107 Security Council resolution 1820, 19 June 2008, para 4.

CHAPTER 7

THE PLACE OF SEXUAL VIOLENCE IN THE STRATEGY OF THE ICC PROSECUTOR

Luis Moreno-Ocampo[1]

1. INTRODUCTION

I have the privilege and the responsibility to be the first prosecutor of the International Criminal Court (ICC). My mandate is to put an end to impunity for the most serious crimes of concern to the international community, including gender crimes as part of genocide, crimes against humanity and war crimes, and to contribute to the prevention of such crimes. The Rome Statute pays particular attention to gender crimes.

Accordingly, since my appointment over nine years ago, the Office has been developing policies on gender crimes.

In doing so, we have benefited extensively from the expertise of international and non-governmental organizations. A number of experts have paved the way, pushing for accountability of gender crimes; the *ad hoc* tribunals' jurisprudence has laid the groundwork for the development of international criminal law in this area.

2. HISTORICAL NOTION

The recognition of "gender violence" or "gender crimes" is relatively recent in international law. For example, the 1979 Convention on the Elimination of All Forms of Discrimination against Women did not address issues relating to violence against women. For a long time, the gender perspective was also not reflected in major international instruments related to international crimes such

1 This chapter is an adapted version of my keynote address given at the Interdisciplinary Colloquium *Sexual Violence as International Crime: Interdisciplinary Approaches to Evidence*, (The Hague, the Netherlands, 16 June 2009).

as the Convention against Torture and Inhuman, Cruel or Degrading Treatment or Punishment.

It was only in the early 1990s that there was greater understanding of gender crimes. In particular, the 1992 General Recommendation No. 19 by the Committee on the Elimination of Discrimination against Women constituted a major step. It defined gender-based violence as a form of discrimination against women. The General Recommendation took the view that "*the definition of discrimination includes gender-based violence, that is, violence that is directed against a woman because she is a woman or that affects women disproportionately.*"

In the field of international criminal justice, the evolution that took place in 60 years is remarkable. Remember that Robert Jackson, the Chief Prosecutor of the Nuremberg Tribunal, decided not to present sexual crimes in the cases against the Nazi leaders.

The efforts since the mid-90s to obtain accountability for atrocities committed against women during the conflict in the former Yugoslavia helped establish how rape and other sexual violence could be instrumentalised in a campaign of genocide. This equally contributed to the expanded understanding of sexual or gender violence as war crimes and crimes against humanity.

Perhaps the most groundbreaking decision advancing gender jurisprudence worldwide is the *Akayesu* judgment delivered by the Trial Chamber of the International Criminal Tribunal for Rwanda on 2 September 1998. For the first time in history, rape was explicitly recognized as an instrument of genocide. As described by the ICTR in the *Akayesu* case, rape is used to "*kill the will, the spirit, and life itself.*" The decision provided a definition of rape – "*a physical invasion of a sexual nature under circumstances which are coercive*" – placing gender crimes in a larger context.

Moreover, the Special Court for Sierra Leone has addressed the issue of forced marriage as a crime against humanity.

It was however only in the Rome Statute that a basis in gender first became an element of a crime in positive law, specifically of persecution as a crime against humanity.

3. GENDER CRIMES IN THE ROME SYSTEM

"Gender violence" or "gender crimes" is a concept that is firmly established in the Rome Statute. Under Article 7(1)(h), persecution against any identifiable group or collectivity on grounds of gender could constitute a crime against humanity if committed in connection with other types of crimes against humanity or other crimes under the jurisdiction of the Court. The term "gender" is defined for the purpose of the Statute as referring to "*the two sexes, male and female, within the context of society.*" Various provisions of the Statute also proscribe what can be characterised as gender crimes, such as rape, sexual slavery, enforced prostitution, and forced pregnancy as a war crime and/or crime against humanity.

Importantly for my Office, Article 54(1)(b) of the Statute specifically provides that in order to ensure the effective investigation and prosecution of the crimes under the jurisdiction of the Court, the Prosecutor shall "*take into account the nature of the crime, in particular where it involves sexual violence, gender violence or violence against children.*"

Sensitivity towards gender issues is even prescribed in relation to the protection of witnesses and victims. According to Article 68(1) of the Statute, "*the Court... shall have regard to all relevant factors, including gender and the nature of the crime, in particular, where the crime involves sexual or gender violence or violence against children.*"

Additionally, Article 42(9) of the Statute requires the Prosecutor to appoint advisers with legal expertise on specific sexual and gender violence. As such, we established the Gender and Children Unit (GCU), comprised of advisers with legal and psycho-social expertise to deal specifically with gender and children issues. The GCU advises the Prosecutor directly and provides support to the Office's divisions, from pre-analysis through to prosecution phases. We also appointed Professor Catharine MacKinnon as Special Gender Adviser in November 2008. Professor MacKinnon has been instrumental in establishing the concept of sexual crimes being gendered and has made a significant contribution to the recognition of gender crimes in international criminal jurisprudence.

My Office ensures that we effectively investigate and prosecute sexual and gender-based crimes by taking a focused and integrated approach. All of the investigators and lawyers receive specialized training on the legal framework and methods for conducting interviews on these types of crimes. An internal operational manual has been developed describing *inter alia* in detail how to approach an investigation on gender crimes and how to treat victims and witnesses associated with such cases. We work also a lot on statistical analysis which can be particularly problematic in cases of gender and sexual violence, since these crimes are often under-reported.

Under our statutory regime, we must present gender crimes in the larger context of an armed conflict, a widespread or systematic attack against a civilian population or genocide. As the Prosecutor of the ICC my challenge is to capture this "gendered" reality in our different cases and present them in connection with the contextual elements of the crimes as defined by the Rome Statute. Our current cases provide examples of how gender crimes are committed today in such contexts.

4. CASE EXAMPLES

In our first case, against Thomas Lubanga Dyilo, we presented the gender dimensions of the crime of enlisting and conscripting children under the age of 15 years. The evidence in this case showed how Mr. Lubanga instrumentalised sexual violations to subject child soldiers of both sexes to his will, and made them tools to further his own violent goals.

In the camps, girl soldiers, some aged 12 years old, were used as cooks and fighters, cleaners and spies, scouts and sexual slaves. One minute they would carry a gun, the next minute, they would serve meals to the commanders, the next minute, the commanders would rape them. They were killed if they refused.

You can still meet many of them in the Democratic Republic of The Congo (DRC), kept as "wives" by the commanders, or in the streets of Kinshasa and Bunia, rejected by their communities and struggling to make a living as prostitutes. These girl combatants are left on the margins of many Disarmament, Demobilization and Reintegration projects.

It is our responsibility to present the gender crimes suffered by the most vulnerable. During the course of the trial, Prosecution has made it its mission to ensure that Mr. Lubanga be held criminally responsible for the atrocities committed against little girl soldiers. In the ICC, girls will not be invisible. The Lubanga ruling could change the life of these girls; never again should they be left out of the assistance provided by demobilization programmes.

In our second DRC case, the ongoing trial against Germain Katanga and Mathieu Ngudjolo Chui, both men are charged with the gender crimes of sexual slavery and rape, as crimes against humanity and war crimes. They are held responsible for alleged crimes committed during the attack upon their order of the village of Bogoro, in the district of Ituri, in 2003. Hundreds of civilians were massacred during this attack, civilian's residences were looted and destroyed, and women and girls were raped.

The decision to open an investigation into the situation in the Central African Republic represented the first time for the international criminal justice system to deal with a situation where allegations of sexual crimes far outnumbered alleged killings. The evidence collected has shown that Jean-Pierre Bemba sent his soldiers to intervene in this country to maintain power in the hands of the then President Patassé, which resulted in widespread acts of rape and other acts of sexual violence. The charges confirmed against Mr. Bemba include counts of rape as crimes against humanity and war crimes. The trial started in November 2010 and is likely to have a huge impact, since the charges are confirmed in Mr. Bemba's capacity as commander, therewith giving a strong signal worldwide to commanders controlling their subordinates.

Our investigation into the situation in Uganda shows how the *Lord's Resistance Army* (LRA) systematically abducted girls for sexual enslavement and rape. We are seeking to prosecute Joseph Kony, who controls all aspects of this, together with other high commanders of the LRA, on several counts, including sexual enslavement and rape as crimes against humanity and rape as a war crime. The arrest warrants against them are still outstanding and need to be implemented.

In the application for an arrest warrant against Sudanese President Al Bashir, we submitted that the crimes of rape and sexual violence committed in Darfur are an "integral part" of his attempt to destroy the Fur, Massalit and Zaghawa groups, and should be charged as genocide under the Rome Statute. Rape of women and girls in and around IDP camps for food or firewood is systematic, and benefiting from total impunity.

Since 2003, thousands of women and girls belonging to the target groups have been raped in all three states of Darfur by members of the Militia/*Janjaweed* and Armed Forces, and this continues today. A third of the victims of rape are children. Rape is a silent weapon used to destroy the communities. The total denial by President Al Bashir of these crimes, stating that rape does not exist in Sudan and that it is not in the Sudanese culture, is another affront to the victimized women.

Following a first arrest warrant, on 4 March 2009, for five counts of crimes against humanity and two counts of war crimes, on 12 July 2009, Pre-Trial Chamber I issued a second warrant of arrest against Omar Al Bashir for three counts of genocide committed against the Fur, Masalit and Zaghawa ethnic groups: genocide by killing, genocide by causing serious bodily or mental harm and genocide by deliberately inflicting on each target group conditions of life calculated to bring about their physical destruction. In the decision the Pre-Trial Chamber considered that *"[t]housands of civilian women, belonging primarily to the Fur, Masalit and Zaghawa groups were subject, throughout the Darfur region, to acts of rape by GoS forces"* during the period covered by the arrest warrant application.

The evidence shows that in the campaign of massive rape is ongoing today. Since the date of the submission of the Prosecution's application, 14 July 2008, the situation has worsened. President Al Bashir ordered the expulsion of those who were helping the victims of rapes. In August 2010, it was reported that the Government of the Sudan expelled UNHCR aid officials for distributing "rape-detection devices" in Darfur. Instead of stopping the rapes, President Al Bashir stopped the information about the rapes.

5. CONCLUSION

Gender crimes are prominent in our prosecutions because they are prominent in the contexts being prosecuted. This only becomes remarkable against the backdrop of the prior and still prevalent norm of denying their existence, ignoring them, shaming their victims, and or defining them in legally improvable ways. In other settings, it has been as if there was a tacit agreement to look the other way as women and children were sexually abused – minimizing, trivializing, denigrating, and silencing the victims, destroying their credibility and further violating their dignity, so abusers can continue unimpeded. The body of the ICC's first cases, however, signals to the world that here, at least, this deal is off.

Addressing such crimes in this manner is ushering in a new era. At the Office of the Prosecutor, in the next years building on the last nine, our hope, our vision, and actually our plan is to pursue the gender crimes the Rome Statute defines and in the process to develop effective procedures and reality-based legal doctrines that respond to the practical imperatives for their effective prosecution. In order to stop these crimes we will give victims a voice – their own.

The mandate of the ICC is to go up the chain of command to those most responsible, to those who ordered and financed the violence; as for the mid-level perpetrators, for the executioners, we need to empower the local courts and authorities.

By setting an example, supporting institution-building, and through multi-levelled interface and cooperation, together we will transform the public response to *les crimes sexistes* in national jurisdictions worldwide, in and outside recognized zones of conflict.

CHAPTER 8

JURISPRUDENTIAL DEVELOPMENTS RELATING TO SEXUAL VIOLENCE: THE LEGACY OF THE SPECIAL COURT FOR SIERRA LEONE

Teresa DOHERTY[1]

1. INTRODUCTION

Sierra Leone is a small country in West-Africa bounded by the Atlantic Ocean, Liberia and Guinea. From approximately 1991 to 2002 the population was subjected to a brutal civil war the hallmarks of which included sexual violence, amputation of limbs and the abduction of children by the warring factions to be "child soldiers."

Following the declaration of peace in January 2002 the Government of Sierra Leone negotiated an agreement with the Security Council of the United Nations to set up a war crimes tribunal to try those responsible for the crimes committed in the course of the conflict. The Security Council had already, on 14 August 2000 passed Resolution 1315 (2000) expressing "deep concern at the very serious crimes committed within the territory of Sierra Leone against the people of Sierra Leone and United Nations and associated personnel and the prevailing situation of impunity."[2]

The resultant treaty setting up the tribunal that became known as the Special Court for Sierra Leone (SCSL or Special Court) was entered into between the United Nations and the government of Sierra Leone on 16 January 2002. It was the first of the treaty-based hybrid international war crime tribunals. Its mandate was more restricted than those of the International Criminal Tribunal for the former Yugoslavia (ICTY) or the International Criminal Tribunal for Rwanda

---

1 The views in this article are entirely those of the author and do not necessarily reflect the views of the Special Court for Sierra Leone.

2 Preamble to the Agreement Between the United Nations and the Government of Sierra Leone on the Establishment of a Special Court for Sierra Leone.

(ICTR) as its powers were limited to try those who bore "the greatest responsibility" for war crimes, crimes against humanity and breaches of international criminal law during the period 30 November 1996 to 18 January 2002 (i.e. less than the entire conflict period). Unlike the ad hoc tribunals it does not have Chapter 7[3] powers and included in its jurisdiction are crimes under domestic law that are: offences relating to the abuse of girls under the Prevention of Cruelty to Children Act, 1926, and offences relating to the wanton destruction of property under the Malicious Damage Act, 1861.[4] The agreement between the United Nations and the Government of Sierra Leone provided for the appointment of judges, the prosecutor and deputy prosecutor with the Government of Sierra Leone appointing one of the three judges in each of the Trial Chambers, two of the five judges in the Appeals Chamber and the deputy prosecutor. Other judges and the prosecutor were appointed by the United Nations.

The court sat in Freetown, Sierra Leone and was the first international war crimes tribunal to hold trials in the place where the alleged crimes were committed.

The Government of Sierra Leone also set up a Truth and Reconciliation Commission to consider and report on the causes leading to the civil war, the events which occurred during it and to make recommendations. The mandate of the Commission was, *inter alia*, to investigate the causes, nature, and extent of the breaches and violations of human rights during the Sierra Leone conflict with view to creating a historical record and to promote healing and reconciliation.[5] The Commission also sat in Freetown and its hearings were contemporaneous with the trials at SCSL.

2. LANDMARK DECISIONS AND CASES ON SEXUAL VIOLENCE

The Special Court for Sierra Leone is noted for several landmark decisions in international law, including the decision on the non-immunity of a Head of State for international crimes,[6] on the non-application of amnesties in peace treaties

3 United Nations Charter, Chapter VII, enabling the Ad Hoc Tribunals to direct governments to implement their orders.

4 Statute of the Special Court for Sierra Leone, Article 5(a) and (b).

5 The Truth and Reconciliation Commission Act 2000 Section 6(1) provides: "The object for which the Commission is established is to create an impartial historical record of violations and abuses of human rights and international humanitarian law related to the armed conflict in Sierra Leone, from the beginning of the Conflict in 1991 to the signing of the Lome Peace Agreement; to address impunity, to respond to the needs of the victims, to promote healing and reconciliation and to prevent a repetition of the violations and abuses suffered."

6 *Prosecutor v. Taylor*, SCSL-03-01-I-059, Decision on Immunity from Jurisdiction, 31 May 2004.

to crimes against humanity and war crimes,[7] and the prohibition on the recruitment and use of children in war (commonly referred to as "child soldiers").[8]

In the preliminary Report of the Secretary General of the United Nations to the Security Council on the Establishment of the Special Court on the 4th October 2000 (S/2000/915) – at Part 111 on the Competence of the Special Court and subject matter Jurisdiction – the Secretary General particularly noted that:

> the subject matter jurisdiction shall include *inter alia*... the most egregious practice of... sexual violence against girls and woman, and sexual slavery and abduction of thousands of children and adults.[9]

Article 15 of the Statute providing for the Responsibilities of the Prosecutor included a provision at Article 15(4) that:

> Given the nature of the crimes committed and the particular sensitivities of girls, young women and children victims of rape, sexual assault, abduction and slavery of all kinds, due consideration should be given in the appointment of staff to the employment of prosecutors and investigators experienced in gender-related crimes and juvenile justice.[10]

Article 15(4) appears to be a unique provision in the Statute of the Special Court and does not have an equivalent in the other ad hoc or hybrid tribunals. The Prosecutor made appointments of prosecutors and investigators with experience in gender related crimes and juvenile justice and throughout the trials a psychologist with experience with assisting victims of sexual violence was appointed and available to witnesses and victims.

In her article "Your Justice is too slow: Will the ICTR Fail Rwanda's Rape Victims", Binaifer Nowrojee noted this distinct prosecutorial intent and suggested that the SCSL illustrated what could be achieved by "a prosecutor with political will." Nowrojee stated:

> Despite significantly fewer resources and staff at his disposal, prosecutor David Crane,[11] made a concerted decision that justice would be delivered to Sierra Leonean victims of sexual violence. Under his watch a prosecution strategy that incorporated

7 *Prosecutor v. Kondewa*, SCSL-04-14-AR72(E), Decision on Preliminary Motion Based on Lack of Jurisdiction/Abuse of Process: Amnesty Provided by the Lomé Accord, 25 May 2004.

8 *Prosecutor v. Norman*, SCSL-04-14-AR72(E), Decision on Preliminary Motion Based on Lack of Jurisdiction (Child Recruitment), May 31, 2004.

9 *Preliminary Report of the Secretary General of the United Nations to the Security Council on the Establishment of the Special Court on the 4th October 2000* (S/2000/915), 4 October 2000, Part 111 on the Competence of the Special Court and subject matter Jurisdiction, para 12.

10 Statute providing for the Responsibilities of the Prosecutor, Article 15(4).

11 David Crane was the SCSL's first Chief Prosecutor.

> sexual violence crimes was devised at the outset *and followed through consistently.* With only 10 investigators in the team, two competent and experienced female investigators were immediately dedicated to sexual assault investigations (twenty percent of investigation team, as opposed to the ICTR, which has never dedicated more than one to two percent of its investigative team of approximately one-hundred persons to this issue).[12]

A total of thirteen indictments were preferred against thirteen men; twelve individuals associated, variously, with the Civil Defence Force (CDF),[13] Armed Forces Revolutionary Council (AFRC),[14] and Revolutionary United Front (RUF),[15] and one against Charles Taylor, then the Head of State of the neighbouring country of Liberia. Nine of the indictments were later consolidated into three cases; and the subsequent trials were commonly referred to as the CDF, the ARFC, and the RUF trials. Two of the remaining indictees, Bockarie and Sankoh, died before coming to trial and one, Johnny Paul Koroma, is still at large.

The initial indictment brought by the Prosecutor against the alleged members of the AFRC and RUF cases included allegations of sexual violence. For the first time the offence of sexual slavery, provided for in Article 2(g) of the Statute, was included in the indictments as a crime against humanity.

In February 2004, the Prosecutor applied to the court (Trial Chamber I) for leave to amend two of the three consolidated indictments – viz. those preferred against the AFRC and RUF indictees – to, *inter alia*, "add one or more new courts of forced marriage" a crime against humanity.[16] The indictments preferred in the AFRC and RUF indictments already included the crimes of rape, sexual slavery and outrages against personal dignity. In support of his application to amend the AFRC and RUF indictments the Prosecutor submitted that the additional charge of forced marriage was based on "the exact same factual context" that was pleaded in the earlier indictments and the defence would not need to make further investigations.[17] The Defence objected arguing that forced marriage was not a crime against humanity and therefore such a charge violated the principles of legality.[18]

---

12 Binaifer Nowrojee, "Your Justice is Too Slow: Will the ICTR Fail Rwanda's Rape Victims," *United Nations Research Institute for Social Development, Occasional Paper* 10 (November 2005): 11–12.

13 Sam Hinga Norman, Monina Fofana, and Allieu Kondewa.

14 Johnny Paul Koroma, Alex Tamba Brima, Brima Bazzy Kamara and Santigie Borbor Kanu.

15 Foday Saybana Sankoh, Sam Bockarie, Issa Hassan Sesay, Morris Kallon and Augustine Gbao.

16 *Prosecutor v. Brima, Kamara and Kanu*, SCSL-2004–16-PT, Prosecution Request for Leave to Amend the Indictment, 9 February 2004.

17 *Ibid.*

18 *Prosecutor v. Brima et al.*, SCSL-04–16-PT, Response to the Prosecution Request for Leave to Amend the Indictment, 19 February 2004.

On 6 May 2004 after a lengthy review of the principles, in particular "the crucial consideration" of "timing and whether the application for the amendment is brought at the stage in the proceedings where it would not prejudice the rights of the accused," the Trial Chamber by a majority allowed the Prosecution to amend its indictments in the two cases – AFRC and RUF – to include charges of forced marriage as a crime against humanity.[19] In *Prosecutor v. Brima et al.* (AFRC) the Trial Chamber also held that forced marriage was a "kindred offence" to those that existed in the consolidated indictment[20] and referred to "the necessity for international criminal justice to highlight the high profile nature of the emerging domain of gender offences with a view to bringing the alleged perpetrators to justice."[21]

The Prosecutor had not preferred any charges involving sexual or gender-based violence against the alleged members of the CDF. In his application to amend the indictment to include counts alleging sexual violence filed on 9 February 2004 in that case, the Prosecutor stated that his initial investigations did not provide sufficient evidence to proffer counts based on gender-based violence.[22]

In its decision on this application of 20 May 2004, the majority of the Trial Chamber considered the impact of adding four counts that were "completely new" on the rights of the accused to be tried without undue delay.[23] The majority noted that it was pre-eminently conscious of the importance gender crimes occupy in international justice given the very high casualty rates of females in sexual and other brutal gender related abuses in conflicts,[24] but held that allowing the amendment would breach the Accuseds' fair trial rights.[25] Therefore, the application of the Prosecutor to amend the indictment to include sexual violence charges was dismissed by the Chamber.

In his dissenting opinion on the Prosecutor's application for leave to appeal that followed that decision, Justice Boutet stressed the right of victims of sexual violence to be heard. He stated:

---

19 *Prosecutor v. Brima et al.*, SCSL-04-16-PT, Decision on the Prosecution Request for Leave to Amend the Indictment, 6 May 2004, paras 6, 88, 12.

20 *Ibid.* at paras 46 and 52.

21 *Prosecutor v. Brima et al.*, SCSL-04-16-PT, Decision on Prosecution Request for Leave to Amend the Indictment, 6 May 2004, para 34.

22 *Prosecutor v. Norman, et al.*, SCSL-2004-14 –PT, Prosecution Request for Leave to Amend the Indictments Against Samuel Hinga Norman, Moinina Fofana and Allieu Kondewa, para 5 and Consolidated Reply to Defence Response to Prosecution Request for Leave to Amend the Indictments Against Samuel Hinga Norman, Moinina Fofana and Allieu Kondewa, 9 February 2004, paras 7, 15.

23 *Prosecutor v. Norman et al.*, SCSL 2004-14-PT, Decision on Prosecution Request for Leave to Amend the Indictment, 20 May 2004, para 62.

24 *Prosecutor v. Norman et al.*, SCSL 2004-14-PT, Decision on Prosecution Request for Leave to Amend the Indictment, 20 May 2004, para 82.

25 *Ibid.* at para 82.

The request by the Prosecution to amend the Indictment concerned essentially serious charges of sexual violence against the Accused persons, in addition to alleged direct participation of the Accused in such crimes. It is my opinion that a failure to grant leave to appeal on such a fundamental issue could prejudice this Court's capacity to fulfill its mandate outlined in Article 1(1) of the Statute, namely, "to prosecute persons who bear the greatest responsibility for serious violations of international humanitarian law," a mandate founded on recognition by the United Nations Secretary General that sexual violence committed against girls and women was one of the most egregious practices committed during the armed conflict in Sierra Leone.[26] Victims of sexual violence have the right to have crimes that are committed against them prosecuted with all due respect to the Rule of Law. I consider these factors to constitute, in themselves, exceptional circumstances within the meaning of Rule 73(B) of the Rules in that not to do so in these circumstances would not be in the interest of justice.[27]

In an earlier opinion[28] Justice Boutet had emphasized the research and increasing awareness that:

When dealing with gender-based crimes a special consideration should be brought to bear in the appreciation of the circumstances. It is now quite widely recognized and accepted that victims of sexual violence will often demonstrate reluctance to come forward and report such actions. Studies, surveys, reports about the effects of gender-based violence on victims demonstrate the difficulty of investigating and gaining evidence about such crimes and the reluctance of victims to discuss these matters.

He then referred to a report of the International Committee of the Red Cross by Charlotte Lindsay:

Woman may be unable or afraid to report such violations because national institutions have broken down or because doing so may endanger women further. In many cultures, the "shame" associated with rape is in a social sense perceived as even worse than the physical act itself.

Survivors of rape or sexual violence may face further problems such as ostracism or retribution (in addition, the perpetrators may have told them that if they report the violation they, or their families, will be subjected to further violence).

---

26 Referring to the *Report of the Secretary-General on the Establishment of a Special Court for Sierra Leone*, UN Document S/2000/915, 4 October 2000, para 12.

27 Dissenting Opinion of Justice Pierre Boutet on Decision on Prosecution Application for Leave to file an Interlocutory Appeal against the Decision on the Prosecution's Request for Leave to Amend the Indictment against Norman, Fofana and Kondewa, 5 August 2004, para 18.

28 *Prosecutor v. Norman et al.*, SCSL-04-14, Dissenting opinion of Judge Pierre Boutet on the Decision on Prosecution's Request for Leave to amend the Indictment, 31 May 2004.

> Women who have been subjected to violence, including sexual violence, need to assess for themselves what constitutes justice, and may not necessarily want to give evidence in criminal proceedings because they do not wish their family to know what happened to them, or because of fears for their own safety and that of their family, and/or because of desire not to live through the ordeal again by retelling it.[29]

And Justice Boutet referred to the preliminary report of the Special Rapporteur on the situation of systematic rape, sexual slavery and slavery-like practices during periods of armed conflicts, where these comments can be found:

> It is clear from the material gathered in this preliminary report that there exists a very substantial body of international law relating to systematic rape, sexual slavery and slavery-like practices during wartime, including internal armed conflict... there is preliminary information about the widespread occurrence of systematic rape, sexual slavery and slavery-like practices during periods of armed conflict...
>
> Reasons for reluctance to report wartime rape may include shame and social stigma, fear of awakening bad memories, fear of reprisals, a lack of trust in the judicial system and the national legislature, and the belief in the absence of remedies.[30]

Clearly there was an awareness in the Special Court for Sierra Leone of both the rights of victims of sexual violence to be heard in the international tribunals and that sexual violence produces fear and "shame" in a social sense which engenders a reluctance in victims to come forward to investigators.

As a result of these decisions one of the three consolidated trials, the CDF trial, proceeded to hearing without any counts relating to sexual violence, and the joint trials of the AFRC and RUF proceeded to hearing with an additional count of forced marriage, a crime against humanity.

In the course of hearing in the CDF trial a further issue relating to evidence of sexual violence arose. The Prosecutor sought to call female witnesses who were prepared to testify about violence but when they started speaking about violence of a sexual nature the Defence objected. According to Staggs Kelsall and Stepakoff: "[a]lthough the judges dismissed the Defence's objection, Judge Thompson noted that allowing any evidence of sexual violence would undermine

---

29 Charlotte Lindsey, *Women Facing* War (Geneva, Switzerland: International Committee of the Red Cross, October 2001).

30 Referring to Linda Chaves, *Preliminary Report of the Special Rapporteur on the Situation of Systematic Rape, Sexual Slavery and Slavery-like practices during periods of Armed Conflict*, UN DOC E/CN.4/Supr. 2/1996/26, 16 July 1996, paras 86–87. Judge Boutet also cited the reports on rape and abuse of women in the areas of armed conflict in the former Yugoslavia, "Women, Peace and Security: Study submitted by the Secretary-General pursuant to Security Council Resolution 1325 (2000)" and "Rape and Sexual Abuse of Women in International Law," *European Journal of International Law* 5 (1994).

the integrity of the proceedings. The prosecution was further cautioned against leading evidence that could be construed as such."[31]

The Prosecutor sought clarification of what evidence of sexual violence could be led.[32] The majority of Trial Chamber I later ruled that all evidence of sexual violence was inadmissible.[33] Justice Boutet dissented and, *inter alia*, restated an earlier opinion:

> as I previously stated in a related but different Dissenting Opinion related to such crimes: Victims of sexual violence have the right to have crimes that are committed against them prosecuted with all due respect to the Rule of Law." And "[t]hat, in itself, would constitute exceptional circumstances within the meaning of Rule 73(B) of the Rules. Failure to do so in these circumstances would not be in the interests of justice.[34]

Of seven women who came forward to give evidence of acts of sexual violence none were permitted to adduce evidence of sexual violence. In the end, four of them to gave evidence of being beaten or detained but not of rape, and three did not testify at all. There is no record in the proceedings of the reasons why these three witnesses were not called.

The decision has been criticized. Staggs and Stepakoff interviewed the witnesses whose evidence had been partly or wholly excluded and concluded:

> ... it is clear that the majority judges' determinations and the silencing that followed resulted in significant psychological distress for the witnesses. This finding is consistent with observations made by the Witness and Victim Section's supervising psychologist as well as the psychosocial counselors who worked closely with the women during their two-week stay in Freetown.[35]

The writers emphasized that Article 2(g) of the statute extended the mandate of the Special Court in the area of prosecution of crimes of sexual violence beyond that of the ICTY and ICTR and cited a Human Rights Watch report:

---

31 Michelle Staggs Kelsall and Shanee Stepakoff, "When we wanted to Talk about Rape: Silencing Sexual Violence at the Special Court for Sierra Leone," *The International Journal of Transitional Justice* 1 (2007): 363.

32 Urgent Prosecution Motion for a Ruling on Admissibility of Evidence, 15 February 2005.

33 Decision on the Prosecutions' Motion for a Ruling on the Admissibility of Evidence, 24 May 2005 (issued on 23 June 2005).

34 Dissenting Opinion of Justice Pierre Boutet on the Majority Decision on Request for Leave to Appeal Decision on Prosecution Motion for a Ruling on Admissibility of Evidence, SCSL-04-14-T, 9 December 2005, para 10.

35 Michelle Staggs Kelsall and Shanee Stepakoff, "When we wanted to Talk about Rape: Silencing Sexual Violence at the Special Court for Sierra Leone," *The International Journal of Transitional Justice* 1 (2007): 373.

> The Special Court appears to be taking its mandate on sexual violence seriously... Investigating and prosecuting crimes of sexual violence have been an integral part of the investigative and prosecutorial strategy... The Court has on staff two full-time gender crimes investigators and has conducted gender sensitivity training for all members of its investigations team.[36]

They concluded, in relation to the CDF case:

> The resulting judgment is yet another addition to the international criminal legal precedents which completely fail to consider violence against women in any real depth and sexual violence at all. It also marks an opportunity missed by the Special Court to lead by example on an important issue that deserves further consideration in Sierra Leone's domestic legal sector.[37]

Despite the criticism of the CDF decisions, Justice Boutet's dissents show that members of the court were aware of the rights of victims of sexual violence to be heard and the Conventions, reports and surveys dealing with crimes of sexual violence in conflict.

The RUF and AFRC trials proceeded to trial charging all the six defendants with rape, sexual slavery, outrages on personal dignity and, forced marriage. Trial Chamber II, appointed in 2005, heard the AFRC trial and was the first to render a judgment and the SCSL was the first international court to give decisions on the offences of forced marriage and sexual slavery.

2.1. SEXUAL SLAVERY

Article 2(g) of the SCSL Statute empowers the Special Court to prosecute persons who committed the crime of sexual slavery as part of a widespread or systematic attack against any civilian population. The Prosecutor charged the defendants in the *Prosecutor v. Brima et al.* (the AFRC case) with "sexual slavery and any other form of sexual violence" at count 7.

The crime of sexual slavery was referred to in the ICTY in the *Kunarac* case. Trial Chamber II of the SCSL adopted the definition of sexual slavery in the Statute of the International Criminal Court, Art 7 (1)g-2, defining the elements of the crime of sexual slavery as:

---

36 *In War as in Peace: Sexual Violence and Women's Status* (New York: Human Rights Watch, World Report 2004), 325.

37 Michelle Staggs Kelsall and Shanee Stepakoff, "When we wanted to Talk about Rape: Silencing Sexual Violence at the Special Court for Sierra Leone," *The International Journal of Transitional Justice* 1 (2007): 372.

1. The perpetrator exercised any or all of the powers attaching to the right ownership over one or more persons, such as by purchasing, selling, lending or bartering such a person or persons, or by imposing on them a similar deprivation of liberty.
2. The perpetrator caused such person or persons to engage in one or more acts of a sexual nature.
3. The perpetrator committed such conduct intending to engage in the act of sexual slavery or in the reasonable knowledge that it was likely to occur.

When adopting this definition Trial Chamber II held:

> The powers of ownership listed in the first element of sexual slavery are non-exhaustive. There is no requirement for any payment or exchange in order to establish the exercise of ownership. Deprivation of liberty may include extracting forced labour or otherwise reducing a person to servile status. Further, ownership, as indicated by possession, does not require confinement to a particular place but may include situations in which those who are captured remain in the control of their captors because they have no where else to go and fear for their lives. The consent or free will of the victim is absent under conditions of enslavement.[38]

The evidence showed that in the course of the civil war the two rebel groups, the RUF and the AFRC, regularly abducted civilians and used them for forced labour such as mining, domestic work and carrying of loads, and abducted women, in particular, for sexual purposes. The women and girls, forcefully abducted from their homes and communities by rebels, were taken to the rebel bases and forcefully marched from one base to another as the rebels moved through Sierra Leone. Some of the women and girls were sent for training in military tactics and fighting and sent to the front lines, others were forced into marriage and may not have been obliged to fight. Those women and girls who were not "wives" were available to all and any fighter as sexual objects. They were frequently raped and frequently gang-raped, they had no right to resist and could not escape.

The abducted women and girls were obliged to perform domestic duties including cooking, laundering, and food finding. Food finding involved looting food from villages and farms as well as looking for food in the bush. Resistance or attempts to escape were met with severe punishment and, often in cases of attempted escape, with death.

Evidence was adduced of women being punished by being beaten, by being locked in a rice box, a wooden box used for storing food, and/or being lashed. The descriptions of the forced marches when women were pregnant, sick, and in

38 *Prosecutor v. Brima et al.*, SCSL-04-16T, Decision on Defence Motions for Judgement of Acquittal Pursunat to Rule 98, 31 March 2006, para 709.

one case giving birth to triplets, showed very severe maltreatment as part of the slavery and sexual slavery of these women.

The Defence in the AFRC case argued that the pleading of "sexual slavery and any other form of sexual violence" was duplicitous as it did not distinguish between sexual slavery and other forms of sexual violence. The Trial Chamber by a majority agreed, that Count 7 was "bad for duplicity and is accordingly dismissed in its entirety."[39] The majority of the Trial Chamber considered the evidence of sexual slavery under count 8, other inhumane acts, and the new count alleging forced marriage, and held that another inhumane act must involve conduct not otherwise subsumed by the crimes enumerated under Article 2 of the Statute.[40]

In a dissenting minority opinion, Justice Doherty considered that the Defence was estopped from raising duplicity as an issue and that the count should have been severed. This view was upheld by the Appeals Chamber which, whilst holding that the rule against duplicity applies to international criminal tribunals and that Count 7 violated the rule against duplicity,[41] held that the Trial Chamber should have proceeded with the count as "sexual slavery"[42] as the offence of sexual slavery had been properly charged and should have struck out the charge of "any other form of sexual violence."[43]

2.2. FORCED MARRIAGE

Prior to the AFRC and RUF cases before the SCSL, forced marriage, as a crime against humanity, had not been considered by any other international tribunal.

The evidence presented in *Prosecutor v. Brima et al.* showed that when women and girls, who were forcefully abducted from their homes, were taken to the rebel camps, fighters could select those women and girls they wanted as "wives." Commanders got the first choice. Very young girls were sometimes allocated to young Small Boy Unit (SBU) fighters. A bureaucratic system of registering the names and allocation of these women was instituted in some camps and fighters were obliged to sign for the women or girls allocated to them as "wives." The captors sometimes kept those women or girls they captured for themselves. The girl or woman was told she was the "wife" of the captor or fighter. She was given no choice in the matter.

39 *Prosecutor v. Brima et al.*, SCSL-04-16T, 20 June 2007, paras 92–95.

40 *Ibid.* at para 703. This decision has been criticised by, e.g., Patricia Sellers, "Wartime Female Slavery: Enslavement?" *Cornell International Law Journal* 44 (2011): 129–143; and the Keynote address at the conference "Gender and Justice" co-sponsored by the American University, Washington College of Law and the American Jewish Congress, 14–16 June 2009.

41 *Prosecutor v. Brima et al.*, SCSL-2004-16-A, Judgement on Appeal, 22 February 2008, para 103.

42 *Ibid.* at para 109.

43 *Prosecutor v. Brima et al.*, SCSL-2004-16-A, Judgement on Appeal, 22 February 2008.

Both the Prosecution and Defence adduced expert evidence. The expert evidence by both parties showed that customary arranged marriage was and still is, a common phenomena in the rural areas throughout West Africa, less so in the urban areas. Girls were and are frequently married or had marriages arranged when they were quite young and were given little say about who they would marry. Whilst the Muslim religion (the majority religious group in Sierra Leone) did not allow for women being married without their consent, it was apparent from the expert evidence that many girls were, and still are, obliged for the good of the clan or the community to conform with the choice made by their elders. There was consent, albeit a reluctant consent or one that was made for the good of the community, rather than the wish of the individual. The vital element is the consent of the families of the prospective spouses.

In separate opinions Justices Doherty and Sebutinde noted the experts' distinction between these traditional customary marriages and the forced marriages described in evidence in the trial. Justice Sebutinde noted both experts drew a distinction between the traditional or customary practice of early or arranged marriages where young girls or minors are forced by their parents or family into early marriages in times of peace and the phenomenon of forced "marriage" during the Sierra Leone conflict.[44] Justice Doherty noted that, according to the experts, girls and young women are commonly coerced into arranged marriages by the bride and groom's kin and "seniors" but the practice is not universal and many men and women marry a person of their own choice. The experts stressed that arranged marriages entailed the involvement and agreement of the families and seniors of the prospective bride and groom.[45]

The majority of the Trial Chamber in the AFRC trial, having heard the evidence, decided that they were not satisfied that the Prosecution was capable of establishing the elements of a non-sexual crime of forced marriage independent of the crime of sexual slavery under Article 2(g) of the Statute[46] but rather that forced marriage was subsumed into the crime of sexual slavery, the separate crime provided for in Article 2(g) of the Statute of the Special Court as a crime against humanity. For this reason the Trial Chamber decided, by majority, that Count 8, other inhumane acts, was redundant.

Justice Doherty dissented from the majority view and issued a minority opinion noting that the evidence showed that women and girls who were made into "wives" had a conjugal status forced upon them. They were immediately stigmatized as "bush wives" or "rebel wives" and they were considered "tainted" by "rebel blood" and refused re-entry into their village communities or their family homes. Their children were stigmatized and, as one expert described it,

44 *Prosecutor v. Brima et al.*, SCSL-04-16-T, 20 June 2007, Separate Concurring Opinion, para 11.

45 *Prosecutor v. Brima et al.*, SCSL-04-16-T, 20 June 2007, Separate Dissenting Opinion, para 25–27.

46 *Prosecutor v. Brima et al.*, SCSL-04-16-T, 20 June 2007, paras 704–714.

were running naked without an education or future. The women were obliged to care for and carry the "husband's" possessions, clean, cook and be loyal and provide sex when and as the "husband" wanted. They had children and often suffered miscarriages; diseases and HIV/Aids were common. Any transgressions were severely punished and a "husband" who was tired of his "wife" could replace her and might send her to the front line as a fighter. However, being a "wife" of a fighter brought with it certain protections. The "wife" was protected from rape by other men, given food when food was available, and depending on the status of the "husband," had a corresponding status, to the extent that evidence showed that some "wives" of commanders were responsible for the distribution of looted goods.

The label "wife" of a rebel caused mental trauma, stigmatized the victims and negatively impacted on their ability to re-integrate into their communities.

In approaching the evidence and the submissions of the parties, Justice Doherty looked to international customary law and internationally recognized norms and standards because, as stated by Professor Werle:

> As part of the international order, international criminal law originated from the same legal sources as international law. These include international treaties, customary international law, and general principles of law recognized by the world's major legal systems. Decisions of international courts and international legal doctrine can be used not as sources of law, but subsidiary means for determining the law. Decisions of national courts which apply international law can also be referred to here.[47]

This led to taking account of the Penal Laws of other countries in Islamic, Christian, Hindu, Common Law and Civil Law systems and international treaties and conventions such as the International Covenant of Civil and Political Rights (ICCPR) and the Convention on Elimination of all Forms of Discrimination Against Women (CEDAW), which Sierra Leone signed on 21 September 1988 and ratified in November 1988, as well as African Charters and Conventions such as the African (Banjul) Charter on Human and People's Rights and the Protocol to the African Charter on the Rights of Women in Africa, both of which had been signed (but not implemented by Sierra Leone). On the basis of those conventions and on the evidence, the minority opinion was that:

> international treaties and domestic law provide that a marriage is a relationship founded on the mutual consent of both spouses. In forced marriage the consent of the victim is absent. In the absence of such consent, the victim is forced into a

[47] Gerhard Werle, *Principles of International Criminal* (The Hague, the Netherlands: TMC Asser Press, 2005), 44, para 123.

> relationship of a conjugal nature with the perpetrator thereby subsuming the victim's will and undermining the victim's exercise of their rights to self-determination.

The minority dissenting opinion further noted that forced marriage did not necessarily involve elements of physical violence such as abduction, enslavement or rape, and the fact that many women accepted their lot and remained with their "husbands" because they had no other choice did not transform a forced marriage into a consensual situation and did not retroactively negate the original criminality of the act of forced marriage.

The Prosecution appealed the majority decision on forced marriage, and the Appeal Chamber reviewed the evidence and both the majority and minority opinions. The Appeal Chamber noted that 'the Prosecution may have misled the Trial Chamber by the manner in which forced marriage appeared to have been classified in the Indictment. The Indictment classified Count 8 'Other Inhumane Acts' along with Counts 6, 7 and 9 under the heading 'Sexual Violence.' This categorization of forced marriages explains, but does not justify, the classification by the Trial Chamber of forced marriage as 'sexual violence.'

After reviewing the history of 'other inhumane acts' in International Criminal Law first introduced in the Nuremburg Charter, the Appeal Chamber held that the category 'other inhumane acts' was intended to be a residual provision so as to punish criminal acts not specifically recognized as crimes against humanity but which, in context, are of comparable gravity to the listed crimes against humanity.'

After considering the evidence and the law, the Appeal Chamber held that the perpetrator intended to impose a forced conjugal association rather than exercise mere ownership over civilian women and girls. They adopted the view in the dissenting opinion that forced marriage involves "the imposition, by threat or physical force arising from the perpetrator's words or other conduct, of a forced conjugal association by the perpetrator over the victims" and noted that:

> Victims were subjected to mental trauma by being labeled as rebel 'wives'; further they were stigmatized and found it difficult to integrate into their communities… causing mental and moral suffering, which in the context of the Sierra Leone conflict, is of comparable seriousness to the other crimes against humanity listed in the Statute.[48]

And the Appeal Chamber further held "that no tribunal could have found that forced marriage was subsumed into the crime of sexual slavery."[49]

The Appeal Chamber then considered whether forced marriage satisfies the elements of 'other inhumane acts' and held that other inhumane acts contained

---

48 *Prosecutor v. Brima et al.*, SCSL-04-16-A, 22 February 2008, para 193.

49 *Prosecutor v. Brima et al.*, SCSL-04-16-A, 22 February 2008, para 195.

in Article 2(i) of the Statute form part of Customary International Law, serving as a residual category designed to punish acts or omissions not specifically listed as crimes against humanity provided these acts or omissions meet the following requirements:

1. Inflict great suffering, or serious injury to body or to mental or physical health;
2. Are sufficiently similar in gravity to the acts referred to in Article 2(a) to Article 2(h) of the Statute; and
3. The perpetrator was aware of the factual circumstances that established the character of the gravity of the act.

The acts must also satisfy the general chapeau requirements of crimes against humanity.

The Appeals Chamber stated that it was firmly of the view that "acts of forced marriage were of similar gravity to several enumerated crimes against humanity including enslavement, imprisonment, torture, rape, sexual slavery and sexual violence," and the Appeals Chamber held that forced marriage is therefore a crime against humanity.[50]

3. CONCLUDING REMARKS

In an article entitled "Impunity for War Crimes against Women," Louise Arbour, then the United Nations High Commissioner for Human Rights, writing about the plight of victims of sexual attacks during conflicts stated that:

> The Special Court for Sierra Leone has made strides in addressing (such) hindrances in the face of a monumental task; as the result of ten years of conflict and the belligerents' methods of warfare in that country, the brutality of sexual violence was extraordinary, and its victims were to be counted in the thousands.[51]

The Special Court decisions have initiated discussions on the nature of gender based sexual violence during conflict, a discussion that is likely to continue both academically and in the development of international humanitarian and criminal law.

---

[50] *Prosecutor v. Brima et al.*, SCSL-04-16-A, 22 February 2008, paras 200.

[51] Louise Arbour, "Impunity for War Crimes against Women," *Spectator Newspaper* (16 May 2007).

CHAPTER 9

VICTIMS OF SEXUAL AND GENDER-BASED CRIMES BEFORE THE EXTRAORDINARY CHAMBERS IN THE COURTS OF CAMBODIA: CHALLENGES OF RIGHTS TO PARTICIPATION AND PROTECTION

Silke STUDZINSKY[1]

1. INTRODUCTION

The Extraordinary Chambers in the Courts of Cambodia (otherwise known as the ECCC or the Khmer Rouge Tribunal) was established pursuant to the Agreement[2] between the United Nations and the Royal Kingdom of Cambodia. The ECCC started in 2006 with the first preliminary investigations by the co-prosecutors. ECC was established to prosecute crimes committed during the period of Democratic Kampuchea between 17 April 1975 and 6 January 1979. The ECCC has personal jurisdiction over senior leaders and those most responsible for serious violations of the Cambodian Penal Code, and the international crimes of genocide, war crimes and crimes against humanity. It is a hybrid court composed of national and international judges and staff, and it follows mainly civil law procedure. It is the first internationalized court dealing with mass crimes that allows victims to apply as civil parties and to become

---

1 This chapter is based on a speech prepared for the 'Interdisciplinary Colloquium on systematic sexual violence and victims' rights' (7–8 April 2011) and reflects the author's work as international civil party lawyer before the ECCC since early 2008. This chapter was concluded at the end of March 2012.

2 Agreement between the United Nations and the Royal Government of Cambodia concerning the prosecution under Cambodian Law of crimes committed during the period of Democratic Kampuchea, 6 June 2003, available at www.eccc.gov.kh/sites/default/files/legaldocuments/Agreement_between_UN_and_RGC.pdf.

party to the proceedings alongside the prosecution and the defense.[3] In Case 001, against Kaing Guek Eav (alias Duch), the former director of the security center, S-21, the Trial Chamber announced a judgment in July 2010.[4] The judgment was appealed by all parties. On 3 February 2012, the Supreme Court Chamber pronounced the final judgment and sentenced Kaing Guek Eav to life imprisonment.[5]

In case 002, against four senior leaders of the Khmer Rouge regime, indictments were finalized in January 2011[6] and the substantive hearing started on 21 November 2011. The case against the accused IENG Thirith was separated due to health reasons.[7]

Cases 003 and 004 are strongly objected by the Cambodian government and are in the investigative phase.[8]

In this chapter I will give (2) an overview on the participation rights and the protection scheme available for victims of sexual crimes, (3) an outline of the current situation at the ECCC with regard to sexual violence, (4) the challenges that victims face and (5) the lessons to be learned.

---

3 See the Internal Rules (Revision 7), as revised on 23 February 2011, in particular Rule 23 and 23 *bis* – 23 *quinquies*, available at www.eccc.gov.kh/sites/default/files/legal-documents/IRv7-EN.pdf. The Internal Rules reflect the Cambodian Procedure Code.

4 *Case against Kaing Guek Eav*, 001/18-07-2007-ECCC/TC, 26 July 2010, available at www.eccc.gov.kh/sites/default/files/documents/courtdoc/20100726_Judgement_Case_001_ENG_PUBLIC.pdf.

5 *Case against Kaing Guek Eav*, 001/18-07-2007- ECCC/SC, available at www.eccc.gov.kh/sites/default/files/articles/03022012Summary-Eng.pdf. By the time of this writing, only the summary is available.

6 *Case against Nuon Chea et al.*, 002/19-09-2007-ECCC/OCIJ, 15 September 2010, available at www.eccc.gov.kh/english/cabinet/courtDoc/740/D427Eng.pdf. The closing order was appealed by the accused and became final with two amendments, available at www.eccc.gov.kh/en/document/court/decision-ieng-thirith-and-nuon-chea39s-appeal-against-closing-order and www.eccc.gov.kh/sites/default/files/documents/courtdoc/D427_1_26_EN.PDF. The reasoning of the Pre-Trial Chamber Decisions on Ieng Thirith and Nuon Chea, available at www.eccc.gov.kh/sites/default/files/documents/courtdoc/D427_2_12_EN.PDF. The Decision on Ieng Sary, available at www.eccc.gov.kh/sites/default/files/documents/courtdoc/D427_1_30_EN.PDF.

7 *Case against Ieng Thirith*, Decision on Immediate Appeal against the Trial Chamber's Order to Release the Accused Ieng Thirith, 002119-09-2007-ECCC-TC/SC(09), 13 December 2011, available at www.eccc.gov.kh/sites/default/files/documents/courtdoc/E138_1_7_EN-1.PDF.

8 See Report of Open Society Justice Initiative, Recent Developments at the Extraordinary Chambers in the Courts of Cambodia, 24 February 2012, available at www.soros.org/initiatives/justice/articles_publications/publications/cambodia-eccc-20120223/cambodia-eccc-20120223.pdf. Previous reports can be found at www.soros.org/initiatives/justice/focus/international_justice/articles_publications/sub_listing.

2. OVERVIEW OF THE PARTICIPATION RIGHTS OF AND THE AVAILABLE PROTECTION SCHEME FOR VICTIMS OF SEXUAL VIOLENCE BEFORE THE ECCC

2.1. PARTICIPATION RIGHTS

Victims of sexual violence, who apply to become a civil party and, therefore, a party to the proceedings, have to a large extent equal rights as appropriate like the prosecution and the defense. The Internal Rules determine the purpose of civil party participation as, "a) to participate in criminal proceedings against those responsible for crimes within the jurisdiction of the ECCC by supporting the prosecution; and b) seek collective and moral reparations."

Participating in this context means that they exercise, as a party to the proceedings, a wide range of procedural rights. In addition, they can be interviewed during the phase of the investigation by the co-investigating judges. In the trial stage they can be personally heard by the Trial Chamber. Given the high number of civil parties, there will be only a limited number of civil parties who will give a statement in court on the facts of the indictment and/or their sufferings.

Civil parties have a right to legal representation, which has been made mandatory in the trial phase.[9] They have full access to the electronic case files, including confidential materials[10], and can respond to all applications submitted by the other parties to raise any legal or factual matters *proprio motu*. Until now the civil parties have not been required to provide reasons as to the extent of their personal interest in the respective matter, unlike victims participating at the International Criminal Court (ICC). Most importantly in this context is the right during the investigation phase to submit investigative requests[11] to the co-investigating judges in order to get cases of sexual violence addressed and investigated at the ECCC to get an appropriate indictment.[12] During the trial

9 Internal Rule 23 *ter* (1). Internal Rule 23 *ter* (2) stipulates that their rights are exercised by lawyers, except when a civil party is interviewed, either by the co-investigating judges during the investigations or before the Trial Chamber. When they testify as civil parties they do not take an oath (like the accused) because they are parties to the proceedings.

10 Internal Rule 86.

11 Internal Rule 55 (10).

12 During the investigations co-lawyers for civil parties submitted various investigative requests to interview or re-interview witnesses and civil parties on forced marriages and sexual violence outside of the context of forced marriages, for example '[Redacted] civil parties' co-lawyers second request for investigative actions concerning forced marriages and forced sexual relationship,' D188, 15 July 2009, available at www.eccc.gov.kh/sites/default/files/documents/courtdoc/D188_Redacted_EN.pdf and '[Redacted] co-lawyers for the civil parties' fourth investigative request concerning forced marriages and sexually related crimes', D268, 4 December 2009, available at www.eccc.gov.kh/sites/default/files/documents/

phase the most important right of civil parties is the questioning of the accused, witnesses, civil parties and experts through their lawyers.[13] Civil parties can also submit their own witness/civil party/expert lists to the Trial Chamber in order to ensure the civil parties are heard.[14] Questioning does not need to be linked to a specific personal interest. Nevertheless this right which is unlimited in its application under both the applicable Cambodian Procedure Code and the Internal Rules was restrained by the Trial Chamber in case 001. The Trial Chamber ruled that civil parties are not allowed to question witnesses who testify on the character of the accused, and experts who examined the mental health of the accused and his culpability. The Trial Chamber determined the role of civil parties as principally to seek reparations and, as a result, limited their participation rights to addressing only the guilt of the accused and not on matters related to sentencing.[15] The Trial Chamber strictly limited the role of civil parties to making submissions only on matters for which they demonstrate a personal interest, i.e. consideration of the proof of guilt of the accused for the crimes which caused their harm and the issue of reparations.[16]

This ruling can be seen as a first step towards the "personal-interest-approach at the International Criminal Court (ICC) where victims are limited in their interventions to matters which affect their 'personal interests.'"[17]

Although this limitation has no legal basis in the Internal Rules or the Cambodian Criminal Procedure Code[18] and affects the participation rights of civil parties, the possibility for civil parties to intervene is still broad, as outlined above.

---

courtdoc/D268_Redacted_EN.pdf. A request for expert opinion was filed with regard to sexual violence and in particular forced marriages under the Khmer Rouges. Additional documents and witness statements were submitted. Most documents are classified as confidential. The co-investigating judges agreed to receive *Amici Curiae* on this issue but it was impossible to submit them within the deadline from 22 December 2009 until 31 December 2009, see 'order on request for investigative actions concerning forced marriages and sexually related crimes', D268/2, 18 December 2009, para 14, at www.eccc.gov.kh/sites/default/files/documents/courtdoc/D268_2_EN.pdf.

13 Internal Rule 90 (1) and 91 (2).

14 Internal Rule 80 (2) and (3).

15 *Case against Kaing Guek Eav*, 001/18–07–2007-ECCC/TC, decision on civil party co-lawyers' joint request for a ruling on the standing of civil party lawyers to make submissions on sentencing and directions concerning the questioning of the accused, experts and witnesses testifying on character, E72/3, 9 October 2009, [sentencing decision] at www.eccc.gov.kh/sites/default/files/documents/courtdoc/E72_3_EN.pdf. Judge Lavergne dissented in parts and stressed that civil parties have the same rights like other parties if not explicitly limited, para 16.

16 *Ibid.* at para 22 (Judge Lavergne, dissenting).

17 Rome Statute, Article 68 (3).

18 Judge Lavergne stated that "the decision taken by Trial Chamber tilts towards a view that is far removed both from Cambodian law and the Internal Rules of the ECCC", at para 32 (Judge Lavergne, dissenting).

2.2. PROTECTIVE MEASURES AT THE ECCC

There are a wide range of protective measures available at the ECCC.[19] They vary from the redaction of the names of victims and witnesses and other identifying facts, to the use of pseudonyms, to testifying in closed court sessions, voice distortion and relocation. However, the threshold for a grant of protective measures remains high and any protective measures will only be granted if an individual can demonstrate *specific* circumstances that would put him/her at risk of harm. A special unit, the Witness and Expert Support Unit (WESU), conducts a risk assessment of witnesses, civil parties and experts who have requested protective measures. Although civil parties are not reflected in the name of this unit, they are not excluded from the unit's work in analyzing potential risks. In each case, the WESU assesses the general danger that an individual faces, including examining whether and to what extent a specific and concrete potential risk exists that might imperil a person and/or his/her family. The co-investigating judges rejected the request of the prosecutors for protective measures for a large number of victims and witnesses in case 002 to whom they referred in their introductory submission.[20] The prosecutors did not provide any specific personal risk and therefore the request was deemed as unnecessary in the investigation phase. In general, this part of the proceedings is considered as confidential.[21] Thus, the question of protective measures arises mainly during the trial phase which is usually a public proceeding.

To provide some background to the developments in Cambodia, early on, at the beginning of 2008, a large number of civil party applicants requested protective measures but subsequently withdrew their requests in the course of the proceedings. Initially, most protective measure requests were based on a general concern that the Khmer Rouge could return to power at any time and seek revenge against the victims who exposed themselves by applying for civil party status. Between 2008 and 2010, the number of civil party applicants increased exponentially and the applicants grew less concerned with protective measures, as they had not experienced any reprisals in their communities. The son of the accused, Ieng Sary and Ieng Thirith, now Deputy Governor of Pailin Province, which is still a Khmer Rouge province, noted during a Public Forum in late 2008 that the victims do not need to have fear because of their sheer numbers.[22]

The fact that many individuals had applied between 2008 and 2010, coupled with the numerous outreach activities country-wide, and the fact that suspected persons, i.e. the alleged senior leaders, have remained in detention, led to a

19 Internal Rule 29 (4)(a)-(e).
20 On file with author, the decision is classified as confidential.
21 Internal Rule 56 (1).
22 Note on file with author.

reduction in fears about participating, and the ultimate withdrawal of most of the initial requests for protective measures. However, this does not apply to all victims: minority groups such as the Vietnamese and the Khmer Krom, who suffered targeted persecution under the Khmer Rouge regime (and genocide, on the part of the Vietnamese), and still suffer from general discrimination in society today, feel a higher degree of intimidation linked with participating in any activities initiated at the state level, such as the ECCC. The majority of these victims raised protective measures concerns. These requests have not yet been decided. So far most of these individuals will have difficulties demonstrating concrete, specific and objective incidents that form the basis for a belief that they and/or their families are at risk of harm. They may also have difficulties linking their fears specifically to their participation as complainants and civil parties at the ECCC. This is because the fears they face are based on the accumulation of violent policies against the groups under various government leaderships in the past, and particularly, the genocidal policy to destroy these groups by the Khmer Rouge regime, rather than specific instances of abuse *resulting* from their participation.

For victims of sexual violence, the situation is different. In my experience, they feel insecure simply submitting their story to the Court. This feeling is amplified with the prospect of testifying in public. However, the reasons behind their fears are not so much intimidation by the accused or the Khmer Rouge, but because of the anticipated stigma and discrimination from their respective communities should they disclose that they were victims of sexual violence. Even today, a victim of sexual violence who speaks out is marginalized, particularly if it is a male victim.

Therefore, some civil parties who are listed by civil party lawyers to testify on details of sexual violence committed against them wish to keep their identity and testimony undisclosed to the public. As their lawyers, we requested that the Trial Chamber impose the following measures: to allow our clients to testify in a closed court session, and to be referred to by a pseudonym. These measures would not infringe upon the accused's rights because they have full access to the identity of these victims via the case file. The requests are still pending and so far no jurisprudence is available for these specific cases.

3. DEALING WITH SEXUAL CRIMES – THE STATUS QUO

The first preliminary investigations by the co-prosecutors which resulted in the introductory submission[23] – binding on the co-investigating judges – did not

[23] At the outset, the introductory submission addressed five Suspects. In 2007, the case against Kaing Guek Eav *alias* Duch was separated and subsequently formed case 001. The other four

include any investigations in cases of sexual violence at all. Although the ECCC was established after the *ad hoc* tribunals and the ICC, the ECCC seems to be far behind these courts with regard to the investigation of sexual crimes. The rationale the co-prosecutors informally gave was that in light of the huge number of victims who were killed, starved and overworked, they focused chiefly on those crimes. In addition, at the beginning, the co-prosecutors adopted the common perception that while the Khmer Rouge acted cruelly against their own population, they exercised the moral high ground when it came to sexual matters. These assumptions by the Prosecution were made without a clear line of questioning to establish this as a fact, and without further investigations.

In case 001, there was only one case of rape, disclosed and admitted by the accused during the investigations, for which he was indicted and subsequently convicted.[24] It concerned the rape of a female prisoner by a male interrogator. The accused did not punish him which was, according to the accused, the agreement with his superior, a member of the standing committee.[25] Although there was more evidence that suggested that other cases of rape were committed, these cases were not investigated, and witnesses were not interviewed in detail. During the hearing, a civil party disclosed facts about being raped during her imprisonment after she saw her perpetrator testifying in court. This evidence was rejected on the basis that it was introduced too late.[26]

In the case 001 Judgment, the Trial Chamber used the narrow definition of rape as *penetration* from the ICTY Appeals Chamber in the *Kunaraca* case.[27] Furthermore, according to this definition the absence of the victim's consent is still necessary to be proved.

The broader concept of "invasion" of the victim's body should be preferred over the narrower conventional reference to "penetration" coupled with a list of body parts. This definition is considered to be gender-neutral.[28]

---

individuals, Nuon Chea, Ieng Sary, Ieng Thirth and Khieu Samphan are now accused in case 002.

24 *Case against Kaing Guek Eav*, 001/18-07-2007-ECCC/TC, 26 July 2010, D188, para 567, available at www.eccc.gov.kh/sites/default/files/documents/courtdoc/20100726_Judgement_Case_001_ENG_PUBLIC.pdf. In the Judgment the single instance of rape is subsumed under torture, see footnote 5. The final judgment is only available as a summary.

25 *Case against Kaing Guek Eav*, 001/18-07-2007-ECCC/TC, 16 June 2009 (accused), 68-69, 79 and 22 June 2009 (accused), 42.

26 *Case against Kaing Guek Eav*, 001/18-07-2007-ECCC/TC, E176, 28 October 2009, E176, para 14, available at www.eccc.gov.kh/sites/default/files/documents/courtdoc/E176_EN.pdf.

27 *Case against Kaing Guek Eav*, 001/18-07-2007-ECCC/TC, D188, 26 July 2010, para 362, available at www.eccc.gov.kh/sites/default/files/documents/courtdoc/20100726_Judgement_Case_001_ENG_PUBLIC.pdf; see also *Prosecutor v Kunarac et al.*, IT-96-23&IT-96-23/1-A, para 127, available at www.icty.org/x/cases/kunarac/acjug/en/kun-aj020612e.pdf.

28 *Model Codes for Post-Conflict Criminal Justice*, United States Peace Institute. The use of the term *invasion* rather than the term *penetration* is suggested. The use of *invasion* was welcomed by the delegates at the drafting of the *Elements* of *Crimes* as it more accurately portrays the criminal offense of rape from the perspective of the victim rather than that of the perpetrator. It is also a more gender-neutral term. *Elements* of *Crimes*, footnote 15, states that

Astonishingly, evidence indicating that under the order of the accused, at least one case of forced marriage among the S-24 staff had taken place, was not included, and the respective witness was even removed from the witness list.[29] Any questioning on the topic of forced marriage among staff members of S-21 or S-24 was immediately interrupted by the President of the Trial Chamber. Further, the Chamber did not consider it worthy to shed light on this aspect of the life and working conditions of staff at the worksite S-24.

All efforts by my legal team to have other sexual violence cases included in case 001, beyond the single admitted rape case, including the request for re-interview of witnesses, failed.

In case 002 – I had, early on, tried to push the issue of forced marriages by seeking further investigations from the Court on this widespread practice of the Khmer Rouge.[30] In my interviews with clients, I had discovered that this was a very common policy and a systematic crime under the Democratic Kampuchea. The purpose of the regime's forced marriage policy was to breed a new population, to be able to contribute to the agrarian work of the country. Pol Pot articulated an objective of the Communist Party to increase Cambodia's population to 20 million within ten to fifteen years, an expected growth of more than threefold of the population. The Communist Party (CPK) also aimed to control the interaction between individuals, such that they were only permitted to marry and have sexual relations in accordance with the CPK. At the beginning the objective was also to match couples with similar political status. The forced marriages were always organized in groups between 2 couples and 300 couples. Often the new couple did not know each other before the marriage. The mass weddings would be followed by a political speech and a declaration of commitment to one another under the orders of *Angkar*, the name for the leaders and standing committee meaning "organization."

The newly wedded couples were then forced to spend several nights together and, often-times, the males were explicitly ordered to have sexual intercourse with their new wives. The couples were monitored by soldiers to check and control whether sexual intercourse took place. In the event that the couple did not engage in sexual intercourse by joint agreement or otherwise, they were sanctioned. This was usually through being assigned to harder work, being sent to re-education, imprisonment or being killed. Several victims committed

"the concept of invasion is intended to be broad enough to be gender-neutral,"229, available at www.usip.org/files/MC1/MC1-Part2Section3.pdf.

29 The discussion of the removal of witnesses from the Trial Chamber's list was held in closed session on 15 June 2009.

30 Press release on first civil party application on gender-based violence, available at www.eccc.gov.kh/sites/default/files/media/PressRelease_1st_civil_party_on_Gender_Based_Violence.pdf. See also Phnom Penh Post, 22 October 2008, reporting the submission of four civil party applications raising forced marriage, available at www.phnompenhpost.com/index.php/2008102122239/The-Post.blogs/new-forced-marriage-complaints-before-eccc.html.

suicide. Through interviews with my clients I could demonstrate a pattern of forced marriages which was imposed on the non-married or widowed population countrywide with only few regional variations.[31]

The practice of forced marriages under the Khmer Rouge regime was common knowledge and most scholars and researchers on Cambodian history have referred to it in their writings.[32] Forced marriage was not *discovered* by the civil parties. And the investigating bodies at the ECCC *ignored* this systematic and widespread crime, even though the impact on the population is significant and continues to this day. Only by actively exercising their participation rights, victims and survivors of forced marriages, female and male, submitted focused civil party applications, and requested investigations into forced marriage. It was due to the courage of our clients to talk, and our own legal efforts, that forced marriage was successfully pushed at the ECCC, with the result that the Court eventually included this attack against the population successfully into the indictment.

In the course of the investigations in case 002, the co-prosecutors filed a supplementary submission for five cases of forced marriages raised by our clients. This was then extended to a countrywide investigation and recognition of forced marriages. It was included into the ECCC's judicial "scope of investigations." 780 out of 3864 admitted civil party applicants, were admitted as civil parties on the basis of the forced marriage claims they raised.[33] This must be seen as one of the biggest successes of the participation of civil parties, many of whom are direct and indirect victims of forced marriages – not only because it was the basis on which 1/5th of civil parties were admitted, but it also introduced the implementation of a significant criminal policy into the closing order. Forcing people to marry was a population policy which was widespread and systematically imposed on hundreds of thousands of victims in order to breed the new revolutionary progeny. The impact on victims, their families and their future generations is considerable.

The investigations resulted in the indictment of forced marriage as rape under crimes against humanity and forced marriage and sexual violence as other inhuman acts under crimes against humanity. According to the Indictment, the

31 Following the submissions and descriptions of our clients and other witnesses, the closing order in case 002 (see *supra* 3) reflects our findings in paras 216–20 with regard to the policy and paras 842–60 with regard to the pattern.

32 See Nakagawa Kasumi, *Gender-based Violence During the Khmer Rouge Regime (1975–1979)*, (2008, 2nd ed. 2010).

33 *Case against Nuon Chea et al.*, 002/19-09-2007-ECCC/OCIJ,15 September 2010, D427, para 861. 48% of the civil party applicants were not admitted by the co-investigating judges. The main reason given was that they could not establish a link with the crimes under investigation. More than 1700 applicants appealed the rejections and were admitted by order of the Pre-Trial Chamber, dated 24 June 2011, available at www.eccc.gov.kh/en/articles/pre-trial-chamber-overturns-previous-rejection-98-appealing-civil-party-applicants-case-002. The Pre-Trial Chamber admitted another 116 individuals as being victims of forced marriage.

unions "were part of the attack against the civilian population, in particular the imposition of sexual relations aimed at enforced procreation."[34]

The accused appealed the closing order (the indictment) *inter alia* with the objection to the charge of rape as a crime against humanity stating that during the relevant time (1975–79), rape was not yet applicable as an enumerated crime under crimes against humanity. The Pre-Trial Chamber agreed with this argument and held in their decisions on the appeals of the accused that rape was not a crime in its own, but ruled that the facts described as rape can be subsumed as 'other inhumane acts.'[35] Accordingly, the Pre-Trial Chamber struck rape as a crime against humanity out of paragraph 1613 (g) of the indictment.[36]

The reasoning was surprising, as rape was already in the Control Council Law 10[37] and in various national legislations[38] listed as a crime against humanity. It was recognized as a war crime since the *Lieber Code* in 1863 and in the regulations annexed to the 1907 Hague conventions.[39] These are strong indicators that it can be considered as customary international law that rape is already recognized as a crime in war times and a crime that is prohibited in the context of war. If committed as part of a widespread or systematic attack against the civilian population, the inclusion of rape as a war crime would seem to support and confirm a categorization of rape as an underlying crime against humanity, already part of customary international law throughout 1975–1979.[40]

---

34 *Case against Nuon Chea et al.*, 002/19-09-2007-ECCC/OCIJ, D427, 15 September 2010, para 1445.

35 *Case against Nuon Chea et al.*, 002/19-09-2007-ECCC/PTC, D427/1/30, 11 April 2011, paras 366–72, available at www.eccc.gov.kh/sites/default/files/documents/courtdoc/D427_1_30_EN.PDF.

36 *Pre-Trial Chamber decision on Ieng Thirith's and Nuon Chea's appeals against the closing order*, 002/19-09-2007-ECCC/OCIJ (PTC145&146), D427/2/12, 13 January 2011, para 11(2); *Pre-Trial Chamber Decision on Ieng Sary's appeal against the closing order*, 002/19-09-2007-ECCC/OCIJ (PTC75), D427/1/26, 13 January 2011, para 7(2); *Pre-Trial Chamber decision on Khieu Samphan's appeal against the closing order*, 002/19-09-2007-ECCC/OCIJ, 13 January 2011, para 2(2).

37 Control Council Law, No. 10, punishment of persons guilty of war crimes, crimes against peace, and against humanity, 20 December 1945, Article II(1)(c), reprinted in Trial of war criminals before the Nuremberg military tribunals under Control Council Law No. 10 (Vol.1).

38 See www.icrc.org/customary-ihl/eng/docs/v2_rul_rule93.

39 *Lieber* Instructions (1863) (Criminalizing rape with capital punishment, "all rape… [is] prohibited under the penalty of death."); The Hague Convention (1907) (Providing for the protection of women under Article 46, "family honour and rights, the lives of persons, and private property… must be respected."). See also, Report of the Commission on the Responsibility of the authors of the war and on enforcement of penalties, 29 March 1919, at 17, based on several documents supplying evidence of outrages committed during the First World War, listing rape as a violation of the laws and customs of war which should be subject to criminal prosecution.

40 See Kelly Askin, "Treatment of Sexual Violence in Armed Conflicts: a Historical Perspective & the Way Forward," in *Sexual Violence as an International Crime: Interdisciplinary Approaches*, eds. Anne-Marie de Brouwer, Charlotte Ku, Renée Römkens and Larissa van den Herik (Antwerp, Belgium: Intersentia), *supra*, for the historical development of the prohibition of sexual violence in situations of conflict.

Civil parties have exercised their participation rights to request expert opinions on this matter, in order to have the crime of forced marriage appropriately addressed and the criminality involved, against females and males alike, fully acknowledged.[41]

Regrettably, the indictment does not hold the accused liable for the few cases of rape in security centers,[42] even where a link up the chain of command could be made out. Instead, it alleged that rape was not one of the common purposes of the Khmer Rouge, and, to the contrary, that the Khmer Rouge had a policy of punishing perpetrators of sexual violence if the conduct was discovered.

Civil party lawyers tried to demonstrate that the examples of alleged punishment provided in the closing order do not support this conclusion. In contrast, we will submit that rapes against a declared enemy were committed, akin to torture, ill-treatment and killing, without being punished. In addition, civil parties will submit additional evidence which clearly demonstrates that rape of an "enemy," who was already targeted for execution, was not punished, although known by the perpetrator's superiors.

Half of the victory that civil parties through performing their participation rights have achieved, by having forced marriages countrywide included into the indictment, is tainted by the exclusion of rapes outside of the context of forced marriage. The problematic definition and offence elements for forced marriage and rape used at the ECCC, and the Pre-Trial Chamber's decision excluding rape as a crime against humanity for the relevant period of time, are backward steps for these issues in international jurisprudence.

Another step back for victims of sexual violence occurred on 22 September 2011: The Trial Chamber severed case 002 in order "to enable the Chamber to issue a verdict following a shortened trial, safeguarding the fundamental interest of victims in achieving meaningful and timely justice, and the right of all Accused in Case 002 to an expeditious trial."[43] Now, the first trial of Case 002 is limited to forced transfers of the population. All other crimes and crime sites, including forced marriage are adjourned. Due to the age of the accused and the expected length it is unlikely that more than this first trial in Case 002 will take place.

This development is disappointing for the victims of forced marriage. Notwithstanding that they constituted the second largest group by crime,[44] forced marriage is not included into the first trial.

---

41 At the trial stage the request for expert opinion is still pending before the Trial Chamber.

42 See *Case against Nuon Chea et al.*, 002/19-09-2007-ECCC/OCIJ, D427, 15 September 2010, paras 1426–29.

43 *Case against Nuon Chea et al.*, Severance Order pursuant to Internal Rule 89*ter*, 22 September 2011, E124, para 8, available at www.eccc.gov.kh/sites/default/files/documents/courtdoc/E124_EN.PDF.

44 The only group larger than that of the civil parties who allege forced marriage are the 781 admitted civil parties on the grounds of the first forced transfer of the entire population of

4. CHALLENGES

At the current stage of the proceedings in the ECCC, with the investigations closed, the indictment issued, and the substantive hearing started in case 002, the planned work of civil parties with regard to sexual violence is indefinitely deferred as a result of the severance order. Therefore, the following thoughts and suggestions are now more theoretical in nature.

They were namely intended to focus on the proper legal qualifications of forced marriage, and persuading the Trial Chamber to reconsider the liability of the accused for sexual violence outside of forced marriages. To achieve the latter, the existing evidence on sexual violence needs to be put before the Chamber, in order to be considered at all.

Witnesses and/or civil parties who testify on sexual violence should do this in an environment where they feel comfortable to speak out. The Trial Chamber should establish guidelines on witness/civil party testimony on sexual violence and guarantee an appropriate environment for their testimony. The experience during the investigations has shown that the interviews for victims of sexual violence were not conducted with the necessary diligence, sensitivity and competence that is required. In addition, only male investigators were employed. In one instance, this contributed to the collapse of a client, who was the victim of a gang rape, when she was overwhelmed by being surrounded exclusively by males during the interview.

Any requests for protective measures by victims, who risk their well-being through testifying on these crimes, and risk negative reaction and stigma, should be granted by the Trial Chamber.

The new legal representation scheme, which now stipulates that one national and one international lead co-lawyer employed with the Court represent a "consolidated" group of civil parties, could reduce, if not hinder, the proper representation of civil parties through their lawyers. Because of the intermediary "lead co-lawyers," deadlines for civil party lawyers are in fact shortened. Further, where the lead co-lawyers do not react in a timely manner on civil party lawyers' submissions, the effect could be a silencing of the civil parties. The scene for civil party representation has indeed changed at the ECCC, and it remains to be seen how civil party lawyers could continue to represent their clients without direct access to the Court, where they have standing to be heard, since the Trial Chamber has expressed that it would liaise only with the lead co-lawyers.

Phnom Penh in April 1975.

5. LESSONS LEARNED

- The prosecutorial strategy at the beginning of an investigation is of crucial importance and largely determines the charges at a later stage in proceedings. Utmost vigilance is required at the investigative stage, and sexual violence has to be considered as a severe and grave crime instead of often being considered as peripheral to other crimes, such as killings.
- The participation of victims vested with strong rights to influence the prosecution has to be included at the earliest point.
- Being familiar with and learning from the achievements and failures of other courts and tribunals is of great importance in order to avoid the same mistakes. Best practices with regard to the inclusion and investigation of sexual violence cases, should be the duty of any future Court, the permanent International Criminal Court and any national prosecution of mass crimes.
- The respective procedural rules should include evidentiary provisions on how to deal with testimonies concerning sexual violence.
- A careful consideration of the alleged sexual crimes against male persons should be included for best practice at international courts. For all sexual crimes the victims should have the option to be interviewed either by female or male investigators and interpreters.
- Competent and appropriate staffing is a prerequisite for investigating cases of sexual violence from all organs of a Court. As such, sensitivity to sexual criminal matters should be a priority criterion for recruitment of staff members. Further, continuous trainings and updates on matters pertaining to sexual violence crimes should be mandatory for all court staff, including judges and prosecutors.

6. CONCLUSION

The ECCC is the first internationalized court dealing with mass crimes that grants victims the role of third parties to the proceedings. This could be a unique chance for the ECCC to have victims become actively involved and to become a model for any future international or internationalized courts.

In the beginning, back in 2008, the ECCC clearly disregarded and ignored cases of sexual violence. What has been achieved thus far has been the direct result of civil party lawyers' work – and of course, the courage and bravery of our clients, in speaking out, amidst risk of stigma and social alienation. The Court itself has, in the past, appeared hesitant about properly and appropriately addressing sexual crimes. For example, the prosecutors' strategy did not include sexual crimes at all, in the earlier stages of investigation. This approach is extremely difficult to change and influence at later stages in the proceedings.

Adequate provisions for dealing with sexual violence in the internal rules and well-trained and competent court personnel are crucial for proper investigations. In addition, although the need for training was, in-principal, foreseen in the budget, adequate training of investigators and court staff has never taken place before the investigations were closed.

More recently, amendments to the Internal Rules have effectively reduced the actual possibilities of civil parties to participate by imposing a lead co-lawyer section, responsible for representing the "consolidated group."

For this and other reasons, the role of civil parties to obtain some remnant of justice through actively participating in this process remains a continuing challenge and one that must be balanced against secondary harm caused to civil parties and applicants by the gaps and inadequacies that have resulted so far in both cases 001 and 002.

To conclude, it has been a huge challenge to ensure that victims of sexual violence have a voice and justice in this jurisdiction at all stages of the proceedings. However, inclusion of forced marriages in the indictment is one visible success story resulting from civil party participation. The inclusion of "forced marriages" under the judicial "scope of investigations," coupled with its inclusion in the indictment, has stirred up much discussion and debate, and raised awareness about the criminal nature of forced marriages under the Khmer Rouge regime. Prior to this, forced marriages were simply not considered to be so much "a crime," as compared with other horrendous acts perpetrated by the regime. It has now been given its proper place in these criminal proceedings. Hopefully, the inclusion of forced marriage in the indictment at the ECCC will give some basis, at the international level, for courts to take gender-based crimes seriously and to draw adequate attention to these types of offences world-wide – particularly at early stages of the criminal process.

However, since the Trial Chamber separated the case and did not include the cases of forced marriage into the first trial, it is unlikely that these charges will be ever tried at the ECCC.

PART 2

SOCIAL, ARCHIVAL AND MEDICAL DATA COLLECTION AND ITS USE FOR THE CRIMINAL LAW PROCESS: METHODOLOGY ISSUES

CHAPTER 10

ETHICAL, SAFETY AND METHODOLOGICAL ISSUES RELATED TO COLLECTION AND USE OF DATA ON SEXUAL VIOLENCE IN CONFLICT

Chen REIS[1]

1. INTRODUCTION

Sexual violence is a pervasive public health and human rights issue with potential serious effects on physical and mental health, and social well-being.[2] Unfortunately, there are often few available data on prevalence, risk and protective factors, and consequences to survivors. This lack of data and the paucity of programming approaches which have been assessed may result in interventions that are not effective and may negatively impact the fight to end impunity and achieve justice for survivors. In settings affected by conflict and other humanitarian crises, the challenges to obtaining data to inform prevention of and response to sexual violence may be magnified.

The increasing attention to sexual violence as a tactic of armed conflict has contributed to increasing demands for data on sexual violence in conflict settings. Data are being requested by a range of different actors for different reasons. Many of the demands and the responses to them do not take into account the limitations of available data and the feasibility of collecting other data. This increased demand for data and the actions taken to respond to it raise methodological and other ethical issues including ethical, safety and methodological issues related to collection, sharing and use of data.

This chapter explores some of the key sources of data which may be available at country level and the limits to what they can tell us about sexual violence in the setting (methodological limitations). It will also identify ethical issues related

---

1 The views expressed in this article are those of the author solely and do not necessarily represent the views, policies and decisions of the World Health Organization.

2 Eds. Etienne Krug, Linda L. Dahlberg, James A. Mercy, Anthony Zwi, & Rafael Lozano, *World Report on Violence and Health*, (Geneva, Switzerland: World Health Organization, 2002).

to data collection and sharing, and discuss the development and content of recommendations to inform those who are collecting, using or supporting the collection of data on sexual violence. These are important for those involved in international criminal investigations and prosecutions both as users of existing data and collectors of new data.

2. BACKGROUND

Sexual violence in conflict is not a new phenomenon nor can it be entirely separated from sexual violence in the setting outside of the conflict. Sexual violence can occur during attacks on civilian populations, while people are fleeing fighting, and among those who are internally displaced or refugees whether in camps, urban settings, or living within host communities.

- Sexual violence may be perpetrated by armed combatants as a tactic of conflict.
- The environment of vulnerability and lawlessness that prevails in many conflict affected settings may contribute to the occurrence and nature of sexual violence, including sexual violence perpetrated by those involved in provision of aid.
- There are likely to be various forms of sexual violence (including rape, intimate partner violence, incest and harmful traditional practices) already occurring in communities. This violence may continue or resume during the conflict and post conflict periods and it may also be exacerbated by the conflict.

The use of sexual violence as a tactic of conflict, once considered as an inevitable consequence of war, is now increasingly the focus of efforts to bring those responsible to justice. Sexual violence, however, doesn't happen in a vacuum. It reflects and may exacerbate existing vulnerabilities in a society, particularly of women and children. Societal and political norms relating to how crimes of sexual violence are addressed, if at all, may also be mirrored in the national legal response to sexual violence in conflict.

Due to legal developments since the second world war and in particular judgements of the International Criminal Tribunals for the former Yugoslavia and Rwanda[3], which are discussed elsewhere in this book[4], there is now official

3 K.D. Askin, *War Crimes Against Women: Prosecution in International War Crimes Tribunals*, (Dordrecht, the Netherlands: Martinus Nijhoff Publishers, distributed by Kluwer Law International, 1997). United Nations Department of Peacekeeping Operations, *Review of the sexual violence elements of the judgments of the international criminal tribunal for the former Yugoslavia, the international criminal tribunal for Rwanda, and the special court for Sierra Leone in the light of Security Council Resolution 1820*, (New York: United Nations, 2009) available at www.stoprapenow.org/uploads/advocacyresources/1284125586.pdf.

4 See for a more elaborate discussion on the historical developments in the recognition of sexual violence as an international crime, *inter alia*, Kelly Askin, "Treatment of Sexual

recognition that sexual violence may be a crime against humanity, war crime or even a form of genocide. This is reflected in the statute of the International Criminal Court.[5]

Sexual violence is also recognized as a critical international security issue as well as an important component of the protection of civilians. Several recent UN Security Council Resolutions mention or are focused on sexual violence, including various Security Council resolutions regarding mandates for UN peace operations[6] and:

- 1325 (2000), Women and peace and security[7]
- 1612 (2005), Children and armed conflict[8]
- 1674 (2006), Protection of civilians in armed conflict[9]
- 1820 (2008), Women and peace and security.[10]
- 1882 (2009), Children and armed conflict[11]
- 1888 (2009), Women and peace and security[12]
- 1889 (2009), Women and peace and security[13]

Violence in Armed Conflicts: a Historical Perspective & the Way Forward," in *Sexual Violence as an International Crime: Interdisciplinary Approaches*, eds. Anne-Marie de Brouwer, Charlotte Ku, Renée Römkens and Larissa van den Herik (Antwerp, Belgium: Intersentia), *supra*.

5 Rome Statute of the International Criminal Court, adopted 17 July 1998 entered into force on 1 July 2002, available at www.icc-cpi.int/NR/rdonlyres/EA9AEFF7–5752–4F84-BE94–0A655EB30E16/0/Rome_Statute_English.pdf.

6 Including United Nations Security Council resolutions 1856, 22 December 2008, available at http://daccess-dds-ny.un.org/doc/UNDOC/GEN/N08/666/94/PDF/N0866694.pdf?Open Element; 1858, 22 December 2008, available at http://daccess-dds-ny.un.org/doc/UNDOC/GEN/ N08/665/59/PDF/N0866559.pdf?OpenElement; 1861, 14 January 2009, available at http://daccess-dds-ny.un.org/doc/UNDOC/GEN/N09/208/44/PDF/N0920844. pdf?OpenElement; 1880, 30 July 2009, available at http://daccess-dds-ny.un.org/doc/UNDOC/GEN/N09/433/60/PDF/ N0943360.pdf?OpenElement; 1881 (2009), 30 July 2009, available at http://daccess-dds-ny.un.org/doc/UNDOC/GEN/N09/433/60/PDF/N0943360. pdf?OpenElement; and 1885, 15 September 2009, available at http://daccess-dds-ny.un.org/doc/UNDOC/GEN/N09/514/01/PDF/ N0951401.pdf?OpenElement.

7 United Nations Security Council resolution 1325, 31 October 2000, available at http://daccess-dds-ny.un.org/doc/UNDOC/GEN/N00/720/18/PDF/N0072018.pdf?OpenElement.

8 United Nations Security Council resolution 1612, 26 July 2005, available at http://daccess-dds-ny.un.org/doc/UNDOC/GEN/N05/439/59/PDF/N0543959.pdf?OpenElement.

9 United Nations Security Council resolution 1674, 28 April 2006, available at http://daccess-dds-ny.un.org/doc/UNDOC/GEN/N06/331/99/PDF/N0633199.pdf?OpenElement.

10 United Nations Security Council resolution 1820, 19 June 2008, available at http://daccess-dds-ny.un.org/doc/UNDOC/GEN/N08/391/44/PDF/N0839144.pdf?OpenElement.

11 United Nations Security Council resolution 1882, 4 August 2009, available at http://daccess-dds-ny.un.org/doc/UNDOC/GEN/N09/442/14/PDF/N0944214.pdf?OpenElement.

12 United Nations Security Council resolution 1888, 30 September 2009, available at http://daccess-dds-ny.un.org/doc/UNDOC/GEN/N09/534/46/PDF/N0953446.pdf?OpenElement.

13 United Nations Security Council Resolution 1889, 5 October 5, 2009, available at http://daccess-dds-ny.un.org/doc/UNDOC/GEN/N09/542/55/PDF/N0954255.pdf?OpenElement.

- 1894 (2009), Protection of civilians in armed conflict[14]
- 1960 (2010), Women and peace and security[15]

Sexual violence, along with other forms of gender-based violence (GBV) has also been recognized as a critical issue to be addressed in humanitarian response operations, with specific responsibilities for all sectors.[16]

Box 1: Definitions

Gender-Based Violence (GBV) is an umbrella term for any harmful act that is perpetrated against a person's will, and that is based on socially ascribed (gender) differences between males and females.

Acts of GBV violate a number of universal human rights protected by international instruments and conventions. Many—but not all—forms of GBV are illegal and criminal acts in national laws and policies.

Around the world, GBV has a greater impact on women and girls than on men and boys. The term "gender-based violence" is often used interchangeably with the term "violence against women." The term "gender-based violence" highlights the gender dimension of these types of acts; in other words, the relationship between females' subordinate status in society and their increased vulnerability to violence. It is important to note, however, that men and boys may also be victims of gender-based violence, especially sexual violence. The nature and extent of specific types of GBV vary across cultures, countries, and regions. Examples include:

- Sexual violence, including sexual exploitation/abuse and forced prostitution
- Domestic violence
- Trafficking
- Forced/early marriage
- Harmful traditional practices such as female genital mutilation, honor killings, widow inheritance, and others

Guidelines for Gender-Based Violence Interventions in Humanitarian Settings: Focusing on Prevention of and Response to Sexual Violence in Emergencies

Sexual violence is "any sexual act, attempt to obtain a sexual act, unwanted sexual comments or advances, or acts to traffic a person's sexuality, using coercion, threats of harm or physical force, by any person regardless of relationship to the victim, in any setting, including but not limited to home and work."

Sexual violence takes many forms, including rape, sexual slavery and/or trafficking, forced pregnancy, sexual harassment, sexual exploitation and/or abuse, and forced abortion.

Etienne Krug, *World Report on Violence and Health, World Health Organization; Guidelines for Gender-based Violence Interventions in Humanitarian Settings: Focusing on Prevention of and Response to Sexual Violence in Emergencies.*

---

14 United Nations Security Council resolution 1894, 11 November 2009, available at http://daccess-dds-ny.un.org/doc/UNDOC/GEN/N09/602/45/PDF/N0960245.pdf?OpenElement.

15 United Nations Security Council resolution 1960, 16 December 2010, available at http://daccess-dds-ny.un.org/doc/UNDOC/GEN/N10/698/34/PDF/N1069834.pdf?OpenElement.

16 *Guidelines for Gender-based Violence Interventions in Humanitarian Settings: Focusing on Prevention of and Response to Sexual Violence in Emergencies.* (Geneva, Switzerland: Inter-Agency Standing Committee, 2005), available at www.humanitarianinfo.org/iasc/pageloader.aspx?page=content-subsidi-tf_gender-gbv.

The term "**conflict-related sexual violence**" is used to denote sexual violence occurring in a conflict or post-conflict setting that has a direct or indirect causal link with the conflict itself. Such a link may be demonstrated by the perpetrator's status as a belligerent party; the proliferation and use of small arms and light weapons; the breakdown of law and order; the militarization of sites of daily activity such as fuel and water collection; cross-border consequences such as displacement, trafficking or economic disruption; the (sometimes deliberate) spread of HIV; and the targeting of ethnic, sectarian or other minorities or of populations in contested territory affording an economic, military or political advantage, including in violation of a ceasefire agreement.

In paragraph 1 of Resolution 1820 (2008), the Security Council stresses that sexual violence, when used or commissioned as a tactic of war in order to deliberately target civilians or as a part of a widespread or systematic attack against civilian populations, can significantly exacerbate situations of armed conflict and may impede the restoration of international peace and security. The Council qualifies the "tactic of war" threshold with the word "including", indicating that this is just one type of case to be addressed alongside sexual violence committed against civilians, in situations of armed conflict, in and around refugee and internally displaced persons camps, and in disarmament, demobilization and reintegration processes.

Report of the Secretary-General on the implementation of Security Council resolutions 1820 (2008) and 1888 (2009) (New York: United Nations 2010), para 5, available at http://daccess-dds-ny.un.org/doc/UNDOC/GEN/N10/653/46/PDF/ N1065346.pdf?OpenElement

3. DATA ON SEXUAL VIOLENCE

The increased attention to sexual violence has also contributed to increased demand for information on the nature and extent of sexual violence during conflict, in its immediate aftermath and in the post-conflict period. These demands for data to inform protection, prevention and response including resource allocations, humanitarian programs and advocacy and justice processes come from a range of actors including UN bodies, governments, the press and non-governmental organizations.

Increased demand contributes to increased efforts to gather information on sexual violence. Data may be gathered in the context of assessments to inform program planning and monitoring and evaluation of ongoing programs. Testimonies and other information may be collected for human rights monitoring and documentation and as part of the justice process. Data may also be collected in response to a specific demand – such as reports of the UN Secretary-General or monitoring and reporting mechanisms in response to UN Security Council Resolutions. Information may also be gathered by academic researchers studying aspects of the issue or as part of surveys on health or justice.[17]

[17] For more discussion of existing data collection efforts see *Report of Meeting on Sexual Violence in Conflict: Data and Data Collection Methodologies, in Geneva on18–19 December 2008* (UN Action/World Health Organization, 2008), available at www.stoprapenow.org/uploads/advocacyresources/1282164411.pdf.

In a given context, several data gathering activities may overlap and co-exist in a non-coordinated manner and without sharing of data or appropriate programmatic follow-up. This may lead to unintended negative consequences including the waste of resources and the exposure of those affected by sexual violence to several encounters with data collectors all requesting similar information. Furthermore, attention to only specific types and contexts of sexual violence to the exclusion of others due to specific mandates, definitions, actors or timeframes of interest may inadvertently contribute to the creation of a false hierarchy of rape or hierarchy of forms of violence.

The collection of data on sexual violence in the absence of health, psychosocial and other services to assist survivors presents ethical and safety issues which are especially relevant in the context of conflict where access to services may be limited. Health and other services are critical for the well-being of the survivor and should go hand in hand with processes for ending impunity.[18] In addition to addressing immediate needs of survivors and helping to fulfil their rights, health, psychosocial and legal services are important entry points to and supports for survivors during the justice process and help provide information that can be used to improve protection and responses.[19]

3.1. LIMITATIONS RELATED TO UNDER-REPORTING

In general, information on sexual violence is based on reports by survivors. Most survivors, however, never report what happened to them. This under-reporting will have an impact on all sources of data on sexual violence and is important to consider when designing the data collection approach, during collection of information and when analysing and interpreting the data.[20]

In conflict affected settings as in relatively peaceful ones there may be a variety of factors that affect reporting by a survivor of sexual violence. Factors which may bar disclosure may be social, security-related or legal. Access barriers may also affect disclosure, especially in conflict affected settings. There may be additional and different social and legal barriers to disclosure for male survivors of sexual violence.[21]

---

18 This is reflected in UN Security Council resolution 1820, 19 June 2008, para 13 wherein the Council "[u]rges all parties concerned, including Member States, United Nations entities and financial institutions, to support the development and strengthening of the capacities of national institutions, in particular of judicial and health systems, and of local civil society networks in order to provide sustainable assistance to victims of sexual violence in armed conflict and post-conflict situations."

19 *Guidelines for medico-legal care for victims of sexual violence*, (Geneva, Switzerland: World Health Organization, 2003), 2.

20 *Ibid.* at 9.

21 *Ibid.*

Social factors may include fear of facing stigma, ridicule, abandonment by an intimate partner, or social exclusion. In some settings a survivor may not disclose due to fear that she will be blamed for the sexual violence or for not preventing it from happening. A survivor may also face adverse legal consequences if she discloses what happened to her. In some settings a woman who survives sexual violence may be considered unfit for marriage and where marriage confers a degree of economic security and social status, concern about this may be a strong deterrent. Feelings of shame may also prevent a survivor from coming forward and may lead a survivor to isolate herself from her family and community. In many settings sexual violence which happens within a marriage or other intimate partnership may be considered a private matter within the family or a normal part of the relationship.

Survivors may also have well-founded concerns about personal safety or fear retribution. This may be true both when the violence happens within an intimate partnership and when perpetuated by community members, combatants or government agents.

For many survivors, there will be no access to legal recourse due to the definition of sexual violence crimes which may be limited to specific acts or which may not recognize sexual violence within a marital relationship as a crime.

Even when a survivor wants to pursue a legal case, disclosure may not lead to justice for her due to discriminatory laws and inadequate application and enforcement due to the complicity of the authority in the violence, weakness of law enforcement and legal infrastructure, or lack of capacity or biases of actors in the system. In some settings, there is a preference to seek justice within traditional community systems, which may not approach cases of sexual violence in compliance with international human rights principles.

Those survivors who are able to pursue a case in the legal system may be subjected to unnecessary invasive exams and may feel that she herself is being put on trial due to prevalent societal norms and attitudes which assign blame to the victim of sexual violence. In some settings, a survivor who reports sexual violence risks being put on trial with charges of adultery. In many settings, there is no formal system for provisions of social, psychological or legal support or protection for a survivor who is engaging with the legal system. Disclosure of sexual violence may therefore result in negative consequences for the survivor in addition to those that are a direct result of the sexual violence.

A lack of reports about sexual violence should not, therefore be interpreted to mean that sexual violence is an unimportant issue. Rather, and especially in humanitarian settings, an absence of data should be understood as a result of the complexity of gathering information about the occurrence and nature of sexual violence in these contexts.

3.2. SOURCES OF DATA

Data that are collected correctly, and analysed and reported appropriately, however, can meet a variety of needs including informing protection and justice processes and, as such, it is important to understand the limits of various data gathering approaches such as collection of medico-legal evidence, recording of testimonies, compilation of case reports from service providers, and conduct of population based studies. It is important to note that in many settings, there may be various forms of data available and these should be used to complement each other.

3.2.1. Medico-legal evidence

An important role of health service providers is collection of medico-legal evidence as appropriate and with informed consent of the survivor. Collection of physical evidence should be done in the context of health service provisions and only evidence that can be processed and used should be collected. Medico-legal evidence should not be collected in the absence of medical and other services for survivors.

Physical evidence may be collected within certain time period. There is a range of physical evidence, which can be collected from the body and clothing of the survivor including foreign material (soil, leaves, etc.), foreign hair, sperm, seminal fluid, saliva, blood or urine and documentation of tearing or stains on clothing.[22] Documentation of what the survivor reports and of any external and internal injuries is also an important aspect of collection of medico-legal evidence,[23] though in most cases of rape there will not be any injuries which can be documented.[24] What evidence may be collected depends on a number of factors including availability of trained staff and trusted services, capacity of the medico-legal system to collect, store, process and use evidence, and when the survivor reports the incident. In general, within 72 hours of the incident and if the survivor has not washed, it may be possible to collect samples of blood, hair, saliva, and sperm.[25] After 72 hours, the amount and type of evidence which can be collected will be limited.[26] Collection of medico-legal evidence must take into account relevant legal and evidentiary requirements, facilities available for storage and analysis of evidence, and the legal responsibility of health care providers.

---

22 *Guidelines for medico-legal care for victims of sexual violence*, (Geneva, Switzerland: World Health Organization, 2003), 57.
23 *Ibid.* at 94.
24 *Ibid.* at 11.
25 *Ibid.* at 59–60.
26 *Ibid.* at 57–58.

While collection of medico-legal evidence is a standard component of post-rape care in some developed settings, even when properly collected and used, this evidence may not be dispositive.[27] Medico-legal evidence should only be collected and released to authorities with full consent of survivors and should, if possible, be collected at the same time as the medical exam, and by the same individual to minimize possibly traumatic invasive exams.[28]

It is important for health professionals to be aware of any relevant laws, policies or protocols which relate to the provision of medico-legal services to victims of sexual violence. These laws, policies and protocols may address specific aspects of medico-legal service provisions including who may provide the services, what procedures must be followed and which forms must be used. Legal and policy documents may also address broader aspects of health service provision to survivors of sexual violence, including which medical interventions may be offered (e.g. emergency contraception) and whether a health provider is legally obligated to report suspected or reported incidents of sexual violence to authorities (mandatory reporting). When the relevant laws and policies are not followed this may have a negative impact on whether the medico-legal evidence collected can be used. In addition, health providers who do not comply with these laws and policies may face professional consequences.[29]

3.2.2. Individual testimonies

Information on the specific experiences of survivors of sexual violence is a standard methodology for human rights and justice investigations. Information may be collected in the context of documentation work by local and international human rights groups or in the context of specific justice processes. Testimonies are often gathered through one on one interviews with the survivor, asking open-ended questions aimed at both documenting the experiences of the survivor as well as getting at specific elements which may be relevant for justice processes. In addition to these testimonies, interviews are often conducted with key informants, which can provide context and critical background information. This approach can provide extensive, detailed and powerful information about individual experiences, identify issues requiring further investigation, and capture important information to support prosecutions and other processes aimed at achieving justice and ending impunity. The individual stories of survivors have also been used in media and other public fora to raise awareness

---

27 J. Du Mont & D. White, *The uses and impacts of medico-legal evidence in sexual assault cases: a global review* (Geneva, Switzerland: Sexual Violence Research Initiative, World Health Organization, 2007), available at www.svri.org/medico.pdf. Other relevant documents can be found at: www.svri.org/medico.htm.

28 *Guidelines for medico-legal care for victims of sexual violence*, (Geneva, Switzerland: World Health Organization, 2003), 18.

29 *Ibid.* at 19.

and advocate for increased funding for programs aimed at prevention of and response to sexual violence.

While testimonial evidence may be an important source of information, testimonies do not provide information that is generalizable to a broader population.[30] As such, when used alone, testimonies are unlikely to show whether sexual violence is widespread or systematic, and cannot be used to estimate prevalence. Furthermore, the experiences of those interviewed may not be representative of the broader population of those who have experienced sexual violence.

3.2.3. Aggregated data from cases reported to services

The data collected by providers of health, psychosocial and legal services to survivors of sexual violence may be a useful source of information. The case files of service providers may include detailed information about the sexual violence incident as well as information about the survivor and the impacts of the incident on her/him.

When data from individual cases are aggregated and properly contextualized they may be used to identify which services survivors approach for assistance and which may need to be strengthened. These data may also help to identify issues requiring further investigation and action, inform prevention and response programming, and support efforts to hold those responsible for sexual violence crimes accountable. When shared and used in an ethical and safe way, the use of these available data may protect the survivor from disclosure of his/her identity and from repeated contacts.

There are, however, key limitations to the use of aggregated data from service providers. Even where these data are available, reporting may be inconsistent. Furthermore, data cannot be used to identify temporal or other trends, estimate magnitude or prevalence or generalize about survivors.

By definition, the information available in the files of service providers represents only those cases which have been reported to service providers. In general, only a small percentage of those who experience sexual violence actually report what happened to them.[31] This may be due to a fear of stigma or retribution, or feelings of shame. In conflict affected settings, the lack of services, disrupted access to services or lack of confidence in available services may further hinder reporting. As such, data from reported cases are unlikely to reflect the totality of those affected by sexual violence in the setting. Those who do report to services

---

30 On this issue, see also Lynn Lawry, Kirsten Johnson and Jana Asher, "Evidence-Based Documentation of Gender-Based Violence," in *Sexual Violence as an International Crime: Interdisciplinary Approaches*, eds. Anne-Marie de Brouwer, Charlotte Ku, Renée Römkens and Larissa van den Herik (Antwerp, Belgium: Intersentia), *infra*.

31 *Guidelines for medico-legal care for victims of sexual violence*, (Geneva, Switzerland: World Health Organization, 2003), 96.

may differ markedly from other survivors in terms of key personal characteristics, key aspects of the sexual violence incident and/or impact of the incident.

It is not appropriate to make assumptions about trends in sexual violence incidents from case reports. Reporting may be affected by a number of factors including awareness of, access to and trust in services. An increase in the number of people reporting sexual violence to service providers may not necessarily mean an increase in sexual violence incidents.[32] This increase may be linked to changes in access to services or may follow campaigns aimed at increasing public awareness about sexual violence and available services. Similarly, a decrease in reporting should not automatically be assumed to reflect a decrease in sexual violence in the setting.

The sharing and use of data from service providers should take into account these limitations[33] and must not put individuals, communities, service providers or access to services at risk. One system designed to facilitate good practice in safe and ethical collection, sharing and analysis of GBV data by service providers is the GBV Information Management System (GBVIMS). The GBVIMS is a system comprised of 4 elements: a standard Intake and Consent Form, an Incident Classification System which includes standardized definitions of GBV types to ensure comparability of data, an Incident Recorder Excel based spreadsheet, and an Information Sharing Protocol Template. It is aimed at improving coordination among service providers and has been used by agencies in Cote d'Ivoire, Ethiopia, Kenya, Liberia, Sierra Leone, Southern Sudan, Thailand, and Uganda. It is currently being rolled out more widely.[34]

3.2.4. Population based surveys

When needed, prevalence estimates and other generalizable data may be obtained through population-based surveys.[35] This information can be used in support of justice processes for example by documenting whether sexual violence is widespread or systematic and can inform allocation of funds for prevention and response programming. These types of studies can be labour and cost intensive, and raise additional safety and ethical considerations. Furthermore, the highly structured nature of most of these studies means that the full range of experiences that a survivor has undergone is unlikely to be captured.

Population based surveys which aim to capture generalizable information about the scope and nature of sexual violence in conflict affected settings have

---

32 On this issue, see also Lynn Lawry, Kirsten Johnson and Jana Asher, "Evidence-Based Documentation of Gender-Based Violence," in *Sexual Violence as an International Crime: Interdisciplinary Approaches*, eds. Anne-Marie de Brouwer, Charlotte Ku, Renée Römkens and Larissa van den Herik (Antwerp, Belgium: Intersentia), *infra*.

33 Additional challenges related to the use of case data are highlighted in Lawry *et al.*, *supra* 32.

34 See gbvims.org.

35 On this issue, see also Lawry *et al.*, *supra* 32.

been conducted in a number of recent and ongoing conflict affected settings including Uganda,[36] Liberia,[37] Sierra Leone,[38] Kosovo,[39] the Democratic Republic of the Congo,[40] Timor Leste,[41] Colombia,[42] and Rwanda.[43] Many of these studies use different methodologies and their findings are therefore not comparable. The purpose and quality of these studies also differ and the findings of some, but not all of these studies, have been subjected to a stringent peer review process and published in academic journals. Others are disseminated through organizational reports and some are not published but rather shared selectively with partner organizations or specific justice processes. It is important when evaluating the findings of a study to understand the background for the survey, the methodology used and its limitations, as well as other factors which

---

36 Akumu Christine Okot, Amony Isabella and Otim Gerald, *Suffering in Silence: A Study of Sexual and Gender Based Violence (SGBV) In Pabbo Camp, Gulu District, Northern Uganda*, 2005; Eugene Kinyanda, Seggane Musisi, Christine Biryabarema, Isaac Ezati, Henry Oboke, Ruth Ojiambo-Ochieng, Juliet Were-Oguttu, Jonathan Levin, Heiner Grosskurth James Walugemb, *War related sexual violence and its medical and psychological consequences as seen in Kitgum, Northern Uganda: A cross-sectional study*, available at www.reliefweb.int/library/documents/2005/unicef-uga-15jun.pdf.

37 See S. Swiss, P. Jennings, G. Aryee, *et al.*, "Violence against Women during the Liberian Civil Conflict," *Journal of the American Medical Association*, 1998; Johnson, Kirsten, Asher, Jana, Rosborough, Stephanie, Panjabi, Raj, Raja, Amisha, Beadling, Charles, Lawry, Lynn, "A Population-based Assessment of Health, Mental Health and Social Functioning of Post-conflict Communities Including Former Child Combatants in Liberia," *Journal of the American Medical Association* 300, no. 6 (2008): 676–90; see also *Research on Prevalence and Attitudes to rape in Liberia September to October* 2008, (New York: United Nation Mission for Liberia), available at www.stoprapenow.org/uploads/advocacyresources/1282163297.pdf.

38 Lynn L. Amowitz, Chen Reis, Kristina Hare Lyons, *et al.*, "Prevalence of War-Related Sexual Violence and Other Human Rights Abuses Among Internally Displaced Persons in Sierra Leone," *Journal of the American Medical Association* 287, no. 4 (2002): 513–21.

39 Michelle Hynes, *Field Tests of a Gender-Based Violence Survey in East Timor and Kosovo: Lessons Learned* (undated), available at www.rhrc.org/resources/general_reports/con03/pdf/michellehynes.pdf.

40 Kirsten Johnson, Jennifer Scott, Bigy Rughita, Michael Kisielewski, *et al.*, "Gender Based Violence and Human Rights Violations in Eastern Democratic Republic of Congo (DRC): The Health Consequences on Individuals, Families and the Community," *Journal of the American Medical Association* 304, no. 5 (2010): 553–62.

41 See Michelle Hynes, *supra* at 39; *Gender-Based Violence in Timor-Leste: A Case Study* (New York: United Nations Population Fund, 2005), available at www.unfpa.org/women/docs/gbv_timorleste.pdf; and Jeanne Ward, *Conducting population-based research on gender-based violence in conflict-affected settings: An overview of a multi-country research project* (United Nations Division for the Advancement of Women, Economic Commission for Europe, and the World Health Organization, 2005), available at www.un.org/womenwatch/ daw/egm/vaw-stat-2005/docs/expert-papers/Ward.pdf.

42 Jeanne Ward, *Conducting population-based research on gender-based violence in conflict-affected settings: An overview of a multi-country research project* (United Nations Division for the Advancement of Women, Economic Commission for Europe, and the World Health Organization, 2005), available at www.un.org/womenwatch/daw/egm/vaw-stat-2005/docs/expert-papers/Ward.pdf.

43 *Ibid.*

may affect the generalizability of the findings. Lawry et al., in this volume provides more information on these types of studies.

4. ETHICAL AND SAFETY ISSUES

As mentioned above, the increased demand for information on the nature and scope of sexual violence during and immediately after conflict by governments, NGOs, and UN bodies (such as the Security Council), have led to increased collection of data on sexual violence in these settings. Regardless of the source of information or reason for its collection and use, and though often motivated by desire to end impunity and help survivors, the ethical safety and methodological issues are not always sufficiently understood by those collecting, sharing and using information.

International community attention to sexual violence in conflict settings is a fairly recent phenomenon. While a number of studies have been conducted,[44] there is still a lack of reliable information about sexual violence including its scope, magnitude and prevalence and risk and causal factors. Furthermore, little is known about the short-term, medium-term and long-term health, psychological and social effects on survivors and their communities. Few prevention and response interventions have been properly evaluated.

Any inquiry into sexual violence must take into account that most survivors remain silent and never disclose what happened to them. This is true even in relatively stable and well resourced settings where services are accessible. In the context of the precarious human rights, political, security, health and legal environment associated with conflict, this reluctance to report is often based on justifiable fears of harmful physical, social or legal consequences. Disclosure may be further affected in conflict and post conflict settings by lack of access to services, disruption of family and community support mechanisms, and ongoing threats to human rights and well-being.

Collection of information about sexual violence requires discussion about a sensitive subject socially, politically and culturally. It often requires those who have experienced sexual violence to recall and speak about a traumatic experience or set of experiences, which may put them at risk of additional emotional, social or even physical harm.

The sensitive nature of the subject matter of sexual violence poses important challenges for anyone aiming to gather data related to this issue and requires that a number of ethical and safety issues be considered and addressed before the start of the data gathering activity. If these issues are not appropriately addressed, there is a very real risk of physical, psychological and social harm to participants. In all settings, it is therefore critical to ensure that there is a legitimate need for

---

44 See *supra* 36–43.

the data and that the information gathering is done in a way that does not cause further harms to those involved in the process including the survivors, families and communities as well as the staff of organizations offering services to survivors, the services themselves as well as those who are involved in the data collection. In a conflict affected setting, the reduction of access to services, the disruption of families and other social support networks, and the context of physical insecurity may exacerbate the likelihood of a negative impact to survivors, their families and communities and those providing critical services and support to them. There are also significant possible additional risks to those collecting the information on sexual violence in these settings.

While there are a number of established ethical guidelines and codes of practice which offer guidance on ethics and safety which can inform gathering of data, which involves human subjects, including the Declaration of Helsinki,[45] the CIOMS-guidelines,[46] and the Belmont Report,[47] there are also a number of guidance documents which address the specific issues that may arise when gathering data on sexual and other forms of gender-based violence.[48] Specific guidance on collection of information about sexual violence in humanitarian including conflict affected settings, however, did not previously exist.

4.1. CONSULTATION

In recognition of the above, and following a 2005 Technical Consultation on Sexual Violence and Exploitation in Conflict Situations,[49] and the Brussels Call

---

45 Declaration of Helsinki (1964), available at www.cirp.org/library/ethics/helsinki/.

46 *International ethical guidelines for biomedical research involving human subjects.* (Geneva, Switzerland: Council for International Organizations of Medical Sciences (CIOMS), 2002), available at www.cioms.ch/frame_guidelines_nov_2002.htm; *International guidelines for ethical review of epidemiological studies*, (Geneva, Switzerland: CIOMS, 1991), available at www.cioms.ch/frame_1991_texts_of_guidelines.htm; *International ethical guidelines for epidemiological studies*, (Geneva, Switzerland: CIOMS, draft April 2007 to supersede the 1991 version (above)), available at www.cioms.ch/070516april_epi_revisions.pdf.

47 *The Belmont Report: Ethical principles and guidelines for the protection of human subjects of research*, (Washington, D.C.: The National Commission for the Protection of Human Subjects of Biomedical and Behavioral Research, 18 April 1979), available at http://ohsr.od.nih.gov/guidelines/belmont.html.

48 *Putting Women First: Ethical and Safety Recommendations for Research on Domestic Violence Against Women* (Geneva, Switzerland: World Health Organization, 2001); Cathy Zimmerman & Charlotte Watts, *WHO ethical and safety recommendations for interviewing trafficked women* (Geneva, Switzerland: World Health Organization, 2003); Mary Ellsberg & Lori Heise, *Researching violence against women: A practical guide for researchers and activists*, (Washington, D.C. World Health Organization, PATH, 2005).

49 Ed. Mendy Marsh, *Report of a technical consultation: methods and systems for the assessment and monitoring of Sexual Violence and Exploitation in Conflict Situations* (New York: Social Science Research Council for the United Nations Population Fund and the World Health Organization, 15–16 December 2005), available at: www.ssrc.org/workspace/images/crm/new_publication_3/%7Bb69cbfd5-da59-de11-bd80–001cc477ec70%7D.pdf.

to Action to Address Sexual Violence in Conflict and Beyond in June 2006,[50] which called on a range of actors including governments, the UN, and civil society to "[u]ndertake comprehensive, ethically and methodologically sound, qualitative and quantitative research on the nature, scope, impact, root causes and contributing factors of sexual and gender-based violence..."[51] The World Health Organization (WHO) convened an expert meeting in late 2006 with participants representing humanitarian, health, and human rights organizations, academic and research institutions, and donors.

The objectives of the meeting were to:

- review experiences, key issues and lessons learned
- develop consensus on recommendations
- identify strengths and weaknesses of different methodological approaches.

During the consultation, eleven case studies were presented in addition to four background and overview presentations about ethical, safety and methodological issues in researching, monitoring and documenting sexual violence in emergencies. Meeting participants identified the scope of existing information gathering activities on sexual violence in conflict settings and discussed a range of ethics, safety, and methodology issues related to this information-gathering. A number of participants raised specific examples of harm resulting from inappropriate collection, sharing and use of data on sexual violence in conflict and post-conflict settings and expressed concerns about worrying practices in the field.

Meeting participants generally agreed that ethical and safety guidance was needed to inform the collection of data on sexual violence in information-gathering efforts, and that those collecting, sharing and using data on sexual violence in conflict settings should be held accountable. They further identified a need for increased information sharing, coordination and collaboration in sexual violence data collection and use.

The draft recommendations of the meeting were shared for consultation with a broader range of stakeholders and the final outcome was a recommendations document – WHO Ethical and Safety Recommendations for Researching, Documenting and Monitoring Sexual Violence in Emergencies (hereafter "WHO recommendations document")[52] – with eight recommendations which related to key aspects of ethics and safety: risks and benefits, methodology, referral to services, safety, confidentiality, informed consent, information gathering team, and special considerations when involving children (see box 2). The WHO

50 *Brussels Call to Action to Address Sexual Violence in Conflict and Beyond* (2006), available at www.unfpa.org/emergencies/symposium06/docs/brusselscalltoactionfinal.doc.

51 *Ibid.*

52 *WHO Ethical and Safety Recommendations for Researching, Documenting, and Monitoring Sexual Violence in Emergencies* (Geneva, Switzerland: World Health Organization, 2007) available at www.who.int/gender/documents/OMS_Ethics&Safety10Aug07.pdf.

recommendations document was further informed by previous work on ethical and safety issues involved in researching violence against women.[53]

Box 2: WHO Ethical and Safety Recommendations for Researching, Documenting, and Monitoring Sexual Violence in Emergencies.

Risks and Benefits
The benefits to respondents or communities of documenting sexual violence must be greater than the risks to respondents and communities.

Methodology
Information gathering and documentation must be done in a manner that presents the least risk to respondents, is methodologically sound, and builds on current experience and good practice.

Referral to services
Basic care and support for survivors/victims must be available locally before commencing any activity that may involve individuals disclosing information about their experiences of sexual violence.

Safety
The safety and security of all those involved in information gathering about sexual violence is of paramount concern, and in emergency settings in particular should be continuously monitored.

Confidentiality
The confidentiality of individuals who provide information about sexual violence must be protected at all times.

Informed consent
Anyone providing information about sexual violence must give informed consent before participating in the data gathering activity.

Information gathering team
All members of the data collection team must be carefully selected and receive relevant and sufficient specialized training and ongoing support.

Children
Additional safeguards must be put into place if children (i.e. those under 18 years) are to be the subject of information gathering.

4.2. THE WHO RECOMMENDATIONS DOCUMENT

The WHO recommendations document resulting from the consultation was designed to be used before the start of information collection on sexual violence in humanitarian settings, and to apply to a range of forms of data collection. It can be used by anyone involved in planning, conducting, funding, reviewing protocols for, approving or supporting information collection on sexual violence in humanitarian settings including researchers, programme planners, funders,

53 See *supra* 48.

ethics review committees, ethicists, managers and staff of humanitarian and human rights organizations, and all those involved in sexual violence inquiries. The eight inter-related recommendations are grounded in core ethical principles including respect for persons, beneficence and justice. The WHO recommendations document is intended to complement and enhance existing professional and ethical standards and guidelines, and inform ethics review processes. It is not intended to be a stand alone document and should be read together with other tools and documents which govern ethical and safe practice related to research and documentation in humanitarian settings.

The following section summarizes some key aspects of each of the recommendations. This summary does not replace the reading of the full WHO recommendations document.

4.3. THE RECOMMENDATIONS

4.3.1. Risks and benefits

Recommendation 1: The benefits to respondents or communities of documenting sexual violence must be greater than the risks to respondents and communities.

It is the responsibility of those who are gathering data on sexual violence in humanitarian settings to ensure that this activity is justified. In order to help users identify whether the information gathering activity is necessary and consider whether the benefits to individuals or communities who will be providing information are greater than the risks to them, box 3 below includes the key questions to be answered by project planners or researchers in the early planning stages. These may also be used by those with oversight or approval responsibilities for data collection activities.

Box 3: Questions to Answer When Planning and Designing Information Collection Activities

- What is the purpose of the proposed data collection activity?
- How likely is it that collecting information in a given way from a given group will achieve the intended purpose?
- What are the likely physical, psychological, social and legal risks to survivors, their families and supporters, and to communities?
- What are the likely physical, psychological, social and legal risks to those involved in collection of the data of the proposed data collection activity?
- How can the above risks be minimized?
- Is it fair to the individuals and the community to ask them to be involved in this activity? Must this population be used? Will they benefit directly?

4.3.2. *Methodology*

Recommendation 2: Information gathering and documentation must be done in a manner that presents the least risk to respondents, is methodologically sound, and builds on current experience and good practice.

A sound understanding of the local context must inform any effort to collect data on sexual violence in humanitarian settings. Those involved in data collection must abide by relevant standards and recommended good practice for data collection and for working with survivors of sexual violence. Before any data are collected, the plan for data analysis and reporting must be elaborated. When compiling existing data (for example information from service providers) this must be done in a way that prevents the linking of data to a specific individual or group of individuals.

There are particular risks that may arise from interviewing survivors of sexual violence or those who are likely to have experienced sexual violence. Several of the recommendations include specific guidance related to directly interviewing survivors of sexual violence. These are summarized in a textbox entitled "Special considerations for interviewing women or other persons who may have experienced sexual violence."[54] Because of the heightened risk associated with interviewing survivors, this should only be considered after all other options have been considered and judged insufficient for gathering critically needed information.

4.3.3. *Referral services*

Recommendation 3: Basic care and support to victims/survivors must be available locally before commencing any activity that may involve individuals disclosing information about their experiences of sexual violence.

In the process of collection of data about sexual violence – especially through interviews with those who may have experienced sexual violence – those collecting the data may encounter individuals who request or who may need specific health or psychosocial services or access to services that can address safety issues. For some these will be issues that arise from the sexual violence but for which they have not been able to seek assistance. In other cases, the participation in the data collection exercise may lead to a need for specific support.

54 *WHO Ethical and Safety Recommendations for Researching, Documenting, and Monitoring Sexual Violence in Emergencies* (Geneva, Switzerland: World Health Organization, 2007), 14, available at www.who.int/gender/documents/OMS_Ethics&Safety10Aug07.pdf.

As such, in any setting where data collection is being considered, it is an ethical imperative that survivors have access to at least basic medical care, psychosocial support and protection from further violence. In order to ensure that these services are available, those undertaking data collection should ensure links with local service providers. If the information collection involves children (i.e. those under 18 years of age) this required basic care and support must include services designed to meet the special needs of children (see recommendation 8, below).

4.3.4. Safety

Recommendation 4: The safety and security of all those involved in information gathering about sexual violence is of paramount concern, and in emergency settings in particular should be monitored continuously.

Given the sensitive nature of an inquiry about sexual violence in a humanitarian setting and the likely inherent insecurity of the setting itself, safety and security must be a paramount concern. The safety and security issues which must be considered relate not just to those from whom information is being gathered but also to anyone involved in or possibly affected by the data collection activity, including the members of the information collection team and the community. A data security plan, which sets out procedures for ensuring that data are protected and which defines principles around data sharing must be in place before the data collection starts. The safety and security issues should be monitored and evaluated throughout the data collection and the data gathering stopped or reconfigured if it is deemed that security has been compromised or that it is unsafe to continue.

4.3.5. Confidentiality

Recommendation 5: The confidentiality of individuals who provide information about sexual violence must be protected at all times.

The right to privacy obligates those collecting personal information to preserve the confidentiality of this information. This means that information disclosed by an individual may not be shared without the specific, explicit and informed consent of the individual. Breaches of confidentiality are not only ethical issues but in humanitarian contexts can lead to serious harm to the survivor, the family, and the community. As such, it is critical that confidentiality be maintained during data collection, when data are stored as well as when they are analyzed. Furthermore, confidentiality considerations must govern whether and how data are shared or publicized. The WHO recommendation document also addresses specific issues related to confidentiality including mandatory reporting requirements, limits to confidentiality in the context of service provisions, and issues related to use of photos, audiotapes and videotapes.

4.3.6. *Informed consent*

Recommendation 6: Anyone providing information about sexual violence must give informed consent before participating in the data gathering activity.

Informed consent is a process which, when applied to gathering of data on sexual violence, aims to ensure that those providing the information understand:

- why it is being collected
- the procedures that will be followed
- the risks and the benefits to themselves if they participate
- their rights to refuse to provide certain information or to participate at all.

It is important to view informed consent as an ongoing process rather than merely a requirement for a form to be signed. To avoid inadvertently coercing people into participating in the information collection exercise, both the content of the information and the way in which it is conveyed must take into account the power dynamics in the local context.

4.3.7. *Information gathering team*

Recommendation 7: All members of the data collection team must be carefully selected and receive relevant and sufficient specialized training and ongoing support.

Careful selection, training and support of those involved in data gathering on sexual violence in humanitarian settings is essential not only for reducing risk for themselves but also for those providing information including survivors. The selection process and criteria for information collection team members should take into account at least age, sex, ethnicity and language skills of team members. All those involved in the information collection activity, whether directly (e.g. interviewers) or in support functions (e.g. drivers) may encounter safety and ethical issues during the process. These issues may differ depending on the role of the team member. As such, all (regardless of role) must be carefully selected, trained and supported.

4.3.8. Children

Recommendation 8: Additional safeguards must be put into place if children (i.e. those under 18 years) are to be the subject of information gathering.

Any information collection activity which involves children must involve additional safeguards to protect them. Every effort must be made to identify possible risks, and anticipate and prevent, or minimize harmful consequences. Children must only be involved if both of the following conditions are in place:

- their inclusion is the only way to get needed information

and

- support services for children are in place.

The recommendation also addresses issues of informed consent specific to children as they may not legally be able to give consent. It also highlights specific additional background information, for example about mandatory reporting rules in the setting, which must be considered by those planning the information collection exercise before starting.

5. CONCLUSION

There are important legal, methodological, ethical and safety issues which must be considered before collecting information on sensitive issues in humanitarian settings. Although many of those seeking information on sexual violence in conflict and post conflict settings are motivated by a desire to end impunity and help survivors, insufficient understanding of and attention to these issues may lead to harm.

When collected, analysed and used correctly and responsibly, data on sexual violence in humanitarian settings can help inform political and justice processes, and prevention and response programming, increase attention to the issue of sexual violence and support efforts to increase resources to address it.

The collection and use of data on sexual violence in humanitarian settings must consider the needs of survivors and should support, rather than undermine or create barriers to the work of those responding to these needs including health and psychosocial support service providers. Efforts to collect, share and use data on sexual violence in conflict affected settings should use appropriate methodological approaches and be based on guidance regarding ethics and safety.

CHAPTER 11

INVESTIGATION OF CRIMES OF SEXUAL AND GENDER-BASED VIOLENCE UNDER INTERNATIONAL CRIMINAL LAW

Maxine Marcus[1]

1. INTRODUCTION

Crimes of sexual and gender based violence are part and parcel of the pattern of international criminal law violations committed in the context of armed conflict and/or mass scale criminal acts constituting crimes against humanity and/or genocide. Yet it is still the case, regrettably, that this category of violation is often approached with greater reluctance, analysed as if it were a separate category unto itself, and not assumed to be a component of every investigation into international criminal law violations. As a result, crimes of sexual and gender-based violence are under-documented and under-included in cases which are brought under international criminal law.

This article dispels myths which may lead to omission of such crimes from the initial investigation plan, or lead investigators and prosecutors to intentionally or inadvertently turn away from such evidence when it is brought to their attention. It will also seek to provide some concrete methods for accessing this evidence, to encourage international criminal investigators and prosecutors to include sexual and gender based violence as a matter of course in any international criminal investigation.[2]

---

1 The views expressed herein are those of the author alone and do not necessarily reflect the views of the International Criminal Tribunal for the Former Yugoslavia or the United Nations in general.

2 This article will be written from the point of view of a prosecutor/investigator engaged in the gathering of evidence of crimes of sexual violence for the purpose of international criminal proceedings. However, it is the author's hope that the perspectives presented herein may be useful to a wide range of practitioners, not only including defence counsel/investigators in international criminal proceedings, but also to others including researchers, human rights researchers and legal practitioners, and litigators in the civil sector who bring cases dealing

2. THE INVESTIGATION PLAN

Every investigation begins with a plan. Ideally, one starts with a clean slate, gathers potential leads, selects from among them, and follows the evidence where it may lead. In reality, due to many factors including most prominently mandate, political, security and resource constraints, there is usually a given starting point. The starting point may be defined by the temporal or geographic jurisdiction of the investigative body, and/or by the management of the investigation. The starting point may be a particular incident, a specific individual, or the leadership of a particular group or groups. It may be a body of information gathered by a particular agency or group which may have been collecting evidence based on techniques which could affect their admissibility in judicial proceedings. As such, it may suggest a certain type of crime or group of alleged perpetrators which may not reflect the reality of events on the ground.

Sexual and gender based violence occurs in all situations of mass violence. This does not mean that the sexual violence will necessarily constitute an international crime – the systematic or widespread nature of the crimes (sexual or non-sexual) may vary, the strength of the available evidence may vary, the strength of the evidence of its nexus to the armed conflict may vary, and the evidence of a link between particular alleged perpetrators and the crimes may vary. This is, however, the case with all crimes/violations; crimes of sexual violence are no different. There is no higher legal standard or higher evidentiary standard which must be reached, or proven, when the subject matter of the evidence involves crimes of sexual violence rather than when the subject matter of the evidence involves non-sexual crimes.

The difference comes in the manner in which evidence of sexual violence violations is considered; the manner in which leads are followed; the manner in which investigative team leaders and decision-makers ensure the investigators follow this evidence and whether they do so in the same manner as they would for evidence of non-sexual crimes.[3] Just as an investigator embarking on an investigation during or following an armed conflict will anticipate receiving evidence of crimes such as killings, torture, arbitrary arrest or detention, persecution through the commission of other criminal acts, an investigator should anticipate that if they look for it, they will discover evidence of sexual violence. When this is presumed to be part of the possible body of evidence, the questioning of witnesses and survivors will ensure that crimes of sexual violence

with large scale criminal acts/human/civil rights violations and who engage with survivors of sexual violence. The author would be pleased to engage in constructive dialogues with anyone engaged in the justice process from any perspective.

3 In other words, all investigation team leaders could ask themselves if they would react in the same way, in terms of instructions to their investigators regarding what leads to follow, to the report of the first account of an act of sexual violence as they would to the report of the first account of an act of non-sexual torture or ill treatment.

are also being investigated as part of the general spectrum of crimes which may have taken place. As a result it will be assumed that each investigative team will comprise individuals with skills enabling them to reach out to survivor-witnesses of sexual violence. It will be assumed that any international criminal investigator will elicit and follow any and all leads in connection with crimes of sexual violence, and will follow those leads just as if they had received evidence of non-sexual crimes.

3. INFORMED PREPARATION

Investigation of crimes of sexual violence under international criminal law poses some challenges, some of which are common to investigation of any international criminal law violation, and some of which are unique to the investigation of sexual and gender based crimes. Some of these challenges are inherent in the nature of conducting investigations in conflict or post-conflict contexts, with the consequent serious security risks to witnesses, investigators, intermediaries and sources; the logistic and infrastructure limitations in which the investigations take place; the political polarisation and sensitivities of the affected communities; the customary and traditional contexts which have often been impacted by domestic or international militarisation and also by the commission of mass crimes; and the post-conflict struggles for basic needs faced by any community – subsistence levels of food, water, shelter, medical care, family reunification, and many more critical needs. In this context international investigators and prosecutors endeavour to bring some hope of accountability, without raising expectations unrealistically. The methods explored in this article are put forward as proposed methods of overcoming some of these obstacles to the gathering of evidence of crimes of sexual and gender-based violence; but most proposals apply equally to investigation of any international criminal law violations.

3.1. INFORMATION

Information is the central way to smooth the path of the investigation and protect the survivor-witness, with the consequent benefit of safely obtaining high quality comprehensive evidence. Prior to conducting any investigation the prosecutor/investigator requires extensive information, preferably from first-hand sources. In general, the more information the investigative team and prosecutors possess during the planning process prior to deployment, the better prepared the team will be. The more information obtained in advance, the lower the security risk to potential witnesses, sources, intermediaries, interlocutors, and the investigative team itself. Field investigators, in practice, make moment-to-moment decisions of all kinds each day. The decision may be which village to visit; which individual to talk to out of a list of scores of leads; which witness is reluctant due to security concerns versus which witness is reluctant due to belligerence which could pose a security threat; which source to accept advice from and which not; which intermediary to engage to contact the witness and which not; which community is too intermingled with potentially dangerous persons in positions of power; which survivor-witness is simply risking too much or too at-risk to be interviewed or approached at all. The decisions taken by investigators on a moment by moment basis can have a profound impact upon the witness, her/his community, and the path of the investigation.

Even the most seasoned international criminal investigator will agree that much of the on-the-spot decision-making which an investigator is obliged to do will be based upon instinct. Relying upon instinct in communities not one's own is exceedingly difficult – and potentially risky. If possible at all, the instinctive ability to make sound judgements calls in foreign contexts can be bolstered by preparing oneself with as much information in advance as possible.

3.2. TOPICS FOR ADVANCED PREPARATION

An investigator would be greatly assisted with as much information as possible at least in relation to the following subjects. The list is intended only as a beginning and is presented in question form, with the suggestion that the more the investigator and prosecutors can be prepared prior to deployment with answers to these and other related questions, the more likely the successful and safe access to hard-to-gather evidence such as evidence of crimes of sexual violence can be secured.[4]

3.2.1. Political structures, affiliations, motivations and methodology

Who are the groups and individuals in positions of power prior to the conflict, during, and after the conflict, and in the current investigative climate? What is the relationship between the different political alliances and the military, police, paramilitary, civilian structures and other persons in authority positions? What are the political platforms, motivations, goals and methodologies employed by the relevant political actors and groups? What is the relationship between

[4] It may be that in certain circumstances where little-to-no information is available from outside sources, an advance mission should be deployed to gather the required information. In fact, the author strongly recommends conducting an advance mission wherever possible. Though resource constraints may not permit this, in practice significant resources are saved due to the advance mission – it may prove far more effective and far safer for witnesses, investigators, interlocutors, and the investigation itself than sending out an investigative team to improvise on the ground.

different societal groups, ethnic, religious, customary leaders, and the political structures, groups and individuals? Which groups played which roles in the conflict and what are their positions in the investigative context?

3.2.2. *Military, police, paramilitary and/or other armed group structures and affiliations, motivations and methodology*

Who are the military, police, paramilitary and/or other armed groups and authorities and what role, if any, did/do they play before, during and after the conflict, and in the current investigative climate? What is their relationship to each other and to other authority and community structures? What are their platforms, motivations, goals and methodologies? What is the relationship between different societal groups, ethnic, religious, customary leaders, and these armed groups and individuals? What were the various roles in the conflict and what are their positions in the investigative context?

3.2.3. *The history and pattern of the conflict*

What was the cause of the conflict and the pattern of its evolution? What factors had an impact upon the manner in which the conflict took place? Who were the parties involved, what was their historical role and position and what was the geographic and temporal scope of the conflict? What are the historical motivations, affiliations and allegiances among the parties and if this changed throughout the conflict, what factors caused these changes?

3.2.4. *Customary and traditional context within which the witnesses/survivors live(d) and within which the crimes took place, and within which the investigation will be conducted*

What is the belief system of the affected community? What are the gender constructs, what role and position does each gender and age group hold in the community? What is the nature of women's and girl's access to education, leadership positions, employment, economic resources, civil and political and economic and social rights? What are the rites of passage, the marital and relationship practices, and customary views on sexuality? What is the traditional and customary response of the community (including the law enforcement authorities and traditional leaders) to sexual and gender based violence (against women/girls or against men/boys) and how did these views change – if at all – in the context of armed conflict or mass violence? Who are the individuals in the community who may serve as advisors or support-persons to the potential survivor-witnesses – whether male or female? What are the consequences which would be faced by a survivor who comes forward within his or her community to say that s/he has survived a crime of sexual violence? Who are those individuals who could facilitate safe access to the survivor-witnesses?

3.2.5. *The security situation from the highest levels of official government or non-state party control levels to the direct communal security situation*

Which groups and individuals might pose a threat to the witnesses, interlocutors and sources, and the investigative team and its information? Why would they pose a threat and what motivates the threat? Is there a way to diffuse this threat through positive engagement? How great is the threat and what is its proximity to the affected community and individuals among whom the evidence will be gathered? What is their network like? How able are they to access the community and individuals being contacted by the investigator? Are there local, traditional, communal mechanisms that might mitigate the security risk? How great is the risk that the survivor-witness or the intermediary takes in engaging in the justice process, beginning with the first interaction with the investigator? (This last question is one which covers not only physical security concerns for the survivor-witness and his or her family and community, but also what other consequences does s/he face as a consequence of coming forward with the evidence)? What steps can the team or individual investigator take to minimize the exposure of the community and/or the survivor-witness due to their interaction with the investigation?

3.2.6. *Presence and mandate of other agencies*

What other local and international agencies and individuals have been present and operating in the zone where the proposed witnesses are – humanitarian, legal/judicial, international and national, political, media, NGOs? What services have been offered to the affected community, and what has been the manner of provision of those services – the criteria and the methodology? What other organisations and individuals may have been present during the commission of certain crimes, and what role did they play in the conflict or protection or security for the targeted community?[5] What information or misinformation may have been shared by these agencies or organisations with the affected community? What if any justice-related outreach activities have been conducted

[5] Often the post-war international presence is completely different in personnel and agencies than those present during the conflict. Information sharing may not have occurred and the post-war institutional memory may not reach back to the conflict itself. International investigators arriving after the conflict may find international interlocutors who do not have much information about what happened; and who may even be inadvertently cooperating with individuals associated with wartime perpetrator groups. In such circumstances extreme caution is recommended, and the more information the investigator has about the mandate of that international agency the better the investigator will be able to weigh the information they have provided.

among the affected community – and to what extent has this outreach impacted upon the community's willingness to engage with the justice process?

3.2.7. *Existence of other research/interviewing/evidence gathering or information gathering activities in which prospective witnesses have engaged*

What other individuals and organisations have been documenting events in the region, whether through observation or through interviews?[6] What has the nature of their interaction been with the affected community and individuals, and what methodology has been employed by those agencies in interacting with these witnesses? Has any of the information been documented and should the investigative team seek to gain access to that documentation? What information have these agencies been sharing with the affected communities, and to what extent has misinformation about the mandate of the investigative team and/or the international justice mechanism been spread? Have there been any negative or positive consequences to the affected community as a result of such contact? Does this prior contact with any of the survivor-witnesses increase or decrease the risk to the witness of contact with investigators? Does the fact that these individuals have previously spoken to other agencies and individuals have an impact on the evidence?[7] Are there groups of survivors who have not been spoken to or have been overlooked for ethnic, religious, cultural or other reasons of bias?

---

6 See also See also Lynn Lawry, Kristen Johnson, and Jana Asher, "Evidence-based Documentation of Gender-based Violence," in *Sexual Violence as an International Crime: Interdisciplinary Approaches*, eds. Anne-Marie de Brouwer, Charlotte Ku, Renée Römkens and Larissa van den Herik (Antwerp, Belgium: Intersentia), *infra*; Chen Reis, "Ethical, Safety and Methodological Issues Related to Collection and Use of Data on Sexual Violence in Conflict" in Sexual Violence as an International Crime: Interdisciplinary Approaches, eds. Anne-Marie de Brouwer, Charlotte Ku, Renée Römkens and Larissa van den Herik (Antwerp, Belgium: Intersentia), *supra*.

7 For example, there are some emergency relief agencies who operate in or near the conflict zones, and whose staff are the very first to make contact with survivors. In providing those individuals with emergency medical care, shelter, food aid, they may receive information – often abundant and in some cases first-hand information – regarding the details of the attacks the in-dividuals survived. During such information-gathering for the purpose of service-provision, much crucial evidence in relation to international criminal law or human rights violations may be received by these agencies. When a justice-related institution seeks such information from a humanitarian organisation, this places the agency in an unenviable conundrum; they have a well-founded reason to fear that their access for service-provision may be hampered if not blocked should they provide this information to any judicial body whether international or national. But yet, they will struggle with the knowledge that they are in a sense observing crimes being committed, are in fact nearly or actually witnesses to those crimes, and they may feel helpless to stop or report the crimes. Many agencies operating in regions of conflict and post-conflict are struggling with this dilemma. International investigators and prosecutors, recognising and appreciating this dilemma, can strive to find methods of constructive engagement, where possible, with such agencies and individuals.

The greater the body of information the investigator possesses prior to engaging in first contact with survivor-witnesses, the more likely the success of the evidence-gathering exercise and the greater the likelihood that the survivor-witness will have a positive experience with the justice process. Some reasons for this are listed below.

a) Each day as the on-the-ground investigation advances, the team gains more information and the path of the investigation needs to be accordingly somewhat adjusted. Much of the initial period of an investigation is spent acclimatising to and familiarising oneself with the context. The direction the investigation takes may well alter numerous times according to many factors as the evidence emerges. However, the more the team knows before heading out to the field, the less time will be lost and fewer resources expended in the early phases of the field work. The team will better navigate the nuances of initial contacts, employing a more refined awareness of the aspects which impact upon initial interactions;
b) The more information the investigator possesses when arriving on the ground, the less chance they will be led astray or fall prey to the suggestions or guidance of "advisors" with their own agenda who can disable the investigator's ability to follow the evidence impartially where it may lead;
c) The investigator can also better avoid inadvertently sharing information with individuals or organisations who may have ill intentions and who may pose a security threat of some kind, either to person, to information or to means of access to witnesses and other sources of information;
d) The investigator can demonstrate to a survivor-witness that they have a familiarity with the context, history, geography, terminology, such that when the witness alludes to or makes reference to a particular political structure or event or group, this knowledge will contribute to the confidence-building process which is so crucial to testimonial evidence-gathering from survivors of sexual and gender based violence crimes.[8]

---

8 Many agencies and judicial institutions may have departments which have specific expertise in obtaining and analysing this and other information relevant to a particular investigation and case. Criminal analysts, leadership research teams, and other researchers and scholars may have particular knowledge of the region in which the investigation is being conducted. Depending upon the resources and infrastructure under which the investigation is taking place, the investigative team itself may not be obliged to gather this information – it may be outsourced and the information may be provided to the investigative and prosecution team by those best equipped to gather and assess this information.

3.3. SECURITY AND ACCESS TO EVIDENCE

Assuming the investigator has done as much pre-mission research as possible and developed a detailed understanding, s/he should have an idea of the contours of the affected community and their proximity to the alleged perpetrators and other affiliated hostile or potentially dangerous influences. An assessment of the method of access to evidence of crimes of sexual violence in these contexts must necessarily be based upon a detailed familiarity with the matters raised in the section above. This is not a part of the investigation – if ever such a part exists – which can just be done through experimentation. The potential to place witnesses and their families and communities in danger is great, and a side effect of such consequences is that the evidence becomes even more difficult to access due to the lack of confidence which will be justifiably felt by any witness or community whose security has been placed at risk by evidence-gatherers. Another side effect of this may be that the survivor-witness who seeks access to justice could face even greater obstacles in coming forward with this evidence; now s/he faces not only her own trepidation but also may risk antagonising or even directly placing at risk her own family or community.

There is no blueprint for safely accessing this evidence which would apply in all contexts. Suggestions for proceeding start with certain recommendations which run throughout this piece. First, questions relating to alleged crimes of sexual violence should be put to all witnesses without assumptions as to who might have such information or who might be the potential victims of such crimes (either men or women may be victims or perpetrators, and the perpetrator/victim group for crimes of sexual violence might not be the same as for other crimes). That said, this body of evidence might not be accessible in depth in the initial phases of an investigation. If such evidence is elusive, this is likely because it has not yet been discovered – not because such crimes have not occurred. At the very early stages of the field investigation much damage can be done through an absence of sufficient information about the affected community within which the survivor-witnesses reside. Once the prosecutors/investigators have gained sufficient information about the survivor witness's community, strategies for access will become quite obvious assuming the investigative team is looking and listening for options for access.

There are some general trends which might apply to a multitude of contexts in terms of methods of gaining access. First, access to survivor-witnesses of sexual violence in conflict or post conflict contexts must most always be done through intermediaries. It is difficult to conceive a situation where an international investigator may simply drive her/his 4x4 up to the tent where the sought witness resides, step out of the vehicle with the interpreter and possibly a psychosocial support person, be welcomed into the tent, ask all others to leave, and start interviewing the survivor. This scenario is not realistic within the context in which these investigations take place. An intermediary is necessary and must be chosen with great care. Some suggestions appear below but it must be emphasised that these are only suggestions and may not be applicable in the particular context of a particular investigation. Investigators should primarily rely upon the information gained through answers to the above and other questions in determining how to proceed.

In approaching a community it may be useful if not advisable to have formal official meetings with community leaders of all kinds to dispel misconceptions, to reach out to them to explain the mandate of your organisation, and generally to start the process of confidence building through transparent information sharing. This is not to suggest that any details of the investigative plan or strategy should be shared in such contexts; that is clearly not advisable. In fact, those who carry out these formal official outreach informational sessions may well need to be staff other than those who will ultimately be interviewing the at-risk witnesses and questioning insiders.

Nonetheless, from formal introductory meetings with communal leaders, information may be obtained regarding the kind of medical care which is provided to male or female survivors of sexual violence in the community, any support mechanisms which exist in the community, who the midwives are, who the teachers are, who the other communal advisors are and where they stay. It can be determined to what extent the community authorities are aware that such crimes have occurred, how the communal authorities and those in power are likely to react to such allegations, and in this way, information can be gathered as to what obstacles any survivor-witness must face in coming forward with such evidence, even where great care is taken.

Following these formal meetings, information can be sought as to the affiliations of the midwives, women community leaders, support persons and teachers, to try to determine whether they would be potentially helpful interlocutors between the investigators and the survivors/witnesses – or rather whether their involvement might increase the risk to the survivor-witness or to the evidence. Later, once the formal official meetings have taken place, a trusted intermediary can be deployed to reach out to the midwife, the women community leaders, possibly teachers (depending upon the affiliations of the above) and arrange for a private meeting with investigators. And such "reaching out" will then be done with substantial information about the context, the resources, the attitude of the communal leadership to both the internationals as well as the consequent obstacles faced by any survivor-witness in coming forward with such information.[9]

---

9 There are some contexts in which official or formal meetings will not be advisable and may even pose additional security risks, and where only covert methods may be employed in accessing evidence. Every context is different and advance preparation with information can assist in making these determinations of how best to proceed.

Identification of potential communal interlocutors: The identification of potential interlocutors and sources is the job of the investigative team, who may need to find other sources for obtaining information about potential safe communal interlocutors. Some of these have been explored above – and it is in the context of these meetings between the investigator and the midwife/female community leader/teacher/support person/nurse or medical staff that key connections can be developed and bridges built. These contacts may themselves turn out to be survivor-witnesses themselves, or may prove to be excellent overview witnesses later on should that be helpful and should they be willing. But regardless of whether they themselves ultimately become witnesses before the court, these relationships can be the key to accessing the survivor witnesses themselves.

This method may not be appropriate in certain communities where relationships of trust are dramatically few and far between. This may have been as a result of a deep seated conflict which has altered alliances and infused fear and distrust into the community and irreparably damaged the social network and individual capacity for trust. Or it may result from unfortunate experiences with post conflict contact with individuals and/or organisations which have negatively impacted on people's trust of outsiders or foreigners. In such cases it may be more difficult to access survivor witnesses.[10]

It is important to bear in mind that international crimes of sexual violence may take place individually against individual victims over the course of a conflict, and/or the crimes may be committed through an organised system such as in the context of detention centres.[11] Yet again, the more information the

---

10 Witnesses should always be interviewed one-on-one. However, there are often large numbers of victims of a particular pattern of crime, and once an investigator gains the trust of a respected intermediary, there may be numerous survivor-witnesses who survived the same crime or the same pattern of criminal acts who are willing to come forward. Building a relationship of trust with such an intermediary can lead to the nearly instantaneous discovery of a large body of evidence of crimes of sexual violence.

11 Crimes of sexual violence – as with crimes of a non-sexual nature – need not be committed in a system-type context such as a detention centre in order to be international crimes. A woman who was harmed by being gang raped by a group of perpetrators using clubs does not have less access to justice in the international context than she would have had had she been "gang beaten" on her head by the same group of perpetrators using the same clubs in precisely the same context. The sexual nature of the crime does not add an additional threshold from a legal perspective. The specific elements of the crime which was allegedly committed must be met. Common elements of war crimes or violations of the laws and customs of war, crimes against humanity, and genocide must be satisfied in order to bring charges in relation to sexual as well as non-sexual acts of violence, and the linkage elements to an Accused must be satisfied as well in order to bring charges in relation to sexual as well as non-sexual acts of violence. As long as the specific, general, and linkage elements can be satisfied, the crime can be charged and with sufficient evidence, may result in a conviction. There are a multitude of considerations for prosecutors in the context of prosecutorial discretion, scope of mandate, there may also be jurisdictional limitations regarding what charges can be brought for what crimes. Certainly if there is less evidence gathered for some crimes than for others, choices about charges may result rightly from the evidence. But from a purely legal perspective, there

investigative team has at its disposal in advance of the field investigation, the greater the likely success of the investigation.

4. THE FIELD INVESTIGATION – EVIDENCE-GATHERING

A witness should be approached with patience and respect; be given whatever time necessary in telling the story – or be given the choice to decide not to tell it in whole or in part, at any point; s/he should be confident that his or her physical and emotional security will be prioritised over the evidence-gathering process, and to anticipate that s/he will be provided with full information prior to consenting and electing to participate in the justice process; s/he should be empowered and not harmed in any way through the investigative and judicial process; s/he should not have any assumptions made on her or his behalf and should not be mislead or promised something that s/he may not or will not receive or experience. There is no simple path toward accessing this evidence while keeping in mind these and other justified expectations that the survivor-witness has. Every investigative context is different, every witness is unique, every investigator will have her/his own refined skills and every dynamic between two or more persons has its own rhythm. This section will contain some thoughts and suggestions regarding practices which have proven effective in a variety of settings, and ideas to consider as possible paths toward maximising the protection of the survivor-witness, while simultaneously accessing evidence of crimes of sexual violence.

4.1. FIRST CONTACT

The first moment of contact between the investigator and the survivor-witness will determine the relationship and the success of the evidence-gathering. In the first few moments of the meeting between investigator and survivor-witness – much as with any first impression one has upon meeting another individual – the path will be set and difficult to alter thereafter.

It is especially critical when determining the method, timing, manner of first approach, in deciding how best to approach the survivor-witness and their community/family environment, or the degree to which to be circumspect, that we rely upon the information we have gleaned from our preparation and initial meetings. All factors are relevant in making this decision – security factors are paramount, but of course other factors play a vital role as well – customary and

is no additional legal requirement or hurdle which must be overcome for crimes of a sexual nature than there is for crimes of a non-sexual nature.

traditional contextual circumstances, political influences and geographic considerations, all contribute to the decision regarding how, when, under what circumstances and through what intermediary, if any, to approach the survivor-witness.

To a certain extent some of this is common sense; if we know that the community in which the survivor-witness lives prepares food for the one daily communal meal from 8-10 A.M., to the extent the survivor-witness is centrally involved in this food preparation, we should avoid asking her to forego a vital daily need for her community to speak to us. Clearly, any time we ask an individual to take time – hours or more – out of any daily routine to speak to investigators, this will require a degree of sacrifice on their part. Our evidence-gathering process should at all times endeavour to minimise the negative impact upon the witness and should require as few sacrifices on her/his part as feasible. The mere act of demonstrating to a witness that an investigator has taken their daily obligations, work schedule, family rituals, seasonal context or religious practices into consideration in the context of the first approach, will raise the confidence of the witness.[12] Doing so will demonstrate that their lives are a priority, that their daily routine is a priority, that they, in fact, are the priority – over the priorities or schedule of the investigator, or the evidence. This will help to pave the way for a positive first contact and interview dynamic.[13]

---

12 For example, if prayer time arrives during an interview, the survivor-witness may already have decided not to attend prayers so as not to show disrespect to the outside visitors. But if the investigator asks the witness whether they would like to take a break for prayers, whether or not they accept, the offer can contribute to confidence building and relationships of trust. This witness will take a lesson from this that this particular investigator – or agency – knows her community, respects her belief systems, and is not as much of an outsider. This may lead the witness to feel more comfortable sharing additional detail highly relevant to the investigation. For example, if there had been ethnic slurs uttered in the context of the criminal acts, the witness may otherwise be reluctant to repeat such phrases so as to not have to explain to the outsider what this means. But now believing the investigator to be familiar with the traditions and terminology of the community, s/he may come forward more easily with such evidence, confident that s/he will not need to resort to a lesson in the community's religion or customs. The more one feels one needs to explain, the more one may be inhibited – the explanation itself can be daunting. The more one feels understood, the more one feels free to speak. This is common sense – but it works successfully in the context of working with vulnerable survivor-witnesses as well.

13 All suggestions contained herein about confidence-building between an investigator/researcher and a witness are contingent upon an understanding that there must always be a professional and objective distancing between these two individuals. Confidence-building strategies must never cross the professional objective boundaries between witness and investigator or prosecutor.

4.2. GREETINGS AND INTRODUCTIONS

The more an investigator/researcher can approach a prospective witness, intermediary or community leader in the local customary manner, the greater the chance that the confidence-building will commence from the moment of first contact. If men do not shake women's hands in that community, or if it is viewed as impolite or inappropriate to make eye contact at first introduction, an offer of a handshake by a male investigator to a female survivor-witness or a meeting of the eyes might serve to offend the survivor-witness and thus block the path toward confidence building and information sharing. A survivor-witness may have met others from different backgrounds and may be aware that there are other methods of greeting – and may even understand this and may even be willing to make exceptions – but the more we place someone in a strange and unfamiliar encounter, the less comfortable s/he will feel. The message that is sent is again that our practices and priorities and customs are of greater priority and that s/he must do the adapting rather than the investigator doing so. The subtlety of these messages – as inadvertent as they are on the part of the international researcher/investigator – can contribute to increasing the gaps between the international investigator and the witness. This in turn can render the information-sharing less likely.

Many communities have customary greetings – whereas it may be common in certain places say hello and then immediately proceed to broach the subject matter of the meeting or encounter, this may be considered inappropriate – and in fact shocking – in some communities. As with the other examples herein, if the investigator knows that one must first sit and discuss the weather, the rains, the harvest, the celebrations or recent traditional events, the family or any other matters first, engaging in these subjects of conversation may serve to put the survivor-witness at ease. Yet again, though s/he may not expect as much from an outsider, this can be done as a matter of course (where it is the custom), setting the stage for trust and confidence. If the investigator/researcher can learn a few words of greeting in the language of the witness, this can further contribute to the building of trust. It shows that the investigator respects the witness, is willing to step outside her/his comfort zone, take risks, expose their outsiderness – and in turn can show immense respect for the community, language and practices of the survivor-witness.[14]

[14] To the extent possible, the investigator should also sit the way the witness is sitting – if the witness is sitting on the floor so too should the investigator. In any case, it is advisable for the investigator to avoid sitting higher up than the witness, such as sitting on a chair while the witness sits on the floor.

4.3. POWER DYNAMICS

Someone who has survived a crime of sexual violence, as with many victims of violent crimes, has been disempowered by the perpetrator. Though everyone who survives violence will have a personal reaction which will differ not only due to context and community but due to character and personality and so many other factors, a victim has survived a violent abuse of their bodily integrity and their control over their own person. As international investigators/researchers/analysts/prosecutors – whatever our position, we have power. This is not certainly the abusive power of the perpetrator – yet it is indeed a power, a power of privilege, a power of resources, a power of decision making, a power of access, a power of information and knowledge. This power is the kind we intend to use for good – to bring justice. But the survivor-witness may not encounter this power as a positive one, in particular to the extent s/he feels in any way disempowered by the process of interaction with the investigator/prosecutor. The more we can do to assist the witness in experiencing a sense of empowerment through the interview – and later on the testimonial and judicial – process, the greater gift we give the witness, the consequent greater the likelihood that s/he will choose to engage in the justice process. Furthermore, the greater the likelihood that s/he will withstand the rigours of testimony and cross-examination – and emerge with a sense that s/he has brought justice and justice has been brought to her or him. There is no formula for empowerment – but to the extent we can take the time for the witness to take the lead in information sharing, to the extent we can show the witness that s/he has a choice of whether to speak, when and in what contexts to share, how to explain what has happened, what terminology to use in the first instance description – the more likely s/he may feel empowered through the interview process. For example, a witness may choose a particular term to refer to the perpetrators. It may be a slang term used by the community, it may be a word in the witness's language which means soldier or police officer or it may even be a pejorative term for an evil person, or a devil. Obviously the investigator hearing the witness's evidence will ultimately need to learn as much as possible about that perpetrator – they will need to know to what armed group if any they belonged; what uniform they were wearing; what words and language they spoke; what equipment they carried; what vehicles they drove; what insignia they bore – the term which will ultimately be used in a courtroom setting will not be the same as the word first used by the witness in the first contact interview process. But there is no need to rush; patience is an investigator's friend in such instances. The witness's choice of word can be echoed back to the witness by the investigator after the first use, to ask a follow-up question. A person hearing back the same word they used may feel heard and reaffirmed and attended to. This may in turn inspire increased confidence, and assist the witness in providing greater detail.[15]

Undoubtedly, in the final judicial context, the witness will be faced with the legal terminology, judicial procedures, and courtroom dynamic that is unavoidable. But to the extent the interaction which precedes the presentation of his or her evidence in court can also serve to empower the witness – or at least minimise additional feelings of disempowerment – the greater our contribution to the witness's protection and as a by product, the more thorough and accurate and effective the information-gathering process may be.[16]

4.4. INFORMED CONSENT

Putting into words the subtle dynamic that takes place between an interviewer and a victim is difficult to do – in situations such as those which international investigators/researchers find themselves, the interviewer must strike a balance. The balance is between on the one hand, building confidence and reasonable trust in the witness such that s/he feels comfortable to share his/her experiences, feels empowered through the telling, and opts to seek justice for the crimes of which s/he was a victim; while on the other hand, taking care to ensure that the witness does not unduly rely upon the ability of the investigator to protect them,

15 The contrary is also true. For example, if a witness describes a perpetrator as a "soldier" and then describes what the "soldiers" did, obviously a witness might not be referring, necessarily, to a member of the armed forces – the term soldier could be a term used for any armed individual with any uniform or even just a weapon-bearing person. The term soldier without further context or description is legally useless. However, it is not advisable for the investigator to answer the witness, just after s/he has used this term in describing an act of violence, to say well what did the rebel say? Now, the investigator may know from prior extensive experience that when witnesses in that community use the term "soldier" they usually mean a member of the rebel forces. But in this case, not only has the investigator influenced the evidence of the witness toward this conclusion – but the investigator has also changed the terminology of the witness immediately after a particular term was used. This interaction can serve to cause a witness to feel unheard – it may even lead to a confrontation – s/he may rightly say, "I did not say rebel, I said soldier" – and returning to a place of comfort and trust from this place is not easy to achieve. These are subtle suggestions – the recommendation is that we use as many of the same terms as the witness uses in the first instance questioning, and then later, we can explain that we need a bit more detail and explanation and ask the witness to explain precisely as possible what she meant when she used the term "soldier." This will lead to the same evidentiary result – through a much more reaffirming and respectful process.

16 International criminal investigations are usually taking place through the use of interpreters. The subject of interpreters deserves an article unto itself – for the purposes of this discussion, it should just be noted that an interpreter's role is critical, that standard guidelines should be followed in working with interpreters, in particular in the context of such sensitive investigations. Selection and preparation of interpreters must be conducted with extreme caution, in knowledge of as much information as possible about the context of the investigation. The significance of the potential influence of an investigator – positive or negative – on the investigation cannot be overstated.

to achieve justice for them, or in fact, to make any even small promise or assurance at all – even the promise to come visit them again. Practitioners in all aspects of the international justice process know well that unpredictable events or matters – legal, factual, procedural – arise at all stages of any trial process. There are no benefits – in fact there are only drawbacks – to making assurances of any kind to a particular witness even where the investigator truly believes that those assurances are based upon matters s/he can control – because in the case that for some unanticipated reason the investigator cannot deliver on those assurances, there may be a potential harm to that witness (and as a by-product to the evidence). The evidence-gathering process is about the experiences of that individual witness, and s/he has a right of control over with what organisations and individuals s/he shares that information. It is our duty as professionals in this field to be clear and direct about what can be done and what cannot be done, what the protections are – and what they are not, what the process involves and what it does not, to the extent possible. This is not to say that at the first meeting with a survivor-witness an investigator must go into precise detail about the courtroom process – this is merely to say that the investigator should endeavour to ensure at all times that any provision of information by the witness is based upon an understanding of what s/he is getting into, of what the potential ultimate use for that information may be, of what the organisation does and what its powers are – and what its powers are not. The seasoned investigator will know that in some circumstances, being forthcoming about matters such as protective measures and their ultimate effectiveness may serve to dissuade a particular witness/survivor from coming forward – in such situations the investigator faces a conundrum. With complete information, the investigator will be equipped to assess how much detail to offer at the first meeting, how much more to provide at the second. Nonetheless, it is the author's view that it is the ethical obligation of any researcher or investigator or prosecutor to ensure that s/he accurately explains what can and what cannot be done to protect a particular witness – so that the witness can make their own decision about whether to proceed. No doubt all practitioners agree that it is better to lose some evidence than obtain it through the raising of false hopes or assurances, whether among individuals or entire communities.

5. ORGANISATION OF THE EVIDENCE-GATHERING TO SUPPORT WHAT NEEDS TO BE PROVEN IN COURT: THE "EVIDENCE CHECKLIST"

This section will briefly introduce a proposed methodology for the organisation of the evidence gathered in the context of an investigation of crimes of sexual violence under international criminal law. The proposed methodology provides a means of testing the information gathered from individual survivor/victims to ensure that the statement taken or information report prepared by the investigator contains sufficient detail and covers as many relevant areas as possible. This testing method allows prosecutors and investigators to clearly identify and fill gaps well in advance of the trial process.

For the survivor-witness, this methodology has benefits as well. The more thorough the content of any interview with a survivor-witness, the fewer times those crisis moments need to be reviewed by investigators and prosecutors with the witness in the future. The fewer times the witness is obliged to repeat in this amount of detail in the context of interviews with investigators and prosecutors, the less the survivor-witness is obliged to relive the tragic experiences.[17] This method could also ensure that the full picture of the witness's experiences is documented as soon as possible, thus preserving the freshness of their memory.[18] In addition, the more thorough the initial interview notes, the better the investigator and prosecutor will be able to assess the likelihood of this witness being called to testify – thus avoiding any possible raising of hopes with later disappointment.[19]

---

17 Ideally, some degree of healing may take place for survivors of serious trauma through the telling and re-telling of their experiences. In the author's experience, some survivor-witnesses do report after the judicial process is over that the process of telling and re-telling has indeed been cathartic for them; whereas others implore the investigator or prosecutor not to oblige her or him to repeat the details yet again. It would be outside the author's expertise to comment upon any psychosocial benefit or detriment to a particular individual of recounting repeatedly their traumatic experiences – though it is common sense that any benefit or detriment may vary for each particular witness. Regardless, however, of how kind, patient, and respectful any individual investigator, prosecutor, victim support person or judge may be in relation to the survivor-witness, it would be inappropriate and inaccurate for one to suggest that an interview with an investigator or prosecutor may in any way be comparable to a treatment process by a trained psychologist or psychotherapist. Furthermore, it would be a conflict of interest and professionally inappropriate for any investigator or prosecutor to act in any way in the role of a psychosocial support person with respect to a particular witness. In an abundance of caution, the author recommends striving for as few requests for recounting of the central details as possible under the circumstances. The proposed methodology may serve to minimise the number of times a witness is obliged to reiterate the description of the traumatic event in the context of an interview with investigators and prosecutors.

18 It is not uncommon in international criminal practice for prosecutors and investigators to return to reinterview witnesses who had been interviewed years prior to try to fill gaps or clarify critical points which only come to light when the trial is being prepared and the witness's testimony approaches. Whereas to some extent this may be unavoidable as the full picture of a particular case only emerges as the case develops in trial, the proposed methodology endeavours to minimise the need for substantive re-interviews years after the first interview with a particular survivor-witness.

19 Making promises or raising hopes of any kind should be avoided to the extent possible in working with survivors of sexual and gender-based violence. In speaking about the possibility of testimony, it is difficult not to raise the hope in that survivor-witness (if they are inclined to wish to testify) that they will indeed be called. The more thorough the notes from the interview with that witness/survivor, the better able the investigator/prosecutor will be to

Simply put, the reality of the current situation is that any information gathered from a survivor-witness, regardless of who gathers it, may ultimately be used in the context of judicial proceedings. From the prosecution point of view, in order to bring a case or present evidence in support of charges, certain elements of crimes must be proven. If any aspect of any element of a crime charged cannot be supported by the evidence, the Prosecution will not succeed in proving its case – the burden is on the Prosecution to prove every aspect of every crime through presentation of evidence, and any Accused will be acquitted of that crime should the Prosecution not meet its burden in any respect.

The elements of international crimes may be broken down into three main groups:

1. **Specific elements** of the specific crime.
2. **Common elements** of the category of international crime into which this specific crime falls.
3. **Linkage elements** which link the commission of each crime to a particular accused person or persons.

Any investigation into international criminal law violations may be broadly organised according to these three categories, and a checklist emerges from this which enables the investigator to test whether s/he has comprehensively documented all the evidence which a particular survivor-witness may bring. Addressing all three categories of information/evidence with each witness will ensure that the witness's evidence is as comprehensively explored as possible; it will also assist the investigator/prosecutor in avoiding serious omissions in the evidence-gathering process.

5.1. SPECIFIC ELEMENTS OF SPECIFIC CRIMES

This is perhaps the most straightforward category – it is focused on the details of the actual act(s) which the survivor-witness experienced or witnessed. This category is also perhaps the most obvious to any person interviewing a survivor-witness. The investigator can be assisted by knowing the elements of the crimes of which the survivor-witness was a victim. If the investigator has at hand the elements which need to be proven, that can serve as a reminder of what questions to ask the witness. Those elements may vary by jurisdiction to some extent and the methodology can be adapted according to the elements which have to be met in the jurisdiction within which the investigation is taking place. For example, in order to prove the crime of rape in court according to the elements of crimes at

assess the likelihood of that individual being asked to bring her/his evidence to court. This can in turn help avoid raising hopes in individuals who are not likely to be called as witnesses.

the ICC, the evidence must demonstrate that there was penetration as one of the elements of the crime of rape. If the survivor-witness does not have evidence of penetration, s/he may still likely be a victim of another international crime under the Rome Statute involving sexual and non-sexual violence – but s/he is not a victim of rape. In the case where the crime was committed long ago, and in fact in most instances in the context of international criminal investigations, the primary evidence for crimes of sexual violence will be witness testimony, as physical evidence is most often no longer available. This renders the witness testimony the main evidence to prove the crime, and thus centrally important to the case which will be presented at trial. The manner in which the original evidence is obtained from the witness/survivor is critical and can impact upon the ultimate weight attributed to his/her testimony in court.

Another example would be with the matter of the coercive or threatening circumstances in which the survivor was attacked. Although the investigator may ask the witness to describe the crime of sexual violence in great detail, s/he may omit to ask about the surroundings or physical circumstances in which this act took place. Does the investigator know after the interview whether any doors were closed/locked? What was the proximity of weapons or other armed troops to the scene of the crime? What threatening words were spoken? The main point of dealing with such matters is to determine the facts supporting the specific element requiring a showing of coercive circumstances as one element of many crimes of sexual violence.

If these subjects are not covered during the interview, a prosecutor later reviewing the evidence will not know if this witness was a victim of rape, or other crime(s). A prosecutor will not know the nature of the circumstances of duress or repression which contextualised the criminal act. A prosecutor will then be faced with two choices upon reviewing this witness's evidence: either re-interview the witness with all the consequences described above, or "drop" this witness from the witness list due to insufficient detail as to what s/he survived.[20] Neither scenario is a positive one for the victim – s/he may well have been raped and may wish to seek justice and accountability but s/he will not be given that opportunity. These were but two simple examples of possible results of not covering all relevant issues in an interview, and this applies to crimes of sexual violence as well as crimes of a non-sexual nature. Most often such investigations are conducted in high risk, high pressure settings, with long hours worked and a certain degree of exposure of the investigator to vicarious trauma. A checklist of elements can protect the survivor-witness as well as the

20 Such questions are not easy to ask nor easy to answer. The way such matters are dealt with during the interview can be critical to the impact on the witness and to the evidentiary value of the information provided by the witness. Careful phrasing, timing, with sensitivity and respect for the wishes of the witness, combined with information so that the witness understands why such questions are being posed, will in most cases result in minimising the harm to both the witness and the evidence.

investigator – and may serve to protect the evidence itself from later misinterpretation.[21]

5.2. COMMON ELEMENTS OF THE CATEGORY OF CRIME – WAR CRIMES, CRIMES AGAINST HUMANITY, OR GENOCIDE

In order to prove international crimes there must be evidence which satisfies the common elements of the category of international crime. It is this additional proof which "converts" a domestic crime into an international crime. If there is insufficient evidence to satisfy the common elements of war crimes, crimes against humanity, or genocide, no charge may be brought for this crime under international criminal law. Keeping these elements in mind should serve to assist the researcher/investigator, rather than to burden them. Again, keeping a checklist of the elements of war crimes, crimes against humanity, and genocide at hand, an investigator may avoid leaving gaps which later need to be filled, and can ensure that the full picture of criminality is included in the case to be brought.

Examples of evidence which could be gathered from an individual survivor-witness which could serve to satisfy the common elements[22]:

- A particular repeated pattern or methodology to the attack(s) (eg. First the village is attacked from the air, then it is surrounded by tanks, and finally the perpetrators on camelback enter and violations are committed.)
- Public statements related to the attacks
- Means and methods used in the attack
- Political or military involvement
- Persecutory or discriminatory remarks which the witness heard spoken by the perpetrator or those with the perpetrator
- Detailed descriptions of the hostilities and their scale and proximity to the incident

21 One more suggestion is relevant here – it is recommended that the researcher/investigator always ask a witness what *else* they saw, what *else* they heard, what *else* they witnessed, did they see anything else, is there anything else they would like to share. It is natural to focus an investigation on a particular incident or particular kind of crime – but every individual survivor may well have information about other crimes or other incidents, and these paths are best explored as soon as possible to enable the investigator to follow the evidence wherever it may lead. If the question is not asked, the information cannot be obtained; a survivor-witness cannot be expected to know what kind of information may be relevant to a particular judicial investigation. This type of question may also serve to elicit exonerating evidence which must be explored alongside the inculpatory evidence. In any case, open ended questions must always be the rule of thumb.

22 This list is illustrative, not exhaustive.

- Evidence of persons in coordinating/superior role suggesting organisation/ system
- Information regarding the scale and nature of the harmful acts
- Patterns of targeting of particular persons (civilian/combatant, ethnic or religious group, etc)
- Geographic scope of the harmful acts
- Information regarding a policy or plan
- Organisation of armed groups involved
- Involvement of national armed groups or foreign forces of any kind

5.3. LINKAGE ELEMENTS

Even with sufficient evidence to satisfy the specific elements of a particular crime and the common elements of war crimes, crimes against humanity, and/or genocide, a charge may not be brought if there is insufficient evidence to satisfy the linkage elements, upon which individual criminal responsibility would be based. In order to bring a case against an Accused for his/her individual criminal responsibility for rape, sexual slavery, cruel treatment, forced pregnancy, or any other specific crime as a crime against humanity, or as a war crime, or as an act of genocide, there must be sufficient evidence that the Accused was either directly (such as through commission, ordering, aiding and abetting, etc) or indirectly (such as through command responsibility) allegedly responsible for the crimes. A checklist including the specific and common elements of international crimes must also include the linkage elements.

Examples of evidence which could be gathered from an individual survivor-witness which could serve to satisfy the linkage elements[23]:

- Descriptions of the perpetrator group and perpetrator "tools" (uniforms, insignias, other distinctive dress, weapons, boots, vehicles, flags or shields, etc.)
- Words spoken by perpetrators or co-perpetrators (in person, to each other, to her, on radio, orders, code words, language used, ethnic/racial slurs)
- Description of other persons present before, during, after attack and their proximity to the incident, presence of persons in more than one relevant location
- Someone taking or sharing command, passing or following orders, enforcing discipline
- Someone passing up daily reports to superiors via radio or other means of communication

[23] This list is illustrative, not exhaustive.

- Existence of a plan, discussion of aspects of this plan, persons involved in the planning and organisation
- Someone helping the direct perpetrator commit the act – telling them "go ahead", or giving them a gun and pointing, using gestures of encouragement
- Description of coordination or methodology before, during, after the attack or incident (did the perpetrators come and leave together? Was there coordination among them?)

5.4. EXAMPLE OF AN EVIDENCE CHECKLIST FOR INTERNATIONAL CRIMINAL INVESTIGATIONS INTO CRIMES OF SEXUAL VIOLENCE

As an example of what such a checklist would look like, please consider the following. Note please that these elements are most closely aligned (though somewhat abbreviated) with the provisions of the Elements of Crimes for the International Criminal Court and/or the ICTY/R, but that any investigator can alter the wording of the elements to accord with elements of crimes or violations in any jurisdiction whether domestic or international. The boxes at the left of each element can be checked during a pause in an interview with a witness to ensure that the investigator has asked questions to elicit evidence satisfying each and every element of what will ultimately need to be proven in court.

Example 1:
Checklist for Interviews:
Evidence needed to support an allegation of
Rape as a War Crime

	Specific Elements of Rape
☐	The perpetrator invaded the body of a person by conduct resulting in penetration, however slight, of any part of the body of the victim or of the perpetrator with a sexual organ, or of the anal or genital opening of the victim with any object or any other part of the body,
	AND
☐	The invasion was committed by force, or by threat of force or coercion, such as that caused by fear of violence, duress, detention, psychological oppression or abuse of power, against such person or another person, or by taking advantage of a coercive environment, or the invasion was committed against a person incapable of giving genuine consent.

AND

Common Elements of War Crimes

- ☐ The crime was committed in context of and associated with armed conflict,
- ☐ The victims were protected persons (international armed conflict) or were taking no direct part in hostilities (internal armed conflict),

AND

- ☐ The perpetrator was aware of the factual circumstances that established the existence of an armed conflict.

AND

Elements of Individual Criminal Responsibility – Linkage Elements

Direct Responsibility:

- ☐ The accused committed, ordered, solicited or induced, aided and abetted or otherwise assisted in the commission (or attempt) of the crime

OR

- ☐ Contributed to a group with a common purpose to commit (or attempt) the crime

OR

Command Responsibility:

- ☐ The accused had effective control over the direct perpetrator
- ☐ The accused knew or had reason to know that the direct perpetrators were committing crimes,

AND

- ☐ The accused failed to either prevent or punish the commission of these crimes.

Example 2: Checklist for Interviews: Evidence needed to support an allegation of Rape as a Crime Against Humanity

Specific Elements of Rape

- ☐ The perpetrator invaded the body of a person by conduct resulting in penetration, however slight, of any part of the body of the victim or of the perpetrator with a sexual organ, or of the anal or genital opening of the victim with any object or any other part of the body,

AND

- ☐ The invasion was committed by force, or by threat of force or coercion, such as that caused by fear of violence, duress, detention, psychological oppression or abuse of power, against such person or another person, or by taking advantage of a coercive environment, or the invasion was committed against a person incapable of giving genuine consent.

AND

Common Elements of Crimes Against Humanity

- ☐ The crimes were committed as part of a widespread or systematic attack
- ☐ The attack was directed against a civilian population
- ☐ The direct perpetrators knew that the conduct was part of or intended the conduct to be part of a widespread or systematic attack against a civilian population.

AND

Elements of Individual Criminal Responsibility – Linkage Elements

Direct Responsibility:

- ☐ The accused committed, ordered, solicited or induced, aided and abetted or otherwise assisted in the commission (or attempt) of the crime

OR

- ☐ Contributed to a group with a common purpose to commit (or attempt) the crime

OR

Command Responsibility:

- ☐ The accused had effective control over the direct perpetrators
- ☐ The accused knew or had reason to know that the direct perpetrators were committing crimes,

AND

- ☐ The accused failed to either prevent or punish the commission of these crimes.

Example 3:
Checklist for Interviews:
Evidence needed to support an allegation of Sexual Slavery as a <u>Crime Against Humanity</u>

Specific Elements of Sexual Slavery

- ☐ The perpetrator exercised any or all of the powers attaching to the right of ownership over one or more persons, such as by purchasing, selling, lending or bartering such a person or persons, or by imposing on them a similar deprivation of liberty,

AND

- ☐ The perpetrator caused such person or persons to engage in one or more acts of a sexual nature.

AND

Common Elements of Crimes Against Humanity

- ❑ The crimes were committed as part of a widespread or systematic attack
- ❑ The attack was directed against civilian population
- ❑ The direct perpetrator knew that the conduct was part of or intended the conduct to be part of a widespread or systematic attack against a civilian population.

AND

Elements of Individual Criminal Responsibility – Linkage Elements

Direct Responsibility:

- ❑ The accused committed, ordered, solicited or induced, aided and abetted or otherwise assisted in the commission (or attempt) of the crime

OR

- ❑ Contributed to a group with a common purpose to commit (or attempt) the crime

OR

Command Responsibility:

- ❑ The accused had effective control over the direct perpetrators
- ❑ The accused knew or had reason to know that the direct perpetrators were committing crimes,

AND

- ❑ The Accused failed to either prevent or punish the commission of these crimes.

Example 4: Checklist for Interviews: Evidence Needed to Support an Allegation of Rape as an Act of Genocide

Specific Elements of Rape

- ❑ The perpetrator invaded the body of a person by conduct resulting in penetration, however slight, of any part of the body of the victim or of the perpetrator with a sexual organ, or of the anal or genital opening of the victim with any object or any other part of the body,

AND

- ❑ The invasion was committed by force, or by threat of force or coercion, such as that caused by fear of violence, duress, detention, psychological oppression or abuse of power, against such person or another person, or by taking advantage of a coercive environment, or the invasion was committed against a person incapable of giving genuine consent.

AND

Common Elements of Genocide

Any of the following acts, committed with the intent to destroy, in whole or in part, a national, ethnical, racial or religious group, as such:

- ☐ Killing members of the group;
- ☐ Causing serious bodily or mental harm to members of the group;
- ☐ Deliberately inflicting on the group conditions of life calculated to bring about its physical destruction in whole or in part;
- ☐ Imposing measures intended to prevent births within the group;

OR

- ☐ Forcibly transferring children of the group to another group.

AND

Elements of Individual Criminal Responsibility – *Linkage Elements*

Direct Responsibility:

- ☐ The Accused committed, ordered, solicited or induced, aided and abetted or otherwise assisted in the commission (or attempt) of the crime

OR

- ☐ Contributed to a group with a common purpose to commit (or attempt) the crime

OR

Command Responsibility:

- ☐ The accused had effective control over the direct perpetrators
- ☐ The accused knew or had reason to know that the direct perpetrators were committing crimes,

AND

- ☐ The accused failed to either prevent or punish the commission of these crimes.

The theory which underlies this methodology is that any witness may have evidence to prove any aspect of a particular international crime. Investigators and prosecutors may be inclined to believe instinctively that victim-witnesses will have only evidence to support the specific elements, and that only insider witnesses will have linkage evidence linking the crimes directly to the accused or the investigative target. However, a victim/survivor witness may well have heard words spoken by the accused or seen documents signed by the accused or his close associates, and may have such information highly relevant to the case.

Questions pertaining to all three categories must be asked from all manner of witnesses and sources.[24]

This recommendation that the investigator or prosecutor implement a kind of a checklist based upon the three categories of elements which need to be proven in court is a way to ensure no gaps remain after the investigation as the case is prepared for trial or a final report. It is as simple as having at hand the elements of crimes which need to be proven in the particular jurisdiction where any case would be brought, and preparing a checklist for reference in the field during interviews. When the case is ultimately reviewed by prosecutors in preparation of an indictment, the collection of evidence will be assessed, in essence, along the lines of the above described structure. It is at that stage often too late, for many reasons, to return to fill any major gaps. This could result in critical aspects of the criminal enterprise or the scope of the violations not being as comprehensively adjudicated as they could have been.

6. STRATEGIES FOR PRESENTATION OF EVIDENCE IN COURT

There are numerous ways in which we can ease the process of bringing this evidence in court, remaining squarely within the applicable rules of procedure and evidence, and without employing extraordinary measures. Several suggestions are included here. However, undoubtedly there are many more examples of ways to facilitate this process in a manner which protects the witness, assists the Chamber, and respects the rights of the accused.

6.1. MEASURES TO PROTECT SURVIVOR WITNESSES IN COURT

Witnesses who have survived crimes of sexual and gender based violence may require particular protective measures, which should be explored providing they are reasonable and not outside the bounds of the proper conduct of courtroom proceedings. These may aim at ensuring witnesses' security and well-being to avoid re-traumatisation when testifying in Court, as well as aiming to conceal the witness' identity from the public since a strong social stigma is attached to crimes of a sexual nature. Evidently, the court will weigh these considerations

24 One question asked in relation to one category may provide answers which satisfy elements from several categories at once. For example, evidence of discriminatory words spoken can serve to prove both common elements of persecution as a crime against humanity or genocide, while also serving to prove linkage elements in relation to an individual accused or member of the joint criminal enterprise.

against the rights of an accused to a fair trial. General provisions such as those which strive to ensure that the prejudice to the witness does not outweigh the probative value of the evidence to the presenting party, can serve as support for submissions seeking remedies for the protection of vulnerable witnesses. For instance, Prosecutors may request that the following measures be taken to protect the witness' identity from the public: use of face and voice distortion and pseudonyms, use of code words or numbers to avoid mentioning identifying names or locations. To prevent re-traumatisation, prosecutors may move a Chamber in order to obtain the following measures to support survivor witnesses during their testimony: the use of a curtain so that the witness does not see the accused; additional breaks during proceedings; presence of support persons in the courtroom during the witness' testimony; protection of the witness from viewing particularly traumatic images unless absolutely unavoidable. These and more proposals can all be explored and used within the proper bounds of courtroom proceedings. In international criminal justice contexts, due to the common absence or paucity of physical and documentary evidence, witness testimony often becomes the central body of evidence. In order to provide sufficient corroboration, often more witness testimony must be presented and in greater detail. Thus, more individuals are exposed and may need protection. Creativity can also be employed through consultation with the witness and with leave of the Court to endeavour to meet his/her particular needs within the bounds of what is appropriate in the courtroom process.

6.2. SUMMARY WITNESSES

A "summary" or "overview" witness is a witness of fact who, due to his/her position, location, role, during the pattern of crimes of sexual violence, is able to bring generalised factual evidence of patterns and scale, nature and gravity of crimes. In the case of sexual violence crimes summary witnesses can serve numerous purposes. Many victims of sexual violence are later killed, either directly as a result of the injuries sustained in the context of the sexual violence crimes, or due to other violent attacks. Many other victims of sexual violence flee and are inaccessible to investigators; still others face a security situation which does not permit them to come forward with this evidence. A summary witness can bring to the court evidence of the pattern, scale, gravity of crimes of sexual violence to assist the Chamber in determining whether the acts were linked to the armed conflict, whether the acts were part of a widespread or systematic attack against a civilian population, or even discriminatory intent for the purpose of demonstrating persecution or genocidal intent. Examples of summary witnesses might be the following: a doctor or nurse who worked in a clinic just across the border from the locations of the pattern of sexual violence, where most of the victims who survived the sexual attacks sought treatment.

This doctor or nurse will have observed first-hand the pattern of victimisation; they would have observed and may have documented how the crimes took place, who perpetrated these crimes, any systematic pattern to how the crimes took place, the kind of victims who were targeted (in terms of gender, religion, ethnicity, etc), in some instances they may have taken detailed notes of first hand information provided by the victims immediately upon arrival at the clinic. The direct first hand evidence given by the doctor or nurse as a fact witness who directly observed the pattern of sexual violations can provide critical additional evidence, placing the evidence of the individual victims of specific acts into the wider context as part of a pattern of violations. This context itself can be a critical component of proving the common and linkage elements of the crimes charged.

6.3. EXPERT OR SPECIALIST WITNESSES

Just as prosecutors bring in experts of all kinds to assist the chamber in its deliberations, so can they offer experts to assist the Chamber in making determinations upon the evidence. In particular where crimes of sexual or gender based violence may have taken place in a customary and traditional context which may have had an impact upon the pattern of violations, an anthropologist or a community leader emerging from the affected community might provide useful and necessary contextual evidence.[25]

7. POST-INTERVIEW AND POST-TESTIMONY FOLLOW UP

The brief nature of this section is disproportionate to its significance. Survivor-witnesses may face all manner of security risks following an interview or following testimony which may not have been foreseen by investigators or victim and witness support personnel, or which may result in spite of best efforts. It is well understood that it is the obligation of international criminal investigators

25 For example, in Sierra Leone the crimes of sexual violence allegedly committed by the Civil Defence Forces or "kamajors" were concealed under the mystical belief system which was the psychological component of the military strategy of the Kamajors. It was said that the kamajors would lose their power to be bullet proof if they touched a woman; therefore, the kamajors claimed that it would not have made sense that they commit any crimes of sexual violence as their military might would be consequently reduced. This was a perversion of the customary belief system associated with secret societies, and in this instance that distortion of a customary belief system was used to conceal crimes of sexual violence. In such instances it may that in order for such constructs to be translated into evidence which may be presented in court (for example to explain why the evidence took so long to elicit from witnesses due to the veil of secrecy surrounding the kamajor society), a particular kind of summary or expert witness testimony might prove useful.

and prosecutors to take into account the security of victims and witnesses before, during, and after their participation in judicial proceedings. This may include direct provision of security protection or referral to other agencies for such security protection, and it pertains not only to those witnesses who ultimately testify in court but also to those who provide information or an interview but do not ultimately testify in judicial proceedings.

In addition to physical security concerns, there is an entire field of expertise surrounding strategies for trauma treatment and psychosocial support mechanisms most appropriate to support and assist survivors of sexual violence before, during, and after their participation in a judicial process. It is now common knowledge that post-testimony follow up has proven critical to the overall emotional and psychological recovery of victim witnesses and can be a decisive factor in whether their participation in the justice process has been beneficial to them. In particular where the courtroom process was challenging – which is most often the case – post-testimony follow up by psychosocial support mechanisms has increased the chance that a survivor-witness will be positively benefited from participation in the justice process.

Furthermore, to the extent possible, survivor-witnesses should be informed of the outcome of the judicial process or investigation to which they contributed. In some contexts this would necessarily automatically happen through media and public information, but in others this may not be the case. In addition, even where there is public information, it may not fully explain the way in which this witness's evidence contributed to the result or was considered by the Chamber. This information can contribute to bringing justice to the survivor-witness directly.

8. CONCLUSION

Where a full-fledged international criminal investigation has turned up no evidence of crimes of sexual violence, it is not because these crimes have not been committed; it is because the investigator has not yet uncovered them. Often investigators and prosecutors inadvertently shy away from investigating crimes of sexual violence or turn away from related evidence, though these crimes have no greater evidentiary burden than do any other non-sexual crimes. As a result, crimes of sexual and gender-based violence are still under-documented and under-included in cases which are brought before international jurisdictions. Evidence need not be more difficult to uncover if investigators are properly prepared, gather knowledge about the context and situation, carefully plan their approach to survivors of these crimes and treat them with dignity and respect while interviewing them.

This article has described some strategies which have been and can be used to bring justice to survivors of international crimes of sexual and gender based violence, and to bring the survivors into the justice process. It has presented the evidence required and has presented methods of obtaining this evidence, and the nature of the evidence gathering process in the unique context of international criminal investigations and prosecutions. Uncovering these crimes requires the investigative plan include and be open to evidence of these crimes as a matter of course. Preparation with as much information as possible in advance of the field investigation is the next step. Throughout the whole process, a checklist of elements needed to be proven can be relied upon. Furthermore, there are endless ways to gather this evidence while prioritising the survivor-witness throughout the process to the extent possible. Gathering evidence of crimes of sexual and gender based violence does not pose any additional legal burden and need not pose any additional investigative challenge. The aim is to include it from the beginning, proceed in an informed and respectful manner, filling gaps as the investigation proceeds, with patient persistence and cautious determination.

Throughout an investigator's interaction with a survivor-witness, the focus must be on the survivor-witness as a *beneficiary* – rather than a tool – of the justice process. Justice is being done on her/his behalf and on behalf of those like her/ him, s/he is a participant in the process. To the extent that the survivor-witness of crimes of sexual violence is sacrificed to the justice process, or is used as a means to an end, or is misinformed and misled, s/he is sacrificed to that process. In such instances, we have cast a pallor on the judicial process. The investigation and prosecution of crimes of sexual and gender based violence is crucial to closing the impunity gap. If it is done with care, with respect and with a consciousness of the dignity and humanity of the people involved in the process, not only we will we be bringing justice to them, but they will know that justice has been done as well.

CHAPTER 12
EVIDENCE-BASED DOCUMENTATION OF GENDER-BASED VIOLENCE

Lynn Lawry, Kirsten Johnson and Jana Asher

1. A BRIEF HISTORY OF THE PROSECUTION OF SEXUAL VIOLENCE AS AN INTERNATIONAL CRIME[1]

Rape and sexual enslavement has been considered for centuries not only as a natural part of war, but in some cases, as part of a romanticized version of war.[2] *The Iliad* depicts a war in ancient Greece, rooted in a conflict between two military leaders over a captured and enslaved enemy woman.[3] Many classical paintings depicting wartime and the atrocities that occurred during war included rape.[4] As the Soviet army moved westward onto German territory in early 1945, large numbers of women were raped.[5] Also during that time, German troops occupying Eastern Europe raped girls and women of various ethnicities and organized brothels in labor and concentration camps.[6] Extensive sexual violence also occurred in the Pacific theater during World War II.[7] The invasion of Nanking became known as the Rape of Nanking, using rape not just as a metaphor, but also because the Japanese troops committed rape

---

1 See Kelly Askin, "Treatment of Sexual Violence in Armed Conflicts: a Historical Perspective & the Way Forward," in *Prosecuting Sexual Violence as an International Crime: Interdisciplinary Approaches*, eds. Anne-Marie de Brouwer, Charlotte Ku, Renée Römkens and Larissa van den Herik (Antwerp, Belgium: Intersentia), *supra*, for a more elaborate historical overview of the recognition and prosecution of sexual violence as an international crime.

2 Peggy Kuo, "Prosecuting Crimes of Sexual Violence in an International Tribunal," *Case Western Reserve Journal of International Law* 34 (2002): 305–21.

3 Homer, *The Iliad*, 800–725 B.C.

4 *Supra* 2.

5 Elisabeth Jean Wood, "Variation in Sexual Violence During War," *Politics and Society* 34 (2006): 307–41.

6 *Ibid.*

7 *Supra* 5.

against the civilian Chinese population on a massive scale.[8] Following this was the widespread implementation of the so-called "comfort women" who comprised more than 200,000 women from across East and Southeast Asia, mostly Korean, recruited by force to serve as on-call prostitutes to the Japanese soldiers.[9] Most recently, rape has become a commonly accepted "weapon of war," employed as a tactic to attack and terrorize civilian populations. Sexual violence has played an important role in the conflicts in Rwanda and the Balkans during the early 1990s, Iraq,[10] Sierra Leone,[11] Liberia,[12] Darfur,[13] and in the Democratic Republic of Congo.[14]

One of the first explicit prohibitions against rape was the Lieber Code, enacted during the American Civil War by President Lincoln to outline the conduct of Union soldiers.[15] Among the prohibitions was that against rape which was punishable by the military commanders who could execute a soldier if that person committed a prohibited act.[16] However, since then, the body of international law of war, which sovereign states had been assembling since the 1860s, has largely neglected rape.[17] Most laws implicitly prohibited rape rather than prohibiting it outright.[18] For example, the Fourth Hague Convention of 1907 implied such a prohibition as respect for and protection of "family honor and rights."[19]

---

8 *Supra* 2; Iris Chang, *The Rape of Nanking: The Forgotten Holocaust of World War II* (New York: Penguin Books, 1998).

9 *Supra* 5.

10 Lynn L. Amawitz, Glen Kim, Chen Reis, *et al.*, "Human Rights Abuses and Concerns About Women's Health and Human Rights in Souuth Iraq," *Journal of the American Medical Association* 291, no. 12 (2004): 1471–79.

11 Lynn L. Amowitz, Chen Reis, Kristina Hare Lyons, *et al.*, "Prevalence of War- Related Sexual Violence and Other Human Rights Abuses Among Internally Displaced Persons in Sierra Leone," *Journal of the American Medical Association* 287, no. 4 (2002): 513–21; Physicians for Human Rights, *War-Related Sexual Violence in Sierra Leone: A Population-Based Assessment*, Physicians for Human Rights and the United Nations Assistance Mission in Sierra Leone (Cambridge Mass., 2002).

12 Kristin Johnson, Jana Asher, Stephanie Rosborough, Raj Panjabi, Amisha Raja, Charles Beadling, Lynn Lawry, "A Population-based Assessment of Health, Mental Health and Social Functioning of Post-conflict Communities Including Former Child Combatants in Liberia," *Journal of the American Medical Association* 300, no. 6 (2008): 676–90.

13 Physicians for Human Rights, *Darfur Assault on Survival: A Call for Security, Justice and Restitution*, Physicians for Human Rights (Cambridge Mass., 2006).

14 Kristin Johnson, Jennifer Scott, Bigy Rughita, Michael Kisielewski, *et al.*, "Gender Based Violence and Human Rights Violations in Eastern Democratic Republic of Congo (DRC): The Health Consequences on Individuals, Families and the Community," *Journal of the American Medical Association* 304, no. 5 (2010): 553–62.

15 *Supra* 2.

16 *Supra* 2.

17 Joanne Barkan, *As Old As War Itself: Rape in Foca. Dissent*, 2002. 60–66.

18 Melina Milazzo, "Military Commissions Act of 2006: A Regressive Step Back from the International Legal Standards of Rape and Sexual Violence," *Florida State University Law Review* 35 (2008): 527–54.

19 *Ibid.*

After World War II, there were two international military tribunals: Nuremburg and Tokyo. The statute under which the Nuremburg trials in 1945–1946 were created did not contain the word "rape".[20] Rape and sexual crimes could have been prosecuted as "ill treatment" under war crimes and as "inhumane acts" under crimes against humanity but they were not.[21] The indictment for the Tokyo Tribunal (1946–1948) where high-ranking Japanese officials were tried and convicted, listed rape as a crime but only included it as part of the greater atrocities committed. Furthermore, the indictment never mentioned the sexual enslavement of the "comfort women". This was a glaring omission given that shortly after, in 1948, a Dutch military court in Batavia prosecuted and convicted twelve Japanese army officers of sexually enslaving thirty-five Dutch women.[22]

The Geneva Conventions, created in 1949 as an outcome to the Nuremburg Trials, expressly prohibit rape in both the Fourth Geneva Convention[23] and the Additional Protocols,[24] but do not specifically enumerate rape as a grave breach.[25]

After the Batavia trial, no court prosecuted rape as a war crime or crime against humanity under international law for almost fifty years.[26] During that time, wartime rape changed along with war. Ethnic conflicts targeted civilian populations; this kind of war lent itself to sexual violence.[27] Military forces in Rwanda, Sierra Leone, Darfur, the Democratic Republic of the Congo, Cambodia, and East Timor, as well as the Balkans used it as an instrument of terror for ethnic cleansing and genocide.[28]

The International Criminal Tribunal for Rwanda (ICTR), created to prosecute those responsible for the genocide in Rwanda during 1994, delivered a ruling that took up where the Batavia trial left off. In the *Prosecutor v. Akayesu* case, sex crimes against Tutsi women were treated as an instrument of genocide and a crime against humanity.[29] *Akayesu's* case was the first conviction ever for genocide and it was the first time that an international tribunal ruled that rape and other forms of sexual violence could constitute genocide.[30] Furthermore,

---

20 *Supra* 19.
21 *Supra* 19.
22 *Supra* 19.
23 Geneva Convention Relative to the Protection of Civilian Persons in Time of War, 12 August 1949, 6 U.S.T. 3516, 75 U.N.T.S. 287.
24 Protocol Additional to the Geneva Conventions of 12 August 1949, and Relating to the Protection of Victims of International Armed Conflicts, art. 76(1), adopted on June 8, 1977, 16 I.L.M. 1391; *id.*, art. 4(2)(e), 16 I.L.M. 1442.
25 *Supra* 20.
26 *Supra* 19.
27 *Supra* 19.
28 *Supra* 19.
29 Kelly Askin, *Analysis: Foca's Monumental Jurisprudence.* International Justice - ICTY, 2005, TRI Issue 226.
30 *Supra* 20.

the Chamber held that rape is a violation of personal dignity and constitutes torture when instigated or consented to by a public official for the purposes of interrogation, information, humiliation or degradation.[31] By likening rape to torture, the Chamber delivered the first conviction of an individual for rape as a crime against humanity.[32]

The concept of "rape as a war crime" was further addressed by the International Criminal Tribunal for the former Yugoslavia (ICTY) which was created after the war in Bosnia to address the Serb-based concentration camps, ethnic cleansing and the systematic rape of Muslim women.[33] The successful prosecution for rape as a crime against humanity and a war crime was assisted through the jurisprudence established by both the *Akayesu* case and the ICTY conviction of a Croatian commander, Furundzija, for torture and outrages upon personal dignity for a single act of rape.[34]

The landmark ruling in the *Foca* case made legal history. On June 26, 1996, the ICTY indicted eight men from Foca on sixty-two counts of crimes against humanity, grave breaches of the Geneva Conventions of 1949, and violations of the laws or customs of war.[35] The charges against them included rape, torture, outrages upon personal dignity, persecution on political, racial and/or religious grounds, willfully causing great suffering, enslavement, and inhuman treatment – all directed against the Muslim women of their hometown.[36] In the end only three were apprehended. All stood trials that involved witnesses recounting descriptions of the horrific rapes, sexual enslavement and torture and were found guilty of rape and torture as crimes against humanity and rape and torture as violations of the laws or customs of war.[37]

For the first time in history, the *Foca* trial, an international war crimes trial, focused exclusively on crimes of sexual assault and found that crimes of sexual assault, under certain conditions, amount to enslavement as a crime against humanity.[38] In addition, the document read by the presiding Judge Mumba established, on the basis of the evidence, that rape was used as an instrument of terror to drive Muslims out of the Foca district.[39]

---

31 *Supra* 20.

32 *Supra* 20.

33 Daniella DeVito, Aisha Gill, Damien Short, "Rape Characterized as Genocide," *International Journal on Human Rights* 10 (2009): 29–51.

34 *Supra* 20.

35 *Supra* 19.

36 *Supra* 19.

37 *Supra* 19.

38 *Supra* 19.

39 *Supra* 19.

1.1. THE INTERNATIONAL CRIMINAL COURT AND SEXUAL VIOLENCE

It is clear that the jurisprudence of the ad hoc tribunals (ICTR and ICTY) influenced the International Criminal Court's (ICC) treatment of rape and sexual violence. The court came into being on 1 July 2002, the date its founding treaty, the Rome Statute, entered into force. The court can only prosecute crimes committed on or after its start date and the official seat is in The Hague, Netherlands, although proceedings can take place anywhere. Unlike the ICTY and ICTR, the ICC is a permanent court with a wider range of jurisdiction, including rape and sexual violence.[40] In the Rome Statute, the ICC explicitly lists rape and sexual violence as war crimes in both international and non-international armed conflict and as a crime against humanity; in addition, the ICC's Elements of Crimes list rape and sexual violence as genocide.[41] As Justice Goldstone writes, "[t]his is significant in that the Rome Statute for the ICC represents the normative benchmark of international criminal law, and gender crimes are now given the recognition they were denied for so many years."[42]

1.2. THE EVOLUTION OF THE DEFINITION OF RAPE AS IT PERTAINS TO THE INTERNATIONAL CRIMINAL COURT

The jurisprudence that informed the International Criminal Court's definition of rape and the Rome Statute's inclusion of rape as a crime against humanity (Article 7, 1(g)) and a war crime (Articles 8(2)(b)(xxii) and 8(2)(e)(vi)) came from the characterizations of rape that emerged from the ad hoc Tribunals. The legal developments of the Tribunals both in Arusha and The Hague had helped to more clearly define rape.

The judges at the ICTR defined rape as "a physical invasion of a sexual nature, committed on a person under circumstances which are coercive."[43] The Chamber held that a showing of physical force was not necessary to demonstrate coercion, but that "threats, intimidation, extortion and other forms of duress which prey on fear or desperation may constitute coercion."[44] It concluded that certain circumstances, such as armed conflict and presence of the military, were inherently coercive and could therefore constitute coercion.[45] Furthermore, the Chamber found that "sexual violence… is considered to be any act of a sexual

[40] *Supra* 20.
[41] *Supra* 20.
[42] *Supra* 20.
[43] *Supra* 20.
[44] *Supra* 20.
[45] *Supra* 20.

nature, which is committed on a person under circumstances which are coercive."[46] Again the Chamber noted physical force was not necessary to show coercion and further held physical contact was not necessary to find a crime of sexual violence.[47]

The Court in the *Foca* trial further expanded the definition of rape created by the ICTR by including the concept of consent. They required that consent would have to be given "voluntarily as a result of free will, taking into account all of the circumstances."[48] This definition took into account all the circumstances in assessing whether the victim could indeed exercise their will freely and voluntarily, including whether they were in detention, subjected to psychological pressure, or any other condition whereby they would not be able to truly consent.[49]

The progressiveness of the definition of rape from the ICTY is re-enforced when taken in conjunction with the procedural aspects of the Tribunal's fight against gender crimes.[50] For example, the ICTY did not require the corroboration of the testimony of a victim of sexual violence, thereby dispensing with the evidentiary distrust of female complainants.[51] Also, the admissibility of prior sexual conduct of the victim was excluded, dispensing with the implication that a woman with a sexual history is an unreliable witness.[52]

Rape, for the purposes of the International Criminal Court, is defined as penetration by force, threat of force, coercion, or where there is no consent in the case of natural, induced or age-related incapacity. Sexual violence is defined as an act of a sexual nature by force, threat of force, coercion, or without consent in the case of natural, induced or age-related incapacity.[53] In the Rome Statute, rape, sexual slavery, enforced prostitution, forced pregnancy, enforced sterilization, or any other form of sexual violence of comparable gravity is considered a crime against humanity and when it occurs in war, a grave breach of the Geneva Conventions.[54]

---

46 *Supra* 20.

47 *Supra* 20.

48 *Supra* 2.

49 *Supra* 2.

50 Richard J. Goldstone, "Prosecuting Rape as a War Crime," *Case Western Reserve Journal of International Law* 34 (2002): 277–285. It is, however, debatable whether the ICTY definition of rape is really that progressive as it includes the element of "lack of consent" which may not need to be included as an element in the cases in which international criminal tribunals are dealing with, such as genocide, crimes against humanity and war crimes, see, *inter alia*, Patricia Viseur Sellers, "The 'Appeal' of Sexual Violence: Akayesu/Gacumbitsi Cases," in *Gender-based Violence in Africa*, ed. K. Stefisyn, (Pretoria, South Africa: University of Pretoria, 2007), 51–103.

51 *Ibid.*

52 *Supra* 52.

53 *Supra* 20.

54 Text of the Rome Statute, circulated as document A/CONF.183/9 of 17 July 1998 and corrected by procès-verbaux of 10 November 1998, 12 July 1999, 30 November 1999, 8 May 2000, 17 January 2001 and 16 January 2002. The Statute entered into force on 1 July 2002.

Academics, individuals and non-governmental organizations contribute to the collection of evidence required by the Office of the Prosecutor to either launch an investigation or to create the body of proof for a case. For the purpose of collecting the evidence to prosecute rape as a crime against humanity and/or a war crime, the definition of rape must therefore be consistent with that of the ICC.

Studies focused on the gathering of evidence to demonstrate human rights violations now employ a standard definition of sexual gender based violence (SGBV) which is far more inclusive of all forms of sexual/gender based violence and not just rape. SGBV is defined as any violence physical or psychological, carried out through sexual means or by targeting sexuality, including rape and attempted rape, molestation, sexual slavery, being forced to undress or being stripped of clothing, forced marriage, and insertion of foreign objects into the genital opening or anus, forcing two victims to perform sexual acts on one another or harm one another in a sexual manner, or mutilating a person's genitals.[55] This definition, decided upon by the United Nations and its partners, is the definition that is recognized by governments, donors and partner organizations.

For the purposes of data collection in sexual violence studies, other definitions concerning sexual violence must also be defined. Gang rape is rape by two or more individuals. Sexual servitude is being forced to be a sexual servant or sexual slave to a government or non-government military or militia group and followed with whom the perpetrator may have been if known. A perpetrator is defined as any person who directly inflicted violence or a reported abuse.[56] Within humanitarian law, SGBV has been recognized and incorporated into the Geneva Conventions (Article 27, paragraph 2, Fourth Convention[57]) which states that SGBV is an attack on personal dignity and honor and therefore forbidden, and in Articles 75[58] and 76[59] of the Additional Protocol I and Article 4 of Additional Protocol II[60] which provide for the protection of women and children against prostitution and rape and now use the term "persons" as a general recognition that men are at risk as well. Finally, torture is defined according to Common Article 3 of the Geneva Convention.[61] Sexual violence is considered torture and/or acute suffering if inflicted for a purpose and by someone in an official capacity. All of the definitions used for research and/or

55 *United Nations Contemporary Forms of Slavery: Systematic Rape, Sexual Slavery and Slavery-like Practices during Armed Conflict*, (Final Report submitted by Gay J. McDougall, Special Rapporteur E/CN.4/Sub. 2/1998/13), 22 June 1998, 7–8.

56 *Ibid.*

57 *Supra* 25.

58 *Supra* 25.

59 *Supra* 25.

60 *Supra* 25.

61 *Supra* 25.

medical purposes may not conform to legal standards of evidence and are not intended to as the purpose for these studies are different. For the most part, medical studies cannot follow rules of evidence and do not need legal specifics. In fact, some of what the legal system would need to conform to their standards would not be ethical to ask in these types of surveys.

2. COLLECTING EVIDENCE THAT IS USEFUL FOR THE ICC FOR CASES OF SEXUAL VIOLENCE

The remainder of this chapter will be dedicated to the description of specific methods of data collection that can be used by the ICC to gather evidence for rape and sexual violence as crimes against humanity and war crimes. The methods described here have been tailored to SGBV population-based studies by the authors, and although individual interviews are conducted to obtain the data, they are anonymous as part of a greater data collection scheme and as such these individuals would not constitute witnesses to the court nor would they be part of the responsibility of the Victims and Witnesses Unit of the Court.

The ICC prosecutes rape in the context of crimes against humanity, war crimes and genocide. As such it must place rape within the group dynamic. However, there has been a tendency of the Court to require higher standards of evidence in cases of sexual violence[62] and moreover, the use for sexual violence charges have been limited.[63] Advocacy campaigns have created an assumption that rape is a "weapon of war" or has some broader strategic design within war, which has led and even misled investigators down a path to find orders or directions that may in fact have never been issued. Rape during conflict can be committed by anyone and at anytime.[64] Even opportunistic sexual violence can come from higher levels of authority but under different liability whereby leaders create opportunity to use sexual violence either by setting an example or by simply allowing sexual violence to happen without punishment. With maturity of the Court, the terms opportunistic versus strategic are evolving, allowing data

62 See Michelle Jarvis and Elena Martin Salgado, "Future Challenges to Prosecuting Sexual Violence Under International Law: Insights from ICTY Practice," in *Prosecuting Sexual Violence as an International Crime: Interdisciplinary Approaches*, eds. Anne-Marie de Brouwer, Charlotte Ku, Renée Römkens and Larissa van den Herik (Antwerp, Belgium: Intersentia), *supra*; Maxine Marcus, "Investigation of Crimes of Sexual and Gender-Based Violence under International Criminal Law," in *Prosecuting Sexual Violence as an International Crime: Interdisciplinary Approaches*, eds. Anne-Marie de Brouwer, Charlotte Ku, Renée Römkens and Larissa van den Herik (Antwerp, Belgium: Intersentia), *supra*.

63 Susana SaCouto and Katherine Cleary, "The Importance of Effective Investigation of Sexual Violence and Gender-Based Crimes at the ICC," *American University Journal of Gender, Social Policy and the Law* 17 (2009): 338–58.

64 Susan Brownmiller, *Against Our Will. Men, Women and Rape* (New York: Fawcett Columbine, 1975).

collected to be used in much broader evidence of sexual violence as an international crime.[65]

This necessitates evidence to be collected that can demonstrate the systematic or even opportunistic nature of the crime directed at many individuals. To date, ICC investigators have invested a significant amount of time in the field, interviewing as many victims and witnesses as they can find, all while trying to protect the identities and ensure safety of these individuals as dictated by the Rome Statute. Although this method of evidence-gathering provides access to witnesses, interviewing of only those individuals willing to come forward has inherent bias. Furthermore, the data collected this way cannot be generalized to the population as a whole. In other words, a small cohort of non-randomly selected individuals cannot speak for everyone else who is also affected by such crimes.

A more effective and scientifically defensible method for providing population-based evidence is to employ validated epidemiologic sampling methods which function to gather data from individuals of the population who represent the population as a whole. A cluster-sample design, or surveying a cluster of households in an area to represent a larger area, is a practical solution for surveys that are conducted in dynamic environments that include difficult access due to terrain and conflict; in such regions a simple random sample of individuals would be practically impossible.[66] Cluster surveys are commonly used in humanitarian emergencies because of their purported simplicity, reasonable validity, and precision.[67] They have been adapted for use in morbidity[68] and mortality[69] studies. They have also been employed to collect important data pertaining to human rights violations, for example, the ground-breaking work done in Sierra Leone that quantified the prevalence of rape in the internally displaced population at the end of the conflict in 2004.[70] Since then other groups have employed this methodology to collect data on sexual

---

65 Xabier Agiree Aranburu, "From the Trenches and Towers: Sexual Violence beyond Reasonable Doubt: Using Pattern Evidence and Analysis for International Cases," *Law & Soc. Inquiry* 35 (2010): 855.

66 *Supra* 25.

67 Paul Spiegel, Peter Salama, Susan Maloney, and Albertien van der Veen, "Quality of Malnutrition Surveys Conducted During Famine in Ethiopia," *Journal of the American Medical Association* 292, no 5 (2004): 613–18.

68 F.T. Cutts, C. Dos Santos, C. Novoa, P. David, G. Macassa, and A. C. Soares, "Child and Maternal Mortality During a Period of Conflict in Beira City, Mozambique," *International Journal of Epidemiology* 25, no. 2 (1996): 349–56.

69 *Ibid*; S. Lemeshow and D. Richardson, "Surveys to Measure Programme Coverage and Impact: A Review of the Methodology used by the Expanded Programme on Immunization," *World Health Statistics Quarterly* 38 (1985): 65–75; Benjamin Coghlan, Richard Brennan, Pascal Ngoy, *et al.*, "Mortality in the Democratic Republic of Congo: a Nationwide Survey," *The Lancet* (2006): 44–51.

70 *Supra* 13.

violations in Darfur[71], Iraq,[72] Liberia[73] and most recently the DRC.[74] Results from those studies have been used to determine intervention strategies, advocate for respect of humanitarian law statutes, and inform decision-makers.

In some instances, the data obtained via quantitative studies have been used by Truth and Reconciliation Commissions and/or for prosecutions in international criminal tribunals such as the International Criminal Court. For example, data on sexual violence during the 10-year civil conflict in Sierra Leone permitted activists to assert that each "story is but one of the more than 64,000 women who experienced such sexual violations." These numbers helped humanitarian aid agencies advocate for health services such as fistula repair and mental health programs for those who have suffered sexual violence, in addition to the Special Court for Sierra Leone using the data for prosecutions of the Revolutionary United Front (RUF) and now Charles Taylor.[75]

In addition to the population based quantitative study providing generalizable information on the prevalence of sexual violence, and its being able to show the systematic nature of the crime, this kind of study also provides statistics to help understand the context of the crime when used in conjunction with other methods such as qualitative studies, focus groups (using a group to discuss issues) and proxy or secondary indicators (for example using mental health parameters to predict sexual violence).[76]

2.1. USING EVIDENCE BASED STUDIES TO ASSESS HUMAN RIGHTS VIOLATIONS INCLUDING SGBV

Assessing the nature and intensity of human rights violations in populations requires ingenuity and adapting to austere, diverse and challenging settings. Population assessments have an advantage over interviews with victims or other types of interviews in that the population level methods and statistical techniques used allow for assessment of the rates and risks associated with rights violations, and can be extrapolated to a much broader and/or larger population. As researchers with now more than a decade of studies completed in such diverse

---

71 G. Kim, R. Torbay, and L. Lawry, "Basic, Mental, and Women's Health among Internally Displaced Persons in Nyala Province, South Darfur, Sudan," *American Journal of Public Health* 97, no. 2 (2007): 353–61. (It should be noted that the publication could not report the sexual violence data collected due to the risk on the ground for humanitarian aid workers and data collectors who assisted with the study).

72 *Supra* 11.

73 *Supra* 14.

74 *Supra* 15.

75 *Supra* 11.

76 M. Anastario, R. Larrance, and L. Lawry, "Using Mental Health Indicators to Identify Post-Disaster Gender Based Violence Among Women Displaced by Hurricane Katrina," *Journal of Women's Health* 17, no. 9 (2008): 1437–44.

and difficult settings as Kosovo, Pakistan, Afghanistan, Sierra Leone, Nigeria, Iraq, Sudan, Liberia and the Democratic Republic of Congo, we will attempt to share what we have learned about ways to adapt research designs to fit locale-specific cultural norms and political conditions on the ground, the need for evidence-based data for policy, human rights documentation, and evidence for ICC cases specifically with regard to SGBV.

2.2. THE LINK BETWEEN HEALTH AND HUMAN RIGHTS

Understanding the methods we use requires an understanding of the health and human rights model. Jonathan Mann first promoted the idea that human health and human rights are integrally and inextricably connected, arguing that those fields overlap in their respective philosophies and objectives toward improving health.[77] Health and human rights is a relationship whereby rights violations result in adverse health effects.[78] Mann's approach treats health as a human rights issue and human rights as a health issue, thereby showing the linkages between the two, and since his first proposal, many studies have verified that association.[79] He created a framework to bridge the gap between philosophies, correspondence and vocabulary, education and training, recruitment, and work methods of the disciplines of bioethics, jurisprudence, public health law and epidemiology.

The investigation of health consequences due to human rights violations is critical for promoting health, for closing service gaps in health delivery, and for documenting human rights abuses for populations at risk in settings of civil chaos or among those living under repressive regimes. The guiding document for the health and human rights movement is the 1948 Universal Declaration of Human Rights[80], which categorizes human rights as either civil and political rights or economic, social, and cultural rights. Within the health and human rights community, "individual freedoms", or civil and political rights, include freedom from discrimination, torture, and arbitrary arrest; freedom of movement; freedom to participate in government and in public expression; the right to asylum; the right to fair trial; the right to privacy; and the rights to life, liberty, and security. Economic, social, and cultural rights, or what may be termed "basic needs", include the right to employment and education, to adequate nutrition, clean water, shelter and health, and to own property and to protect one's interests. It is the economic, social, and cultural rights violations

---

77 L. O. Gostin, "Public Health, Ethics, and Human Rights: A Tribute to the late Jonathan Mann," *Journal of Law, Medicine & Ethics* 28 (2001): 121–30.

78 R. W. Schusky, "Jonathan's Mantle," *The Lancet* 352, no. 9145 (1998): 2025.

79 *Supra* 11; *Supra* 14; *Supra* 16.

80 The Universal Declaration of Human Rights, available at: www.un.org/en/documents/udhr/index.shtml, last visited 29 June 2010.

that are most critical in conflict settings. The health consequences from those violations can be severe, long lasting, and devastating to populations in conflict and post-conflict environments.[81]

Rights violations against women in societies where they are subordinate can include early and forced marriage, the inability to negotiate the terms of sex including the use of contraception and birth spacing, and the inability to access a health serves unescorted in times of extremis.[82] The health consequences of those violations include malnutrition with subsequent anemia. Additionally, chronic malnutrition in childhood can produce stunted growth, including the development of a smaller than normal pelvic outlet, increasing the risk of obstructed births with devastating consequences for both mother and baby. Lack of appropriate shelter, absence of clean water or sanitation, and lack of access to education including health education further contribute to infection and complications to pregnancy and childbirth.[83] In such instances, maternal mortality can be the result of abrogating rights as defined by the Universal Declaration of Human Rights. Simply put, maternal morbidity and mortality are indicators of the economic, social and cultural rights afforded or not afforded to women.[84]

But as we have learned through our research, women and girls are not the only ones who are vulnerable to rights violations and specifically SGBV. Our research has shown that men and boys, especially former combatants, are a vulnerable group not addressed at the United Nations level and programmatic or policy level.

Our methodology uses multiple measures of health status, as opposed to single indicators such as mortality, to document the association between a rights violation and the ensuing health consequence. By using population-based sampling, we obtain prevalence data and generate more valid denominators for rights violations and health outcomes. Finally, by framing research questions within the international definition of human rights described in the 1948 Universal Declaration of Human Rights and other United Nations documents and resolutions, we can document health impacts of human rights violations on populations, conduct effective advocacy, promote accountability at the local and international levels, and provide a strong public voice for people who otherwise cannot advocate effectively for their needs. The use of evidenced-based data and statistics has been a powerful tool for policy makers and the ICC to better

---

81 M. Mann, S. Gruskin, M. Grodin, and G. Annas, *Health and Human Rights* (New York: Routledge, 1999), 8.

82 Lynn L. Amowitz, Vincent Iacopino, Hollie Burkhalter, S. Gupta, A. Ely-Yamin, *Women's Health and Human Rights In Afghanistan: A Population-Based Assessment*, (Cambridge, Mass.: Physicians for Human Rights, 2001).

83 J. Reldman, D. Makuc, J. Kleinman, J. Cornoni-Huntly, "National Trends in Educational Differentials in Mortality," *American Journal of Epidemiology* 129 (1989): 919–33.

84 *Supra* 12.

understand the scope of violations. The empirical or evidence-based approach is largely devoid of agenda and more scientific and/or impartial than advocacy-collected data.[85] Advocates must focus on the gravity of the crime and the urgency to act, but the Court must establish the truth in accordance to due process. The evidence-based approach gives the Court a more impartial and far more scientifically rigorous approach to elucidate the facts.[86] This has become increasingly important in cases of SGBV.

3. RESEARCH METHODS

There are many places in the world where rights and health problems intersect and where scientific investigation could elucidate the issues more clearly, particularly where rates of violations may be needed for accountability. Policy implications, timing and funding must be weighed against risk and benefit of conducting these types of studies to ensure ethical guidelines are followed for all involved. Finally, it is helpful to understand each of the methods of data collection to better understand what each method can offer to the impartiality, truth and facts.

Both quantitative and qualitative research methods have been adapted to the task of assessing the health consequences of human rights violations.[87] Qualitative approaches have been used as primary data collection tools, and as formative tools to better develop quantitative instruments. Quantitative studies are more highly structured approaches meant to capture specific data in an empirical or evidence-based approach, while qualitative studies tend to rely on semi-structured interviews with open-ended questions designed to capture testimonies and give a face to the issues on the ground. Such stories often are powerful and can provoke emotional responses to situations that later translate into increased media and public attention and funding for health needs in addition to important context to population gathered data.

Our research has demonstrated that both qualitative and quantitative methods are both complementary and also more individually powerful when used together. For example, semi-structured interviews in Iraq collected poignant testimony that documented horrendous cases of torture perpetrated by the regime of Saddam Hussein against the Shi'a in Southern Iraq during 10 years

85 On NGO advocacy, see Brigid Inder, "Partners for Gender Justice," *Prosecuting Sexual Violence as an International Crime: Interdisciplinary Approaches*, eds. Anne-Marie de Brouwer, Charlotte Ku, Renée Römkens and Larissa van den Herik (Antwerp, Belgium: Intersentia), *infra*.

86 *Supra* 67.

87 M. Q. Patton, *Qualitative Evaluation and Research Methods* (Newbury Park, Cal.: Sage Publications, 1990), 169–283.

preceding the war in 2003.[88] We conducted numerous interviews with torture victims and presented these findings in public reports. One such example was that of a mechanic imprisoned in Baghdad in 2002 who told us:

> One afternoon, several of us were brought into a yard. Other prisoners were brought out as well. One was chained with arms out stretched to a wall and a tire was placed around his head and neck. They set it on fire. The other prisoner was brought in as the one with the tire burned. They took out a sword and cut his hands off at the wrist...

However, while publication of this kind of testimony provides a firsthand understanding into the horrors people endured under Ba'ath rule, it does not give statistically valid numbers as to how many people were similarly victimized – how widespread these abuses really were. A follow up quantitative population-based study documented that nearly every other household in Southern Iraq had a family member who suffered something similar to this account.[89] The melding of qualitative and quantitative data is an effective way to portray the extent of rights abuses and make them real, and helps service providers better assess the medical and psychological services needs of survivors and families.

The choice of whether to seek quantitative population-based or qualitative case documentation data as a primary method is based on factors such as the feasibility of travel and access to subjects, the urgency of the situation, safety considerations for data collectors and participants, advocacy goals, resource constraints and the timetable of programmatic needs. Within the remainder of this chapter, we will discuss each as a stand-alone research option, but we prefer to combine research approaches whenever possible.

3.1. INITIAL PLANNING

Deciding on where to go and what to study are determined by factors such as the political landscape, security on the ground, infrastructure and logistics, funding, and the potential remedies and/or policy implications that might result from the investigation. Weighing these components permits an assessment of the risks involved and the ability to complete the work. The fact that data *could* be obtained does not necessary mean it *should* be obtained if the risks outweigh any potential benefits to recipients of the study. It is certainly not ethically defensible to collect data, especially SGBV data, with no policy endpoint or possible solution to issues on the ground.[90] This is especially the case with field research

---

88 *Supra* 11.

89 *Supra* 11.

90 *WHO Ethical and Safety Recommendations for Researching, Documenting, and Monitoring Sexual Violence in Emergencies.* (Geneva, Switzerland: World Health Organization, 2007).

in conflict zones because the very nature of the setting and the work can put investigators, data collectors, participants, and partner organizations (NGOs) at risk. Benefits gained from research to consider include heightening public awareness, fostering changes in policy, and improving funding possibilities that thereby promote increased provisioning for human needs of those subject to the very violations we are researching. A positive outcome of effective health and rights research includes radio, television, print and electronic media coverage, as well as publications in professional peer-reviewed journals. However, in some cases, political conditions and cultural sensitivities made it unwise to release data or made it necessary to withdraw scientific publication of work in order to protect staff, data collectors and participants.[91]

3.2. QUALITATIVE METHODOLOGY

Sometimes, as in active conflict or environments where respondents may be at risk, it is not feasible or warranted to conduct quantitative research, so well designed qualitative research is the appropriate approach. Well conceived and executed qualitative studies can provide accurate and useful information and usually can be accomplished in less time and with more limited resources than more statistically powered quantitative work but will not give the same data as a study that is population-based.

Qualitative investigations typically consist of semi-structured interviews of key informants such as victims, witnesses, religious or community leaders, government officials, military leaders, assistance providers, local and international policy makers, and/or other stakeholders including donors. The primary strength of the qualitative approach is that it can provide compelling, emotional, first-hand accounts of abusive practices and their consequences in the voices of victims and witnesses. This is a social sciences-based approach and attempts to elicit from those interviewed their sense of the "who, what, where, when, why, and how" of rights violations and health outcomes. This type of interview can be among individuals, or groups within communities (focus groups), with community leaders who might have a different view from individuals, and key informants such as government, police, United Nations personnel, NGO workers and advocacy personnel.

Qualitative interviews provide insight into the individual's experience of human rights abuses and thereby offer the human face and voice to the statistical numbers that are obtained from quantitative work. The impact of these data is particularly powerful when the research captures the unique words of victims and witnesses. The impact of each story is further amplified by descriptive detail, including the identity of perpetrators, graphic descriptions of events and

91 *Supra* 75.

firsthand details not reported elsewhere. Accurate detail melded with additional sources of evidence serves to corroborate individual accounts.

An example from our research involves female perpetrators of SGBV, a poorly understood phenomenon. Within the DRC, some rebel groups use female perpetrators and others do not. Discussions with Mai-Mai leaders revealed that male Mai-Mai culture requires a cleansing ceremony after any sexual act and during that ceremony they are not allowed to touch women (as they may be on their menses). In addition, the Mai-Mai ascribe to *"Utu,"* a morality code that, if broken, can make them less bullet proof and/or invisible, resulting in a greater likelihood of harm in battle. The cleansing takes three days, leaving this rebel group without male members to perpetrate SGBV for extended periods of time. However, these cultural taboos do not apply to female Mai-Mai combatants; note that 17% of survivors of SGBV perpetrated by the Mai-Mai name females as the perpetrators.[92] Such complex social reasons for patterns of gender for perpetrator are extremely difficult to obtain via quantitative research methods.

An additional strength of qualitative data collection is a reduction in assumptions related to the data to be collected. Because semi-structured interviews involve open-ended questions, unexpected details related to the phenomena being captured might be obtained; such information is not as easily obtained via quantitative surveys, where a set series of questions restricts the possible answers given. As a result, qualitative data can uncover events and needs not documented by a quantitative survey. For example, our quantitative work in Sierra Leone did not document the need for fistula repair among women victimized by sexual violence, but this issue was uncovered during semi-structured interviews.[93]

The preliminary weakness of most qualitative case documentation is that alone it does not document the prevalence of abuses, attitudes, or experiences. In other words, in most cases qualitative data cannot be generalized to populations beyond the individuals from which they are gathered. However, this limitation is due to qualitative assessments being based on non-probability and biased sampling, causing an inherent potential bias to the population studied. Typically the bias in the qualitative data is generated by the goals of the data collectors; for example, sampling only the worst cases of abuses for legal casework or only those individuals willing to come forward for truth and reconciliation commission hearings. Relying on data collected in these circumstances and extrapolating those data to the population will overstate the severity of the issue. Alternatively, sometimes the most severely victimized do not come forward, causing extrapolation to the population of interest to understate the severity of the issue. In any of these situations, obtaining a study population through valid sampling techniques might be necessary in order to generalize findings.

---

92 *Supra* 16.

93 *Supra* 12.

Qualitative data can require considerable effort to review, transcribe, analyze and interpret, including the task of identifying exemplar themes that emerge out of diverse narrative information. This is a complicated activity requiring training and skills. Often there are language barriers to overcome that create time delay, increase costs to accurately transcribe interview material and sometimes difficulties in interpreting meaning in the context of cultural differences. It also is not easy to summarize these data into concise and effective reports and publications. And it may take more time to train local data collectors to do qualitative data gathering than to administer a quantitative survey. Despite the impediments and costs, the firsthand experiences of victims and witnesses can be compelling and informative for quantitative studies that may follow and serve as a useful adjunct to quantitative studies.

3.3. QUANTITATIVE METHODOLOGY

The goal of a quantitative study is to credibly document the full scope of abuses and elucidate patterns and predictors of abuse. Good quantitative work often reveals previously hidden patterns and underlying issues and can identify targets for intervention. Proper sampling techniques for obtaining respondents allow the findings of quantitative studies to be generalized to larger populations, which case documentation does not permit. Solid quantitative research also can be a source of future leads for case documentation efforts and provide essential information for program planning and funding requirements.

Quantitative studies often are the only method available to determine the prevalence of a phenomenon previously not understood. During our recent study in the DRC, anecdotal data revealed that women were coming forward to discuss their roles in rape and sexual violence as female combatant members. And although female perpetrators were known to exist,[94] the scope of the problem was unknown. By simply asking respondents to report the sex of the perpetrator, we found that of female survivors 40% reported the perpetrator as female, and among male survivors 10% reported the perpetrator as female. This context and scope will change how policy programming addresses SGBV. The paradigm of female victim/male perpetrator is now turned on its head and requires rethinking when it comes to health care, policy, guidelines for response to SGBV, and advocacy.

Developing a good survey requires extensive background research that includes a thorough understanding of the political and cultural context on the ground, including cultural sensitivities, and a clear-eyed assessment of risks. For example, background research informed us that women in Sierra Leone who became sexual slaves to Rebels faced the horrendous practice of hand and foot

---

94 *Supra* 16; Joanna Bourke, *Rape: Sex, Violence, History.* (Virago Press, 2007): 209–16.

amputations.[95] Therefore, we included questions about amputation in the sexual violence survey. As another example, in Southern Iraq abuse, torture and killings were rumored to have occurred within households in addition to torture centers. Based on that preliminary understanding, we included questions on this in the survey instrument. The result was that we learned that more than 60% of abuses were reported to have occurred at home and that household members were commonly forced to witness them. This informed mental health programming to deal with an exceptionally high suicide attempt rate among household members (not just victims of the abuse) that had witnessed rights abuses of loved ones.[96]

Surveys on SGBV require additional specialized knowledge of culture issues and training in survey methods to counter those concerns. A clear example is provided by our work in Sudan. Despite government claims of denial, preliminary investigation revealed that rape was being perpetrated against Sudanese IDPs (internally displaced persons) in Darfur. Therefore, an aid organization, felt it would be important to identify ways of improving conditions and decreasing behavior that can lead to rape and other forms of sexual violence. Because of the sensitivity of the government and the risk to humanitarian aid workers who try to investigate rape/sexual violence, we were left to identify risk patterns for sexual violence based on other reports from the field and the use of secondary indicators as a proxy for SGBV rates (see 4.4 for discussion of the use of secondary indicators). In addition, in our background research, we found that many women were raped when foraging for wood. Our survey then looked at the percent of foragers, need for fuel (wood, grass or dung) and how best to supply this to eliminate the risk women were taking to find fuel. The analysis showed that more than 62% of the foragers were women and that fuel distribution in the camps was infrequent (1%). Simply supplying fuel to the women in the camp could eliminate the need to forage and thus decrease the risk of sexual violence.[97]

Quantitative studies should follow basic epidemiological techniques for designing instruments and conducting surveys. Instructions for local surveyors should be clear and easy to follow. After training, local surveyors should find the survey instrument easy to administer and easy for survey respondents to understand. These requirements are complicated by circumstances of severe violence, during which it seem infeasible to conduct quantitative fieldwork. However, even in very challenging situations we, and others, have successfully conducted population-based assessments. Examples include during the post-conflict but violent time of authoritative rule in Kosovo, in war-torn Sierra Leone, in Afghanistan under Taliban rule, in Iraq before and during the U.S.

95 *Supra* 12.
96 *Supra* 11.
97 *Supra* 15.

occupation, during the humanitarian disaster in Darfur Sudan, and in the Democratic Republic of Congo. In addition to the backdrop of violence and insecurity, or even fear of arrest for talking about SGBV for researchers and participants, a major impediment to conducting quantitative population-based surveys is that they typically require more time, resources and funding than qualitative studies.

4. BEST PRACTICES FOR QUANTITATIVE STUDIES OF SEXUAL VIOLENCE

Over the years, members of our team have both researched existing best practices for quantitative studies, and also further developed those techniques for the contexts in which we have worked. We share our experiences here.

4.1. SURVEY/INSTRUMENT DESIGN

Good questionnaire design is a multi-step process that involves both vetting by cultural experts and questionnaire designers, as well as testing with the study population. Questionnaires intended for multi-language, multi-cultural use require even more rigorous design standards. Research on such surveys exists[98], but best practices, especially in conflict areas, are still under development.

Survey instruments used by our team have evolved over the years as our experience has widened. Since 1999, our goal has been to advance strategies in survey development that may be adapted and used across geographic regions and political contexts in order to make comparisons among disasters and conflict affected regions. Frequently, studies have occurred in populations that speak multiple different languages; in such situations best practices require that survey instruments be in the language of the respondent, not translated "on the fly." These are first written, proofread and edited in English, then translated into the relevant language(s), and then back translated into English by two or more independent people. Typically that step must occur prior to researchers being in the field; therefore, the survey is again translated in the field by a trustworthy translator or several translators *with local cultural knowledge*. The process of forward and back-translation is designed to ensure accuracy of translation; the additional step of translation in the field is designed to both ensure *functional* equivalence of the questions across the two languages as well as adjust for

98 Janet A. Harkness, Fons van de Vijver, J. R. Mohler, and P.H. Peter, *Cross-Cultural Survey Methods*, (New York: J. Wiley and Sons, 2002); Janet A. Harkness, Michael Braun, Brad Edwards *et al.*, *Survey Methods in Multicultural, Multinational, and Multiregional Contexts*, (New York: J. Wiley and Sons, 2010).

cultural issues. Cultural sensitivity, especially around sexual and psychological terminology, is very important. For example, in our Afghanistan survey, psychological terms were translated into neurological terminology because it is not acceptable in Afghan culture to admit one has a psychological problem. Although this caused the structural meaning of the questions to change, the cultural differences required that difference to allow the function of each question to be as identical as possible across languages and cultures.

Sometimes there is no simple English equivalent for direct translation into a local language, and a question must be rewritten in the English version without changing its essential meaning or intent in order for it to be successfully translated back into the local language for the survey. This may be due to cultural context, such as for rape, sexual violence and domestic violence; sometimes a local or regional term will be more effective than the legal one. In our recent study in the Democratic Republic of Congo, the professional translation service translated sexual violence terminology into crude and vulgar terms. The problem was discovered by our field team as we were training our data collector supervisors. Note that as the number of languages and cultures covered by the study increases, the need for simpler and clearer questions in the original language becomes more pronounced. Also, as the number of languages for which translated instruments are required increases, the efficacy of the forward/back translation paradigm decreases, and even more rigorous translation methods become more essential.[99]

Survey questions also must be checked carefully for switched numbers and scales. For example, we have had instances in which the scale from poor to excellent is reversed in a language that reads right to left instead of the left to right in English.

4.2. SAMPLE DESIGN

The power of extrapolation to an entire population from a sample of individuals is created by the *random* selection of those individuals to participate in the quantitative study. A sample is random if there is an element of chance as to who is selected into the survey, and every member of the population has some chance, however, small, of being selected. Random sampling allows researchers to make valid inferences for large populations by studying much smaller sets of individuals. However, because only a subset of the population is studied, a margin of error exists for all statistics created from that subset. That margin of error is typically described via a *confidence interval* around the statistic of interest. Selecting an appropriate random sample in the context of a conflict or

99 Jana Asher, *Methodological Innovations in the Collection and Analysis of Human Rights Violations Data*, (unpublished dissertation, 2010).

post-conflict setting presents many challenges, including locating and accessing a sample frame, determining a sample plan (i.e., whether to stratify, cluster, and/or systematically select the sample), and calculating a sample size.

A *sample frame* simply is a list of the units/individuals to be sampled. Typically a direct list or registry of the individuals to be interviewed does not exist, and an *area frame* is used instead. Such a frame is based on the residence of the individuals rather than the individuals themselves, and often is in the form of a set of maps rather than a list *per se*. In the best case, the maps clearly delineate each physical residence of the population of interest. When each member of the population has *equal* probability of being selected, the sample is called a *simple random sample*; this can only occur when a well-defined, comprehensive and readily accessible list of the members of the population exists. For example, a study of health professionals' views of patients with HIV/AIDS[100] used a simple random sample. Accurate and easy-to-use random number generation tables and electronic programs are available to randomly sample the lists.

Unfortunately conditions on the ground in conflict, post-conflict, and complex humanitarian disaster situations rarely permit simple random sampling. In conflict and post-conflict settings, typically the government has ceased or has never maintained an appropriate sample frame for the population. In those situations, maps are often available from a local Office for the Coordination of Humanitarian Affairs or other relief-oriented agency. Such maps typically show locations of local villages, but do not provide detail as to their size. In such cases, *multi-stage cluster sampling* is typically employed. Cluster sampling is the random selection of clusters of individuals rather than the individuals themselves, and multistage cluster sampling occurs when there are several levels at which only clusters of individuals can be selected. For example, if the sample frame available is a map with villages, each village is treated as a cluster and a simple random sample of those villages is randomly chosen. Then, within a village, each household is treated as a cluster and a simple random sample of those households is taken. Finally, one individual might be selected from each household to participate in the survey.[101] Such was the case for our studies in both Liberia[102] and the DRC.[103]

When no maps are available for a region, satellite imagery might be used as a sample frame instead. For example, during a study in urban areas of southern

100 C. Reis, L. Amowitz, M. Heisler, R. Morel, J. Mafeni, C. Anyamele, and V. Iacopino, "Assessment of Discriminatory Clinician Attitudes and Practices toward Patients with HIV/AIDS in Nigeria," *PLoS Med.* 19, no. 2(8) (2005): 246.

101 A general description of cluster sampling can be found in: William G. Cochran, *Sampling Techniques, Third Edition* (New York: John Wiley and Sons, 1977).

102 *Supra* 14.

103 *Supra* 16.

Iraq, satellite maps were used to randomly select households to interview.[104] To create clusters, researchers first partitioned the cities into blocks, which were then randomly sampled. Households were then sampled from the blocks.

Use of cluster sampling (or multi-stage cluster sampling) has many advantages, even outside of the difficult settings we typically encounter during our studies. As well as allowing a wider selection of sample frames to be used, cluster sampling is typically cheaper than a simple random sample, as multiple individuals all within close geographic proximity are easier to interview than randomly selected individuals across a large space. However, there is a statistical "price" for the relative ease of cluster sampling: the resulting statistics have greater error associated with them, leading to wider margins of error and confidence intervals. As a result, more individuals must be interviewed to allow the same level of precision as would be obtained by using a simple random sample.

When possible, an option that somewhat counteracts the increased error caused by clustering is to *stratify* the population of interest prior to selection of the sample. Stratification is the partitioning of the population of interest so that all members of the population appear in exactly one stratum. Typically strata are geographic in nature; for example, for our study in the DRC, districts were treated as strata. When stratification is used, it is the first step in the sample selection process; in other words, first the strata are determined, and then a sample is selected within each stratum. This is an important characteristic of stratified samples; every stratum must contain at least some sampled units.

A version of sampling that mimics the effect of stratified samples without requiring explicit stratification is called *systematic random sampling*. In systematic random sampling, a random starting point is selected in an ordered list of the units to be sampled (whether clusters or individuals), and then every *n*th unit (3rd house, 4th person etc.) on the list is selected into the sample. Systematic random sampling generally is the more practical and effective technique for conducting rights and health investigations in settings like IDP and refugee camps, in that geographic location within the camp might be associated with personal characteristics. Specifically, there often are subgroups of people that reside in pseudo-villages within an IDP/refugee camp that have different characteristics from that of the larger population in the camp with regard to important factors such as duration of exposure to the conflict, arrival time, and socio-demographics. These differences need to be researched and understood prior to determining the sampling frame, in order to ensure that the sampling interval (*n*) is set appropriately.

The primary disadvantage of systematic random sampling is that it requires *accurate* mapping of the entire camp or village prior to conducting the study. When no map is available it may be necessary to construct a map of an entire

104 *Supra* 11.

village or camp with the help of village elders; even drawing maps in the sand.[105] The most useful maps available for systematic sampling are the US satellite maps at a 1:100,000 or 1:50,000 resolution, available from the US Department of State. However, obtaining those maps takes time and patience. If obtaining maps is impossible, systematic sampling can also be accomplished by using a list of GPS coordinates of housing units and now with on-line GIS resources, the task is easier.[106]

Once the sample frame has been obtained and the sample plan (i.e., stratification and levels of clustering, use of systematic sampling) has been determined, a *sample size*, or number of individuals to be interviewed, can be calculated. Quantitative studies require calculating the minimum sample size needed to ensure with some degree of confidence that the final result can be generalized to larger populations. Please note that the sample size also determines whether the study will have the statistical power to allow determination of differences among men and women or among vulnerable groups such as former combatants. One must also consider budget and field needs, such as the number of data collectors, sites (distance) and transportation.

Calculation of sample size requires the size of the population to which the resulting statistics will be generalized, such as the total refugee population in the area of interest. More than not, the size of the population has to come from older or less rigorous population estimates. In conflict, post-conflict, and complex humanitarian settings, populations typically move frequently and security in these settings changes even more frequently. It is not uncommon to adjust sample size before or during a study, or to use migration statistics to adjust for in and out migration of populations. Also required to calculate sample size is the relative proportion of individuals out of the entire population that are likely to be impacted by the question of interest. Input from activists in the field, partner organizations, and previous studies can be used to estimate that proportion. As our work has progressed through several countries, for example, we have developed prior estimates of levels of post-traumatic stress disorder and major depressive disorder – 0.5 and 0.4 respectively – for populations that have recently experienced conflict.

Finally, calculation of sample size depends on the *significance level* desired for the margins of error and/or confidence intervals to be calculated for the statistics derived. Most researchers select 0.05, which results in 95% confidence intervals; however, some studies might require values of 0.03 or even 0.01,

---

105 L. Lawery, "Maps in The Sand: Documenting Health and Human Rights," in *Public Health and Human Rights: Evidence-Based Approaches*, eds. Chris Beyrer and Harry F. Pizer, *Public Health and Human Rights: Evidence-Based Approaches* (Baltimore, Md.: Johns Hopkins University Press, 2007): 243–67.

106 National Academies Press. Demographic Assessment Techniques in Complex Humanitarian Emergencies: Summary of a Workshop. Committee on Population, 2002 available at: www.nap.edu/books/0309084970/html/18.html, last accessed 22 September 2005.

particularly when the population under study is poorly understood. Note that the significance level selected will affect greatly the sample size needed to conduct the study, with smaller significance levels resulting in larger sample sizes and smaller levels of sampling error. However, increasing sample size can produce diminishing returns while increasing the resources needed to conduct the study. For our work, we exclusively use a significance level of 0.05.

A final note: it is possible to use a non-random sample for a quantitative study, just as it is possible to use a random sample for a qualitative study. Intentional, non-probability sampling (for example snowball sampling) should be considered when the primary concern is not to generalize from the sample to the larger population, or when it is simply not possible (due to security or conflict concerns among others) to use a more randomized sampling method. Selection of a specific sampling technique will depend on a number of factors and will be driven most by security conditions on the ground.

4.3. USE OF CLINICAL DATA FROM HEALTH FACILITIES

One of the easiest ways to collect data is to do so in a healthcare facility where patients with abuses including SGBV present for care. Care should be given to the interpretation of these data as this is a highly biased population due to under-reporting of sexual assault. Women who experience GBV often do not readily admit to having been abused when directly screened, and estimates of the rate of underreporting range as high as 70 percent.[107] Under-reporting may be due to numerous factors including fear of retaliation; stigma and fear of rejection by family, spouses or communities; loss of inheritance rights in some countries; and/or lack of adequate medical care. Underreporting across medical settings has been attributed to such factors as sensitivity to interrogation, protection of the perpetrator, and physician-patient communication in clinics that screen.[108]

---

107 C. L. Kothari and K. V. Rhodes, "Missed opportunities: Emergency Department Visits by Police-Identified Victims of Intimate Partner Violence," *Annals of Emergency Medicine* 47 (2006): 190–99.

108 C. Zimmerman and C. Watts, "Violence Against Women: Global Scope and Magnitude," *The Lancet* 359 (2002): 1232–37; R. L. Fischbach and B. Herbert, "Domestic Violence and Mental Health: Correlates and Conundrums Within and Across Cultures," *Social Science of Medicine* 45 (1997): 1161–76.; H. L. MacMillan, C. N. Wathen, E. Jamieson *et al.*, "Approaches to Screening for Intimate Partner Violence in Health Care Settings: A Randomized Trial," *Journal of the American Medical Association* 296 (2006): 530–36.; S. B. Plichta, M. M. Duncan, and L. Plichta, "Spouse Abuse, Patient Physician Communication, and Patient Satisfaction," *American Journal of Preventative Medicine* 12 (1996): 297–303; B. Gerbert, K. Johnston, N. Caspers, T. Bleecker, A. Woods, and A. Rosenbaum, "Experiences of Battered Women in Health Care Settings: A Qualitative Study," *Women's Health* 24 (1996): 1–17.; B. Gerbert, N. Caspers, A. Bronstone, J. Moe, and P. Abercrombie, "A Qualitative Analysis of How Physicians with Expertise in Domestic Violence Approach the Identification of Victims," *Annals of Internal Medicine* 131 (1999): 578–84.; G. S. Feder, M. Hutson, J. Ramsay, and A. R.

Screening is not necessarily done in non-Western societies, but the lack of justice and the factors listed above are likely to impact disclosure and presentation to care. As an auxiliary observation, the tendency toward not reporting sexual violence might result in only the most severely physically traumatizing cases presenting at the clinic. The joint result is that while the *prevalence* of sexual violence can be underestimated by relying on clinical data, the *severity* of sexual violence might be highly overestimated.[109]

A recent study by OXFAM and the Harvard Humanitarian Initiative used clinical data from Panzi Hospital to describe cases of rape presenting to Panzi Hospital in South Kivu.[110] Besides the data being over generalized to the South Kivu province and then further to the entire country by the media, the United Nations and others, even the title of the study was misleading, in that it portrayed the study as an *"Investigation of Sexual Violence in Eastern Democratic Republic of Congo."* The study begins by stating the goals are to determine 1) When, where and how are women being attacked; and what makes them vulnerable to sexual violence; and 2) How has the rape epidemic in South Kivu evolved over the last five years. However, because the study only uses data from Panzi hospital, the data and subsequent generalization are restricted to those presenting to the hospital for care. The language of the study leads readers to assume the study is generalizable to the entire Province; for example, in the conclusions, "in South Kivu" is repeated without stating "in South Kivu, *among those presenting to care at Panzi Hospital...*" leaving readers to assume the study is representative of the entire province. The methodology of this study does not allow such generalization. Finally, the study's finding that "the number of civilian rapes increased by an astounding 1733% or 17-fold, while the number of rapes by armed combatants decreased by 77%" is not borne out by our later population-based study, which incorporates results across a wider geographic range and includes individuals that did not present to the hospital for treatment.[111] The media, donors and United Nations used the results of the Panzi hospital study to align resources for a gap and a problem that did not bear out in population-based data; thus misaligning resources.

Taket, "Women Exposed to Intimate Partner Violence: Expectations and Experiences When They Encounter Health Care Professionals: A Meta-Analysis of Qualitative Studies," *Archives of Internal Medicine* 166 (2006): 22–37; M. A. Rodriguez, W. R. Sheldon, H. M. Bauer, E. J. Perez-Stable, "The Factors Associated With Disclosure of Intimate Partner Abuse to Clinicians," *Journal of Family Practice* 50 (2001): 338–44.

109 See Chen Reis, "Ethical, Safety and Methodological Issues Related to Collection and Use of Data on Sexual Violence in Conflict," in *Prosecuting Sexual Violence as an International Crime: Interdisciplinary Approaches*, eds. Anne-Marie de Brouwer, Charlotte Ku, Renée Römkens and Larissa van den Herik (Antwerp, Belgium: Intersentia), *supra*.

110 See www.oxfamamerica.org/files/HHI-Oxfam%20DRC%20GBV%20report.pdf, last accessed 1 August 2010.

111 *Supra* 16.

That being said, in some instances, clinical data may help to provide clues to patterns of SGBV. Clinical/medical data can be useful especially for assessing surges in violence. An increase in presentations to the clinic for rape or other human rights abuses may be an indicator of a larger problem in the community; however, caution and restraint should be used when using the statistics to describe that problem. Other methodologies can elucidate the larger problem; these data are representative of those coming to care only.

4.4. USE OF SECONDARY INDICATORS IN THE DOCUMENTATION OF SGBV

In some situations, the ability to directly ask individuals about SGBV may be limited or dangerous to the respondent, data collectors or ongoing humanitarian aid programs in the area of interest. Such was the case in Darfur in 2005. A study in Sudan was changed less than 24 hours prior to departure due to the arbitrary arrest and incarceration of aid workers accused of assessing sexual violence violations in Darfur. The local police had interrogated data collectors and even internally displaced persons in and around the IDP camps in Darfur. The protocol and survey were changed immediately to ensure safety of the staff on the ground and the participants to be interviewed. Fortunately, the ethics review committee (also known as an Institutional Review Board or IRB) understood the complexity and emergent nature of the changes and responded within less than 48 hours.

Because of the sensitivity of the government and the risk to humanitarian aid workers who try to investigate rape/sexual violence, we were left to identify risk patterns for sexual violence based on other reports from the field. As we describe above, background research suggested many women were raped when foraging for wood, and our survey showed that more than 62% of the foragers were women. Although we used other secondary indicators of rape in the study such as vaginal tears or trauma unrelated to child birth, we were unable to use these statistics in a publication and had to withdraw the manuscript from a major medical journal to avoid the media that would follow the study and might put the respondents, aid staff and data collectors at risk. Local government officials oversaw the hiring of local data collectors and as a consequence several data collectors were "given to us" by local authorities. This was not negotiable. These individuals were unqualified obvious "minders" who fed information back to the local authorities. They could not be fired nor could we trust the data collected. Data from these "minders" that appeared incongruent with that from other data collectors was either cleaned or not included in our final analysis. This was unavoidable in order for the work to go forward and posed a risk to all if there were any mention of SGBV.

As a result of this experience, we developed a method for identifying SGBV without asking the question directly and using a simple 9-question mental health screening tool for identifying individuals at risk for symptoms of Major Depressive Disorder[112] which is useful in estimating SGBV in settings where direct questioning may be hazardous.[113] Specific depressive symptoms (appetite or sleep dysregulation, low self-esteem, and suicidal ideation) indicate greater odds of exposure to SGBV post-disaster in female internally displaced persons (IDPs). This alternative screening method will help researchers and clinicians counteract the effects of underreporting when determining SGBV exposure among women in disaster-affected populations. At this time, we can only state this to be true among women in IDP settings; however, planned post-hoc analysis of several data sets will be used to determine its value and accuracy in other settings and among men.

4.5. PROTECTING HUMAN SUBJECTS

In the United States and many other countries, research designs involving human subjects must go for approval to an independent IRB or ethical committee made up of scientists, doctors, non-scientists and community members. During more recent studies, we have also been required to use local in-country IRBs prior to the start of the study as well as gain permission from the country Ministry of Health and the US Department of State. The IRB reviews the research methodology and the consent form as well as determining whether the risks of the study are reasonable when compared to the potential benefits. The IRB process involves submitting a research proposal in a standardized form that addresses the ethical issues relating to the proposed research and survey instruments. The IRB will review and discuss the proposal, and may request additional information. The final step is to approve or reject the research plan with or without changes to the consent statement, surveys, and, or protocol.

Appropriate IRBs or their Ethical Committee equivalents can be difficult to identify in some countries. In some settings, these are government entities that might be unwilling to approve studies that would identify government collusion in rights violations. In others, it may be unsafe to notify a national committee of in-country investigator's participation, so other forms of human subjects review may be necessary or ethical. Members of the review board might use bribery to approve the study instead of seeing their primary responsibility is to protect human subjects, as has been the case in DRC. It is incumbent upon researchers

112 K. Kroenke, R. L. Spitzer, and J. B. Williams, "The PHQ-9: Validity of a Brief Depression Severity Measure," *Journal of General Internal Medicine* 16 (2001): 606–613; D. S. Brody, S. R. Hahn, and R. L. Spitzer, *et al.*, "Identifying Patients with Depression in the Primary Care Setting: A More Efficient Method," *Archives of Internal Medicine* 158 (1998): 2469–75.

113 *Supra* 80.

to be familiar with international ethical standards and apply them as best as possible to the situation at hand, meeting the spirit of the guidelines and being flexible to context.

Our work has always been Human Subjects reviewed, and although that review involves a fairly lengthy process, the comments and suggestions have been helpful in ensuring the safety of respondents, data collectors, and the entire research team. However, sometimes issues and specific nuances involved in our research may not be well understood by an Institutional Review Board. Generally the panel participants will not have firsthand experience conducting field research in the context of civil strife or under repressive regimes. The educational gap, including basic literacy, between human subjects in developed nations and the developing world is likely to be enormous, so the kind of signed informed consent employed by researchers in developed nations is not likely to be appropriate in human rights challenged situations, especially in situations where the literacy rate is quite low. Even the implications of signing an informed consent are different in conflict or developing country contexts. We have found that once a thumbprint or signature is put on a form there often is an expectation that special assistance will follow, especially if the research is administered by a known humanitarian aid organization. And no matter what is said, we are unable to dissuade the individual that assistance is not forthcoming. We therefore substitute verbal informed consent for the signed informed consent. The language of the informed consent must be fully understandable to the respondent and there must be sufficient time to consider whether or not to participate.

Unfortunately, individuals that participate in studies designed to document the health impacts of rights violations rarely will benefit directly or immediately from the research. That is because the research likely will be used to guide policy only. And there may be negative consequences from members of their community and the government in power. To comply with the Declaration of Helsinki, as revised in 2000, every effort must be made to ensure protection and confidentiality, and to minimize potential adverse consequence to participants.[114]

4.6. BUILDING A RESEARCH TEAM

Team members must be committed to the goals of the research. Each member of a team must be committed to the functional integrity of the team and dedicated

[114] US Department of Health and Human Services, Title 45 CFR Part 46: Protection of Human Subjects, available at: http://ohsr.od.nih.gov/mpa/45cfr46.php3, last accessed 4 April 2003; World Medical Association, Declaration of Helsinki: Ethical Principles for Medical Research Involving Human Subjects, 5th rev. (Edinburgh, Scotland: World Medical Association, 2000).

to the success of the study. It is essential to work with impartial, non-partisan data collectors in countries that have extremely volatile political issues. Even so, overseeing local staff is essential; local staff may have been subject to the abuses that one is investigating. In such instances personal agendas and motives can cloud impartiality and potentially put others at risk or bias data collection, whether qualitative or quantitative. Data collectors must also be able to address and be flexible in the face of conflict, logistical obstacles and other problems, while maintaining priorities and focus and flexibly adjusting the research plan in the field. It is not uncommon for the research plan envisioned before the study to require repeated adjustments in the course of the research. In the DRC study of SGBV, inaccessible villages, funding shortfalls and conflict required a changing sampling strategy. In some cases, data collectors had to "wait out" the armed combatants before entering a village to sample.

Finally, where feasible the data collection team should include local people to minimize cultural misunderstandings and maximize buy-in. Training them effectively is essential for the study to be successful, to limit systematic errors and misunderstanding, and to ensure the data collected are as intended by the protocol. Standardized training guidelines[115] have helped us limit errors and minimize differences between data collectors, allowing for more standardized interviews.

4.7. CULTURAL CONTEXT

Proper understanding of culture context will determine the validity and reliability of the data collected and the ease at which a study can be conducted. It is also essential for getting the community to buy-in to the study. For example, researchers in Muslim or even conservative countries must wear appropriate modest clothing, and women must cover their heads. It is imperative to use the right words, such as "Dauya" to describe an untrained birth assistant in Afghanistan, or culturally appropriate terms for sex, rape, and other abuses. Most importantly, the team should make every effort to meet and court village elders, camp Sheiks, and regime leaders in order to gain access to the communities of interest. It takes time, but it may be necessary to spend a day or more having tea with local leaders, graciously accepting gifts or even giving tokens of appreciation (small sums of money or fruit/nuts), and being respectful. We have found that translators and local drivers often are the best resources for learning to navigate cultural rules.

Female data collectors usually are more effective than men for interviewing women or mixed groups of men and women, especially if not trained well.[116]

115 *Supra* 12.

116 *Supra* 13.

However, cultural norms sometimes can be bridged. In the Shia areas of southern Iraq, we were unable to recruit enough female data collectors and had to include men as data collectors. The protest that "it was impossible" for men to interview women did not pan out, and after extensive training on gender sensitivity and developing strategies for having men interview women without ignoring local culture, male data collectors were able to interview women independently and ask questions about rape and sexual and domestic violence with little to no difficulty. When the data was analyzed it seemed clear that male and female interviewers produced similar results.

4.8. TRAINING DATA COLLECTORS

Over the years we have developed a standardized protocol for training data collectors that could be used in and adapted to a variety of settings.[117] Because effective research depends on the quality of interviews by local interviewers, effectively training locally based interviewers is a key contribution to data quality. Qualified individuals should train locally hired interviewers in coordinated program of classroom teaching and experimental role-play, followed by several days of field observation. In general, the training takes anywhere from 3–8 days to complete and is dependent on the complexity of the survey instrument and the educational level of the data collectors. The style of the program is participatory and interactive with the trainers. At the end of the training, trainees are tested on content and their ability to conduct an interview using a mock survey that incorporates difficulties they may encounter in the field. A good training curriculum enhances the data collector's understanding of the survey.

We evaluate data collectors on the basis of education, language skills and their experience and knowledge about the specific topic under study. Although data collectors should be fluent in English and at least one other language, we have worked with large groups of data collectors who do not speak English with a translator present throughout training. Data collectors need to be literate and, where possible, have at least a high school level of education. Experience with survey instruments and methodology is preferable, but clearly not always possible. Sudan and Afghanistan posed significant problems in finding educated female data collectors. Not all could read Arabic/Farsi well and even fewer were versed in speaking and writing in regional languages and dialects. We use two to four Field Supervisors (local and/or expatriate) on a project to oversee and provide training for data collectors as well as review surveys daily to limit systematic errors.

---

[117] *Supra* 13; *supra* 105.

4.9. ENTERING AND CLEANING DATA

Surveys in developed country contexts have moved toward computer-assisted interviews, during which data are entered directly into a laptop or computer. In that context, data entry has become somewhat obsolete. However, the majority of our studies have used paper-and-pencil data capture in the field for multiple reasons, including expense of laptops, lack of electricity in conflict and post-conflict contexts, and lack of computer proficiency of data collectors.

Data entry personnel should be both training in proper data entry techniques and also cognizant of the cultural context from which the data are derived. Data entry is greatly enhanced by a sophisticated interface that mimics the look of the survey form and controls values that can be entered for each variable. Such an interface can be developed for Microsoft Access or for other more sophisticated database tools. When translation of responses to open-ended questions is required, it should be completed prior to the data entry whenever possible by translators that understand the cultural context. For example, the data entry step for our DRC study relied on speakers of Kiswahili and French for translation. The quality of the data entry can be measured by double data entry or by entering the data from a questionnaire by more than one person. Although the gold standard would be complete double data entry, a good rule of thumb is to re-enter about 10% of the total surveys collected. A measure of reliability of the data entry, called the interrater reliability, can then be calculated.

Once the data are entered, some level of data cleaning will be required prior to analysis. For example, in Sudan it was discovered that food units were entered in many forms: cups, cans, and *Melawas* (tin cans from international food distribution that were used as a measure in the market). Each *Melawa* was approximately 9 cups, but the actual amount sold could vary significantly from merchant to merchant. Because of this, we developed a dichotomous variable to indicate food availability; i.e., meat present in household or not.[118] As another example, for many of our studies we provide an "other" option for questions such as identity of perpetrator, available health care options, etc., and request the respondent describe what they mean by "other." Typically at least some of the "other" responses fit in one of the pre-determined response categories for the question, and can be edited as such. In other cases, there might be enough similar descriptions to warrant a new response category. Finally, if a controlled data entry interface is not available, there will be data entry errors that cause out-of scope values, such as an age of 150. If this is the case, each variable must be meticulously studied to clean the clearly incorrect responses, and reference back to the original questionnaires might be required.

---

118 *Supra* 75.

5. CONCLUSIONS

There is general agreement in the public health community that forcibly displacing populations, subjecting them to conflict and violence, and/or violating their rights can have significant health consequences measureable as excess morbidity and even mortality. Sexual violence has been shown to be prevalent in many, but not all,[119] conflict settings, including natural disasters. In conflict, however, SGBV perpetrated by armed combatants is a war crime, and those who perpetrate it should be and are prosecuted to the full extent of international law. We also can expect that changing trends in international conflicts and funding priorities will also impact what, where and how we conduct population-based health and human rights research. Regardless, accurate numbers based on reliable and indefensible data will remain an essential tool toward understanding sexual violence.

This chapter has discussed sexual violence as an international crime, described the essential role of quantitative data in elucidating patterns of sexual violence, and provided a basic overview of field methods for assessing sexual violence. Those methods, derived from epidemiology and the connection between health and human rights, require high research standards while relying on adaptive and creative techniques in the field. Our studies have become more rigorous, more complex and less disputable over the years. We spend considerable time making sure that we do not over generalize our results and that limitations are well documented.

Looking back, the data we collected helped to make modest but important changes for the populations we studied. While no one advocacy argument always works, it is clear that quantitative research efforts have their place in making broad and powerful arguments against the forces of government-sponsored violence, negligence, inaction, and discrimination. And although both researchers and prosecutors use similar words to describe the data needs, it is clear that communication, collaboration and scholarly discourse is needed between the two to bridge the gap between understandings as *evidence*-based data may not follow Rules of *Evidence*. However, using data that are impartial and scientifically defensible will be important for the ICC to consider as it considers evidence sources for cases involving human rights abuses and sexual violence war crimes cases. Although these data have been used by the ICC for cases where sexual violence has been part of an indictment, it is not as well used as it could be. The ICC, future tribunals and researchers are beginning to collaborate. It is important to continue the dialogue and to better understand the different needs between the lawyers, the social scientists and the survivors of sexual violence.

---

119 E. Wood, "Armed Groups and Sexual Violence: When Is Wartime Rape Rare?" *Politics & Society* 37, no. 1 (2009): 131–62.

CHAPTER 13
"REASONABLE GROUNDS" EVIDENCE INVOLVING SEXUAL VIOLENCE IN DARFUR

John Hagan, Richard Brooks and Todd Haugh[1]

1. INTRODUCTION

1.1. THE CALL FOR A NEW TYPE OF EVIDENCE

In remarks to The Hague Colloquium on Sexual Violence as International Crime, Luis Moreno-Ocampo, Prosecutor of the International Criminal Court (ICC) observed that cases of gender and sexual violence committed during conflict are "particularly problematic" because "these crimes are often underreported."[2] U.N. High Commissioner on Human Rights Navanethem Pillay similarly observed in her remarks to the Colloquium that, "we [the international community] are only addressing the tip of the iceberg... merely scratching the surface" in prosecuting sexual violence perpetrated during conflict.[3] Both Prosecutor Moreno-Ocampo and Commissioner Pillay spoke to what those victimized during conflict know directly: under the surface of internal and international conflict is a massive level of impunity that allows sexual violence to persist unchecked by military and political leaders. As seen in

---

1 Special thanks to Michael Brower, DePaul University College of law student, for his expeditious and diligent work on this chapter. Portions of this chapter appeared as "Reasonable Grounds Evidence Involving Sexual Violence in Darfur," *Law and Society* 35 (Fall 2010): 881–917.

2 Luis Moreno-Ocampo, Prosecutor, Int'l Criminal Court, Keynote Address at the Interdisciplinary Colloquium on Sexual Violence as International Crime: Interdisciplinary Approaches to Evidence (16 June 2009) (transcript available at www.grotiuscentre.org/files/SexualViolence-speechOcampo.tif.pdf) (hereinafter Moreno-Ocampo, Keynote Address).

3 Navanethem Pillay, High Commissioner, U.N., "Address at the Interdisciplinary Colloquium on Sexual Violence as International Crime: Sexual Violence: Standing by the Victim (16 June 2009)" *Case Western Reserve Journal of International Law* 42 (2009): 459 (hereinafter Pillay Address).

conflicts such as Darfur, the sexual violence is also often left unchecked by international law.

Commissioner Pillay nonetheless highlighted the work of international tribunals in the 1990s and insisted that the prosecution of sexual violence committed during conflict was "a triumph for women who had previously been considered 'collateral damage.'"[4] Prosecuting sexual violence "has to be done," she said, "even in situations where women cannot identify perpetrators."[5] Commissioner Pillay insisted that "a good prosecutor should be able to argue a case without individual testimony by establishing the planning, the modus, and the effects of the crime."[6] Prosecutor Moreno-Ocampo made a similar declaration. "Our goal is to go... further: a case with no witnesses, no victims."[7] He expressed a desire for a new kind of evidence available to those prosecuting the most serious of international crimes: "We want to use methods [social scientists] are developing, such as statistical analysis. We must refine how to use your tools."[8]

Xabier Agirre, Senior Analyst from the ICC's Office of the Prosecutor, echoed Prosecutor Moreno-Ocampo's call for a new type of evidence. Agirre spoke to the Colloquium more specifically regarding what role social scientists could play in developing this evidence.[9] He identified three social scientific needs: "[1] to get a level of description of the patterns of the crime; [2] then, to correlate the crime with command structures that produced it; [3] then to explain what caused it."[10] Agirre also gave social scientists a specific directive: "[w]e need descriptive statistics to show that the crime is grave, that its scope warrants the International Criminal Court, which intends to take on only the most serious cases."[11]

The remarks of these three speakers preceded a commentary by Law Professor Harmen van der Wilt.[12] Professor van der Wilt spoke regarding the

---

4 Pillay Address, *supra* 3 at 460; see also Press Release, *International Criminal Court Prosecutor and U.N. High Commissioner on Human Rights: The World Community Denies Severity of Rape as War Crime* (Chicago: Center on Law & Globalization, 17 June 2009) available at www.americanbarfoundation.org/news/186.

5 See Pillay Address, *supra* 3, at 466; see also Press Release, *International Criminal Court Prosecutor and U.N. High Commissioner on Human Rights: The World Community Denies Severity of Rape as War Crime* (Chicago: Center on Law & Globalization, 17 June 2009) available at www.americanbarfoundation.org/news/186.

6 Pillay Address, *supra* 3 at 466.

7 Moreno-Ocampo, Keynote Address, *supra* 2.

8 Moreno-Ocampo, Keynote Address, *supra* 2.

9 See Press Release, *Innovations in Evidence Gathering Can Help Hold Leaders Accountable for Sexual Violence and Genocide* (Chicago: Center on Law Globalization, 22 June 2009) available at www.americanbarfoundation.org/news/192 (hereinafter Press Release, Innovations in Evidence Gathering).

10 *Ibid.*

11 *Ibid.*

12 Professor van der Wilt has also published the substance of her commentary. See generally Harmen van der Wilt, "The Continuous Quest for Proper Modes of Criminal Responsibility,"

ICC's decision to issue an arrest warrant for Sudan's President Omar Al Bashir for war crimes and crimes against humanity, including rape, as well as the Prosecutor Moreno-Ocampo's denied application on the charge of genocide.[13] Van der Wilt's central point was that in prosecuting high-level officials, international criminal law has oscillated between ideas about "joint criminal enterprise" to the concepts of "co-perpetration" and "participation."[14] He concluded that a "huge challenge of judges and prosecutors alike is to portray men like Al Bashir as 'spiders in the web,' demonstrating how they interact and communicate with others in order to accomplish their devious goals."[15]

All four speakers' parallel messages – the necessity of developing new types of evidence to aid in the investigation and prosecution of international crimes – were highly relevant to the evidentiary issues addressed in recent actions of the ICC Appeals Chamber. On 3 February 2010, the Appeals Chamber reversed the Pre-Trial Chamber's decision not to issue an arrest warrant for President Al Bashir on the crime of genocide.[16] The Appeals Chamber reasoned that the Pre-Trial Chamber had applied an erroneously high "beyond a reasonable doubt" standard of proof when it decided whether an arrest warrant to issue for President Al Bashir.[17] According to the Appeals Chamber, consistent with the Rome Statute,[18] the "beyond a reasonable doubt" standard only applies at the

---

Journal of International Criminal Justice 7 (2009): 307.

13 See Situation in Darfur, The Sudan, ICC-02/05-151-US-Exp, Prosecutor's Application Under Article 58(7), 14 July 2008, 1.

14 Van der Wilt, *supra* 12 at 308.

15 Van der Wilt, *supra* 12 at 308.

16 See *Prosecutor v. Al Bashir*, ICC 02/05-01/09, Judgment on Prosecutor's Appeal, 3 February 2010; *rev'g Prosecutor v. Al Bashir*, ICC-02/05-01/09, Decision on Prosecutor's Application for a Warrant of Arrest, 4 March 2009.

17 See *Prosecutor v. Al Bashir*, ICC 02/05-01/09, Judgment on Prosecutor's Appeal, 3 February 2012, paras 30-33. The Pre-Trial Chamber concluded that an arrest warrant could only issue if the existence of genocidal intent was the *only* reasonable conclusion to be drawn from the evidence. See *Prosecutor v. Al Bashir*, ICC-02/05-01/09, Decision on Prosecutor's Application for a Warrant of Arrest, 4 March 2009, para 159.

18 The applicable section of the Statute of Rome provides:
At any time after the initiation of an investigation, the Pre-Trial Chamber shall, on the application of the Prosecutor, issue a warrant of arrest of a person if, having examined the application and the evidence or other information submitted by the Prosecutor, it is satisfied that:
(a) There are reasonable grounds to believe that the person has committed a crime within the jurisdiction of the Court; and
(b) The arrest of the person appears necessary:
  (i) To ensure the person's appearance at trial,
  (ii) To ensure that the person does not obstruct or endanger the investigation or the court proceedings, or
  (iii) Where applicable, to prevent the person from continuing with the commission of that crime or a related crime which is within the jurisdiction of the Court and which arises out of the same circumstances.
Rome Statute, Article 58(1), 17 July 1998.

trial stage of a prosecution, not at the investigation and arrest stage.[19] The Appeals Chamber ruled that the standard of proof at the pre-trial stage is the lesser standard of whether there were "reasonable grounds to believe" that President Al Bashir committed genocide.[20] Because the Pre-Trial Chamber misapplied the legal standard in addressing the genocide charge, the Appeals Chamber remanded the issue for a "new decision, using the correct standard of proof."[21] Prosecutor Moreno-Ocampo has already vowed to introduce new evidence of President Al Bashir's genocidal intent sufficient to meet the reasonable grounds standard.[22]

1.2. THE ROLE OF SOCIAL SCIENCE EVIDENCE

Prosecutor Moreno-Ocampo's and Commissioner Pillay's comments at the Colloquium have set a bold and far-sighted agenda. They have embraced the innovative use of social science evidence to supplement traditional legal approaches in gathering evidence and prosecuting crimes of sexual violence committed during international and internal conflicts – crimes that are often precursors to and acts of genocide. The tools of social science are uniquely able to develop the type of "reasonable grounds" evidence necessary to support such charges. Social science evidence, unlike traditional modes of evidence, can demonstrate the roles of the physical perpetrators of genocide acting together in horizontal relationships, as well as establish the indirect participation of perpetrators through vertical relationships, linking higher-level defendants in a chain of command of superior responsibility.

It is just this type of evidence that is now being called for in the ICC. Commissioner Pillay noted that joint criminal enterprise, a key concept when prosecuting joint participation in sexual violence, refers to any individual who

---

19 See *Prosecutor v. Al Bashir*, ICC 02/05–01/09, Judgment on Prosecutor's Appeal, 3 February 2010, paras 30-33.

20 See *Ibid.* at paras 30, 42.

21 See *Ibid.* at para 42.

22 Prosecutor Moreno-Ocampo told Reuters that he would present new evidence to the ICC to support his application to have Al Bashir charged with genocide. Specifically, Moreno-Ocampo noted Al Bashir's expulsion of humanitarian assistance from Darfur. "When he expelled these people who were providing the water and the food he confirmed his intention to destroy his people." "ICC Appeals Panel Wants Fresh Ruling on Bashir," *Arab News* (4 February 2010) available at http://archive.arabnews.com/?page=4&section=0&article=132385&d=4&m=2&y=2010. Victims from Darfur recently joined Prosecutor Moreno-Campo's appeal that successfully reversed the decision by the Pre-Trial Chamber. The victims supported the argument that a lower standard of proof applied at the pre-trial investigation stage. They argued, and the Appeals Chamber agreed, that the Pre-Trial Chamber erred in applying "an overly critical evaluation of the evidence." See Situation in Darfur, The Sudan, ICC-02/05–01/09–65-Red., Second Victims' Request for Participation, 4 January 2010, para 32; see also *Prosecutor v. Al Bashir*, ICC 02/05–01/09, Judgment on Prosecutor's Appeal, 3 February 2010, para 39.

plans, instigates, commits, orders or abets the execution of crimes. It does not require the direct hand or the physical participation of the accused in the perpetration of the criminal act. Rather, it applies when this individual participates in criminal conduct with a plurality of actors.[23]

Commissioner Pillay emphasized that "[t]he responsibility lies not just with the military leaders, but with their political masters as well."[24] In Darfur, Prosecutor Moreno-Ocampo charged that this chain of command ran through Sudan's governing hierarchy, including President Al Bashir and Deputy Minister Ahmed Mohammed Harun.[25]

Evidence of joint participation in crimes of sexual violence, especially that which rises to the level of genocide, is difficult to develop, however. As van der Wilt commented, "[t]he choice of a proper concept of criminal responsibility sustaining the charge against high-level perpetrators like President Al Bashir is not obvious, especially not at the early stages of investigation."[26] Yet joint enterprise evidence must be developed if case investigation and preparation for the prosecution of crimes of genocide is to proceed.[27]

---

23 Pillay Address, *supra* 6, at 463.

24 Navanethem Pillay, High Commissioner, U.N., *Draft of Address given at the Interdisciplinary Colloquium on Sexual Violence as International Crime: Sexual Violence: Standing by the Victim*, (Leiden, the Netherlands: Grotius Centre for International Legal Studies, 16 June 2009), 8 available at www.grotiuscentre.org/files/SexualViolence-speechPillay.pdf.

25 See Situation in Darfur, The Sudan, ICC-02/05–151-US-Exp, Prosecutor's Application under Article 58(7), 14 July 2008, 8. Legal scholars call these hierarchical forms of participation "indirect co-perpetration," "perpetration-by-means," "perpetration by another person," and "control over an organization." See, e.g., Van der Wilt, *supra* 12 at 308. All ultimately involve the superior responsibility invoked by Hugo Grotius when he wrote centuries ago that, "we must accept the principle that he who knows of a crime, and is able and bound to prevent it but fails to do so, himself commits a crime." Hugo Grotius, 2 *De Jure Belli ac Pacis* (1625), 523 (Francis W. Kelsey trans., 1964).

26 Van der Wilt, *supra* 12 at 307.

27 David Scheffer, the first U.S. Ambassador on War Crimes, recommended distinguishing between "mass atrocity law" and "mass atrocity crime" as a way to address this difficulty. David J. Scheffer, "Genocide and Atrocity Crimes," *Genocide Studies & Prevention* 1 (2006): 229, 237-48; David J. Scheffer, "The Future of Atrocity Law," *Suffolk Transnational Law Review* 25 (2002): 389, 398. At early stages in cases, Scheffer prioritized establishing patterns of atrocity crime over resolving issues of atrocity law. See Scheffer, Genocide and Atrocity Crimes, *supra* at 237-44; Scheffer, The Future of Atrocity Law, *supra* at 399-400. According to Article II of the Genocide Convention, genocide consists of any of the following five acts "committed with intent to destroy, in whole or in part, a national, ethnic, racial, or religious group, as such:
(a) Killing members of the group;
(b) Causing serious bodily or mental harm to members of the group;
(c) Deliberately inflicting on the group conditions of life calculated to bring about its physical destruction in whole or in part;
(d) Imposing measures intended to prevent births within the group;
(e) Forcibly transferring children of the group to another group."
Convention on the Prevention and Punishment of the Crime of Genocide, Article 2, 9 December 1948, 78 U.N.T.S. 277. Any one of the five specified elements can legally constitute genocide. The third act – with its reference to "group conditions of life" – is perhaps the most

In this paper, we present this evidence – evidence sufficient to meet the "reasonable grounds" standard required by the Rome Statute and recently enunciated by the Appeals Chamber – as to President Al Bashir's joint participation in the crime of genocide. The evidence is developed from the U.S. State Department Atrocities Documentation Survey (ADS).[28] The specific evidence we present is based on the uniquely detailed ADS data set that includes reports of sexual victimization as well as other forms of violence.[29] The method of analysis we apply to the ADS data – hierarchical linear modeling (HLM) – allows us to document the targeting of groups of persons identified in the ethnic and racial terms protected under the Genocide Convention.[30] HLM analysis additionally allows us to focus on group or village clusters, as well as on the individual level, to document occurrences of violence that are aimed at the destruction of ethnic groups in whole or in part.[31] Our analysis further examines the joining of government of Sudan (GoS) troops with local Arab militias in attacks on Black African villagers, indicating the responsibility of government leaders, including President Al Bashir, in a joint enterprise chain of command.[32] Our ultimate conclusion is that, through the documentation and analysis of the ADS data, "reasonable grounds" evidence exists sufficient to charge and arrest President Al Bashir for the crime of genocide in Darfur.

2. DEVASTATION, IMPUNITY, DENIAL, AND OBSTACLES TO RESEARCH INVOLVING SEXUAL VIOLENCE COMMITTED DURING CONFLICT

Before elaborating on our analysis, we will first discuss why the evidence gleaned from the ADS is so important, why such evidence is so rarely developed and so scarce, how the scarcity of this evidence allows for the continued denial of sexual

all-encompassing and meaningful element in understanding how genocidal violence denies sustainable life to entire villages, communities, or populations.

28 See *Documenting Atrocities in Darfur*, (Bureau of Democracy, Human Rights, and Labor & Bureau of Intelligence and Research, U.S. Department of State, 2004), available at http://2001-2009.state.gov/g/drl/rls/36028.htm (hereinafter U.S. Department of State, ADS). The information gathered as part of the ADS, which was collected for then-Secretary of State Colin Powell from 1,136 refugees across Sudan's Darfur border in Chad, became the foundation for Powell's charge before the U.S. Senate Foreign Relations Committee that genocide occurred in Darfur. See *The Crisis in Darfur: Testimony Before the Senate Foreign Relations Committee*, 9 September 2004 (statement of Colin Powell, Secretary of State).

29 See U.S. Dep't of State, ADS, *supra* 31.

30 See *infra* Part III.

31 See *infra* Part III.

32 See *infra* Part III.

violence committed during conflict to continue, and how obstacles to research on mass atrocities can be overcome.

2.1. DEVASTATION

Public health scholars have studied the devastating physical, mental, and social consequences of the epidemic occurrence of rape and sexual violence in conflict zones.[33] Health scholars conceptualize this violence within their study of "complex humanitarian emergencies."[34] The most obvious near-term health consequences to victims of sexual violence include physical injury, reproductive trauma and harm, the spread of sexually transmitted diseases (including HIV), and unwanted pregnancies.[35] Long-lasting health consequences include traumatic fistula, a medical syndrome resulting from sexual violence that causes continuing urinary incontinence, leaving victims traumatized, shamed, and socially ostracized.[36] These feelings of helplessness and humiliation persist as post-traumatic stress disorders long after the conflict has ended.[37]

2.2. IMPUNITY

Despite the devastation caused by sexual violence, history records centuries of impunity for such acts committed during conflict. Historians estimate that Russian soldiers raped nearly two million women in eastern Germany during World War II.[38] Japanese occupiers raped, assaulted, or killed approximately 20,000 women in Nanjing during the first months of 1937. Japan also kept approximately 200,000 Korean and other women in sexual slavery from about 1931 to 1945.[39] Yet the Charters for the International Military Tribunals for

---

33 See generally eds., Barry S. Levy & Victor W. Sidel,*War and Public Health,* (Oxford, UK: Oxford University Press, 1997); Eds., Holly E. Reed & Charles B. Keely, *Forced Migration and Mortality, National Research Council* (Washington, D.C.: National Academy Press, 2001).

34 See generally Ronald Waldman & Gerard Martone, "Public Health and Complex Emergencies: New Issues, New Conditions," *American Journal of Public Health* 89 (1999): 1483 (discussing "complex emergences" in the context of humanitarian efforts).

35 See "Traumatic Gynecologic Fistula as a Result of Sexual Violence," *Acquire Technical Update* (2006): 1, available at http://pdf.usaid.gov/pdf_docs/PNADF980.pdf.

36 See *Acquire Technical Update, supra* 35 at 1.

37 See *Acquire Technical Update, supra* 358 at 1.

38 See Sabine Mandl, "Krieg Gegen Die Frauen," in *Frauenrechte*, ed. Elisabeth Gabriel, (Vienna, Austria: Neuer Wissenschatlicher Verlag, 2001).

39 Judith G. Gardam & Michelle J. Jarvis, *Women, Armed Conflict and International Law* (The Hague, the Netherlands: Kluwer Law International, 2001); Eds., R. John Pritchard & Sonia Magbanua Zaide, *The Tokyo War Crimes Trial* (New York: Garland, 1981).

Germany and Japan that followed World War II did not explicitly include rape in their charges of crimes against humanity.[40]

Following World War II, international criminal law's failure to recognize sexual violence as a crime left victims without redress or remedy. States continued to treat rape as "collateral damage" and the "spoils of war."[41] Veronique Zanetti writes that, "[n]ot only was it not condemned with the same severity as other equivalent violations of rights, but it was long considered as a 'side effect' of war or even, more cynically, as a bonus to soldiers, regardless of allegiance."[42] Denial, neglect, allowance, instigation, organization, and cover-up all played their roles. Social science failed victims of sexual violence too: it provided neither sufficient data collection nor an adequate theoretical conceptualization to expose state responsibility for sexual victimization during international and internal conflicts. This is finally changing along with the laws of war.

In 1993 and 1994, the International Criminal Tribunals for the Former Yugoslavia (ICTY) and Rwanda (ICTR) explicitly included rape and sexually violence in their charters.[43] After years of indifference, international criminal law began to recognize the social consequences of rape and sexual violence associated with conflicts. For example, inter-group sexual violence can be a means of controlling reproduction – a powerful physiological and sociological weapon used to destroy social groups. Rape can also be a means of absorbing as well as eliminating enemy populations.

The ICTR verdict in the *Akayesu* case in Rwanda, adjudicated by then-ICTR Justice Pillay, identified rape as "an integral part of the process of destruction."[44] The ICTY verdict in *Kunarac, Kovac & Vukovic* also recognized rape as an element of crimes against humanity and established sexual enslavement as a war crime.[45] *Akayesu* defined rape as a "physical invasion of a sexual nature, committed in circumstances which are coercive."[46] The ICTY *Furundzija* case defined rape in terms of human vaginal and anal penetration or with objects, thereby facilitating the inclusion within the prosecution of rape acts perpetrated against both male and female victims.[47]

---

40 Frank Askin, *Defending Rights* (Atlantic Highlands, Jersey: Humanities Press International, 2007), 163.

41 Ed., Igor Primoratz, *Civilian Immunity In War* (Oxford, UK: Oxford University Press, 2007), 219.

42 *Civilian Immunity In War, supra* 41.

43 See Statute of the International Criminal Tribunal for the Former Yugoslavia, Security Council Resolution 827, Article 5, U.N. Doc. S/RES/827, 25 May 1993; Statute of the International Criminal Tribunal for Rwanda, Security Council Resolution 955, Article 3, U.N. Doc. S/Res/955, 8 November 1994.

44 *Prosecutor v. Akayesu*, ICTR-96-4-T, 2 September 1998, para 731.

45 See *Prosecutor v. Kunarac, Kovac & Vukovic*, IT-96-23-T, 22 February 2001, paras 436, 542.

46 *Prosecutor v. Akayesu*, ICTR-96-4-T, 2 September 1998, para 688.

47 See *Prosecutor v. Furundzija*, IT-95-17/1-T, 10 December 1998, para 185.

Despite the ICTY and ICTR cases, states and international institutions still lagged in recognizing the role of *state participation in* and *state responsibility for* protection from rape and sexual violence in conflict situations. The United States officially repudiated state-led sexual violence when it presented a resolution in October 2007 at the United Nations condemning government use of organized rape and sexual violence to achieve political or military objectives.[48] The response of other nation states temporarily succeeded in removing references to government responsibility in the resolution.[49] However, in June 2008, the UN Security Council finally adopted a follow-up resolution sponsored by the United States that *implied* the role of states. The resolution stated that "rape and other forms of sexual violence can constitute a war crime, a crime against humanity, or a constitutive act with respect to genocide."[50] The organizing role of governments in sexual violence during war-making became more difficult to ignore.

2.3. DENIAL

Nonetheless, high officials, such Sudan's President Al Bashir, still unequivocally deny the occurrence of rape and sexual violence during both war and peacetime. President Al Bashir insisted in an internationally-reported interview that rape *never* occurs in Darfur. According to Al Bashir, "[i]t is not in the Sudanese culture or people of Darfur to rape. It doesn't exist. We do not have it."[51] President Al Bashir's statements were strikingly similar to that of another head-of-state charged with war crimes: Saddam Hussein. When confronted with testimony about rape at his trial for the Anfal genocide in Iraq, Saddam Hussein told the Iraq High Tribunal (IHT) that he could not "sit down and remain silent when it's said that an Iraqi woman was raped... This couldn't happen while Saddam Hussein is alive."[52] In a significant sense, the IHT vindicated Hussein's claims because in spite of the evidence of rape and sexual violence heard in the *Anfal* trial, the IHT did not explicitly charge Saddam and his co-defendants with

48 H. Warren, "Measure Against Rape Fails at the U.N.," *N.Y. Times* (17 November 2007): A10.

49 "UN Denounces Rape as 'War Crime,'" *Agence France Press* (19 June 2008).

50 See Security Council Resolution 1820, U.N. Doc. S/RES/1820, 19 June 2008, para 3; see also Security Council Resolution 1888, U.N. Doc S/RES/1888, 30 September 2009, (reaffirming Security Council Resolution 1820 and noting the need for greater state involvement in implementing the resolution).

51 Interview by NBC News with Omar Hassan Al Bashir, President, Sudan (20 March 2007), reprinted in Randy James, "Sudanese President Omar Hassan al-Bashir," *Time* (5 March 2009).

52 Edward Wong, "Prosecutors Detail Atrocities in Hussein's Genocide Trial," *N.Y. Times* (22 August 2006): A6.

rape.[53] Instead, the IHT charged the more general crime of torture, which subsumed the charges of rape.[54] The failure of the IHT to explicitly charge rape against Hussein is significant because Iraq is a country where national courts still legally and socially marginalize rape victims, likening them to offenders for 'dishonoring' their families and even the perpetrators of the crime.[55]

This kind of legal neglect – if not outright denial – of rape continues in many traditional legal systems. Researchers have not yet challenged these denials with enough quantitative studies of rape and sexual violence in conflict zones. As noted by Prosecutor Moreno-Ocampo and Commissioner Pillay, it is difficult to systematically record and analyze sexual violence, especially in conflict zones and repressive regimes. Although even a small amount of sexual violence creates widespread havoc that disrupts and displaces households and communities, the societal taboos and shaming that often surround rape and sexual violence also effectively suppress its reporting.

2.4. OBSTACLES TO RESEARCH

Ideally, in order to break through the public and legal denials detailed above, social scientists would use population-based random sampling of communities that incorporate self-reports of personal sexual victimization to provide the foundation for the study of sexual violence in conflict settings. However, the large-scale displacement of population groups by attackers in conflict situations makes ordinary household probability sampling misleading. Instead, much more targeted samples are required. For example, systematic quantitative analysis of mortality has been conducted using survey data collected in special high-risk settings, such as displacement and refugee camps.[56] These analyses demonstrate that in the rare instances where specific survey questions reveal rape, the prevalence of reports among women is as high as seven percent.[57] An important aspect of rape is its capacity to terrorize a population.[58]

---

53 *The Anfal Decision: Breaking New Ground for Women's Rights in Iraq* (Center for Global Justice, 2007), 9.

54 Center for Global Justice, *supra* 536 at 9-10.

55 See Center for Global Justice, *supra* 536 at 2.

56 John Hagan & Wenona Rymond-Richmond, "The Collective Dynamics of Genocidal Victimization in Darfur," *American Sociological Review* 73 (2008): 875, 889; John Hagan & Alberto Palloni, "Death in Darfur," *Science* (15 September 2006): 1578–79.

57 Lynn L. Amowitz *et al.*, "Prevalence of War-Related Sexual Violence and Other Human Rights Abuses Among Internally Displaced Persons in Sierra Leone," *Journal of the American Medical Association* 287 (2002): 513, 520 (hereinafter Amowitz *et al.*, *Sierra Leone*).

58 See the discussion of rape as an instrument of terror in John Hagan, *Justice in The Balkans: Prosecuting war crimes in The Hague Tribunal* (Chicago: University of Chicago Press, 2003), 199–200.

Societal taboos and stigma in Arab and Muslim culture further restrict reporting of sexual victimization. In post-invasion Iraq, Lynn Amowitz led a systematic household survey in three highly-affected southern cities.[59] The survey revealed only four of 1,057 respondents who reported a pre-invasion regime-related rape or sexual assault involving an extended family member since 1991.[60] Displacement of many of the victims and normative concerns about family honor likely suppressed truthful responses.[61] When Amowitz and her colleagues reframed the question to include community members, beyond and without attribution of family membership, 87 respondents reported rapes.[62] These findings encourage a new focus on the larger community, while earlier work in displacement and refugee camps encourages sampling in concentrated populations of human rights victims. Despite the potential obstacles and regardless of the tools ultimately used, it is clear that social science has a particular role in identifying sexual violence committed during conflict.

3. A NEW APPROACH

Our research – published in *Science*, the *American Journal of Public Health*, the *American Sociological Review*, and in *Darfur and the Crime of* – sought to build on the lessons of the past outlined above.[63] Here, we bring together the core findings of this research to set a social science foundation for the development of "reasonable grounds" evidence of rape and sexual violence as support for charges of crimes against humanity and genocide in Darfur.

As noted earlier, previous survey research encourages moving beyond the reported rape of respondents themselves to reports of rape in the larger communities from which they come. The predictable legal objection to evidence regarding the reported rape of others is its hearsay aspect. The similar concern from the social science perspective is the reliability and validity of these "second-hand" reports. However, international criminal law allows hearsay evidence and provides special accommodations to insure anonymity and confidentiality of

59 See Lynn L. Amowitz *et al.*, "Human Rights Abuses and Concerns About Women's Health and Human Rights in Iraq," *Journal of the American Medical Association* 291 (2004): 1471 (hereinafter Amowitz *et al.*, *Iraq*).

60 *Ibid.* at 1475.

61 *Ibid.* at 1476.

62 *Ibid.* at 1474.

63 See Hagan & Palloni, *supra* 56; John Hagan, Wenona Rymond-Richmond & Alberto Palloni, "Racial Targeting of Sexual Violence in Darfur," *American Journal of Public Health* 99 (2009): 1386; Hagan & Rymond-Richmond, *supra* 56; John Hagan & Wenona Rymond-Richmond, *Darfur and the Crime of Genocide* (Cambridge, UK: Cambridge University Press, 2009).

witnesses.[64] Social science in this case involved the use of a Hierarchical Linear Modeling methodology (HLM), which allows for the cross-validation of aggregated respondent reports (for example, in villages or settlements), while also taking into account individual-level sources of variation and bias.[65] Below, we summarize our use of this method to analyze central tendencies in the aggregation and concentration of the ADS reports of sexual attacks at the community or settlement level in Darfur.[66]

3.1. BUILDING THE DARFUR CASE

We conceive the mass atrocities in Darfur as follows: the leadership of the government of Sudan knowingly allowed a racially constructed outbreak of violence to emerge and escalate between the Arab and Black African groups in Darfur, which resulted in rapes and sexual violence during the death, destruction, and displacement of those Black African groups. Although documentary evidence thus far is limited, below we link this scarce evidence to the social science evidence indicating that there was superior responsibility – and therefore participation – from the highest levels of the Sudanese government. The data shows coordinated and racially-targeted attacks on African farms and villages by Government of Sudan (GoS) military forces acting with Arab Janjaweed militias. As one refugee in the survey reported: "[t]hey come together, they fight together, and they leave together."[67]

Prosecutor Moreno-Ocampo identified three individuals – President Al Bashir, former Deputy Minister of Interior Ahmad Harun, and the militia leader

---

64 Hearsay evidence is generally admissible in ICC cases, but judges may exclude hearsay evidence if they believe it is unreliable. The reliability of hearsay evidence is evaluated on an item-by-item basis. In addition, victims of sexual violence receive heightened protection under ICC procedural rules. See International Criminal Court, Rules of Procedure and Evidence, U.N. Doc. ICC-ASP/1/3, 9 September 2002, available at www.icc-cpi.int/NR/rdonlyres/F1E0AC1C-A3F3-4A3C-B9A7-B3E8B115E886/140164/Rules_of_procedure_and_Evidence_English.pdf.

65 Stephen W. Raudenbush & Anthony S. Bryk, *Hierarchical Linear Models: Applications and Data Analysis Methods* (London: Sage Publications, 2002).

66 The previous survey work on violence in displacement and refugee camps also encourages data collection in concentrated human rights victim populations where rape and sexual violence are likely to be more common. The World Health Organization conducted previous work with the Sudanese Ministry of Health in internal displacement camps in Darfur and focused on mortality resulting from disease and malnutrition. The foundation for this work was focused on mortality in "complex humanitarian emergencies." The researchers did not consider violence resulting from attacks on settlements in Darfur. In order to focus on the mass atrocities, including sexual violence, involved in these attacks, it was necessary to conduct the research with refugees outside Darfur. This is one reason why the U.S. State Department, in cooperation with the Coalition for International Justice, collected the ADS data across the border from Darfur in Chad.

67 U.S. Department of State, ADS, *supra* 28.

Ali Kushayb – as joint participants in the mass atrocities in Darfur.[68] In addition to these individuals, Figure 1 names three other militia leaders identified in the ADS data who participated in mass atrocities in connection with Deputy Minister Harun.[69] This "chain of command" is evidenced by the documentation and analysis of the U.S. State Department survey of refugees in Chad (the ADS), which we discuss below.[70] "This brings us," Commissioner Pillay observed, "to the concept of the duty of [i]nquiry which lies with anyone in a superior position, military or civilian, who knew or had reason to know that crimes were being perpetrated or about to be committed, and failed to take necessary and reasonable measures to prevent them and to punish those responsible."[71] This also raises the question: What level of evidence is required to advance an investigation of and proceed to a lawful arrest pursuant to that duty of inquiry?

Figure 1. Sudan-Darfur Chain of Command 2003–4

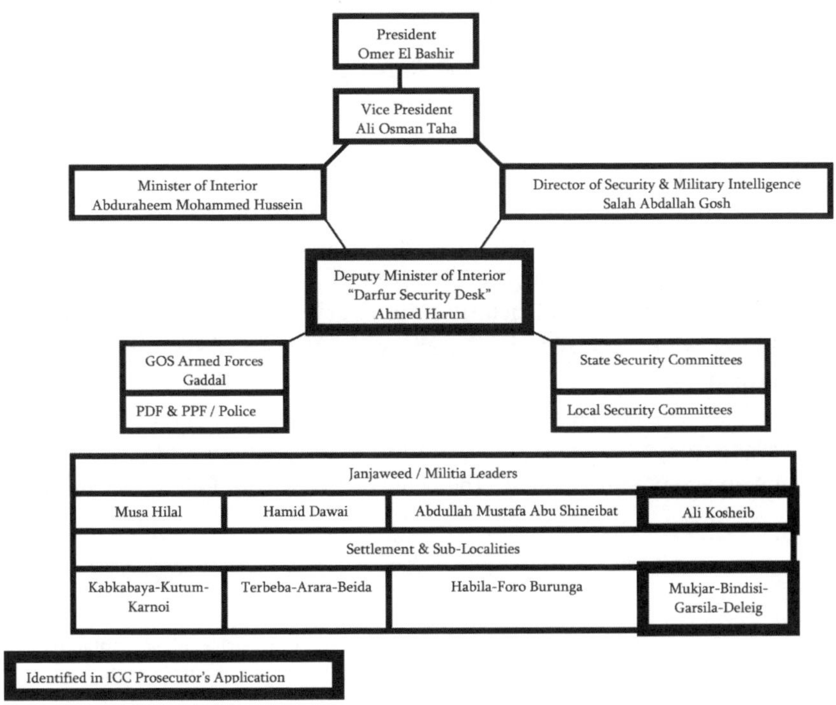

68 Hagan & Rymond-Richmond, *supra* 63 at 116 (quoting *Sudan: Peace But at What Price?: Hearing Before the Senate Commitee On Foreign Relations*, 108th Congress (2004), 52–62 (statement of Julie Flint, Darfur field researcher, Human Rights Watch)).

69 Figure 1.

70 See *infra* Part III(B).

71 Pillay Address, *supra* 3 at 463.

We do not assert that the evidence presented in this paper rises to the level of "substantial grounds to believe" President Al Bashir committed the crime of genocide, or that the evidence reaches the even higher standard of "beyond reasonable doubt" necessary for a conviction. As the Appeals Chamber recently held, these higher thresholds constitute "an erroneous standard of proof" at the pre-trial investigation and arrest stage.[72] Instead, we focus on the "reasonable grounds" standard as explained by the Appeals Chamber. This standard does not require that there be "absolute certainty that the evidence exclude all hypotheses inconsistent with the requisite statutory elements of the alleged crime" – if it did, the "lower threshold of 'reasonable grounds' would be meaningless."[73] As such, the kinds of testable hypotheses and social science evidence presented in this paper are aimed at furthering "reasonable grounds" evidence that will support the determination that President Al Bashir committed the crime of genocide.[74]

3.2. THE ADS SAMPLE AND INTERVIEWS

In June 2004, a U.S. official placed the Sudan government on notice that it was observing and recording its coordinated attacks on villages in Darfur with satellite and aerial imagery.[75] Although these attacks were at a minimum signs of ethnic cleansing (if not outright genocide), the official cautioned "that the images are not hard evidence until they are corroborated by testimony of witnesses on the ground."[76] Therefore, during the following July and August, the U.S. State Department, at the direction of then-Secretary of State Colin Powell, fielded the Atrocities Documentation Survey.[77] The ADS was a survey of 1,136 refugees who witnessed and experienced attacks in Darfur, but were now living in Chad.[78]

An eight-page summary of the ADS, which included a table of descriptive statistics and maps, formed the background for Secretary of State Powell's testimony on 9 September 2004 to the U.S. Senate Foreign Relations Committee

72 *Prosecutor v. Al Bashir*, ICC 02/05–01/09, Judgment on Prosecutor's Appeal, 3 February 2010, para 3.

73 *Ibid.* at para 12.

74 The Appeals Chamber made clear that under the Rome Statute such evidence is a prerequisite for Al Bashir's lawful arrest or detention. Indeed, at the earlier investigation stage, the Appeals Chamber cites the Prosecutor in its decision as making the crucial point that requiring the higher trial standard of proof "beyond reasonable doubt" might actually endanger witnesses. See *Prosecutor v. Al Bashir*, ICC 02/05–01/09, Judgment on Prosecutor's Appeal, 3 February 2010, paras 10, 18.

75 Monica Amarelo, "Using Science to Gauge Sudan's Humanitarian Nightmare," *American Association for Advancement of Science, New Release* (26 October 2004), available at www.aaas.org/news/releases/2004/1026sudan.shtml.

76 *Ibid.*

77 U.S. Department of State, ADS, *supra* 28.

78 U.S. Department of State, ADS, *supra* 28.

stating that genocide was occurring in Darfur.[79] This summary report, however, was only the first step. We report next how we have used the ADS to document and analyze rape and sexual violence in Darfur. The point is to illustrate how a social scientific analysis of these mass atrocities involving rape and sexual violence can establish a foundation for "reasonable grounds" evidence of genocide.

The U.S. State Department contracted with the Coalition for International Justice to conduct the ADS from 12 July through 18 August 2004.[80] The ADS used a randomized multi-stage probability sample of 1,136 Darfur refugees in 20 sites in Chad.[81] The UN used lettered grids to sub-divide refugee camps into sectors, each led by a recognized chief, umda, sheikh, or other leadership figure.[82] The ADS team identified all sectors of all camps and proportionately sampled them by size and ethnicity.[83] The team similarly sampled informal villages by using landmarks as sector boundaries.[84] Interviewers set out on random routes from the leaders' households and selected every tenth occupied space in each sector.[85] Using a Kish grid,[86] a team member randomly selected an adult for interview in each fully enumerated household.[87]

The State Department's Bureau of Intelligence and Research developed the questionnaire used by the ADS team with input on the victim and perpetrator crime codes from international law advisors.[88] Using cartographers and translators, interviewers located 90 percent of the villages from which refugees fled.[89] We thus located 932 respondents clustered in 22 originating village clusters ("villages") with 15 or more respondents each. Population pyramids from this refugee sample and samples from displacement camps inside Darfur are similar with regard to age and gender composition.[90] In both Chad and Darfur there is a disproportionate absence of fighting-age men (18 to 29 years of age), which increases the average age of respondents.[91] There are no indications the Chadian refugees differ in significant ways from internally-displaced Darfuris in the bordering areas.[92]

---

79 U.S. Department of State, ADS, *supra* 28.

80 *Ibid.*

81 *Ibid.*

82 *Ibid.* An "umda" is a considered a community leader in Darfurian culture.

83 *Ibid.*

84 *Ibid.*

85 *Ibid.*

86 A Kish grid lists individuals within a sampling unit (e.g., family) to equalize chances of selection.

87 U.S. Department of State, ADS, *supra* 28.

88 *Ibid.*

89 *Ibid.*

90 *Ibid.*

91 *Ibid.*

92 We can note several possible limitations of the data. First, the interviewers did not speak the languages of the Darfur refugees, so interpreters were required. However, the interpreters

The ADS data uniquely and extensively documented victimization during the attacks on Black African settlements in Darfur. We know of only one other systematic quantitative study of pre-camp violence in Darfur, and none that includes sexual violence.[93] As part of the ADS survey, interviewers asked refugees, since the beginning of the conflict approximately 18 months earlier: (1) when, how, and why they had left Darfur; and (2) if, when, how, and by whom they, their family, or their fellow villagers were harmed.[94] The survey's structure mixed the closed-ended format of health and crime victimization surveys with the semi-structured format of legal witness statements. We cross-checked and supplemented the ADS data by rereading and recoding the extensive narratives recorded in the interviews.

The ADS refugee sample, as introduced above and as documented in Table 1, provides a descriptive picture of the results of attacks on farms and villages in Darfur. About 40 percent of the ADS respondents are male and they are on average 37 years old.[95] Female refugees probably outnumber males because in Darfur males are more likely to be killed while females are more likely to be raped and survive, at least in a physical sense. Just over half of the Africans in the sample are self-identified as Zaghawa, approximately a quarter Masaleit, and about five percent each are Fur and Jebal.[96] The largest concentrations of the Zaghawa fled from North Darfur, while most of the Masaleit and Fur fled from West Darfur, with the Jebal previously concentrated in one town, Seleya, in West Darfur.[97] The identification of the groups is important in establishing the protected status of the victims of the atrocities.

---

contributed to the study in an important way: they greeted and introduced interviewers to the refugees, using knowledge of local customs and rules of politeness to establish trust. The investigators expressed high satisfaction with the interpreters' work. Second, shared method bias may result from reporting by respondents of both predictor variables and sexual violence outcomes. However, aggregated reports of sexual violence across villages yielded highly reliable reporting. We also controlled for the respondents' reports of their own sexual victimization to minimize potential common sources of bias and heterogeneity. Third, an indirect survey of Darfur villagers who fled from Sudan could introduce selectivity bias. Yet the Chad survey displays demographics similar to those from Sudanese camp surveys. The refugee survey allows questions about sexual victimization unasked in the latter camps. An adjustment for months since fleeing to Chad introduced below is a partial control for selectivity.

93 See Evelyn Deportere *et al.*, "Violence and Mortality in West Darfur, Sudan (2003–2004): Epidemiological Evidence from Four Surveys," *Lancet* 364 (2004): 1315.

94 U.S. Department of State, ADS, *supra* 28.

95 Hagan & Rymond-Richmond, *supra* 63 at 93.

96 Hagan & Rymond-Richmond, *supra* 63 at 173.

97 Hagan & Rymond-Richmond, *supra* 63 at 173.

Table 1. Individual and Settlement Level Profiles, Atrocities Documentation Survey, Darfur Refugees, July-August 2004

Individual Level Characteristics	**Mean[a]**	**(SD)**
Respondent Attributes		
Age, Mean (SD)	37.100	14.634
Male	.400	.491
African Group Membership		
Zaghawa	.527	.550
Fur	.055	.288
Masalit	.275	.447
Others (Reference Group)	.143	.330
Attacking Groups		
GoS or Janjaweed (Reference Group)	.328	.345
GoS & Janjaweed Militia	.672	.470
Ethnic Protection		
Report Arab Villages Spared	.063	.244
Racial Intention		
Heard Racial Epithets	.343	.475
Reported Sexual Victimization		
Own Reported Victimization	.04	.205
Others Reported Victimization, Mean (SD)	1.184	2.539
Village Level Characteristics		
Racial Intention Mean Racial Epithets Heard (SD)	.312	.144

Abbreviations: GoS, Government of Sudan forces.
[a] N=932 individuals (level-1) and 22 village clusters (level-2).
Data are expressed as percentage of respondents unless otherwise indicated.

We read and coded each narrative to designate the attacking group as Janjaweed, Sudanese, or combined Sudanese and Janjaweed forces. We distinguished GoS forces and Janjaweed militia by their clothing and equipment. About two thirds of the attacks were joint Sudanese and Janjaweed operations; nearly a fifth of the attacks involved Sudanese forces acting alone (usually in bombing attacks); and about one tenth involved the Janjaweed alone.[98] The remaining ten percent of cases are uncategorized and were used as a comparison group in some of our

98 Hagan & Rymond-Richmond, *supra* 63 at 173.

analyses.[99] The documentation of when the attacks included Sudanese military forces is important to establishing the responsibility of Sudanese government leadership in the mass atrocities.

During the second two week period of the ADS interviews, a question was added asking if there were rebels actually staying in the respondent's town or village.[100] Less than two percent of the respondents in the sample reported a rebel presence.[101] These reports were disproportionately located in several northern settlements, such as Karnoi, near Tine, and Girgira, with the reporting of rebel presence still low, but ranging from six to thirteen percent.[102] The documentation of rebel involvement in the settlements that were attacked is important to refuting the Sudanese government's defense that it was acting in proportionate self-defense against an organized insurgency.[103]

There were two waves of attacks in Darfur, and these predictably corresponded with the peak periods involving violent and health-related death and displacement. About a quarter of the sample fled during the first three months of the first wave attacks, about half fled during the four months of the second wave of attacks, and the remaining quarter fled during the other thirteen months.[104] The second wave of attacks was obviously the most costly in terms of the physical destruction of the group conditions of social life for Black Africans in Darfur. It was during the second wave of attacks, in December 2003, that President Al Bashir vowed to "annihilate Darfur rebels."[105] Figure 2 shows monthly death counts from January 2003 to August 2004, encompassing the two waves of attacks as well as the months before and after. The two sources of death counts are the ADS interviews and a separate survey based on news and NGO reports of deaths in attacks on 101 villages.[106] The parallel patterns in the two studies provide a source of convergent validation for the data collection in both research efforts.

There are more than a dozen frequently-cited estimates of the death toll in Darfur.[107] Prosecutor Moreno-Ocampo estimated that 35,000 African villagers

99 *Ibid.*

100 U.S. Department of State, ADS, *supra* 28.

101 *Ibid.*

102 *Ibid.*

103 For a discussion of the idea that the attacks in Darfur analyzed in this research were organized in response to organized insurgency, see Alex de Waal, "Counter-Insurgency on the Cheap," *London Review of Books* 26 (2004): 25.

104 Hagan & Rymond-Richmond, *supra* 63 at 173.

105 See "Sudanese President Vows to Annihilate Darfur Rebels: Report," *Agence France Press* (31 December 2003); Hagan & Rymond-Richmond, *supra* 63 at 139–40.

106 Andreas Hofer Petersen & Lise-Lotte Tullin, *The Scorched Earth of Darfur: Patterns of Death and Destruction Reported by the People of Darfur, January 2001 – September 2005* (Copenhagen, Denmark: Bloodhound, 2006).

107 Olivier Degomme & Debarati Guha-Sapir, "Patterns of Mortality Rates in Darfur Conflict," *Lancet* 375 (2010): 294, 294-95.

were killed outright in Darfur and 100,000 died overall.[108] The higher estimate includes deaths from disease and malnutrition associated with forced displacement following from the attacks. *Science* and *Lancet* published peer-reviewed lower to upper bound confidence interval estimates of Darfur mortality from the conflict in the range of 170,000 to 255,000 and from 178,000 to 461,520, respectively.[109] Although President Al Bashir and the Sudanese government estimate that 9,000 have died in Darfur, there are reasonable grounds to believe that the total is over 100,000. And there is a growing convergence based on the research literature outlined above on estimates of approximately 300,000 deaths.[110]

Figure 2. Chronology of Key Events and Monthly Death Estimates from Survey and News Counts of Killings, January 2003 – September 2004

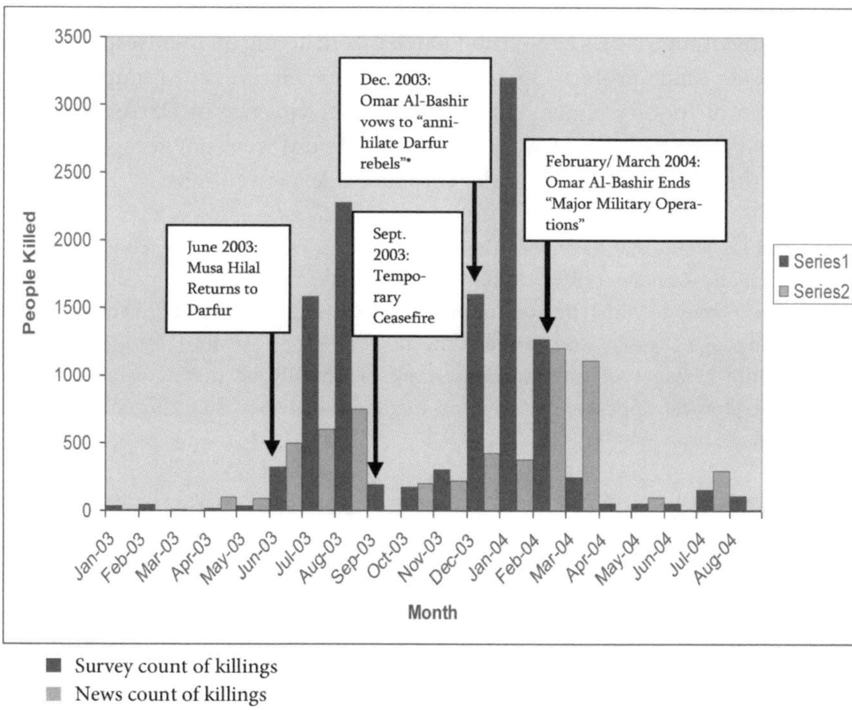

[108] Situation in Darfur, The Sudan, I.C.C.-02/05-01/09, Prosecutor's Application Under Article 58(7), 14 July 2008, 7.

[109] Compare Hagan & Palloni, *supra* 56 at 1578–79 (estimating deaths in the range of 170,000–255,000) with Degomme & Guha-Sapir, *supra* 106 at 298 (estimating deaths in the range of 178,000–461,520).

[110] Hagan & Rymond-Richmond, *supra* 63 at 102.

3.3. THE REPORTING OF RACIAL EPITHETS

The ADS interviews are highly detailed in recording the shouting of racial epithets, our measure of racially targeted intent, during the attacks.[111] The epithets are important, in part, because they provide evidence of explicit targeting that focused the attacks in a way that went beyond the multiple ethnic tribal identities indigenous to Darfur (*i.e.*, the Zaghawa, Fur, and Masaleit). The effect of these epithets was to identify an explicit binary racial division. As we see next, although both ethnic and racial groups are protected under the Genocide Conventions, ethnic attributions are more easily dismissed as subjectively and internally adopted by the groups themselves.

The U.N. International Commission of Inquiry on Darfur approached the distinction between subjective and objective identity as an important issue of atrocity law. This is an example of how David Scheffer argues that the exclusively legal framing of such issues can inhibit parties from acting on their responsibility to investigate and protect against attacks on victimized groups.[112] The Commission of Inquiry concluded that victims of violence in Darfur were not *objectively distinct* from their attackers and therefore were not recognizable as *protected ethnic or racial groups* under the Genocide Conventions:

> The various tribes that have been the objects of attacks and killings (chiefly the Fur, Massaleit and Zaghawa tribes) do not appear to make up ethnic groups distinct from the ethnic group to which persons or militias that attack them belong. They speak the same language (Arabic) and embrace the same religion (Muslim). In addition, also due to the measure of intermarriage, they can hardly be distinguished in their outward physical appearance from the members of tribes that allegedly attacked them.[113]

The U.N. Commission failed to acknowledge that racial distinctions are often socially constructed and forcefully imposed with little regard to actual physical differences. Racial epithets are important for both criminological and legal analysis because they capture the motivation and intent of attackers. The frequently quoted *Akayesu* decision in Rwanda and the *Jelisić* decision in Bosnia both emphasize the importance of spoken language in documenting genocide.[114] Social science evidence regarding the influence of racial epithets is shown below to have an important bearing on violence and genocidal intent in Darfur.

---

111 U.S. Department of State, ADS, *supra* 28.

112 Scheffer, *Genocide and Atrocity Crimes*, *supra* 27 at 229.

113 U.N. International Commission of Inquiry, *Report of the International Commission on Darfur to the United Nations Secretary-General*, U.N. Doc. S/2005/60, 1 February 2005, para 129.

114 See *Prosecutor v. Akayesu*, ICTR-96-4-T, 2 September 1998, para 145; *Prosecutor v. Goran Jelisić*, IT-95-10-T, 14 December 1999, paras 73-77.

We examined the narrative accounts of the attacks on a case-by-case basis to find reports of victims and refugees hearing racial epithets. We recorded the content of the epithets, detailing as exactly as possible the wording of the epithets. Each surveyed individual was assigned a code indicating whether or not they heard racial epithets. We argue that the racial epithets combine elements of motivation and intent, and that they were raised to compelling collective levels in the village settings where they were most frequently heard.

Refugees often reported hearing the incoming forces shouting racial slurs, such as "this is the last day for blacks," "[w]e will destroy the black skinned people," "kill all the slaves," "kill all the blacks," "you are black, you deserve to be tortured like this," and "we will kill any slaves we find and cut off their heads."[115] The mixture of ethnicity and racial markers in the expressed motivations for the sexual violence during the attacks is illustrated in the additional ADS reports of the speech used during the attacks. The surveys noted the following statements indicating violent action based on ethnic and racial motivations:

- Masalit – you are dirty; you deserve to be raped. You are black – you deserve to be tortured like this.
- Janjaweed said to women they raped after cutting their arms to brand them, 'You are now Arab wives. There are no men here.'
- In August, some women return and were raped by Arabs who said to them, 'You will have Arab babies.'
- Arabs said that they would kill as many Masalit as they could and that the rest would never live there again. They also said, "We will take your women and make them ours. We will change the race."
- Ten men raped a Black African woman and said, "You are black people's wives and you bear black children but now you have to bear white people's children.[116]

These words and phrases shouted by the perpetrators of sexual violence provide insight regarding the attackers' motivation and intentions during the raids on Darfurian villagers.

We used village level proportions of respondents hearing racial epithets to measure the aggregation and concentration of racial targeting. These scores ranged from zero to 50.2 percent, indicating wide variation across villages. We shorten the reference to "collective racial intent" below, but it is noteworthy that both motivation and intent are involved in the reported racial epithets. We also include as a further measure of the "us/them" dynamic of ethnic cleansing the respondents' reports of other nearby Arab villages being spared from attacks.

---

115 See U.S. Department of State, ADS, *supra* 28.

116 See U.S. Department of State, ADS, *supra* 28.

Figure 3. Moving Average Percentage of Refugees from Darfur who Reported They Heard Racial Epithets During Attacks by Date of Departure, Atrocities Documentation Survey, Summer 2004

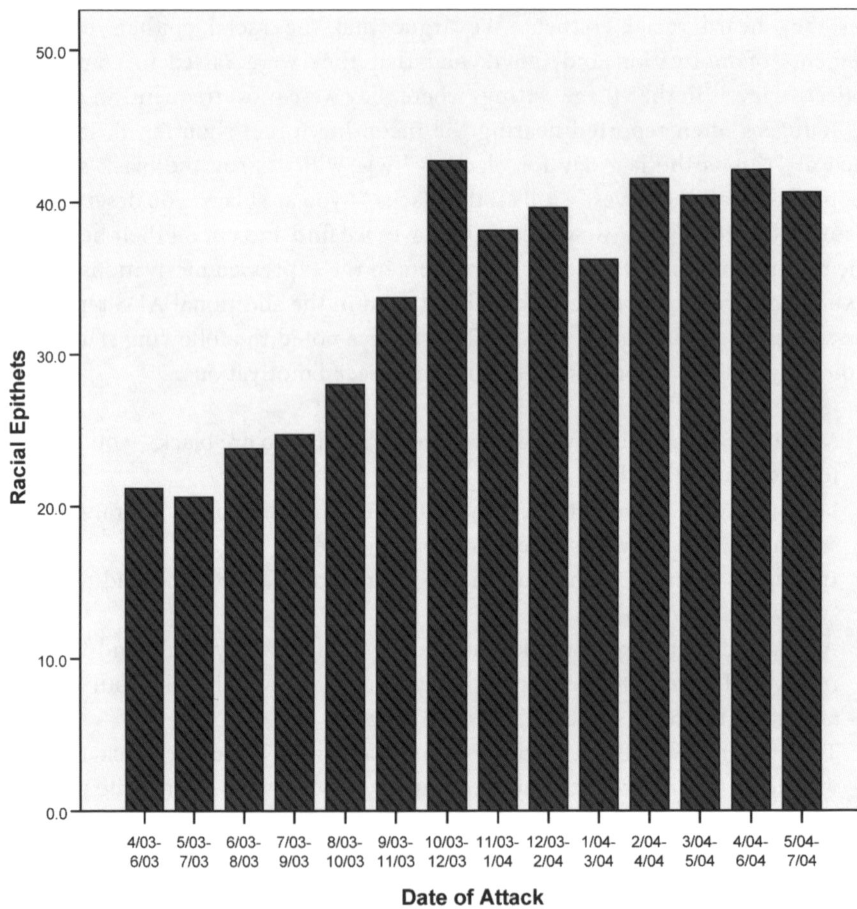

Figure 3 presents a bar graph based on a three month moving average of refugees from Darfur in the ADS who reported hearing racial epithets during attacks. The dating indicates when the refugees reported that they departed from their farms and villages in Darfur. The upward ascent in reports of hearing racial epithets begins in June of 2003, the month when Musa Hilal returned to Darfur after a period of detention elsewhere.[117]

[117] Julie Flint & Alex de Waal, *Darfur: A Short History of a Long War* (London: Zed Books, 2005), 98. Flint and de Waal explain that in June of 2003, Hilal flew back to Darfur and organized the Janjaweed with government support, reportedly due to the intervention of Vice President Ali Osman Taha.

This is also the time period the Office of the Prosecutor indicates Deputy Minister Harun visited Darfur numerous times to lead a major recruitment drive with local leaders such as Hilal.[118] Harun spoke at meetings across Darfur, repeating the message that he held the power "to kill or forgive whoever" he wanted and that he possessed the authority "to kill three-quarters of Darfur in order to allow one quarter to live."[119] The Office of the Prosecutor reports the testimony of a witness about a specific July 2003 speech in Al Geneina: "On that day, Harun's speech was preceded by that of the notorious Milita/Janjaweed leader Musa Hilal. Hilal's speech was characterized by the witness who heard it as 'very racist.' Hilal was enthusiastic about unifying to fight the enemy and characterized the conflict as 'holy war.'"[120]

3.4. ENUMERATING SEXUAL VIOLENCE AND MASS ATROCITIES

The final pieces of our descriptive portrait from the ADS sample consist of the reports of mass atrocities. The classical understanding of genocide emphasizes the intentional *taking of lives* that characterizes the destruction of a group.[121] A more contemporary approach to genocide also focuses on the deliberate infliction of *conditions of life* on a group calculated to bring about its destruction.

Both the taking of lives and the conditions of life are crucial components of the Genocide Convention's definition of what constitutes genocide. According to Article II of the Genocide Convention, genocide consists any of the following five acts committed with intent to destroy, in whole or in part, a national, ethnic, racial, or religious group:

1. killing members of the group;
2. causing serious bodily or mental harm to members of the group;
3. deliberately inflicting on the group conditions of life calculated to bring about its physical destruction in whole or in part;
4. imposing measures intended to prevent births within the group; or
5. forcibly transferring children of the group to another group.[122]

---

118 Situation in Darfur, The Sudan, I.C.C.-02/05–56, Prosecutor's Application under Article 58(7), 27 February 2007, paras 47, 122.

119 *Ibid.* at para 67, 141.

120 *Ibid.* at para 155.

121 The classical focus in defining genocide on loss of life likely derives from the massiveness of mortality in The Holocaust and from the customary importance attached to human life in common law.

122 Convention on the Prevention and Punishment of the Crime of Genocide, Article 2, 9 December 1948, 78 U.N.T.S. 277.

Any one of the five specified elements can legally constitute genocide. The third act, with its reference to "group conditions of life," is perhaps the most all-encompassing and meaningful element in understanding how genocidal violence denies sustainable life to entire villages, communities, or populations. There is little doubt that sexual violence can undermine conditions of group life and lead to the destruction of that group.

Our measurement approach involved using a report section from each survey that recorded incidents of victimization. Respondents reported attacks on themselves, their families, and their settlements, which involved bombing, killing, rape, abduction, assault, property destruction, and theft. Each respondent therefore reported for him or herself together with his or her settlement. Our most specific interest was in systematic counts of the number of sexual attacks reported by the respondents. However, for comparative purposes, we also created a total victimization severity score, which we describe first, based on the common law seriousness of the incidents reported for attacks on the settlements. Commissioner Pillay noted the importance of measuring the link between the sexual violence and other mass atrocities when she observed: "The case law of the tribunals has given us direction as to how to conduct investigations. We know that commanders have been found responsible for the 'incidental murders and rapes' that were deemed to be the 'natural and foreseeable consequences of an ethnic cleansing campaign.'"[123]

We aggregated reports of specific incidents experienced or witnessed by each respondent in the settlement. To create the total victimization score, we assigned the following values to the incidents: five to reported killings; four to sexual attacks; three to assaults; two to property destruction or theft; and one to displacement.

To illustrate the coding of the incidents in the severity scale, consider the example of a 35-year-old Masaleit woman with a total severity score of 52. The attack reported by this woman occurred in a village near Masteri. Sudanese government troops and Arab Janjaweed militia attacked her village on 1 September 2003. Her report included 20 incidents during the attack that occurred that day. Her report includes herself, her family, and others in the village. During the attack, she was beaten (severity score of 3) and raped (4). Her father was severely beaten (3) trying to protect her, and he was subsequently abducted (4). Some women from her village were abducted (4) and held for two hours. They were beaten (3) and raped (4) before being released. Another group of women, ages ranging from 16 to 20, were raped (4), and she personally witnessed one of the rapes and heard about the rapes from other victims (4). Additional villagers, including her brother, were

beaten (3), shot (3), and stabbed (3). She witnessed dead bodies (5), all male, some of whom had their throats cut, and others that were shot in the head. Her

[123] Pillay Address, *supra* 3 at 463.

village was completely destroyed (2), except for three huts that were on the far edge of the village. Theft occurred (2), included that of livestock, food, and water pots. She reports that there was no rebel activity in or around her village. The only defense the villagers had was a few spears, which were no match for the attackers' guns, knives, pickup trucks with mounted guns, and aircraft. She entered Chad in February 2004, becoming one of the two to three million Darfurians displaced (1) from the mass atrocities.

We defined sexual victimization as including rape, sexual assault, acts of sexual molestation such as insertion of foreign objects into the genital opening or anus, and sexual slavery. Four percent of the full sample and seven percent of women refugees reported personal victimization.[124] Nearly a third of the Darfur refugees (29.1%) indicated that other villagers were sexually victimized during attacks. Others' sexual victimization is coded from one to 10 other persons victimized, with a mean of 1.18. As noted above, others' sexual victimization is our ultimate outcome variable, while we used self-reports of personal sexual victimization as a control variable for unmeasured heterogeneity and/or reporting bias. Map 1 indicates that sexual violence was most common in West Darfur villages where Fur and Masalit tribal groups were concentrated. This map further reveals that the villages ranking highest in reports of sexual violence were also usually the same villages ranking highest in total victimization, which included killings as well as other forms of physical and sexual violence. This overlapping of sexual and other forms of violence is consistent with the finding in the ICTR *Akayesu* case in Rwanda. The *Akayesu* case found that rape is "an integral part of the process of destruction."[125] The ICTY *Kunarac, Kovac & Vokovic* case also recognized rape as part of crimes against humanity.[126]

4. APPLYING AN APPROPRIATE ANALYTIC METHOD

The above-described data was then analyzed using the HLM methodology designed for multi-level clustered samples.[127] HLM allows analysis within and between villages, as explained below. We analyzed the combined roles of GoS forces with Janjaweed militias in the racial targeting of sexual violence – as well as in the sparing of Arab villages – in an "us" and "them" dynamic of targeted violence and ethnic cleansing.

124 The latter approximates reporting of sexual assaults in Sierra Leone. See Amowitz *et al.*, *Sierra Leone*, *supra* 57 at 518.

125 *Prosecutor v. Akayesu*, ICTR-96-4-T, 2 September 1998, para 731.

126 *Prosecutor v. Kunarac, Kovac & Vukovic*, IT-96–23-T, 22 February 2001, paras 436, 542.

127 Stephen W. Raudenbush & Anthony S. Bryk, *Hierarchical Linear Models: Applications and Data Analysis Methods* (London: Sage Publications, 2002).

First we used a logistic regression to model binary reports of whether individuals heard racial epithets during the attacks. Then we estimated joined individual and village level Poisson regression equations of others' sexual victimization (adjusted for dispersion, months of exposure before flight, and own sexual victimization).[128] The dependent variable, sexual victimization, is the count of the number of other persons reported by each individual (*i.e.*, other than this individual) in the village to have been sexually attacked, as described above. HLM allows simultaneous analysis of outcomes within and between villages. Thus, our within-village Poisson model first regresses the individual level reports of sexual victimization by the 932 respondents on their individual reports of racial epithets and other independent variables defined below. Our between-village Poisson model then regresses the average sexual victimization scores for the 22 villages – after the individual level variables are taken into account – on the proportion of the respondents who report they heard racial epithets in each village. The averaging of victimization scores within villages avoids the over-counting of overlapping reports.[129]

Poisson models assume independence of the modeled events. Reports of others' sexual victimization could be as problematic as hearsay evidence and as well be dependent on the respondents' own sexual victimization. To minimize such dependence and the violation of this assumption, we include in our Poisson model of the sexual victimization of others an independent variable that is the individual's report of personally being sexually victimized.

We learn from the joint analysis not only about individual sources of reported sexual victimization in Darfur, but also about the influence of aggregate differences in the distribution of racial epithets between villages on sexual victimization, with individual level variables controlled. We ultimately show in Map 1 how these joint GoS and Janjaweed attacks are associated with aggregated and concentrated racial intent at the village level in the prediction of sexual victimization in Darfur. We also include on this map a parallel indication of total victimization scores.

The models we estimate thus consider: (1) whether during attacks ethnic group members of the Fur, Masaleit and Zaghawa tribes report more often hearing racial epithets, our indicator of intent to victimize a protected group; (2) whether the joining of government and non-government forces in attacks, and

---

128 Poisson regression is a kind of regression analysis that is most often used to analyze data that takes the form of counts, in this case counts of rape and sexual assault.

129 The equations for the hierarchical Poisson model are as follows:

$$\ln\lambda_{ij} = \beta_{oj} + \Sigma_k \beta_{kj} X_{kji} + \varepsilon_{ji}$$

$$\beta_{oj} = \pi_{oo} + \pi_{o1} Y_j + \delta_j$$

where λ_{ij} is the rate of sexual victimization of others reported by individual i in settlement j, β_{kj}'s are regression coefficients for variables k in settlement j, X_{kji} individual level covariates, Y_j represents the proportion of individuals in settlement j that heard racial epithets, π_{oo} is a constant term for the entire sample, π_{o1} is the effect associated with the proportion hearing racial epithets, and ε_{ji} and δ_j are Poisson and normally distributed errors.

sparing of nearby Arab villages, further predicts reports of hearing racial epithets; (3) whether reports of hearing racial epithets are unequally distributed across villages, and whether this is an important determinant of the effects epithets have on reported sexual violence; and (4) whether joined government and non-government attacks in conjunction with higher prevalence of racial epithets at the village level predict higher sexual victimization.

The HLM reliability score resulting from the partitioning of the variance of others' sexual victimization within and between villages is 0.906, indicating precision at the village level. This high score not only speaks to, but should almost completely eliminate concerns about the unreliability of the hearsay nature of the ADS evidence of sexual victimization. The surveys, as analyzed above, are therefore strong pieces of the new type of social science evidence called for by Prosecutor Moreno-Ocampo and Commissioner Pillay.

4.1. MAPPING THE RACIAL TARGETING

We can summarize important aspects of our analysis on two maps. We begin with the distribution of the racial epithets heard during attacks by the ADS respondents. First, we consider how the reporting of these epithets varies across the *settlements* – that is, we answer the question: *where* were these epithets heard most often? Second, we consider how racial epithets were distributed in terms of the characteristics of the *individuals* who heard them – that is, we answer the question: *who* heard these epithets most often?

Map 1 portrays the variation in reported racial epithets across the settlements. It indicates variation in the proportion of respondents reporting epithets with circles of increasing sizes (calibrated in quartiles) in the settlements. About half of the respondents in the top quartile heard racial epithets during the attacks. Thus, 45 percent of the respondents heard racial epithets in Kabkabiyah, where early attacks are reported to have included Musa Hilal, and from 43 to 50 percent of respondents heard these epithets in settlements in southwestern Darfur – in Al Geneina, Masteri, Habilah, Garsila, Foro Burunga, and Benesi – the sites of attacks reported in the media and in the ADS data as led by three other Janjaweed militia leaders. The latter sites are in the more fertile and densely settled areas of Darfur.

Map 1. Settlement Cluster Map of Racial Epithets and Total Victimization and Sexual Victimization

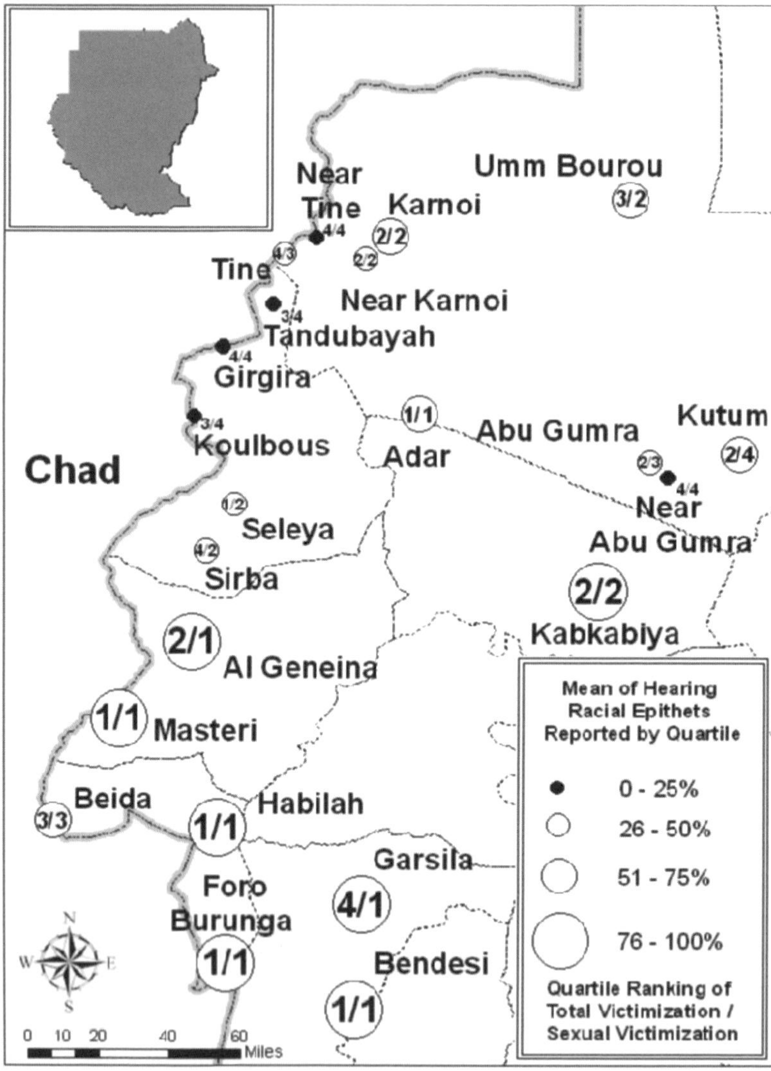

Map 2 outlines the locations where news media and human rights groups reported attacks occurred that were led by four militia leaders – Musa Hilal, Hamid Dawai, Ali Kushayb, and Abdullah Shineibat. We designate the approximate areas of these leaders' operations with triangular-shaped markings on Map 2. These are also the areas with high reports of racial epithets and attacks in Map 1.

Map 2. Janjaweed Militia Leaders' Areas of Operation

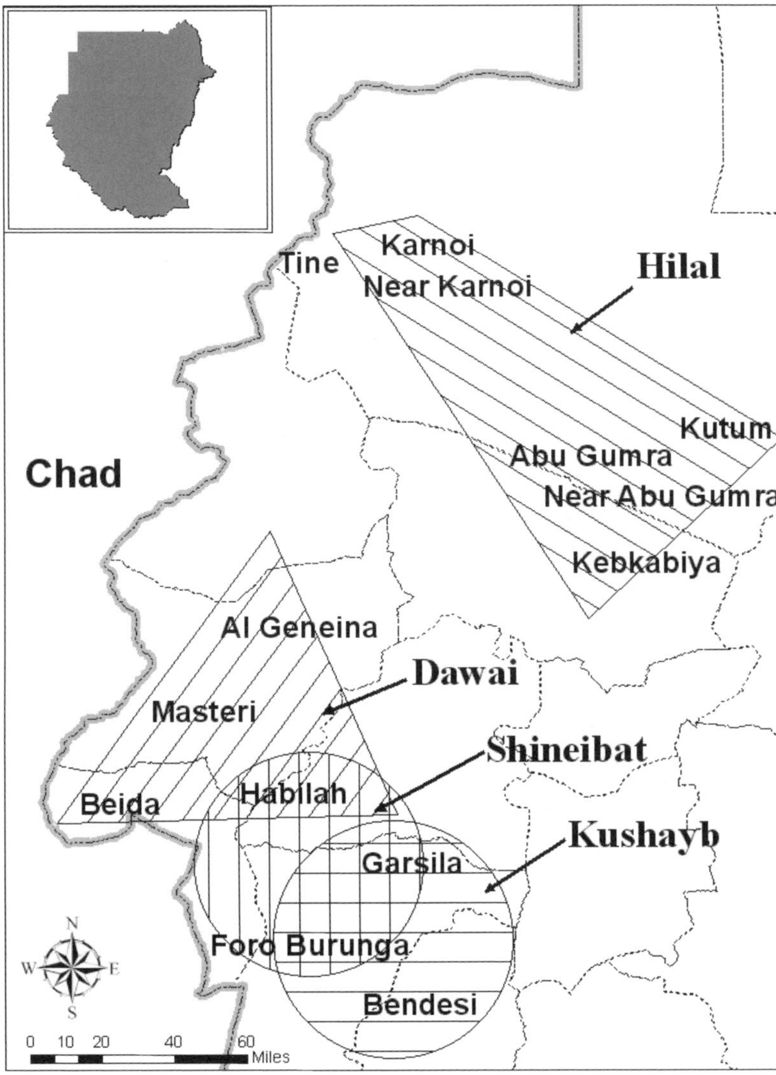

4.2. MODELING THE RACIAL EPITHETS

Table 2 presents a logistic regression model of hearing racial epithets during attacks. The model indicates men were more likely than women to hear epithets. Nearly three quarters (72.8%) of the women refugees had no schooling and less than five percent (4.5%) had attended Islamic school, while just over one third

(35.6%) of men refugees had no schooling and more than a quarter (26.0%) had attended Islamic school. Men were thus more likely to understand and report racial epithets shouted in Arabic.

The model further indicates Fur, Masalit, and Zaghawa were also more likely than others to hear the racial epithets. The Zaghawa experienced more bombing than ground attacks, which may explain why they were somewhat less likely to report hearing racial epithets. There has been much attention paid to the specific targeting of the Fur in Darfur. An additional finding of the model is that respondents who reported that nearby Arab villages were spared also were more likely to report hearing racial epithets. The final important finding in the model is that racial epithets were more likely to be heard during *joint* Sudanese government and Janjaweed attacks, suggesting government involvement in elevating the racial epithets.

Table 2. Documentation Survey, Darfur Refugees, July-August 2004[a]

Individual Level Characteristics			
	b(se)	*OR*	*95% C.I.*
Respondent Attributes			
Age	-.005(.005)	.995	(.985,1.005)
Gender	.655 (.185)***	1.925	(1.339,2.766)
African Group Membership			
Fur	.679 (.252)**	1.973	(1.206, 3.231)
Masalit	.727 (.200)***	2.070	(1.398, 3.064)
Zaghawa	.384 (.192)*	1.469	(1.008, 2.141)
Attacking Groups			
GoS & Janjaweed	.652 (.165)***	1.920	(1.389, 2.653)
Ethnic Protection			
Arab Villages Spared	1.123(.231)***	3.074	(1.957, 4.830)
Intercept	-1.737 (.288)	.176	(.097,.320)

a

N aN= 932 individuals (level-1) and 22 settlement clusters (level-2).

*

*p p<.05, **p<.01, ***p<.001, and in following table

	Model 1 Fixed Effects, Exposure Adjusted	Model 2 Fixed Effects, Exposure Adjusted, Own Victimization Included	Model 3 Fixed Effects, Exposure Adjusted, Own Victimization Included, Robust Standard Errors	Model 3 Fixed Effects, Exposure Adjusted, Own Victimization Included, Robust Standard Errors, Over dispersion Adjusted
Individual Level	*b(se)*	*b(se)*	*b(se)*	*b(se)*
Age	-.022(.003)***	-.018(.003)***	-.018(.006)**	-.019(.006)**
Gender	.043(.065)	.228(.071)**	.225(.186)	.235(.183)
Fur	.754(.183)***	.503(.184)**	.503(.497)	-.235(.379)
Masalit	.058(.151)	-.002(.153)	-.002(.379)	-.380(.335)
Zaghawa	-.033(.178)	-.079(.177)	-.079(.553)	-.514(2.85)
GoS and Janjaweed	.270(.072)***	.329(.073)*	.329(.165)*	.345(.164)*
Arabs Spared	.222(.103)	.190(.104)	.190(.153)	.196(.165)
Own Victimization		1.124(.095)***	1.124(.230)***	1.180(.229)***
Racial Epithets	.300(.063)***	.294(.063)***	.294(.183)	.290(.188)
Village Level				
Mean Racial Epithets	3.564(1.157)**	3.367(1.082)**	3.367(1.298)**	2.518(.905)**
Intercept	-3.778(.147)	-.3.807(.136)	-3.867(.159)	-3.660(.100)

It is possible that the combined forces shouted the epithets in several languages, thereby increasing the likelihood that racial epithets would be understood by respondents. Yet this could account neither for an effect of combined forces on sexual victimization, nor for the persistence of an effect of racial epithets on sexual victimization after statistically controlling for combined attacks. The latter relationships are the focus of Table 3.

4.3. MODELING THE SEXUAL VICTIMIZATION

To the extent that ethnic cleansing and genocide victimization encompasses a group "in whole" – as, for example, a "scorched earth" policy would imply – there might be little within- or between-settlement variation in numbers of deaths or severity of victimization of the kind whose quantitative measurement we have just described; all would be victimized. On the other hand, to the extent that this group victimization is "in part," there should be variance in both within and between-settlement outcomes. For the criminological and legal reasons we have indicated, we were particularly interested in determining the role that racial intent played in explaining variation in Sudanese state organized victimization along with the Janjaweed militias of the Black African groups and settlements.

Our interest was thus in the settlements as much as the individuals who are the victims of the Darfur conflict as represented in the ADS sample. The hypothetical process examined in our analysis is expressed in Figure 4. We analyzed the combined roles of GoS forces with Janjaweed militias in racially-targeted mass atrocities, as well as in the selective protection of nearby Arab villagers. Selective protection as well as predation can be an instrumental way of separating "us" from "them" in an organizational dynamic of violence and ethnic cleansing resulting in mass atrocities.

Figure 4. Combined Roles of GoS and Janjaweed with Ethnic Protection in Racial Targeting of Ethnic Cleansing and Mass Atrocities in Darfur

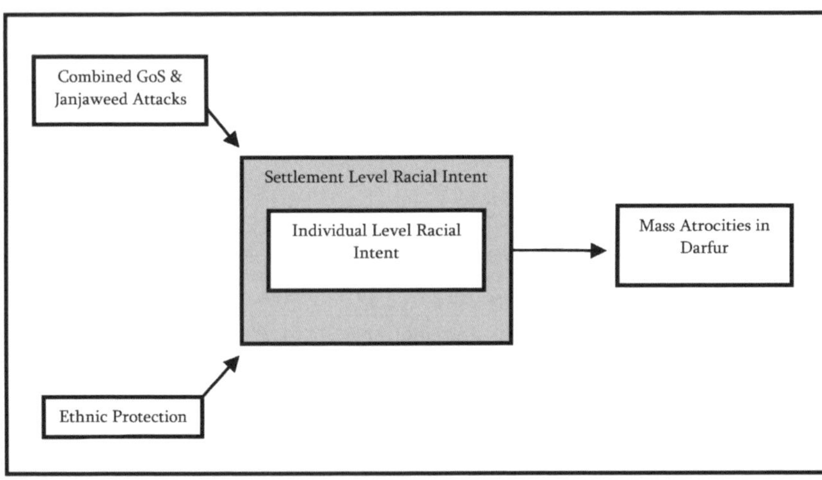

Table 3 presents Poisson models of sexual violence, with robust standard errors and successively adjusted for dispersion and for months of exposure before fleeing, as well as controlling for respondents' own reported sexual victimization. The results are strikingly consistent across the columns. A significant age effect indicates that younger respondents reported more sexual victimization. More striking is the direct and significant role of the combined government and Janjaweed forces in explaining sexual victimization. More striking still is the simultaneously significant role of racial intention when measured as a proportion hearing racial epithets at the village level. This effect is net of all other variables in the table, including racial epithets measured at the individual level, as well as respondents' own reported sexual victimization. As expected, the latter self-reports have a highly significant effect on the reported sexual victimization of others. The effects of combined GoS and Janjaweed attacks and village level racial intention remain statistically significant, withstanding controls for bias and unmeasured heterogeneity in reports of sexual victimization.

The fact that ethnic group memberships exercise statistically significant effects on the hearing of racial epithets (Table 2), and in turn that these racial epithets measured at the village level exercise statistically significant effects on sexual victimization (Table 3), is consistent with the causal inference that ethnic group membership and racial intentions directly and indirectly lead to sexual victimization.[130] This sequence of findings is an important part of the "reasonable grounds" evidence indicating that the protected group statuses of ethnicity and race are associated with sexual violence in ways that violate the Genocide Convention. A more detailed discussion of checks on the further sources of causal dependency in the Poisson models we have presented in Table 3 is provided in the Appendix to this paper.

Table 3. Alternative Individual and Village Cluster Models of Sexual Victimization, Atrocities Documentation Survey, Darfur Refugees, July-August 2004
N=932 individual (level-1) and 22 village clusters (level-2)

Individual Level	Model 1. Fixed Effects, Exposure Adjusted b(se)	Model 2. Fixed Effects, Exposure Adjusted, Own Victimization Included b(se)	Model 3. Fixed Effects, Exposure Adjusted, Own Victimization Included, Robust Standard Errors b(se)	Model 4. F Fixed Effects, Exposure Adjusted, Own Victimization Included, Robust Standard Errors, Over Dispersion Adjusted b(se)
Age	-.022(.003)***	-.018(.003)***	-.018(.006)**	-.019(.006)**
Male	.043(.065)	.228(.071)**	.225(.186)	.235(.183)
Fur	.754(.183)***	.503(.184)**	.503(.497)	-.235(.379)
Masaleit	.058(.151)	-.002(.153)	-.002(.379)	-.380(.335)
Zaghawa	-.033(.178)	-.079(.177)	-.079(.553)	-.514(2.85)
GoS & Janjaweed	.270(.072)***	.329(.073)*	.329(.165)*	.345(.164)*
Arabs Spared	.222(.103)	.190(.104)	.190(.153)	.196(.165)
Own Victimization		1.124(.095)***	1.124(.230)***	1.180(.229)***
Racial Epithets	.300(.063)***	.294(.063)***	.294(.183)	.290(.188)
Village Level				
Mean Racial Epithets	3.564(1.157)**	3.367(1.082)**	3.367(1.298)**	2.518(.905)**
Intercept	-3.778(.147)	-3.807(.136)	-3.867(.159)	-3.660(.100)

N = 932 individual in twenty-two village clusters.
* $p < .05$, ** $p < .01$, *** $p < .001$.

The results from the Poisson model of sexual victimization are summarized graphically in Figure 5. The lines in this figure show the predicted number of other persons sexually victimized in the villages that result from the proportion

130 See Reuben Baron & David Kenny, "The Moderator-Mediator Variable Distinction in Social Psychological Research: Conceptual, Strategic, and Statistical Considerations," *Journal of Personality & Social Psychology* 51 (1986): 1173, 1180-81.

of respondents who reported hearing racial epithets, and that the attacking forces were a combination of GoS and Janjaweed forces.[131] Thus, the top line in this figure indicates that an average of more than one and as many as two persons were reported sexually victimized when half or more of the respondents reported hearing racial epithets during attacks by combined GoS and Janjaweed forces. Sexual victimizations were reported less often when the attacks were described as by separate GoS or Janjaweed forces and without racial epithets. The combined weight of the described analyses paints a compelling picture of GoS and Janjaweed joint participation in sexual violence against Black Africans. As the statistically controlled analysis of the use of racial epithets indicates, this joint violence appears to have been intended to destroy the targeted group's way of life.

Figure 5. Additive Effects of Combined GoS and Janjaweed Attacks in Village Level Racial Targeting of Sexual Victimization in Darfur

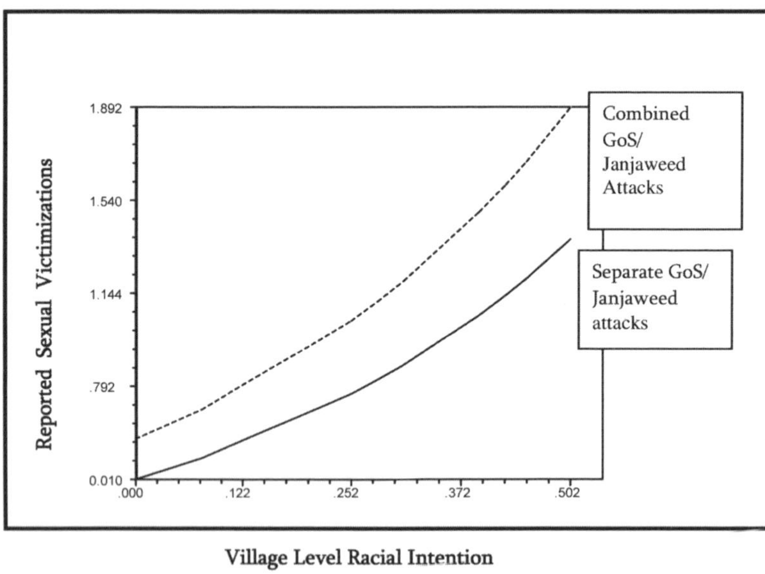

5. CONCLUSIONS

Commissioner Pillay reminded The Hague Colloquium that the prosecution of grave sexual attacks in international criminal law is not merely an option, but rather it is a responsibility:

131 Other variables in the Poisson model are set at their mean values.

> Let me reiterate and summarize the key elements of the cases I have just discussed. To begin with, international justice deemed rape as a natural and foreseeable consequence of a lack of discipline in cases involving other violations of international humanitarian law. Further, it established command responsibility and upheld the duty of inquiry to reflect the obligation of persons in a position of responsibility and authority to prevent violations from occurring, and to punish perpetrators when such crimes are committed. In addition, it considered that culpability could involve all those engaged in sexual violence crimes, directly or indirectly.[132]

Not to prosecute gender and sexual violence that occurs in conflict zones is an evasion of the responsibility to protect those victimized and is a legally unacceptable form of denial. Prosecutor Moreno-Ocampo put the matter squarely when he said that, "It is normal that President Al Bashir denies the crime, but the question is: why is the international community joining in the denial?"[133]

In July 2008, the ICC Office of the Prosecutor led by Prosecutor Moreno-Ocampo applied to the Judicial Chambers of the ICC for charges including rape and genocide against Sudan's president.[134] In March of 2009, the ICC judges issued a warrant for the arrest of President Al Bashir on charges of crimes against humanity, extermination, and rape – but not genocide.[135] This last decision is under appeal.[136] We submit that the decision of the ICC judges not to charge genocide ignores the importance of social science evidence demonstrating the racial targeting of protected groups in Darfur for acts of sexual violence. We further submit that this charging decision constitutes a legal denial of a key part of the racially-based *mens rea* that led to rape and sexual violence in Darfur, and in this way is a failure of the international community to provide protection to racially identified groups in Darfur.

The evidence we have presented indicates that Fur, Masalit, and Zaghawa farmers and villagers in Darfur heard racial epithets with increasing frequency during attacks in the summer of 2003. This was the period when the Sudanese

132 Pillay Address, *supra* 3 at 463-64.

133 Moreno-Ocampo, Keynote Address, *supra* 2.

134 See *Situation in Darfur, The Sudan*, I.C.C.-02/05–01/09, Prosecutor's Application Under Article 58(7), 14 July 2008, 1 ("[Al Bashir] bears criminal responsibility for the crime of genocide...").

135 See *Prosecutor v. Al Bashir*, ICC-02/05–01/09, Decision on Prosecutor's Application for a Warrant of Arrest, 4 March 2009, para 206 (finding insufficient evidence of genocidal intent). But see *Prosecutor v. Al Bashir*, ICC-02/05–01/09, Separate and Partly Dissenting Opinion on Decision on Prosecutor's Application for a Warrant of Arrest, 4 March 2009, para 105 ("I am satisfied that there are reasonable grounds... to believe that Omar Al Bashir has committed the crime of genocide.").

136 See *Situation in Darfur, The Sudan*, I.C.C.-02/05–01/09, Prosecutor's Application for Leave to Appeal, 10 March 2009; see also *Prosecutor v. Al Bashir*, ICC 02/05-01/09, Judgment on Prosecutor's Appeal, 3 February 2010 (granting Prosecutor's appeal and remanding to the trial court).

central government reinstalled militia leader Musa Hilel in Darfur and when the Deputy Minister Ahmad Harun held public meetings in Darfur with Hilal. The Fur, Masalit, and Zaghawa villagers heard racially-motivated shouts and slurs more often when GoS forces joined with Janjaweed groups in attacks on their farms and settlements. When these villagers heard these epithets they more often also experienced violent victimization. This victimization included mass atrocities in general and sexual attacks in particular. The unfolding pattern of events was both undeniable and foreseeable upwards through the chain of command, reaching to the highest level of Sudan's government and ending at President Al Bashir. It was his responsibility to protect the citizens of Darfur from these attacks, and in the absence of this domestic protection, it is the responsibility of the International Criminal Court to prosecute President Al Bashir for crimes against humanity, extermination, rape, and genocide. The data and analyses described above provide "reasonable grounds" evidence adequate to do so.

APPENDIX: THE ISSUE OF DEPENDENCY IN MODELING THE REPORTED SEXUAL VICTIMIZATION OF OTHERS IN DARFUR

The Poisson model assumes that reported events of sexual violence occur independently. Yet there may be sources of dependence. There are two possibilities: (1) a single source is responsible for the reports of each person but the sources are independent (that is they are not the same); (2) a single source is responsible for reports of each person and the source is correlated across persons.

If (1) is the case, then the number of acts of violence reported by each individual within a fixed time period could be considered Poisson, if the events occur independently of each other. But if (2) is the case and there is a single source, say a single battle or attack and/or clustered sampling of respondents in villages, then the number of violent events reported may not follow a Poisson. Controls for the respondent's own victimization which we include in our model help to purge for dependency but do not completely explain it away. Fortunately, the hierarchical linear model (HLM) we have used further addresses the second set of possibilities.

HLM allows the calculation of robust standard errors that are adjusted for the increased within-group homogeneity resulting from sampling of clustered respondents. HLM further allows the adjustment of coefficients and standard errors for increased heterogeneity resulting from correlated sources of over-dispersion. For example, the correlated targeting of attacks on selected villages can result in increased heterogeneity or variance in reported events across villages. HLM allows a relaxation of the independence assumption by not imposing distributional assumptions on the extra-Poisson variance parameter. The result is a negative binomial model yielding estimates that can better capture the underlying process: the adjusted coefficients are efficient and the standard errors are unbiased.

Table A1 presents coefficients and standard errors in four different models, all of which include adjustments for length of exposure to risk before fleeing. However, Model 1 does not include reports of personally being sexually victimized in estimating the reported sexual victimizations of others. Five variables significantly predict sexual victimization of others in this model– younger age, being Fur, combined attack by Government of Sudan (GoS) forces and Janjaweed militia, individual level reports of hearing racial epithets, and village mean level reports of hearing racial epithets.

Model 2 adds the control for self-reports of own sexual victimization, which is statistically significant and strong. The biggest change in Model 2 is that gender is now statistically significant. This makes sense because in Darfur women more often than men report themselves being raped, while men more often report others being raped. The latter effect is suppressed in Model 1 and revealed in Model 2 by the inclusion of the measure of own sexual victimization. In addition, the five variables previously found statistically significant remain so. The effect of being Fur declines by about one third in strength, while the effect of combined GoS and Janjaweed attacks increases by more than 20 percent.

The final two models, Models 3 and 4, respectively introduce two further adjustments: robust standard errors and adjustment for over-dispersion. These models yield similar results. The effects of gender, being Fur, and individual level racial epithets now are reduced below significance, while the following four variables retain their strength and statistical significance: younger age, combined attack by GoS forces and Janjaweed militia, own sexual victimization, and village mean level of hearing racial epithets. The latter village level effect of hearing racial epithets is reduced by about one quarter in size, but the standard error of this coefficient is similarly reduced, so the statistical significance of this effect remains stable.

The essential point is this: across the four models the key variables in our analysis – combined attacks and village level racial epithets – remain stable in their significant effects on the reported sexual victimization of others.

PART 3

SURVIVING SEXUAL VIOLENCE, STORY TELLING AND CREATING AWARENESS

CHAPTER 14
PARTNERS FOR GENDER JUSTICE

Brigid INDER[1]

1. INTRODUCTION

Throughout history, women's rights organisations and advocates have been instrumental in every social change and justice initiative. They have influenced international conventions, provoked ground-breaking jurisprudence and driven legal reform. Non-governmental organisations (NGOs) led by women have also created global movements, adapted communication tools and established innovative services. Although sometimes invisible, women have often been at the forefront of democratic and political liberation struggles, anti-war and peace movements, and national emancipation efforts.

These initiatives continue with women advocates leading strategies to shape international gender justice and the work of the International Criminal Court (ICC), the only permanent Court with the potential to try individuals anywhere in the world for war crimes, crimes against humanity and genocide.[2]

On 17 July 1998, the Rome Statute was adopted by 120 States and opened for signatories. The Statute came into force on 1 July 2002 upon receipt of sixty ratifications at which time the Court's jurisdiction became active. Since then it has established itself as a 698 person institution[3] with 18 elected Judges, an independent Office of the Prosecutor, and Registry with oversight of the administrative and operational functions of the Court. The ICC includes a feature unique in international criminal justice, which is the Trust Fund for Victims mandated to provide rehabilitation assistance and reparations to victims and their families.

---

1 The author would like to thank Jessie Kenmore for feedback on early drafts of the chapter as well as the staff of the Women's Initiatives for Gender Justice for their support. This article is dedicated to victims/survivors of armed conflicts around the world and to all those courageously working for gender justice.

2 RC/10-11062010, Adopted 12 June 2010 at the Closing Plenary of the ICC Review Conference of the Rome Statute.

3 *Gender Report Card on the International Criminal Court 2011* (The Hague, the Netherlands: Women's Initiatives for Gender Justice, 2011), 12.

The key elements, which eventually gave rise to the ICC, have their roots in:

- Past conflicts and two world wars
- Previous efforts towards accountability and deterrence for grievous crimes and
- The voices of victims, civil society and in particular women's NGOs, who have shown themselves to be significant partners in the pursuit of accountability and peace.

Advocates for gender justice are asserting a stake in the process of designing a new international justice system, one that effectively prevents and addresses gender-based crimes and other forms of brutality most pervasive in conflict situations as well as developing a cohesive peace and security framework capable of deterring armed conflict itself.

It has been clearly documented that the commission of rape and other forms of sexual violence intensify and increase in both scale and brutality during violent civil unrest and armed conflicts. Rape is an effective strategy in war because it relies on pre-existing norms, standards and belief-systems regarding gender inequality to create a breakdown within the community; to fracture individual and family networks; to splinter social and cultural connections; and to assert ethnic and political supremacy through the use of acts already legitimized as a means of expressing dominance, that is – through sexualized violence, most commonly rape – predominantly against women. Violence committed against women during armed conflicts is multi-faceted and systemic, multi-purposed and gendered. Therefore, accountability for such acts is often complex and always crucial. The role of the ICC, a Court with an explicit mandate to prosecute gender-based crimes as war crimes, crimes against humanity and genocide, is of paramount importance to ending both sexualised violence and the violent contexts within which these acts occur.

Partnerships between local and international NGOs and the International Criminal Court hold credible prosecutorial potential. The interplay between experts in the justice process, including women's NGOs, can contribute in positive, reliable and material ways to the pursuit of truth and in describing, with greater human voice, the form and extent of victimization and the perseverance of communities until justice is satisfied.

As partners in the pursuit of justice, women's organisations and the ICC have much to gain from each other's leadership, expertise and mandates.

Historical Context. There are at least three crucial elements which inform the history and backdrop to the emergence of the ICC, and the infusion of gender provisions within the Rome Statute.

1. International Humanitarian Law and the First Tribunals – historical treatment of gender-based crimes in armed conflicts and war.

The Law of The Hague (1907) and the Geneva Conventions (1949) largely ignored gender-based crimes, although rape and enforced prostitution were explicitly mentioned in the Fourth Geneva Convention (1949) and Additional Protocol II (1977), where they were described as 'outrages upon personal dignity'. Rape and other forms of sexual violence do not appear to have been taken seriously by the Tribunals following the end of World War II where they were categorized as an offence against 'honour'. Rape was considered indecent rather than violent.

For example, no one was charged with gender-based crimes at the Nuremberg Tribunal (1945–1946). In the International Military Tribunal for the Far East (IMTFE) (1946), there were convictions for rape in only one case where rape was charged as 'inhumane treatment,' 'failure to respect family honour and rights' and 'ill treatment.'[4]

2. Women's human rights advocacy and the global women's movement

In the early-to-mid 1990s, a series of global conferences convened by the United Nations (UN) ignited an array of simultaneous civil society movements. The conferences included:

- The Earth Summit, Rio de Janeiro, 1992
- The World Conference on Human Rights, Vienna, 1993
- The International Conference on Population and Development (ICPD), Cairo, 1994 and
- The Fourth World Conference on Women (FWCW), Beijing, 1995.

These conferences triggered a decade-long international mobilisation of women's rights activists and created a momentum for change, which gathered pace as the 1990s progressed. Women advocates organised caucuses during the conferences and seized the opportunities to influence global negotiations and international policy. The size and sequencing of the conferences held over a four-year period facilitated the exchange and deepening of analysis, the building of strategic capacity, and the formation of a global feminist advocacy agenda on a scale experienced by few other social movements at that time. These were new opportunities to demonstrate a collective ability to influence international political, policy and resource decisions.

Advances in communication technology helped to facilitate the impact of this social movement. With the Internet and mobile phones becoming more widely accessible during the early 1990s, women's rights advocates were able to

[4] For an authoritative analysis of the history of gender-based crimes in international tribunals see Kelly D. Askin, *War Crimes Against Women: Prosecution in International War Crimes Tribunals* (The Hague, the Netherlands: Kluwer Law International, 1997).

share information instantly between locations, regions and time zones thus enabling the development of cohesive strategies in multiple policy-making settings. The use of the newly available forms of technology by networks of women's rights activists enabled simultaneous monitoring of a range of UN negotiations, and allowed advocates to impact political developments in real time. The ICPD process, including the Preparatory Committees and Conference, was the first time this type of technology was deliberately used by feminist advocates as a strategic tool in global advocacy and policy-making.

The work of women's rights advocates created watershed agreements at the Vienna, Cairo and Beijing Conferences, and strengthened the recognition of autonomy and women's rights as the cornerstones for human progress, development, equality and justice. The overdue declaration of women's rights as human rights, and the recognition of sexual and reproductive health and reproductive rights concepts were transformative at the policy and political levels. Similarly, the ideological shift in population debates, historically framed solely in developmental terms to notions of women's rights, self-determination and human aspiration, and the articulation of violence against women as a global and preventable epidemic, were amongst some of the most profound advancements.

However, States, UN agencies and NGO advocates underestimated at least two major thematic issues during this period. Although both the HIV/AIDS pandemic, and the experience of women in armed conflict, were recognised within the Beijing[5] and Cairo Agreements[6], the respective policy and programmatic frameworks proved to be grossly inadequate as the scale and complexity of the HIV/AIDS -related challenges unfolded and the armed conflicts in Rwanda and the former Yugoslavia were fully revealed.

3. The conflicts in the former Yugoslavia and Rwanda, and the United Nations Tribunals established in 1993 and 1994, respectively, to prosecute those responsible for genocide, war crimes and crimes against humanity.

The Statutes for the ad hoc Tribunals[7] established in response to the conflicts in the former Yugoslavia and Rwanda both recognized rape as a crime against

5 *United Nations Report of the Fourth World-Conference on Women,* (A/CONF.177/20/Rev.1), 4–25 September 1995, available at www.un.org/womenwatch/daw/beijing/pdf/Beijing%20full%20report%20E.pdf (last visited 12 April 2012): HIV/Aids herein: 14, para 37; 37, para 98; 44–46, para 108. The experience of women in armed conflict is recognized herein: Strategic Objective E. Women and armed conflict, 56–64, paras 131 to 149.

6 *United Nations Report of the International Conference on Population and Development,* (A/CONF.171/13/Rev.1) 15–13 September 1994, available at www.unfpa.org/webdav/site/global/shared/documents/publications/2004/icpd_eng.pdf (last visited 12 April 2012): HIV/AIDS herein: 47–48, paras 7.27 to 7.33; 59–61, paras 8.28 to 8.35; The experience of women in armed conflict is recognized herein: 24, para 4.10.

7 International Criminal Tribunal for the Former Yugoslavia (ICTY), International Criminal Tribunal for Rwanda (ICTR).

humanity. The Statute for the International Criminal Tribunal for Rwanda (ICTR) also recognized rape and enforced prostitution as war crimes, although neither the ICTR nor the Statute for the International Criminal Tribunal for Yugoslavia (ICTY) recognized rape or sexual violence as genocide specifically. While the Statutes were considered a significant improvement on the earlier classification of gender-based crimes they still contained limited provisions addressing the range of violence committed against women including in armed conflicts.

Despite these constraints, the initial jurisprudence from the Tribunals established historic benchmarks in international criminal law for the prosecution of gender-based crimes.[8] In addition, the timing of the first judgment by the ICTY,[9] the developments in trials inclusive of gender-based crimes underway at both Tribunals during 1997–1998,[10] and the charges contained in the arrest warrants issued in this period,[11] all occurred during the negotiations of the Rome Statute and indisputably influenced the dynamics and chemistry of the debates regarding gender-based crimes at critical moments in the process.

In many respects, the ICTY is perhaps the unsung institutional hero in the development and practice of international justice for conflict-related violence against women.[12] The ICTY created the largest collection of international jurisprudence addressing gender-based crimes produced by a single institution. The work of the ICTY provided the field of international criminal law, with unprecedented jurisprudence for rape as torture and sexual violence as a crime against humanity and a war crime.

---

8 *Prosecutor v. Tadić*, IT-94-1-T, 7 May 1997; *Prosecutor v. Akayesu*, ICTR-96-4-T, 2 September 1998; *Prosecutor v. Delalić, Mucić, Delić and Landžo* ("Čelebići Camp"), IT-96-21-T, 16 November 1998; *Prosecutor v. Furundžija*, IT-95-17/1-T, 10 December 1998.

9 *Prosecutor v. Tadić*, IT-94-1-T, 7 May 1997.

10 *Prosecutor v. Akayesu*, ICTR-96-4-T; *Prosecutor v. Delalić, Mucić, Delić and Landžo* ("Čelebići Camp"), IT-96-21-T; *Prosecutor v. Furundžija*, IT-95-17/1-T; *Prosecutor v. Blaškić*, IT-95-14-T.

11 See *Prosecutor v. Zelenović* ("Foča"), IT-96-23, 18 June 1996 (Initial Indictment: including thirteen charges of rape constituting torture as a Crime Against Humanity under Article 5(f), sixteen charges of rape as a Crime Against Humanity under Article 5(g), thirteen charges of rape as torture constituting a Grave Breach under Article 2(b), thirteen charges of rape constituting a Violation of the Laws or Customs of War under Article 3, one charge of willfully causing great suffering as a Grave Breach under Article 2 (c), two charges of outrages upon personal dignity constituting a Violation of the Laws or Customs of War under Article 3, two charges of enslavement constituting a Crime Against Humanity under Article 5(c), and one charge of rape as inhumane treatment constituting a Grave Breach under Article 2(b)).

12 See, on the ICTY, Michelle Jarvis and Elena Martin Salgado, "Future Challenges to Prosecuting Sexual Violence Under International Law: Insights from ICTY Practice," in *Sexual Violence as an International Crime: Interdisciplinary Approaches*, eds. Anne-Marie de Brouwer, Charlotte Ku, Renée Römkens and Larissa van den Herik (Antwerp, Belgium: Intersentia), *supra*.

The ICTR record for the prosecution of gender-based crimes does not appear to be as rich, despite the widespread commission of rape during the conflict and genocide in Rwanda.[13] There have been significantly fewer convictions for sexualised violence when compared with the ICTY. In addition, sexual violence charges were often dropped by the Prosecution in exchange for a guilty plea on other charges. However, the Tribunal's most profound contribution to jurisprudence in this area was the ground-breaking conviction of Jean-Paul Akayesu[14] for acts of rape as genocide. The Akayesu decision provided an insightful articulation of the ways in which rape and other acts of sexual violence were integral to the overall genocide. The Akayesu decision was the first judgement to reflect the experience of women victims/survivors and accurately capture the meaning and purpose of rape in armed conflict. It provided criminal law, both international and domestic, with a better understanding of rape and other forms of sexualized violence, and therefore, suggested a more effective way of prosecuting these crimes.

Building on the successful strategy developed by feminist advocates for international conferences, a women's caucus was formed to influence the Rome Statute negotiations. The Women's Caucus for Gender Justice,[15] catapulted by the policy advances for women's rights during the 1990s and the momentum of the early jurisprudence and trials underway at the ad hoc tribunals, brought together women's legal rights advocates to ensure that the principles of gender justice and accountability for crimes of sexual and gender violence were infused within the Rome Statute.

The inclusion of rape and other forms of sexual violence as amongst the gravest crimes committed in war and armed conflict is one of the milestones of the Rome Statute. For the first time, rape, sexual slavery, enforced prostitution, forced pregnancy, enforced sterilization, gender-based persecutions, trafficking and other forms of sexual violence were codified as war crimes, crimes against humanity, and in some circumstances, as genocide.[16] In addition the Rules of Procedure and Evidence and Elements of the Crimes also integrated explicit gender provisions. Indisputably, women advocates demonstrated their efficacy as partners in the development and adoption of a Statute with the most advanced articulation in history of acts of violence against women recognized in international criminal law.

---

13 See, on the ICTR, Linda Bianchi, "The Prosecution of Rape and Sexual Violence: Lessons from Prosecutions at the International Criminal Tribunal for Rwanda," in *Sexual Violence as an International Crime: Interdisciplinary Approaches*, eds. Anne-Marie de Brouwer, Charlotte Ku, Renée Römkens and Larissa van den Herik (Antwerp, Belgium: Intersentia), *supra.*

14 *Prosecutor v. Akayesu*, ICTR-96-4-T, 2 September 1998.

15 The Caucus was the forerunner to the Women's Initiatives for Gender Justice. For information about the work and history of the Caucus (1997–2003) please see www.iccwomen.org/aboutus/history.php.

16 Rome Statute, Article 8(b)(xxii); Rome Statute Article 7(g); and Rome Statute Article 6(b).

2. COMPLEMENTARITY AND POTENTIAL OF THE ROME STATUTE FOR GENDER JUSTICE

Since the Statute came into force and the ICC was established, the Court has been learning, testing and defining how to interpret this visionary treaty and operationalise its jurisdictional mandates.

Today, the ICC has opened investigations into seven situations[17] and is working in some of the most violent territories in the world. The work of the Court is compounded by the realities of ongoing conflicts, the limited role states are able and willing to play in securing the arrest of ICC indictees residing on their territory, and by an international system of justice and security which is fragmented and still in the process of developing as a cohesive, mutually reinforcing set of policies and body of law. The ICC also suffers from bi-focal support from amongst its own 'members' with 41% of States Parties to the ICC, (47 States[18] out of 115[19]) also having agreements with the United States of America guaranteeing protection for US service men and women active on their soil from any ICC prosecution.

The Court operates in countries with limited functional state institutions and little public sector accountability. Unsurprisingly, the ICC is working in some of the most corrupt political systems around the globe. According to the 2011 Corruption Perceptions Index published by Transparency International,[20] Uganda, the Democratic Republic of the Congo, the Central African Republic, Libya, Sudan, Kenya and the Ivory Coast, all countries under investigation by the ICC, rank in the top 25% of the most corrupt countries in the world.

According to the Division for the Advancement of Women, "the United Nations Secretary-General's 2006 in-depth study on all forms of violence against women notes that in 2006, only about half of United Nations Member States [88 states] had in place legislative provisions that specifically addressed domestic violence, and fewer than half had legislation on sexual harassment or on trafficking. Even where legislation existed, it was often limited in scope and

---

17 Situation in Uganda (ICC- 02/04); Situation in Democratic Republic of Congo (ICC- 01/04); Situation in Darfur, Sudan (ICC- 02/05); Situation in the Central African Republic (ICC-01/05); Situation in Kenya, (ICC- 01/09); Situation in Libya (ICC-01/11); Situation in the Ivory Coast (ICC-02/11).

18 Georgetown University Law Library, *International Criminal Court – Article 98 Agreements Research Guide*, 2009, available at www.ll.georgetown.edu/guides/article_98.cfm (updated 8 September 2010).

19 UN Treaty Collection Database, *Rome Statute of the International Criminal Court*, available at http://treaties.un.org/pages/ViewDetails.aspx?src=TREATY&mtdsg_no=XVIII-10&chapter=18&lang=en, (last visited 10 June 2011).

20 Transparency International, *Corruption Perceptions Index*, 2011, 1 December 2011, accessed at http://cpi.transparency.org/cpi2011/results/; retrieved 29 March, 2012.

coverage."[21] Honour killings, dowry murder, marital rape, and a range of other forms of gender-based violence continue to fall outside most domestic legislative coverage, and even where anti-violence laws exist, they do not guarantee deterrence, safety or justice.

In many of the situations where the ICC is exercising or could exercise its jurisdiction, there is limited recognition of the human and legal rights of women especially in relation to physical integrity and the prevention of violence. The principle of complementarity under the Rome Statute allows for the ICC to investigate and prosecute crimes within its jurisdiction in situations where the State is unable or unwilling to provide credible accountability for such crimes. This principle provides a strong basis for the Court to investigate and prosecute gender-based crimes in an array of countries and entities with recognised Statehood,[22] if there is a widespread unwillingness or inability of States to genuinely conduct domestic prosecutions of these crimes.

Violence against women is enabled and assured through the absence of effective legislation preventing such acts, and by laws which actively condone certain forms of gender-based violence. The low number of convictions for rape, discriminatory corroboration requirements and masculinised constructions of 'consent' contribute to the ongoing impunity for gender-based violence. Similarly, inadequate police investigations, gender-biased attitudes on the bench, and the stigma associated with rape, all conspire to create a state of unwillingness and inability to genuinely prosecute gender-based crimes. In such circumstances, the commission of these crimes in the absence of a system able, willing and likely to prosecute such acts is a justifiable criterion, on its own, for the ICC to open an investigation.

Such prosecutions would demonstrate that the ICC recognises the legal rights of women even when the laws and practices of their own country deny these rights. It is possible these prosecutions may also inspire national legislation for sexual and gender-based violence, stimulate judicial and security sector reform, and provide a template for future domestic prosecutions of rape and other forms of sexual violence.

Empowered by its mandate, the International Criminal Court can be an important partner in addressing violence against women and modelling gender-inclusive justice.

21 *United Nations Report Offers Guidelines for Legislation on Violence Against Women, Division for the Advancement of Women*, (Press Release WOM/1704), 11 November 2008.

22 For example, the Holy See.

3. DOCUMENTING GENDER-BASED CRIMES

Documenting and reporting on human rights abuses have been effective strategies employed by human rights groups and women's human rights defenders around the world to spotlight under-reported violations, massacres and humanitarian crises. Human rights reports help to surface and magnify injustice, and focus the interventions by governments, the United Nations and humanitarian organisations to where they are most needed. Legal institutions have sometimes relied upon human rights reports as the basis for considering investigations into possible criminal acts.

Documentation programmes strengthen the advocacy for justice, including gender-justice, in tangible and compelling ways. Such initiatives contribute to the fullness of information publicly available, engage victims/survivors in locations often difficult to reach and personalise the impact of violence within the justice process.

The Women's Initiatives for Gender Justice has been working in armed conflict situations since 2004. Currently it has extensive country-based and advocacy programmes in Uganda, the Democratic Republic of the Congo (DRC), Sudan, the Central African Republic (CAR), Kenya, Libya, the Ivory Coast and Kyrgyzstan. The organisation has over 6,000 members and partners who are predominantly grassroots women's rights and peace organisations and advocates, victim/survivor groups, transitional justice networks, and development and human rights organisations across these conflict areas.

Documenting gender-based crimes is one of the organisation's strategic initiatives towards domestic and international prosecutions for these acts. In 2009, the Women's Initiatives trained 30 women's rights advocates from the DRC (20) and CAR (10) as future partners in the documentation of these crimes in their respective countries. In particular, those selected from the DRC were all from North and South Kivu in response to the announcement by the Office of the Prosecutor (OTP) that the third DRC investigation would focus on these provinces.[23]

The ability of women's organisations to access victims/survivors of gender-based crimes, to conduct interviews, gather a collection of experiences, move safely amongst the community, and the willingness of women victims/survivors to trust the intentions and goals of such a documentation programme, make these organisations valuable partners in justice and truth-telling mechanisms.

---

[23] Deputy Prosecutor Fatou Bensouda, Speech, 'Update on judicial proceedings: a focus on charging and prosecuting sexual and gender crimes', *Semi-annual Meeting between the ICC and NGOs*, (The Hague, the Netherlands, 30 September 2008), 3, available at www.icc-cpi.int/NR/rdonlyres/EF316814-2FF4-44E3-9FC6-8C4CB33CB310/280605/300908TheHagueNGOs2.pdf.

In 2006, the Women's Initiatives carried out its first two documentation missions in eastern DRC.[24] The purpose of the missions was to gather information about the gender-based crimes reportedly committed by the Union des patriotes Congolais (UPC) given the absence of charges for these acts in the ICC arrest warrant[25] for Thomas Lubanga Dyilo, President of the UPC and its militia wing the Forces patriotiques pour la libération du Congo (FPLC).[26]

Thomas Lubanga was taken into ICC custody on 17 March 2006, charged with the war crimes of enlistment and conscription of children and using them to participate actively in hostilities.[27] Despite reports by the United Nations and human rights organisations documenting the widespread commission of gender-based crimes by the UPC/FPLC, this category of crimes had not been prioritised by the Office of the Prosecutor (OTP) in its case hypothesis nor in the subsequent investigations.

The two field missions conducted by the Women's Initiatives were carried out in May and July 2006 over a period of 22 days and focused on interviewing women victims/survivors of gender-based crimes committed in Ituri, the provincial base of the UPC/FPLC and the geographic focus of the first ICC investigation. The intention of the missions was to gather information about the scope of crimes, the type of attacks, the modes of commission, the range of perpetrators, the availability and willingness of women victims/survivors to be interviewed, and assess the relevant security issues.

On the first mission, 41 interviews were conducted including 17 women victims/survivors of rape and other forms of sexualised violence allegedly committed by the UPC/FPLC. Non-UPC victims were also interviewed and were able to identify perpetrators from a range of other militia groups and armed

---

24 The organisational methodology for the field missions included hiring three local activists as consultants to locate victims/survivors and implement the interview questions designed by the organisation specifically for these missions. The consultants received online interview support before the first mission and in-person interview and documentation training from the Women's Initiatives prior to the second mission. The interview data was translated, fact checked and analysed for inclusion in the dossier submitted to the Office of the Prosecutor in August 2006. Documentation equipment was also provided in the form of laptops and a camera. Given the high levels of insecurity in eastern DRC, the local activists preferred to operate as 'consultants' rather than to have a formal partnership between their organisations and the Women's Initiatives thus limiting the number of people who knew about the missions. In addition, a security protocol was developed including an evacuation policy, provision of a satellite phone, funds for immediate escape should any member of the team be threatened and daily check-ins during the missions. Funds and logistical support were also made available for interviewees who required urgent medical and psychosocial assistance.

25 *Prosecutor v. Thomas Lubanga Dyilo*, ICC-01/04-01/06-2, 10 February 2006.

26 Brigid Inder, *Making a Statement* (The Hague, the Netherlands: Women's Initiatives for Gender Justice, Second Ed. 2010), 23.

27 *Prosecutor v. Thomas Lubanga Dyilo*, ICC-01/04-01/06-2, 10 February 2006; Rome Statute, Article 8(2)(b)(xxvi); or Rome Statute, Article 8(2)(e)(vii).

forces including the FNI,[28] FARDC,[29] UPDF[30] as well as other perpetrators from unidentified militia and forces.

The second field mission focused solely on interviewing victims of alleged UPC/FPLC crimes. Some of the original UPC/FPLC related interviewees were selected for follow-up interviews in order to clarify important details and to seek additional information relating to the specific attacks, location, time frame, the identification of perpetrators and other relevant and substantial information. In addition, the team interviewed 15 'new' victims/survivors of gender-based crimes allegedly committed by the UPC/FPLC.

4. MISSED OPPORTUNITY

In August 2006, the Women's Initiatives submitted a confidential report documenting gender-based crimes committed in Ituri to the ICC Prosecutor, urging his office to immediately open investigations into the alleged commission of these acts by the UPC/FPLC.[31] Of the 55 victims/survivors whose interviews were included in the report, 51 were victims/survivors of gender-based crimes, including 48 women and three men who had been forced to rape women. In particular, 31 interviewees alleged the sexualised violence had been committed by the UPC/FPLC.[32] The report submitted to the OTP by the Women's Initiatives was redacted for victims' names and other identifying information but included detailed accounts of their horrifying experiences.

The documentation indicated that more than 40% of those who reported sexual violence had been gang raped, with several interviewees reporting that they had been gang raped on more than one occasion either by the same perpetrators or by members of the same militia group.

The UPC was allegedly responsible for 10 of the 22 incidents of gang rape reported by interviewees in this research. More than half of those who experienced gang rape specified the number of offenders involved in the incident, indicating a range of 2–10 perpetrators. Analysis of the interviews indicated that more than 90% of the victims/survivors of gender-based crimes had experienced multiple attacks, meaning they had been subjected to more than one sexual or non-sexual attack including gang rape, beatings, abduction, torture and forced labour.

---

28 Front des nationalistes et intégrationnistes.

29 Forces armées de la République Démocratique du Congo.

30 Ugandan People's Defence Force.

31 Brigid Inder, *Making a Statement*, (The Hague, the Netherlands: Women's Initiatives for Gender Justice, 2010), 23.

32 The interview with one victim/survivor of an alleged attack by the UPC/FPLC was not included in the report due to the inability to verify some details of the incident.

Approximately half of the 51 interviewees reporting sexual violence were abducted and enslaved mostly in camps, although around 13% reported that they had been enslaved in houses outside militia encampments. In both locations, interviewees reported that they were exposed to frequent and repeated rapes. The length of time held in captivity was indicated by 35% of those abducted. Of these, 16% were held captive for one year or more, 50% were captive for less than one year but more than one month, and 33% were held captive for more than one day but less than one month.

Seven senior-level militia were identified as direct perpetrators by interviewees, all from the UPC/FPLC; and 80% of the ten senior militia alleged by interviewees with knowledge of rape committed by combatants under their command, were reportedly also from the UPC/FPLC.

The injuries reported were extensive.[33] Interviewees expressed a range of mental and psychological injuries including the inability to work, memory lapses, anxiety, inability to look people in the eye, and constant fear. Physical impairments included genital wounds, vesi-covaginal fistula, mutilation of limbs, and pain in the hips, chest and abdomen. Only 27% of interviewees reported receiving medical assistance despite the severity of the medical, physiological and material needs following their brutalization.

The report indicated that women were victims/survivors of gender-based crimes committed by several militia groups and armed forces, and that interviewees could identify perpetrators by militia group, and in some instances by name. The documentation also indicated that rape and other forms of sexualised violence, including those allegedly committed by the UPC/FPLC, appeared to be widespread and systematic and that women were willing to be interviewed regarding the attacks.

Alongside the report, the organisation submitted a letter to the ICC Prosecutor in which the Women's Initiatives specifically noted their concern that "no investigations appear to have been undertaken in this case into allegations of child soldiers being raped given especially the only crimes included in the arrest warrant relate to child soldiers. We are aware of information regarding the rape of girls abducted by the UPC for the purposes of induction into the militia group. Several reports exist on gender-based crimes committed against girls abducted by militia groups in the DRC."[34]

Despite the submission of the documentation report to the OTP in 2006 only 5 months after Lubanga was taken into ICC custody, the Office of the Prosecutor did not follow-up on leads or open investigations into gender-based crimes allegedly committed by the UPC/FPLC. This crime base in relation to the UPC

---

33 Including, but not limited to, vaginal pain; wounds or scabs (including in one case an arrow wound); inability to walk; vaginal discharge; inability to urinate or defecate; sexually transmitted diseases, recurrent headaches; loss of teeth; and hypotension.

34 Brigid Inder, *Letter to the Prosecutor*, (The Hague, the Netherlands: Women's Initiatives for Gender Justice) 4.

has never been, and is now unlikely to ever be, the focus of an ICC investigation.[35]

In September 2006, 25 local women's and human rights organisations from eastern DRC released the Beni Declaration,[36] in which they expressed their support for the arrest of Thomas Lubanga and their "[ ] deep regret that the only charges brought pertain to the enlistment and conscription of child soldiers. Without minimizing these charges, as human rights organisation we stress that the UPC has committed several other crimes falling under the jurisdiction of the International Criminal Court, for which details have been submitted to the Office of the Prosecutor by national and international NGOs. In particular we draw attention to the widespread commission of rape and other forms of sexual violence by the UPC and the responsibility of the ICC to address impunity for gender-based crimes."[37]

Despite consistent indications from women's organisations that they would be willing to assist the ICC, the Court has regularly overlooked the importance of establishing contacts and forging collaborations with credible local and international women's organisations. Investing in these relationships within a coordinated investigation strategy could benefit the ICC in gaining greater access to witnesses and an entree into community knowledge regarding specific militia, armed forces, the cultural context of the conflict, and incidents of interest to their investigations. It may also support their ability to effectively follow up with victims/witnesses given the high levels of displacement common in armed conflicts.

5. LUBANGA – LEGAL PROCEEDINGS

After six years in custody, on 14 March 2012 the Trial Chamber found Mr. Lubanga guilty as a co-perpetrator of the crimes of enlistment and conscription and using children under the age of 15 to participate actively in hostilities.[38]

---

35 On 15 March 2012, in a press conference following the trial Judgment issued in the case against Lubanga on 14 March 2012, the Prosecutor announced his intention to amend the charges against Bosco Ntaganda to add charges for rape and murder. The original Arrest Warrant against Bosco Ntaganda, issued on 22 August 2006, charges Ntaganda with the war crimes of enlistment, conscription and using children under the age of fifteen to participate actively in hostilities. While sexual violence may now be included in the case against Ntaganda, the larger scale of sexual violence crimes committed by the UPC/FPLC against individuals other than child soldiers is unlikely to be the subject of an ICC investigation. See 'Lubanga case: Press conference by ICC Prosecutor', 15 March 2012, available at www.youtube.com/watch?v=eoj_qCwHePk&list=UU183T5VoMh5wISSdKPaMgRw&index=4&feature=plpp_video.

36 Brigid Inder, *Making a Statement*, (The Hague, the Netherlands: Women's Initiatives for Gender Justice, Second Ed. 2010) 21.

37 *Ibid.*

38 *Prosecutor v. Thomas Lubanga Dyilo*, ICC-01/04-01/06-2842, 14 March 2012.

Despite not addressing gender-based crimes in its original investigation, nor seeking an amendment to include these crimes in the indictment against Mr. Lubanga during the three years the accused was in custody, during the trial the Office of the Prosecutor presented evidence of sexual violence.[39] It appears that this material was intended to describe the experience of children enlisted and conscripted by the UPC/FPLC and to demonstrate the co-existence of sexual violence within each of the specific crimes for which Mr. Lubanga was charged. The strategy adopted for the trial appeared to be in response to external advocacy critiquing the absence of explicit charges for sexual violence as well as a realisation within the OTP itself of the enormity of this oversight. More than 15 prosecution witnesses offered testimony about sexual violence committed against girls within the militia group.[40] In addition, victims' legal representatives also described the experience of girls enlisted by the UPC/FPLC including the commission of rape and other forms of sexual violence during the enlistment and conscription process.[41] However, in its judgment, the Chamber did not recognize sexual violence acts as components of the charges for which the accused was convicted, and stated that it would be impermissible for them to do so because facts regarding sexual violence were not included in the Document Containing the Charges, and thus they were not included in the Confirmation Decision.[42]

However, the Majority did not make any definitive legal finding as to whether sexual violence could or should be properly included within the scope of the crime of using children to actively participate in hostilities. In addition, the Judges left the door open to considering whether evidence of sexual violence "ought to be taken into account for the purposes of sentencing and reparations."[43]

---

39 *Lubanga*, ICC-01/04-01/06-T-107-ENG, 26 January 2009; *Lubanga*, ICC-01/04-01/06-T-356-ENG, 25 August 2011.

40 The following Prosecution witnesses testified about sexual violence committed against girl soldiers by the UPC in open court: Witness 38: ICC-01/04-01/06-T-114-ENG, Witness 299: ICC-01/04-01/06-T-122-ENG, Witness 298: ICC-01/04-01/06-T-123-ENG, Witness 213: ICC-01/04-01/06-T-133-ENG, Witness 8: ICC-01/04-01/06-T-138-ENG, Witness 11: ICC-01/04-01/06-T-138-ENG, Witness 10: ICC-01/04-01/06-T-144-ENG, Witness 7: ICC-01/04-01/06-T-148-ENG, Witness 294: ICC-01/04-01/06-T-151-ENG, Witness 17: ICC-01/04-01/06-T-154-ENG, Witness 55: ICC-01/04-01/06-T-178-Red-ENG, Witness 16: ICC-01/04-01/06-T-191-Red2-ENG, Witness 89: ICC-01/04-01/06-T-196-ENG, Witness 31: ICC-01/04-01/06-T-202-ENG and Witness 46: ICC-01/04-01/06-T-207-ENG.

41 The Legal Representatives of Victims detailed the specific abuse of girl soldiers in their opening statements and closing statements. *Lubanga*, ICC-01/04-01/06-T-107-ENG, 26 January 2009 and *Lubanga*, ICC-01/04-01/06-T-356-ENG, 25 August 2011. In addition, in a Joint Application filed on 22 May 2009, the Legal Representatives of Victims also sought to change the legal characterisation of facts to include inhuman and cruel treatment and sexual slavery to the existing characterisation. *Lubanga*, ICC-01/04-01/06-1891, 22 May 2009.

42 *Lubanga*, ICC-01/04-01/06-2842, 14 March 2012, para 630.

43 *Ibid*, para 631.

Judge Odio Benito issued a dissenting opinion specifically on the evidence of sexual violence, where she found that the Chamber had "a responsibility to define the crimes based on the applicable law, and not limited to the charges brought by the Prosecution against the accused."[44] She argued that:

> [b]y failing to deliberately include within the legal concept of 'use to participate actively in the hostilities' the sexual violence and other ill treatment suffered by girls and boys, the Majority of the Chamber is making this critical aspect of the crime invisible. Invisibility of sexual violence in the legal concept leads to discrimination against the victims of enlistment, conscription and use who systematically suffer from this crime as an intrinsic part of the involvement with the armed group.[45]

As a result, Judge Odio Benito considered it "necessary and a duty of the Chamber to include sexual violence within the legal concept of 'use to participate actively in the hostilities,' regardless of the impediment of the Chamber to base its decision pursuant to Article 74(2) of the Statute."[46]

6. IMPLEMENTING GENDER JUSTICE PROVISIONS IN THE ROME STATUTE

The lack of explicit charges for gender-based crimes in the Lubanga case, and the struggle to sustain the sexual violence charges brought by the ICC in other cases, is proving to be an ongoing challenge. Overall, gender visibility in warrants of arrest is high with charges for gender-based crimes included in all situations where indictments have been issued except Libya;[47] and in nine out of fifteen cases[48] brought by the Office of the Prosecutor. In the eight cases for which confirmation hearings have been held,[49] four have included charges for sexual

44 *Lubanga*, ICC-01/04–01/06–2842, 14 March 2012 (Judge Odio Benito, dissenting), para 15.

45 *Lubanga*, ICC-01/04–01/06–2842, 14 March 2012 (Judge Odio Benito, dissenting), para 16.

46 *Ibid.*

47 Uganda, ICC- 02/04; 2004; Democratic Republic of Congo, ICC- 01/04, 2004; Darfur, Sudan, ICC- 02/05, 2005; Central African Republic, ICC- 01/05, 2005; Kenya, ICC-01/09, 2009; and the Ivory Coast, ICC-02/11, 2011.

48 *Prosecutor v. Kony, et al.*, ICC-02/04–01/05; *Prosecutor v. Harun and Kushayb*, ICC-02/05–01/07; *Prosecutor v. Katanga and Ngudjolo*, ICC-01/04–01/07; *Prosecutor v. Bemba*, ICC-01/05–01/08; *Prosecutor v. Al Bashir*, ICC-02/05–01/09; *Prosecutor v Callixte Mbarushimana*, ICC-01/04–01/10; *Prosecutor v. Muthaura, Kenyatta and Ali*, ICC-01/09–02/11; *Prosecutor v Gbagbo*, ICC-02/11–01/11; *Prosecutor v Hussein*, ICC-02/05–01/12.

49 *Prosecutor v. Lubanga*, ICC-01/04–01/06; *Prosecutor v. Katanga and Ngudjolo*, ICC-01/04–01/07; *Prosecutor v. Bemba*, ICC- 01/05–01/08; *Prosecutor v. Abu Garda*, ICC-02/05–02/09; *Prosecutor v. Mbarushimana*, ICC-01/04–01/10; *Prosecutor v. Banda and Jerbo*, ICC-02/05–03/09; *Prosecutor v. Ruto et al*, ICC-01/09–01/11; *Prosecutor v. Muthaura et al.*, ICC-01/09–02/11.

violence crimes.[50] Disappointingly, more than 50% of these charges have been dismissed before trial. This figure is predominantly due to the dismissal by Pre-Trial Chamber I of the entire case against Callixte Mbarushimana, the alleged Executive Secretary of the *Forces démocratique pour la libération du Rwanda* (FDLR), in which eight out of thirteen charges related to sexual violence.[51]

The Chamber's decision indicates that there appears to have been substantial grounds to believe that several of the war crimes alleged by the OTP had indeed been perpetrated by the FDLR.[52] The dismissal of the case hinged upon the ICC not proving sufficient linkage between the accused and the commission of the crimes themselves.[53] In a dissenting opinion, Presiding Judge Monageng found that the evidence presented did establish the requisite standard of proof regarding an organizational policy to attack the civilian population and that Mbarushimana facilitated the commission of several of the crimes contained in the indictment.[54] The OTP is seeking leave to appeal the Pre-Trial Chamber's decision with an intention to reassemble the case and revive the charges. However, even setting aside this result, in the three other cases for which confirmation hearings have been held and in which gender-based crimes have

---

50 *Prosecutor v. Katanga and Ngudjolo*, ICC-01/04–01/07; *Prosecutor v. Bemba*, ICC- 01/05–01/08; *Prosecutor v. Mbarushimana*, ICC-01/04–01/10; *Prosecutor v. Muthaura et al.*, ICC-01/09–02/11.

51 In the Arrest Warrant against Mbarushimana, seven out of 11 charges were for gender-based crimes. Between the issuance of the Arrest Warrant and filing the Document Containing the Charges, which forms the basis for the confirmation of charges hearing, the Prosecutor added two further war crime charges (mutilation and pillage as war crimes), which he can do pursuant to Article 61(4). The charges for gender-based crimes were: torture as a crime against humanity, torture as a war crime, rape as a crime against humanity, rape as a war crime, other inhumane acts (based on rape and mutilation of women) as a crime against humanity, inhuman treatment (based on rape and mutilation of women) as a war crime, persecution (based on gender) as a crime against humanity, and mutilation as a war crime.

52 The Pre-Trial Chamber found substantial grounds to believe the following war crimes were committed by the FDLR: (i) attacks against civilians; (ii) murder; (iii) mutilation; (iv) rape; (v) cruel treatment; (vi) destruction of property; and (vii) pillaging. These charges were limited geographically to only five of the 25 incidents referred to by the Prosecution. *Prosecutor v. Callixte Mbarushimana*, ICC-01/04–01/10–465-Red, 16 December 2011, paras 133, 151, 160, 164, 168, 175, 178, 191, 192, 196, 203, 208, 219, 225. For a detailed analysis of the confirmation of charges decision *see* "Pre-Trial Chamber I declines to confirm charges against Mbarushimana and orders his release" in *Legal Eye on the ICC eLetter*, (The Hague, the Netherlands, Women's Initiatives for Gender Justice, March 2012), available at www.iccwomen.org/news/docs/WI-LegalEye3–12-FULL/LegalEye3–12.html#2.

53 The majority of the Pre-Trial Chamber did not find that Mbarushimana "provided any contribution to the commission of… crimes, even less a 'significant' one," *Mbarushimana*, ICC-01/04–01/10–465-Red, para 292.

54 *Mbarushimana*, ICC-01/04–01/10–465-Red, (Judge Monageng, dissenting opinion). See also "Pre-Trial Chamber I declines to confirm charges against Mbarushimana and orders his release" in *Legal Eye on the ICC eLetter*, (The Hague, the Netherlands, Women's Initiatives for Gender Justice, March 2012), available at www.iccwomen.org/news/docs/WI-LegalEye3–12-FULL/LegalEye3–12.html#2.

been charged, one third of these charges were dismissed.[55] There is no other category of crimes before the ICC which faces these persistent prosecutorial and judicial challenges.

Prosecutor v. Katanga and Ngudjolo. On 30 September 2008, following the Confirmation of Charges Hearing in the case of Prosecutor v Katanga and Ngudjolo, Pre-Trial Chamber I issued a decision confirming charges against each accused for three counts of crimes against humanity and seven counts of war crimes[56] for the attack on 24 February 2003 of Bogoro village in Ituri, eastern DRC.

The crimes against humanity charges confirmed included murder, rape and sexual slavery;[57] and the war crimes charges confirmed included wilful killing, sexual slavery, rape, using children under the age of fifteen years to participate actively in hostilities, intentionally directing attacks against the civilian population of Bogoro village, pillaging and destruction of property.[58]

However, the gender-based charges were confirmed by a majority of the Judges, not by unanimous decision. Judge Ušacka wrote a partly dissenting opinion dealing with the charges of rape and sexual slavery. Concerning these charges, the Judge noted that, although there were substantial grounds to believe these crimes had been committed by FNI/FRPI[59] members in the aftermath of the attack on the village, the Prosecutor's evidence was "insufficient to directly or closely link [the accused] to these crimes."[60]

Rather than declining to confirm the charges, however, the Judge noted that in her view, "a better course of action would have been for the Chamber to adjourn the hearing on these charges pursuant to Article 61(7) (c)(1) of the Rome Statute and request the Prosecutor to provide further evidence which links the suspects with the crimes charged under counts 6, 7, 8, and 9."[61]

Despite this dissenting opinion, the trial has proceeded with few major challenges and based on a review of the publicly available witness testimonies, the charges for sexual violence appear to be substantiated.[62]

---

55 *Prosecutor v. Katanga and Ngudjolo*, ICC-01/04-01/07, *Prosecutor v. Bemba*, ICC-01/05-01/08, and *Prosecutor v. Muthaura et al.*, ICC-01/09-02/11.

56 *Prosecutor v. Katanga and Ngudjolo*, ICC-01/04-01/07-717, 30 September 2008. See also *Gender Report Card on the International Criminal Court 2008* (The Hague, the Netherlands: Women's Initiatives for Gender Justice, 2008) 47, 48.

57 Rome Statute, Article 7(1)(a); Rome Statute, Article 7(1)(g).

58 Rome Statute, Article 8(2)(a)(i); Rome Statute, Article 8(b)(xxii); Rome Statute, Article 8(b)(xxvi); Rome Statute, Article 8(b)(i); Rome Statute, Article 8(b)(xvi); Rome Statute, Article 8(b)(xiii).

59 Front des Nationalistes et Intégrationnistes/ Force des Resistance Patriotique d'Ituri.

60 *Katanga and Ngudjolo*, ICC-01/04-01/07-717, (Judge Ušacka, partial dissenting opinion), paras 13–29.

61 *Ibid.*, para 29.

62 See further *Gender Report Card on the International Criminal Court 2010*, (The Hague, the Netherlands: Women's Initiatives for Gender Justice, 2010), 160–178; *Gender Report Card on*

Prosecutor v. Bemba. On 15 June 2009, in the case Prosecutor v. Bemba, Pre-Trial Chamber II confirmed the charges against Jean-Pierre Bemba but decided not to confirm three charges based on acts of rape – torture as a crime against humanity and a war crime, and outrages upon personal dignity as a war crime – because, it reasoned, these counts were cumulative to the charges of rape itself, and therefore, prejudicial to the rights of the accused.[63] The Chamber confirmed rape as a crime against humanity and rape as a war crime.[64]

In July 2009, the Women's Initiatives for Gender Justice, working with scholar and former ICTY Prosecutor Patricia Viseur-Sellers, filed a "Request for leave to submit Amicus Curiae observations pursuant to Rule 103 of the Rules of Procedure and Evidence",[65] in support of the Prosecution's request for leave to appeal the confirmation decision regarding the rape charges.

Pre-Trial Chamber II granted leave to the Women's Initiatives to file observations as amicus curiae;[66] and on 31 July 2009, the organisation submitted its brief in which Viseur-Sellers argued that the Pre-Trial Chamber improperly dismissed crimes of torture and outrages upon personal dignity on the grounds that cumulative charging was detrimental to the rights of the accused. While the Chamber used the appropriate test for cumulative charging,[67] the brief argued that the Chamber's application of the test was too narrow, at least with respect to three categories of victims – the child of ten years who was raped, the brother of a rape victim who was beaten while his sister was raped, and the persons who watched the sexual assault of their relatives. The Chamber's holding that these victims were not also tortured is at odds with the precedent established in the case of Prosecutor v. Furundzija,[68] which recognised the torture, and therefore,

the International Criminal Court 2011, (The Hague, the Netherlands: Women's Initiatives for Gender Justice, 2011), 225–233.

63 *Prosecutor v. Jean-Pierre Bemba Gombo*, ICC-01/05-01/08-424, 15 June 2009, para 501 (e) (i)-(iii).

64 *Bemba*, ICC-01/05-01/08-424, para 501(d)(ii), 501(a)(iv).

65 *Bemba*, ICC-01/05-01/08-447, 13 July 2009, request for leave to submit Amicus Curiae observations pursuant to Rule 103 of the Rules of Procedure and Evidence, available at www.iccwomen.org/news/docs/WIGJ-Amicus-Curiae-Submission-in-Jean-Pierre-Bemba.pdf. See also, *Legal Eye on the ICC eLetter – Special issue on amicus curiae filing*, (The Haguc, the Netherlands, Women's Initiatives for Gender Justice, August 2009), available at www.iccwomen.org/news/docs/LegalEye_Aug09/index.html; *Gender Report Card on the International Criminal Court 2009*, (The Hague, the Netherlands: Women's Initiatives for Gender Justice, 2009), 142–144.

66 *Bemba*, ICC-01/05-01/08-451, 17 July 2009, Decision on Request for Leave to Submit Amicus Curiae Observations Pursuant to Rule 103 of the Rules of Procedure and Evidence. The Single Judge noted that 'the proposed amicus curiae brief tends to provide legal information that the Chamber may find useful in the context of the present case' and that granting the request is "both desirable and appropriate for the proper determination of the case", therefore meeting the requirements for Rule 103.

67 Set forth by the International Criminal Tribunal for the former Yugoslavia Appeals Chamber in *Prosecutor v. Delalić, Mucić, Delić and Landžo* ("Čelebići Camp"), IT-96-21-T, 20 February 2001.

68 *Prosecutor v. Furundžija*, IT-95-17/1-T, 10 December 1998.

the broader victimisation, of those who were forced to watch their relatives being raped.

On 28 August 2009, the International Women's Human Rights Law Clinic (IWHRC) also requested leave to file amicus curiae observations in the same case on "the negotiating history and applicability of key provisions of the Rome Statute and Elements of Crimes as well as developments in international law, which compel the cumulative charging of rape and torture."[69] The applicants called the attention of the Court to "the universal acceptance and treatment of rape as torture, and the reasoning therefore, in the human rights system."[70]

They identified the recognition of rape as torture by several human rights bodies and concurred with the Women's Initiatives and the Office of the Prosecutor regarding cumulative charging. Their conclusion was that "the charging of both torture and rape are correct under cumulative charging rules, which were misapplied in this case."[71] The International Women's Human Rights Law Clinic indicated their Amicus would show that treating rape as torture was essential for the full gravity of rape to be properly understood and preserved in international law.[72]

Their request was denied by the Pre-Trial Chamber[73] which ruled that, while the proposed brief may provide information useful to the Chamber, granting the request would cause unnecessary delay in the proceedings, given the right of the parties to respond to the observations.

In what has been interpreted as a surprisingly defensive position by the Pre-Trial Chamber, in September 2009, the Chamber denied the Prosecution's request for leave to appeal the confirmation decision to dismiss charges of rape as torture and outrages upon personal dignity.[74] Although the filings in this instance did not persuade the Chamber to allow a review of its decision, recognition of the Women's Initiatives as amicus curiae and the request filed by IWHRC reflect the high level of engagement of gender justice advocates and their willingness to assist the Court in areas of specific expertise.

---

69 *Bemba*, ICC-01/05-01/08-488, 31 August 2009, Counsel for Amici: Rhonda Copelon, Professor of law and Director of the International Women's Human Rights Law Clinic and Pamela Spees, International Women's Human Rights Law Clinic.

70 *Bemba*, ICC-01/05-01/08-488, para 14. See also *Gender Report Card on the International Criminal Court 2009*, (The Hague, the Netherlands: Women's Initiatives for Gender Justice 2009), 143.

71 *Bemba*, ICC-01/05-01/08-488, para 11.

72 *Ibid.*, para 17.

73 *Bemba*, ICC-01/05-01/08-504, 4 September 2009.

74 *Bemba*, ICC-01/05-01/08-532, 18 September 2009. See also *Gender Report Card on the International Criminal Court 2009*, (The Hague, the Netherlands: Women's Initiatives for Gender Justice 2009), 66–67.

7. LEGAL FILINGS AS A STRATEGY FOR GENDER JUSTICE

The Bemba case before the ICC was not the first time women's rights advocates have sought to shape the contours of international criminal law. Earlier filings before the ICTY and ICTR, both those invited by Chambers and those unsolicited by the Tribunals, have contributed to the discourse on gender justice.

The first filing on gender-related issues before the ICTY was in its first case, *Prosecutor v. Dusko Tadic*. Christine Chinkin, Dean and Professor of International Law, University of Southhampton, requested and was granted leave to prepare observations on issues of anonymity and protective measures for victims and witnesses, especially in relation to issues of sexual violence.[75]

In the same case, the Chamber also granted leave to Professor Rhonda Copelon, Jennifer Green, Felice Gaer and Sara Hossain as joint applicants, to submit an *amicus* brief addressing the "legal protections for victims and witnesses who might present information" to the ICTY. This included those who may have long-lasting trauma as a result of attacks such as women "who were subjected to rape and other sexual and reproductive abuse."[76]

As the Tadic case dealt with issues of sexual violence, the Chamber sought relevant expertise on issues of trauma, security, and threats to witnesses and their families, in its consideration of appropriate protection measures while also balancing the rights of the accused.

The first filing by women's rights advocates before the ICTR was also in its first case, *Prosecutor v. Jean-Paul Akayesu*. The filing by Co-counsel,[77] supported by Rwandese and international women's rights organisations, requested "the Trial Chamber to exercise its supervisory authority under the Tribunal Statute and the Rules to call upon the Prosecutor to amend the indictment against Jean-Paul Akayesu to charge rape or other serious acts of sexual violence as crimes within the competence of the Tribunal."[78]

Although the applicants were not granted leave, their request stressed that sexual violence charges should be brought in this case due to the " testimony and evidence presented thus far in the Akayesu trial, as well as the documentation

---

75 Christine Chinkin, "Amicus Curiae Brief on Protective Measures for Victims and Witnesses," *Criminal Law Forum* 7, no. 1 (1996): 179, available at www.iccwomen.org/publications/briefs/index.php.

76 *The Prosecutor v. Tadić*, IT-94-1-T, 15 June 1995, Amicus Brief.

77 Joanna Birenbaum and Lisa Wyndel, Working Group on Engendering the Rwanda Tribunal; Rhonda Copelon, International Women's Human Rights Law Clinic; Jennifer Green, Centre for Constitutional Rights.

78 *Prosecutor v. Akayesu*, ICTR-96-4-T, Amicus Brief Respecting Amendment of the Indictment and Supplementation of the Evidence to Ensure the Prosecution of Rape and Other Sexual *Violence Within the Competence of the Tribunal*, available at: www.iccwomen.org/publications/briefs/docs/Prosecutor_v_Akayesu_ICTR.pdf.

carried out by human rights investigators, indicating that further probative evidence is available to prove these charges."[79]

The Women's Initiatives for Gender Justice was the first NGO to file before the ICC, and its legal advocacy also related to the first case before the Court.[80] As noted earlier, the *Prosecutor v. Lubanga* case, contained charges of enlistment and conscription of child soldiers and using them to participate actively in hostilities.[81] Although the organisation's request to provide observations was denied by Pre-Trial Chamber I; the request itself, prepared by victims legal representative and former ICTY Prosecutor, Sureta Chana, acting as legal counsel for the Women's Initiatives, served to enter into the public record of the trial important issues regarding the commission of gender-based crimes by the militia group led by the accused, and the impact on victims of impunity for acts of sexual violence. Its advocacy surrounding the case also sought to highlight two aspects of the unfortunate and regrettable signal sent by the ICC in not bringing charges for gender-based crimes in its principal case.

Firstly, women around the world, especially those in conflict situations, and in particular women in eastern DRC (the site of the first two ICC cases), were watching to see whether the ICC would treat violence committed against women seriously and prosecute these crimes. Secondly, the DRC has been called the 'rape capital of the world' by Margot Wallström, the United Nations Secretary-General's Special Representative on Sexual Violence in Conflict, largely due to the prolonged conflict in the east of the country.[82] The *Prosecutor v. Lubanga* case is the first international criminal trial ever held on the conflict in the DRC. Therefore, the decision by the Court to not include charges for gender-based crimes sent a powerful and surely unintended message, that despite having the Statute obliging it to prosecute such acts, crimes of gender-based violence remained in the margins and perpetrators could continue to rely on impunity.

In February 2008, the Lubanga Trial Chamber granted leave to the United Nations Special Representative on Children in Armed Conflict, Radhika Coomaraswamy, to provide observations regarding the definition of 'conscripting and enlisting' children by armed groups, bearing in mind any distinction which could be made between the two formulations; and secondly, the interpretation of the term 'using them [children] to participate actively in hostilities.'[83] The Special Representative drew on her knowledge of children in

79 *Ibid.*, at 2, para 6.

80 www.iccwomen.org/publications/briefs/index.php.

81 *Lubanga*, ICC-01/04-01/06-803-tEN.

82 Margot Wallström, Statement, *United Nations Security Council Open Meeting on 'Women, Peace and Security: Sexual Violence in Situations of Armed Conflict'*, (New York, 27 April 2010), available at www.stoprapenow.org/uploads/features/StatementofSRSGWallstrom SecurityCouncilOpenMeeting27April2010.pdf?v=h1wnEb3xrBE.

83 *Lubanga*, ICC-01/04-01/06-1175, 18 February 2008, para 11. See also *Gender Report Card on the International Criminal Court 2008*, (The Hague, the Netherlands: Women's Initiatives for Gender Justice, 2008), 87.

armed conflict as well as her experience as a former Special Rapporteur on Violence against Women, to provide the Court with analysis of the multiple roles children are assigned during war, and that 'the use of girl children in particular includes sexual violence.'[84]

Legal advocacy for gender justice from external parties, and the concomitant receptivity of Chambers to this skill-set, is vital for deepening understanding of the purpose and impact of sexual violence; for demonstrating that such acts are worthy of prosecution; and for strengthening the ability of the legal system to respond effectively.

8. CONTINUING EFFORTS

In its first decade, the desire on the part of the OTP to charge gender-based crimes has not been matched by its ability to secure and sustain these charges through the legal process.

Three possible reasons are suggested for why these charges in particular are fragile and disputed. Firstly, one of the specific factors implicated in the difficulties facing the ICC in sustaining charges of sexual violence, is the quality of the evidence – which relates to the source of the evidence. In 2010, the Women's Initiatives raised concerns about what appeared to be a liberal use of open-source or secondary material upon which the Office of the Prosecutor was constructing its sexual violence charges. Concurrently, the Office was embarking on a strategy of reduced investigation days.[85] This reduction, coupled with the emerging pattern regarding the construction of charges, appeared to indicate that the OTP intended to reply upon secondary sources – such as UN reports, NGO reports, newspaper articles and media reports – to substantiate the sexual violence charges, rather than a solid reliance on witness testimonies and other primary evidence.

In 2011 the Women's Initiatives conducted a review of the five publicly available applications for arrest warrants and summons to appear containing charges for gender-based crimes,[86] and found what appeared to be a ready use of open-source material to verify the sexual violence charges. In some instances

---

84 *Lubanga*, ICC-01/04-01/06-1229-AnxA, 18 February 2008, para 25. See also *Gender Report Card on the International Criminal Court 2008*, (The Hague, the Netherlands: Women's Initiatives for Gender Justice, 2008), 88.

85 See *Gender Report Card on the International Criminal Court 2010*, (The Hague, the Netherlands: Women's Initiatives for Gender Justice, 2010), 83.

86 *Prosecutor v. Harun/Kushayb*, ICC-02/05-56, 27 February 2007; *Prosecutor v. Bemba*, ICC-01/05-01/08-26-Red, 9 May 2008; *Prosecutor v. Al'Bashir*, ICC-02/05-157-AnxA, 14 July 2008; *Prosecutor v. Mbarushimana*, ICC-01/04-01/10-11-Red2, 20 August 2010; *Prosecutor v. Muthaura, Kenyatta and Ali*, ICC-01/09-31-Red2, 15 December 2010.

open-source material appeared to be the *only* evidence supporting specific counts of sexual violence.

In addition, the review found that it was only the sexual violence charges, which were being dropped from the warrants of arrest and summons to appear. More recently, Judges from several Pre-Trial Chambers have described open source material as hearsay evidence and therefore of a lower probative value than direct evidence.[87] The Judges have stated that they wish to be presented with evidence arising from investigations rather than evidence based on reports.

It is hoped, as part of the internal learning process within the OTP, that such strategies will not continue as normative and that future charges will be more secure.

Secondly, narrow interpretations of existing jurisprudence for gender-based crimes, and perhaps the unconscious application of limited notions of sexual violence still prevalent in many national jurisdictions, may play a heavier hand than expected in ICC judicial determinations.

Judges elected to the ICC come from a variety of domestic jurisdictions with a range of sexual violence laws and legal practices which may differ from the progressive definitions and rules described in the Rome Statute and the Rules of Procedure and Evidence. It is reasonable to expect that in some instances a transition period may be required for Judges, with years of domestic legal practice regarding sexual violence, to effectively apply the unfamiliar principles of gender justice articulated in the Statute. In addition, the international jurisprudence for gender-based crimes is still relatively new in criminal law-years; and although there is a credible volume of law on these matters, it is not widely enough known nor understood by prosecutors and judges, and thus regularly contested and far from assumed, unlike many other areas of international criminal law. Unfamiliarity with the Statute and the existing jurisprudence on sexual violence have had a negative impact at the ICC particularly at the confirmation of charges stage of proceedings in both the Bemba case as discussed; and the Kenya case where Pre-Trial Chamber II found that forced male circumcision was not a form of sexual violence deciding instead to re-characterise this as 'other inhumane acts'.[88] Such decisions force a replay of legal concepts argued and settled in other tribunals, and undoubtedly make the work of the OTP even more challenging.

---

87 *Prosecutor v. Callixte Mbarushimana*, ICC-01/04–01/10–465-Red, 16 December 2011, Decision on the Confirmation of Charges, para 78; *Prosecutor v. Ruto et al.*, ICC-01/09–01/11–373, 23 January 2012, Decision on the Confirmation of Charges Pursuant to Article 61(7)(a) and (b) of the Rome Statute, para 74; *Prosecutor v. Muthaura et al.*, ICC-01/09–02/11–382-Red, 23 January 2012, Decision on the Confirmation of Charges Pursuant to Article 61(7)(a) and (b) of the Rome Statute, para 86.

88 *Muthaura et al.*, ICC-01/09–02/11–382-Red, 23 January 2012, paras 265–266. See also *Gender Report Card on the International Criminal Court 2011*, (The Hague, the Netherlands: Women's Initiatives for Gender Justice, 2011), 179–181.

And finally, judges across different Pre-Trial Chambers have consistently raised issues with the OTP about the quality of their filings; and in some instances, the incomplete information included in the Document Containing the Charges. The Judges have at times also expressed concern at the insufficient volume of evidence they are presented with, not only for sexual violence crimes, but in general. The ICC Judges are encouraging the Prosecutor to provide more witness statements and witness summaries in support of specific counts.[89] Without such issues being addressed, charges including those for gender-based crimes are likely to continue with partial success.

The Rome Statute places the ICC in an ideal position to advance justice for sexual violence as it refines and enhances its practices. The inclusion of gender-based crimes within indictments is a necessary first step, but gender visibility must be partnered with evidence and a well-crafted strategy to successfully argue the gender dimensions of the crimes within the Court's jurisdiction. The ICC will in time be capable of delivering convincing prosecutions and solid jurisprudence that will shape the way gender-based violence is understood, and ultimately contribute to the accountability and deterrence of violence against women worldwide.

89 *Gbagbo*, ICC-02/11–01/11–9-Red, 20 December 2011, Public redacted version of "Decision on the Prosecutor's Application Pursuant to Article 58 for a warrant of arrest against Laurent Koudou Gbagbo," para 59.

CHAPTER 15
"HOW CAN YOU MEET YOUR RAPIST AND SHAKE HIS HAND?": THE ROLE OF DOCUMENTARIANS IN CREATING AWARENESS ABOUT SEXUAL VIOLENCE

An Interview with Filmmakers Ilse and Femke van Velzen

Rachel IRWIN[1]

Near the end of the documentary 'Weapon of War' (IF Productions, 2009[2]), a young woman agrees to meet with the man who gagged, raped and beat her.

They meekly shake hands and sit down at a table together. She looks right at him and says calmly: "I'm not sure you understand that you are now responsible for my life."

Her fiancé left her after she was raped and now she has to live with her parents, she says. "I've lost all of my chances."

"Please forgive me," responds the lanky man, a former member of the Mai Mai militia group in the Democratic Republic of Congo (DRC).

He looks down, avoiding the young woman's persistent gaze. "I know now what I did," he says softly. "We have to forget and forgive each other."
After speaking for a few minutes, she says: "I can forgive you now."

---

1 This interview was conducted in February 2010, with a follow up in May of that year, after the documentary 'Weapon of War' had travelled around to various festivals throughout the world.

2 For more information on the documentary and how to purchase it, see www.weaponofwar.nl.

Then, in an apparent effort to further atone, he gives her a small piglet, which she accepts.

"I'm very pleased he realizes we're human beings, too," she says shortly afterwards.

The extraordinary scene – like much of the documentary – upends commonly held notions of what it means to be a perpetrator and a rape victim. It also complicates the idea of what exactly constitutes justice in a country where sexual violence has reached epidemic proportions and impunity continues to reign.
Since war began to rage in 1996, it is estimated that hundreds of thousands of Congolese women have been raped and often viciously brutalized. While numerous articles, reports and films have explored the issue of sexual violence in the DRC, 'Weapon of War' is unusual because it is told mainly from the point of view of the perpetrators. Most of the rapists are portrayed not as faceless monsters, but as men haunted and often severely traumatized by what they have done.
Dutch filmmakers and twin sisters Ilse and Femke Van Velzen have for several years concentrated their work on Africa, previously making films about Angola and South Africa. Their first film about the DRC, Fighting the Silence, focused on rape victims who were abandoned by their husbands.
In this interview, they explain their motivation for making Weapon of War, and argue that until organizations "wake up" and develop comprehensive programs for perpetrators, the problem of sexual violence in the DRC is likely never to be solved.

Q: You've made two films on sexual violence in the DRC. The first one, Fighting the Silence, focused on rape victims abandoned by their husbands. Your most recent film, Weapon of War, is more unusual in that it is from the perspective of the rapists. Why did you decide to focus the film on perpetrators?

Femke: While we were making 'Fighting the Silence,' and after making it, we still had questions, like, who are these men and why are they raping? And then we asked organisations to give us answers, and most people had no idea. This is the first film that looks at the point of view of the perpetrators and there's so much less research done on the topic. We thought, 'Ok, no one will give us answers, so we'll go ask the perpetrators ourselves.' In the beginning, we never thought we'd get such an intimate portrait.

Ilse: Femke and I are fighting against sexual violence, but we have this open minded approach. You can't turn your back to one party if it affects the other one as well. We were frustrated after making 'Fighting the Silence' because everyone was only focusing on the victims. If you keep focusing on victims – and it's of course very important and needed – you never solve the problem because you just exclude a whole group. You have to look at the source of the problem in order to put a halt to the rapes in Congo.

Q: Given the sensitive nature of the film, what has the reaction to it been among NGOs and other organizations?

Ilse: In a human rights film, you normally have good guys and bad guys, but in our film, we make it difficult for the viewers and organisations, because suddenly this is a film where you see the human side behind this 'monster', this perpetrator, and for a lot of people who are used to thinking in black and white, that is difficult.

Femke: Some people find it difficult to see perpetrators as human beings because what they are doing to women is unbelievable. In that way, it will always be a challenging film. If you make a film about victims, everyone is on the same side. Everyone knows how horrible it is for victims.

Q: The sexual violence is so horrific that I can see people thinking that if you humanize those who are doing it, you're somehow condoning the behavior.

Femke: I spoke with some women who said, I don't want to feel sorry for these guys. But you don't have to. We show a very complex situation within the problem of sexual violence in Congo. It sometimes says more about people who struggle themselves with watching the film and don't want to feel sorry for the perpetrators, but maybe they do a little bit. Maybe they are afraid that the focus on women will disappear.

Q: What has been the reaction from general audiences so far? You've travelled quite extensively to film festivals around the world.

Ilse: The audiences are great. We've had fantastic screenings. For example, at one screening in Belgrade, women's groups pointed out how the men in the film say they became animals when they raped, so it's almost like they disconnect themselves from their actions, like they were not human beings when they did that. It was a really interesting observation.

Femke: We have done so many Q&As with audiences who knew nothing about Congo, but nobody had the feeling that the perpetrators are the victims. Everyone understands that women are victims. People who are not familiar with Congo, what they pick out of the film is how easily human beings can transform from normal people into these animals. There are so many layers in the film, but people are very smart and they get it.

Q: Let's talk more about the film itself now. How did you find these men and how did you get them to talk to you in such a candid way on camera? I was especially struck by Captain Basima, a soldier turned pastor – who now spends all of his time fighting against sexual violence. It was shocking to learn that he was a rapist himself. He said he raped six women – even his own wife.

Ilse: We found Captain Basima because he was working on the mobile cinema project we set up for our first film. We weren't looking for him, but he was there, and he really believed in the fight against sexual violence. We slowly got to know him, and we had a friendship going, although we didn't know everything. The way you as a viewer experienced him, that's how we got to know him. We found out that he raped his wife after we had gotten to know his wife and his children. They were such a loving family. Then on the last day of the filming period, we did an interview with him that was postponed the whole time, because the locations were very difficult. He suddenly told us everything.

Femke: We were shocked. We knew him, and his wife, and how they were together. In the beginning, we had no idea that he had raped. But we did wonder, why did a guy who was in the military when he was 15 become a pastor fighting against sexual violence in the national army? We thought, something happened, but he said, 'No, no.' Later on, he was very open, but maybe he wanted to know us a little bit better, which is fair enough.

Q: I remember the scene where he describes seeing his wife for the first time, and how he liked the look of her, and I thought, Oh, how sweet – and such an antidote to the rest of the film. And then you saw her, cleaning his shoe, and she starts talking about how he raped and beat her, and I thought, is she talking about the same person?

Femke: It's unbelievable with him, how he changed. He's so driven by his fight against sexual violence. It didn't really matter if we were filming or not, every single person who would listen, he would talk to about rape being bad. It's amazing.

Ilse: And Captain Basima can explain this to other military people because he did it himself. It's really powerful that he's using his own example the whole time. I think that's also amazing, to tell about what you did to your wife and children – I would be so ashamed and would never tell anyone. He is truly a role model who can inspire other soldiers.

Q: Why do you think he could talk so openly given that this topic is still something of a taboo?

Ilse: The thing is, rape is so common there. A lot of times we asked very personal questions to some of the rebels we interviewed, and they know what they did was bad, but it's so common that they can just talk about it apparently. At the same time, they feel it's their right to claim sex with a woman, because they see women as second class citizens. To change this behavior, lots of education is needed so that men and boys understand they don't have that right and need to treat women with respect. On the other side, women in Congo need to claim their rights and fight.

Femke: It is a taboo, so I have no idea why we were successful. We have a good network and they trust us, so if the people in our network look for perpetrators, then the perpetrators can trust us. Because we have a very open approach and attitude that we didn't condemn the rebels and soldiers, they talked openly. Every interview we went in with this approach in the hope that they wouldn't feel threatened and would tell us everything. Of course this was difficult for us, but we knew this would be the only way that they would talk to us.

Q: Do you think it's less of a taboo for men to speak out than women?

Femke: For men, they don't see it as a huge deal. The biggest reason for them not to talk about it is that they are afraid of being arrested. But there is a huge taboo in general, so there are a lot of women who are not talking openly about being raped. But on the other hand, because there are so many women who are raped, there are a lot who are talking about it. The problem is just so widespread. There are so many women and there are always women who are speaking out. There's been a little bit of movement for some years, and organizations who are helping victims. Women understand it's good to ask for help.

Q: There is a man in the film who used to fight with the Mai-Mai rebel group. He raped a young woman and then seeks her out to ask for forgiveness. How did you find him?

Ilse: We were very impressed with a small organization that organises reconciliation between the rebels. We asked if they knew anyone, and they knew him. This guy really needed to talk to someone. He suffered from PTSD [post traumatic stress disorder] and he couldn't tell his story to anyone because when he did tell a tiny bit to his friends, they said they didn't want to hear about it and rejected him as a friend. We learned that as soon as soldiers are confronted with their acts and they are dealing with it, then there is no way back. They start thinking about it, and they are haunted by their past and they have to do something. Captain Basima will spend his life fighting against sexual violence, that's his way of making up with the past. With the rebel, he was so desperate to do anything, and that's why he was so open.

Q: One of the most fascinating and troubling scenes in the film is when this former rebel meets with the woman he raped and gives her a little piglet as a sort of trinket of his apology. There is so much going on in that scene and I imagine that many people will have trouble with it.

Ilse: Yes, some people got really angry about it, and especially people from the NGO world. I think they get frustrated because the justice system is not working, but it's not fair to get angry at the film, because this is what's happening. Because the legal system doesn't work, people solve these matters in traditional way by talking and sharing. The girl doesn't have a chance to bring him in front of a court. A rough figure stated that it costs the victim about 200 U.S. dollars to do so and most people don't have that money. The second thing is that nobody trusts the justice system because it's corrupt. We are making a new film about this topic called 'Justice for Sale.'

Femke: I think for this victim, the meeting maybe helped her more than if she would have tried to get the case to court. At least she could express all of her feelings and heal her heart – which are the words they use to express it. I really think that this helped her, because it's good to see that he really regrets what he did. In a country where victims hardly get the chance to win a case in court, getting back her dignity was a good option for her and she was happy with it. I have to state that not all reconciliations work out well for the victims. A lot of times parents want this because their daughter is 'damaged goods' and they want her to marry the perpetrator. In this kind of situation she is a double victim.

Q: Tell me more about your experience filming the scene.

Ilse: We knew the reconciliation was that day and the social worker had told us he didn't know what to expect because this girl is not saying much to him, so he had no idea what would come out of this reconciliation. Then the minute we met her, she was just so powerful. This session lasted maybe half a day, but we could only show a little part, because afterwards they went to eat together. It's very difficult for a western audience to understand, how can you meet your rapist and shake his hand?

Q: Yes, I can see why viewers might have a problem with this scene, because it's almost like he can give her the piglet and go on his way, whereas she has to live with the consequences for the rest of her life.

Ilse: If you have experienced war after war after war, people are living in a different mentality than we are. For us it's so difficult to understand how you can forgive your rapist. I know that here in the Netherlands, there is for example a woman who chose to reconcile with her husband's killer. They started up a project together and a lot of people sort of disapproved of that. But on the other hand, it's very brave and it's also mature.

Femke: If you forgive someone, at least you can move on with your own life. I think in Congo, that's the only thing they can do. You can't put all perpetrators in prison, because there would be almost no men left in Congo. We believe that almost every soldier has raped, because they have a gun and they have the power.

Q: Did anyone close to the young woman know she was doing the reconciliation?

Femke: She told her family, because they are sort of taking care of her, but she decided she didn't want her parents there at the reconciliation. Also, no one in her village knew she was doing it. It was her choice to do the reconciliation outside of the village.

Q: I noticed he couldn't look at her, but she looked straight at him and said "You're responsible for my life."

Femke: The thing is, he knew what he did was wrong. He got smaller by the minute, and she was the stronger one. For him, what could he do? He could say sorry, but what else?

Q: You interviewed other soldiers for the documentary and everyone was incredibly forthcoming, almost shockingly so.

Ilse: We went to Goma to these reintegration camps, with all these different rebels, and everyone was answering every single question. I think the reason why they did was firstly, no one had asked them before, and we didn't go in there with this attitude of "You are bad." We went very openly and didn't judge them. I don't know how we did it, but we were doing this to learn more about why and how, and the only way to think about it was, we are human beings, they are human beings, and they were. They were very vulnerable and they were like little boys in a way, but everything that they told us was just unbelievable. However, we did take these rebels out of the group, so it was a private one-on-one meeting that we planned with them in secret. None of the other rebel members knew about it. In this way, they could talk more openly and also protect themselves as they were revealing secrets of group tactics.

Q: Some reports have indicated that rape is also increasingly on the rise among the civilian population in the DRC.

Femke: A lot of young guys who are ex-rebels are now back in society like normal civilians, but they still have that war mentality. What you see in the DRC, is that in the communities, there is more and more rape. If for example a man in a community is raping girls, most of the time he has a military background. People don't look at it that way, they see him as only a civilian. You have to look further and see that these are all ex-combatants who are now in society and continuing to rape because that's what's in their system.

Ilse: They don't get detraumatised or demobilised properly, that's what was really clear to us. We did this exercise in the film where the men are sitting in a circle and Captain Basima is talking to them, and it's so sad. The guys were in a way quite desperate and really wanted to be normal again, but they don't know how, because psychological help is not provided, and they don't know how to deal with it. There are many sick men walking around who form a dangerous 'bomb' in society that is going to explode and make things worse.

Q: So what do you hope to accomplish with this film?

Femke: To change the mentality of organisations and wake people up. Our way of doing that is to get as intimate as possible with the people we follow. It fits us and with the films we make. Also on the political level – United Nations people and people in political office – they are the ones making all the policies. We have to wake them up and confront them with images.

Q: Why do you think there is such a hestitation to provide programs for the perpetrators?

Ilse: The problem now is that a lot of NGOs don't have the backbone yet that they can stand up and set up programs for perpetrators as well, so they can cure the problem. It's difficult because of course the victims will say, 'These perpetrators destroy our lives and now they are getting projects and help?' Of course, you need to be very strong as an organization to explain it well, but it's just a matter of being brave enough to do this because otherwise the situation won't change.

Q: Obviously what also has to change is the justice system. As much as Captain Basima seems like a changed man, he should have been held accountable for his crimes.

Ilse: Yes, definitely, and actually the film we are making now is about corruption in the justice system. We are going to set up a nation wide campaign when we launch the film, probably around mid 2012.

Femke: And with 'Weapon of War', we are going to set up a huge project in DRC which we've been working on for a year now. There will be a lot of military guys trained for the project, and we will make a reedited film. We will never bring the whole film 'Weapon of War' back to the Congo, but we will make a reedited educational version and use footage from both 'Weapon of War' and 'Fighting the Silence.' We travelled twice to Kinshasa to do presentations there, and everyone is really enthusiastic about it – including the Congolese government.

Ilse: Our aim is to make strong educational films for the military. So, in the military camps there will be a cinema, and after the film they will go deeper into the problems. For example, one theme will be to explain to the military how they destroy womens lives by raping and what the consequences are for society and Congo. For example, another film edit will show what the consequence is for the military itself – if you rape and murder it will hunt you down in the end. I think that's also important for them to understand – that it also destroys their own lives.[3]

Q: Why do you think film is such an effective tool with this particular topic?

A. Film works really well because you can talk about characters in the film and then easily move on to personal stories. Film just breaks open conversations. That's what we see in Q&As after our screenings. You can't heal people straightaway, but maybe after several months of seeing the films, doing workshops, and group discussions, there will be a moment when perpetrators remember what they have done, and what they have seen. We will also include a part where we show the damage it does to the men themselves. People react to their own interests, so if they don't care about women, at least they will think, 'Gosh, I don't want to be hunted down with nightmares for my entire life.' This will be quite a process. We are going to develop it with the national army and have lots of experts on board to put something together that can work.

---

3 For more information, please visit http://mobilecinemafoundation.com/website/?p=39.

Q: Tell me more about the mobile cinema project you set up for your first film, 'Fighting the Silence.'

Ilse: It's one big mobile cinema that's been running for one and a half years and travels from village to village in South Kivu, and we hope to start up a second one in North Kivu. The mentality towards women has to change in Congo, and the only way to change people's mentality is by education. We brought 'Fighting the Silence' back to Congo to break the stigmas, open a debate and to give people role models that actually take back their wives after they have been raped. If they do a question-and-answer session afterwards, you hear men say: 'Well, I never looked at it that way, that you can actually take back your wife.' That was not an option, but if you give people examples then they can also follow it. That's our believe in the power of film.

Femke: But we thought this wasn't enough, so we designed these mini-mobile cinema kits. The big mobile cinema will drive from village to village and then drives off. We thought, why shouldn't people there be able to use the films all the time? So we designed mini mobile kits – hand luggage with a beamer, speakers, screens, and the films. Ten different organizations are using it already. That's just our thing – if it's there then everyone should start using it.

Q: I noticed that neither of you appears in the films. Can you explain why not?

Femke: That's our choice. No white people, no experts, and no voiceovers. Just the people. Let them explain the story. We do that in all our films.

Ilse: We, with our big western world and our muscles, we always tend to speak for other groups. They know it so much better than we do – give them a chance to tell the story. It is a decison. It doesn't always make it easier. We want to give all the words to them.

Femke: And because we don't use voiceovers, the films are so good to bring back to Congo. For example, with 'Fighting the Silence,' a lot of organisations and womens' groups asked us if they could use the film when it was finished. But to hand out DVDs is pointless because there is no electricity and no DVD players, so that's why we decided to do a mobile cinema. That way, we can reach the countryside where there are few NGOs. Everyone loved the film because it's their story. It's not us saying, 'What you do is bad' – it's the story of real people of Congo. That makes it suitable to bring the films back.

Q: So would you say that you are using the medium of film to inspire change in Congo?

Ilse: Yes. We are filmmakers and we want to make good documentaries that will reach a large audience. But as soon as the film is launched we become activists and try to do more with it.

Femke: With film, you can confront people with images and real stories – and in Congo, perpetrators have never been confronted by victims, because they never have to talk to their victims, or think about them. I think the power with film is that it will be stuck in your brain. Maybe they go back to the front after the whole session we're planning and go back into their old habits, but there will be a point when this little door opens in their minds. As soon as that happens, as soon as people are emotionally caught by the image on screen, that's the point when it's too late for them. Then they will be haunted by what they've done and have to start doing things with it, and then you need programs to make sure that these men can be rehabilitated.

Q: Right, because if men become socalized to think that rape is normal and without consequences, how is it ever going to change?

Ilse: The biggest key is to change the attitudes of men. Sometimes it's so strange to see all these organisations and the government trying to set up programs for the military, where they retrain them on how to use guns, but they all forget what the basic principle is, which is to protect the population. Will the men be better behaving towards each other and the population? For the army to be better, they have to change their mentality.

Q: Rape is a horrific weapon used in so many wars, but the level of violence involved is just so mind boggling. In Lisa Jackson's film on sexual violence in Congo, 'The Greatest Silence,' there is a small part where she asks rapists why they do it, and they say they are in the bush for a long time, so there is a need. But when you consider the mutilation and torture involved, that explanation makes very little sense.

Femke: It's a very cheap way to engage in battle, because in Congo the rebel groups don't have enough ammunition, and raping is just a really strong weapon. When you take down the women, then you sort of terrorize a whole area and destroy the total community. That's why it works so well. The woman is the root of the family, so if you damage her, you damage the whole family. If you systematically do this with all the women in the village, then you destroy a whole community.

Ilse: Also, there is such a big percentage of people who have grown up as child solders, and child soldiers have their minds completely destroyed and they are capable of anything. We were in rebel camps and that's what you felt. The day before we filmed in these rebel camps, we went in at four o'clock in the afternoon, which is not a good time to go because everyone will be drunk and stoned. The biggest aggression you felt there was from the youngsters.

Q: I'm just thinking about how one of the rebels interviewed in 'Weapon of War' says that sexual violence gave their group negotiating power with the government. That literally, women's bodies are used as pawns. Especially when he talked about cutting off the woman's breasts. I'm glad you included that, because I think a lot of people don't understand the level of violence involved – that womens bodies are actually destroyed.

Ilse: Even for us doing this film, it doesn't answer all the questions. I think the biggest thing is that war changes people into the worst possible version of themselves.

Femke: Captain Basima is living proof that you can change. I mean, he was a monster, he terrorised his whole family, and raped his own wife and beat up his children.

Q: I think part of it is being able to acknowlege your actions and show remorse, which Captain Basima was able to do. I'm curious, how have your own attitudes evolved while making this film?

Ilse: We learned that judging is very easy. When we were making 'Fighting the Silence,' if we even saw a soldier, we felt uncomfortable, but now we were surrounded by them. We do not approve of rape at all, and hold every person responsible for these brutal acts, but if you are so against an entire group, you will never understand the problem.

Femke: The problem can grow bigger and bigger if you don't start looking at these men. In addition, there are hardly any organizations focused on children. Everyone is very focused on women – which is good – but why not also focus on their husbands and children. Children have witnessed their mothers being raped and often the husbands are traumatized because they were not able to save their wives. The whole society is so traumatized in Congo. We tried to raise more awareness by not only focusing on the women, because that way you won't solve any problem.

Q: So how did people react to you while you were making this film?

Ilse: I think they underestimated us. It was a big advantage for us to be young. People didn't take us too seriously, but at the same time, we weren't a threat. I think that helped.

Femke: After working in Congo for so many years, we also understand the conflict and all the layers so well, and that's really an advantage. Plus, we do really take our time making the films, about two and a half years on each one.

Q: Do you do this all yourselves?

Ilse: If we don't do it, no one else will. That's what drives us. To make a film is great and what we love to do, but it's also about spreading this awareness and actually going back to Congo to create change.

The Van Velzen sisters latest film about the DRC, 'Justice for Sale,' premiered in November 2011.

CHAPTER 16

VOICES OF COURT MEMBERS: A PHENOMENOLOGICAL JOURNEY

The Prosecution of Rape and Sexual Violence at the International Criminal tribunal for the Former Yugoslavia (ICTY) and the Bosnian War Crimes Court (BIH)

Sara Sharratt

"You know, during my whole life I have been surrounded by love of women, firstly my mother, my grandmother, my aunts. As for aunts, I have many; then my daughters, I have two of them. That's why I don't make the difference between women and men. I don't even accept that division. I don't see a difference between men's perception of rape and women's perception of rape. What matters is our attitude towards women or the attitude of women towards men. It is just the way I see things. I'm not sure that any woman would have more sensitivity towards that matter than I do."
Male Judge, BIH court (personal interview 2008).

1. INTRODUCTION

Written from the point of view of a Clinical Psychologist, this chapter takes a social/psychological/phenomenological approach to the prosecution of rape and sexual violence in international courts. The central assumption is that the affective/cognitive/behavioural aspects of human beings determine to a large degree how we see the world, how we judge, how we think and, especially in this case, how court members and all actors perceive and react to rape. Attitudes towards rape survivors, and more broadly toward sexuality, as well as stereotypes of both the survivor and the perpetrator can and have affected the judgments of court members. Bias is frequently denied, and holders of such bias hide behind legalism and illusions of objectivity.

The discriminatory practices against women are the ever present context in this globalized world, and what takes place within courts is no exception. Feminist scholars, during the second wave of feminism, struggled to challenge the assumption that law is objective and uninfluenced by gender, race, class, personal beliefs, and country of origin. This continues to be an ongoing struggle. Considerable progress has been made in the recognition of rape as a war crime. Yet, in the actual practice of the prosecution of rape and sexual violence crimes, the personal/subjective nature of the law and the impact of the gender of its practitioners too often remain unexamined and unchallenged. This chapter presents the results of an emipirical study, based on interviews with a wide range of court officials at the International Criminal Tribunal for the former Yugoslavia (ICTY) in The Hague and the World Criminal Court (WCC) in Sarajevo. Central focus of this chapter is if/how gender-bias affects the prosecution of sexual violence in war and conflict situations.

2. METHODOLOGY

In the current study, in-depth semi-structured interviews[4] were conducted with court members.

Together with a local coordinator in Bosnia Herzegovina, I have interviewed court members in two courts: the ICTY in The Hague and the WCC in Sarajevo. Court members were selected because of their experience with cases involving charges of rape and sexual violence against women. In-depth interviews were conducted with a sample of 14 judges (seven females and seven males) and 12 prosecutors (seven women, six men) in both courts. It is important to point out that the samples reflect most of those court members who had been involved in the most prominent cases of sexual violence in ICTY, as well as those conducted up to 2009 in BIH. Numerous interviews with the Gender Legal Expert at ICTY were also conducted. Additional interviews (total of 8) were carried out with 3 investigators in BIH (one female) and two investigators in ICTY (one female and one male) and with members of Victim and Witnesses Units (VWU) in both courts, including the directors (females). Additional interviews were conducted with members of Organization for Security and Cooperation (OSCE) in Europe, which monitors the work of the WCC in Sarajevo and the Office of the High Commissioner for Human Rights (OHCHR). Among these, there was only one male trial monitor.

---

4 In my book: *Gender, Shame and Sexual Violence: The voices of witnesses and court members at War Crimes Tribunals* (Farmham, UK: Ashgate 2011), this and related material has been elaborated. Questionnaires with closed and open questions were also distributed to court members and supplemented the interview data. A total of 61 questionnaires were analyzed.

With the semi-structured in depth interviews, we attempted to cover more personal issues and challenges faced in these trails, including level of evidence required to convict, attitudes toward women and sexuality, effects of protective measures on stigmatization, ways in which the court could address stigmatization, etc. This is also a central part of the study, as this research assumes that those who deliver justice are an integral part of a socially constructed world and no amount of so-called objectivity can overcome an unexamined mind. Court members were asked about their feelings about working with these cases; where they saw themselves as not adequately prepared to meet these challenges, attitudes towards the survivor, and questions such as: Do women lie more than men? Is rape harder to prosecute? Why?

The data were analyzed by the use of by Maqxsda 10[5] for qualitative analysis, especially for grouping common themes and diverse answers to main categories needed for the objectives of the project.

This chapter provides data supporting the findings that the prosecution of rape and sexual violence in two international courts is often marked by misogyny, biases, and rape-myth acceptance (RMA) by court members. In order to protect the confidentiality and anonymity of court members, no reference is made to specific cases, but the gender and the formal position of the interviewee is indicated.

Results of this phenomenological journey, in which the attitudes of court officials are captured in their own words taken from personal interviews as well as from published statements and courtroom interventions, are recounted.

3. REVIEW OF THE LITERATURE

In a 2000 study designed to assess attitudes of judges and prosecutors in Bosnia toward the ICTY and the prosecution of war crimes, one of the following conclusions was that:

> All participants used the term "politics" or "political" primarily to distinguish between a legal process – a process governed by a fixed set of rules that can be applied in a neutral manner – and a process by which decision-makers exercise discretion to achieve a particular policy goal or desired outcome. Frequently, judges and prosecutors adamantly reiterated the distinction between themselves, as legal professionals, and politicians. In addition, participants repeatedly expressed their personal distaste for politics and politicians and vigorously criticized the overt and indirect influence of political parties on the legal system.[6]

5 See www.maxqda.com/products/maxqda10.

6 H. Weinstein and L. Fletcher, "Justice, Accountability and Social Reconstruction: An Interview Study of Bosnian Judges and Prosecutors," Berkeley Journal of International Law: the Human Rights Law Clinic (2000): 10.

In an ideal world judges would sit aloof from the tainted world of politics, conferring judgment and legal opinion only according to a tightly ordered set of rules.[7] Yet courts are inevitably part of political systems; human beings develop legal systems and rules that reflect their own socialization and power positions. As individuals, judges and prosecutors are also subjected to these biases, myths and distortions. Claims of objectivity and rationality clash with the evidence to the contrary.[8] Specifically, rape law, states Kaspiew[9], reflects a construction of sexuality which discounts women's subjectivity and privileges the male perspective.

Psychologists, sociologists and other social scientists[10], have illuminated the issues surrounding rape myths and rape-myth acceptance: lack of awareness of the subjectivity of perception, misogynistic influences of psychodynamic factors in decision making, impact of race, age, class on attitudes and perceptions. Yet, a large number of judges, prosecutors, and legal officers focus only on not contaminating the "truth" (which presupposes the existence of only one truth) and the importance of maintaining objectivity and professionalism in examining the evidence. These two artificially separated worlds must be brought together if justice is to wear a gender-inclusive garment. Laws reflecting political power and the illusory dichotomy personal vs. political are as arbitrary as other tightly bound dichotomies: objective/subjective; rational/emotional, or private/public. The private, as many feminists claimed in the 1970's, is political.

Social psychology research on attitudes surrounding sexual violence offers a wide spectrum of possibilities for studying the presence of rape myths among a broad range of subjects. Yet, Gavey, for example, criticizes how much this approach could contribute to "an implicit, if not always explicit, diagnosis of the problem as located within people's minds, rather than in the cultural fabric itself."[11] I, however, hold that individual widespread responses certainly reflect cultural prescript ability and endorsements of such myths. As many other feminists have done, I point out the social construction aspects of the biological and dismiss the dichotomy between the biological and the cultural.

7 D. Terris, C. Romano and L. Swigart, *The International Judge: An introduction to the men and women who decide the world cases* (Oxford, UK: Oxford University Press, 2007).

8 Binaifer Nowrojee, *Your justice is too slow. Will the ICTR fail Rwanda's rape victims?* (New York: United Nations Research Institute for Social Development (UNRISD), 2005), Occasional Paper 10.

9 N.R. Quenivet, *Sexual Offences in Armed Conflict and International Law* (New York: Ardsley Park, 2005), 20 quoting R. Kaspiew.

10 V. Helgeson, *Psychology of Gender* (New Jersey: Prentice Hall, 2005), 194–204; Judith Herman, Trauma and Recovery: The Aftermath of Violence-from Domestic Abuse to Political Terror (New York: Basic Books, 2005); G. Bohner, F. Eyssel, A. Pina, F. Siebler, and V. Tendayi, "Rape myth acceptance: cognitive, affective and behavioural effects of beliefs that blame the victim and exonerate the perpetrator," in Rape: Contemporary Challenges, eds. M. Horwath and J. Brown (Oregon: William Publishing, 2009).

11 N. Gavey, *Just Sex?: The Cultural Scaffolding of Rape* (New York: Routledge, 2005), 45.

Bohner *et al.* characterize rape myths as "descriptive or prescritive beliefs about rape, (i.e. about the causes, context, consequences) perpetrators, victims and their interaction that serve to deny, downplay, or justify sexual violence against women."[12]

Psychologists developed a scale to measure Rape Myth Acceptance (RMA) Lonsway and Fitzgerald consisting of no fewer than 24 discrete statements encapsulating rape myths.[13] Respondents are asked whether they agree or disagree with each statement. In general, regardless of the scale or methodology used, there are several consistent findings.

- Those with a higher RMA score attribute greater responsibility to the survivor, rate the trauma suffered by the survivor less severely, and were likely not to recommend that the survivor go to the police.[14]
- Rape myths are more widely accepted in males than in females[15] and men are more disposed to blame the survivor than women blame the survivor.[16] For a complete review of all relevant literature see Temkin and Krahé[17] and Horvard and Brown (eds).[18]
- Ward, using her own scale, found worldwide support for rape myths, but with considerable variation among countries.[19]
- Individuals who subscribe to traditional gender-role beliefs show greater acceptance of rape myths and adopt narrower definitions of what constitutes rape than those who are comfortable with more flexible gender roles.[20]

---

12 G. Bohner, F. Eyssel, A. Pina, F. Siebler and G.T. Viki, "Rape myth acceptance: cognitive, affective and behavioural effects of beliefs that blame the victim and exonerate the perpetrator," in *Rape and Challenging contemporary thinking*, eds. Horvath, and Jennifer Brown (Devon, UK: Hart publishing, 2009), 19.

13 K.A. Lonsway and L.F. Fitzgerald, "Rape Myths," *Psychology of Women Quarterly* 18 (1994): 133–64.

14 B. Frese, M. Moya, and J.L. Mejias, "Social Perception of Rape: How rape myth acceptance modulates the influence of situational factors," *Journal of Interpersonal Violence* 19 (2004): 143–61; B. Krahé, J. Temkin, S. Bieneck, and A. Berger, "Prospective lawyers rape stereotypes and schematic decision making about rape cases," Psychology, Crime and Law 14 (2008): 461–79.

15 S. Hinck and W. Thomas, "Rape myth acceptance in college students: how far have we come?" *Sex Roles* 40 (1999): 815–32; L. Morri, J. Benart and L. Dyanuro, "Attitude towards rape: Gender and ethnic differences across Asian and Caucasian college students," Sex Roles 32, no. 7–8 (2000): 457–67.

16 M. Morry and E. Winkler, "Student acceptance and expectation of sexual assault," *Canadian Journal of Behavioural Science* (2001): 188–92.

17 J. Temkin and B. Krahé, *Sexual assault and the justice gap: A question of attitude* (Oregon: Hart Publishing, 2009).

18 Eds. M. Horvath and J. Brown, *Rape: Challenging contemporary thinking* (Oregon: Hart Publishing, 2009).

19 C. Ward, *Attitudes Toward Rape* (London: Sage, 1995).

20 J. Temkin and B. Krahé, *Sexual assault and the justice gap: A question of attitude* (Oregon: Hart Publishing, 2009), 36.

- Attitudes tolerant of rape were significantly correlated with other beliefs detrimental to women.[21]
- Men attribute less blame to the perpetrator, even in cases where the perpetrator is female.[22]

While these studies were mostly conducted during "peace times," war rapes have a long history whose occurrence and significance has been ignored until relatively recent times. These rapes have been seen as part of "collateral damage" or as a reward for winners. It is important to examine if the attitudes toward rape differ when they happen during wars or conflicts, especially given the brutality of the assaults and that most of them are committed by strangers (see stranger myth below).

Temkin and Krahé (2009) found that among the 74 undergraduate law students in the study, the closer the relationship between complainants and defendants, the less certain they were that a rape had occurred their study also measured perceptions of female precipitation (i.e., how much women were believed to have provoked the rape by teasing men or allowing men to touch them intimately prior to the rape). Male study subjects were more willing to blame the survivor and saw the defendant as less blameworthy than did female study subjects. The authors attribute this to an underlying difference of the acceptance of female participatation beliefs, shown to be greater in men than in women.[23]

In another study conducted by Temkin and Krahe (2009) amongt 17 judges (mostly men) and seven barristers (three women and four men), all were specially licensed to try rape cases. Most balked at the suggestion of a justice gap, but did allow that improvements were needed in the areas of effective policing, competent prosecuting counsel, and vigorous defense counsel.[24] However, none of the judges acknowledged that *they also* may contribute to the existing problems. The findings of this article confirm that although judges may be aware of some of the problems in obtaining justice in rape cases, they are certainly not themselves immune to the myths of rape, as shown in the present study.

The attitudinal difference, based on gender, that was found in student samples is true also for police officers. The findings in earlier research provide suppport of rape myths accepted by among police officers, alongside lack of awareness of a justice gap (many of the investigators in ICTY and WCC were former police officers). Female officers tend to hold a more positive attitude toward victims than do male officers (see Schuller and Stewart 2000).[25] Several

21 *Ibid.* at 45.
22 *Ibid.* at 43.
23 *Ibid.* at 85.
24 *Ibid.* at 126, 141.
25 R.A. Schuller and A. Steward, "Police responses to sexual assault complaints: The role of perpetrator/complainant intoxication," *Law and Human Behaviour* 24 (2000): 535–51.

studies found police officers endorsed the "real" rape stereotype (stranger-rape scenario).[26] Ward found that 51% of police officers and doctors, 37% of lawyers, and 27% of counsellors endorsed the statement: *"Many women claim rape if they have consented to sexual relations but changed their minds afterwards."*[27]

A study in England found the highest attrition rates (the point at which the decision not to prosecute a case occurs) are at the police investigation stage (74% of the cases).[28] High levels of RMA among police officers (the majority of whom are male), and investigators at both courts (many of whom were former policemen), account for so many cases being dismissed as lacking evidence, before ever getting to the Office of the Prosecutor. A most comprehensive recent study[29] finds, along with that of numerous researchers on rape cases and attrition rates (that is, cases that are reported, but dropped before trial), that gains have been modest. They find that the "good" character of the witness and stranger relations are less important than they once were, but witness evidence, physical injuries and in general issues of nonconsent continue to predominate in court proceedings.[30] While it is also imperative not to generalize and specific results have to be contextialized, legal reforms are insufficient and may even worsen the situation. Yet, the generalized finding is clear: gains have been modest. The high attrition rate of rape contribute to the often unsubstantiated assumption that women who have been raped or sexually assaulted do not *want* to speak out. Yet those who do appear in court to seek justice, may eventually wonder why they agreed to testify in the first place.

A related myth is the "stranger-rape" myth, typified by the stereotypical rape scenario: a psychopathological stranger, seizes and rapes women in dark streets.[31] This scenario generally is contrasted with acquaintance rape or partner or ex-partner rape.

It make sense to assume that a great many rapes that occur during war are stranger rapes, which logically would suggest that it should be easier for women who have been raped in wartime to get convictions, and less likely to be subjected to RMA behaviour.

26 See J. Temkin and B. Krahé, *Sexual assault and the justice gap: A question of attitude* (Oregon: Hart Publishing, 2009) for a summary of all relevant studies.

27 C. Ward, *Attitudes Towards Rape* (London: Sage, 1995), 59.

28 J.M. Brown, C. Hamilton, and D. O'Neill, "Characteristics associated with rape attrition and the role played by scepticisms, or legal rationality by investigators and prosecutors," *Psychology, Crime and Law* 13 (2010): 355–70.

29 Kathleen Daly and Brigitte Bourhours, "Rape and attrition in the Legal Process: A Comparative Analysis of Five Countries," in *Crime and Justice: A review of research* 39, no. 1, ed. M. Tonry (Chicago: University of Chicago Press, 2010): 565–650.

30 *Ibid.*

31 S. Lees, *Carnal Knowledge: Rape on trial* (London: Women's Press, 2002), 8.

4. A PHENOMENOLOGICAL JOURNEY

"The international community made a mistake in exaggerating the power of laws to deal with the aftermath of war. The trials are not for victims and often work against them." Court member, both ICTY and WCC (personal interview 2007).

4.1. CREDIBILITY AND GENDER INJUSTICE: A NO-WIN FOR SURVIVORS

Judges are required to consider mitigating, as well as aggravating, circumstances before delivering a sentence. In 2008, a presiding judge (male) in Sarajevo read the judgment in a sexual assault (rape) case. The judge offered as a *mitigating* circumstance the following: *"One of the mitigating circumstances is that he* [the convicted rapist on trial] *is a family man."* This assertion made no sense. Immediately several questions arose: Shouldn't his family-man status be more appropriately considered as an *aggravating* circumstance rather than as a mitigating circumstance? How does having a husband or a father who is known in the community as a rapist affect the wife and children of such a man? Are courts implicitly giving the message to rapists that being married and having children will ensure them of a lighter sentence? Does the rape victim feel less injured if her attacker was married and had children? The basis for considering a rapist's family status as a mitigating factor appears to center around the man's role as the provider for his family and the need for him to resume his functions as fast as possible. The judge conveyed the attitude that a man's role as primary family provider renders his rape as worthy of a lesser punishment than a rape by a single man without family responsibilities.

One female ICTY judge involved in major cases of sexual assault reacted very differently when she considered the same set of circumstances. *"It* [family-man status] *should be an aggravating one* [circumstance]." All other female judges and prosecutors in major sexual violence cases who were asked agreed that a rapist's family-man status is an aggravating circumstance, *not* a mitigating circumstance. Furthermore, not one rape survivor, whom I also interviewed for a different project,[32] believed that being married and fathering children should be a mitigating circumstance for rape. On the contrary, some witnesses told of attempting to avoid their rape by telling their rapist that they could be the rapist's daughter or mother or wife. It never worked.

"I knew he was married and had three children. One of his daughters was one year younger than me. I asked him how he could rape someone who is the same

[32] Forthcoming publication see footnote 1.

age as his daughter. That made him really angry. I was too afraid to insist on an answer."[33]

In one of the trials at ICTY, a rape survivor testified that she begged her rapist not to rape her, as she was alone, having no knowledge of the whereabouts of her family. However, the man said: "*We won't talk about that. Let's talk about sex.*" Then he raped her.[34]

In the previously mentioned Serajevo case, the reading of the sentence continued with an additional mitigating circumstance cited: the alleged previous relationship with her rapist (which she denied). When victim and rapist were acquainted prior to the rape, that too is considered a mitigating circumstance. Furthermore, the victim being aquainted with her attacker gave rise to doubts about the credibility of the witness. The defendant in this case did in fact receive a lesser sentence than he would have if the rape had fit the stranger-myth stereotype. This substantiates evidence already provided by the literature. In a private interview the research investigator asked one of the judges presiding over this case (a good friend) what was the rationale for the relatively lenient sentence.

"*This was only one rape and cannot be compared with Jankovic or Stankovic* [rapists convicted of numerous rapes in WCC], *because he raped a woman with whom he had a former relationship. He doesn't have the character of a rapist.*"[35]

The clear message sent by this judge is that when a rapist has had a previous relationship with his victim and is accused of "only" one rape, he is viewed as less culpable. Once again, the perpetrator is judged as not fitting either the pathological stranger myth or the severely mentally disturbed rapist profile (another rape myth).

On the other hand, the rape survivor's credibility is constantly questioned.

"*I am interested in the law and being objective, and I wouldn't convict a woman based on only her testimony. They need witnesses, they need more proof. I think that prosecutors don't ask enough questions and they need to ask even more.*" Male judge, BIH.

Another experienced male judge (BIH-court) said in a personal interview:

"*The witness said the rapist had done to her what her father does with her mother. No word for rape. It is hard to listen to the witnesses and try to ascertain the veracity of their testimony.*"

Witnesses are often in a no-win position illustrated by the following observation: "*They* [survivors] *should fight for their rights. Yet, at the same time, when members of the public* [referring to women's support groups] *complain loudly, then they are too agressive and make everyone look bad.*" Female VWU, WCC.

---

33 Balkan Ivestigative Reporting Nework, RN Report # 3 (2006), available at http//birn.eu.com/en/1/200/5/.

34 *Celebici case*, CC/ PIU/364-E, November 1998, 525–27, available at the ICTY webpage.

35 Personal Interview, 2008. Male Judge BIH.

Another example of the no-win position of rape survivors expressed by prosecutors, judges, and legal officers is their willingness to use *whatever* the witness says as justification for doubting her. If the female witness offers too many details, that is reason to suspect she may be making it up. If she does not give enough details, that too is reason to believe she made it up, or to judge her story worthless because it lacks sufficient detail. If she cries too much, she is judged too traumatized to be believed; if she doesn't cry and is composed, then it did not happen. If she behaved passively and was unable to defend herself, she is partially blamed for what happened to her. If she appears too aggressive, that too is suspect, citing the characteristic behavior of trauma is lack of outward expression, which means silent. Every conceivable demeanor a rape witness may display is scrutinized and judged and used to discredit the witness.

Witnesses are usually flooded with unnecessary questions. True, there has been progress on legal issues of consent. In the International Criminal Court (ICC)[36] Statute for example, it explicitly states in Rule 70 that consent cannot be genuine in a coersive environment and therefore not be an issue in cases of rape and or sexual violence during wars and conflicts. This was also true in the Rules of Evidence and Procedures for ICTY and WCC.[37] When it comes to issues of rape and sexual violence, however, the rules and laws are clearly often ignored or interpreted with a clear gender bias. However, this relative improvement in the legal arena clearly highlights the need for input from other relevant disciplines. Laws alone are just not enough; women must also look in other directions. Psychology and social sciences must be brought into the realm of justice, in this context to undrestand what hampers the implementation of the law and what is the deeper source of gender bias.

Hence these legal truths are not necessarily internalized by members of the court. Almost all pray for witnesses to the rapes. In WCC, the rape survivor needs to testify in an open session, or her ordeal must be validated by a witnesss to the crime who must testify in an open court. When I asked a female judge if so many questions and details are necessary, she responded:

> *"I don't think so. The right questions should be asked. The prosecutor and defense attorneys should ask important, crucial questions. They shouldn't ask all the details. I don't think that any presiding judge would allow it, and they are not allowing it, as far as my council is concerned. We don't allow going into details and asking about every*

36 Rome Statute and Rules of Evidence of the International Criminal Court.

37 At first Rule 96 of the ICTY Rules of Procedure and Evidence passed because of the insistence of the female judges present at the time, Judges Gabrielle McDonald and Elizabeth Odio, strictly stated that consent was not an issue. It was later modified so that in some cases the judges in Chambers (privately) could hear the defence present the justification for using the issue of consent. In a private interview, a female judge shared with me that she agreed to this change so that in the case where she was one of the judges, the two other male judges would agree to a conviction of a man accused of rape.

segment. She was raped or she wasn't raped. Other details¾when, what, how, in what order, etc. – are not needed." Female judge, WCC.

One judge told me that it is difficult to rule on rape cases because there are fewer details. On the other hand, judges are afraid to ask more questions because they do not want to "retraumatize the victims."

4.2. PERCEPTIONS AND RELATIONSHIPS AMONG COURT MEMBERS

The more sensitive approach expressed by the female judge in the previous section is not shared by other court members, especially other prosecutors or trial monitors who were interviewed in WCC for this research. They saw numerous prosecutors and judges as poorly trained, unprepared, and unable to deal with rape testimonies and witnesses. Moreover, they viewed judges as ineffectual and passive and often not able to control the courtroom participants, resulting in abusive behaviours towards the women witnesses.

Judges were seen as being either "good" or "incompetent" by the prosecutors, and this was true in both courts. Judges had the same opinion of the prosecutors. The VWC members interviewed for this study did not hold a good opinion of all judges and prosecutors, and it is fair to say that they blame each other for missteps. The three following citations illustrate this point:

"*Judges do not trust prosecutors to have explained protective measures to witnesses properly. The prosecutors are my worst enemies. We can't trust the prosecution. I tell them they are my enemies and avoid them in hallways.*" VWU, BIH.

"*Part of the problem is that prosecutors do not meet with victims before trial, and when they say they do, they are lying.*" Male judge, WCC.

"*I am angry with Prosecutors. Some bring in witnesses with horrendous stories of rape, and witnesses go on and on but they are irrelevant for the charges. For example, one woman spoke about terrible rapes, but didn't know the perpetrator.*" Male judge, WCC International.

One might wonder, how many rape victims actually do know their rapist? This fragmented vision of the three chambers is illustrated by the following answers I received from three female officers when I asked them how the court could improve the situation for witnesses.

"*I am NOT working for VWU or their parties. I believe that the fairness and impartiality of the chamber is, in part, granted by a certain neutrality towards the actors of the trial. Getting involved with challenges of victims and such subjective considerations is dangerous for the court.*" Female legal officer, ICTY

"Who am I to interfere with victim witnesses and give them recommendations? Again, I work for chambers. Do you understand the rules of procedure of the ICTY?" Female legal officer, ICTY

"This is simply shocking to me; this is not the victim's justice. Justice is for all, towards all working there, for chambers. I am not serving the purpose of one actor or party over another; and doing so would be a violation of my professional obligations. What does this have to do with data?" Female Legal officer, ICTY (my underlines).

Only those judges and prosecutors most experienced with gender-related issues, as well as the Gender Legal advisor, identified as important challenges the prejudices and biases that victims have to face.

Laws and procedures are presented as neutral, and the welfare of the victim is relegated to psychologists and social workers who are there to ready the witnesses for testifying. There is always a psycho-social component that is separate and equally important as legal skills. However, the psycho-social component remains in the shadows, relegated to levels below the purely legal realm. All agree that the witnesses must be better prepared, and yet, conversely, often blame her for the crime. The following quotations taken from the research interviews are good examples of this:

- "They just do not get their lives organized." *Female VWU, WCC.*
- "It is very important that witness support plays a role in managing the witness." *Male investigator, ICTY* (my emphasis).
- "If she *[the witness]* is not able to give objective statements and not to present it *[the rape]* the way she likes it, it is very hard to prove before the court. The entire proceedings depend on her statements." *Male prosecutor, WCC.*

In the court members' view, the challenges in their profession are squarely on the survivor. Their most common request for the future was *"continuing education,"* without ever specifying exactly its proposed content or purpose.

4.3. RAPE MYTHS AND STEREOTYPES OF SURVIVORS

Interviews revealed that even the most experienced judges and prosecutors held rape-myth beliefs. One of the most senior male trial judges, who has been a champion for women's issues in the ICTY, shared the following during an interview in the privacy of his office:

"I do not understand the cruelty of the rapes, the mutilations, the markings, the killings. I can see that if a group of men were fighting in the bush for weeks, when they come, they rape. That I understand."

A male prosecutor told me:

"I had a very strong woman; she had a lot of strength. Such women are rare." WCC.

One of the most experienced female judges in ICTY told me:

"I had to struggle with male colleagues who often saw the victims as so frail that their testimony needed to be abbreviated."

This final quotation by a female judge contrasts with other judges who wanted survivor's to provide extensive details of their rape. In general, males tended to see the survivors as more traumatized than their female counterparts saw them. More female court members showed greater empathy and concern for the survivor than did their male colleagues. There is, on the one hand, the notion that survivors are too fragile and so should not be asked too many questions. On the other hand, is the belief that women are liars and should be asked for every detail of their alleged ordeal. The latter attitude is more prevalent among men judges. A woman's veracity may be questioned because because of her inability to remember every detail. The notion that women lie is very common among court members. Many questioned why the women did not come forward earlier, why there is a the lack of material evidence (supposedly to be gathered in the midst of a war), and/or could they possibly have lied to get a state pension as a rape survivor.

4.4. ATTITUDES AND FEELINGS ABOUT CASES INVOLVING SEXUAL VIOLENCE

Most prosecutors who were interviewed clearly do not like to prosecute rape cases. The exceptions were often female prosecutors. The most reluctant ones stated that rape cases require much sensitivity and time. Their lack of competency on gender issues and the time pressure makes their reluctance understandable. As of June 2009, in WCC there were 18 prosecutors with 21 legal advisors working on war crimes with around 4,000 cases pending. A recent (April 2011) conversation with a male prosecutor in WCC confirmed that that the overload is on the increase and the budget is also tighter. One (male) prosecutor pointed out:

"Due to overload the prosecutors usually do not have enough time needed to dedicate to victims of rape, to prepare them for testimony."

The exceptions were always some gender-competent female prosecutors and a few of the males:

> *Rape is difficult to convict and prosecutors, especially when time constraints are present, prefer to prosecute other crimes as they want to invest their time where they have more probability of getting a conviction. It is also the case that victims/witnesses require more time and patience, again making the cases more demanding. This is*

especially the case in prosecuting higher-ranking persons. In the case of Milosevic, for example, rape charges in Croatia were dropped. This was also due to the pressure put on the OTP by the bench to speed up the trial. Female Prosecutor, ICTY.

The tendency to want to avoid rape cases is not only because of the difficulty in winning them. Rape intrudes on deeper issues, colouring the picture for both the prosecutors as well as the judges, who have no stake in "winning."

"*It is so hard to look into their eyes (survivor/witness's).*" Male judge, BIH.

More male than female judges mentioned that looking into the perpetrators' eyes must also be the most difficult task for the survivors. However, in interviews with survivors,[38] there was no evidence of this. On the contrary, many saw the opportunity to face their rapist as empowering. Some court members, mostly male, viewed looking into the eyes as revealing the visibility of sexuality, of dishonor for the survivor, and the collective shame of the violation of purity and chastity, which in their own minds they so needed for women to possess.

It's harder to deal with rape cases because you have to meet victims when they come to testify. You see all the terror that she had to go through. She has to live with all that dread and despair. You can feel it, perceive it. While in murder cases you don't have to deal with victims. That's completely another thing. Male judge, BIH.

One of the most experienced male prosecutor said in an interview:

"*I often have more weeping men sitting in the box recounting torture than women recounting rape.*"

When it comes to rape and sexual violence against women, many judges and prosecutors project very different attributes onto the female who has been brutalized than they do onto the tortured male. As Engle comments, it is "*the tranformation of the spectator into lewd voyeur.*"[39]

When interviewed about why men have particular problems with rape, a senior prosecutor was very cautious. He agreed with a statement recounted to him by the interviewer that a judge in WCC had made: "*as men we could be the perpetrators.*"

The senior prosecutor conceded: "*It is too close.*" Senior prosecutor, BIH.

Others acknowledged the connection with sexuality implying also the differential impact of sexual violence on women and men.

- "I would prefer only murder cases. I am also more sensitive with women who have been raped." Male prosecutor, WCC.

[38] See footnote 1 for references to my book about this study. The description of witnesses' experiences are fully discussed there.

[39] Karen Engle, *Seeing Ghosts: 9/11 and the Visual Imagination*, (Montreal: McGill-Queens University Press, 2009), 31.

- "They hardly talk about sex in front of strangers, even when as prosecutors they have to talk to victims." *Female judge, BIH.*
- "I get embarrassed asking questions to rape victims." *Male Prosecutor.*

This discomfort is confirmed by a female prosecutor, BIH:

"Only in last few years the talk on sexuality has appeared in the public discourse, on TV. The families rarely talk about it, especially when men are in question. So they hardly talk about sex in front of strangers, even when as prosecutors they have to talk to victims."

Judges also recognize their relief about not being prosecutors in cases of rape as in the following example:

"I acknowledged that I would rather be a judge than a prosecutor, because prosecutors have to ask questions that are very delicate and I would feel uncomfortable. Yet, I am comfortable in dealing with rape. Male judge, BIH.[40]

4.5. PRESENCE OF WOMEN

The effect of being male was mentioned only by two members of the court: one male prosecutor saw it as "a disadvantage." Another male investigator recognized the need for an investigator of the same sex as the victim.

Most male court personnel asserted that they were competent to handle the cases; but it is interesting to note that the female judges once again felt they needed to protect the survivor at times from male judges and prosecutors. Female judges behaved as traditional engendered females i.e., protecting other women.

- "I always can react and control my colleagues somehow, for example, by saying, ask gently; lower your tone; make a break; let her speak for herself; leave her; be careful about the way you ask; lower your voice, etc." *Female judge, WCC.*
- "I always worry how my colleagues are going to act, how the attorneys going to pose the question or how the prosecutor is, if he isn't a woman, because women are more subtle. For example, one or two months ago, I had to warn one attorney. He usually spoke very loudly and he is massive, so whenever he asked her something, she would draw back. I asked my colleague to warn that attorney. He warned him. However, he continued asking her the same way he did before. Then I turned my microphone on and I said: 'Attorney, she is a victim of sexual abuse. Don't ever forget that. The way you are posing your questions, your tone, the way you gesticulate, isn't appropriate for

40 Emphasis added.

examination of this witness." After that, the attorney was more careful. That was one positive experience I had." *Female Judge WCC.*

- "I often found myself tutoring my male colleagues of what it means to a woman to be raped. You have to be insistent that this was a serious crime and they could not have consented it to it under the situation that they were in [captivity]." *Senior Female Judge, ICTY.*

Most court members recognized that the presence of a woman may be comforting for the witness, and the presence of women has had a clear impact on some of the most important cases involving sexual violenece in the ICTY.[41]

5. CONCLUDING REMARKS

When it comes to rape and sexual violence against women, international criminal courts have barely begun to open their eyes, especially when it comes to the specific application of the laws in their Statutes. The majority of court members, especially males, function in a world filled with rape myths, stereotypic notions about women, discomfort with the perverse sexuality involved in rape, and differential standards about male and female sexuality. There is very little recognition of structural gender arrangements, the subjectivity of laws, the context in which the prosecution of rape takes place, and the barriers that the women have to face and overcome. These are mostly mentioned by the most experienced females from ICTY. There also remains strong constraints on what can and cannot be spoken about publicly. Most rape cases are often closed to the public, increasing voyeurism towards female sexuality ("behind closed doors") when sexual violence paradoxically dissappears from the public view. For a clinical psychologist who has worked with many trauma survivors, including those involving rape and sexual violence,

[41] I want the women in ICTY who in the past have been too often rendered invisible to be present, recognized, and known. (WCC women will be recognized when more cases are completed). The women in ICTY include: Judge Elizabeth Odio Benito in Celebici, Judge Gabriele McDonald in Tadic, Judge Florence Mumba in Foca and Furundjiza, Judge Carmen Argibay in Bragojevic and Stakic, Judge Patricia Wald in Kvocka. Prosecutors included Hildegard Uertz-Retzlaff in Kunarac, Peggy Kuo in Foca, Theresa McHenry in Celebici, Brenda Hollis in Tadic and Furundzija, with Patricia Sellers; Joanna Korda (Brjdanin) with Ann Sutherland, Nancy Patterson who prepared the Nikolai indictment and the eventual sexual violence evidence that appeared in Tadic, Kvocka, and Milosevic; Michelle Jarvis Senior legal Officer; Maxine Marcus currently in ICTY advising on gender issues for the Office of the Prosecutor; Wendy Lowein for years acting Director of VWU; Trudie Garrison the investigator in The Furundijza case. Other female investigators, Jan Pfundheller, Rita Pradham, Tej Thapa, Annette Murtagh, Brigette St. Germain, Agnes Inderhaug Plony Bos, Brid O'Toole worked on sexual violence cases. Patricia Sellers, the Gender Legal Advisor was present in most these cases; her contribution is/was invaluable. These women generously acknowledged the cooperation of their male colleagues.

the most personally traumatic experience for me was talking to many court members and experts. I hope that I have made it possible for the readers to understand my despair.

In our attemtps to bring justice to victims of sexual violence in war time, we must strive for a judicial institution that accepts that all stakeholders are imperfect engendered human beings. Both mandatory gender competence and psycho-social capacity building must be the core of any court, if we define justice as including women in its institutions and processes.

CONCLUDING REMARKS

CHAPTER 17

HOW TO MOVE FORWARD? INTERDISCIPLINARY APPROACHES TO RECOGNIZING, INVESTIGATING AND PROSECUTING SEXUAL VIOLENCE AS AN INTERNATIONAL CRIME

Anne-Marie de Brouwer, Charlotte Ku, Renée Römkens and Larissa van den Herik

Although the explicit criminalization and efforts to prosecute sexual violence as an international crime are relatively new when compared to the long historic presence of these crimes in times of conflict, the international judicial response to such crimes is already breaking new ground in attending to the needs of individual survivors even while trying to establish a trail of mass brutality. The stories represented in this volume are very human whether of the survivors of these crimes or of those advocates dedicated to the prosecution of such violations or of the countless others who become involved as field workers or judicial officials. What this volume highlights is, amongst other things, that the issue of sexual violence is not an academic or theoretical subject far removed from people, but is very much an issue of individuals and communities caught up in waves of violence. An issue that concerns and affects us all, and that therefore needs to be recognized and addressed on multiple levels in order to be prevented and prosecuted. It further underscores the need to involve survivors and others in the peace-building process following a conflict beyond judicial process and the punishment of the perpetrators of these acts.

The juxtaposition of single acts of extreme violence against a backdrop of mass brutality of course is one of the reasons why these crimes have been difficult to address. For one thing, a conflict environment is not congenial to the systematic gathering of evidence and the carrying out of orderly judicial and legal process. Yet, strides have been made to prosecute those responsible for war crimes, crimes against humanity and genocide, but less so when the focus has been on sexual and gender based crimes.[42] As stated by Maxine Marcus, who has more than thirteen years of experience as an international criminal prosecutor, in this volume: "crimes of sexual and gender-based violence are under-documented and under-included in cases which are brought before international jurisdictions."[43] This, she argues, is however remarkable in light of the fact that the gathering of evidence of such crimes does not pose any additional legal burden and need not pose any additional investigative challenge when compared to other international crimes. The key to include sexual violence crimes in the indictments requires the investigative plan to include and be open to evidence of these crimes, preparation with as much information as possible in advance of the field investigation, and, throughout the whole process, a checklist of elements of crimes to be proven, need to be relied on. Furthermore, while gathering the evidence, the needs of the survivor need to be prioritized to the extent possible. According to her "[t]he investigation and prosecution of crimes of sexual and gender-based violence is crucial to closing the impunity gap."[44] At the ICTR, in light of the seemingly low conviction rate for sexual violence crimes compared to the high conviction rate for other crimes, the Prosecutor of the ICTR set up a "Committee for the Review of the Investigation and Prosecution of Sexual Violence" in 2007. The work of this committee resulted in a "Best Practices Manual on the Investigation and Prosecution of Sexual Violence Crimes in Situations of Armed Conflict."[45] The Manual provides recommendations on how to improve the investigation and prosecution of sexual violence and Linda Bianchi elaborated upon these recommendations in her chapter in this volume. Bianchi refers, *inter alia*, to other innovative ways of dealing with witness testimony that can be considered, such as using more written statements in lieu of oral testimony.[46] Furthermore, she refers, amongst other things, to the important role of management, that is to have a clear and comprehensive global strategy to address sexual violence crimes, a strategy that

42 See Susan Brownmiller, *Against Our Will: Men, Women and Rape* (New York: Fawcett Columbine, 1975). See also Patricia Viseur-Sellers, "Gender Strategy is Not a Luxury for International Courts," *American University Journal of Gender, Social Policy & Law* 17 (2009): 301–25. For the advancements in the substantive and procedural law concerning sexual violence crimes in the statutes of the Tribunals, see the introduction to this book.

43 Maxine Marcus, "Investigation of Crimes of Sexual and Gender-Based Violence Under International Criminal Law," in *Sexual Violence as an International Crime: Interdisciplinary Approaches*, eds. Anne-Marie de Brouwer, Charlotte Ku, Renée Römkens and Larissa van den Herik (Antwerp, Belgium: Intersentia), *supra*.

44 *Ibid.*

45 The Manual is available at http://lexglobal.org/files/Renifa%20Madenga-ICTR%20Practice%20Manual.pdf. During the second Hague Colloquium Renifa Madenga, Appeals Counsel at the ICTR and member of the ICTR Sexual Violence Committee, presented on the lessons learned.

46 Also minimizing the number of victims to establish certain facts could be considered, see Marie-Bénédicte Dembour and Emily Haslam, "Silencing Hearings? Victim-Witnesses at War Crimes Trials," *European Journal of International Law* 15, no. 1 (2004): 151–77.

needs to be communicated to the entire office from the outset. She also refers to the lack of understanding, know-how and training to elicit the necessary evidence that would support a conviction for sexual violence among the investigators. Cultural aspects of the region and victims, having several interviews with victims and approaching them with the necessary level of respect and care, as well as a better coordination between the investigators and prosecutors on the evidence required to fulfill the legal requirements, are all important factors to have sexual violence included among the charges. Whereas the ICTY and the ICTR had to grapple with the fact that they had no real precedents, the lessons learned today from these and other courts has unfortunately not yet led to a coherent investigation and prosecution policy concerning sexual violence crimes among and within the different international criminal courts. Silke Studzinsky in her contribution to this volume, for instance, elaborates on the experiences before the ECCC concerning the interviews with victims of sexual violence during the investigation phase and argues that these are often times not conducted with the necessary diligence, sensitivity and competence that is required. She mentions the example in which a female survivor of gang rape during the interview collapsed because she was overwhelmed by the all-male interviewers, while experience before the ICTR had already taught us that women may feel a greater willingness to talk to other women than with men.[47]

Many of the authors in this volume have posed the question where this reluctance to prosecute sexual violence and gender based crimes comes from? Why sexual violence crimes often seem to be considered as secondary or peripheral to other crimes, such as killing, or sometimes even viewed as byproducts of the conflict, private acts not meriting criminalization and prosecution at all? Some do not even see how rape and sexual violence can amount to the crime of genocide. Although sometimes the argument is raised that survivors of sexual violence do not want to come forward out of shame and stigma surrounding these crimes, the experience of many of the authors in this book and others is that oftentimes survivors of sexual violence are willing to talk about their experiences. Perhaps the reluctance to take up cases of sexual violence should be found elsewhere? Sara Sharratt in this volume stated that interviews with judges, prosecutors, investigators, and victim and witnesses unit members of the ICTY and the Bosnian War Crimes Court (BIH) in fact revealed that many of them accept rape myths, hold misogynistic views about women, and are ambivalent and uncomfortable when dealing with rape and sexual violence. According to Sharratt, the ghost of sexuality, with its accompanying

---

47 Linda Bianchi, "The Prosecution of rape and sexual violence: Lessons from Prosecution at the International Criminal Tribunal," in *Sexual Violence as an International Crime: Interdisciplinary Approaches*, eds. Anne-Marie de Brouwer, Charlotte Ku, Renée Römkens and Larissa van den Herik (Antwerp, Belgium: Intersentia), *supra*.

notions of chastity and purity required of women, permeates the proceedings and judgments. To overcome such attitudes, a mandatory training in gender competence and psycho-social capacity building should therefore be obligatory for all parties involved in the judicial system.

Some other challenges and lessons learned in the prosecution of sexual violence as an international crime that, at the moment, can be foreseen include the prosecution of sexual violence in highly complex cases involving high level officials and/or crimes that require linking sexual violence with a broader campaign of crimes, as elaborated upon by Michelle Jarvis and Elena Martin Salgado in this volume. They mention that before the ICTY, the bulk of sexual violence cases today include direct perpetrators of sexual violence crimes or others close to the scene of the crime. Prosecuting sexual violence in high level complex cases where the perpetrators are more remote from the crime scene could, however, be based on the basis of superior responsibility and joint criminal enterprise theories, they argue. While convictions based on these liability modes are necessarily complicated, Jarvis and Salgado point out that in cases of sexual violence crimes where prosecutors and fact finders may mischaracterize sexual violence as non-violent crimes that are incidental to the conflict, these prosecutions will definitely be bound to fail. The challenge in establishing superior responsibility for sexual violence cases is to satisfy a fact finder that an accused person at least had reason to know of the risk that his subordinates would commit sexual violence crimes specifically, as opposed to other types of mistreatment. While establishing a generalized level or risk of the prevalence of sexual violence in conflict is unlikely to be sufficient for establishing superior responsibility, many of the factual situations in international prosecutions disclose more concrete indicators of the risk of sexual violence crimes, including the detention of women in camps where subordinates have uncontrolled access to them. The authors also push for sexual violence prosecutions on the basis of joint criminal enterprise categories I, II and III. Although it is generally considered easier for a prosecutor to prove that a crime was a natural and foreseeable consequence of a joint criminal enterprise (category III) than to prove that it formed part of the common criminal purpose to which all JCE members subscribed (categories I and II), the ICTY Appeals Chamber has recognized that sexual violence can constitute part of a common criminal purpose, either at the outset of the joint criminal enterprise or over time. Before the ICTR, prosecutions based on command responsibility and joint criminal enterprise theory for sexual violence crimes have proven to be very difficult and rare and in its more recent prosecutions, prosecutors have been putting more emphasis on putting the rapes *within* the context of the genocide so as to help the judges accept that the rapes were within the sphere of the genocidal campaign, and not outside.[48]

Another challenge facing the prosecution of sexual violence as an international crime before international tribunals concerns the prosecution of gender-based persecution as a crime against humanity, for the first time codified in the Rome Statute of the ICC. Valerie Oosterveld explores this topic in this volume and lists three potential areas of difficulty that the ICC will need to address in order to ensure a comprehensive consideration of gender-based persecution. She warns against the risk of not coming to a clear interpretation in the Rome Statute's definition of the term "gender" in relation to persecution, which could possibly lead the prosecutor to abstain from gender-based persecution charges to begin with. In addition, the intersection of other forms of persecution with gender-based persecution must be properly contextualized within each prosecution. This will help the Court to understand persecution on the basis of gender and the harm flowing there from, but will also help the Court to understand the wider picture of where targeting on the basis of gender fits within the particular conflict or oppressive situation under consideration. Finally, she argues that specific conduct could be charged in several different ways, for example as rape, torture, enslavement and gender-based persecution, because the conduct was multilayered in its function and in its range of harms. The current approach by the ICC to "cumulative charging" – that is that specific conduct can only result in one type of crime and therefore harm – is, according to Oosterveld, unsatisfactory and diminishes the effective access of victims to justice and reduces the proper contextualization and breadth of gender-based crimes. Furthermore, it is also contrary to earlier jurisprudence on this issue from the ICTY and the ICTR. In particular in the case of sexual violence crimes which are less developed in jurisprudence to date because they are either criminalized for the first time (such as in the case of gender-based persecution) or not at all criminalized as crimes in itself because the international community is not yet in agreement whether these are crimes having different elements from other (sexual violence) crimes (such as in the case of forced marriage[49]), caution is needed that these crimes are not overlooked by investigators and prosecutors.

A third challenge involves the participation of victims generally and that of victims of sexual violence in particularly. While victims can before certain international tribunals now participate in the proceedings to express their views

---

48 See Linda Bianchi, "The Prosecution of rape and sexual violence: Lessons from Prosecution at the International Criminal Tribunal," in *Sexual Violence as an International Crime: Interdisciplinary Approaches*, eds. Anne-Marie de Brouwer, Charlotte Ku, Renée Römkens and Larissa van den Herik (Antwerp, Belgium: Intersentia), *supra*.

49 See Teresa Doherty, "Jurisprudential Developments Relating to Sexual Violence: the Legacy of the Special Court for Sierra Leone," in *Sexual Violence as an International Crime: Interdisciplinary Approaches*, eds. Anne-Marie de Brouwer, Charlotte Ku, Renée Römkens and Larissa van den Herik (Antwerp, Belgium: Intersentia), *supra*.

and concerns (such as before the ICC and ECCC), the challenge for the tribunals is how to inform victims of their rights and how to streamline these participatory rights of victims in light of the often numerous victims wishing to participate. Before the ICC the practice has been that victims' views and concerns were represented through their legal representative(s). For example, in the *Katanga and Chui* case, the Court consolidated victim representation by merging legal representation from eight victims' legal representatives into two legal teams.[50] Each legal representative is responsible for representing the common interests of the group assigned to him or her and for acting on behalf of specific victims when their individual interests are at stake.[51] Given the diversity of experiences of survivors of sexual violence, it may be difficult for legal representatives to represent the unique interests of victims of sexual violence in addition to the interests of other victims. The question that comes to mind is to whom or what section of the Court victims of sexual violence in that case can find recourse to. In her chapter on the ECCC, Silke Studzinsky states on the issue of participation that "the new legal representation regime, which now stipulates that one national and one international Lead Co-Lawyer employed with the Court represent a "consolidated" group of Civil Parties, could reduce, if not hinder, the proper representation of Civil Parties through their Lawyers."[52] Since the judges of the ECCC will now only liaise with the Lead Co-Lawyers, in her view, it remains to be seen how Civil Party Lawyers can continue represent their clients without direct access to the Court.

Only recently, the international community is becoming aware of the brutality of sexual violence perpetrated against men in conflict situations, and that the number of these atrocities is much higher than we always assumed. Sadesh Sivakumaran, who focuses in his chapter on sexual violence against men and boys committed by other men, furthermore mentions that male sexual violence is sometimes also committed by female perpetrators and that there are also female perpetrators who commit sexual violence against women. He therefore takes off the table the once presumed idea that sexual violence is always committed by men against women only. Sexual violence against men by men in conflict situations often takes the form of rape, enforced sterilization, beatings to the genitals, enforced nudity and enforced masturbation, sexual slavery and forced marriage (such as in Cambodia in 1975–1979 under the Khmer Rouge[53]).

---

50 *Prosecutor v. Katanga and Chui, Situation in the DRC*, ICC-01/04–01/07–1328, Order on the Organisation of Common Legal Representation of Victims, Trial Chamber II, ICC, 22 July 2009.

51 *Ibid.* at para 13.

52 Silke Studzinsky, "Victims of Sexual and Gender-Based Crimes Before the Extraordinary Chambers in the Courts of Cambodia: Challenges of Rights to Participation and Protection," in *Sexual Violence as an International Crime: Interdisciplinary Approaches*, eds. Anne-Marie de Brouwer, Charlotte Ku, Renée Römkens and Larissa van den Herik (Antwerp, Belgium: Intersentia), *supra*.

53 On forced marriage in Cambodia, see *Ibid.*

The problem of sexual violence against men remains hidden and lack of reporting by the victims (due to shame, issues of masculinity, etc.) is a problem as is the lack of knowledge or uncomfortability with the issue with the people on the ground, including investigators. While Sivakumaran understands the reasons why until now the focus of lobby groups and others has been on sexual violence committed against women, he also calls for the recognition, investigation and prosecution of sexual violence committed against men and boys. Although the legal framework is in place to prosecute sexual violence against men, as the legal framework for prosecuting sexual violence is no different for men than for women, investigations and prosecutions of male sexual violence have to date been rare, and in case they did take place, where prosecuted under other non-specific sexual violence crimes, such as cruel treatment. His chapter informs us that we should not turn a blind eye to sexual violence crimes committed against men as sexual violence can be perpetrated by anyone (men, women) against anyone (men, women) and is therefore an issue that involves us all and should therefore be tackled by us all (men, women), which requires that all parties concerned – in and outside the judicial setting – to have knowledge and experience in dealing with crimes of sexual and gender based violence.

It is largely because of advocates for gender justice who pushed hard to raise awareness of the gap to hold perpetrators of sexual and gender based violence to account and to be punished for their crimes. In her chapter, Brigid Inder, for example, elaborates on the still valid and needed partnerships between local and international NGOs and the ICC that hold credible prosecutorial potential. The interplay of experts in the justice process, including women's NGOs, can contribute in the pursuit of truth and the larger experience of victims, including by documenting gender based crimes and filing *amicus curiae* submissions to the court to influence the charging practice related to sexual violence crimes. In addition to the lobbies of advocates for gender justice, long overdue in this area, the individual dignity and personhood recognized by the post-World War II human rights conventions demanded awareness and action. As the pages of this volume however have shown, action has not been simple. Although sexual and gender-based crime is not new, international judicial proceedings against these crimes were. This reality required dedication and innovation to establish appropriate procedures of investigation that not only respected the rights of the individual survivor, but also complied with the standards of due process appropriate to orderly judicial proceedings. This meant that the first prosecutions of crimes of sexual violence would be responsible for setting future standards and procedures. Successful and effective work in prosecuting acts of sexual violence therefore required the simultaneous development of practices in a variety of fields including traditional criminal and forensic investigation, psychology, and sociology. This also requires those working on the trying of these crimes to gain sufficient awareness to handle the evidence generated by these different fields.[54]

Recognizing the need for those working in different fields to have an opportunity to gain greater familiarity with each other, the first Hague Colloquium on "Sexual Violence as an International Crime: Interdisciplinary Approaches" was convened in June 2009 and the second Hague Colloquium on "Systematic Sexual Violence and Victims' Rights" took place in April 2011 and was organized by the Center on Law and Globalization, a partnership of the American Bar Foundation and the University of Illinois College of Law; The Grotius Centre for International Legal Studies, Leiden University/Campus The Hague; and the Department of Criminal Law and the International Victimology Institute Tilburg (INTERVICT), Tilburg Law School, Tilburg University. On both occasions, more than 150 individuals from international and national courts, government officials, NGO and advocacy groups, survivor groups, and academics came together to note milestones, to share experiences, and to provide perspective. International courts now take sexual violence seriously, said Kelly Askin, of the Open Society Institute, conference participant, and chapter contributor.[55] After World War II the international tribunals heard much testimony on rape but did not pursue it in its own right. A Dutch military court in Batavia in 1948 did prosecute and convict twelve Japanese army officers of sexually enslaving thirty-five Dutch women, but there were no prosecutions by international tribunals.

This has changed and since the mid-1990s, the *ad hoc* international tribunals for the former Yugoslavia and Rwanda have incorporated rape directly and indirectly in more than forty cases. The permanent International Criminal Court has sexual and gender based violence as a focus with twelve of seventeen individuals before the ICC now charged with crimes of sexual violence.[56] Crimes of sexual violence comprised a central component of the 2010

---

54 See, for example, the standard set out for U.S. judges by the 1993 U.S. Supreme Court case, *Daubert v. Merrell Dow Pharmaceuticals, Inc.*, with regard to the use of expert testimony in court. Writing for the majority, Justice Harry Blackmun wrote: "[f]aced with a proffer of expert scientific testimony, then, the trial judge must determine at the outset, pursuant to [Federal Rules of Evidence] Rule 104(a), whether the expert is proposing to testify to (1) scientific knowledge that (2) will assist the trier of fact to understand or determine a fact in issue. This entails a *preliminary assessment of whether the reasoning or methodology underlying the testimony is scientifically valid and of whether that reasoning or methodology properly can be applied to the facts at issue.* We are confident that federal judges possess the capacity to undertake this review." (Emphasis added). *Daubert v. Merrell Dow Pharmaceuticals, Inc.*, 509 U.S. 579, 1993.

55 See Kelly Askin, "Treatment of Sexual Violence in Armed Conflicts: a Historical Perspective & the Way Forward," in *Sexual Violence as an International Crime: Interdisciplinary Approaches*, eds. Anne-Marie de Brouwer, Charlotte Ku, Renée Römkens and Larissa van den Herik (Antwerp, Belgium: Intersentia), *supra*.

56 Elisabeth Rehn, *Second Hague Colloquium: Systematic Sexual Violence and Victims' Rights: Opening Address, April 7, 2010*, available at www.lexglobal.org/?q=node/1105&nid=1105.

indictments against Sudan's President Omar al-Bashir and others. But, said International Criminal Court Prosecutor Luis Moreno-Ocampo, "our goal is to go even further." He has welcomed the interventions of social scientists to push forward the frontiers of international criminal justice and writes: "[o]ne of our goals is a case with no witnesses, no victims. We want to use methods that you are developing, such as statistical analysis. We must refine how to use your tools."[57]

The Colloquia heard several ways that social science evidence can build cases and international justice institutions and this volume includes them. One important example is the work of Lynn Lawry, Kirsten Johnson and Jana Asher using epidemiologic sampling methods "to gather data from individuals of the population who represent the population as a whole."[58] Lawry *et al.*'s chapter shows how cluster surveys are used to provide generalizable information in circumstances where a comprehensive study could not be done because of terrain or safety concerns in conflict situations. Such studies do not rely on interviews, but rather on population assessments and can be used "to demonstrate the systematic nature of the crime."[59] This approach was developed from the four-step impact assessment framework developed by public health official and scholar, Jonathan Mann, "to bridge the gap between philosophies, correspondence and vocabulary, education and training, recruitment, and work methods of the disciplines of bioethics, jurisprudence, public health law and epidemiology."[60]

As Lawry, Johnson and Asher show, however, the preparation and gathering of usable data faces unique challenges requiring detailed focus on local mores, languages, and practices that need to be incorporated into the survey instruments. Chen Reis notes in her chapter that increased awareness of these crimes have also increased the demand for data "to inform protection, prevention and response including resource allocations, humanitarian programs and advocacy and justice processes coming from a range of actors including UN bodies, governments, the press and non-governmental organizations."[61] This increased demand puts a premium on producing good data and sound analyses

---

57 See the speech of Luis Moreno-Ocampo during the first Hague Colloquium on "Sexual Violence as an International Crime: Interdisciplinary Approaches," (June 2009), available at https://www.law.illinois.edu/news/article/1061.

58 Lynn Lawry, Kirsten Johnson and Jana Asher, "Evidence-Based Documentation of Gender-Based Violence," in *Sexual Violence as an International Crime: Interdisciplinary Approaches*, eds. Anne-Marie de Brouwer, Charlotte Ku, Renée Römkens and Larissa van den Herik (Antwerp, Belgium: Intersentia), *supra*.

59 *Ibid.*

60 *Ibid.*

61 Chen Reis, "Ethical, Safety and Methodological Issues Related to Collection and Use of Data on Sexual Violence in Conflict," in *Sexual Violence as an International Crime: Interdisciplinary Approaches*, eds. Anne-Marie de Brouwer, Charlotte Ku, Renée Römkens and Larissa van den Herik (Antwerp, Belgium: Intersentia), *supra*.

of those data that are based on findings and not on assumptions or foregone conclusions. These same concerns continue to be present when conducting the survey. This includes providing appropriate training for the individuals collecting and coding the data all of which requiring close supervision and awareness of culture specific and local conditions. This has meant that development of the surveys have relied on qualitative information in order to identify and to capture key indicators. For example, knowing that in the Democratic Republic of the Congo, Mai Mai culture required a cleansing ceremony of males following a sexual act revealed that female Mai Mai combatants were responsible for a portion of sexual and gender based violence in that area. Through their methodology they therefore discovered that, not only men, but also women can be perpetrators of sexual violence in conflict and that not only women and girls are victims of such crimes, but also men and boys, and came up with shocking percentages. Although this phenomenon was not completely unknown, the scope of the problem was and now requires rethinking when it comes to health care, policy, guidelines for responses to gender based violence, advocacy, but also investigation and prosecution of these crimes, as also highlighted by Sivakumaran. As Lawry and colleagues noted, "Qualitative interviews provide insight into the individual's experience of human rights abuses and thereby offer the human face and voice to the statistical numbers that are obtained from quantitative work."[62] Qualitative and quantitative data therefore play essential and complementary roles in providing evidence of sexual violence crimes, according to the researchers. This form of evidence-based documentation has been important in placing rape within an overall group dynamic of violence and has helped to overcome the assumption that acts of sexual violence committed during wartime necessarily follows orders or directions from higher authorities. Lawry, Johnson and Asher caution that rape during conflict can be committed by anyone and at anytime and therefore should be searched for more broadly beyond a chain of command. These methods adapted from epidemiology are becoming "more rigorous, more complex and less disputable over the years", but this evidence-based data may differ from the Rules of Evidence developed by the ICC, and there remains a need for training and orientation as to the use of the information.[63] As Reis's chapter points out, data is derived from and corroborated by individual testimonies, aggregated data, and wider population-based surveys. Depending on the initial purpose for gathering the data, it may not be immediately applicable to a judicial proceeding so that the significance and appropriate use of such data also needs to be well understood. As Lawry, Johnson and Asher conclude in their chapter: "[i]t is important to continue the dialogue and to

62 *Ibid.*
63 *Ibid.*

better understand the different needs between the lawyers, the social scientists and the survivors of sexual violence."[64]

In their chapter on reasonable grounds evidence, John Hagan, Richard Brooks and Todd Haugh demonstrated how hierarchical linear modeling (HLM) using the data collected by the U.S. Department of State's Atrocity Documentation Survey (ADS) could document a chain of command connecting the government of Sudan to acts of sexual violence and genocide in Darfur. HLM allows "for the cross-validation of aggregated respondent reports (for example in villages or settlements), while also taking into account individual-level sources for variation and bias."[65] Using this technique allowed Hagan and colleagues to determine who the attackers were and to map the distribution of racial epithets heard during attacks.

ADS information revealed that two-thirds of the attacks were carried out by joint Sudanese and Janjaweed forces. ADS information further revealed the use of racially charged epithets that provided evidence of explicit racial targeting – an important element in establishing the crime of genocide.[66] It was further found that when racial epithets were present, sexual assaults were linked to race. Working with the data of the Atrocity Documentation Survey in this way, Hagan and colleagues established a pattern of events that reached through the highest levels of the government of Sudan.[67]

But, how can these statistical analyses be useful for international criminal prosecution? Xabier Agirre, Senior Analyst in the International Criminal Court's Office of the Prosecutor, has written: "[w]e need descriptive statistics to show that the crime is grave, that its scope warrants the International Criminal Court, which intends to take only the most serious cases."[68] Agirre reminds that pattern evidence has been used to investigate large-scale killings, destruction, and displacement, but much less for sexual violence.[69] As Agirre noted:

> International crimes often comprise a large number of incidents that can be characterized as a pattern as long as they show common features on all or most of the following aspects: (1) the profile of the perpetrators; (2) the profile of the victims; (3) the geographical and chronological distribution profile of the victims; and (4) the modus operandi in the commission of the crime.[70]

---

64 *Ibid.*

65 John Hagan, Richard Brooks and Todd J. Haugh, "'Reasonable Grounds' Evidence Involving Sexual Violence in Darfur," in *Sexual Violence as an International Crime: Interdisciplinary Approaches*, eds. Anne-Marie de Brouwer, Charlotte Ku, Renée Römkens and Larissa van den Herik (Antwerp, Belgium: Intersentia), *supra*.

66 See a sample of such epithets in *Ibid.*

67 *Ibid.*

68 As quoted in *Ibid.*

69 Xabier Agirre Aranburu, "Sexual Violence beyond Reasonable Doubt: Using Pattern Evidence and Analysis for International Cases," *Law and Social Inquiry* 35 (Fall 2010): 855.

70 *Ibid.* at 856.

The Elements of Crimes of the International Criminal Court explicitly mentions the "context of a manifest pattern of similar conduct" in the definition of genocide. However, for those planning to use statistical evidence in a legal proceeding, such evidence must follow methodologies accepted by the scientific community, be subject to peer review, be properly sourced and justified. Impartiality of the findings will be important. Agirre has noted that there are challenges to using pattern evidence on at least three levels: (1) the tendency of law enforcement and judicial institutions to ignore sexual violence requires direction from the top of these institutions to correct; (2) sexual violence continues to be under-reported; and (3) whatever evidence is provided needs to stand up to the scrutiny of experts and others who are not directly involved in the conflict.[71]

The need for interdisciplinarity is not just one for the gathering of evidence and the development of sound international judicial proceedings. It is also essential to the treatment of the survivors of this violence and ultimately to the development of durable peace. As Maxine Marcus noted, "the focus must be on the survivor-witness as a *beneficiary* – rather than a tool – of the justice process."[72] The Statute of the International Criminal Court explicitly provides for the well-being of survivors. Concerns that need to be addressed range from the psychological and physical needs of the survivors to providing for child care during a legal proceeding and to explaining the judicial process to those generally unfamiliar with court proceedings.[73] According to Sharratt there is, however, still "very little recognition of structural gender arrangements, the contact in which the prosecution of rape takes place, and the barriers that the women have to face and overcome (...). There also remains strong constraints on what can and cannot be spoken about publicly: but the absence only makes then ghost of female sexuality ever more present."[74] Psychology and social sciences should therefore be brought into the realm of justice. In addition, the Trust Fund for Victims is able to provide both reparation (through a court order) and assistance to survivors of sexual violence, which may help survivors some way towards recovery after conflict. In its assistance mandate, the Trust Fund for

---

71 *Ibid.* at 875–76.

72 Maxine Marcus, "Investigation of Crimes of Sexual and Gender-Based Violence Under International Criminal Law," in *Sexual Violence as an International Crime: Interdisciplinary Approaches*, eds. Anne-Marie de Brouwer, Charlotte Ku, Renée Römkens and Larissa van den Herik (Antwerp, Belgium: Intersentia), *supra*.

73 See Summary Report of Working Group C, *Colloquium on Sexual Violence as International Crime: Interdisciplinary Approaches*, 17 June 2009, available at www.lexglobal.org/?q=node/90&nid=90.

74 Sara Sharratt, "Voices of Court Members: A Phenomenological Journey – The Prosecution of Rape and Sexual Violence at the International Criminal Tribunal for the Former Yugoslavia (ICTY) and the Bosnian War Crimes Court (BIH)," in *Sexual Violence as an International Crime: Interdisciplinary Approaches*, eds. Anne-Marie de Brouwer, Charlotte Ku, Renée Römkens and Larissa van den Herik (Antwerp, Belgium: Intersentia), *supra*.

Victims has 29 approved projects operational in the DRC and Uganda, benefitting some 75,000 people, including survivors of sexual violence.[75] Based upon the Trust Fund's work so far, the Chair of the Board of Directors Elisabeth Rehn concluded that three important lessons concerning reparation and assistance to victims of sexual violence have already been learned, which include: (1) that a gender dimension related to the impact of violence needs to be included as violence impacts men and boys differently than women and girls (victims of sexual violence repeatedly expressed more severe psychological trauma and social stigma stemming from the violence they suffered, especially girls who had babies from their rapists); (2) that victims of sexual violence, both men and women, experience an extremely diverse range of atrocities and consequences which requires different reparation and assistance approaches (individual and/or collective); and (3) that victims of sexual violence are consulted and engaged in the process of reparation and assistance.[76]

There is also growing awareness that sexual and gender-based violence reaches deeply into communities not only to destroy individual lives, but also to destroy communities and social mores. This leaves these populations and areas vulnerable to ongoing attacks and can fuel renewed violence and fighting, including the use of sexual violence. Addressing sexual and gender based crimes provides an important reminder that women and others who have survived such atrocity need to have their individual dignity restored – sometimes in a society that has been profoundly changed by violence. This includes actions that "shift the stigma from the victims to the perpetrators and empower the victims to reclaim their dignity and rebuild their lives."[77] Victims sometimes also prefer to be called survivors rather than victims, as survivors better captures the agency they have over their lives. It should be mentioned here that international criminal legal responses are naturally not the only means available for survivors of sexual violence and national and local courts, Truth and Reconciliation Commissions, community based victims' groups, symbolic reparations (e.g., commemoration memorials), cultural forms of recognition (e.g., theatre), media (e.g., journalism, documentaries, movies), Victims' Tribunals (in a similar vein to the 2000 Women's Tribunal in Tokyo created to address the crimes committed against women who were held as sexual slaves by the Japanese during World War II) and education (e.g., schools, museums, books) are some other measures through which victims of sexual violence could obtain some form of justice and reconciliation.[78] The example of filmmakers Ilse and Femke van Velzen,

75 Elisabeth Rehn, "Second Hague Colloquium: Systematic Sexual Violence and Victims' Rights: Opening Address, 7 April 2010," available at www.lexglobal.org/?q=node/1105&nid=1105.

76 *Ibid.*

77 *Ibid.*

78 See, inter alia, Julie Mertus, "Shouting from the bottom of the well: The impact of international trials for wartime rape on women's agency," *International Feminist Journal of*

interviewed by journalist Rachel Irwin in this volume, is exemplatory in this regard. The Van Velzen sisters made two films on sexual violence in the DRC (one from the perspective of the victims and one from the perspective of the rapists) and confronted the perpetrators of sexual violence with their films in the DRC itself. Showing these films to the people who were actually involved in sexual violence did provoke change among the perpetrators and understanding of the crimes they had committed. In their opinion, the biggest key to change the culture of rape with impunity is to change the attitudes of men, of those who commit the rapes, which can be done through filmmaking. What is important therefore is that the diversity of victimization requires similarly diverse and multi-faceted responses and more research on the appropriate measures and how current legal and non-legal mechanisms can be improved is needed.[79]

Addressing sexual and gender based violence provides also a further reminder that durable and lasting peace in any conflict area can only be created with the full participation of *all* those most directly affected and closest to the situation.[80] The international recognition of sexual violence is but a first step towards justice for survivors of sexual violence, and it is vital that the next steps include an understanding for their needs and their direct participation. If they are no longer to be silenced, their participation in preventive strategies[81], justice

---

Politics, 6, no.1 (March 2004): 110–128; Marie-Bénédicte Dembour and Emily Haslam, "Silencing Hearings? Victim-Witnesses at War Crimes Trials," *European Journal of International Law* 15, no. 1 (2004): 151–177; Jamie O'Connell, "Gambling with the Psyche: Does Prosecuting Human Rights Violators Console Their Victims?" *Harvard International Law Journal* 46, no. 2 (Summer2005): 295–345.

79 See for some research on this for the ICTR, the Best Practices Manual 2008 (available at http://lexglobal.org/files/Renifa%20Madenga-ICTR%20Practice%20Manual.pdf); for the ICTY, Eric Stover, *The Witnesses: War Crimes and the Promise of Justice in The Hague* (Philadelphia: University of Pennsylvania Press, 2005); for the Special Court for Sierra Leone, Rebecca Horn, Saleem Vahidy and Simon Charters, "Testifying in the Special Court for Sierra Leone: witness perceptions of safety and emotional welfare," *Psychology, Crime & Law* (2010): 1–21; on transitional justice mechanisms for sexual violence generally, see Estelle Zinsstag, *Sexual Violence against Women in Armed Conflicts: Towards a Transitional Justice Perspective*, (Antwerp, Belgium: Intersentia 2012) (forthcoming).

80 See UN Security Council resolution 1325, 21 October 2000. See also Elisabeth Rehn, "Second Hague Colloquium: Systematic Sexual Violence and Victims' Rights: Opening Address, 7 April 2010," available at www.lexglobal.org/?q=node/1105&nid=1105.

81 "International responses which focus on preventing sexual violence and providing victim support have only recently emerged, though they are promising. The appointment of a UN Special Rapporteur on Sexual Violence in Conflicts provides a champion and focal point to develop these preventive and support efforts more coherently. Governments have also increasingly made a commitment to speak out and take action against sexual violence, including by actively training military to prevent it. Nevertheless, the development of training and educational interventions directed at strict prohibition of sexual violence is still in their infancy. This is particularly complicated in light of the legacy of sexual objectification and denigration of women within the military. Much work remains to be done, and given this legacy active monitoring, reporting and sanctioning structures within the UN system are vital. NGOs are also crucial as independent watchdogs to help realize victims' rights and encourage a shift in attitudes that condone sexual violence against civilians in times of

and reconciliation efforts will be imperative to any meaningful form of such initiatives. As stated by Navi Pillay, UN High Commissioner for Human Rights, during the opening of the First Hague Colloquium in June 2009: "(...) I am heartened by the progress made so far regarding the prosecution of sexual violence. The jurisprudence and methodology developed by international justice mechanisms, as well as national tribunals or regional courts, has made great strides. Yet we are still wanting in our capacity to fully describe, understand and address the real experience of sexual violence from the victim's perspective."[82] Building awareness was a recurring theme throughout this volume – awareness of these acts of violence and crime, of the conditions that lead to the crime, of the people who survive the crimes, of those who work to investigate and to prosecute the crimes, and of those who work with survivors. This volume shows that we have made some progress in cultivating awareness about the crime, but much more needs to be done on understanding the needs of the individuals and communities affected by these crimes and of those working with them. It is clear that the needs of all the individuals involved in this issue are not the same, but this does not mean that their work cannot help some other facet of the issue. To do this effectively, however, requires awareness of the purpose and limits of each effort including of judicial process itself. As we heard during the first Hague Colloquium, some survivors just wanted their stories told and were less interested in initiating or participating in judicial proceedings taking place very distant from home.

Such awareness is important after crimes have taken place and is key to preventing them. We have seen in this volume the steps taken to bring this crime out of the sidelines and directly into international judicial proceedings. Increasingly, we now see awareness of this issue as a facet of rebuilding society and efforts to restore stability and peace in conflict regions. The national legislation of States implementing the sexual violence crimes laid down in the Rome Statute of the ICC can also be seen as part of the change in countries towards viewing sexual violence crimes as serious crimes warranting prosecution. This volume records the more than two decades of experience and development in criminalizing sexual violence and recognizing it as a war crime, crime against humanity and genocide. What the volume reveals is not only how much more needs to be done, but also underscores the urgency of understanding the individual and group dynamics that produce these savage acts of violence to start. It is also clear that only with this understanding and the active involvement

---

conflict." See further: Sandra Ka Hon Chu, Anne-Marie de Brouwer and Renée Römkens, "Survivors of Sexual Violence in Conflict: Challenges in Prevention and International Criminal Prosecution," in *Victimological Approaches to International Crimes: Africa*, eds. Rianne Letschert, Roelof Haveman, Anne-Marie de Brouwer and Antony Pemberton (Antwerp, Belgium: Intersentia, 2011), 527–560.

82 For Navi Pillay's keynote speech, see: http://lexglobal.org/files/SexualViolence-speechPillay_0.pdf.

of those most affected can we hope for lasting and durable peace. This study further bears eloquent witness to the fact that the basis for peace ultimately must be respect for the dignity for every person in society. The work done to prosecute the crime of sexual violence is an important step towards building this into the international judicial process. We must continue efforts to develop this awareness as part of strengthening the capacity and knowledge to prevent sexual violence crimes from recurring and from taking place at all on this globe.

ABOUT THE CONTRIBUTORS

Jana Asher, M.S., is a statistician who specializes in the collection and analysis of human rights violations data, as well as the Executive Director of StatAid, a nonprofit statistical consultation firm.

She has worked on projects for the International Criminal Tribunal for the Former Yugoslavia, the Peruvian Truth and Reconciliation Commission, Physicians for Human Rights, Human Rights Watch, the East Timor Truth and Reconciliation Commission, the Sierra Leone Truth and Reconciliation Commission, the American Bar Association, the Science and Human Rights Program of the American Association for the Advancement of Science, and the U.S. Census Bureau.

In 2009, the American Statistical Association selected her as a Fellow for her contributions to the profession, and for excellence in the application of statistical methodology to human rights and humanitarian measurement problems.

Kelly Askin, B.S., J.D., Ph.D. (law) is senior legal officer for International Justice in the Open Society Justice Initiative. She was also 2004–2005 Fulbright New Century Scholar on the Global Empowerment of Women. Since 1995, Askin has taught or served as a visiting scholar at Notre Dame Law School, American University's Washington College of Law, Harvard's Kennedy School of Government, Yale Law School, and Oxford University. She also served as executive director of the International Criminal Justice Institute and American University's War Crimes Research Office.

Askin served as a legal advisor to the judges of the International Criminal Tribunal for the former Yugoslavia and for Rwanda from 2000–2002, and for over ten years has also served as an expert consultant, legal advisor, international law trainer to prosecutors, judges, and registry at the International Criminal Tribunal for the former Yugoslavia, the International Criminal Tribunal for Rwanda, the Serious Crimes Unit in East Timor, the International Criminal Court, the Special Court for Sierra Leone, and the Extraordinary Chambers in the Courts of Cambodia.

Her books include *War Crimes Against Women: Prosecution in International War Crimes Tribunals* (1997) and the three-volume treatise *Women and International Human Rights Law* (1999, 2001, 2002, co-editor), and she has authored dozens of law review articles and book chapters.

Her op-eds have appeared in the *New York Times*, *International Herald Tribune*, and the *Washington Post*. She has testified before the U.S. Senate Committee on the Judiciary and she has appeared on CNN, BBC, and NPR. She serves on the executive board of the American Branch of the International Law Association, the International Judicial Academy, and International Criminal Law Services.

Linda Bianchi was an Appeals Counsel in the Appeals and Legal Advisory Division for the Office of the Prosecutor at the ICTR from 2003 to 2010. She acted as Chairperson and was a founding member of the Committee for the Review of the Investigation and Prosecution of Sexual Violence which was set up in the OTP in June 2007 to review the work of the OTP in its investigations and prosecutions of sexual violence crimes and report its findings and recommendations. This Committee published a Best Practices Manual which formed the basis of this paper. Since 2011, Linda has been working as a Crown Counsel for the Public Prosecution Service of Canada in Ottawa, Canada.

Richard Brooks is Professor of Law at Yale Law School. He previously taught law at both Cornell University and Northwestern University. His expertise is in law and economics, contracts, business organizations, and race and the law.

Professor Brooks has a B.A. from Cornell, an M.A. and a Ph.D. from the University of California at Berkeley, and a J.D. from the University of Chicago.

Anne-Marie de Brouwer (Ph.D., LL.M.) is an Associate Professor in international criminal law at the Department of Criminal Law of Tilburg University, the Netherlands, and a research fellow with the International Victimology Institute Tilburg (INTERVICT). Previously, she was an associate legal officer at the Women's Initiatives for Gender Justice in The Hague.

Her main areas of research and interest include international crimes, international criminal law and procedure, victims' rights, victimology, sexual violence and transitional justice.

She is the author of the book *Supranational Criminal Prosecution of Sexual Violence: The ICC and the Practice of the ICTY and the ICTR* (Intersentia, 2005), for which she received the Max van der Stoel Human Rights Award 2006. She also co-edited the book *The Men Who Killed Me: Rwandan Survivors of Sexual Violence* (Douglas & McIntyre, 2009) / *De mannen die mij hebben vermoord* (Wolf Legal Publishers, 2011), which features seventeen testimonials of survivors of sexual violence. She has published numerous articles in the field of international (criminal) law, and edited several collections of essays in this field, including *Victimological Approaches to International Crimes: Africa* (Intersentia, 2011).

She is the chair of the *Mukomeze* Foundation, which aims to improve the lives of women and girls who survived sexual violence during the Rwandan genocide.

Teresa Doherty (Hon. Justice) C.B.E. is from Northern Ireland. She returned to study law in Belfast after working as a civil servant and as a volunteer in Zambia and worked in legal aid clinics in "no go areas" of Belfast as a student in early 1970s. She was called to the Bar in 1978. She worked in Papua New Guinea from 1976–1987 first in the Public Solicitor's (public defence) office and as provincial legal officer for Morobe Province. While Provincial legal officer she continued to do legal aid work and made several Constitutional rights challenges in the courts. She was the first woman to be elected as a councillor of the Papua New Guinea Law Society. She was appointed as the Principal Magistrate for the Momase region of Papua New Guinea in 1987 and as National and later Supreme Court judge in 1988, the first woman to hold any high judicial office in the South Pacific Islands Region and the first Northern Irish woman to be made a judge.

She returned to the Bar in Northern Ireland in late 1997. At the request of the Commonwealth she went to Sierra Leone at the end of the civil war and has worked as a judge of the High Court and Court of Appeal of Sierra Leone from 2003. She was appointed by the United Nations in January 2005 as a judge of the Special Court of Sierra Leone (the international war crimes tribunal for Sierra Leone) and is presently dealing with the Charles Taylor trial in The Hague, the Netherlands.

She is a Parole Commissioner for Northern Ireland, part time chairman of Appeal Services, member of the Commonwealth Reference Group for the promotion of the Rights of Women and the Girl Child and has worked on consultancies in various countries in Africa and Asia. She has received several awards for her work including CBE and an honorary doctor of laws degree from University of Ulster.

John Hagan is Professor of Sociology and Law at Northwestern University and Co-Director of the Center on Law & Globalization at the American Bar Foundation in Chicago. He received the Stockholm Prize in Criminology in 2009 and was elected in 2010 to the American Academy of Arts and Sciences. Hagan is the Editor of the Annual Review of Law & Social Science. His research with a network of scholars spans topics from war crimes and human rights to the legal profession.

He is the co-author with Wenona Rymond-Richmond of Darfur and the Crime of Genocide (Cambridge University Press 2009), which received the American Sociological Association Crime, Law and Deviance Section's Albert J. Reiss Distinguished Publication Award and the American Society of Criminology's Michael J. Hindelang Book Award.

His most recent book is Who are the Criminals?: the Politics of Crime Policy in the Age of Roosevelt and the Age of Reagan, Princeton University Press, 2010.

Todd Haugh is a Legal Writing Instructor at DePaul University College of Law. Prior to joining DePaul, Professor Todd Haugh practiced white collar criminal defense and commercial litigation at Winston & Strawn LLP and Stetler & Duffy Ltd. While in private practice, he represented a variety of clients in matters ranging from fraud, false statements, obstruction of justice, and conspiracy to criminal sentencing, appeals and forfeiture.

From 2006 to 2007, Professor Haugh served as a law clerk to the Hon. Suzanne B. Conlon, senior district judge, Northern District of Illinois.

Professor Haugh presents on topics including litigation tactics, criminal procedure and associate life, and writes on issues related to money laundering, criminal procedure and international criminal law.

He received a B.A. with honors in political science from Brown University and a J.D., cum laude, from the University of Illinois.

Brigid Inder is the Executive Director of the Women's Initiatives for Gender Justice. She has 25 years of experience working in the international justice, human rights and health fields as a strategic leader and activist for women's human rights and gender equality.

Ms. Inder has led the development of the organisation's strategic initiatives including its legal programme, peace negotiation efforts, documentation programme on gender-based crimes in armed conflicts and assessing the impact of violence on women and girls. Ms. Inder is an internationally recognised expert and political adviser to numerous United Nations conferences, global negotiations, election campaigns, political and legal advocacy strategies for accountability before the International Criminal Court, domestic Courts and other transitional justice initiatives. She has worked in the Asia-Pacific and Africa regions particularly in Bangladesh, the Central African Republic, Democratic Republic of the Congo, Sudan and Uganda.

Ms. Inder is the immediate past President of the Association for Women's Rights in Development (AWID) and served on its' Board of Directors from 2004 – 2010. Brigid Inder has authored and co-authored numerous women's rights articles and publications including the Gender Report Card on the ICC (2005–2011, co-authored).

Rachel Irwin is a journalist who writes about international justice for The Institute for War and Peace Reporting (IWPR) in The Hague. She has penned in-depth articles about issues relating to cases at the International Criminal Court and covered numerous trials at the International Criminal Tribunal for the Former Yugoslavia. Most recently, she traveled to Bosnia to write a special report on war atrocity denial in the eastern town of Visegrad.

She holds a Bachelor's degree in English literature from the University of Wisconsin-Madison and a Master's degree from the Medill School of Journalism at Northwestern University.

Michelle Jarvis is an Australian lawyer who has worked at the International Criminal Tribunal for the Former Yugoslavia for the past ten years. She is presently Senior Legal Adviser to the Prosecutor and Senior Appeals Counsel in the Office of the Prosecutor.

Previously, she worked as a Legal Officer in Chambers, as a consultant for the United Nations Division for the Advancement of Women and as a solicitor for a community legal service focusing on women's legal justice issues in Australia.

Her prior publications include: S. Brammertz and M. Jarvis, "Lessons Learned in Prosecuting Gender Crimes under International Law: Experiences from the ICTY", in C. Eboe-Osuji (ed.) Protecting Humanity: Essays in International Law and Policy in Honour of Navanethem Pillay, Martinus Nijhof 2010; and J. Gardam and M. Jarvis, *Women, Armed Conflict, and International Law* (Kluwer 2001).

She has lectured on international criminal law and international humanitarian law topics in many countries throughout the world, including: Australia, Canada, Bosnia and Herzegovina, Croatia, Macedonia, the Netherlands, Serbia, Sweden and the United Kingdom.

Kirsten Johnson (Ph.D.) is a Lecturer at the McGill University Faculty of Medicine in Montreal, Quebec, and works as an attending staff in the Emergency Department at the Royal Victoria Hospital which is one of the McGill University Health Centres in Montreal. She also provides medical care to Canada's northern Cree and Inuit communities, working at the Centre Hospitalier de Chisasibi and the Ungava Bay Tulattavik Health Center respectively. Dr. Johnson received her M.D. from the University of Calgary and specialized in Family Medicine and Emergency Medicine at McGill University. She subsequently obtained her M.P.H. from the Harvard School of Public Health and a diploma from the Humanitarian Studies Initiative, a collaborative program between HSPH, Tufts, and MIT.

Dr. Johnson's extensive international health experience includes infectious disease and tropical medicine training in Peru, instructing backpack medics in refugee camps on the Thai-Burmese border and working at the MaeTao clinic for Burmese refugees, establishing women's health programs with the Campaign for Female Education (CamFed) in Ghana, setting up health services in rural Nepal with Helping Hands Health Consortium and Cambodia with the University of Toronto-ROSE medical outreach program, performing rapid needs assessments for Samaritan's Purse in Uganda, and a program audit for the Red Cross in Kenya. She has also worked as a Critical Care Flight Physician for Skyservice Air

Ambulance in Montreal, providing transport and repatriation of critically ill patients worldwide.

Over the last two years, Dr. Johnson has focused her interests on humanitarian relief, disaster response and human rights. Most recently she participated in an investigation conducted by Physicians for Human Rights into the destruction of Darfurian livelihoods by the government of Sudan. In her role as a human rights investigator with PHR during the summer of 2005, she performed interviews with refugees from Darfur's three main ethnic groups in camps along the Chad-Sudan border and subsequently co-authored a report on the Destruction of Livelihoods that is being used by the United Nations Special Representative for the Secretary General on Genocide Prevention and the International Criminal Court.

Charlotte Ku is Professor of Law and Assistant Dean of Graduate and International Legal Studies. She is also Co-Director of the Center on Law and Globalization at the College of Law. Prior to that, she served as Acting Director of the Lauterpacht Centre for International Law at the University of Cambridge in England following a twelve year tenure as Executive Director and Executive Vice President of the American Society of International Law in Washington, DC. Dr. Ku has taught on the faculties of the University of Virginia, American University, and the Johns Hopkins-Nanjing University Center for Chinese and American Studies in Nanjing, China. Dr. Ku specializes in issues of global governance and international law. Her publications include International Law, International Relations, and Global Governance (Routledge, 2012), (with Professor Paul F. Diehl), The Dynamics of International Law (Cambridge University Press, 2010), and (with Harold K. Jacobson, co-editor), Democratic Accountability and the Use of Force in International Law (Cambridge University Press, 2002).

Lynn Lawry, M.D., M.S.P.H., M.Sc. acts as Senior Health Stability/ Humanitarian Assistance Specialist, International Health Division, Office of the Assistant Secretary of Defense (Health Affairs); Director, Initiative in Global Women's Health, Brigham and Women's Hospital; Associate, Department of International Health, Bloomberg School of Public Health, Johns Hopkins University.

Dr. Lawry is a specialist in internal medicine, disaster research, and epidemiology. She earned her medical degree at East Carolina University School of Medicine, a Master's of Science in Public Health from the University of North Carolina Chapel Hill, and a Master's of Science in Epidemiology from the Harvard School of Public Health.

Her humanitarian aid experience includes direct care as medical director for several humanitarian aid organizations, advocacy and research. In her 16 years in humanitarian aid she has been in more than a dozen complex humanitarian disasters/conflicts and has researched health and human rights issues in Taliban-controlled Afghanistan, Sierra Leone, Iraq, Nigeria, Darfur, Liberia and Hurricane Katrina communities.

Dr. Lawry is the author of many publications including book chapters and journal articles relating to these health and human rights issues. She has developed a model for research for health and human rights issues to gain a broader sense of policy changes needed to make governments responsive or accountable for the needs of their people.

Maxine Marcus is an international criminal prosecutor and investigator who has worked for the past fourteen years in the ICL field, in Chad (for Darfur), Sierra Leone, Bosnia and Hercegovina, Hungary, Kosovo, Ingushetia/Chechnya, Ivory Coast, Ethiopia (Gambella), and Guinea.

For the past six years she has served as a prosecuting attorney at the International Criminal Tribunal for the Former Yugoslavia, on the Dragomir Milosevic, Lukic, Stanisic and Simatovic, and now Mladic cases. From 2003 to 2005 she served as lead investigating attorney for the Civil Defence Forces prosecution team in the Special Court for Sierra Leone. She regularly serves as legal counsel and trainer for judges, prosecutors, police, military, international and local IGOs and NGOs, and community-based organisations in international criminal law, international criminal investigations and prosecutions, evidence in war crimes trials, international human rights law, and international and hybrid tribunals, and she has particular expertise in the

investigation and prosecution of crimes of sexual violence under international criminal law.

Her experience includes work in the context of NGOs (International Rescue Committee, Human Rights Watch, Coalition for International Justice, Article 19, Open Society Institute, Aegis Trust), UN agencies (UNICEF, UNHCR, UNIFEM) and International Criminal Tribunals (ICTY and Special Court for Sierra Leone). In November and December 2009 she was seconded by ICTY through UNIFEM to the UN Commission of Inquiry for Guinea as the gender and international criminal law advisor.

Elena Martin Salgado is a Spanish lawyer who has worked at the International Criminal Tribunal for the Former Yugoslavia for the past ten years. At present she is an Appeals Counsel in the Office of the Prosecutor, where she has been involved in prosecuting sexual violence.

She previously worked as a Legal Officer in the Chambers of the ICTY and at the Special Court for Sierra Leone, and as a researcher in King's College London and the University of Durham.

She has written on international criminal law and human rights law topics for the *Leiden Journal of International Law* (2003), the *European Human Rights Law Review* (2001) and the *Yearbook of International Humanitarian Law* (1999).

Luis Moreno-Ocampo as elected as the first Prosecutor of the International Criminal Court on 21 April 2003. In 1985 Dr. Moreno-Ocampo was the deputy prosecutor in the "military juntas trial" in his home country, Argentina, the first case against top commanders responsible for mass atrocities since the Nuremberg trials.

He had a distinguished career as national prosecutor and lawyer. He also worked pro bono for national and international NGO and was visiting Professor at Stanford University and Harvard University. His mandate today is to investigate and prosecute the most serious crimes of concern to the international community, namely genocide, crimes against humanity and war crimes.

He has opened investigations into the Democratic Republic of Congo, Uganda, Darfur (the Sudan), and the Central African Republic, and analyzed alleged crimes under the jurisdiction of the Court and the existence of genuine national proceedings in Georgia, Colombia, Kenya, Afghanistan and Cote d'Ivoire.

Valerie Oosterveld is a Professor at the University of Western Ontario Faculty of Law. Before joining Western Law in July 2005, Valerie served in the Legal Affairs Bureau of Canada's Department of Foreign Affairs and International Trade. In this role, she provided legal advice on international criminal accountability for genocide, crimes against humanity and war crimes, especially with respect to the International Criminal Court, the International Criminal Tribunals for the Former Yugoslavia and Rwanda, the Sierra Leone Special Court, and other transitional justice mechanisms such as truth and reconciliation commissions.

She was a member of the Canadian delegation to the International Criminal Court negotiations and subsequent Assembly of States Parties. From May 31-June 11, 2010, she served on the Canadian delegation to the Review Conference of the Rome Statute of the International Criminal Court in Kampala, Uganda.

She teaches International Criminal Law, International Human Rights Law, International Organizations and Public International Law. Her research and writing focus on gender issues within international criminal justice.

Chen Reis works with the World Health Organization's Department of Emergency Response and Operations.

She has researched and published extensively about women's health, gender and sexual violence in humanitarian contexts including on ethical and methodological aspects of research on sexual violence in humanitarian settings.

She received her J.D. from Colombia University and her M.P.H. from the Johns Hopkins School of Hygiene and Public Health.

Renée Römkens is the Director of the Dutch National Institute on Gender Equality and Women's History (as of May 2012). She contributed to this book in her capacity as Professor of Interpersonal Violence (INTERVICT International Victimology Institute – Tilburg University Law School, the Netherlands). (B.A. Law; M.A. Criminology; Ph.D. Psychology, 1992, University of Amsterdam, *cum laude)*.

She has worked internationally in South Africa (Visiting Professor at University of the Western Cape, Cape Town, and has been involved in the development of the SANPAD programme (South African Netherlands Research Programme on Alternatives in Developments), and in the United States (New York University Law School/Program of Global Law (2000–2001), and at Columbia University of New York (Visiting Professor/Institute for Research on Women and Gender, 2001–2004).

She has published widely on gender and victimization, notably on domestic violence and its regulation. She conducted the first national survey on domestic violence and marital rape in the Netherlands (1989). Her current research focuses on socio-legal issues regarding victimization, gender and the role of legal regulation, notably on European developments in regulation of VAW. In 2010 she was part of an international consortium that conducted an EU-wide comparative study on legislation and policy based measures in the field of violence against women, children and sexual orientation based violence. As expert on gender based violence she serves regularly for the European Commission (Fundamental Rights Agency), the United Nations (for the Special Rapporteur on Violence Against Women) and for the Council of Europe, she was appointed as scientific expert to the Commission that has drafted the CoE *Convention on Violence Against Women and Domestic Violence* (2011).

Sara Sharratt (Ph.D.) is Emerita Professor of Psychology from Sonoma State University in California and Professor of Gender and Peace Building at the University for Peace in Costa Rica. She is on the Board of Directors of the *Women and Therapy Journal* published in USA.

She was an official member of the Costa Rican delegation to the Preparatory Meeting of the ICC in Rome which participated actively on the inclusion of gender issues in the Statute.

She is an international consultant on gender issues and co-authored in 1998 the book entitled *"Assault on the Soul: Women in the Former Yugoslavia."*

Dr. Sharratt has conducted numerous training and workshops worldwide on gender issues, trauma and its aftermaths for members of national and international courts. Since the establishment of the ICTY, she has monitored many of the proceedings there as well as In Bosnia Herzegovina and currently at the International Criminal Court in Den Haag.

Sandesh Sivakumaran is a lecturer in law at Emmanuel College, Cambridge (B.A., double first class honours; M.A.) and New York University School of Law (LL.M., Hauser Global Scholar). Sandesh's research interests are in the area of public international law, particularly international human rights, international humanitarian law and international criminal law.

He is a co-editor of *International Human Rights Law* (Oxford University Press, 2010) and his book *International Law in Internal Armed Conflict* is forthcoming with Oxford University Press. His work has been cited by the Supreme Court of Israel and awarded the Giorgio La Pira Prize and the Antonio Cassese Prize by the Journal of International Criminal Justice.

Sandesh has acted as expert for the United Nations Office for the Coordination of Humanitarian Affairs, served as international legal advisor to the Appeals Chamber of the Special Court for Sierra Leone and advised on international law aspects of peace processes. He is a member of the International Law Association Committee on International Human Rights Law and Practice, teaches on the annual UK Foreign and Commonwealth Office International Law Course and is a member of the Bar of the State of New York.

Prior to taking up his lectureship, Sandesh's professional experience included: Fellow, previously Research Fellow, at the Lauterpacht Centre for International Law, University of Cambridge; Fellow of the International Bar Association and Associate Legal Officer to Judge Mohamed Shahabuddeen at the Appeals Chamber of the International Criminal Tribunals for the former Yugoslavia and for Rwanda; Law Clerk to Judges Dame Rosalyn Higgins and Peter Tomka at the International Court of Justice; Intern for former President of Ireland and UN High Commissioner for Human Rights, Mary Robinson, at Realizing Rights: the Ethical Globalization Initiative.

Silke Studzinsky has been working with the support of the Civil Peace Service of the German Development Organization DED (now GIZ) in Cambodia to represent Civil Parties before the Extraordinary Chambers in the Courts of Cambodia (ECCC) since February 2008. Until 2009, she was the Senior Legal Advisor to the Khmer Rouge Tribunal program of the Cambodian Human Rights Organization ADHOC, and she currently holds the same position in another Cambodian NGO "Legal Aid of Cambodia." She has been the only international lawyer who has been permanently based in Phnom Penh since the beginning of civil party participation.

Since 1990, Silke has been working as a criminal defense lawyer and as a legal representative for civil parties before criminal courts in Germany and elsewhere in Europe. One of her main working areas is fostering the rights of victims of sexual violence, sexual abuse, trafficking and racial discrimination in and outside of courtrooms.

She joined the "Association of European Democratic Lawyers" in 2000 and acted as their Secretary General from 2005 until the end of 2007. She organized and participated in several human rights missions and trial observations and delegations in Turkey, Spain, Greece, Israel, South Korea and Kashmir. In 2006, she was admitted as counsel at the International Criminal Court at The Hague.

Larissa van den Herik is Professor of Public International Law at Leiden University and Editor in Chief of the *Leiden Journal of International Law.*

She has previously worked at the Vrije Universiteit Amsterdam, where she defended her Ph.D. thesis on *The Contribution of the Rwanda Tribunal to the Development of International Law* (Martinus Nijhoff) in 2005.

She was awarded the Bulthuis Van Oosternieland Prize for this academic work. In 2007, Larissa received a three-year grant from the Netherlands Organization for Scientific Research to do research on illegal trade during times of armed conflict: the responsibility of corporations and individual businessmen.

Prof. Van den Herik is a member of the Editorial Board of De Internationale Spectator and a commentator of the Dutch International Crimes Act (Militair Straf- en Tuchtrecht, losbladige editie, Kluwer) and annotator for the *International Law in Domestic Courts* Project (OUP, University of Amsterdam).

She is the author of several articles and annotations in the field of public international law, international criminal law and the law on peace and security, as well as co-editor of collections of essays in the field of international criminal law (*Future Perspectives on International Criminal Justice*, T.M.C. Asser Press – Cambridge University Press, 2009 and *Fragmentation and Diversification of International Criminal Law*, in preparation).

She coordinates the Marie Curie Research Course and Top Summer School on International Criminal Law (together with Dr. Carsten Stahn).

Patricia Viseur Sellers was the Legal Advisor for Gender and a prosecutor at the Yugoslav (ICTY) Tribunal from 1994 until February 2007. Ms. Sellers is a presently a Visiting Fellow at Kellogg College the University of Oxford. Throughout 2007 she was a Special Legal Consultant to the Gender and Women's Rights Division of the United Nations High Commissioner for Human Rights. As an Independent Legal Expert she lectures on international criminal law and advises organizations, such as WNET- 13/WIDE ANGLE, the producers of the upcoming PBS series, Women, War and Peace.

As the Legal Advisor for Gender, Ms. Sellers developed the legal strategies that led to successful prosecutions of sexual violence under international criminal law. Ms. Sellers tried the first international case, the *Prosecutor v. Furundzija*, wherein rape and sexual torture were recognized as war crimes under the 1949 Geneva Conventions. At the Rwanda Tribunal (ICTR), she was co-counsel and a legal strategist in the *Prosecutor v. Akayesu*, the first international case to prosecute the perpetrators of the Rwanda genocide and to hold sexual violence as an act of genocide and rape as a crime against humanity. Ms. Sellers was the legal advisor on the *Prosecutor v. Kunarac*, the first international case that led to a conviction of enslavement as a crime against humanity, based in part on acts of sexual violence.

Ms. Sellers also served as the Acting Head of the Legal Advisory Section and represented three successive Prosecutors of the ICTY at governmental, international organizations or non-governmental organization meetings on legal matters concerning gender.